Making Music

for the

Joy of It

Making MUSIC for the JOY of It

*Enhancing Creativity, Skills,
and Musical Confidence*

Stephanie Judy

Jeremy P. Tarcher/Putnam
a member of
Penguin Putnam Inc.
New York

Most Tarcher/Putnam books are available at special quantity
discounts for bulk purchases for sales promotions, premiums,
fund-raising, and educational needs. Special books or book excerpts
also can be created to fit specific needs.
For details, write Putnam
Special Markets, 375 Hudson Street
New York, NY 10014

The author thanks the following for permission to reprint from copyrighted works.

Excerpts from *Growing Without Schooling*, © 1990 by Holt Associates, Inc., reprinted by
permission.
Excerpt on page 8 reprinted by permission, Ann Landers/Creators Syndicate and The
Vancouver Sun.
Excerpt on page 262 from *Never Be Nervous Again*, © 1987 by Dorothy Sarnoff,
reprinted by permission of Crown Publishers, Inc.
Excerpts from *The Recorder Book*, © 1962, 1982 by Kenneth Wollitz, reprinted by
permission of Alfred A. Knopf, Inc.
Excerpt on page 270 from *With Your Own Two Hands*, © 1981 by Seymour Bernstein,
reprinted with permission of Schirmer Books, a division of Macmillan, Inc.
Excerpts from *Never Too Late: My Musical Life Story*, © 1974 by John Holt, reprinted
with permission of Holt Associates, Inc.
"Teeter Totter" by Joan Hansen from *Music of Our Time, Vol. III*, © 1977. Reprinted by
permission of Waterloo Music Company Limited.
"So Long, It's Been Good to Know Yuh" (Dusty Old Dust). Words and music by
Woody Guthrie, © 1940, renewed in 1963. Reprinted on page 126 by permission of
Folkways Music Publishers, Inc.
Photograph on page 1 by Hansel Mieth, LIFE Magazine, © Time Warner, Inc. Used by
permission.
Photograph on page 29 by Roger Katz, courtesy of Apple Hill Center for Chamber
Music, Inc.
Photograph on page 89 by Clemens Kalischer, Image Photos, Stockbridge, MA.
Photograph on page 191 by Clemens Kalischer, Image Photos, Stockbridge, MA.
Photograph on page 245 by Sandra Pilotto.

Jeremy P. Tarcher/Putnam
a member of
Penguin Putnam Inc.
375 Hudson Street
New York, NY 10014
www.penguinputnam.com

Library of Congress Cataloguing-in-Publication Data

Judy, Stephanie.
    Making music for the joy of it: enhancing creativity, skills, and musical
confidence / Stephanie Judy.
        p.   cm.
    Includes bibliographical references.
    ISBN 0-87477-601-5—ISBN 0-87477-593-0 (pbk.)
    1. Music—Instruction and study. I. Title
MT6.J85M3 1990   90–36789 CIP
781.4'2—dc20

Design by Gary Hespenheide
Cartoons by Shyamol Bhattacherya
Spot Art illustrations by Maria Reeves

Manufactured in the United States of America
11 13 15 17 19 20 18 16 14 12

*To an inspiring teacher,
an enthusiastic colleague,
and a beloved friend—*

*this is for
Agnes Herbison*

*You will jump to it someday. Then you'll fly. You'll really fly.
After that you'll quite simply, quite calmly make your own
stones, your own floor plan, your own sound.*

Anne Sexton

Contents

Acknowledgments

I am grateful to many wonderful people for their help with this project. First of all my thanks go to all the amateur musicians across the United States and Canada who so willingly and heartfully answered my questions by letter, by phone, and in personal interviews. Any sense of richness and community in this book belongs entirely to them.

Librarians are wonderful people, too. I appreciate the warm welcome I received in the public libraries of Portland, Oregon; Spokane, Washington; and Castlegar, Nelson, and Vancouver, British Columbia. Very special thanks go to the Music Library at the University of British Columbia, especially to Ken Morrison and Kirsten Walsh, and to the Selkirk College Library in Castlegar, especially to Kate Enewold, Norman Fields, Judy Laret, and Ron Welwood.

My life has been blessed with the most loving and hospitable friends: Louise Dunn, Susan and Herb Hammond, Janet and Bryan King, Suzanne and Steve Kulik, Linda and Nick Morris, Ruth and Julian Ross, Sally and Tom Seymour, Jim Whipple, and especially Bette Tanasovich. Heartfelt thanks to all of you and to your lovely children.

My own musical colleagues have been a constant source of positive support and lively experiences. Thank you so much April Anderson, Gail Bearham, Kathryn Chapman, Christine Cowern, Bob Eddy, Rachel Grantham, Ian Hartline, Bruce Hunter, Lynelle Inwood, Jack McDowall, Lem McGinnes, Evan McKenzie, Don Mitchell, Vic Neufeld, Dick Pollard, Don Wild, the Nelson Choral Society, and the Selkirk Chamber Orchestra.

I accept complete responsibility for any foolishness or inaccuracy you find in these pages. However, for the fresh ideas about teaching, about musicality, and about the very human side of making music, I am grateful to these generous professional musicians and friends: Andrew Inglis; John Payne; David Rogosin; Rebecca Shockley; Dale Topp; Happy Traum; John Trepp; the faculty and staff at the Apple Hill Center for Chamber Music in East Sullivan, New Hampshire, especially Harriet Feinberg and Eric Stumacher; the faculty and staff at CAMMAC's Lake MacDonald Music Centre in Lake MacDonald, Quebec; and the Purcell String Quartet.

Many thanks, as well, to Shannon Hammond, the world's best babysitter; Tonnie Wickens, travel agent *extraordinaire*; and all the other generous individuals who contributed their own special talents to this project: Jim Brennan, Patrick Farenga, Roeddy Green, John Holt, Dan Joy, Doug Kennedy, Terry and Jim Mayor, Dr. Keith Merritt, Fred Rosenberg, Ted Rust, Marguerite Sailor, and Mable Wishlow.

Behind my own enduring love for music are some wonderful teachers: Chuck and Audrey Bisset, Philippe Etter, Everett Fetter, Wendy Herbison, Jane Hill-Daigle, Ellen Tolson, and Marlena Tureski.

To my friend, Tom Lowry, who kindled the spark; to my gracious agent, Barbara Kouts; to my sensitive editor, Robert Shepherd; and to my splendid publisher, Jeremy Tarcher, and all of the Tarcher staff, especially Daniel Malvin, Dianne Woo, and Paul Murphy—thanks to all of you for your help, your wisdom, your generosity, and your patience. Thank you for believing in me and in this project.

And finally to my dear ones—my partner, Jerry, and our daughter, Tessa—thank you for the sandwiches, for the uninterrupted hours, for the errands, for the encouragement, and for the music in your hearts.

Prelude

Stop! Before you read any further, please answer three questions.

1. TRUE or FALSE? You make music now. You play an instrument or you sing.
2. TRUE or FALSE? You used to make music. You took lessons once or you belonged to a group or you fooled around a bit on your own. You'd like to make music again, but you don't have time or you're afraid you're rusty or you've run out of talent (or someone said you have no talent).
3. TRUE or FALSE? You've never really had a chance to make music, but you'd like to be able to play or sing. You fantasize about it, but you think maybe you're unmusical or you're tone deaf or it's too late to learn.

If you answered TRUE to any question, then keep reading. This book is for you. Whether you dream of playing clarinet or castanets or classical guitar, whether you're drawn to Baroque or big band or barbershop, you'll find in these pages both encouragement and practical advice for reaching your musical goals. You'll find ideas for empowering yourself as a musician, for finding and relating to a teacher, for practicing effectively, for making music with others, and for performing confidently and skillfully.

Some of you probably have musical horror stories left over from childhood. Maybe someone told you that you were tone-deaf or that you were unmusical. Maybe a piano teacher rapped

My idea is that there is music in the air; the world is full of it, and you simply take as much as you require.

♪ Sir Edward Elgar

your knuckles, or maybe the kids in the third grade laughed at your singing. That's over now. This book recognizes that you're an adult. *You can take charge of your own music making.* You can decide what to play and how to play. The ideas and practical advice in these pages will help you nurture your skill, your knowledge, your confidence, and your joy in the music you make.

We are all born to music. Very few of us earn a living playing music, but many of us include music as an important part of our lives. Ralph Vaughan Williams speaks of a great pyramid of music makers with the virtuosos at the top, the "general practitioners" in the ranks below, and the amateurs "at the foundation of the pyramid, sustaining those above them and at the same time depending upon them for strength and inspiration."

And yet, for every amateur standing boldly in that foundation, there are many others standing apart, wishing to join, but feeling excluded from the company, perhaps because they lack time, information, or courage, or perhaps because they think of themselves as "unmusical" or "untalented." This book is here to say one thing to all that: *Begin.* Because you are a human being, you have a claim to music. You have a rightful place in the great human company of musicians. Making music is a lifelong calling. What's important is to begin—it doesn't matter when.

This book is not here to tell you that making music will always be easy. At times it helps to have, as amateur jazz pianist David Sudnow puts it, "an ambitiousness of the aim unmindful of the difficulties." But through the words and experiences of many amateurs, this book is here to tell you that it is possible and that it is important for you to make music. The saying is true: *It's never too late to begin, and it's always too early to give up.*

Being an amateur does not mean being inept or being forever a novice. Some of the amateurs who speak on these pages are skillful enough to make, if they wanted to, professional careers in music. But they have chosen instead to share the calling of *amateur,* of "one who loves." All amateur musicians embrace a common task: We are not here to play music perfectly but to love music deeply.

My own research for this book has proved to me that amateur music making is very much alive and vigorous in North America. As I traveled around the United States and Canada, attending camps and workshops and meeting musicians in their

There are some disabling myths about what art is, how to do it, what is good art, and what art is for, that have gagged generations, depriving them of a significant and natural means of expression. This is a terrible loss and an unnecessary one.

♪ Peter London, *No More Secondhand Art*

Talent is the capacity to project life.

♪ Lili Kraus

homes, I found everywhere more people willing to share than I could possibly talk to, more events taking place than I could attend in a hundred lifetimes, and more books and music to read and study than I will ever have time to explore.

I found a world of amateur music full of thriving subcultures—ragtime enthusiasts, Renaissance consorts, Suzuki families, *a cappella* gospel ensembles, Irish duos, jazz trios, barbershop quartets, woodwind quintets, brass choirs, symphony orchestras, rock bands, madrigal singers, and soloists playing everything from accordion to zither. I have been endlessly delighted and surprised as I looked over the shoulders of this great throng of fellow musicians.

My own musical story began in Topeka, Kansas, in a family of music lovers. My mother was a decent pianist and a rather good singer, and my father had a turn at the clarinet and a soft, warm bass voice (which I heard only in church). My first piano lessons were at age three, and my first teacher was my brother, Tom, who was then five. He hurried home from each of his own lessons and proudly showed his awestruck little sister how to play.

At five I, too, started "real" lessons on the piano, and a few years later followed brother Tom once again, this time into the Randolph Elementary School Band. This proved less successful. I had to share his instrument—the tenor sax—though I could never muster anything like enthusiasm for it. Meanwhile, we had a neighbor who was an unfailing source of wooden cigar boxes. With my school ruler, some rubber bands, and a dowel filched from my father's lumber supply, I manufactured in the basement (secretly, I thought) pretend violins.

When I was eleven, my mother finally asked The Question: Do you want to play the violin, or what? The violin, I said. A real instrument was procured (a sensational improvement over a cigar box), along with a fine teacher. I came fully under the spell, willingly practicing two or three hours a day during the school term and always looking forward to summers when I could practice four or five. Just before leaving home, in the final year of high school, I first put a viola under my chin, and with some fellow students I discovered the inexpressible joys of chamber music.

A heavy academic load and a part-time job at the university soon crowded music off the stage. I took violin lessons for a year and played in the Washington University Symphony for two, but I had no piano and little time and finally, regretfully, I packed all that away. Three liquor boxes full of music and two odd-shaped cases followed me—but were never opened—as I traipsed about North America in my twenties.

One day in October of 1970, in Huntington, New York, I ran out of money. With no misgivings, I put an ad in *Newsday* offering a good violin for sale. A gentleman phoned and wanted to see it at once. I thought I should dust it off and tune it if I really wanted to make the sale. When I put it under my chin, for the first time in five years, the smell of Hill's violin polish—like Proust's *madeleines*—flooded my senses, and I knew, instantly and absolutely, no matter how poor I was, that I couldn't sell my violin. The man knocked at that moment, and I told him the truth: The violin had just been sold—to myself, for the price of the ad. He shook my hand warmly and said that he understood.

So began my own renaissance of amateur music making. I joined a string quartet so eager for a viola that they would take even me, as rusty and inhibited as I was then. I bought a guitar. I borrowed a banjo. I learned to play the recorder and toyed with the flute for a few weeks. I bought my own piano (my first purchase on credit) and began to cart *that* around with *eight* liquor boxes full of music and I've-lost-count-how-many odd-shaped cases, all opened as often as I could steal time from the unpredictable course of my "real" life.

I came to rest in the mountains of southeastern British Columbia (adding a cello to my collection on the way), in a home already outfitted with a harpsichord, a clavichord, and a string bass (and bassist). I signed up for voice lessons and discovered to my wonder that I am a soprano!

When my parents' piano was shipped from Kansas to Canada, there was no place in our house to put another big instrument, so we moved our only table to the garage, put the piano in the kitchen, and ate from our laps for the next five years. It was during that tableless time that we added to our family a new musician, who has proved that musical vagrancy is inherited. She has played, in her first eight years, piano, cello, violin, guitar, and recorder, and she is developing into an indefatigable madrigal singer.

Through all of this, I have met the most wonderful people, the community of musicians—amateurs and professionals, young and old, people who teach, who share, who encourage, who struggle, who exult, who love what they do. Beginning with the musicians I know and reaching out to the musicians they know and to the musicians those musicians know and so on and on, I have compiled this book to share with you whatever advice and inspiration I have been able to collect. I gathered the advice and information in these pages not by consulting my experience alone but by observing and interviewing hundreds of helpful, generous amateurs.

I mean this book to be as inclusive and inviting as possible. My own classical background has slanted my research to some extent, though I have tried to invite other forms and styles to speak in these pages, too. The text mentions "players" often and "singers" somewhat less, but this is in no way intended to exclude singers, who are the most numerous and steadfast of any musical community. It is simply a fact that we are all born singing, but those who want to play have to learn how first. It also becomes awkward to say, in every relevant sentence, "play or sing," so I have said simply "play," trusting that singers will recognize their voices as their instruments. (By the way, if you long to make music but feel you can't because you are tone-deaf, please turn—*right now*—to page 9.)

I have centered this book on Western acoustic music. Perhaps something here will be useful to amateurs drawn to non-Western traditions or to electronic music. Because my task was so large, I had to set some arbitrary boundaries and stay within shouting distance of my own experience. I apologize for this shortcoming.

Leonard Marsh, an avid amateur cellist, once said that music making is a kind of distilled happiness. I believe he is right. If you are a musician now, you already know that. If you are what my colleague Dale Topp lovingly calls a "not-yet-musician," I hope you will know it soon.

As this book neared completion, my daughter observed that my work on it is like planting flowers. These pages are here in the hopes that readers will bloom.

Thank you.

I've always had this idea from the day I started to play music: that not only is it alive, but that it's endless and has no ego in it. There's something about creativity that every human being gets an equal share.

♪ Ornette Coleman

Stephanie Judy
Slocan Park, British Columbia
September 1990

How to Use This Book

Adult amateur musicians come in a great and glorious variety of skill levels and musical interests. There's something in this book for everyone, but some topics are more appropriate for some readers than for others. Here's the overall plan of the book:

- Part One, "Starting from Where You Are," examines patterns of musical development in adult life, considering separately beginners, returnees, and active amateurs.
- Part Two, "Learning," looks at the separate skills of music making and at all the various ways of learning those skills.
- Part Three, "Playing and Practicing for Yourself," discusses attitudes about practicing and offers some practical suggestions for where, when, and how to practice effectively.
- Part Four, "Playing and Practicing with Others," looks at musical groups of all sizes and makes specific suggestions for playing or singing effectively in an ensemble.
- Part Five, "Playing and Performing: Making Music for Others," examines in detail the process of preparing to perform and gives extensive advice for coping with stagefright.

If you are a beginner, you will probably find these chapters to be the most useful ones to read first: chapter 1, "If You Are a

Beginner," chapter 4, "Ways to Learn," chapter 6, "What Is There to Learn?" and chapter 11, "Inside Ensembles: The Musical View."

If you are an active amateur or have made music before, you will probably find these chapters especially relevant to your situation: chapter 2, "If You Have Played Before," chapter 10, "Beyond the Notes: Musicianship, Mapping, and the Music You Play," and chapter 12, "Inside Ensembles: The Social View."

If you are a music teacher with adult amateur students, you may be especially interested in these chapters: chapter 1, "If You Are a Beginner," chapter 2, "If You Have Played Before," chapter 3, "Growing as a Musician," and chapter 5, "Learning with a Teacher."

The rest of the book contains information of interest to all amateur musicians at any level of development.

Part One

STARTING FROM WHERE YOU ARE

I believe the world of music to be a true democracy. I am convinced that our chief need is to make music ourselves. I believe that under the right conditions we should enjoy doing so. . . . That we all are more musical than we are thought to be; that we are more musical than we get the chance to be—of this there is no doubt whatsoever.

Thomas Surette, *Music and Life*

CHAPTER 1

♪♫ If You Are a Beginner

All I can see is music, lots of it, simply dying to get out.

Welcome! You've chosen a wonderful time to start making music! As an adult beginning musician, you have many advantages over a child in the same situation. Your primary advantage is that you are in charge. No one else will direct your musical education. No one else will decide what instrument you'll play, choose a teacher for you, or decree which style of music you learn. No one else will determine how long you practice or under what conditions, if any, you will perform. You are moving into music not by coercion but by desire.

Maybe you regret that you didn't start sooner, but that regret is a pale rival to your freshness and enthusiasm. You are not just fulfilling a personal fantasy; you are answering a great human longing. If you ever worry about what other people will think, rest assured that many will envy you for actually doing what they only dream about. Because you are in control, because you are not being coerced, you can begin to feel at ease with the idea of being a musician.

Feeling at ease with music making is, perhaps, the most important thing that an adult beginner can learn. As with riding a bicycle or learning to swim, once you feel at ease your natural abilities take over, enabling you to perform with a competence that surprises you. How, then, do you learn to feel at ease? Many adult beginners blame their lack of ease on the physical challenges that accompany taking up an instrument or learning to sing. However, feeling at ease has more to do with clearing away self-doubts than it has to do with learning how to hold an instrument, how to move your lips or fingers, how to sit or stand, or how to breathe. Once you are rid of doubts about your musical self, you clear the path for progress. The purpose of this chapter is to dispel the most common doubts that plague beginning musicians by showing how unfounded they actually are.

WHAT ABOUT MUSICAL APTITUDE?

Musicality is a gift, the birthright of human beings, one of the qualities that marks us as human. A few individuals—very, very few—have a rare neurological disorder called *sensory amusia*, which is the inability to comprehend music. But if you can tell the difference between "Happy Birthday" and the national anthem, you can relax. It's unlikely that you have sensory amusia.

As humans we are innately musical. And yet, as music educator Dale Topp points out, "by adulthood most of us feel rather clearly sorted *into* or *out of* music." Those who are sorted out tend to think of themselves as "unmusical." In nearly every case, however, it is not aptitude but opportunity that is lacking. Some adults have simply had no chance yet to develop their musical abilities, whereas others were systematically excluded from music making in childhood, usually by some tactless or misinformed "authority"—a teacher, a parent, an older sibling. If you have ever been given the label "unmusical," or if you have applied this label to yourself, you are hereby granted full and official permission to stop using it. If you'd like to verify your musicality, here's a quick test.

The Making Music for the Joy of It Test of Musical Aptitude

Answer every question with a YES, with a NO, or with as much explanation as you'd like.

To be human is to be capable of music, just as to be human is to be capable of speech.

♪ Rosamund Shuter-Dyson, *The Psychology of Musical Ability*

This is precisely the unique thing about music: it speaks a language that is understood without learning, understood by everyone, not just by the so-called musical people.

♪ Victor Zuckerkandl, *The Sense of Music*

3

1. If you hear someone play or sing a familiar tune, and if the person hits a wrong or unusual note, do you notice it?
2. If you hear some music but can't see the musicians—when you listen to the radio, for example—can you tell, in general, what instruments are playing? Can you tell strings from a brass band? A piano from a trumpet? Can you tell the difference between humming and whistling? Can you identify bagpipes when you hear them?
3. Can you recognize styles of music just by hearing them? Can you tell the difference between rock and classical music? Can you tell the difference between a march and a lullaby? A jazz band and a church choir?
4. Would you like to make music yourself?

If you answered YES to any of these questions, then you are musical enough to make your own music. Did the questions seem too easy? If so, consider this: Attempts to model human behavior on computers have shown that the most complicated behaviors to reproduce are those that humans do most easily and naturally—things like walking on two legs, holding a conversation, and perceiving musical structures. If the questions seemed easy, it is because, being human, you are born with the basic skills that you need to become a musician!

Can you tell the difference between rock and classical music?

Let's consider the skills addressed by the aptitude test. The first three questions reveal your skill at recognizing musical structures, an all-important ability because music is a structure, like a house or a cathedral, except that the material of musical structure is not wood, stone, and glass, but time. Music is organized time—vibrations, frequencies, pulses, patterns—moving across your consciousness. The first three questions deal with your intricate, largely unconscious skill at processing, mentally organizing, and so understanding musical structures. These are skills that everyone has but that most of us take for granted.

Think again about the skill addressed by the first question. If you are able to detect a wrong note in a familiar song, you have obviously internalized the structure of that song, and while you listen, you are able to anticipate the oncoming sounds and match them against the mental model you have created. You do this matching of the actual sound against your mental model quite well—so well, in fact, that you can probably detect the most trivial deviations. It is likely that you could even listen to a tune that you didn't know and still detect wrong notes. If you have musician friends, and if you are curious about this, ask them to try it on you.

Now consider the skills addressed by the second and third questions. When you distinguish one instrument from another, you are mentally categorizing complex physical phenomena— the unique acoustical properties specific to each instrument. When you recognize the style of a piece, you are not only using cues about musical structure and acoustical properties, but you are also applying an intuitive knowledge of the types and histories of musical form. Very heady stuff. You probably do these things well and think that they're easy. They're not. You are able to do these things only because of your passive musical experience and because of your genetic inheritance. All the listening that you have ever done has trained you to be a musician, and as a member of the human community you have inherited a fantastically complex neural organization that makes music as natural an activity as speech.

The fourth question is the telling one. Almost all people inherit the ability to understand music. What really determines musical aptitude is, therefore, desire. If you have read this far in this book, and if you really want to play or sing, you are musical.

We often don't give ourselves credit for what we can already do, for how much we already know, for the untapped power of our minds and spirits. John Payne, who teaches beginning sax to Boston-area adults at the John Payne Music Center, puts it this way:

> I start from the assumption that the people who walk in here and want to learn to play music must have an interest in music, and if they have an interest in it, they must have some feeling about it, and if they have some feeling about it, it must make sense to them, and if it makes sense to them, then they obviously have some ability. That doesn't mean they can play already. It just means that as musicians, basically they're all there. You just have to get some technical things down and draw that out.

People like to speak of music as a language (and it is), and

In music education we deal with talent better than desire. We need to believe in that desire and rescue it from beneath the mountains of bad experiences that some students carry.

♪ Dale Topp, professor of music, Calvin College

people like to say that when you're learning music you're learn-ing a language (and you are), but you're not learning a whole new language. You're learning more about a language that, to a large degree, you already understand! You may not know how to describe the grammar of it, and you may not yet have the small muscle skills that you need to speak the language. But you do have an innate understanding of "musical grammar," and you can learn the muscular coordination that you will need. So, musical potential comes to a matter of training your muscles and opening your heart.

BUT DON'T YOU HAVE TO START WHEN YOU'RE A CHILD?

The fact is, you did start learning music when you were a child. All those childhood experiences, with some adult experiences added in, brought you through our *Making Music for the Joy of It Test of Musical Aptitude.* It is true that if you begin learning to make music as an adult, you are unlikely to become a virtuoso or even a professional. So what? Most children who study music don't become virtuosos or professionals either. It is no shame to fall short of virtuosity. Our task as amateurs is not to play music perfectly but to love it deeply. If you have a real desire to play or sing, you have all the preparation you need.

Author and educator John Holt, who started playing the cello at age fifty, labeled as "musical folklore" the notion that one must begin music making as a child. Unfortunately, this bit of folklore, which is rather widely accepted, begets the plainly absurd idea that only those who already know how to make mu-sic are musical. Much closer to the truth is the old joke about the fellow who was asked if he could play the violin. "I don't know," he said. "I've never tried."

This is not meant to dismiss the concerns that adult begin-ners feel about their lack of experience. New musicians often worry about having either inadequate knowledge or poor coor-dination and dexterity. Yet in terms of knowledge, children have few advantages over adults. Adults often help themselves along the road of musical understanding more quickly than children because of their deeper experience, both of music and of life. The real "mental block" is not our capacity to under-

Untrained musicians have implicit knowledge of that which musicians can talk about explicitly. In this respect, music is similar to language. Ordinary people speak their natural language according to the same gram-matical rules as professional linguists even though they may have very limited conscious knowledge of those rules.

♪ John A. Sloboda,
The Musical Mind

6

stand but rather our doubts and expectations—a topic we'll look at again in chapter 3. As far as mental equipment goes, it's not important to have "had" music as a child. It's only important to maintain, or rediscover if necessary, a childlike curiosity, openness, and awareness.

In regard to physical dexterity and coordination, you will find that playing music is apt to make unfamiliar demands on your body—but the word is *unfamiliar*, not *impossible*. Dr. Frank R. Wilson, neurologist, amateur pianist, and author of a reassuring book called *Tone Deaf and All Thumbs?* is unequivocal on this issue: "I am convinced that all of us have a biologic guarantee of musicianship. This is true regardless of our age, formal experience with music, or the size and shape of our fingers, lips, or ears. . . .We all have music inside of us and can learn to get it out, one way or another."

A beginning adult may indeed have problems with dexterity, flexibility, coordination, or breath control. But some accomplished adults have these problems, too, as do some children. These are problems encountered by people in general, not by adult beginners in particular. Many older musicians actually find that the joint stiffness that accompanies aging is somewhat improved by musical activities that exercise the affected joints.

WHAT ABOUT LEFT-HANDEDNESS?

Research by Stanley Schleuter at Kent State University showed no relationship between instrumental achievement and the tendency to favor one hand, eye, or foot. In fact, it's hard to la-bel most instruments with any quality of handedness. Percussion and keyboards certainly use both hands equally, and right-handed pianists often bemoan their weak left-hand technique. Most woodwinds—flute, sax, recorder, and clarinet, for example—make equal demands on both hands. Stringed instruments make equal but very different demands on each hand—the left hand selects the pitch, and the right produces the sound by bowing, plucking, or strumming. Some strongly left-handed players—especially those who are self-taught—reverse the position of their stringed instrument. Charlie Chaplin played the violin left-handed; Harpo Marx rested his harp on his left shoulder; and Elizabeth Cotten, a close friend of the Seeger family

There's a wonderful childlike feeling of experiencing something and understanding something for the very first time.

♪ Ann MacNab, retired librarian and amateur pianist

Differences in the problems of young and adult students are commonly exaggerated. We tend to underestimate both the intellectual and interpretative powers of the child, on the one hand, and the ability of the adult to learn new skills, on the other.

♪ William S. Newman, *The Pianist's Problems*

7

and the composer of "Freight Train," played her guitar "the other way 'round," fingering with her right hand and strumming with her left. She kept the strings in the same order as a "right-handed" guitar, and the result was a beautiful, unique, and difficult-to-duplicate style.

Only the brass instruments might be considered right-handed, but with those, finger technique is straightforward. Lip and breath control pose the challenges here.

Far from causing trouble, left-handedness can give an edge on some valuable musical skills. Some teachers speculate that left-handed students play by ear and memorize more easily than right-handers. The one potential source of difficulty is the left-handers' habit of substituting the word *left* when they hear or read the word *right*. Playing music is like driving a car. Directions have to be taken literally (unless the instrument itself is reversed).

MAYBE I'M TOO OLD

Balderdash! After three years of voice lessons, Pat Farenga, president of Farenga Brothers Funeral Home in the Bronx, stepped into a new career. At the age of fifty-eight, he released his first record—fittingly titled *The Time is Now*—and launched a new enterprise, O-Kay-Pat Record Company, to distribute his recording. Though no longer strictly an amateur, Pat exemplifies the extraordinary energy and commitment so often shown by older adults who take up music. Several dozen amateurs interviewed for this book began their studies in their fifties and sixties. One retired teacher bought herself a piano for her seventy-fifth birthday. She laughingly reported that her piano lesson book is called *Teaching Little Fingers to Play*. "I love it," she says. "It doesn't have a word in it anywhere about 'golden agers' or 'senior citizens' or—heaven forbid—'the elderly.'"

There's simply no evidence that artistic potential declines with age. Quite the reverse. Biographies and autobiographies of distinguished individuals are generally testaments to maturing and deepening of any artistic tendency, whether pursued on a professional or amateur basis. A study conducted by Alicia Clair Gibbons at the University of Kansas found no significant decrease in musicality in an over-sixty-five population.

Dear Ann Landers:

May I say a few words to the senior citizens in your audience? Do any of you have unfulfilled dreams or ambitions? If so, go for them! It is NOT too late.

All my life I wanted to play in an orchestra. Three years ago I began to take clarinet lessons. I was 64. I now play second clarinet in our community orchestra. It is one of the most thrilling experiences of my life. My blood pressure has dropped dramatically and my medication has been cut in half. It is no exaggeration to say I have never been healthier, happier, or more energetic.

♪ *Tootsie*

Dear Tootsie:

Beautiful! I love it! I hope your letter encourages others to take on new challenges. Age is only a number, folks.

♪ *Ann Landers*

8

"Older people are too cautious sometimes," according to Lucy Melzack, a special education teacher from Montreal who took up the cello when she was fifty. "If you want to play or sing, you should just take the plunge. It gives you something of your own that you can do when your family is grown up and busy with their own lives. It gives you a real feeling of independence." No matter how long it has been postponed, it is never too late to take your rightful place as a doer of music.

BUT I CAN'T CARRY A TUNE

Many—far too many—people feel condemned to musical silence for life because they believe themselves to be "tone deaf," or unable to carry a tune. Around this issue there is some confusion and a great deal of heartache. If, as we've said, music is one of the things that makes us human, then any person cut off from music becomes somehow less than human. The truth is that individuals who are labeled "tone-deaf" not only are musically isolated and demoralized but are almost never "tone-deaf"! The label is untrue, unfair, and inaccurate. Any condition that appears to be "tone deafness" can almost certainly be reversed.

The issue here revolves around what we'll call *pitch sensitivity* and we'll define that as the ability, present in different degrees in different people, to recognize and produce accurately tuned musical tones, either by singing or on an instrument. There are three varieties of pitch sensitivity:

1. absolute pitch
2. relative pitch
3. pitch matching

These three types of pitch sensitivity, which are also three distinct musical skills, are frequently confused and erroneously lumped together as a single skill called *perfect pitch*. We'll look at these skills one by one, and then we can look closely at the so-called problem of "tone deafness."

Absolute pitch. Most people who use the term *perfect pitch* mean *absolute pitch*, which is the ability to name any pitch heard and to play or sing any pitch named, and to do so "out of the

M*y definition of youthful enthusiasm had to be revised after teaching the most fired-up group I have ever encountered: an Elderhostel beginning piano class.*

♪ Eric Street, professional pianist and teacher

blue," so to speak, without reference to any other pitch. Absolute pitch actually means more than simply being able to name a given pitch, because the names of pitches are themselves arbitrary, just as the names of colors or trees or hats are arbitrary. An individual with absolute pitch hears each tone as having distinct qualities—called *pitch chroma* or *pitch class*—always identified with that pitch, just as certain qualities are always identified with the color we call *red* or the tree we call a *maple* or the hat we call a *beret*. Even if we called it something else, it would still have the same qualities that make it recognizable to us.

People who can recognize pitches in this way very accurately are said to have "absolute pitch"—also called "perfect pitch." Some people have a kind of "imperfect pitch," recognizing only certain pitches or only pitches produced on their own instrument. *Not all musicians have absolute pitch and not all people who have absolute pitch are musicians.* Until recently, absolute pitch was considered a rare and remarkable trait. Current research now seems to indicate that, like color recognition, absolute pitch is probably a natural ability, present in nearly everyone, but it is either unrecognized, undeveloped, or perhaps "unlearned" at a very early age by most people. There is also evidence that absolute pitch can be learned or retrieved. Pianist David Burge has developed a self-teaching cassette course to help musicians do this (see the Resources list in appendix 2).

Though it may seem surprising, absolute pitch is not a musical skill that is considered very important. Absolute pitch has been shown to contribute substantially to long-term memory, but it also proves at times to be an impediment. If, for example, an ensemble must tune to match a piano that is tuned low, any musician in the group with absolute pitch may become somewhat disoriented. Absolute pitch can certainly enrich a musician's experience, but it is not essential. Many accomplished amateurs and many professionals as well lead satisfactory and contented musical lives without it.

Relative pitch.   As absolute pitch is a way to identify an isolated tone, so relative pitch is a way to identify the relationship between tones. The musical distance between any two pitches is called an *interval.* A trained musician with good *relative pitch* can name any interval heard and can play or sing any interval

A *singer can adjust unless he has perfect pitch, and then it can be painful. Relative pitch allows the singer to move back and forth with the instruments, but if he has perfect pitch and has to work with whatever instrument is put before him, it can be exceedingly frustrating.*

♪ Cleo Laine

named. Untrained musicians can have good relative pitch, too, without knowing the formal names of the intervals. Once again, the names are arbitrary, but the quality of each interval is unique and musically significant.

Relative pitch is a wonderful skill for any musician and it is especially valuable for singers, string players, trombonists, and those who play by ear or improvise. *Relative pitch can be learned.* It's not at all necessary to have absolute pitch in order to have good relative pitch. The usual method for teaching relative pitch is called *ear training*. It comes more easily to some than to others, but with practice nearly everyone can develop good relative pitch.

Pitch matching.   *Pitch matching* is the ability to tell whether two pitches are the same or different. Someone with good pitch matching skills can find, with her voice or on her instrument, a pitch that she has heard. We say that she has "good intonation"—she can sing or play in tune. She can't necessarily tell you the name of a tone (that's absolute pitch), or how far it is from some other tone (that's relative pitch), but she can clearly "carry a tune," especially in a group or with accompaniment.

Of the three kinds of pitch sensitivity we've described here, pitch matching is the most important for a beginning musician, and, like the others, *pitch matching can be learned.* It's not an elusive talent, bestowed on a lucky few and withheld from the rest. It's not even very difficult to learn. It requires patient listening, and sometimes the help of another musician, but improvement after even a very short time can be truly dramatic. There's more information about this in the next section on "Tone deafness" and in appendix 1.

It's interesting that among instrumental musicians, pitch-matching skills tend to be a bit "instrument specific." For example, an experienced clarinetist can easily tell if a clarinet tone is in tune, but he may feel more doubtful about judging tones from a trumpet or a string bass. Some instrumentalists actually have rather dreadful singing voices, with very limited range and poor vocal intonation. They simply have not had enough practice at vocal pitch matching. But as long as they play their own instruments in tune, no one really cares. Singing experience is not required in order to play an instrument.

I think of myself as a terrible singer, and I've always been very inhibited about singing. But when I started to play the cello, I thought, yes, here is my voice.

♪ Kathryn Chapman, mother, tree planter, and amateur cellist

11

"Tone deafness." Very shortly, we will stop saying "tone-deaf" in this book, simply because there is virtually no such thing. A truly tone-deaf person would obviously be "tune-deaf" as well—able to make no sense whatever of the music he hears. Most people who believe they are "tone-deaf" simply have undeveloped pitch-matching skills. Anyone in this situation who really wants to change and who can find a patient and gentle helper can almost certainly overcome his "tone deafness." Psychological studies have proved that training and practice can substantially increase pitch-matching accuracy. Jim Gear, of Komoko, Ontario, proved it to himself:

"Because I'm in outdoor education, I'm often part of groups that are singing. I do a lot of leadership, and so it's just natural that in singing I'd be a leader, too, except that I couldn't sing. People would say, 'Oh, come on and join us,' and I'd say, 'I can't sing.' But they'd keep at me, so finally I'd join in and then they'd say, 'You're right. You can't sing!'

"I had a friend who was a very good pianist. She showed me how to play some tunes on the xylophone—I thought that might help me. She encouraged me to take guitar lessons, so I joined a class at Fanshawe College, and by the end of ten weeks, I could play some songs. I couldn't tune my guitar—I had to get someone else to tune it—but I learned to play it.

"But that was no good if I still couldn't sing, so I went to another friend and started doing some ear training with her. She found that I couldn't hear the difference between a note up here and a note way down there on the piano. I couldn't tell which was higher or lower. If she gave me the first note of 'Mary Had a Little Lamb,' I couldn't figure out any of the rest of the notes. I had been faking before, singing louder and softer instead of higher and lower.

"So we worked together every week. She would play notes on the piano, and I would try to match them. She would tell me whether I was high or low.

"When my son was born, I played guitar for him from the day he arrived home. I still wasn't singing in tune at the time, but I played for him anyway. I played him to sleep every night.

"I went through a stage where I would never play guitar in front of anyone else. Then I started doing that, but I wouldn't play guitar and sing. And then I started doing that—not always in tune, but I did it. That was a major step.

"Going to a CAMMAC summer music camp was a big step, too, because whatever I do, I'm used to doing it well. And I know that when I do music, relative to other musicians, I'm not doing it well.

"Some people have helped me, and some have blocked me. A friend once, trying to give me a compliment, made a joke out of it. He said, 'You sound fine, Jim. When you sing "Oh, Canada," it sounds just like "God Save the Queen." That set me back. But then at CAMMAC, Pierre Perron came up to me after the first day of *a cappella* and said, 'Great! You're really singing well.' And that helped so much.

"I still can't read music, so I *have* to listen. I'm fairly good now at matching notes, so I know when I'm out of tune. I know when I haven't hit the right note.

"For me there's been real satisfaction in doing something that I never believed I could do. If I can do music, I can do anything."

Though true "tone deafness" is extremely rare, the label is handed out unsparingly to children, usually by well-meaning classroom teachers, choral directors, and even parents. The children who escape this category are the ones who develop good pitch-matching skills naturally and early, by age six or seven. Teachers and parents comment that these children have a "good ear" and often single them out for special music activities or lessons. But many children develop pitch-matching skills at a later age, and some need help and a bit of practice before they get the hang of it. Unfortunately, too many teachers and parents are unwilling to wait and unable to help. Consequently, these late-bloomers are called "tone-deaf" or "monotone" or "unmusical." On the basis of this one criterion, they are often excluded from musical activities, especially group singing, in order to spare them (and their teachers and parents) any disappointment or embarrassment. Some are told "just move your lips" instead of being allowed to sing with their class. Others are strategically given tambourines or triangles instead of a place in the choir. Still others are passed over in auditions for choral groups, without ever knowing why. Writer Michael Rossman's experience is typical:

"I remember as vividly as shame the day the county music teacher came around to my fourth-grade classroom to test our aptitudes. She sat at the old piano and plunked out chords; we were supposed to tell her which notes were 'higher' and 'lower.' I was one of three in the whole class who flunked, even with prompting, and was classed as musically uneducable. . . .

"As I puzzle it out now, what happened was that I just couldn't connect with her spatial metaphor for pitch, though I had my own sense of melody and enthusiasm for sound. But her judgment was momentous, the more so for being delivered in public ritual. From that day on I grew acutely self-conscious . . . my singing got more and more uncertain, until the teacher and class were glad to excuse me to listen with the other musical dummies."

Responding to "a blind longing that refused to be stilled," Rossman became in his adult years a founding member of the Recorder Society of the University of Chicago and a fine amateur flutist.

If you were ever barred from the musical community because you "couldn't carry a tune," or because you "failed" some kind of aptitude test, you are the victim of two serious errors. The first error is the assumption that something called *musical aptitude* can be detected at an early age by a simple test. Musicality is not a single ability; it is a complex array of experience, potential, inherited traits, and learned behaviors. Any quick procedure that pretends to screen an entire group in a matter of minutes is without question inaccurate and unfair.

The second error, which usually follows closely on the heels of the first, is the policy that musical activities and instruction should be offered only to those who can demonstrate musical aptitude. Music belongs to the human community. If a school system includes music in its curriculum, it ought to be equally available to everyone and taught in a self-affirming way that enhances each student's musical growth. Excluding those who appear "unmusical" is like excluding from health and physical education all those who seem to be unhealthy or out of shape.

Sadly, it often takes only *one* incident to silence an individual for the rest of his or her life. Our musical selves are vital but vulnerable. When we are told that we are inadequate, some of us experience so much pain that we simply give up. It is important to know this: having been told that you are "tone-deaf" does not make it true, although it does create a powerful psychological block to singing or playing.

I'm not a born tenor. It was really a fight for me to get the high notes. I am not one of those singers who opened his mouth and found a high C right away.

♪ Placido Domingo

Among adults who say they are "tone-deaf" are many who subsequently outgrew their childhood pitch-matching problems. Some of these people can sing quite decently, although perhaps in a limited range or with a voice quality they think is unpleasant. Singing is not always a "natural" or intuitive skill. Most people sing much better if they have some training in how to make music with their voice. But because those who call themselves "tone-deaf" had no opportunities to acquire any skills, because they learned to doubt themselves, and because their contribution was unwelcome, they now feel shut out of the music-making community. The claim of "tone deafness" becomes a lifelong apology, excusing them from any further risky or hurtful situations.

Miraculously, many people in this situation love music, and many are avid listeners. Provided that the desire to make music has not been extinguished, there is nothing but an emotional obstacle to hold them back. Eugene Dykema, an economist from Grand Rapids, Michigan, faced his own personal obstacle by taking singing lessons. "It was a kind of rebirth," he says. "I was determined to put aside forty-five years of negative experience and give it my best and—who knows?—maybe I could accomplish something. In the early stages, I was in very unfamiliar territory. But I tried it and I worked at it. I was a long way from being good, but I found out that I could sing."

Other adults who claim "tone deafness" are like Jim Gear on page 12; their pitch-matching skills have yet to be developed. Professor Dale Topp, of the Calvin College Department of Music in Grand Rapids, Michigan, has given great love and enthusiastic devotion for fifteen years to rescuing individuals in this situation. In addition to his regular teaching duties, he has initiated a college course called "Music for the Absolute Beginner." Working from a strong base of mutual encouragement and loving support, Topp turns the "tone-deaf" into capable and confident singers. His students—many of whom have not sung in years—present a closing public recital that features every class member in a solo song. Topp describes a typical student:

> At first, Derk could not match pitches, but he quickly developed a resonant bass voice and could accurately follow melodic lines. . . . At the final recital, he sang "Every Night When

The trouble with predictions of failure in music is that they normally go unchallenged. They then take a foothold in the mind, as it were, as a rationale for inertia. For most children, a diagnosis of tone deafness becomes the basis of a lifelong conviction that music is out for them. And it is a great loss.

♪ Frank R. Wilson, neurologist and amateur pianist, *Tone Deaf and All Thumbs?*

the Sun Goes In" with a bass quality coveted by choir directors. He joined the college male choir within a week after this
class ended.

Topp, who gently refers to his new students as "not-yet-singers," has found that most can learn to match pitches accurately
in about three half-hour sessions. His method, offered with his
kind permission, is described in appendix 1 on pages 291–297.
If you are a "not-yet-singer" and would like to learn to sing,
please show the instructions in appendix 1 to a teacher or
friend who meets the description given there of an appropriate
helper—someone who can work with you to overcome this obstacle. Any time you're ready, you can trade in your "tone-deaf"
ticket for one that says "musician."

SO HOW DO I START?

Coming to music as a beginner is a bit like going to the ocean
for the first time. Far away, out there, it is *much* bigger than you
imagined it would be; but right here, where you are, it feels
marvelous to get your feet wet. The best place to begin is where
you are, doing what you most want to do.

Don't fall for any "old musicians' tales." Don't let anyone
tell you that the French horn is too hard or that you shouldn't
be singing in your sixties or that you can't play the piano with
small hands. If you want to play the French horn, get a French
horn and begin. If you love to sing, there's almost certainly a
choir or choral society near you that would welcome your contribution. And if you yearn to play the piano, you can observe
for yourself that pianists come in all shapes and sizes. The best
kind of hand for a musician, according to composer Ernst Bacon, "belongs to the person of good musical mind. . . . To judge
a hand, one would have to measure the heart and head."

CHAPTER 2

If You Have Played Before

If you made music when you were a child, you may still be on the path, playing and practicing and finding your adult way on a journey begun years ago. Or you may have quit, dropped out, given up, only to find something inside you still yearning to play or sing. Whatever the character of your previous music making, you can think of this chapter as a kind of helicopter trip. We'll hover briefly over some difficult terrain that you are already familiar with and then catch a glimpse of the open land beyond it.

The first part of this chapter is addressed to *returnees*—to people who gave up music making at some earlier time but have recently started again or would like to start again. Then we'll look at the experiences and problems of *active amateurs*, those who have been with us and around us, making music all along—the ones who can teach us all so much.

FOR RETURNEES

People who studied music as children and then stopped playing or singing fall into two general groups. In the first group are

I hadn't studied for thirty years. I hadn't read music, I hadn't really played, I hadn't even listened to much piano music in all that time. And as soon as I played those first chords in a Chopin Prelude, it blew me away. Every chord blew me away. All I wanted to do was get more, get more. I felt as if I had had a thirty-year famine and I wanted to be fed. It was that basic.

♪ Anna Hamel, teacher and amateur pianist

those lucky ones who enjoyed their childhood music, who had skilled and caring teachers, and who had support from their families. But as they grew into adolescence or adulthood, music making was crowded out by other activities—by the basketball team, the paper route, a full load at college, a family, a job. For such people, music making is a fond memory, and often, if the circumstances are right, music is taken up again. Old skills return, perhaps slowly, but with expanded and deepened understanding.

In the second group are those who consider themselves failures. Often they quit before adolescence, sometimes after only two or three years of music study. Lots of them played the piano. These are the people who feel untalented and guilty. Yet often, though memories are bitter, the desire to play is still strong.

What follows here concerns primarily those who dropped out after negative childhood experiences with music. If your experience was positive and wholesome, you have much to be grateful for and a solid departure point. Nevertheless, you too might find some interesting ideas here.

If you feel that you "failed" at music as a child, take a moment to sift your memories *without any regard to your own musical ability.* Consider whether any of the situations described below apply to you.

1. You had a serious personality conflict with your teacher. You felt you could never please him or her, and your best efforts drew nothing but criticism, belittling remarks, or even physical pain. (Some piano teachers really did rap students on the knuckles with a ruler.)

It was an unfortunate coincidence that you had this experience in conjunction with music lessons. The outcome has nothing to do with your musical ability. The teacher could have been giving you lessons in painting, tennis, driving, or ballet. With someone so lacking in sensitivity, you might well have floundered no matter what the subject matter. You did not have a musical problem; your teacher had a human relations problem. You were not "lazy" or "unmotivated" or "ungrateful" or "unmusical." If anyone stuck a label on you, it's time to tear the label off and throw it away. You didn't deserve it.

2. You had to play—once or many times—in public. You were frightened, and maybe you played badly.

I was not yet six years old when they placed me under the tutorship of Don Francisco Rivera, a violinist of hard ear and stiffer fingers. He managed to convert my music lessons into my martyrdom. He pinched me and made me cry at the first sign of faulty intonation or rhythm so that I came both to fear the teacher and hate what he was trying to instill in me. . . . I could not remember my lessons and he declared me to be inept: "Neither memory, measure, nor ear" was his verdict.

♪ Andrés Segovia, *Segovia: An Autobiography of the Years 1893–1920*

18

Learning and performance psychology are better understood today than in generations past. Many of us were taught to
rely exclusively on "muscular memory." That is, if we had to
memorize a piece, we just played it so many times that we finally
knew it "by heart." Unfortunately, that type of memory is fragile
in a stressful situation and has probably accounted for more
messed-up recitals than all other memory problems combined.
Again, the outcome had little to do with your musical ability.
You did your best, and your embarrassment was very real. It was
scary and unrewarding to perform under those conditions. You
may or may not have had support from your parents or teacher.
But you have changed. You have choices now that you didn't
have then. You don't ever have to play in another recital unless
you choose to. You don't have to play from memory unless you
choose to. And if you do, you no longer have to rely on muscular memory. (If you're curious about the options, see pages
154–158 for some new ideas on memorizing.)

*3. As far as music making in your home went, you (and perhaps
your siblings) did most of it. Your practice sessions were boring and
lonely. You couldn't really see the point of studying music.*

If you came from a home where "practice your music lesson" had the same status as "mow the lawn" and "change your
socks," no wonder you didn't stay with it! Music thrives in a musical environment. In a family where music is valued for its own
sake, the children do not have to carry the burden of fulfilling
their parents' musical longings. In a household where people
sing or improvise (even with pot lids), where people make music together, where music is a shared joy and not a solitary burden, it is easier for a child to see the point of individual practice.
Childhood lessons also tend to be more fruitful if the style of
music being learned is one that is familiar and valued at home.
Susan Raccoli, a piano teacher and parent, said, "My theory is
that piano lessons are a little bit like religion. Children do as we
do, not as we say."

*4. Your parents pushed you in one direction and your friends pulled
in another.*

The disgruntled child at the piano with a baseball glove and
bat leaning on the bench is a cliché but not a joke. As children,
lots of us felt very isolated with our music, especially if we played

In high school we had to choose—either play or sing. The "hip" thing to do was to sing. Cello was "not hip," and also it was very hard. So I let it go. I didn't touch it again until I was out of college, married, and about to have my first child.

♪ Joann Alexander, arts administrator and amateur cellist

instruments that made us feel like oddballs. It might have been cool to play the trombone in the marching band, but playing the violin (especially if you *liked it!*) usually amounted to self-imposed exile from the in-crowd. Parents swelled with pride as you polished your Mozart, but let your fingers twitch to "Mr. Bojangles" and you were in hot water. William Newman, a generous and perceptive pianist and teacher, discusses this in his book *The Pianist's Problems:* "Often, when a child shows an interest and ability in some direction, the adults around the child take pride and begin to press for productivity. The parents look good, the teachers look good, and the victim, while looking good, is losing himself to others. A spiritual crime has been committed, the effects of which the child may suffer well into adulthood. . . . There are too many adults who, instead of being enriched by their experiences with an instrument, carry within them feelings of failure and resentment."

5. You never really liked your instrument, or you never felt comfortable with it. Your first (or second or third) attempt at music making was unsuccessful or unsatisfying.

A musician in the making needs not just a good instrument, but the right instrument. After a ten-year study of the musical progress of several thousand British schoolchildren, Atarah Ben-Tovim and Douglas Boyd concluded that *"choosing the wrong instrument was the most common factor in musical failure—not lack of musicality, or musical potential."* They could find no evidence that children who gave up music were in any way less musical than those who persisted!

Some people, even very young children, seem to *know*, with absolute conviction, what kind of music they were born to make. Others, like carpenter Dick Pollard of Argenta, British Columbia, have had to search: "I spent a lot of time as a child feeling my way around, trying to find my own music. I had lessons on lots of different instruments—piano, violin, oboe, trumpet—all with mediocre results. Somewhere in there I got a guitar, and that was a turning point. My desire to make music was always very powerful, and the guitar finally opened that window for me."

Pollard's experience was unusual. Most of us were severely limited in our musical explorations, especially compared to

20

other activities. Children are commonly encouraged to try several recreational sports—swimming, volleyball, skating—or several crafts—woodworking, pottery, sewing. As long as they find something they enjoy doing, no one worries too much in the early stages about "aptitude." But if a child loses that first skirmish with the piano, the violin, the choir, or the bagpipes, someone in authority is usually quick to issue a dishonorable discharge to the recruit.

If you are ready to start making music again, you don't have to play the same instrument you used to play. The musical training you've had will stand you in good stead (as your parents always told you it would!), but now it's your turn to choose. What instrument do you love to listen to? What kind of sound moves you? What catches your eye when you pass a music store? When you know for sure you're all alone, do you sing? Do you pretend to play some particular instrument? (It's OK. We all have fantasies like that.) Why not take what you can get for that old clarinet in the closet and make a down payment on a string bass?

As you step into adult music making, you may have to find along the way a sense of release from your negative childhood experiences. Perhaps you need to write a letter to your old teacher and then burn it. Perhaps you need to speak to your own parents, in a calm and forgiving way, and find out their thoughts and feelings about your musical education. Perhaps you're ready to let go of teenage values that no longer fit your adult vision.

You will certainly discover that the face of music can change for you. You can now decide how you want to learn, and you can set your own pace. You can start over with a new instrument. You can decide to teach yourself, join a class, or organize your own group. If you choose to work with a teacher, you can search for one whose approach suits you best. (More about this on pages 59–63.)

You may have to shop around and experiment before you find a comfortable musical niche. "Failed" musicians can suddenly blossom in a shape-note singing group, an improvisatory percussion ensemble, a recorder class, a barbershop quartet, a bluegrass band, a learning support group, a beginning orches-

The difficulty I had in returning to music was dealing with assumptions from childhood—for example, that improvisation is not practice, that practice is something very serious. It's rewarding to be free of those limitations and judgments.

♪ Mitchell Kurker, massage therapist and amateur pianist

tra, or a gospel choir. No one else can define how you can best grow as a musician or how you can most openly express your musical self.

FOR ACTIVE AMATEURS

Active amateurs are the ones who have thrived as musicians, whether they started in childhood or adulthood. They are not beginning, or beginning again; they are carrying on. They already know something about the snares and something about the rewards of music making. But even established musicians, even very capable or experienced musicians, encounter obstacles that diminish their satisfaction or their growth. Giving a name to the problem is often the first step in finding a remedy. See if you recognize yourself in any of the descriptions below.

1. You feel dissatisfied with your skills or frustrated by your technical limitations.

Chapter 3 in this book will look more closely at these difficulties as they affect all amateurs. But the experienced player who feels frustrated by technical limitations needs specific self-help. He or she can often benefit enormously from a self-analysis of musical goals and purposes. Begin by asking yourself hard questions like these: "What am I making music for? What part of music making gives me pleasure? What kinds of challenges do I welcome, and what kinds of challenges are pointlessly frustrating?" The purpose of such questions is to discover which musical experiences provide, for you, the greatest meaning, the deepest connection, the most nourishing environment, the most direct route to your musical self. Some amateurs find their greatest reward as a member of a group, making a unique contribution to a collective voice. Some amateurs are drawn to plumb the solo works of great composers, seeking something of themselves in the visionary spirits of others. Some amateurs find their lives most enriched by musical tradition—by English ballads, American jazz, Hungarian folk song, African drums, capstan shanties, or calypso.

By seeking and trusting the kind of music that touches us deeply, our skills, however limited, find welcome soil. "The power of the content makes up for the simplicity of form" is how

*M*usic is, first and foremost, self-expression; without that it is a falsehood. I feel sure that a man marooned for life on a desert island would continue to make music for his own spiritual exaltation even though there were no one to hear him.

♪ Ralph Vaughan Williams, *The Making of Music*

the *I Ching* puts it. "Even with slender means, the sentiment of the heart can be expressed." Those musical endeavors that are most satisfying can become the rock on which the rest of your musical development is built.

2. You are frustrated by the lack of time for you to accomplish your musical goals.

People at either end of the experience continuum—the new musicians and the professionals—tend to be specialists, concentrating on one instrument and one style. Many experienced amateurs, in contrast, play several instruments or play in several styles or belong to several different groups. Music can easily become one of those insidious pursuits, like gardening or childrearing, where no matter how much effort you expend, you never feel as though you've done quite as much as you hoped you would.

Especially at times when other parts of their lives are busy or stressful, experienced amateurs need to think in terms of goals and priorities. It may be necessary to continue with one or two satisfying groups and let others go or to approach a major new work in very small steps or to concentrate on the trumpet for now and plan to make time for the banjo next summer. Musical time management is looked at more fully on pages 94–101.

3. You are dissatisfied or even bored with your current playing opportunities and musical outlets.

Some musicians happily play the same set of tunes year after year, whereas others in this situation grow restless. Some musicians who have studied for a long time with one teacher find themselves stagnating and need to move on. Some players with advanced skills, however much they enjoy encouraging newcomers, yearn to dig into a challenging repertoire with others who are at a comparable skill level.

You're entitled to have some musical wanderlust, to explore new terrain, and to seek your own level. Taking this sort of step, however, is not always simple. It can be hard to withdraw gracefully from a teacher you respect or from a group that has come to rely on your expertise (though rarely will a group flounder because a single individual leaves, unless that person is the leader or unless the group's future was already in doubt). Changes such as these sometimes mean weighing your commit-

When I started lessons, my life began to accelerate. I bought a ninety-year-old Steinway grand, and I took a job working permanent evenings so I could practice every morning.

♪ Andrea Bodo, nurse and amateur pianist

ment to a musical community against your own personal goals and desires. It's important not only to make changes responsibly, giving adequate notice to others who might be affected, but also to make changes compassionately, without expressing bitterness or antagonism or criticism. A musical experience that is no longer suitable for you may still be gratifying for others.

If you're ready for a change, you may have to spend some time "shopping" among groups or teachers to find one that fits your musical needs, or you may have to take the initiative to get like-minded musicians together to create something new. The effort can be well worth it, though, in terms of your own musical well-being and growth.

4. You are dissatisfied with the kind of music you make or with the instrument you play.

It's common to be strongly attracted to a particular instrument or a particular style of music. Beginners and returnees are free to choose the instrument and style that suits them best. Many experienced amateurs, though, started making music in childhood on an instrument and in a style that their parents selected. For some, as adult musicians, the drive to make music is satisfied, but the means is not always rewarding. Patrick Farenga, a publisher in Boston, started playing the saxophone at age twenty-five. He had studied piano for eight years as a child and continued playing piano as an adult but finally reached a time when, according to Farenga, "it no longer filled my musical needs. I thought about my situation and realized what an influence horn players and especially the saxophone had on my piano playing. My favorite pianists are Bud Powell, Horace Silver, and Thelonius Monk, who play a lot of their solos like horn players—one note, snakelike, bebop blues solos. Though I began the piano with classical lessons, I soon became a hard-core jazz lover, and the sax always struck me as THE jazz instrument. . . . I finally decided to take the risk."

Teachers sometimes discourage students from pursuing several instruments. Success in professional music nearly always demands specialization and a single-minded commitment. *However, amateurs need not play by professional rules.* Adding or switching instruments can open playing opportunities and answer new personal and musical needs. Beginning a new instrument is almost certain to give you a new perspective on music.

A**pril 8, 1668 . . . *thence I to Drumbleby's and there did talk a great deal about pipes and did buy a Recorder which I do intend to learn to play on, the sound of it being of all sounds in the world the most pleasing to me.*

♪ Samuel Pepys

24

Writer and political activist Michael Rossman first taught himself the recorder and then moved on to flute: "Switching to the flute freed me to improvise . . . learning to play it was learning music on a fresh ground."

By valuing our own preferences and intuition, we can discover the musical style or environment that brings out our best. Gail Bearham grew up in Edmonton, Alberta, taking classical piano lessons as a young child and then switching to pop and folk in her teens. "In the last ten years," Bearham says, "I've realized how much I love to play the piano to facilitate group singing. I'm not enough of a perfectionist to want to play for someone to listen to. My interest in music has led me to play in situations that bring people together to sing and enjoy themselves."

Making major changes in your musical focus may require that you wrestle to the ground some shadows from childhood. You may have only the vaguest sense that there's something else you'd like to try. It's all right to test things out, to make small forays into new territory. Rent a trombone for six months. Buy a self-instruction tape on blues improvisation. Find out the date of the next Old Time Fiddlers Club meeting, and show up with your violin. Sign up for a weekend workshop on madrigal singing.

5. You are dissatisfied with your amateur status and entertain regrets that you didn't enter music professionally.

The distinction between professional and amateur music is vague. Some professionals who earn too little at their music must sideline in other work. Some amateurs who work at non-musical jobs accept money for their music making. There are mediocre professionals who play with carelessness and apathy and serious amateurs who play with great depth and freshness. According to Jacques Barzun, "By applying rigorously any test of pure talent, one would find many an amateur high up among the professionals and many a professional down among the duffers."

We can idealize the professionals who stand at the peak of musical achievement; we can acknowledge the inequities that divide work-a-day professionals from accomplished amateurs; we can admit the stresses of a professional life in music; and we can fully appreciate the freedom we have as amateurs to play

My parents chose the violin and the piano for me. I picked up the viola in high school when I discovered that there were few violists and that I could get into better groups. I started singing in university because I was curious about the repertoire. And I took up the string bass when I was forty because I wanted to play something really badly and still have fun. (I succeeded on both counts!)

♪ Jane Wilson, nurse and amateur string player and singer

Music is your own experience, your thoughts, your wisdom. If you don't live it, it won't come out of your horn.

♪ Charlie Parker

The whole idea of professional music, of course, ought to be just the cream on the musicianship of the nation, what we listen to to hear how we might aspire to play.

♪ Jack McDowall, retired engineer and amateur pianist

what we wish, when we wish. And still we can have regrets. Had we decided sooner, worked harder, lived elsewhere, or had more money or a better teacher, we might have been professionals, too. Sometimes these thoughts amount to a "grass-is-greener" kind of feeling, unlikely to arise when we're actually making music, but creeping up on us when we're dissatisfied with other aspects of our lives.

The very word *amateur* has several connotations, some of them openly derogatory. *Amateur* is often used to mean the same thing as *amateurish*—"unskilled, incompetent, in poor taste." (We have a similar confusion with the words *child* and *childish*, saying "Don't be a child" when we mean "Don't be childish.") To the well-meaning who comment that a performance was "surprisingly good for an amateur," we can apply the same treatment that our professional colleagues accord simple-minded critics: *ignore them.*

It's worth remembering that professions as such are recent inventions. If you search back far enough in any culture, you will find that musicians were traditionally unpaid, just as artists, dancers, athletes, healers, teachers, and spiritual leaders were unpaid. In most ancient or traditional cultures, accepting pay for these activities was dishonorable. Only when money begins to change hands, when noble or divine callings become services or products, does the idea of "the professional" arise. Without the amateur, the professional does not exist. Professionalism in all these fields encompasses more than the issue of pay, of course, but the worthiness of the endeavor has not changed. To be a musician is still a sublime calling, amateur or not.

Among the amateurs who contributed to this book are many who actively seek new challenges and new uses for their abilities, as well as a few who have crossed over—some only temporarily—onto the professional side of the continuum.

Jennifer Davis, of Nepean, Ontario, joined a beginning recorder class twenty years ago "to have a night out when the children were small." She now shares her skill by teaching recorder part-time in local elementary schools.

Ida Kowit, of New York City, returned to her flute after a twenty-year lull and subsequently enrolled as a part-time student at Mannes College of Music, studying harmony, counter-

The amateur is the source of all culture and art . . . in the apartments of Vienna and Budapest, or on the African veldt, the plantations of the New World, the streets of Rio de Janeiro or New Orleans, it has always been the amateur around whom the living culture of the day grew up.

♪ Yehudi Menuhin, *Theme and Variations*

26

point, and ear training to prepare herself for a new career as a music teacher.

Don Mitchell, a college biology professor and accomplished violinist from Nelson, British Columbia, has used his sabbaticals to augment his musical experience. During a year at Washington State University, he supplemented his biology studies with a music history course and private lessons. While studying at the University of Saskatchewan, he joined the Saskatoon Symphony Orchestra for an eighteen-concert season.

Under the auspices of the Lafayette Arts and Sciences Foundation, amateur musicians in Lafayette, California, join with teachers and professionals to reinforce a thinly financed public school music program, working as aides and ensemble coaches in the schools.

A nurse who took a year's leave to fill a temporary post as a church organist summarized her experience by saying, "I learned a lot. Most of all I learned that I'm glad I'm a nurse. The professionals may get the money and the glory, but the amateurs get all the deep, quiet pleasure."

To be an amateur is to be, literally, a lover. An amateur pursues a thing for itself alone, not for profit, recognition, or perfection in others' eyes, but purely, as an end in itself. In many ways, there is no higher calling than that of amateur. So, be proud of your amateur status. Like politics and religion, music is too important to be left in the hands of professionals.

I would hate to think that I am not an amateur. An amateur is one who loves what he or she is doing. Very often I'm afraid the professional hates what he is doing. So I'd rather be an amateur.

♪ Yehudi Menuhin, *The Compleat Violinist*

Part Two

LEARNING

Musical form is not a series
of mysteries or trade
secrets but is simply the
development of a power
natural to the human ear
and the human mind.

Ralph Vaughan Williams

CHAPTER 3

Growing as a Musician

Music making is like happiness—it's not a place to get to but a way to go. Each of us has, as Mildred Chase says, "the right to know joy at each level of growth." This chapter will look at the ways adults grow as musicians—at their particular problems and their special rewards. First, we'll discuss the single biggest obstacle that many amateurs encounter—their own expectations. Then we'll look at the path of musical development—at patterns of progress and plateaus. Finally, we'll consider some ideas for charting your own musical journey, bearing in mind that music is a path, not a destination.

FACING OUR EXPECTATIONS

Whether we are new musicians or old hands, many of us let ourselves be frustrated by our own expectations. We feel that we should progress *faster*, that we should play *better, now*. We listen to James Galway or Kathleen Battle or Chick Corea, and we hear how short we fall. We sometimes feel we are struggling mightily to do badly something that other people do well and with ease.

It's useful to remember that a century ago we would have been fortunate to hear, even once or twice in our lives, the quality of performance now instantly available at any hour on any home sound system. Because we hear virtuosity so often, it has come to seem normal to many of us. We have several opportunities a day to realize that we will probably never sound like that. Most likely, we're right. But it's no disgrace to fall short of virtuosity. Professional ensembles and virtuoso soloists bestow on us some of the most sublime experiences of our lives. We may never equal their skill, but we can drink from the spring that is the source of their power—a spring that is fed not by spectacular technique but by a deep love for the making of music.

Comparing yourself to others misrepresents the task. Everyone's experience is different, but everyone's experience is valid. Everyone is entitled to learn, to join, to work hard, and to thrive. It's not necessary to be a world champion in order to enjoy swimming or tennis or fly fishing. It's not necessary to be a celebrated chef in order to enjoy cooking. It's not necessary to be a distinguished political analyst in order to follow global affairs. Your own music is the child of your heart and you are entitled to love it, not because it's good but because it's part of you.

As amateurs, however, many of us are distressed by our limitations, especially if we play in a competitive environment or build goals around external approval or rewards. One violinist interviewed for this book, looking back over nearly fifty years of musical experience, expressed great personal disappointment: "I wish I could agree that music making is an undiluted joy. In my case it has been a love-hate, pleasure-pain relationship which I have often contemplated abandoning. But always, like a moth drawn to a flame, I have returned, hoping to reach a level of performance I could be proud of and which would be esteemed by other musicians. I have taken lessons and practiced carefully. I have worked and I will continue to work, but I feel thwarted."

To one with distant and unreachable expectations, it may seem a distant and meager consolation, but this remains true: The honesty and love that you bring to your work is more significant than how close you come to lofty goals. "Sometimes," according to April Anderson, a forester and amateur pianist, "you realize that you're never going to be able to play the way you wish you could play. But if you think about it, you realize

Don't get frustrated comparing yourself to other musicians. The only useful comparison is yourself now to yourself last week or last year. Then you notice progress, even if it's only a little.

♪ Ron Pulcer, computer systems analyst and amateur guitarist

I've never had any professional ambitions, so anything that I do with music is for my own satisfaction. There's no sense of disappointment in that.

♪ Lynelle Inwood, homemaker and amateur flutist

Gustav Holst used to say that if a thing was worth doing at all, it was worth doing badly. I entirely agree, with this proviso—that this "doing" must be a sincere attempt toward self-expression. Superficiality, halfheartedness, sham, and swagger must have no part in the scheme.

♪ Ralph Vaughan Williams,
The Making of Music

that that's irrelevant, because you're getting so much satisfaction out of doing what you're doing right now. It doesn't have to be monumental. There's so much pleasure in doing something simple very beautifully."

It is admittedly frustrating when our feelings and knowledge far outrun our skills. We find ourselves like the traveler who has something important to say but has only a tourist's command of the language. Daniel Fredgant, a college English teacher in Milpitas, California, began to learn classical guitar when he was twenty-five. "What's hard in the beginning," he recalls, "is that your ability comes nowhere near your desires and goals. At first you can hardly even make a decent sound. But if you give it a fair chance, then every small increment of progress is rewarding—the first chord, the refinement of tone on just one note. Those successes keep you going." The joy we derive from making music as amateurs is sometimes more like finding a single wildflower in the woods than like strolling through an extravagant formal garden in full bloom.

As adults, we expect to get things done quickly. We're the generation of instant communication, fast food, rapid transit, and speed-reading. Those who persevere as musicians usually have to take stock and slacken the pace. With a background in popular piano, Yvonne McDonald, of Jamestown, North Dakota, wanted to learn to play ragtime. "I started taking lessons when I was forty-six," she says, "and I assumed that within a year I'd be able to do everything I wanted to do. Hah! Little did I know! I realize now that this is a lifelong project, but I've never regretted it. Nothing else compares to the joy I get from this music and from knowing that it will be with me for the rest of my life."

If we are beginners, we are sometimes frankly surprised at how *hard* it really is. In *The Recorder Book*, Kenneth Wollitz compares the beginning musician to the beginning ice skater. Especially if you've been watching the pros, your first time on the ice is usually "a cruel disappointment." Educator and ardent amateur musician John Holt wrote a wonderful book about his musical life called *Never Too Late*. Yet Holt actually gave up after his initial attempt at learning the flute: "To some extent I was still not psychologically or emotionally ready to play a musical instrument. I was too frightened and ashamed of my mistakes, and the possibility of making mistakes, to be able to give myself wholly to the music." He later started again, this time on the cello, and grew for himself a sustaining fascination with music that lasted the rest of his life.

The obstacle, of course, is not "out there" in that instrument or in that technique but "in here," in the way we understand and imagine the whole process. David Rogosin, a young Canadian pianist and a thoughtful teacher, encourages his adult students to realize that "it's not dumb me sitting here in front of this piano, which is holding all the music. It's rather that I'm sitting in front of this dumb instrument and all the music is in me."

ON PROGRESS

The idea of "making progress" is not equally important to all musicians. Geologist June Ryder, for example, a member of Vancouver's amateur recorder ensemble T'Andernaken, says, "I don't think of myself as progressing any more, and I don't worry about it. I am at the level where I can play the kind of music that I enjoy, and I don't have time to practice regularly." Other amateurs, however, actively seek new levels and build new repertoire, some constantly and some intermittently. Naturally, many of those who seek progress also find along the way frustration, stress, and discouragement. ("If it's so hard," asked the wife of one amateur tenor, "why does it make you so happy?")

In one way, learning music is like losing weight. If it were really easy to lose weight, everyone would be thin. If it were really easy to learn to play or sing, everyone would play or sing well. It's not always easy. But because it is a great challenge and sometimes a great struggle, it can also be a great joy.

The process of learning music and getting better at it usually seems slow. It's almost always the case that the road ahead looks ever so much longer and more tortuous than the narrow little footpath we've put behind us. What we have already accomplished usually seems ridiculously easy to us while what lies ahead seems immensely difficult. There is never an end to possibilities for musical development. The path, in fact, is a distinct spiral; we meet the same skills again and again, at progressively more complex levels.

The music is not in some instrument. The music is in you.

Technically, I'm not progressing right now, but it's obvious that as I get older, I think of music in a very different way. The experiences that I've had and just the process of maturing make me play better.

♪ Lynelle Inwood, homemaker and amateur flutist

Trying to learn how to do something that really matters to me is worth it, and if I suffer a little bit, it's still worth it.

♪ Ann MacNab, retired librarian and amateur pianist

33

Perhaps musicians can teach the rest of the human race that life is a struggle but not a war.

♪ Pete Seeger,
Henscratches and Flyspecks

One problem that many of us have with "progress" is our tendency to judge ourselves by our difficulties, by what we cannot do, by the ground we have not yet covered. When faced with a difficult passage, we think of ourselves as "bad" players, rather than as decent players facing a strenuous task. We overlook how far we have come and how well-equipped we are to continue. Barbara O'Keefe, of Cleveland, learned something about playing the harp while she was sewing her daughter's wedding dress:

> Some parts of the dress were fast and easy, but other parts, usually small inconspicuous parts, took a long, long time— the buttonholes, the hem, the hand-sewn trim. Before I made that dress, when I was learning a new piece of music, I was used to thinking, "Well, gee, I can play this whole piece except for the hard parts." But what I realized is that that's like saying, "I can make this whole wedding dress except for the hard parts."
>
> It's not that I *can't* do the hard parts. It's just that they take time. When I'm sitting at the harp, I'm making something by hand, something beautiful, something full of promise. Some parts just naturally take longer to finish than others.

The paradoxical nature of music itself can create another kind of obstacle to progress. As complete musicians, we are expected to function simultaneously in two modes—to demonstrate both control and spontaneity, both analysis and synthesis, both immaculate detail and meaningful whole. There is, in fact, some neurological evidence that an apparently low "aptitude" for music, as measured by standardized tests, may result from clinging too firmly to a single mode. This is not a simple case of "right brain" versus "left brain," since it does not appear that musical perception and behavior, especially among trained musicians, divides itself so neatly in half. According to Rosamund Shuter-Dyson and Clive Gabriel in *The Psychology of Musical Ability*:

> The former distinction between the "verbal" and the "musical" hemispheres [of the brain] is untenable. Musical stimuli of various kinds seem to be processed sometimes in one, sometimes in the other, and mostly in both hemispheres. . . . [O]n the face of it, the need is to train the student not only to

operate successfully in those two modes but to gain the practice (and pleasure) of frequently switching between them.

Some musicians imprison themselves in the analytic mode when they try to find their way into music bit by bit, perfecting one tiny task at a time. This is what some educators call *mastery learning*, where complex behaviors are broken into many discrete steps, each to be mastered individually. Although some of this kind of work feels like progress, it doesn't usually feel much like music. We also need to seek the mode of synthesis, approaching our work boldly, not in safe and tidy tidbits but as one great sweeping and sometimes reckless whole (better known in some circles as "full speed ahead and damn the torpedoes"). We might call this approach the *approximation mode*, as each complete attempt approximates the whole we are seeking more and more closely. (For some specific ideas about doing this, see the section on *mapping*, pages 178–186.) In his book *On Singing Onstage*, Broadway singing coach David Craig compares the process of learning to sing to the process of learning to drive. When you drive, you cannot decide to practice only steering or only shifting or only windshield-wiper operation. As soon as you pull into traffic, you must do it *all*. Craig continues sympathetically: "If you are a beginner, this onslaught of activities can be shattering, and everything you do seems to be poor form. Inevitably, what feels awkward will seem less so until a coordinated performance slowly emerges from the mass of discordant acts."

ON PLATEAUS

As with any other subject or skill, progress in music is never smooth and never completely gradual. For days, weeks, sometimes months at a time, you fly—you mine your talent, refine your skills, and expand your repertoire at a dizzying rate. And then comes the plateau—the days, the weeks, the months, when no matter how hard you work, no matter how aware and careful and patient and self-forgiving you are, nothing seems to change. Sometimes you feel yourself going backward, you begin to wonder why, and you get discouraged and think of taking up something else.

The most critical thing to remember at this point is that a plateau is a time of integrating and absorbing what you have previously learned and a time of preparing your body, your ear, your mind, and your spirit for the next great leap ahead. It is a time of gathering in, a harvesting rather than a growing.

Most discouraging of all are the very early plateaus when you have little repertoire to fall back on. Later you can return, review, rest, and enjoy your previous accomplishments. But with few accomplishments yet behind you, the first plateau can be a severe trial. Some teachers talk of the "three-lesson adult"—the enthusiastic beginner who quits after three lessons. In music we hit the wall fairly soon.

Sociologists say that people tend to pursue those activities that create or enhance self-esteem. It's important, therefore, to keep your plateaus in perspective. Anticipate them, and be ready to take good care of your musical self (and your other selves) while you're in the thick of one.

Here are a few tactics that amateurs who contributed to this book have found helpful for riding out plateaus:

- Spend extra time going more deeply into material that you can already play. Send search parties to the horizon. Spreading out at your current level can ease the frustration of reaching for a new one.
- Don't let a teacher push you more quickly than you are willing to go. The fact of hitting plateaus should be known and obvious to your teacher, and most sensitive teachers will offer encouragement and support. Often, a teacher who hears you only once every week or two will perceive results from your practicing that you have overlooked.
- Learn with friends. Organize a musical support group that meets regularly to share works-in-progress and to provide mutual encouragement. Find a "phone buddy"—someone you can call when you're discouraged or stuck.
- Find ways to have fun. Play by candlelight. Practice in the dark. Have an amateur potluck-and-performance party. Use a tape recorder to play duets with yourself. "What helps get through the frustration," according to amateur guitarist Max Henschen, of Indianapolis, "is to

Relieve the severity of your musical studies by reading poetry. Take many a walk in the fields and woods!

♪ Robert Schumann, *Advice to Young Musicians*

The return I get after teaching a student for a year is what I hear from the person when he or she plays the next year. You work and the student works and there seemingly is no progress, but with release from the learning process come those marvelous jumps and the next year we are working on a new level.

♪ John Perry, professor of piano, University of Southern California

find a new way to do something that you've been doing the same way forever."

- Work hard on a particularly challenging goal or piece and then leave it alone for several weeks or months. When you return to it later, some difficulties will resolve easily, and you can often bring a fresh perspective to those that remain. Many, many amateurs mentioned the value of this tactic.
- Sign up for a workshop, a master class, or a music camp.
- Treat yourself to a new music book, a new recording, or a pair of concert tickets.
- Spend an afternoon in a library browsing through books and back issues of music magazines. If you can get to a conservatory or university music library, you can probably find there journals or newsletters about your specific musical interests. (See the list in appendix 2.)
- Go shopping for a better quality instrument. You don't have to buy one, but it's fun to look, and you might collect some information you can use in the future when you're ready to trade up.
- Never underestimate the power of gold stars.
- Find someone with whom you can share what you know. Play duets with a friend. Encourage a beginner.

"Yes, I think that one suits you just fine."

KEEPING A MUSIC JOURNAL

If goals and progress are important to you, one of the most helpful documents you can keep is a music journal. This is not only a place to record when and how long and what you practiced and played—although that is certainly an important function of this kind of journal—but, more importantly, it's a place to keep insights, discoveries, feelings, frustrations, solutions, hopes, and dreams. It's a place to watch yourself grow. Kept near your practice or playing space, with a pen close by (perhaps attached to the book itself), it is ever ready to catch those "Aha!" moments as often as those "Oh drat!" ones. Why not treat yourself to a handsome blank book? Or, after looking at the suggestions on pages 97–100 for planning your practice sessions, you might decide on a three-ring binder with sections for plans, lists, ideas, principles, and—in a section by itself—your journal.

Another way to measure your progress is simply to pencil a date (include the year!) on the top corner of any page in any book you use, whether a teach-yourself theory text, a songbook for sight-reading, or a set of études. When you begin to wonder whether or not you're getting anywhere, look back at last month's or last year's dates and play through some of the work you were doing then. You'll probably be surprised.

A different sort of journal, and one that is easy to combine with a written one, is a taped log of your playing. If anything will convince you that you are making progress, a tape log will probably do it. You can keep an ongoing log by accumulating on a single tape samples of your work recorded at regular intervals, perhaps taping a portion of a practice session every week. Or you might present a miniconcert to your automated audience once a month. On ordinary home equipment the sound quality will not be outstanding, but the accuracy, fluency, and some of the expression will come through.

Many amateurs and families make tapes to share with friends and relatives, especially at holiday times. Cy Rosenthal, a mental health counselor and amateur Irish folk musician in Sturgeon Bay, Wisconsin, says, "I enjoy having tapes to show other people what I've been doing, and it also sometimes helps me realize that I'm farther along than I thought I was."

Any method we choose for marking our progress can never tell the whole story, because the real breadth of our learning defies any attempt at summary or description. As John Holt says in *Never Too Late*,

> We don't have to ask ourselves every day, "What have I learned? am I learning anything? am I learning enough?" If we're working, doing our best, challenging ourselves . . . if we are fully involved in our music making, interested in it, excited by it, then we are learning. We may not and probably cannot know all of what we are learning. We are almost certainly learning more than we think.

When we have been touched and renewed by our work, we have the surest sign that we are making the kind of progress that matters the most.

CHAPTER 4

𝅘𝅥𝅮𝅘𝅥𝅮 *Ways to Learn*

At an amateur recorder workshop in Seattle, the instructor asked how many of the thirty-five players in the room had learned to play when they were children. A few hands went up. He asked how many had taken private lessons as adults. A few hands went up. How many had taught themselves? A large number of hands. How many had learned in a class? A few hands. How many in the room were beginners, enrolled in the workshop to learn how to play? A few hands. Any other possibilities not covered? Yes. Several players had learned in music camps or other workshops, one had learned from a cassette tape series, two had learned with friends, two from a spouse, and one from her twelve-year-old daughter.

Amateur musicians have known for a long time what educators in general are now recognizing: each of us has a unique learning style, and we learn best when we learn in a way that suits our style. Some of us learn best alone, and others learn best in groups. Some of us like to find our own way, and some prefer to have a guide.

No one can learn for you, any more than a surrogate can love for you or eat for you. "To learn" is an active verb, and you as a learner are unique.

♪ Ronald Gross,
The Lifelong Learner

Most amateurs discover through the years that their musical needs and preferences change, sometimes in unexpected ways. In the course of an active life, we find a time to pick up our instrument, and a time to lay it down; a time to move ahead, and a time to look back; a time to play alone, and a time to play with others; a time to work hard, and a time to rest.

Many of us have found that it works best to begin learning in one way and to carry on in another—yet even then we don't all take the same path. For example, a string bass player interviewed for this book started with a teacher: "I thought it was important to get help at the very beginning, so I would feel sure that I was doing the basic things right. I stopped taking lessons after a year. I felt ready by then to experiment more and follow directions less." In contrast, another beginner—this one a guitarist—started by teaching himself: "I was really curious to see how much I could figure out on my own. I wasn't sure what I wanted from a teacher, so I practiced with cassette tapes until I started feeling real itchy—until I had a few good ideas and a whole lot of questions. That's when I went to a teacher."

The great advantage we have as adult musicians is the freedom to choose our own way of learning, and the great challenge is to know and accept our own learning style and our own musical desires so that we can make a fruitful choice. This chapter will look at some of the ways of learning open to us when we have decided that it's a time to learn.

LEARNING FROM YOUR INSTRUMENT

Playing an instrument is a sport in which we are dancing with an object that has a life of its own, partly yielding and partly resistant.

♪ Stephen Nachmanovitch,
Free Play

Your first and best teacher is the instrument in your hands. With no books, no tapes, no teachers of any kind, you can discover an enormous amount through patient listening, watching, and attending to the messages of your body. A teacher or a video can begin to tell you how to produce good tone, but the act of making that tone is entirely between you and your instrument, and only you have ears. Among the many ways of learning, a childlike curiosity with a willingness to experiment is one approach that benefits everyone. It's OK to "play"—to ask, "What will happen if I do this?" and then to find out.

We probably hear far too much about "conquering" our difficulties and "controlling" our instrument and "training" our bodies, as if we'd been given a whip and a chair and introduced to a surly lion. It's been helpful to many amateurs to see their instrument as their ally and to look for practical and comfortable ways of relating to this ally.

When author and educator John Holt began to teach himself to play the violin, he realized that it was "not an impenetrable mystery or a fierce enemy, but a very 'user-friendly' instrument." With often only fifteen minutes a day to practice, Holt nevertheless made pleasing progress by watching in a mirror or reflecting window as he guided his bow in a straight line. "I try to make my right arm and hand in motion *look* as much as possible like what I see when I look at the wonderful violinists of the Boston Symphony," Holt said. "At the same time, I try to keep the sound as musical and even as possible. It seems to work."

Listening *does* work. It works so well that it's strange that so many musicians do so little of it. Many of us, though, learned *not to listen* when we were children, and decades later we still find ourselves needing a teacher or a tape recording to tell us how we sound. Lynelle Inwood, a mother and homemaker in Winlaw, British Columbia, bought herself a flute when she was nineteen and learned to listen from the very beginning:

> There was no teacher where I was living, so I really had no choice. What I did was listen to a lot of flute music and get a feel for what I thought was good tone, what a good sound was. Then I'd try to figure out how to get it on my own instrument. I'd imitate the sounds that I liked. I had no theory and no technique at that time. Listening had to be the focus.

One way to deepen your own listening is to give your sounds a name. Not "this is a good one" and "this is a rotten one," but rather "this one is narrow," "this one is pointed," "this one is silky," and "this one is fat." Observe what you are doing with your body—your hands, lips, breath, spine—when you hear these different sounds.

When you listen to other people's sounds, don't be distracted by flurries of notes or feats of memory. Form a mental image of a sound and then see if you can imitate it. When you experiment with sound, the notes you're playing don't matter at first. The sound matters.

I just followed the sound that I liked. You just follow your body; I liked my instructor's sound when I was a kid in St. Louis.

♪ Miles Davis

41

If you can find some information, read about your instrument. (*Scientific American* has had good articles, now available as reprints, on the physics of various instruments. Another good source is *Horns, Strings, and Harmony* by Arthur H. Benade.) Understand, in as much detail as you can, exactly how your instrument makes sound—what is vibrating and how it is set in motion. Jesse Salazar, a lab technician and amateur jazz pianist from New York City, puzzled for months over his teacher's comment that his playing was "surfacy":

> Then I found a book about piano construction in the library. I got fascinated studying the key and hammer mechanism. It suddenly hit me that I had been aiming my fingers for the *tops* of the keys. I didn't stop to think that the sound can't begin until the key is part-way down. I was putting out the right amount of energy, but I was misjudging the distance it had to travel. I ran home and took the lid off my piano and spent the next couple of days playing with all kinds of weight, pressure, speed, angles—I just went crazy experimenting. And suddenly the thing started to feel alive under my fingers.

A superb activity for building good relations between you and your instrument is improvisation. (We'll come back to this topic on page 149.) A wonderful warm-up, which many musicians do anyway without really thinking about it, is just to wander at will around the instrument. Play your lowest notes. Play your highest. Make big sounds and small sounds. Play a lot of short fast notes and then some long, languid ones. Robin Lamb, an editor in Needham, Massachusetts, varies his warm-up routine as a way of exploring his guitar's capabilities and his own relationship to the instrument. "You can learn a lot," Lamb says, "just by trying a lot of different things systematically and listening to the result." For example, Lamb might do right-hand experiments such as these in a typical warm-up:

- Play with the right hand first close to the bridge and then close to the fingerboard.
- Play with the right hand at various angles.
- Use more or less curvature of the fingers when striking notes, on a continuum between a complete rest stroke and a complete free stroke.

Understand, in as much detail as you can, exactly how your instrument makes sound.

- Play a run or a scale several times on a continuum from legato (smooth and connected) to staccato (short and detached).
- Start with right-hand fingers resting on the strings and then start with fingers poised above the strings.
- Move the right-hand fingers from the middle knuckle and then from the knuckle where the fingers join the hand.

It's interesting to realize that when you play in this exploratory kind of way, you frequently produce passages and riffs that are technically much more difficult than anything else you usually play.

As you explore your sound, do not cling too tenaciously to techniques, ideas, or information you picked up years ago or to ways that you think it's "supposed" to be done. Be willing, always, to make your own observations, draw your own conclusions, and apply any information you collect experimentally.

TUNING: LEARN THIS FIRST

All acoustic instruments must be tuned in some way. When you tune, you select one or more pitches that your instrument can produce and match that to a standard pitch. Pianos, of course, are usually tuned by someone other than the player. Wind players don't always tune for individual playing sessions, but they do have to know how to tune to a standard pitch if they want to play with other musicians. Stringed and fretted instruments (violin, guitar, cello, string bass, harp) must be tuned accurately *every* time they're played, or the results will be disappointing.

As eager as you might be to learn how to make music, you must learn how to tune accurately at the very beginning. A more experienced player can help you. If you have persistent difficulties (not unusual for string players), a tuning lesson with a good teacher is an excellent investment. Though it can seem tedious and fussy to learn, the process of tuning your instrument can eventually become a restful, calming transition into your music making, a ritual of greeting between friends, a kind of "Hello, how are you today?"

The standard pitch you need for tuning depends on your

I picked up the fiddle again when I was twenty-seven. I just started over, right from scratch. I threw all the technique I'd ever been taught out the window, and I just played fiddle tunes. I played them too fast and out of tune and everything else. When I came up against a limitation, I'd back up and reorganize until it sounded better. Working in this way, I've learned to play the fiddle over and over and over through the years.

♪ Dick Pollard, carpenter and amateur fiddler

instrument. The common tuning notes are B♭ and F for most winds and A for strings. The standard pitch can come from a variety of sources: a pitch pipe, a tuning fork, a well-tuned piano, another instrument that's already in tune, or an electronic tuner. You can also take your own tape recorder to a teacher or another player to get a tuning tape made. This is especially useful for string players. (It's best to make your tuning tape on the recorder you will be using at home when you tune. If you make the tape on someone else's recorder, you won't get a true pitch on playback unless the speed of both recorders is identical.) The advantage of a tape or an electronic tuner is that you can get a sustained tone that doesn't fade away, as a piano or a tuning fork does, and that doesn't get impatient, as another player might.

The most accurate way to tune to a sustained tone is to listen for beats. When two tones that are slightly out of tune with each other are sounded together, they produce, in addition to their own two sounds, a third sound called *beats,* caused by the frequencies of the two tones being slightly mismatched. When two tones are perfectly in tune with each other, there are no beats. This may sound puzzling when you read about it, but you can probably learn to hear beats fairly easily. You'll need a friend to help you, or else a tape or a tuner that generates a sustained tone. Get a steady tuning pitch from your friend or from the tape or the tuner. Then match that pitch as closely as you can on your own instrument. (You can do this with voices, too.) Now begin moving your own pitch very slightly closer and very slightly farther away from the steady pitch while listening for beats. Relax your attention; don't listen to the pitches. What you're listening for is not a tone but more like a pulse or throb or fast "wah-wah-wah-wah" sound. As the pitches get farther apart—become more out of tune with each other—the beats get faster. As the pitches come nearer each other, the beats get slower until finally the two pitches are identical and perfectly in tune, producing a "beatless unison." Hearing beats is one of those things, like riding a bicycle, that comes to you all at once. You think you'll never hear it, and then suddenly there it is. A string player—violin, viola, or cello—can easily demonstrate beats for you.

Of the tuning aids available, a *pitch pipe* is inexpensive but the least reliable. An *electronic tuner* is the most expensive but also the most accurate. There are actually two very different kinds of gadgets, which are both called electronic tuners. One kind of electronic tuner does not generate a tone at all, but rather indicates the discrepancy between your tuning pitch and a selected standard pitch by means of an indicator light or a dial. Tuning by referring to a light or a dial rather than to another pitch gives the most accurate results, but this method does not train your own ear, and it doesn't build your own internal accuracy at tuning. The other kind of electronic tuner generates a tone that you listen to and match on your own instrument. You can buy simple tone-generating tuners that produce only the standard tuning pitches (A, B♭, and F) or more sophisticated ones that produce a whole range of pitches. Tuners are also available with both features—tone generation and an accuracy indicator. (Electronic tuners that generate a tone can be used in some other interesting ways. See pages 152 and 168.) Many *electronic metronomes* have a tone-generating tuner built in.

Once you're skillful at tuning, a *tuning fork* is just about the ideal tuning aid. Tuning forks are portable, accurate, and inexpensive (if you buy a small one). They don't have to be plugged in or supplied with batteries, they last a lifetime, and they're easy to find—all music stores have them. They require no maintenance, only careful use. Always strike a tuning fork against a soft surface, like your palm, never against a chair or a music stand. The biggest disadvantage to a tuning fork is that the tone produced is very quiet. It's usually easy, however, to amplify the sound by touching the stem end of the vibrating tuning fork to something resonant or hollow—try a wall or a tabletop. String players can touch the tuning fork to the bridge of their instrument.

LEARNING ON YOUR OWN

Can you really teach yourself to be a musician? Of course you can!—especially if you like to figure things out for yourself, if you think of unexpected developments as "side trips" and not "wrong turns," if you like to putter and fool around, if you enjoy not only making your own discoveries but finding ways to use them. In addition to being well-suited to a hectic or unpredictable schedule, learning on your own offers some musical

Adults who take command of their own learning often master more things, and master them better, than those who rely on being taught.

♪ Ronald Gross,
The Lifelong Learner

advantages. Self-taught guitarist Barry Kahn is now a guitar teacher himself. According to Kahn, "The good aspects of being selftaught are that I developed a very good ear, which I didn't have in the beginning; that I have an excellent musical memory, which comes from playing everything I know thousands of times; and finally that I can improvise very easily, which comes from thousands of hours of doodling aimlessly around the fingerboard."

Learning on your own does not mean learning all alone, of course. Reinforcement and encouragement are important for all musicians, and for newcomers a little bit of direction at the beginning can save you a lot of anguish by getting you started in doable steps that might not otherwise be obvious. For example, for every instrument, there's a good "beginning" key or scale— one that's easier to play in than others. One amateur fiddler started teaching herself by picking out on the piano simple fiddle tunes she knew and then finding the same notes on her fiddle. To make it easy, she played everything in the key of C because for her, as a pianist, that was the easy key. "I never felt so defeated by anything in my life," she recalls. "I was in tears over this time after time. I expected that learning to fiddle would be hard at first, but this was ridiculous. What really puzzled me was that I didn't seem to be doing anything obviously wrong." She finally phoned a local square-dance fiddler who reassured her that she was on the right track but in the wrong key. The "easy key" on the fiddle is the key of A.

Your most important ally as a musician is, of course, your own instrument. The next most useful resource for many self-taught musicians is, as this fiddler discovered, the community of other musicians—not only musicians you hear on recordings and in clubs and concert halls but also the ones who live and practice and play in your own hometown. You don't have to take formal lessons, although many amateurs alternate periods of learning on their own with periods of learning from a teacher. It's likely, though, that you'll save yourself a great deal of frustration if you're in touch with at least one sympathetic and competent player who you can turn to if you get really stuck, someone who can answer questions about tuning, fingering, tone production, instrument maintenance, and the like. Musicians on the whole are generous people and usually enjoy

Nobody ever became a great musician by reading a book. All great musicians got that way by listening to music, playing music, and talking music with fellow musicians.

♪ James Galway, flute

sharing encouragement and nuggets of practical advice, especially in settings like folk clubs, informal jam sessions, and workshops. To supplement the learning he did on his own, Michael Rossman helped organize a casual weekly gathering of recorder players (which later became the official Recorder Society of the University of Chicago): "Together we learned the simple co-operations of group effort, shared our explorations of the literature, picked up trills, alternative fingerings and niceties of phrasing from the more advanced or more recorder-literate. So we all were wrapped in a community of learning, unself-conscious, open and supportive, whose fruit was not only good fellowship but the rapid development of consort skills, the power of collective work."

When it functions this way, the musical community strongly resembles what author Frank Smith calls a "learning club," an environment with no admission fees, no papers to file, no grades, and no exams. According to Smith's model of a learning club, the more experienced members show new members what to do, what's interesting, and what's useful—all without coercion or restriction.

Other major resources for self-taught musicians—and another part of the "learning club"—are books, audiotapes, and videotapes. Most music magazines for specific instruments—such as *Clavier, Keyboard Musician, Downbeat, Guitar Player,* and *American Recorder*—carry reviews evaluating educational materials, including books and tapes for self-teaching. You can also ask a friend or a clerk in a music store to recommend materials.

Evaluating Self-Teaching Materials

It's exciting to see more and more self-instruction media being produced for all kinds of musicians. With so much to choose from, it helps to have some general guidelines for evaluating any book, system, or tape method you're interested in. The first rule of thumb is to be skeptical—or at least realistic—about extravagant claims. Becoming a skillful musician is a rewarding process, but it's a gradual one. A method that offers "music made simple" usually means exactly what it says—what you learn how to play is simple music, and that can be a wonderful way to begin. However, common sense tells us not to expect a windfall when we set out to gather skills. "Music made easy" really means the same thing as "music made simple," and we all have enough experience with instant coffee and instant banking to know what "instant music" means: something has been sacrificed, or at least postponed, in exchange for quick results.

If you want some help deciding what kinds of skills you need to learn, see chapter 6. The following criteria might be useful in evaluating self-teaching materials and matching them to your own needs:

Appropriate teaching level. If it's a method for absolute beginners, does it really start from scratch? Does it teach you how to assemble your instrument? How to tune it? How to put your body and hands in playing position? If any music-reading skills are required, does the method teach them, or does it assume you know how to read already? A method that omits a basic skill is not necessarily a poor choice, but it does mean that you'll have to look elsewhere for some help if you need it. A well-done method will be explicit about any skills you're assumed to have already. For example, Ward Cannel and Fred Marx have written a deservedly popular book called *How to Play the Piano Despite Years of Lessons.* The book's introduction is called "Who Is Allowed to Read This Book," and it specifies that the book is intended for people who can find middle C and "pick out a single-note, one-finger tune—no matter how badly."

Playable music at the beginning. The pieces or songs given early should be selections that you can actually play fairly soon. If it's a beginning-level method, the music should look or sound very simple at first. If it's a more advanced method, it should begin with something reasonably within your reach. Initial success is crucial for building confidence and motivation. If Lesson One requires six months of hard slogging before attempting the first piece, not many people will ever get to Lesson Two.

Accessibility of information. Some methods teach you how to play; some methods show you how other people play. This distinction is most important at the beginning level. Someone who already plays the guitar pretty well can listen to a tape or read a sheet-music transcription of a great blues performance and pick up some useful tips. But a course called "How to Play Blues" that is full of taped or transcribed performances should really be called "How Other People Play Blues" and is of limited use to a beginner. Hundreds of instructional videotapes are available featuring well-known jazz, blues, rock, and pop musicians. Many of these tapes are entertaining and provide an hour's worth of revealing glimpses into how one performer plays and thinks about music. But a fabulous player is not necessarily a fabulous teacher. Many of the tapes by famous musicians assume a fairly sophisticated level of knowledge, even though the tapes themselves may be advertised as suitable for "beginners to professionals." That tag in itself should alert you to proceed with caution, especially if you're a beginner looking for instruction in basic skills. You need models, of course, and there's a great deal to learn from the masters of any art. But a beginner's teach-yourself method has to do much more than display the finished product.

Emphasis on principles and skills.   Good teaching shares freely with the student the principles and skills that the student needs to carry on independently. If a book, tape, or method mainly teaches pieces by rote—that is, by asking you to imitate and memorize pieces note by note—you will eventually be able to play only the method's pieces (although you may become very skillful at rote learning in the bargain). Rote learning is not wrong, but a steady diet of it sometimes results in dissatisfaction later on. "I didn't feel like a musician" is the way one amateur pianist put it. "I felt like a music box. Wind me up and I could play six different tunes." However, if you are learning some technical skills, and perhaps some improvisational techniques, and perhaps some note reading or theory or principles of harmonization, then you are being set free from the boundaries of the method to pursue your own music. (See the section beginning on page 82 for a discussion of specific musical skills.)

Book, Audiotape, or Video?

The quality of self-teaching materials is definitely improving, so the medium you choose really depends on your own learning style, budget, and personal preferences. If you relate comfortably to books and written instructions in general, and if you're especially interested in learning to read music, then a book is a good choice. Compared to other options books are inexpensive, and they're also the easiest to evaluate, since you can stand in a music store and leaf through them—something you can't usually do with a tape. The big disadvantage of books is that they can never give you a sample of the sound you're after, and so they can fall too easily into what William Newman, in *The Pianist's Problems*, calls "glib generalizations that cannot be translated into practicalities."

If you're selecting a book for self-teaching, be sure that you get one that's written for that purpose, or else be sure that you can get help if you need it. *Most instructional books sold in music stores are intended to be used with a teacher.* Many of these books don't tell you enough to let you proceed on your own with confidence. Books designed for self-teaching usually state the fact explicitly on the cover or in the first page or two.

Learning from an audiocassette or a video has the enormous advantage of giving you a model to hear. With a book, you sometimes never feel completely sure that you have it right. A video adds the further reinforcement of a visual model, so you get a clear idea of posture, position, and how movements on the instrument relate to the sounds and to the printed music.

One disadvantage of taped methods is that they're hard to evaluate in advance, except by reading reviews or asking others. Some companies, like Homespun Tapes, will sell separately the first tape of a set, so that you can see if you want to carry through with the whole series. Another problem with tapes is inconvenience. It is rarely enough to listen to or watch a tape once through. Really using a tape means constantly rewinding and replaying very short sections. Some people don't mind that, but it drives others wiggy. Also, books and audiotapes can be used anywhere, but video players are usually fixed in one spot, which may or may not be a good one for your learning sessions.

Self-teaching materials in general are endlessly patient—you can always go at your own speed. However, they are notoriously unresponsive. You can reread or rewind all you like, but you can never ask a question. The person on the tape will never witness your puzzled look and say, "Well, then, let's try that another way." Music, like mathematics, can be explained in many,

many ways. There's a tendency to take a book, a cassette voice, or a video personality as being more authoritative than is the case. The author or performer may be an authority, but there is always another way to do it, another way to explain it, another way to play it.

One way to sidestep some of the individual limitations of self-teaching methods is to use more than one. Work from two books or with one book and one tape series, for example, on the same level and style. You'll likely learn things in a different order from each, and there may even be a stretch of time when all seems confused and in conflict. Chances are good, though, that if you stick with it, they'll catch up with each other and meet you in the middle, and you'll probably bag an "Aha!" big enough to last you for a week or more.

If you're budget conscious, you might like to do a cost comparison of music teaching methods. Costs for tapes, books, and lessons vary widely, of course, but it's possible to come up with a rough measure of the relative cost. The following brief guide is based on prices current at the time this book was written:

- Audiotapes cost about one-third to one-half as much per hour as private lessons.
- Videotapes range in cost from about the same price per hour to about about 50 percent more per hour than private lessons.
- Self-teaching books are equal to or much less than the cost of a single private lesson.
- Group lessons are usually substantially less per hour than private lessons—somewhere between one-half and one-tenth the hourly cost.

A relative cost comparison doesn't tell the whole story, though. You must also weigh the *value* per hour or per dollar. The video- and audiotapes that are truly suitable for complete beginners tend to cover about as much or slightly more material per hour than could be covered in an hour of private lessons. Therefore, it's roughly accurate to say that instructional audiotapes cost, at the most, about half as much as private lessons, and instructional videotapes cost about the same as private lessons or somewhat more.

Self-teaching books, however, tend to cover "more ground per dollar" than either lessons or tapes. In other words, they contain more information between their covers than a private teacher could get through for an equivalent cost. A good self-instruction book, such as Ann Collins's *Lead Lines and Chord Changes* for piano or Frederick Noad's *Solo Guitar Playing*, could easily keep a diligent student busy for a year, which makes each book an unparalleled bargain.

On the whole then, it appears that audiotapes and books are cheaper than private lessons—*but only if you use them.* Just as they will patiently repeat material many times over, they will also patiently sit on your shelf, doing you no good whatsoever. Any motivation to use them comes from your own success with them. Self-instruction materials work for some amateurs, but for others there's nothing quite as motivating as a regular appointment with a teacher or a group.

LEARNING FROM LESSONS

Among the amateurs who contributed to this book, the ones who take lessons nearly all chose that route for the same basic reason. In the words of Daniel Fredgant, "Taking lessons is important for an undisciplined person like me because it's an external force that encourages me to practice." Many lesson-takers felt that their teachers' standards were probably higher than the standards they themselves would accept if they worked on their own.

Taking lessons means choosing a teacher, of course, and that's discussed in chapter 5. The choice is an important one because of the second good reason for taking lessons: modeling. Even for self-taught players, modeling goes on whenever they see or hear someone else playing. You might have experienced for yourself the deep impact of another person's influence if you've ever gone on a binge of listening to one artist or reading one author or watching one athlete and then found that person's style creeping into your own behavior.

Modeling happens constantly, and whether it's good modeling or poor modeling, it's irresistibly effective. That's one reason why your choice of teacher is so important. If you study with

More than any single experience, it was listening to Jimmy Rowles play the piano that marked the crucial turning point in my progress toward competent play in the fourth year. . . . His special sense of time was sufficiently distinctive to make him a difficult player to readily imitate. But I found that I could get much of his breathing quality into a song's presentation by trying to copy his ways.

♪ David Sudnow,
Ways of the Hand

one person for very long, you will begin in some ways to sound, sit, breathe, and phrase like that person. A skillful teacher takes advantage of modeling without taking advantage of the student. Never be afraid to imitate a model you respect. As your own powers grow, you will know when to leave the imitation behind. Beware only of feeling *obliged* to imitate.

Next to discipline and intense modeling, the third quality that amateurs appreciate about regular lesson-taking is guidance. Many amateurs said they relied on their teachers to organize and encourage their progress, to "know what I need to know next and make sure it gets done."

Lessons with a private teacher usually require a substantial commitment of time, money, and energy. Group lessons, however, are an informal, inexpensive, and short-term way to test your interest, as well as a fine place to meet other musicians. Check catalogues of courses offered by city recreation departments, school districts, college and university continuing education programs, Elderhostels, music schools and conservatories, and organizations such as recorder guilds, folk clubs, and jazz societies.

Most group classes are at the beginning or elementary level. The most commonly offered courses are guitar, recorder, fiddle, voice, and keyboards. Some communities also have a preparatory band or orchestra where people of any age can come to learn an instrument. Ken McDougall, a farmer and retired accountant from Appledale, British Columbia, found the regular Tuesday night Winlaw Community Band repertoire too difficult during his first year on the clarinet:

> I finally told the band director that I just couldn't keep up and he said, "Well, if you won't feel too out of place, why don't you come in the afternoon and play with the Junior Band." So I did that. I didn't feel out of place at all, going to the school and sitting in with the kids. We were all beginners together. The music was very easy. They didn't go fast. I really got into it. I was finally playing notes. A year later I moved up to the Intermediate Band. I kept progressing, playing harder music and making more sense of it all. Last spring I went with the Intermediate Band on their trip to Spokane—three other adults and I played with them—and we just had a ball.

The invitation to take the first steps should be presented in such a way that everyone can take that step; in other words, it should present the lowest threshold to participation.

♪ Peter London, *No More Secondhand Art*

A friend of mine plays the oboe and she told me about CAMMAC. Until then I had no idea that there was an organization of people who were doing music at all kinds of levels. It had always seemed a very elitist thing in my mind—you had to start young and you had to be very good at it. Then I visited her at a CAMMAC camp one summer, and I saw these—well—ordinary people doing these extraordinary things.

And now I'm coming to CAMMAC and playing with those people. They don't even mind if you're not very good! This is my week away, by myself, doing what I love to do.

♪ Lucy Melzack, special education teacher and amateur cellist

I came away from that workshop with a few hot tips and a whole lot of inspiration. It's made me realize that the way to keep the music going is to keep going to workshops.

♪ Dick Pollard, carpenter and amateur fiddler

The main disadvantage to group instruction is that all students must move along at about the same pace, and some inevitably spill over on the sides of "too fast" and "too slow." Group instructors are aware of this and can usually think up more challenging work for some, while making life easier for others. This disadvantage is far outweighed by the camaraderie that a group offers, especially to uneasy beginners, and also by the price, which is likely to be far below private lessons. If you decide you don't like the instrument, it's usually easier to withdraw from group instruction than it is to leave a private teacher. But if you do like it, group instruction is a good jumping off place. If you want to go on, the instructor may organize a continuing class or recommend a teacher. You'll also have ensemble partners to call on.

OTHER WAYS TO LEARN
Workshops, Camps, and Master Classes

For any amateur musician—rank beginner through near-professional—a workshop, summer camp, or master class can be a wonderful place to make new contacts, learn new technique and repertoire, and generally soak up a rich musical atmosphere. You can find out about workshops by checking magazines for your instrument or for your kind of music (see appendix 2). Lists begin to be published in late winter, and many workshops fill up quickly, so you may have to make plans early.

Workshops and camps have various offerings and requirements. Some are for advanced players, and some are for beginners. Some are open to all, some require an audition (usually submitted on cassette tape), and some ask for a "placement tape"—a sample of your playing level so that workshop organizers can select appropriate music and arrange groups.

Weekend and daylong workshops are generally intense and music-packed, but weeklong or longer camps and workshops vary tremendously in their focus. Some are high-octane; others are leisurely. You can get an idea of the focus by studying the course offerings and schedule. Lots of time devoted exclusively to music making and coaching plus long hours and multiple spaces available for practice are good clues to a musically intense camp, whatever the level. A leisurely schedule, with nonmusical offerings such as crafts and sports, a long afternoon break for relaxation, and limited hours available for practice, points to a more social atmosphere. Homemaker Rochelle Stoddard was surprised—and at first unnerved—by the intensity of a five-day vocal workshop:

> On the second evening I skipped supper so I could hide in my room and cry—"I don't want to be here. I can't do this. The music is too hard. They expect too much. I wanna go home. Wah!"
>
> On the last evening, I was in tears again, but this time it was, "I don't want to go home! I want to stay here forever. I want to live like this and sing like this for the rest of my life!"
>
> It was hard—*very, very hard*. I've never been so challenged, so desperate, so wrung out, so ecstatic. I leapt up five years in just five days.

A workshop or camp can transform your way of music making by pushing you hard within a totally supportive environment. Eric Stumacher, pianist and executive coordinator of the Apple Hill Center for Chamber Music in East Sullivan, New Hampshire, talks about a blend of "challenge and safety"—the stronger the safety net, the more challenge you can accept. Other musicians know better than anyone else what you're going through, and the encouraging spirit at a music camp's final student concert is often electrifying.

Correspondence Courses

Isaac Stern once said that learning music by reading about it is like making love by mail. Let's not ask what he would say about actually learning music by mail! However, if you look in the most recent edition of *Peterson's Independent Study Catalog*, found in the reference section of many libraries, you'll find listings from the U.S. colleges and universities that offer correspondence courses in music. The course offerings change from year to year, so we can't include an up-to-date list here, but in the past Brigham Young University has offered beginning guitar, the University of Minnesota has offered ear training and sight-singing, the University of Nebraska has offered beginning piano, and the University of Wisconsin has offered music the-

I was in Calgary for eight days, and while I was there I had four lessons on the clarinet and four lessons on the saxophone. I got so much help, so much information from this fellow. He watched me as I played, and he could see where my fingers weren't covering the holes. He showed me how to change the presentation of my hands on the instrument, and that made such a big difference. He gave me lots of encouragement on the saxophone.

♪ Ken McDougall, retired accountant, farmer, and amateur clarinetist

ory. Many institutions offer courses in music appreciation and music history. Some courses carry college credit, and some are noncredit.

The One-Chance Lesson

At times, you may have a chance to have a single lesson or a group of closely spaced lessons, perhaps as part of a workshop, perhaps with a private teacher. Musicians who live in small towns and rural areas with no teacher nearby sometimes arrange to meet with a teacher for a lesson whenever they are in a city.

Setting some kind of agenda is a good idea at the beginning of this sort of lesson. You might also want to keep a notebook and pen handy or to take a tape recorder and a blank tape. In the days before your lesson, jot down some topics you'd like to cover. For example, you might consider asking for

- basic help with your instrument—assembly, adjustment, simple repairs. (Mention any problems you've had. Ask the teacher to check your tuning technique.)
- an assessment of your tone quality and some ideas for improving it.
- help with your playing position, posture, embouchure, breath control, hand shape, or bow hold.
- suggestions for books, tapes, music, and study material.
- suggestions for practice techniques and routines.

Ad Hoc Learning

Sometimes, someone with an intense desire to learn will begin with one or two special pieces, asking a teacher or musical friend to show how they're played, or learning them note-by-note from a recording. For lack of a better name, we'll call this *ad hoc learning*. The process of learning to play these special pieces is often a rewarding, if frustrating, task. Alan Kay, a Fellow with Apple Computer and an amateur keyboard player, began that way: "I think it's what lots of adults do. You take some pieces that you really like and just concentrate like mad on them. You can wind up learning how to play them, but you actually haven't learned how to play, and in fact you're generally

Once I was approached with an extraordinary request from a young Canadian. . . . She wanted piano lessons. I said very well, but what for? She said she would like to play the A-flat Ballade of Chopin. I agreed and asked her to play it. She said she did not know how to play the piano. I was amazed. She said she would practice until she knew it. . . . She knew she could never play it well, but wanted to play it the best she could. . . . So I played it for her, note by note, finger by finger, phrase by phrase. I told her every finger to move. It was a long way, but she finally played it. It was a representation of great love, great confidence.

♪ Nadia Boulanger

very stiff and mechanical. Anything will throw you off. It's like a total house of cards."

Ad hoc learning is pure rote learning, and the limitations are the same as described on page 49—an absence of the essential basic skills and principles that allow the musician to play independently. Yet, as limiting as an ad hoc beginning is in many ways, it is still a beginning, and if it draws you into a wider realm of music making, the music has done its work admirably.

CHAPTER 5

🎵 Learning with a Teacher

After the birth of our sixth child, I started thinking, gee, I'd like to sing again. I started taking lessons with a teacher my parents knew. I had another child after that—we've raised seven children—and I've studied music without a stop ever since. My youngest is twenty-three now.

♪ Julianne Kelly, fabric store owner and amateur singer

Most amateurs are self-taught some of the time, and some are self-taught all of the time, but many of us who have tried learning to play on our own end up agreeing with James Galway: "There are certain things which you can teach in a book, and there are certain things which you can't teach in a book. And one of these last is music."

The decision to start taking lessons isn't always a simple one, especially for people with busy lives. Eric Stumacher, a concert pianist and teacher, asks four questions of prospective students. Try these on yourself:

1. Do you love music?
2. Are you willing to practice consistently? (Stumacher suggests one to two hours a day, five days out of seven. A beginner would practice less initially.)
3. Are you willing to make a commitment to study for at least six months, and preferably for two years?
4. Are you willing to be patient with very gradual progress?

If you've answered YES to these four questions, then answer one more before you start looking for a teacher:

5. What are your goals in studying music?

All teachers have their own particular musical strengths and specialties. When these match the student's goals, the relationship is more likely to start off on the right foot and go in the right direction. Here's a list of a dozen goals to start you thinking:

1. To play for your own enjoyment.
2. To make music with others—to play duets, to accompany others, to join a band or orchestra.
3. To improve your current level of playing.
4. To work on specific problems—intonation, tone production, relaxation, breath control.
5. To enlarge your current repertoire.
6. To explore the repertoire (a respectable goal for an amateur with some skill but limited practice time—a kind of guided sight-reading).
7. To prepare for a concert, recital, or audition.
8. To learn to read music.
9. To improve your sight-reading ability.
10. To learn to play in a particular style—blues, folk, popular, classical, ragtime.
11. To learn to improvise.
12. To play by ear—to be able to pick out tunes without sheet music.

If you're a beginner and feel as if you don't know what your goals are yet, remember that beginning is a goal in itself, and there are teachers who specialize in teaching beginners.

FINDING A TEACHER

Eastern wisdom says that when the student is ready, the teacher appears, and Western musical life often bears this out. For a surprising number of music students, the right teacher materializes at the right moment. If you've been this lucky, you can skip this section (for now—you may want to change teachers someday). But if you're ready and there's no teacher on the horizon, here's how to give providence a nudge.

Making Contact

Word-of-mouth has long been the customary way of finding a teacher, and reasonably so. Music thrives in a social network: musicians know other musicians and are happy to make recommendations. Try asking a member of an orchestra or band, another amateur, a school or church music director, or parents of children who study music. Read the notices and talk to the staff in instrument repair shops and music stores. (Music store proprietors often still know their clientele in the way that good tailors and butchers used to.) Some college and university music departments and conservatories have extension services for nonprofessional students and ensembles.

Many private music teachers put ads on bulletin boards and in the papers in August and September, when they enroll their school-age students. A few private teachers are listed in the Yellow Pages, under Music Instruction, along with private music schools and studios. As you consider possibilities, remember that not everyone who can play music can teach music. The supply of good teachers is surprisingly large and varied, but it pays to probe a little before you decide.

Wherever you look, look for the best. Never settle for mediocre teaching because you're an amateur or "just a beginner." You deserve to take yourself as seriously as any parent takes a musical child. You and the teacher both know that you probably won't become a virtuoso or even a professional, but most children who study don't reach that level either. Very few teachers teach because they want to polish stars.

When you phone a prospective teacher, explain briefly your musical level and goals. You may find that the teacher is booked up (ask if she has a waiting list) or specializes in some area that isn't appropriate for you (ask for a referral to another teacher). When you find someone who has an opening, set up a lesson if you know the teacher or if you've had good reports from the musical grapevine. If you don't know anything about the teacher, though, set up an appointment for an interview rather than a lesson. You might also ask if it's possible to observe another student's lesson. (Don't be offended if this request is turned down. A music lesson can be a very private, personal time between a student and a teacher.)

Music lessons are costly—not only in money, but also in time and personal energy. The relationship between a music teacher and a student is often a peculiarly intense one, and once it begins it can be awkward to change it or end it. By conducting an interview before committing yourself to lessons, you can often avoid making a mistake. You can also make discoveries you might not make for a long while once you step into the role of student.

The Interview

Before you meet a prospective teacher, jot down some questions you'd like to discuss. Here are a few to consider, along with some ideas for evaluating the teacher's responses.

What are your goals as a teacher? What musical styles, skills, and values does this teacher emphasize? Do the teacher's goals match your own? Does the teacher seem flexible or dogmatic about these goals?

What is your training? Framed diplomas from important institutions may mean a great deal or nothing at all. Listen for the teacher's attitude about his own training, the value he gives it, the respect and enthusiasm you detect for the teacher's teachers. Those who teach well have almost always been well-taught themselves. The best teachers tend to be individuals who have had to work especially hard. According to Yehudi Menuhin,

> Someone who has been accustomed to playing well all his life, who has had great talent from childhood onwards, may rely mainly on instinct and intuition. He may never have had to analyze and eradicate defects of technique, and so has never discovered intellectually the basic principles. . . . A performer of modest ability who has had to analyze and struggle to achieve technique . . . may turn out to be one of the best teachers.

I loved the sound of the cello, and my friend Dorothy kept saying, "When you're ready, I've got a teacher for you." This went on for two years, and one day—I was turning fifty—I decided I didn't want to be old and full of regrets and say, gee, I should have done that. So I said, "Dorothy, I'm ready. If it doesn't work out, I'll stop."

I spoke to him on the telephone. I wanted to make sure he knew how old I was and that I was an absolute beginner. He was the most charming guy. He had coffee waiting for me at my first lesson.

I'm not very good. But I practice, and I always come to my lesson prepared. And I love it.

♪ Lucy Melzack, special education teacher and amateur cellist

What is your performing experience? A musician can lack the technique and confidence for a performing career and still be a virtuoso teacher. Nevertheless, some performing—either as a soloist or in ensembles—is an asset; it indicates a level of preparation and thoughtfulness about music that a nonperformer may not have.

Do you follow any particular method or approach? Some teachers follow a highly systematized method of instruction. The Suzuki method is the most familiar example. If your prospect uses a specific method, ask about the method's philosophy. Ask why the teacher uses it, what kind of training she's had, and how appropriate it is for an adult learner. If you already know how to play, ask if you can enter the method at your current level or if it's better to start at the beginning. If the method is a logical route to your goal, if you feel comfortable with the structure and receptive to the philosophy, then the match can be a fine one. But if you, as a learner, work best in a flexible setting and like to be a partner in planning your own path, you might prefer a teacher with a more flexible approach—one who fits her teaching to the student and not the other way around.

What is your teaching experience? How long and how many students? Any experience teaching adults? Experience alone is no guarantee of quality, since experience benefits only those who learn from it. If your prospect has taught for many years, listen for a corresponding openness to growth and change. A young or new teacher can be a delight if both parties have an open and collaborative spirit, so don't base your judgment on this criterion alone.

What other musical activities are you involved in? Does the prospective teacher study with anyone, take master classes, or attend summer workshops? Is he engaged in any personal research, repertoire study, or preparation for a performance? Does he direct or play in any ensembles, play in clubs, compose, give recitals, make music with his family or friends? Musicians who love music do more than teach. Listen here for the message that music is not just a way to make a living.

Why are you teaching? Do you like to teach? How do you feel about teaching adults? These are trick questions, in a way. The fact is that many musicians would rather not teach. Some are born teachers, but many are made teachers by necessity—by the mortgage, the car, the kids' shoes. This doesn't mean that a teacher-by-default is a poor choice. Just listen for a sense that the person loves music, likes to see other people learn, and knows how to help that happen. That's enough.

In addition to the questions listed above, ask questions about practical details.What times are available for lessons? (Many teachers reserve weekday afternoons for children. If you can come at another time, you may be able to study with someone who is otherwise booked up.) Is the teacher willing to make flexible arrangements to fit your schedule? Although most children have weekly lessons, many adult students have lessons every other week, once a month, or in "clusters" at a time when they're most able to practice.

What are the fees, how are they paid (weekly, monthly, by the term), and what is the policy about missed lessons? Do a little checking around to find out the going rate for music lessons in your area. Don't expect to get a bargain. As a matter of fact, be wary of someone who charges substantially less than the going rate. Ask—tactfully—for an explanation.

Making a Choice

When you evaluate your prospective teacher, take seriously your intuitive impressions. Did you like the person? Did you detect enthusiasm, a sense of humor, and imagination? Did she communicate clearly? Was she interested in your goals, your needs, your preferences? Did you find the kind of personality you respond to well as a learner? Remember that there's no such thing as an ideal teaching personality. Amateurs have given top-notch marks to every kind of teacher, from the "cream-filled cupcake" to "Attila the Hun."

If you had a chance to observe a lesson, was the teacher patient and positive? Were explanations clear? Is he, as far as you can tell, competent at his instrument?

Of all the titles applied to me, I like "teacher" best of all.

♪ Gregor Piatigorsky

I would play better today if I had liked my first piano instructor.

♪ Maureen Forrester, *Maureen Forrester: Out of Character*

I wanted to find somebody that wasn't too threatening. The teacher I started with wasn't a fabulous cellist, but she was really good for me. She was so encouraging.

♪ Joann Alexander, arts administrator and amateur cellist

63

LESSONS BEGIN—A TRIAL PERIOD

Consider suggesting to your new teacher that you commit yourself initially to a set of trial lessons—four to six would be a good number—to see if this is something you'll like and to see if you'll be able to fit lessons and practicing into your schedule. In fact, six lessons are not enough to make firm judgments about these matters. However, if you initially commit to only six lessons, you'll have a way to make a graceful exit if you change your mind or if the relationship is an obvious mismatch.

A lot of musical work can take place during this trial period, and the success of it depends heavily on the rapport between you and your teacher. One dictionary defines *rapport* as "a relationship marked by harmony." How apt. As the student, your tasks right now are obvious:

Practice.   Do your best to practice for the amount of time you and your teacher decide is appropriate, and practice specific points in the way your teacher suggests. If the purpose of some practice assignment is unclear, ask about it. Don't assume it's unimportant.

Communicate.   If you don't understand, ask. If you don't remember, ask again. If you're upset, worried, confused—speak up. Share information about any physical difficulties—poor vision, joint stiffness, respiratory problems. This is the time to express both your long-term goals and your immediate needs.

Stay open.   Have faith in your teacher's skill and in your potential. Give it a real try before giving up.

Be patient with gradual progress.   In this initial period, you may strain to detect any progress at all. If you're a beginner, you might find that music making is more difficult than you expected. If you've played before, and if your teacher begins by suggesting major changes in your technique, you might feel that you're going backward. However, don't be discouraged. Spend extra time on those musical tasks that you especially enjoy, and for the rest of it—well, be patient. As composer and bassist Jerry Walker says, "Don't fear *slow*. Just fear *stop*."

I tell students that there's no quick fix here. But there is something about the gradual process of learning to make music that is profoundly important and rewarding.

♪ Eric Stumacher, concert pianist and teacher, Apple Hill Players

I was worried at first. I figured, this might be a little too much for me. I didn't know, at my age, if I could handle it. Would I have the inclination? Would I have the musical ability and the discipline? I guess I've made it this far because I'm someone who just doesn't give up. Anything I do, I give it a pretty good whirl.

♪ Ken McDougall, retired accountant, farmer, and amateur clarinetist

Your teacher actually bears the major responsibility for rapport building in this initial period, especially in the case of an apprehensive or self-conscious student. (Many adults, by the way, fall into this category. Don't be hard on yourself if it happens to you.) The teacher's tasks are listed here in the form of questions; use them to do an informal evaluation at the end of the first four or six weeks, or whatever period seems reasonable to you.

Does the teacher help you feel at ease?   Is the atmosphere calm and unhurried? If you're a beginner, has the teacher explained your instrument and demonstrated assembly, care, basic maintenance, and tuning? Does the teacher encourage your own questions and input? Does he treat you like an adult— with dignity, courtesy, and no condescension?

Does the teacher create a supportive atmosphere?   A skillful teacher knows how to evaluate without being discouraging. You should hear positive messages right from the beginning: "Your tone was brighter that time. Play it again with your elbow here, and see how that changes it." If you're going home from your lessons feeling humiliated, something is wrong. Talk it over if you can. If things don't improve soon, shop for another teacher.

Does the teacher give you opportunities to succeed?   In the early stages—especially for a beginning student—a good teacher will concentrate on things that you can do well right away. Initially, your assignments may seem disappointingly simple—one easy tune, one phrase, one note. The point of such an instructional approach is to seek out the skills you already possess and draw you forward from there.

Are you getting clear information about posture, playing position, breathing, and release of tension?   It is much easier to build good playing habits than to change poor ones. A teacher who does not help students play in a comfortable, natural, and tension-free way is negligent.

Does the teacher show you how to play?   Be sure you're going to a lesson and not a recital. There's a big difference

He was an ideal teacher for me then. He saw that for all my lack of musical knowledge, experience, or skill, I loved music and was ready to fall in love with the cello, and that it was his task as my teacher to help me do it. How welcome he made me feel!

♪ John Holt, *Never Too Late*

Sometimes you play a passage and you think, "This is no good because I'm no good and I can't do this," but that's never the truth. The truth is, "There is a way I can do this if somebody could explain it to me." That's where a good teacher will step in and say, "It can sound like this. You can play it this way."

♪ Joann Alexander, arts administrator and amateur cellist

between a demonstration and a display, between showing how and showing off.

AN EVALUATION: YOUR TEACHER, YOURSELF, YOUR RELATIONSHIP

By the end of six months or a year, it's time for a serious evaluation. Even long-standing teacher-student relationships benefit from periodic review. Many musicians, including those at the beginning level, move on to a new teacher at some point, not because their old teacher is inadequate but because the student is ready for a new challenge, a new approach. The questions you asked during the trial lessons (pages 65–66) are still appropriate, but now there are some additional ones:

Are you growing musically? Your progress may be slower than you expected, but after six months to a year you should have a clear sense of achievement. This issue is often delicate and needs goodwill and open communication from both of you. A teacher who goes too fast eventually takes students out of their depth technically and creates needless frustration. A teacher who goes too slowly offers no challenges and no rewards. If you think you haven't made any progress, try playing some music that you were working on when your lessons began. If you made a tape of yourself then, listen to it now. You may be surprised at how far you have come.

Does your teacher continue to recognize and help you realize your goals? You may not have fulfilled your goals yet, but it should be clear that you're on your way and that your teacher continues to be receptive to your ideas. Terry Mayor, of Damascus, Maryland, reflecting on several years of piano study, asks, "If you hire someone to help you learn something, who's in charge? Should the student look over the teacher's store of knowledge and focus on what seems meaningful? Or should the teacher dictate completely what is learned and how and when? Somewhere in the middle? I don't know, but I do know that learning can't be forced. Students have to be accepted for who

You don't have to be ruthlessly ambitious but it's essential not to stand still. The ones who succeed are the ones who can pick up and move on to the next teacher they need to learn from.

♪ Maureen Forrester, *Maureen Forrester: Out of Character*

they are and for what they're willing to do."

Sticky dilemmas sometimes come up when the teacher is teaching a style that doesn't match the student's goal—classical style, for example, when you want to play rock or ragtime. No teacher *intends* to hold you back. However, it may be that the teacher's skills at your preferred style are not well-developed. Music teachers love best the music they know how to make, and that kind of music is also what they know how to teach and what they think is important. This issue arises most frequently when students taking classical lessons know, or discover later, that they want to work in some other musical style. Classical study can do a lot to help establish your basic musical skills and knowledge, but if classical style is not your preference, the time will come when you will either want to supplement your lessons with other activities or else move on to a different teacher. There's no point in blaming either yourself or your teacher if you're not getting what you want. It is ultimately your responsibility to assess the value of your lessons in light of your goals. Try consulting with someone who plays well in the style you prefer. If you can be candid with your teacher about this, ask for some suggestions for extra materials you might work with or for the name of another musician who could give you some guidance.

Do you feel capable and optimistic most of the time? Laying aside your worst periods of discouragement (they happen to everyone), you should have a sense of solid accomplishment behind you and of new possibilities ahead. No matter what your playing level, you should never feel you're "no good." Bryan King, second violinist with Canada's Purcell String Quartet, spends several weeks each summer with his colleagues coaching amateur players in music camps and workshops. In his approach, King expresses a confidence in adult players that sets a standard for good teaching:

> Amateur musicians are wonderful people. It's the people we like—it doesn't matter how they play. Personally, I'm finding out that if people can't do something, there's a reason why they can't do it, and it's not because they're bad or they haven't practiced or they don't want to. People want to do

It took me a while to leave my first teacher. I thought, "She's been so nice to me. Who am I to think I need a better teacher?" We'd become friends. It all felt very awkward. But when I finally told her that I wanted to study with this teacher at Ohio State, she said, "That's fine. You're ready. It makes sense." She was very gracious about it.

♪ Joann Alexander, arts administrator and amateur cellist

The idea that a classical background will somehow prove detrimental to a musician's expressiveness and inventiveness is a myth; after talking with the likes of Oscar Peterson and Jo Zawinul I would hate to try and convince them that studying classical music has prevented them from expressing their souls.

♪ David Paich, keyboard player with L.A. band Toto

The more consultation with the adult student about goals, methods, and repertoire, the better. Successful in their lives away from the piano, most adults prefer to feel they have some voice in the learning process, even while being guided through unfamiliar territory.

♪ Eric Street, professional pianist and teacher

I have great respect for anyone who chooses to learn a musical instrument, for it is a process which makes him vulnerable to himself and to the rest of the world. This is something that should be understood by any good teacher. A student gives a teacher his trust and the teacher must respond with all the tact, sensitivity, and patience at his command. It is a very rewarding relationship.

♪ Kenneth Wollitz, *The Recorder Book*

things well, and there's no reason to get annoyed with them because they can't. It's our job to figure out how to make it easier for them to do what they want to do.

Does your teacher teach in a way that helps you solve your own problems? Are you acquiring skills and attitudes that make you independent and capable of approaching music on your own? Cellist William Pleeth, a great performer and teacher, says, "The student must learn how to look at himself; to develop the craft of investigation into his own problems. The teacher should be showing his students the inner secrets of how to cope with themselves, how to listen and count, to conceptualize and discriminate—not just carry out orders."

Does your teacher take seriously any pain or discomfort you have when you play? Does she help you develop a natural, tension-free playing position? At the beginning, some instrumentalists contend with small aches or fatigue as their bodies learn new ways to move (and, for string players, as fingertips get used to the pressure of strings). At this stage, however, if you are in pain and your teacher says, "You'll get used to it," think about finding a new teacher who is more sensitive and more knowledgeable about playing positions and use of energy.

EMPOWERING YOURSELF AS A STUDENT

As adult musicians, many of us feel peculiarly vulnerable when we find ourselves on the student side of a teacher-student relationship. Our vulnerability is expressed in many ways, but one of the most common is the tendency to feel inhibited and nervous in front of our teacher and to play poorly at our lessons, especially in the early stages. Debra Tompkins, a dance teacher from Castlegar, British Columbia, followed a lifelong desire to make music by starting violin lessons with her children's teacher: "I knew that she was a wonderful teacher and a nice person, and I was eager to learn, but I felt so embarrassed in front of her. It was hard to be on an equal level with her as an adult and yet be so terrible at the violin. At my lessons, my heart would pound and my hands would shake. Wendy would say, 'You're all right. You're doing just fine,' but I'd have times when I didn't think I could go on. It was that hard, especially in the beginning. I only stuck with it because, for me, it's a heart thing. In my heart I want to be a musician."

The distress we feel in front of a teacher seems to come from three sources. First, nearly all of us find it hard to do something well when someone else is hovering over us, watching critically. Second, as adults we are accustomed to being—or at least appearing to be—efficient and capable. Music making calls our grown-up bluff: if we're to endure as musicians, our desire to make music has to be stronger than our need to appear competent. Finally, for those of us who, like Debra Tompkins, make music out of a heartfelt desire, a lesson becomes a time of laying our hearts open. The emotional turmoil we go through may be disabling at times, but it is also a testament to the very real intensity and human significance of music itself.

If we are to draw the very best from our music lessons, it is important to accept our strong emotional involvement, but it's also important to avoid falling into patterns of guilt and dependency, to avoid the dilemma that Eloise Ristad describes in *A Soprano on Her Head*:

> Music lessons—or lessons in anything—can be dangerous to us, for the weekly guilt can become addictive. We can come to believe that we . . . really can profit from being told repeatedly how to do it, from being given "right" answers. Gradually we lose our childlike enthusiasm for music or tennis or roller-skating or tightrope walking and substitute an intense yearning to do it "right" for the teacher. The pat on the back becomes more important than the music or the skating. One part of us becomes ever more committed to earning the pat on the back, while another subversive part— that we try to ignore—kicks and screams and resists the teacher's authority. This is the part that gives us all kinds of excuses for not practicing.

We don't want to be driven by guilt or recalcitrance or manipulation or even, in spite of the power of modeling, by compliance. "What we can learn best from good teachers," according to John Holt, "is *how* to teach ourselves better." The goal, as

*W*hen I play alone in my bedroom, it's easy to open up and let tender, inner things come out of me. But it's hard to do that when someone is listening critically. It's very risky.

♪ Kathryn Chapman, mother, tree planter, and amateur cellist

*I*t's very important that beginners come to that first lesson realizing that no one expects them to know how to play. People sometimes feel that they have to know something already in order to go in there. In truth, beginners are much easier to teach than someone who already plays, because you know exactly where to start.

♪ John Payne, professional saxophonist and teacher

many teachers say, is to eliminate the teacher by developing our own powers and resources.

So how do we steer around dependency traps and still maintain our own emotional freedom and a productive relationship with our teacher? How do we use our knowledge and skill honestly to make the music that we want to make and not just to please another grown-up?

We need to check with ourselves regularly and ensure that we are keeping our perspective intact and our attitude healthy while at the same time giving the teacher the chance to teach. It can be a difficult balance. As philosopher Allen Ross Anderson puts it, "We should have our minds open, but not so open that our brains fall out."

A student-teacher relationship marked by discord is not necessarily an unproductive one. Biologist Don Mitchell remembers a distinguished violin teacher he had at a workshop: "It was only for six lessons, which was a good thing for both of us. He was so cynical! But strangely enough, I changed my entire bowing technique because of what we did, and it was a very important change."

Nagging discontent and an absence of growth, however, mean that there's trouble somewhere. Of the amateurs interviewed for this book who reported unproductive relationships with teachers, many tolerated the situation for a long time, blaming their lack of progress on themselves. Raye Miller, of Center Moriches, New York, spent six years with her first flute teacher:

> I really liked her and believed she was a good teacher, but I thought there was something wrong with me or something wrong with my hearing. I never learned to sight-read. I didn't understand rhythm. I had no sense of where the beat was. I joined a band and had to memorize all the music because I couldn't keep up any other way. I honestly believed that I was at fault and just kept thinking, well, maybe someday I'll catch on. Finally someone in the band said, "Raye, I have a teacher for you." I tried this other teacher, and it was a revelation.

Self-blame not only contributes to a troubled relationship but often makes it difficult to acknowledge the problem at all. Some amateurs who have found themselves at a real impasse with their teachers discovered the impetus for change by going

There's something about education that builds confidence. If anything, that may be its strongest force—the confidence that you feel when you've got some background and education. . . . There is a fear that people have, that it's going to kill their creativity, or it's going to kill their soul. It will only kill your soul if you allow it to—if you get caught up into believing that everything the teacher says is the only thing that exists and that the rules they tell you about are not meant to be broken. They're all meant to be broken. They get broken every day.

♪ Herbie Hancock

to a workshop, joining an ensemble, or meeting another student—getting some kind of nonlesson input. Looking back, the students could easily name symptoms, even though they didn't seem significant at the time. Here are seven common "danger signals" of a nonproductive teacher-student relationship:

1. **The teacher is chronically impatient.** We all have our "off" days and our harried weeks, but if impatience is the teacher's style, it is the teacher's problem and not the student's. Some musical difficulties, such as rhythmic instability, can take a long time to correct. A good teacher is able to acknowledge partial improvement.

2. **The teacher talks about results and not causes.** "Your tone is weak" and "Your rhythm is all wrong" are not helpful statements. At the very least, a student needs to know what steps to take in order to correct the specific problem at hand. Better still is to be learning the principles of good tone production, a secure method of rhythmic analysis, or whatever musical foundations are needed to support growth in the long run.

3. **The same—or similar—assignments are given week after week.** "Lockstep" teaching requires little input from the teacher, and does not address a student's goals or needs. A teacher who uses only one book or one method, who doesn't adapt the approach to the student, and who progresses doggedly one page or one unit per week is not teaching a student but is teaching a book.

4. **The teacher belittles the kind of music the student wants to play.** A teacher does not have to share everyone's musical tastes, but there is no room in a respectful relationship for condescension. A teacher may not be able to teach the kind of music a student wants to play, but that does not mean it has no value.

5. **Most of the teaching is by rote or imitation.** Modeling has its limits. When it robs the student of any opportunity for growth or input, it's being turned to a negative purpose. Rote learning is a wonderful way to "get something in your pocket" so that you can actually be making music as you expand and explore your skills. But an unchanging diet of imitation and note-by-note

memorization denies the learner the chance to be independent. During rote-based instruction, a skillful teacher explains why a particular passage is played in a particular way or demonstrates why a specific technique is appropriate in a specific circumstance. Even while learning by rote, a student can be developing technical and analytical skills to apply in other musical situations.

6. **The teacher encourages dependence and discourages initiative.**   The lessons are for your benefit, and so it's obvious that your ideas, your contributions, and your questions are important.

7. **The teacher is unapproachable.**   A teacher who closes off verbal avenues of communication can easily close off musical ones as well. It's important to feel safe to express yourself, in words and music.

In many instances, if good communication is possible, a troubled teacher-student relationship can be improved, and it's well worth the effort to do so. But it's also important to admit that sometimes the wisest remedy is to find another teacher. As guitar teacher Barry Kahn explains, that's what makes the system work: "People come to me willingly, I tell them what I can and cannot do, and if they like what I have to offer, they start giving me money, and I give them enjoyable work. It's the greatest system in the world, gives pleasure to all concerned, requires no fancy apparatus, and it's self-regulating: if I do a poor job, I don't have students after a while; if I'm good, I thrive."

Although there's no point in blaming yourself for a bad situation, it's also true that a student's attitude contributes to the stress or the success of a teaching relationship. Vancouver pianist and teacher David Rogosin talks about the "student syndrome"—the feeling that you don't know anything but that if you're diligent, then someday you might. "When you buy into this syndrome," Rogosin says, "you feel like a nobody doing your best." It can help us avoid the student syndrome if we think of our music teacher not as a parent (he will take care of me) or as a mechanic (she will fix what's wrong) but more as a travel agent. We welcome information, guidance, and assistance with many small details, but it is finally our trip.

The teacher who is rigid, who believes there is only one approach, who imposes it and wants unquestioning compliance—such a teacher misses a great deal of the enrichment that comes from the student.

♪ Yehudi Menuhin,
Conversations with Menuhin

72

As students, we make our contribution to a productive relationship in three basic ways:

1. Put criticism in perspective. Many of us tend to inflate the value of negative comments and dismiss praise. If we're paying a teacher to help us change, then we need to find a way to accept the teacher's observations and suggestions without feeling crushed, defensive, or skeptical. It's hard. As vocal coach David Craig says in his book *On Performing,* "If singing can be said to present you in full view, criticism of what you are doing—when you sing—can be misinterpreted as criticism of who you are." In the intensity of the moment, teachers do not always coin graceful phrases. Even the gentlest teachers sometimes say things that strike us as tactless and harsh. We might have to remind ourselves to listen to the caring spirit inside these messages and to ignore the words they are wrapped in.

2. Be willing to take risks. Photographer and Greenpeace founder Rex Weyler was once asked why he took so many risks just to photograph an eagle. "If you don't go out for it," Weyler replied, "you don't come back with it." As musicians, we have to risk being wrong, making mistakes, and sounding foolish, or we'll never grow. All a teacher can work with is what we offer, so it's to everyone's advantage if we pour out our work boldly rather than hold it back fearfully.

3. Be an active learner. Think for yourself. In *Just Being at the Piano,* Mildred Chase says, "As knowledgeable as they are, [teachers] may not always be able to articulate their knowledge. You may have to teach yourself by listening to them play, by analyzing, by watching the way they move, and by asking yourself questions." Being active means working out solutions to our own problems rather than carrying them to the teacher for a fix. Even if our solution is faulty, the effort we've made better prepares us to understand the teacher's point of view. Being active also means doing our own listening. Letting a teacher do the listening for us is a habit many of us picked up in childhood. We finish our piece and then turn to ask, "How did I do?" as if we hadn't even been there while the music was going on. A teacher is only a resource. The learning has to come from us.

Being me, I tend to remember those times when my teacher says, "Well, it helps to know the notes," and I forget the times when she says, "You've made progress—you've accomplished something."

♪ Ann MacNab, retired librarian and amateur pianist

Taking music lessons can be a very humbling experience, but if you want to make music, you just have to put that aside.

♪ Kathryn Chapman, mother, tree planter, and amateur cellist

I think we adults expect far too much of teachers, and we do not demand enough of ourselves.

♪ Leonard Marsh, social scientist and amateur cellist, *At Home with Music*

73

You might expect to see a fourth item here: "Practice, practice, practice." It's obvious that you will progress faster at any level if you practice. But what's not always obvious—at least from the teacher's point of view—is that lessons can be of great value to an adult *even in the absence of progress.* Many adult students have weeks and months at a stretch when it's virtually impossible to "practice enough." The regular lesson, though, can still be worthwhile. It can still be a time of discovery, of self-actualization, of communication—even if progress is minimal. There's no point in students being torn up by guilt and teachers being worn down by aggravation over the issue of practicing.

It's important for both student and teacher to communicate clearly about practicing, though you as the student may have to take the initiative. For instance, you may have to tell your teacher how much work you can handle or what you have been able to prepare for the current lesson. You shouldn't have to be demoralized by taking home assignments larger than you can reasonably do and then fearing that you'll get "caught" by a request to play something you were unable to prepare. Teachers can sometimes be overly enthusiastic and neglect to calculate the amount of practice time they are committing you to. You will have to speak up.

It may also help to discuss in advance a "Plan B" for the weeks when you cannot practice very much. There's no shortage of fruitful things two musicians can do together for an hour—play duets, improvise, do some ear training, review some theory, listen to and discuss recordings, sight-read new material.

If you're practicing very little, or not at all, does that mean you should withdraw from lessons? You may value the lessons in any case, while your teacher feels that you're wasting his time or your money. But what's to keep us from inventing a relationship between a professional musician and an amateur in which progress is not the objective? It's a question worth hashing out honestly with your teacher. Perhaps paying for a "consultant" rather than a "teacher" would clarify this situation somewhat.

Teachers are understandably distressed sometimes by what appears to be the inconstancy of adult students who take lessons but don't practice, or who take lessons for a few months and then stop. But behavior that looks fickle from a teacher's point of view may well be a completely logical step for the student. As amateur pianist Terry Mayor suggests, "Music teachers need to *think* a bit about how they treat adult students. After all, adults aren't taking music lessons because their parents are making them do it. If they're spending the time and money, then they must be truly interested in playing. Teachers might have to make concessions to the fact that adults may be very sensitive to criticism and may not always have time to do everything the teacher wants them to do."

What we all have to remember is that the way into music is never smooth or predictable. A relationship with a music teacher is one of the really unique human bonds, and at some point, even with an "ideal" teacher, you will likely go through some emotional turmoil. A good teacher, though, will always be a catalyst for your personal relationship to music. If you loved music when you started your lessons, you should love music more fiercely after six months and more yet after a year, two years, twenty years. It is the urge to make your own music and the joy you get from it that must endure.

M*ay I have the power to exchange my best with your best.*

♪ Nadia Boulanger

CHAPTER 6

♪♪ *What Is There to Learn?*

Being inside music is like being inside a house with many windows opening onto a lush and varied landscape. The more windows you look through, the more you see and the more the
whole of it makes sense and draws you toward itself. In this
chapter, we'll look at some ways in which the whole idea of
music gets divided up and categorized, from the point of view
of the music maker. We'll talk about *style*, such as jazz, rock,
classical, and blues; *activities*, such as playing in a band or singing in a choir; and *skills*, such as technique, sight-reading, and
improvisation.

The idea of "music in general" is a lot like the idea of "home
in general." Most of us are naturally partial to some aspects of
homekeeping and not to others. We may be good at repairs but
uninterested in architecture. We may like our surroundings upbeat and daring or we may frankly prefer the shabby and familiar. Home may be a place of high energy and social enterprise,
or it may be a soft chair and a good book.

Similarly, when it comes to music, we're mesmerized by this
style and indifferent to that one, a natural at some skills and a

born klutz at others. Even among professional musicians, competence at *everything* is unusual. Musicians, in fact, tend to be a little astonished at what *other* musicians can do. A violinist marvels at how a pianist can play all those notes at once, while the pianist is amazed that the violinist can find the right notes without keys. Someone who plays by ear may envy a good sight reader's comfort with written music, while the sight reader may be mystified at how the "ear player" knows what to do.

Very few musicians can do everything.

Unfortunately, you'll also find condescension among some musicians, professional and amateur alike—jazz players who scoff at classical music, classical players who belittle country, country musicians who put down jazz.

But these categories are arbitrary and artificial. Behind them, there is only music, and *all generous and imaginative musicians know that instinctively.* Tchaikovsky made masterful use of folk songs, Gershwin took jazz to the symphony and the opera, Paul Simon collaborated with Ladysmith Black Mambazo, and Yehudi Menuhin recorded with Ravi Shankar and Stéphane Grappelli. We can call it "borrowing" or "crossover" or "fusion" —the label doesn't matter. The message is that the spirit of music frees us to express our nature but *does not abide arrogance.*

What you need to know, if you're beginning or ready to cross over yourself, is that every style of music picks and chooses from the skills of music rather selectively. In other words, you don't have to learn how to do everything. Everything you learn will be of use to you somehow, but you don't have to learn it all. You can even compensate for a lack of skill in one area by strength in another. If your sight-reading is marginal, for example, the ability to play by ear will pull you through much of the time.

To help readers who may be taking up music for the first time, there's a chart on page 80 that lists several musical skills across the top, and the most common musical activities that amateurs participate in down the side. The skills across the top are defined starting on page 82, but we need a word here about the activities. This chart could well have listed musical styles in the first column—rock 'n' roll, pop, folk, jazz, classical, Dixieland, country, sacred, and all the offshoots and fusions of these. However, such a list would inevitably be full of gaps and overlaps. A concert band, for example, can play jazz numbers, but concert band members don't need the same skills as musicians in a

I play classical music because I love and respect the music; I play jazz because that's what I am—a jazz musician.

♪ Wynton Marsalis

When I started playing guitar, I had no "natural" abilities. I couldn't tune my guitar, I couldn't tell if it was out of tune, and I couldn't sing. But after eighteen years of practice and persistence, I can now play by ear, sight-read, improvise, sing, and compose music and lyrics.

♪ Ron Pulcer, computer systems analyst and amateur guitar player

77

small jazz ensemble. So instead of styles you'll find musical activities divided into three general categories:

Scored. Groups and individuals that play or sing from printed music (a *score*), performing the music as close to the written form as possible. Examples include a symphony orchestra, a concert band, an early music consort, and any soloist or small ensemble playing classical repertoire or arrangements.

Lead Line. Groups and individuals that play or sing from a lead line, whether written, played by ear, or learned by rote. A *lead line* is a melody or song and a series of chords that form an accompaniment. The lead line and chords are usually written down in a songbook, in a fake book, or on sheet music, though many lead line players know their melodies and chords by ear and don't refer to written music very often. Most lead line groups allow some room for improvisation as the piece goes through multiple verses and choruses. Examples include a folk song sing-along, a rock 'n' roll dance band, a bluegrass band, and a gospel choir.

Improvisatory. Groups and individuals that create music spontaneously, usually in a recognizable style. The distinction between this group and the lead line category is slippery, because much improvisatory music is based on a lead line. Musicians in a jazz ensemble, for example, will begin with a lead line for "How High the Moon" and then take turns improvising new material over that melody's chord series, or *progression.* Other groups in this category work their own original material, either composed in the form of a lead line or totally improvised. Music in the improvisatory category includes almost all jazz and blues, as well as some new wave and rock.

On the chart, a big *X* in a square means that that skill is basically indispensable for that activity—if you want to play in a recorder consort, for example, you have to be able to read. A small *x* means that the skill is extremely useful, but you can get along, for a while anyway, without it. A blank square doesn't mean that the skill isn't needed, just that it's not one of the first that you need to acquire. The individual skills are defined after the chart. (Do be aware that musicians may argue with this chart. It was compiled from the information and advice of active musicians and students, and there was some variety of opinion.)

Perhaps this chart can help you find your way into the kind of music you want to make. It's useful to think this through for yourself from time to time because you will find that every instructional text, every self-help video, and every teacher makes assumptions about what kind of music the student is being prepared to play and what skills that music requires. Once you know the boundaries or the context within which you'd like to work, you're in a better position to evaluate opportunities and resources.

So how do you choose which way to go? There's a good argument for going after as many skills as possible, since each reveals a different aspect of music, and each reinforces and complements the others. But you don't have to learn everything all at once. As your skills develop and your life goes on, your interests and goals tend to change. Your best guide is your own desire. David Turner, a business administration student from Dallas, used his daydreams to initiate his own "crossover":

"One day I 'came to' after a music-making fantasy and realized that the kind of music I'd been playing in my daydream was totally different than the kind of music I was learning and practicing. I *never* daydream myself on a stage, performing Chopin, though I'd be capable of doing that. In my daydreams, I'm always at a club or a party, surrounded by people who feel happy but haven't especially come to hear me. I play in a dreamy and sort of sloppy kind of way. I don't even *play well* in my daydreams!

"The reality of it then—at the moment I 'woke up'—was that I could play the Bach *Inventions* very nicely, but I couldn't play 'Happy Birthday' if somebody asked me to.

"So, I'm making changes. I still love Bach, and I still love Chopin. I still play them, but I've stopped taking lessons for the summer, and I'm working my way through some teach-yourself books on improvisation and pop piano. First off, I learned how to play 'Happy Birthday' without the music, and then I moved on to 'Smoke Gets in Your Eyes' and 'Misty' and 'Blue Moon.'

"I know I'll never leave classical music entirely, but that's always been a kind of solitary pleasure, and I'm actually a gre-

There is no prescribed curriculum that everybody must or should or can learn in order to be "well-educated." In fact, a narrow academic notion of what constitutes education can be a major block to growth. . . . The worth to you of any particular subject or field is for you to decide on your own terms.

♪ Ronald Gross, *The Lifelong Learner*

79

MUSICAL ACTIVITIES/MUSICAL SKILLS

	Technique	Reading Music	Sight-Reading
Scored			
Large instrumental ensembles (orchestra, concert band)	X	X	X
Large or small vocal ensembles (chorus, choir, madrigal)	X		x
Small instrumental ensembles (string quartet, brass choir, recorder or early music consort)	X	X	X
Solo instrumental or vocal—any classical repertoire	X	X	
Lead Line			
Small instrumental/vocal ensembles (pop, rock, folk, gospel, country, etc.)	X	x	
Solo instrumentalists or vocalists (pop, rock, folk, gospel, country, etc.)	X	x	
Accompanists for group singing (keyboard or guitar)	X	x	x
Improvisatory			
Small instrumental/vocal ensembles (jazz, blues, new wave, rock, or any innovative music)	X		
Solo instrumentalists or vocalists (jazz, blues, new wave, rock, or any innovative music)	X		

MUSICAL ACTIVITIES/MUSICAL SKILLS

Playing by Ear	Improvisation	Memorization	Harmonization	Transposition
		x	X	
		x		
X	x	X	X	x
X		X		
X		(in lieu of reading) x	X	X
X	X	X	X	X
X	X			

garious person. What I'm doing now makes me feel like I'm moving outward with my music, becoming a kind of asset in the community . . . so invite me to your birthday party, OK?"

MUSICAL SKILLS

Technique

Basic technique has the same meaning for the beginner and the experienced player. It is something you must renew each time you begin to play.

♪ Kenneth Wollitz,
The Recorder Book

Scales. Arpeggios. Études. Trilling. Tonguing. Tone production. Classical musicians call it "technique," jazz players call it "chops and licks," and Broadway vocal coach David Craig calls it "the imprisoning means to liberating ends." Technique is what lets you do the things you want to do. Technique is the nimble servant who coordinates the physical activities that your instrument and your kind of music require.

Technique is not sterile or removed from music itself. Appropriate technique is instantly transferable to the music you want to make. Nor is technique the province of the expert or the virtuoso. Any time you are learning or refining the physical control of your instrument, you are developing technique. Although the result displays itself in physical proficiency, the route to secure technique demands intelligence and imagination in full measure. You'll find more about learning and practicing technique in Part Three of this book, starting on page 89.

Reading Music

Robert J. Silverman: If you were to start your career over, what do you think you would do differently?

Marian McPartland: (Laughs) Well, I think I would have learned to read better for one thing.

The ability to read music is a skill completely distinct from the ability to sing or play. Being musically "literate" is not the same as being "musical." Many fine musicians cannot read. Reading is simply a tool, essential to some kinds of music and irrelevant to others.

Virtually all classical musicians (except for some singers) are able to read, which makes sense, because their art consists of interpreting the written creations of others. Jazz, pop, rock, and folk musicians rely on reading far less than on memory, and they rarely use printed music at a rehearsal or a performance. And yet reading ability among musicians in these fields is common—Billy Preston, Leon Russell, and Elton John all read music. Learning to read does not in any way hamper your style or your creativity. You'll find specific details about learning to read beginning on page 134.

Sight-Reading

Reading music, alas, is not the same as sight-reading music. A good sight reader can take an unfamiliar piece of music and play it off "at sight," reasonably up to tempo, in a fluent, musical-sounding way (though not necessarily without errors). Given the same task, someone who only reads music would—if the piece were difficult—proceed haltingly, getting through it eventually, but not up to tempo, and with much hesitating and stopping to figure things out. Like so many musical skills, sight-reading is not an all-or-nothing ability. Some people sight-read easily, some with difficulty, some not at all. Everyone who can sight-read can read, but the reverse is not true. Developing sight-reading skill requires sustained practice, but once you learn how to do it, it tends to stay with you. See page 144 for specific ideas.

Good sight readers are musically useful people. They're naturally essential in any reading ensemble, such as a community band (though in most rock, jazz, or improvisatory groups, the ability may go unappreciated). Anyone who can sight-read vocal music is a big asset in a choral group. Keyboard sight readers are especially welcomed by community and children's organizations, churches, and school groups for rehearsals and sing-alongs. (Playing by ear will get you by—until someone requests a tune you don't know.)

Playing by Ear

Playing by ear is the ability to play, without printed music, a composition or song that you have heard before. It is a skill distinct from memorization, which usually implies that the music has been consciously studied and learned, either from a printed score or from a recording. (Although playing by ear is different than playing from memory, the ability to play by ear greatly enhances the ability to memorize securely.)

Playing by ear is essential in most small ensembles that play

One of the great pleasures of playing the piano is sitting down with an unrehearsed piece of music simply to make its acquaintance.

♪ Mildred Portnoy Chase,
Just Being at the Piano

jazz, pop, rock, country, gospel, and folk but is rarely required in a full band, an orchestra, or in any classical or early music setting. It's an unusually satisfying activity to many musicians and is a fine way to sharpen listening and awareness of musical design.

Unlike many other musical skills, playing by ear is often *easier* than most people expect it to be. Fear and inhibition are the biggest obstacles. It definitely gets easier with practice and experimentation. Ideas for learning to play by ear begin on page 146.

Improvisation

Improvisation is in some ways the great divide. Many musicians brought up on conventional classical lessons can't imagine how it's done, have no idea where to start, and basically look on improvised music as a kind of never-never land for which their passport is invalid. Yet other musicians—often the ones who are self-taught—use improvisation as their main route into the musical world and look with perplexity at those who need a road map to find their way around such homelike terrain.

David Sudnow, a sociologist and jazz pianist, has written an extraordinary book called *Ways of the Hand*, which chronicles his journey from membership in the first group—the nonimprovisers—to full-fledged membership in the second group. He worked with a teacher and kept detailed notes of his progress. He told his teacher at the beginning, "I don't know where to go, how to start this making up melodies as you go along; tell me where to go." Even while working earnestly, with a teacher who took his goals seriously, he still says, "I got the feeling he was keeping secrets from me."

Improvisation, at a simple and unorganized level, is within the reach of anyone who can make a stream of sound with an instrument or a voice. Organized and expressive improvisation is the real challenge, requiring a strong, intuitive command of both the structure of music and the instrument in hand. Learning how to improvise requires patience, awareness, and some musical daring, but it's not impossible to learn as an adult. David Sudnow did it. After five years of careful work, he found that "good notes were everywhere at hand, right beneath the fingers." It came at first only in short bursts, but Sudnow had no doubt about his experience. "I could hear it. I could hear a bit of that language being well-spoken, could recognize myself as having done a saying in that language . . . particularly said in all its details: its pitches, intensities, pacing, durations, accentings—a saying said just so."

The advantages of knowing how to improvise are many and mostly obvious. Not only is it the ticket to many kinds of music and ensembles—jazz in particular—but it is also an intense experience at the border between music and imagination. No one who improvises, even at the most rudimentary level, can ever think of music in quite the same way again. More information about learning to improvise can be found in the section that begins on page 149.

Memorization

The natural ability to memorize is capriciously distributed in the musical population. Some do it with enormous ease, the most remarkable cases being the concert artists who learn an entire concerto on the flight to their next appearance. The rest of us *can* learn to memorize, probably more securely than we might think possible. Turn to page 154 for ideas.

Among those who need memory skills are solo singers and musicians of any style who learn parts by rote, whether from another musician or from a recording. Classical musicians always have the option of using the printed music (except for singers—some singers don't read, and some choral groups elect to perform without music). But classical players often choose to work from memory anyway, in spite of the anguish they may experience in the process. They take on, perhaps, the greatest challenge when they memorize because they commit themselves to reproduce faithfully what someone else has written.

Harmonization

Harmonization means two different things. For singers or players of melody instruments, harmonization is the the ability to carry, often spontaneously, a stylistically appropriate harmony line above or below a melody. For keyboard players, guitar players, and musicians who play bass instruments, harmonization is a form of playing by ear—the ability to fit an appropriate se-

85

quence or progression of chords to a given melody. Musicians in small, lead line ensembles draw heavily on both types of harmonization. You'll find a bit more about this in Part Three, under "Playing by Ear," on page 148.

Transposition

Transposition is the ability to play a musical line or accompaniment in a different key than the one in which it is written or has just been played. It's a worthy skill for keyboard and guitar accompanists who play for singers, as well as for any solo instrumentalist. If "Grandfather's Clock" is pitched too high for the assembled throng, a good transposer can knock it down a few tones with no panic and not many wrong notes. In Part Three of this book, the skill of transposing comes up in "Playing by Ear," on page 148. (The other clan that needs transposing skills are those who play transposing instruments. You probably know who you are.)

Other Musical Skills

All the skills listed in the chart on page 80 have been defined above, but we haven't yet exhausted the collection of musical skills. We'll look briefly at *music theory* and *style* in a moment, but first we'll briefly define two other skills not discussed specifically in this book:

Composition is the creation of original music, recorded either in written form or electronically so that it can be performed by other musicians. If you'd like to try your hand at composition, an excellent resource is William Russo's book *Composing Music: A New Approach*.

Repertoire development is a process of building and maintaining at performance level a list of pieces, songs, or compositions that you or your group is prepared to perform. Musicians who enjoy performing—amateurs and professionals alike—can build a repertoire thoughtfully so that they have variety and balance in their list. When a repertoire is well-tended, performing opportunities can be welcomed with the confident feeling that you're approaching the occasion with an old, familiar, and well-liked friend.

MUSIC THEORY

Music theory is the analytical study of the structure of scales, modes, melody, harmony, rhythm, chords, and musical form. It is inexhaustibly interesting in and of itself. (Professionals who indulge in this interest are called *musicologists*.) A basic command of theory not only makes it easier to understand how music is structured but also makes it easier to talk to other musicians. Its usefulness in this regard spreads right across the spectrum of musical styles.

That being said, it is also true that music theory is to music as knitting instructions are to a sweater—the sweater exists beyond them and can be enjoyed and used with never any reference to them. Anyone with good "knitter's intuition" can make a nice sweater with no instructions at all. The analogy becomes farfetched at some point, and musicologists are likely quibbling already, but the point is that music exists without theory. Theory is an attempt to explain how music that has already been made is constructed. You don't need theory to make music, but you do need music to make music theory.

Some musicians know a lot of theory, and some know little; some find it easy, and some find it hard. Many find it genuinely fascinating. It's the only musical skill of which it's rarely said that anyone has a "gift" or a "natural talent." Your own experience, needs, and attitude probably determine your ease of learning as much as any native ability. Of the amateurs interviewed for this book who started learning theory as adults, virtually all of them found it unexpectedly rewarding. Violinist Debra Tompkins said, "I'd never done any theory until my daughter had to take a theory exam as part of her piano class. I had to sit down and help her and *I loved it!* It all suddenly started making sense to me."

No matter what kind of music you do, a knowledge of relevant theory is likely to help you do it better. Knowing some theory reveals shortcuts in learning to improvise and play by ear. Knowing some theory makes the process of memorization more logical and reliable. Knowing some theory helps you select technical exercises that will benefit your overall playing.

You're likely to pick up a bit of theory as you go along, whether you mean to or not, especially if you learn to read. The key thing about learning theory is that if it is to be useful to you, as opposed to an empty exercise, it has to be done alongside actual music making, preferably at your own instrument or with your own voice. Music theory explains and augments actual music making. If there's no music, there's no theory. You can find out more about learning music theory by turning to page 158.

STYLE

page 158.

A good musician in one idiom or style may be hopelessly over his head in another. To know the notes doesn't mean one knows the style.

♪ Pete Seeger

When we come to style, we finally bring all our skills directly into the heart of music. *Style*, musically speaking, actually means two different things. One meaning is label: Baroque, big band, boogie-woogie, barbershop. Every musical style develops its own peculiar treatment and interpretation of musical events— rhythmic stress, tone quality, phrasing, chordal harmony. Individual performers usually contribute heavily to the development of a style. Style in this sense is largely absorbed by listening and, initially anyway, by imitation.

The other kind of style is your own. It is not learned or practiced—it just is. Canadian choral director John Trepp insists that all of his singers seek and treasure their own voice quality. You can fruitfully imitate a musical style, but imitation of personal style is a violation of your best musical self. "No one else," Trepp tells his singers, "can contribute what you can contribute."

When you value your own personal style, your joy in music making comes into full bloom, regardless of what other musical skills you have or at what level you play. As Lynelle Inwood explains: "Every time you pick up an instrument or open your mouth to sing, you are communicating heart to heart. What you're putting out at any moment is so much you. It's always you right then. It doesn't have to be great music to have that. It just has to be that feeling in your heart that you're trying, that you're feeling the music. It doesn't mean you're in a rapturous state where you're unconscious of the technical stuff, where it's flowing without any impediment. It's always there. That's the tremendous advantage of being an amateur, because you always have that opportunity to love music, no matter how it comes out."

Part Three

PLAYING AND PRACTICING FOR YOURSELF

All one's life is music, if one touches the notes rightly, and in time.

John Ruskin

I was obliged to work hard. Whoever is equally industrious will succeed just as well.

Johann Sebastian Bach

CHAPTER 7

♫♪ Practicing: A Time and a Place

September 16, 1660 Home; and after supper and a little at my lute, I went to bed.

So ended many a workday for the world's best-known bureaucrat, Samuel Pepys (1633–1703). Though his life was crowded with naval affairs, political affairs, and a few other kinds of affairs, Pepys confided to his diary that "[M]usic is the thing of the world that I love most." He was neither moderate at his music making—he played at least ten different instruments—nor was he bashful:

November 21, 1660 [A]nd so to the office all the afternoon. And at night to my viallin (the first time that I have played on it since I came to this house) in my dining roome; and afterwards to my Lute there—and I took much pleasure to have the neighbours come forth into the yard to hear me.

But Pepys loved the theatre, too, and during the peak of the season he had to accommodate his music making to his night-life:

> *December 3, 1660* This morning I took a resolution to Rise early in the morning; and so I rose by candle, which I have not done all this winter. And spent my morning in fiddling till time to go to the office.

And like many amateurs, he arranged not only his schedule but also his residence around his musical appetite:

> *August 3, 1664* Up betimes and set some Joyners to work to new lay my floor in our Wardrobe, which I intend to make a room for Musique.

Music has a way of starting simply—an instrument we pick up somewhere, an instruction book we borrow from someone, a bit of practicing we do now and then—but it also has a startling way of growing, like that little bundle who turns into a ravenous teenager or that scant handful of seeds that becomes ten-foot-tall sunflowers. A little planning never hurts. Keep a grocery list for the teenager, draw a garden plan to accommodate the sunflowers, and make space in your days and your surroundings for your music. This chapter shares some ideas for shaping your own musical space and time.

A PLACE TO PRACTICE

A good place to practice won't guarantee "good practice." An inviting space, however, can be a source of motivation, reinforcement, and pride. An ideal music space provides not only room enough to play freely but also a place to store instruments and music, a permanent place to leave your music stand, if you use one, and privacy, if that is important to you.

In most homes, however, we can rarely achieve a perfect environment, unless we have enough space to set aside a whole room for our music. (Don't be surprised if music takes over in this way. What was once considered "the laundry room" or "the den" has been turned to musical uses in many households.) Al-

We had a leak in the basement and had to move the piano upstairs. It meant putting the sofa in the bedroom, but what a change in my life! Suddenly I had light and air—no more shadows and cobwebs. I polished the piano, alphabetized my music books, bought a nice vase and a big bunch of daffodils . . . but best of all, I started playing every day.

♪ Heather Swope, student and amateur pianist

though it may be private and quiet, you might prefer not to practice in the basement, at least not if it's damp, cold, poorly lit, and stuffed with ice skates, Halloween decorations, and fifteen years of old magazines. However, a basement nook can be turned into an inviting and climate-controlled music studio with a modest investment in materials and time. (You can get a complete set of instructions for building a ventilated and reasonably soundproofed practice booth from common materials by sending five dollars to acoustical consultants Barron, Kennedy, Lyzun and Associates, 250-145 West 17th, North Vancouver, British Columbia V7N 3G4. Ask for a reprint of *The Design and Construction of a Practice Booth*, by Doug Kennedy.)

However modest or small, if you have a music space, make an effort to keep it special, orderly, and inviting, even if that means barring nonparticipating family members. Set some ground rules—no coffee cups on your music pile, no paper-doll families on your chair, no wool knee socks drying on your music stand. Keeping the place neat makes it easier to practice "on the fly"—to pick up your instrument when you have only five minutes (a tactic almost guaranteed to still find you at it thirty minutes later).

If you have the kind of instrument that can be safely left out of its case, set up and ready to go (which depends in part on what kind of housemates and pets you have), then include a place for that ready instrument in your practice space. A recorder, trumpet, or flute can go on a shelf or a dresser top; a violin or guitar can hang on a wall. Do all you can to increase the chances that you'll be able to play at least a little bit, even if your day's schedule is crowded.

If motivation is a problem for you, include a talisman in your music space and incorporate rituals into your routine. Enjoy getting out your instrument, assembling it, tuning, collecting your music, adjusting your chair. Light a candle or put on a special scarf or stand on a special rug as a signal, both to yourself and to others you live with, that this is your practice time. With these small acts you pass from the distractions and concerns of work and family life and enter your own music-making haven.

For some of us, our music space cannot be at home. There are too many interruptions, or the neighbor in the next apartment works nights and sleeps during the day, or there is no adequate instrument available. A few musicians—organists in particular—are accustomed to practicing elsewhere. Many others manage it successfully, using their office at work after hours, an empty classroom in a school or church, or a friend's house. If you have to make an arrangement like this, be alert to motivating techniques that will help you to counteract any sense of inconvenience.

"Why can't you just go jogging at lunch time like everybody else?"

Conservatories, private music schools, and music stores often rent practice rooms by the hour for a nominal charge. Anna Hamel, an amateur pianist from Toronto and the mother of three teenage boys, does her concentrated practicing in a rented studio. "When I'm at home," says Hamel, "the phone rings, the dishes are there, or the kids bring friends over for lunch. So when I *really* want to practice, I go to the conservatory and rent a practice room for four hours. Before my last recital I rented a practice room almost every day for a month." The act of going to a special place can put you in a special frame of mind. There's something peculiarly inspiring about the din in the hallway of a music school.

Some musicians aren't especially fussy about their surroundings. They can easily adapt their posture to the furniture at hand and rivet their attention to the music. Others, called by psychologists *low screeners*, are sensitive to every slight discomfort and every small distraction. Don't fight with your own personality in this regard. Spend, if you need to, an entire practice session finding the one chair in your house that suits you and the ideal place to put it.

If you feel distracted while you're practicing, see if you can catch your attention in its wanderings. Often something in the environment pulls us away from the music—a splashy image on the cover of a music book, a pile of unpaid bills on the desk, a clock that needs watching. Turn the book over, put the bills in a drawer, and—if you must watch the time—set a kitchen timer (where you can't hear the tick!), an alarm clock, or a watch alarm.

Seated musicians are justifiably picky about their furniture. If you play sitting down, and you can't seem to get comfortable, experiment with your chair. You might prefer a higher seat for playing than you use at other times. If you don't have a chair that's high enough, sit on one or two thick books or catalogs. (Don't use cushions or pillows.)

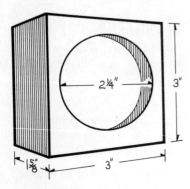

Figure 7–1a

Partially drill a hole to
3/4" depth on one side and
3/8" depth on the other side.

If you keep feeling that you're sliding backward, and you don't have a chair in your home with a level seat, experiment with propping up the back legs of an otherwise acceptable chair. The trick is to keep the legs from slipping off your "proppers." You can ask a woodworking friend to duplicate a pair of blocks that some professional musicians carry with them (see Figure 7–1a).

Figure 7–1b

If you're just beginning and haven't settled into a preferred playing position, you might consult with a teacher or an experienced player about the height of your chair and your stand, the distance between them, and the angle of your arms and hands. Take a tape measure and get "ideal" measurements, and then work to recreate that ideal in your own space. If you wear glasses for music reading, jot down the measurements and take them to your next eye exam. Your eye doctor might suggest special lenses for extended periods of close work.

A TIME TO PRACTICE

Some of us can fit our music making in and around our family and work responsibilities, and some of us can do it the other way around. But almost all amateurs feel that they just don't have the time to practice and play as much as they'd like. If you're

Morning is for labor, afternoon for routine, and evening for the imagination. These may vary, but experience shows that the critical and energetic faculties come soonest after rest; while the mind is dullest in midday; and evening is when the spirit is mellowest, and most charitable to new thoughts.

 Ernst Bacon, *Notes on the Piano*

yearning for more playing time, it could be useful to work with one of the good time-management and goal-setting systems available, such as Alan Lakein's *How to Get Control of Your Time and Your Life*, Neil Fiore's *The Now Habit*, or Barbara Sher's *Wishcraft*.

Among the amateurs surveyed for this book, the two favorite times to play were mornings, usually after other household members left for school or work, and early evenings, just after supper. Efficient practicers schedule their time, if at all possible, to take advantage of their own internal clocks. They look for times of quiet concentration (in the early morning or late at night) or for times when they are ready for a physical and emotional release (in the afternoon or evening).

At some times in our lives, it can be an almost insurmountable challenge to find *any* time to play, much less a psychologically advantageous one. Terry Mayor, of Damascus, Maryland, reports trying to schedule her piano practice at every possible time of day. "I've tried breakfast, lunch, and dinnertime," she says, "as well as before and after. For a while, whenever I woke in the middle of the night, I'd get up and practice for an hour or two. That was *awful* ! Lately, I've been getting up as early as I can, usually between 6:30 and 7:30, and practicing until the kids get up. Sometimes I can get in an hour before Kevin wobbles into the room half asleep, throws himself in my lap, and that's that." (There's more on page 106 about practicing when your children are young.)

Some of us need to find not only time but also privacy. In the beginning we may feel as conspicuous as the new jogger in the bright red sweatsuit and immaculate running shoes. For some the novelty and nervousness wear off, and playing in front of housemates becomes one more normal, noisy activity, like typing or woodworking. But others always prefer to play in an empty house. "I just feel more comfortable practicing alone," says Ken McDougall. "I try to get the chores rigged around just right so that I can be in the house practicing while Phyllis is outside."

In contrast to *finding* time, a few of us have to remember to limit our musical time, especially out of consideration for others we live with who enjoy our company or who need our attention. But whether our time is limited by choice or circumstance, many of us can benefit from tailoring our musical time to meet

*G*et used to hearing yourself making music, even if it strikes your ear as something less than song. Don't allow yourself to be hurt by others' assessment of your vocal adequacy, and if that is not easy for you, sing when you are alone.

♪ David Craig, *On Singing Onstage*

*A*lgernon: *Did you hear what I was playing, Lane?*

Lane: *I didn't think it polite to listen, sir.*

♪ Oscar Wilde, *The Importance of Being Earnest*

our musical goals. In the next section, we'll look more closely at "musical time management."

PLANNING YOUR PRACTICE: TODAY AND TOMORROW

Planning Each Practice Session

A few moments spent at the beginning of each practice session is a good investment for a musician who has clear ideas about goals. A quick assessment of the time available and the work at hand will save you from spending most of your time on one task while neglecting others that you'd like to cover. If you're not pressed for time, you can just make a list of what you'd like to do and then either assign priorities or alternate the work you enjoy best with the work you need a little motivation for.

If your time is limited—you have to leave for work by 8:10, or the kids get home from school in forty-five minutes—then you might sketch out a practice plan that assigns so many minutes to technique, so many to sight-reading, so many to improvisation, so many to working on a new piece, and so forth. Over time, you can accomplish a surprising amount doing even a brief practice every day. (Think how quickly a bucket fills even under a small drip.)

Use your own best psychology on yourself as you plan your playing time. Warm up with something easy and pleasing. Then go on to do your most difficult work in the early part of your session, before you get fatigued or distracted. Plan breaks if you're working in a long session. It's especially important for wind players to pace their practicing. Patrick Farenga still recalls the effects of an overenthusiastic week of tenor sax practice. At his next lesson, Farenga says, "My mouth was so tired, I kept letting air escape from the sides. The muscles just wouldn't work!" His teacher noted on Farenga's assignment sheet, "Don't wear out your chops!"

As you tune into your musical self, you'll find that you have days when anything seems possible and days when nothing seems possible. In *The Recorder Book*, Kenneth Wollitz encourages musicians to recognize and accept their state of mind at

I always want to practice, but some days I am more uncoordinated than other days. If it is a bad day, I don't push it.

♪ Hilliard Bennett, retired commercial artist and amateur pianist

the outset of practicing: "Sometimes we are in the mood to pay attention to tiny details, and sometimes we are not. It is only realistic to acknowledge our state of mind as we begin a session of practice."

You can help sustain your own momentum by using the quit-while-you're-ahead tactic. Every skillful playground director knows to end a game when everyone is a little tired but still having fun, and every good novelist knows to end a chapter when the reader is eager to find out what happens next. Quit when you've had a good workout but while your energy is still high, and you're eager to go on. Leave something good unfinished so that you look forward to getting back to it. Never press on until you're discouraged and exhausted; *plan* to end on a positive note.

If you find it hard to quit before you run out of steam, then set a timer and *stop* exactly when it goes off. The frustration of stopping in the middle of something good is much more tolerable and motivating than the frustration of discouragement. (Let's make an exception for the times you're on a roll. Packing up after a really fine workout is worth savoring, too.)

Keeping a Musical Logbook

On page 37 we discussed briefly using a music journal to build motivation and measure progress. Here are some additional ideas for a more complete musical logbook. Pick and choose from any that appeal to you. If you decide to experiment with a logbook, give it a try for at least three weeks, refining it as you go.

A three-ring, loose-leaf notebook—especially the kind with pockets on the inside covers—gives you maximum flexibility. Using a three-hole punch, you can store in the logbook pages of music, notes you take at a lesson or from a book, and any written exercises you do. Alternatively, you could use several books together—a book of music manuscript paper if you do any music writing, a notebook for your plans and log, and a separate journal. Possible divisions of a musical logbook include the following:

1. A daily log. This is simply a list or record of what you did each day, probably written in some kind of shorthand that will

When you have done your musical day's work and feel tired, do not exert yourself further. It is better to rest than to work without pleasure and vigour.

♪ Robert Schumann, *Advice to Young Musicians*

97

make sense only to you. When you look back over this, you can see what you've been spending time on and what you've neglected. You might begin your log each day with a brief plan and then check off the items as you cover them. Anything that needs more attention can get a star or a check mark in a different color.

2. A journal.   This might be part of the log, or it might be a separate section. Here you jot down feelings, discoveries, highs, lows, questions, and goals. It's a place for you to record not the growth of your skills especially but the growth of your mind, of your spirit, of your attitude toward your music. Looked at on a later date, a journal can reveal to you new directions to go and "obvious" solutions to knotty problems (which you couldn't see when you were too close to them).

3. Your own list of hints, tips, and guidelines for music making.   When you practice with awareness, you frequently come across tidbits of information that make your work easier and your playing more musical. Some things you discover on your own; some you read in a book or hear at a lesson; some you deduce from listening to others or seeing printed music. If these ideas are buried in your journal or your log, they can be hard to find later when you want to review them. But if you group them under headings in a separate section of your logbook, you'll soon find yourself writing your own self-instruction text. A violinist, for example, might have a section on bowing that includes notes like, "Play fast passages with as little bow as possible" and "Take a single upbeat on an up bow." A pop pianist might want reminders to try substituting a major seventh chord for a sixth chord from time to time or to use the longer fingers on the black keys and save the thumb and pinky for the whites.

4. A repertoire list.   As you polish a piece to the point at which you might play it for a performance or for your own progress tape, add it to a repertoire list. Then include in your practice plans special times to review the items on this list. If someone suddenly asks you to play, you probably won't have to open your notebook—you'll know what's on the list. Date the entries, and watch your investment take wings! Computer systems analyst Ron Pulcer, of Haslett, Michigan, plays a weekly guitar gig in a local restaurant. To expand his repertoire, he tries to work on one new song each week, putting songs he wants to learn onto a goal list. When he's learned a new song to his satisfaction, he transfers it to his repertoire list. An improvisor could keep a similar list describing especially satisfying directions for improvisation—the key, the mood, the structure, rhythmic patterns, harmonic progressions, and melodic fragments or motifs.

5. A calendar. Snag a free wall calendar from your insurance agent in December and add it to your book. Record lessons, rehearsals, upcoming workshops, and concerts. Write a congratulatory note to yourself on the calendar for every day that you meet your practice goals.

6. Notes and exercises from written study. If you take a course in theory or note reading or composition, you'll begin to accumulate papers with written exercises on them. Stash them in a separate section of your notebook.

7. Long-range plans. On page 100 are some ideas for long-range planning. If you try this, you can assign a section of the logbook for these notes.

8. A loaned-to and borrowed-from list. If you loan out music or borrow it from others, then either write down the details (name of music, name of lender or borrower, phone number, and date) or else adopt the attitude of Toronto pianist and computer programmer Doug Woods: "I lend sheet music only on the understanding that I will probably never see it again."

9. Miscellaneous. You'll find your own categories to include in this book—things like programs from performances you're in, notes from lessons and workshops, drawings for your dream music room, shopping information for your next instrument, a phone list for likely ensemble partners, a wish list for accessories and sheet music, or an index to your collection of recordings. It's your book!

The idea behind keeping a logbook is not to make you a compulsive record keeper or to suggest that every musical gesture has to be written down and every practice hour accounted for. Use the ideas that you like and forget the rest. The point is that we often underestimate the richness of our experience and the depth of our progress. It can be a big help, in dark moments, to turn back several pages in a logbook and say, "Well look at that—a year ago today I was learning 'Good Night, Irene' in the key of C!"

Making Long-Term Goals

If you like to make long-term plans, music suits itself neatly to a planning scheme. Working with your own ideas, or consulting with a teacher or friend, you can probably come up with a dismayingly long list of things you'd like to do. A pianist interviewed for this book had these goals in her journal:

- Learn scales—major and minor, all keys, four octaves
- Learn arpeggios—major, minor, and dominant sevenths, all keys, four octaves
- Practice Hanon exercises—one every two weeks
- Learn standard chord progressions most useful in pop tunes
- Learn one new song a week from fake book and figure out left hand
- Learn to play easy folk songs by ear, hands together
- Practice sight-reading from camp songbook—be ready to play for sing-alongs at church camp in August
- Learn how to do simple blues improvisations
- Review Bach *Little Pieces* and Bartok *For Children*
- Learn accompaniments to daughter's flute pieces

With the help of a calendar, a folk song list, a fake book, a camp songbook, the Bach and Bartok collections, and a few weeks' worth of old practice journals, this pianist sketched out a plan for a year that let her progress evenly toward all her goals. She discovered quickly that progress in one area bolsters progress in another (since all music meets at the front anyway). Minor arpeggios came in handy when the campers requested spirituals, Hanon helped her Bach, and the chord progressions she learned fit neatly under her blues improvisations.

In *The Inner Game of Music*, Barry Green outlines an excellent long-range system of goal setting for professionals and pre-professional students. A useful adaptation of Green's plan is to label sections in your notebook *Today, This Week, Next Week, This Month, Next Month, Short Term* (three to six months), and *Long*

Term (six months to two years). Goals coming up are shifted from section to section, and new goals are added in the appropriate place as they become needed, desired, or postponed. Green recommends listing the long-term goals near the front so that you see them often.

A part of your long-term planning should be a schedule for "retiring" certain pieces or activities from time to time. Although you are not actively working on it, anything that has commanded your awareness deeply continues to progress even when you lay it aside, and when it resurfaces weeks or months later, it becomes a fresh experience.

Subconscious activity never ceases. Muscles develop after exercise; and the mind, apparently resting, assimilates material provided during the practice hour.

♪ Lilias Mackinnon,
Music by Heart

PRACTICING UNDER SPECIAL CIRCUMSTANCES

All amateurs have peak times in their nonmusical lives when outside demands disrupt their best intentions. The accountant comes up against tax deadlines, the teacher has final exams to mark, the kids all get chicken pox at once, or the family is planning a move or a wedding. That's the time to rest on your laurels and cash in on all your hard work.

Brief Practice Routines—When You Only Have a Few Minutes

If you have even a little time to practice or play, consult your music log and see what's been the most constant, the most rewarding, or the most motivating activity. Perhaps you've discovered your own *sine qua non*: the scale or warm-up routine that makes everything else go better or the licks or trills that tend to deteriorate if you don't stay on top of them.

You might even take on something entirely new while other things go on hold. See what small tasks you've jotted down to get to "some day." It might be time to learn to transpose, for example, which can be mentally exhausting if you think you have to do it for an hour. But if you only have five minutes a day to do one folk song in one new key, you can be well on your way to transposing with ease when the nonmusical dust settles.

It's important not to feel that music must wait until you "have the time." Even a very little time spent with your instrument can be rewarding, especially if you keep your goals and expectations in proportion. Though he was self-taught and played only a few minutes a day, educator and writer John Holt was still pleased with his violin skills: "[T]hough learning to play the violin well may take years of intense concentration and effort, learning to have fun with it, to make interesting and agreeable sounds and even a little simple music, takes almost no time at all."

Unpracticing

Sometimes you just can't practice, even a little bit. Our lives are naturally turned in many directions at once, and few of us can afford the luxury of guaranteed, uninterrupted hours with our music every day. Sometimes when you don't practice, it's because you don't want to. More about that in a moment. But sometimes you're unable to. Still, your music and your development as a musician carries on.

When you can't get your hands on your instrument, you can still pursue other musical projects:

Listening. Many of us naturally fill more time with listening when the time available for playing is diminished. Recordings of your own current repertoire played frequently, even in the background, will usually increase the security and overall cohesiveness of your own playing. Listening to outstanding performances in your favorite style helps to build your intuitive knowledge of tone quality, phrasing, and musical structure.

Conducting. If your break from music is a brief one, and if you have some works underway, you might have a go at conducting them. With a score in front of you or from memory, with recorded music or with just the sounds in your mind, imitating Sir Georg Solti in front of your hall mirror or conducting in a daydream on a transcontinental flight—it doesn't really matter how you do it. Conducting the pieces you play will give you a new perspective. When you don't have individual notes to produce, your attention can be drawn to purely musical characteristics. When all technical demands are removed, you are free to concentrate on tempo, phrasing, dynamics, and interpretation.

The day my daughter was born, a friend gave me a record of piano works by Satie. Aside from Gymnopedie, I really knew nothing about Satie. I listened to that record over and over, many times a day—a kind of listening I hadn't done since I was a teenager with Aretha Franklin. It was three years before I got back to the piano, and the first thing I started with was a book of Satie. How exciting—and how nostalgic—to hear myself play it!

♪ Alinda Brown, travel agent and amateur pianist

Visualization. Here's another good one for airports, dental appointments, traffic jams, and sleepless nights. Visualize yourself playing confidently, with ease, with good position, coordination, and tone. Make your visualization as complete and vivid as you can—really *hear* the exact sounds you want to make and really *feel* yourself playing the way you want to play. Vivid visualization can teach us not to work so hard and help to reduce overall tension as we actually play.

Muscular maintenance. Some people like to think of musicians as athletes specializing in small-muscle activities, and in some ways they're right. When you're not able to play, there is probably some kind of exercise you can do to help maintain muscular coordination and strength for fingering, tonguing, or breathing. Next time you get a chance, ask a teacher, workshop leader, or experienced player for some ideas.

Reading. You'll find a book list in appendix 2, starting on page 298. Any library will have books about composers and performers of every age and genre. Look in the biography section, where books are arranged in alphabetical order, by the subject's name. For other music-related books, look on the shelves labelled 780 to 790, if your library uses the Dewey decimal system, or in the M's, if it uses the Library of Congress system.

The Infrequent Player

For many amateurs, music making is only a sometime thing. We might not touch our instruments but a few times a year, once or twice a month, only in the summer, or only on special occasions. We slip music on and off as we do a familiar coat. We may lose dexterity and accuracy if we don't play very often. Some instruments make physical demands that make infrequent playing uncomfortable. Brass players lose their lip; string and guitar players lose the calluses on their fingers. But if the basic skills have been carefully and lovingly laid down, those skills will return if gently summoned.

If you can anticipate an event coming up—a summer workshop or a production of the *Messiah*, for instance—start getting ready with small doses of playing as far in advance as you can. Play easily and lightly. Stick to easy material at first, and forgive

> **O**ne wants when playing or practicing to have an idea of the perfect position of the bow, fiddle, and body; an idea of the perfect motion, the perfect ellipse or circle or of whatever it is we seek. When we have this picture in our mind's eye, it will eventually produce its embodiment in our movements.
>
> ♪ Yehudi Menuhin, *The Compleat Violinist*

The infrequent player

103

yourself for any problems. Listen right away for the best that you do. Recapture the joy of playing. Fall in love with your instrument again so that when the time for woodshedding arrives, you're willing to give it.

Endurance can be a problem for someone out of playing trim who is suddenly thrust into a marathon—a weekend reunion of your old band or a long-awaited summer music camp. Give yourself frequent breaks to loosen up. Just stroll out of a rehearsal if you need to. Take some deep breaths and do some long stretches. If your muscular action is free, there is little need to "build endurance," and if your body is well-balanced, you have little need for "strength." Players of instruments that put the arms in raised positions—flute, violin, and viola, for instance—can remember that slight movements will keep muscles from going rigid. Whenever you have the least opportunity, put your instrument down, let your arms dangle, and vividly imagine the tension draining out your fingertips and pooling on the floor. Above all, stay very relaxed. Play lightly. Be aware of any tension beginning to concentrate and shed it quickly.

When You Don't Want to Practice

What about the times when you "ought" to practice but really don't want to? In the first place, you know, of course, that you don't "have to practice." It's OK just to play, to go through things you know, to get out favorites from your repertoire list, to do some easy reading or relaxed improvising. If your "don't want to" feeling is fleeting or infrequent, it's obviously nothing to be concerned about. But if it's entrenched and becoming a habit, and if the result for you is guilt or frustration or disappointment, then the situation deserves a closer look.

You know for yourself what it means if you don't practice, and you can also probably put your finger on a reason for your unwillingness. You may feel that the music you're making is no longer rewarding. Perhaps there's too much emphasis on someone else's goals or tastes. Perhaps you feel a vagueness of purpose or an absence of direction. Writer Michael Rossman found that using a flute that he didn't like "slowly sealed over the urge to play."

The problem is that the habit of not practicing can easily reinforce itself and turn into a cycle of frustration and guilt. As

He used to play violin and piano at school, and he took some private lessons. The trouble was getting him to practice; when it was a choice between a game of rugby and playing the piano, rugby always won.

♪ John Dankworth's mother

a beginner, Andrea Kelly-Rosenberg, of Portland, Maine, struggled between the difficulties of practicing and the consequences of not practicing:

> I found that developing my own practice discipline on an instrument as new and as difficult as the violin was unexpectedly troublesome. I would get impatient and push myself too hard, then rebel and not practice for days. Only with great effort could I get back on the horse, so to speak, and pick up the instrument again. I would get discouraged. But gradually, slowly, and with the help of my enthusiastic and loving teacher, joy took over, and I started to love it, love the instrument, love even the mistakes and the hard work it took, and takes, to make each small step forward into music.

As an incentive for practicing, some of us respond well to a specific future goal or commitment such as a recital, a band concert, a workshop, or a weekly lesson. Debra Tompkins decided to take a violin exam after her first year of lessons: "I filled out the application form and sent in the fee right away so I wouldn't change my mind. That gave me a goal, and that's when I really started to practice. I made sure I practiced every day. And of course, when you practice every day, you accomplish a bit more, and then you start to feel a little bit better about it."

Sometimes only an attitude change is needed. In a helpful book called *The Now Habit*, Neil Fiore explains the power of saying, "I choose to," rather than, "I have to." If we are willing to accept the consequences, we can freely choose to do or not to do anything we like. Some musicians experience resistance to practicing when the stakes are raised—when we have a band rehearsal tomorrow or a lesson in three days or a recital next week. We can choose to walk into those events unprepared and to accept the consequences, or we can choose to practice. A tactic recommended by Fiore is to agree with yourself to do a task for thirty minutes without interruption. At the end of that time, reward yourself by doing something you will really enjoy— plunge into a novel, go for a bike ride, or watch some sports on TV. Most musicians find anticipation of practice to be more daunting than practicing itself. Once we're actually playing, the novel or the bike ride or the game is easy to postpone. And

People can stand balanced on two feet very well because they do it all the time. But if you stay in bed for three weeks, you'll be wobbly when you get up. It's the same thing if you draw or play guitar or keyboards or write. You have to keep it alive by doing it all the time.

♪ Peter Max, visual artist and keyboard player

What do I do when I don't want to practice? I practice! It just takes a little longer to warm up, and it may not go as smoothly as other times. But I bet even James Galway doesn't feel like playing all the time.

♪ Ida Kowit, student and amateur flute player

once we're practicing regularly, the activity usually becomes self-rewarding.

ESPECIALLY FOR MOTHERS

Fathers are welcome to read this section, too, of course—especially those wonderful fathers who are genuinely involved in caring for their young children. This section focuses on women, though, because in most families the tasks of childcare that involve interruptions of other activities fall primarily on the mother. "It's not," as one mother put it, "that children need you twenty-four hours a day. They just need you three minutes out of every five."

Mothers who contributed information to this book fall neatly into two camps over the issue of playing music around young children. About half of the mothers found that their babies and toddlers made a wonderful audience. Some women made major strides in their musical development when their children were young. Linda Hecker, a teacher and amateur violinist from Guilford, Vermont, found she got "a musical boost" when her daughter was born: "I only worked part-time that year, and the baby slept a lot, so I was able to practice two or three hours a day. It was wonderful! When she was older, I convinced her that when I took out my violin, it was her time to take a nap. We worked it into a routine, and she *knew*—this was my time to play music and her time to nap. I was pretty insistent on that."

The other half of the mothers surveyed have had to limit their music making drastically around their very young children. Many of their children are light sleepers or non-nappers, and many react forcefully to being shut out of such a highly charged activity. Making music demands total awareness, and their children know this. It is no use thinking, "Well, I'm here if they need me." As soon as Mommy starts to play, they need her. Many of these mothers have children who derive security from frequent physical contact. Many instruments, however, block a child's access to the mother's body. "As far as a kid is concerned," according to amateur cellist Kathryn Chapman, "a cello is about the worst thing a mother can play. It's resting on your knees! *My place!*"

Mothers with more than one child often find that different

I was practicing one day when my son was two. I'd taken my wedding rings off and put them on the stand, and he picked them up and swallowed them.

♪ Joann Alexander, arts administrator and amateur cellist

children react to music making in different ways. One tolerates it, from the beginning, with grace (or at least indifference); another requires years to learn to share a parent with music.

If you have children who will not tolerate your music making, it seems at first that your only choices are either to ignore the wails and play anyway or else to play when they are asleep or out of the house, thus keeping your music virtually a secret from them. It's a tough choice—as soon as you let them in on your music making, they don't want you to do it.

Go gently and thoughtfully through this phase. You are—to such an extent you'll never know—shaping your children's attitudes toward music making. This is no time for a punitive approach. It take years for some children to develop the maturity and self-control that will allow you to sit down and practice without interruption. Meanwhile, do what you can to keep the experience of music making joyful and participatory.

The one absolutely certain solution is to remember that they will grow up. With every passing year, they will tolerate your playing with more grace, and they'll very likely begin to imitate you. It's worth thinking out a tactful, sensitive solution. Here are ten suggestions that have worked for other musician-mothers.

1. Be philosophical.   Realize that this is a time in your life when you probably won't make great musical strides. If you're taking lessons or building your own repertoire, choose short, simple works, and take on small challenges. Ruthann Baker, of Kansas City, continued taking lessons after her children were born. "My piano teacher had three children of her own and knew exactly what I was going through. We gave up on the pages-and-pages-long Mozart and Debussy, and she introduced me to Schumann's *Scenes from Childhood* and Beethoven's *Bagatelles*."

2. Be prepared.   Keep your instrument as handy as possible so you can play even for *very* brief intervals. One mother moved her piano into the kitchen. Another tied a leather thong around the scroll of her cello and hung it on the living-room wall.

3. Find ways to play that acknowledge the child.   You might

I love playing at night as my two children fall asleep. My mother did that for me when I was growing up. I feel a continuity, a tradition.

♪ Judith Musco, amateur pianist and singer

I do not wait until the kids are out of the house or busy or in bed to practice. I practice every morning, during my and their prime time. They play or draw or work with clay or look at books—or sometimes ask to practice, too. If they ask, I stop my practicing to practice with them.

♪ Andrea Kelly-Rosenberg, amateur violinist

play along with the child's favorite recording—great for developing your ear. Try playing for him while he's in his high chair—as long as he's really hungry. Simply maintaining eye contact can help a surprising amount. Perhaps you can play from memory or improvise some jaunty dance tunes while you are looking at your child.

4. Be a little crazy and inventive. Play in the bathroom while your young one is in the tub. (The acoustics are *fantastic!*) Serenade her in her sandbox or her wading pool.

5. Hire a helper. Have a neighborhood youngster come over every day to do something with your child that you'd never do—finger paint, make mud pies, splash in a sprinkler—anything so irresistible that it will buy you an hour of practice time.

6. Trade off. Alternate childcare sessions with another mother, or get a guaranteed hour on regular days from your partner or an older sibling. Reserve this time for practice and playing.

7. Think through the "don't touch" issue. When he's calm, let him explore your instrument. Even a very little child can learn respect for a delicate instrument. He can hold it "like a baby bird." At the first sign of boisterousness, you can swiftly (but nonpunitively) put it away. "Banging" on the piano, by the way, is a definite *yes-yes*. The phase does not last long, and it won't hurt the piano.

8. Encourage participation. Get a yard-sale guitar or autoharp, a pennywhistle, ocarina, or plastic recorder (put a piece of tape across the thumbhole), a slide whistle, or a real tambourine, and be willing to play with accompaniment. Don't offer "toy" instruments—little plastic trumpets or color-coded pianos. The tone quality is awful, and kids are rarely interested in them for long.

9. Do something new. Learn to play accompaniments on the piano or guitar, for example. Even if you've never played these instruments before, you can learn very quickly how to accompany simple songs with basic chords. "Old MacDonald" and

"Mary Had a Little Lamb" are still appealing, even to the Star Wars generation of pre-schoolers.

10. Try music making in a group setting. Children who are upset by a mother's practicing at home are sometimes more at ease away from home, with the novelty of a new setting and new faces. Lynelle Inwood took six-month-old Alicia to a gospel music workshop: "She had never been so quiet for so long. For two hours she sat there totally mesmerized."

As children get older, you can begin to set ground rules for your practice time. How many rules and how long you can practice will depend on the child's age, maturity, and previous experience with your practicing, but expect, most of all, that the situation will change constantly, and largely for the better.

School-age children can rely on a kitchen timer or an easy-to-read clock. Tell them, "When the big hand gets to the six, I'll be finished practicing. You can use your Legos until then"; or, "When the timer goes off, come into the living room, and we'll sing some songs from your book."

When your child is old enough to have good judgment about it, you can use the "blood-or-fire" rule: "You can only interrupt me for matters involving blood or fire." (This really does require some maturity. If the neighbor's dog is digging up your prize dahlias or you get a long-distance collect call from your best friend, you'll want to know. The blood-or-fire rule doesn't cover *every* urgent possibility. The child has to be old enough to understand "the spirit of the law.")

If you want to use a reward system, you can put some pennies, nuts, fish crackers, or poker chips in a dish. For every interruption, take one out of the dish and put it in your pocket. This is most effective if done with the least explanation. When the child asks what you're doing, just mention offhandedly that when you're done practicing, she can have the contents of the dish. (This becomes complicated with siblings! If you use one dish for all, they'll eventually figure out how to cooperate to prevent interruptions so as to maximize their share in the reward.) If you use poker chips or counters of some kind, explain that they can be traded in at the end of the day or end of the week (depending on the child's age) for something you've thought up in advance—a game of Go Fish with you, an extra bedtime story, a trip to the swimming pool, or a new matchbox car. Keep the reward scheme fairly simple, though, or you'll spend more time negotiating the terms of the agreement than you will making music.

The day will finally come (really, it will!) when your children will respect your music time. Even this achievement may take patience from you, but trust that it can happen. The mother of three teenagers expected—and got—the cooperation she needed: "When I started taking piano lessons again, I *made* the kids learn how to do their own laundry. They were very bitter about it, but I just said, 'I don't have time to do that any more because I have to practice.' Now, three years later, they're supportive and proud of me, although they still hate doing their laundry."

No matter how stiff the odds, it's important for you, as a mother, to continue your musical life or to resume it as soon as possible. Peter G. Hanson, a family physician and author of *The Joy of Stress*, talks about the value of *alternate stress*, an activity that engages us intensely but in a very different way from other sources of stress in our lives, "something that requires full concentration but that involves *different* circuits of the brain and body." Agnes Herbison, a pianist from Argenta, British Columbia, remembers "all the years I wasn't learning anything serious about music but was learning a great deal about bringing up a family":

> I could usually regain my sanity by playing the piano at night after everybody had gone to bed. After a hectic day of running hither and yon doing all I had to do for five children, I'd go to the piano exhausted at nine o'clock, and I'd just play. By midnight I'd feel ready to start another day's work.

Despite the difficulties, the interruptions, and the discouragement, most of the musician-mothers who contributed to this book spoke also about the necessity of making music—how music is "something just for me" and how it "nourishes the soul." As Terry Mayor put it, "I get a sense of accomplishment from playing the piano and progressing, however slowly, that is all mine and somehow different from the sense of accomplishment that I get as a wife and mother. Not better, just different."

The piano was in the living room, but we didn't walk in or out. We grew up with an appreciation for concentration. There were no rules, but we knew better than to distract or disturb him while he worked.

♪ John Rubinstein (Arthur Rubinstein's son)

CHAPTER 8

♪♪ *Working to Play: Principles of Effective Practice*

Among some musicians, practicing has a dirty name, implying grim, resentful toiling at dull tasks. Lon Sherer sees it differently. He calls practicing "a musician's personal liturgy." Sherer, professor of music at Goshen College and a professional violinist, had the extraordinary experience of learning to play the violin all over again after an illness left him without muscular control on the right side of his body. It took seven years to regain his former skills, and during that time, Sherer says, "I had to figure out how to take pleasure in the act of learning itself rather than in finished achievement." Practicing, according to Sherer, "opens a window that enables us to observe ourselves in the act of learning. It is an amazing opportunity!"

In this chapter, we'll take a closer look at this "amazing op-

Practice will benefit greatly from an understanding of two facts about the learning process: that falling back is unavoidable, and that there is no finish line marked "perfection."

♪ Donald Payne, professor of music, Case Western Reserve University

portunity" called *practice*, first exploring some attitudes about practicing and then looking at three important principles of effective practice: awareness, release, and chunking.

PRACTICING OR PLAYING?

Some amateurs take issue with the concept of practicing. John Holt, for example, said,

> I'm really serious about getting rid of this word "practice." For a professional performer, the distinction between "playing" and "practicing" is perfectly clear. "Playing" is when you perform before other people, and "practicing" is when you get ready to do it. But this distinction is nonsense for amateurs. What I do is, I play the cello. I don't spend part of my time getting ready to play it, and the rest of the time playing it . . . all of the time I am playing the cello.

Holt's perspective points up an ambiguity in the word *practice*. Perhaps it would clarify the issue if we use *practice* here not in Holt's sense of "preparation for something else" but in the sense of doing something customarily, as we might *practice* tolerance or *practice* courtesy. When we practice music in this way, we seek to make it a natural part of our lives, to apply what we know with an open mind, to renew and refine our skills, to sharpen our own edges, to meet our own genius, to open our own gifts.

All practicing is playing, though not all playing is practicing. Amateur violinist Andrea Kelly-Rosenberg says, "I love to *practice*. There is a deep satisfaction to the work I call 'practicing' that I do not get from what I would call 'playing.'" Kelly-Rosenberg's *practice* is obviously a very different matter from that dreary and mechanical kind of practice that some of us remember vividly from childhood. The fact is that productive practicing—even the repetitive, small-bit-at-a-time kind—can be restful and releasing, withdrawing our minds from our large-size worries and concerns and wholly engaging us in small details of beauty and skill.

It's especially important for amateurs to find ways to make

When I'm challenging a certain problem, I follow very traditional practice habits and focus a lot on technique. But when I'm learning pieces or just playing, then I do whatever I feel like doing.

♪ Lynelle Inwood, homemaker and amateur flute player

Practice doesn't really make perfect, but it sure as hell makes for improvement.

♪ Pete Seeger,
Henscratches and Flyspecks

practice rewarding and satisfying, for two reasons. The first reason goes to the heart of what it means to be an *amateur,* in the root sense of that word: as amateurs we have the special charge always to build the love for what we do into the way we do it. Practice that frustrates and discourages us will eventually erode our own joy in music making. Practice that leads to growth, skill, and insight will nourish our love.

The second reason for thoughtful practice is obvious but easy to forget: the quality of our practice determines the quality of our playing. Only in our fantasies, and once in a great while under the influence of adrenaline, can our playing abilities exceed what we have laid down during practice. For the everyday sort of music most of us make, like our everyday meals, the preparation determines the outcome.

Some of the general dislike and distrust of practice seems to come from the feeling that practice estranges us from actual music by fragmenting it and distorting it into meaningless units. At this point we come to the real distinction between practicing and playing. When we're "just playing," or performing, we cannot spread our consciousness in enough directions to encompass everything we must do—to govern every movement, to tune every interval, to fit every rhythmic unit into the tempo, to shade every tone, to express every interpretive detail. There are too many events and decisions happening simultaneously. Practice lets us consider musical details in isolation, gradually combining them and finally turning many of them over to automatic pilot. Our attention is then free once more to encompass the music in the largest possible sense. As Kenneth Wollitz explains it, "The aim of good practice is to use repetition efficiently by isolating and solving problems one at a time mechanically so we don't have to think of everything at once."

Far from removing us from our music, good practice draws us closer. When we practice scales, arpeggios, chord progressions, and other technical patterns, we are assimilating the primary elements of musical design. These are the mantras of a musical being. When we practice the details of an actual piece of music, we are coming to know that music better—we're not just doing it again and again. Donald Payne, professor of music at Case Western Reserve University, likens practice on a piece to editing an essay. In this "editing" stage we correct our small er-

*N*ever play carelessly, even when there is nobody listening, or the occasion seems unimportant.

♪ Ferruccio Busoni

*P*ractice is not self-expression; it is the exercise that precedes and prepares for self-expression.

♪ Kenneth Wollitz,
The Recorder Book

*T*o know a work fully is to have formed a large habit compounded of many lesser ones.

♪ Ernst Bacon, *Notes on the Piano*

113

The purpose of practice is not to reduce consciousness but to heighten it.

♪ Ernst Bacon, *Notes on the Piano*

rors, and then we reread, rephrase, experiment, and finally come to examine our meaning more closely.

If you are bored or frustrated by practicing, you can change that. The way to begin is to appreciate what you can already do. No matter at what stage you are, your accomplishments and skills are an amazing combination of coordination, love, care, attention, and hard work. Mildred Chase speaks of "taking heart from your best playing," of paying close attention to what you do and finding that one tone, that one phrase, that is the best one you make, of holding that sound and impulse in your mind and spreading it out slowly through all the rest that you do. Chase is talking here about awareness—the first of the three principles of effective practice that we'll look at next.

AWARENESS

Playing and practicing with *awareness* means listening without judging, doing without trying, being fully present in the moment when your body, your instrument, and your music interact.

Professional bass player Barry Green has written a book about musical awareness that deserves a place of honor on every musician's bookshelf: *The Inner Game of Music*. Modeled after Timothy Gallwey's *Inner Game of Tennis* and co-authored by Gallwey, this helpful book is full of advice and exercises to help musicians become aware and stop "trying." "Many musicians," according to Green, "find there is a big difference between the way they play when they are trying and when they are simply being aware. The awareness mode encourages the conscious mind to listen to what's happening, and this increases the a-mount of feedback we receive, which allows positive changes to occur almost without effort."

Practice enables us to observe ourselves in the act of learning.

Here's an example of "trying" versus "awareness." Suppose your teacher or ensemble partner points out a passage where you haven't been holding the sustained notes for their full value. In the trying mode, when you see the passage coming up next, you begin to think: "OK. Here it comes. Now you gotta count. Hold this for three—one and two and three and. Whew! Uh-oh—here comes another one. Ohmigosh, this one gets six! Now don't forget to count. One and two and . . ." At the end of the passage, you naturally turn to your teacher or colleague and ask, "Was that right?"

In the awareness mode, you simply listen: "Listen to the long notes. . . . Listen to this one. . . . Now listen to this one." At the end of the passage, either you know it was better, or you know that you don't know how the passage ought to sound and that you need more information. Both kinds of knowledge are equally valuable, and you are well on your way to owning the passage in the most musical sense.

Awareness is not a frantic thinking but rather a kind of deliberate and unruffled observation. By directing your consciousness toward the music, your self-consciousness is lifted from you. (We have already said that practicing determines playing. Practicing with awareness is the best possible preparation for playing with awareness, which is one of the best ways to cope with stagefright.)

It's easy to talk about awareness, but how do we do it? How do we "try not to try"? Here are some ideas you can experiment with as you practice and play.

Listen

In music, first and foremost, awareness arises from listening. Reminding a musician to listen always seems a bit odd. Isn't that what music is all about? Isn't that what musicians do? Well, not always. Some musicians let a teacher or a tape recorder do their listening. Some let the listening mind be crowded out by the sergeant-major mind, which gives orders when there's trouble coming up: "Watch out for that diminished chord—you always miss it" and "Here comes the high note—now get it in tune" and "Don't mess up the fingering on the fast part." In contrast, when things are going all right, our minds sometimes—come on, admit it—fill with fantasies about how well we're playing—until we make a mistake. Then we begin to thrash ourselves: "You idiot! You blew it again. How many times? . . ." Flutist and recorder player Michael Rossman has observed keenly the effects of listening on his musical awareness:

> If I am anxious for the next note, or about it, I do not listen to the one I am in. *Be where I am.* If I am anxious to hang on to the goodness of where I am, for fear any change may make

Sound is the most important thing a musician can have. . . . If a musician is interested in his sound, then you can look for some good playing.

♪ Miles Davis

Learning to listen means listening with concentration and practising this every day.

♪ Cleo Laine

115

the note more sour, my body translates this into frozen fingers and lips that cannot move. *Don't be afraid to let go; learn to have nothing to lose.*

It is important, if your listening is to be useful to you, that you listen without judgment, that you hear not *what is wrong* but simply *what is.* We've touched a bit on this kind of listening already, in the section on "Learning from Your Instrument" on page 40. As you get to know your instrument or your voice, you become aware of a huge array of possibilities. Every note available to you is available in a fantastic range of volumes, attacks, durations, and tone qualities. This range of possibilities is one of the things that is both frustrating and liberating about making your own music. It's frustrating because, until you develop some technique, it seems that the instrument is making most of the choices. You aim for a clear, soft, ringing A, and you got back a noisy *blat* of indiscriminate pitch. Yet with nonjudgmental awareness, the means will open to you. Each possibility that you accept makes more things possible. Each possibility that you reject as "no good" closes off part of the path. It is not a question of "getting more control" but of "finding more ways."

We may have to stare down some inhibitions on the way to awareness. (Awareness is all fine and good, but we'd rather not be embarrassed or surprised by what we hear.) Improvisation and playing by ear can build awareness by helping us get used to listening to ourselves with open ears and accepting minds.

Watch

Another path for awareness is through the eyes. You may have been told by a teacher that you mustn't watch your hands when you play, and by and large your teacher is right. Your ultimate goal is to feel as comfortable when you play your instrument as when you brush your teeth or button up your overcoat. You could do it with your eyes shut. (Research has shown that musicians who must look at their hands are generally poor sight readers.) However, as an awareness technique, watching yourself play can be very revealing.

By studying your body in action, you can see the musical effects of various postures, embouchures, and hand positions.

There is a continuous dialogue between hand and instrument, hand and culture. Artwork is not thought up in consciousness and then, as a separate phase, executed by the hand. The hand surprises us, creates and solves problems on its own. Often enigmas that baffle our brains are dealt with easily, unconsciously, by the hand.

♪ Stephen Nachmanovitch,
Free Play

You can sometimes easily detect the source of problems with tone quality or tension just by watching yourself play. (If you can't see what you're doing, use a mirror.) You may even find that your intelligent body can outwit your bumbling brain. For example, pianists sometimes cringe at playing in the key of B major. Five sharps! But play a B-major scale and watch your hands. See how the long middle fingers sit comfortably on the black keys and the short fingers—thumb and pinkie—always fall on the same two whites? It is, in fact, a wonderfully genial key for the hand, if not for the mind.

Besides, watching is pleasurable. Every time we watch our hands do something intricate, we are justifiably enchanted. As of this very moment, you have permission to be enchanted by your music-making hands for the rest of your life.

Think Ahead

Careful carpenters have a rule that says, "Measure twice, cut once." Liszt had a sign over his piano that said, "Think ten times, play once."

You are responsible for what you think about as you make music. There are the divine moments when the music draws you after itself, and you simply follow. But there are moments, too, when you feel that you are pursuing it, trying to corner it and tame it. If you are calling yourself names or concentrating on unmusical content (naming notes, for example, or calculating numbers of beats), or if you are fearfully anticipating the next hard passage, then you are missing the place where your mind and the music connect in a beneficial way.

The alternative is to think about what you are going to play and then to listen—simply listen—to the sounds you make, with no judgments, with complete acceptance: this is how it is this time.

In developing awareness, the thinking-about and decision-making step is crucial. When we simply open the book and begin to play, we give our minds no direction. There is no inhale before we exhale, so what comes out is sometimes stale and puny. Taking thought before you begin is like perusing a program before a concert: "This étude, number seven. It's in the key of D and has lots of scale passages. It starts here. I'll listen for it to be not too loud—about a mezzo forte would be right—and a fast walking pace, about *ta ta ta ta*—detached but not too short. I'll listen to see how even the eighth notes are today." You now have a place to go and a way to get there, and your mind has something more important to do than to hurl abuse at you.

One of the simplest but most helpful ways of maintaining awareness is to set a specific objective for every practice effort. For example, if you are just beginning to practice the F-minor melodic scale, your initial goal might be to learn the fingering. Once the fingering is secure, perhaps after several days, your next goal might be to listen to see how many notes have a full, even tone. Once your awareness of tone quality is established, your new goal might be to play the scale for two octaves, listening for a steady tempo, and so forth. You can apply the same process to a fragment of a piece that needs work, deciding to listen to dynamics, to rhythmic accuracy, to intonation, or to the initial sound quality of each note.

Another way of building awareness by thinking ahead is to use your imagination to "pre-hear" a tone or a passage before you play it. As you play, listen to find out how your actual sound resembles or differs from the sound you imagined. Keep your awareness light and easy, and make only observations, no judgments.

The point of thinking ahead, of setting goals, and of pre-hearing is not to set yourself up to succeed or to fail but rather to give your mind appropriate work to do. Practice often involves repetition, but mindless repetition is pointless busywork. As one pianist put it, "It's like trying to teach the piano how to play."

Choose Your Words with Care

No one imagines that a symphony is supposed to improve in quality as it goes along, or that the whole object of playing it is to reach the finale. The point of music is discovered in every moment of playing and listening to it.

♪ Alan Watts

"Now try this" puts you into the trying mode. There's a famous demonstration of the futility of trying that comes to us from the Gestalt psychology of Fritz Perls. A volunteer is asked to try to lift a straight chair from the floor—not actually to lift it but only to try to lift it. The act of trying produces a lot of strain and sweat and what looks for all the world like work, but it never gets the chair off the floor.

In our musical practice, instead of "Try this scale" we can tell ourselves something like "Play this scale" or "Listen to this scale" or "Sing this scale" or "Watch this scale." If you're a person who enjoys using words, you might start a list in your music log of all the things that a musical passage can do: *glisten, throb, melt, bloom, murmur, ooze, thunder, shrug,* and *bound,* for starters.

Be Aware of Being Aware

Our awareness is never perfect, of course. Our attention does wander, but we can learn to be aware of that, too, and simply stop playing. Stopping at the point where you "wander off" or begin to give yourself orders can sometimes reveal a pattern of your own awareness, providing you with more information to use. You become aware of being aware. (If all of this sounds terribly like a course in meditation, that's exactly what it is. If you meditate, you will no doubt bring those skills with you when you play, to your benefit. If you don't meditate, you'll find music a most pleasant way into the well.)

When we are aware, we no longer have to chase perfection. Our practices do not become one disappointment after another. We learn that the opposite of perfect is not failure. We can use awareness to pull ourselves out of the practicing trap—the feeling that "I can't get to the good stuff until I get through this boring stuff." Awareness shows us that it's all "good stuff," that every act of learning is enjoyable for itself. As Barry Green says, "Not only can awareness help us through technical musical challenges of many kinds, it can also enhance our ability to be swept up in the music, to become one with it."

RELEASE

"I ached for years," says Chicago saleswoman Suzanne McGrath, "with all kinds of muscle cramps and pain from playing the viola. I started lessons with a new teacher last year, and I poured out my story one more time. I can't find a comfortable way to hold this instrument, I told her. 'Hold it?' she said. 'You don't have to hold it. Just stand under it.' I won't say that it got easier right away, but this teacher's way of thinking about things helped me get rid of a lot tension over the next few months."

McGrath's new teacher introduced her to our second principle of effective practice: release. *Release*, for a musician, means "letting go." Some musicians use the word *relaxation* to mean the same thing as release, but it's important from the beginning to clarify that we don't mean "limp and lifeless." Using the principle of release means directing energy to its most efficient use, expending no more and no less energy than is required and avoiding pointless tension.

It's hard to have a general discussion of release because every instrument uses the principle in a different way. A pianist, for example, does not have to "hit" a key—the weight of a single finger on a relaxed arm is enough to produce a tone. A recorder player doesn't have to "blow"—it is enough to release the breath in a sigh. A guitarist doesn't have to "lift" the fingers. As one amateur guitarist put it, "They'll just spring back by themselves if you let them. It's a great discovery to get so much for so little. The body will do a lot on its own if you just let it."

We can apply the concept of release to music making in two distinct but interrelated ways. We can think, on the one hand, of "tonal" release—of finding the most efficient and tension-free way of producing a tone or of simply letting a tone happen. And we can think, on the other hand, of what we might call "inter-tonal" release—the relaxed, tension-free state our body returns to when we are not actively preparing or producing a tone.

If we're tense at the moment of tonal release, we're likely to have all kinds of technical problems—inaccuracy, lack of speed, poor dynamic and tonal control—because our muscles are too rigid to respond in the ways the music requires. If we hold tension in our bodies between tones, neglecting inter-tonal release, we're likely to suffer from fatigue or pain as well as to experience a host of technical problems. Otto Ortmann has proposed, in *The Physiological Mechanics of Piano Technique,* that talent for piano playing can be determined in part by "the readiness with which relaxation sets in between [hand] movements."

Ultimately, we are seeking a coordinated pattern of movement, a pattern of alternating contraction and release, which springs from and expresses the rhythm of the music under our hands or through our breath. The rhythm is truly what moves us. In a state of contraction we take it in; in a state of release we let it go. Here are some ideas for applying the principle of release in more specific ways to your own practicing and playing.

I operate on the principle that inside every not-so-beautiful note there's a beautiful note trying to get out. I want to figure out a way to get it out. Free that note!

♪ John Holt, *John Holt and Cello at Home*

I relax my hand after striking every note.

♪ Pablo Casals

Breathe

This is for those musicians "who don't have to breathe as they play." Well, of course you have to breathe! But it's easy, under the stress of mental exertion, to let breathing become shallow or even to hold your breath. This is a significant point for anyone who performs. Breathing freely as you practice will help you breathe freely as you perform, which is a priceless advantage in quelling stagefrights. Remember that *all music springs— way back there—from song.* Experiment using a breathing pattern to accompany a practice pattern. Perhaps you could inhale on a scale going up and exhale going down, or inhale for four bars and exhale for four. Another wonderful exercise is to sing along with your playing (sing *la-la-la* or make up silly words), and observe where you breathe naturally.

Be Aware

Awareness is a close companion of release. You can discover your own principles of release by being aware of the movements you make as you play and the space through which you move. You can be aware of exactly how much effort is really required to release a tone. How much weight do you really have to put down on a piano key, a trumpet valve, or a banjo string? How much air do you really have to move through a clarinet, a trombone, your larynx? Suzanne McGrath, the violist we met on page 119, weighed her viola on her kitchen scale one day. "I had to laugh," she says. "Here I was struggling to hold up something that weighs a pound and a half! I started to think of it as something light and easy to hold. I started letting it just rest on my shoulder, and I suddenly realized that it felt just like a friend putting a hand on my shoulder. It's not heavy, and it's not hard."

During both tonal and inter-tonal release, many musicians have gravity on their side. Any musical gesture that incorporates a downward movement—putting down a key or a string, strumming downward, drawing a bow down, striking with a mallet or a stick—all of these movements can derive virtually all the energy needed from gravity so that the musician can *let* the movement happen rather than *make* it happen. In fact, it usually requires more energy from a player to make a small sound

When we are trying to do something with our fingers, it is very easy to try too hard, to use too much muscular force in the effort to make the fingers move the way we want them to.

♪ Kenneth Wollitz,
The Recorder Book

121

in this way—that is, when the force of gravity must be resisted—than to make a big sound, when gravity can function freely. After a bit of experimentation, we may be surprised at the remarkable efficiency of most musical instruments. All of our squeezing and huffing and pressing and hitting is usually just so much wasted effort.

Be Watchful When You Work on Something New

On his audiotape *Put Your Hands on the Piano and Play*, Daniel Abrams advises students to take four slow, deep breaths before starting something new. It's so easy to let our physical body absorb tension from our feelings ("I really want to do it right") and from our mind ("I really want to figure this out"). Sometimes it doesn't even seem intuitively possible that we can achieve the volume or the speed or the coordination required by a new task unless we put a lot of effort and force into it. This is the time when we need to trust our body, know our instrument, and be willing to let go. Approach a new task with the intention to "let it happen" rather than the need to "make it happen."

Beginners at music sometimes tend to use excessive physical force and activity, like the new driver who oversteers every corner and slams on the brakes at every stop. Most teachers, though, agree that it is easier to refine overly forceful playing than it is to energize or embolden timid, tenuous movements. If your teacher tells you to "lighten up," he's talking about release.

Seek a Playing Position that Encourages Release

Our capacity to release the small movements we use to make music is rooted in our overall posture and position. In this sense playing music is a bit like pouring from a pitcher. With a firm but flexible grip on the pitcher, we can pour smoothly, in just the right place and in just the right amount. Hold firmly and let go.

Most teachers and most instruction books have something to say about posture, and you can get a version of the general ideas that apply to your instrument from almost any accomplished player. Be forewarned that you're likely to find a few widely accepted principles and many specific disagreements. Ultimately, you will have to do your own thinking and observ-

Seek a playing position that encourages release.

ing. A good playing posture for you is one that enables you to feel balanced and safe, to release tones freely, to release tension between tones, to move freely, and to play for as long as you want to play. If your posture "makes all things possible," then it's all right for you, for now at least. If a teacher suggests a change, find out the reasons behind her idea and give it a try if it makes sense to you. It's the result that matters. Your playing will ultimately reflect your posture.

In establishing your playing position, be receptive to new information, to feedback from your body and your sound, and to your own changing needs. Most musicians would love to find The Perfect Position, and some musicians fervently believe that such a position exists. Interestingly, though, a research study on double bass players done by Allan Dennis at the University of Southwestern Louisiana showed no significant difference in overall muscle tension among three very different ways of supporting a double bass. It is probably more useful to be willing to change and experiment than it is to seek fervently for The Truth or to cling tenaciously to one posture forever. Every body is unique; common sense tells us that there's unlikely to be one position that will meet everyone's needs at every stage of musical growth. Alan Spencer, a Boston violinist-turned-fiddler, found the position he learned in childhood much too tension-producing. At a workshop, he evolved to a new position that

felt just right for about a year. Then I started to fiddle, and I wanted to be looser—always looser. Finally, the position that had seemed just right a year before evolved again into something completely new.

And then I changed jobs. My new job took all my attention for many months, and I almost never had my fiddle out. Things finally calmed down in the summer, and I took it on vacation with me. The first time I played it, I tried to re-create the position I had worked so hard for. But because I hadn't fiddled for a long time and maybe was no longer as keenly attuned to my body, that position felt way too insecure. I had to start over, looking for a way to hold it that suited my needs then.

I've finally decided that it's something I have to learn over almost every day. What am I like today? What do I need? What does this music need? As soon as I detect tension or stiffness, I go to the root of it, but I no longer have the expectation that someday I'll find the right way to hold the thing.

If you're troubled by posture or position problems, or if you experience pain or muscular fatigue, you might ask around to locate a teacher who specializes in this aspect of playing and arrange for some lessons on this topic. You might also ask someone to videotape you as you play. Or you might consult an Alexander Technique teacher. (Alexander Technique is a system of movement analysis and education that seeks to make efficient and harmonious use of the body. Many musicians and singers find Alexander Technique lessons very helpful.) For severe problems, some doctors who specialize in sports medicine also treat musicians, and a few doctors practice "music medicine" exclusively, specializing in injuries and stress-related conditions.

Keep Moving

This doesn't mean to wander about the room or to weave on your chair like a punching doll. But try this experiment. Stretch your arm out to your side, at shoulder level, and hold it perfectly still. After thirty seconds, lower your arm and immediately jot down any sensations you've experienced in your arm—burning, tingling, trembling, aches, pressure. Wait for about ten minutes and do the experiment again. But this time, instead of holding your arm perfectly still, let it make continuous "micro-movements"—very small, slight adjustments, a little forward and a little back, a little up and then down, a little bent and then straight, turned a bit in and then turned back. After thirty seconds of this, lower your arm, jot down your observations again, and compare the results. Most people find that with micro-movements they can keep their arm "afloat" far more comfortably than with a rigid arm. Rigidity builds tension. Slight movements, slight continuous adjustments, allow release.

In playing music, we frequently sit or stand in one basic position for long periods of time, making repetitive motions. This is a perfect formula for creating stress, tension, aches, and pain, and for building a clientele for the music-medicine specialists. We can release substantial amounts of this "frozen energy" by incorporating micro-movements into our playing posture and by taking frequent short breaks, perhaps just long enough to shake out the hands and stretch the back, setting a released starting position for the next passage.

Play Lightly

Especially during long practices, when playing very fast passages, or when working on "big" passages or works, play lightly. Both the ear and the muscles are quickly fatigued, and then tension sets in. Work, as singers do, with "half voice" some of the time so that sustaining your focus does not become an effort in itself.

Separate the Idea of Music from the Idea of Performance

We may successfully eliminate every physical cause of tension but still fail to play in a released way because we are so used to associating music making with performing. Nearly all childhood music lessons lead to a recital or to a competition or an exam. Nearly all school music leads to a concert. All the music we hear on our sound systems, on the radio, on TV, and in movies is in a context of performance. Workshops and summer camps end with a performance, and it is a rare ensemble that plays together very long before beginning to seek an audience. It's naturally hard for some of us to shake off the association between music of any kind and performing—especially those of us who were constantly "on stage" as children, trying to please an ambitious parent.

Performance, for most people, gives birth to anxiety and tension. As long as we equate playing with performing, we invite tension and are unable to feel released. If we can come to music to make its acquaintance and not merely to display it, we free ourselves to play in a more released way. As amateurs, we owe it to our fellow humans to rescue music making from the performance arena and return it to a path into our selves and out to the world.

People who don't understand why amateurs make music are confused about this very issue. To some nonmusicians, it appears that the only reason for making music is to perform. If we are obviously not "good enough" to be in demand as performers, then what's the point?

The point is that music is first of all for knowing and for reaching inside ourselves, next it's for sharing, and lastly it's for performing. In the greatest artists and the humblest amateurs these endeavors shine gracefully together.

CHUNKING

The third principle of effective practice is a concept that psychologists call *chunking*. Chunking means grouping data into meaningful units. It has been proved many times by psychological researchers, beginning with Hermann Ebbinghaus in 1885, that it is easier to remember a meaningful series of numbers, letters, or words than it is to remember a random or meaningless series. For example, it's easier to memorize the number series 2, 4, 6, 8, 10, 12, 14 than to memorize the number series 17, 3, 51, 20, 9, 13, 62. It's easier to remember the sequence of sharps—F C G D A E B—by the silly but meaningful phrase "Father Charles Goes Down And Ends Battle" than by a random list of words such as "Fin Canasta Gelatin Declare Acorn Empire Bobsled."

When we apply the principle of chunking as musicians, we perceive and practice our music in meaningful units, even if those units are very short. This principle is especially important for those who read music. The eye easily misleads us into perceiving music as single units called "notes" or as small fenced-off units called "measures" or "bars." Focusing as you play on one note at a time or on one bar at a time is like typing a text in a language you don't know. The exercise has little value except as a feat of mental and manual dexterity.

As an example of how written music can mislead us into playing unmeaningful units, let's look at the first line of the chorus to Woody Guthrie's "So Long, It's Been Good to Know Yuh." If we perceive the line measure by measure, stopping at every bar line, it looks like this:

An experience is an isolated moment, life is a continuity. For music to come to life in the mind, experience must somehow connect with experience, one musical experience with another, musical experiences with experiences of different kinds, the whole thing must develop, must grow in scope and depth.

♪ Victor Zuckerkandl,
The Sense of Music

Figure 8-1

126

But if we ignore the bar lines, apply the principle of chunking, and perceive the music in meaningful units, we get:

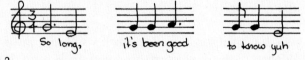

Figure 8-2

Many amateurs have a great love of music and an intense desire to make music, but they feel unfulfilled and dissatisfied with the music they make themselves. Sometimes these feelings are due not so much to limitations of technique as to this fragmentation of attention and meaning whereby the single note or beat or chord or measure gets the complete focus while the relationship between these units is neglected.

Music provides us with endless natural opportunities to apply the principle of chunking. The difficulty is that we are often so deep inside the minute details of what we are doing that the "chunks" escape us. We need to find ways to detect the meaningful units—rhythmic units that belong together, melodically meaningful groups of notes, standard chord progressions, phrase structures, and finally compositional structure itself. Here are some ideas for applying chunking in your playing and your practice.

Always Think in Groups, Never in Single Units

If you are learning to read rhythms, read groups of quarters, groups of eighths, mixed groups of quarters and eighths and dotted notes, and so forth. Knowing that a quarter note gets one beat is not useful information unless there are other notes to which you can relate a quarter note. Similarly, if you are learning to read chords, think of them as single units, not as a collection of three or four or five separate notes. Let your eye see a C-major triad and let your hand make one gesture to take that chord rather than reading and playing three separate items—one finger on C, one finger on E, and one finger on G. (For a bit more on this, see the next chapter on practicing the skills of music making.)

As a general rule, it is almost never useful to stop and repeat, for the sake of practice, a single note. If you have a technical problem or need to fix a mistake, put the troublesome note into a "chunk" and practice that chunk.

Sing

Even if you don't sing very well, even if you are a pure instrumentalist, learn to think of everything you do as song. Listen to good singing in your preferred style of music—Kathleen Battle or Billie Holiday or Loretta Lynn. With the words and the breath to guide them, good singers are natural interpreters, which means they are naturals at chunking.

If you are puzzled by a passage and can't seem to make musical sense of it, make up some words and turn it into a little song. Experiment with different sets of words to see what nestles most comfortably into the musical context. "Mary Had a Little Lamb" would come out quite awkwardly if the lamb were handed over to "Doreen."

Dance

Or at least move. Chunking applies not only to sound but also to movement. A meaningful musical unit is produced by a single gesture. If we forget to apply chunking, and . . . play . . . instead . . . one . . . note . . . at . . . a . . . time, our music turns into something like a film viewed frame by frame. Get the film running, even if you see only short clips.

Once again, if you are puzzled by a passage, see if you can make up a dance step or a hand gesture that captures the sense and direction you think you need. If you are working to fit separate notes together, consider the complete gesture your hand must make to produce them rather than the individual note-by-note movements. Think fluid. Let a scale or a long run become a smooth wave rather than so many separate drops.

Apply Any Music Theory You Know to the Music You Make

The really interesting part of music theory has to do with the relationships of note to note, chord to chord, phrase to phrase. If you study any theory, see how many ways you can use what you know to help you in your practice. (As a general introduction to understanding musical relationships, an excellent book is Victor Zuckerkandl's *The Sense of Music*. It was written for listeners but is a wonderful resource for active musicians as well.)

A major goal for any musician at any level is to be able to "just play" with that kind of effortlessness that makes it look so easy—to reach, in fact, that place where it *is* easy! Another name for this is *musical fluency*, which is just like language fluency. We are aiming to make music a language that we speak—in whatever dialect we choose—with ease and confidence. The principles of practice we've discussed in this chapter—awareness, release, and chunking—are also the keys to musical fluency. They are tools that let us understand and execute music as patterns, as designs, as continuous and meaningful statements.

It may have occurred to you that pursuing practice with these three principles in mind is going to slow you down a bit. You're right about that. Freff, a columnist for *Keyboard* magazine, put it this way: "Anger never forced a chord into your hand. Impatience never taught you a part. Pain never brought you a new idea. These are the enemy. They shut you down, not open you up. And closed minds don't learn anything except avoidance."

Like any other musical skill, these three principles will take time to develop. The skills of practicing have to be practiced too! The reward for this practice, though, arrives at the moment that we just *play*—the word is such a good one!—when we lean into the music and let the world very briefly fall away, when we travel inward and return renewed.

The high-octane approach is a mistake in music. A thoughtful, ambling pace seems to work best.

♪ Frank R. Wilson, *Tone Deaf and All Thumbs?*

Practicing is an act of faith. The practicing that you do now is your down payment for next year and years to come.

♪ John Perry, professor of piano, University of Southern California, Los Angeles

CHAPTER 9

Working to Play:
The Skills of Music

Stop! Look around! This is the farmer's market of musical endeavor. There's something different in every stall, and you probably don't want to carry home too much at one time. Did you bring your list?—the one you made in chapter 6 when we went through the skills of music making? If not, you may want to look back at pages 76–88 before continuing.

In this chapter we'll take a detailed look at ways of learning and improving basic musical skills: technique, reading music, sight-reading, playing by ear, improvisation, memorization, and music theory. We'll end with a discussion about solving musical problems—sticky bits, hard parts, mistakes, and the like.

The best way to use this chapter is to browse through it once to find out what's here and then come back to it later when you need specific information about a particular skill. Even if you're not the practicing sort, you may find ideas here that you can use when you have a tricky ensemble bit to work out, when you want to revive an old skill, or when you're ready to open another window.

TECHNIQUE

We meet some musical patterns so often that it makes sense to learn them separately so that we don't have to scuffle with them every time they come up. This is one of the best reasons for practicing *technique*, the actual movements that you make with your body when you sing or play. When practicing technique we meet and experiment with our instrument or voice to forge strong bonds among mind, muscles, and the means of making sound. As Kenneth Wollitz says, we "learn to play *ourselves* in the mode dictated by our instrument." If you look at the chart on page 80, you'll see that technique is the one musical skill that *every* musician requires.

Certain technical skills are common to all styles of music: these include scales, chromatic scales, chords and chord progressions, arpeggios, and "long tones" (long, sustained notes played to develop tone quality). Other technical skills are associated only with certain musical styles, such as Baroque embellishments or blues turnarounds. When learning these we acquire a special vocabulary for the style of music that we like best—we learn the idioms, the clichés, the figures of speech that give the style its special flavor. There's also technique that is specific to each instrument—vibrato, register changes, flutter tonguing, double stopping, and chord barring, for example.

At the heart of technical development for most musicians are *scales* and *tone quality*. A knowledge of scales and their associated arpeggios and chord forms helps us approach music making with confidence. As scale playing becomes second nature, musical terrain seems less rugged and chaotic. We internalize what musicians sometimes call "key feeling." As our hands, lips, and ears assimilate the shape of various scales and their related key signatures, we develop a natural impulse to reach for either the right note or at least a logical note in any given passage.

The ability to control and vary our tone quality helps us approach music expressively. As our tone quality develops and matures, our music making can carry an ever-expanding scope of meaning and depth. Tone quality and intensity are close relatives. Good tonal technique means knowing the difference between *volume* and *intensity*. It means knowing how to make a big

Attend to your technical apparatus so that you are prepared and armed for every possible event; then, when you study a new piece, you can turn all your power to the intellectual content; you will not be held up by the technical problems.

♪ Ferruccio Busoni

For me, I am hungry to learn about different kinds of scales. It's all a vocabulary that I use and I need as much as possible.

♪ Carlos Santana

For centuries I carried around my first forty pages of Klosé that my teacher gave me and used it faithfully. It got so tattered that I keep it at home now. I still play it. Yesterday, for instance, I played at the Portland Jazz Festival. So I practiced the first few pages of Klosé—scales, basic scales. And legit. I don't play them in a jazz style. Absolutely straight tone, absolutely legit and even. In fact I call it "cleaning out." . . .

My experience is that if you play jazz, every night, without practicing legit fundamentals, you'll erode your technique. But if you stay with those basics, those scales and thirds and chromatics and everything, and tonguing exercises, your jazz is better. Easier to play.

♪ Buddy de Franco

Experiment to find the right time of day to practice technique.

sound that is rich and full, and how to make a small sound that is also rich and full. That's intensity.

To acquire and maintain technique, many musicians like to use standard books of scale studies, technical exercises, and études—Hanon and Czerny for piano, Sor and Giuliani for classical guitar, Kreutzer and Mazas for violin, Hering and Tyrrell for trumpet, Cavally and Köhler for flute, and hundreds and hundreds more. Most books of technical studies were written by nineteenth-century performers who were considered great teachers. Most include a preface by the composer that is worth reading. Many études are actually lovely small pieces all by themselves, and if you play very many, you are likely to develop some favorites. The disadvantage of études is that some require more time and effort to learn than can really be justified in musical—or even technical!—returns. Very few musicians study "every étude in the book." An experienced player who has "done" the standard étude collections for your instrument can likely itemize the names and numbers of the really useful ones.

If you practice technique, it's worth experimenting to find the right time of day and the right time in your playing sessions to do it. Technique requires patience and a forgiving attitude toward yourself, the ability to go slowly and to do only a little at a time. (There are twelve major scales. If you learn only one a month, you will still get through them all in a year.)

Technical points that are specific to particular instruments and particular styles are too numerous to detail here, but these seven general principles apply to everyone:

1. Practice technique with awareness. Before you begin an exercise or an étude, ask yourself *why* you are playing it this time. It could be to learn the fingering, to check intonation, to experiment with hand positions, to improve control of dynamics, to develop even tone. There are dozens of possible reasons, but if there is no reason, then there is no point in doing it.

2. Work in patterns and contexts. Apply the principle of chunking. It is never worth stopping technical practice, or practice of any kind, to fix a single note. Every note lives in a musical context. Always practice musically meaningful groups of notes, including a preparation and a follow-through.

3. Avoid mindless repetition. If you need to repeat a passage many times, introduce some variety so that you stay alert and involved. Small variations are sufficient—a bit softer this time, a bit slower the next, now smooth and connected, now short and detached, now listen to the center of the tone, now close your eyes.

4. Play with a very steady rhythm, even if it's slow.   Playing technical material in a secure rhythm exposes weak spots very quickly. Some parts of scales, for example, are easier to play than others. If you habitually rush the easy parts and "give in" to the difficulties, you will either fumble the same passage when you meet it in a piece of music, or you will alternately rush and drag the tempo where it makes no musical sense to do so.

5. Emphasize efficiency and effortlessness rather than speed. Apply the principle of release. The purpose of some technical practice is to get our speed up—to play runs, trills, and riffs at a musical tempo. Going for speed itself, though, usually gives less reliable results than going for efficiency. If speed is your goal, analyze the sequence of movements you're making. find out where effort is really required and where effortlessness will do. For example, holding a finger down on a violin or a flute requires less effort than lifting a finger up. Excess effort fed into "down" can turn into fatigue and diminished control, leaving the muscles poorly prepared for "up." In his book *The Clarinet and Clarinet Playing*, David Pino offers advice that's valuable to all musicians:

> Very rarely, if ever, is the problem an inherent lack of speed. You *may* lack speed, but if you do, that lack comes from poor control and coordination. It is a mistake to *say* that you lack speed because that lack is only a symptom of some other and more basic lack. The real problem is usually in the areas of airflow, relaxation, rhythmic steadiness, or in the simple coordination of the fingers with the tongue. . . . Work for control, coordination, relaxation, but not for speed!

6. Be fearless.   Vague, flimsy, unfocused playing will not disclose the problems that need attention, nor will it allow your strengths to shine.

7. Be musical.   Technique is drawn out of a musical context and must finally return there. It makes sense, then, to take up technique musically and not mechanically. In *Notes on the Piano*, Ernst Bacon says, "The moment you approach *technique in a musical spirit*, it will begin to yield, and its obstacles will re-

It is infuriatingly difficult sometimes to attain the lack of strain a good technique displays. The perfect juggler does his juggling act effortlessly. . . . To be sure a great deal of effort went into mastering the technique, but the whole object of mastering it is to render it effortless.

♪ Yehudi Menuhin, *The Compleat Violinist*

Technical work should be performed with an impelling sense of risk. Learn to dare; do what is asked for and do it full out, larger than life. You can always make smaller what is too big, but it is often impossible to make larger what has stiffened into too small.

♪ David Craig, *On Singing Onstage*

The HOW of interpretation is technical . . . in most cases, the technical solution to a problem is also its musical solution.

♪ Dorothy Taubman

solve into music, in which spirit they must have been conceived. It's the difference between Sir Edmund Hillary, whose life-dream was climbing Everest, and a Sherpa porter for whom climbing is but a livelihood. The end gives wings to the means."

There is no arguing that technique is plain hard work most of the time. It's like a steamroller—slow and steady, smoothing out everything it travels over. If we approach our work with curiosity and patience, and if we let go of our resistance and our judgments, then acquisition of technique will slowly but reliably strengthen all our musical abilities.

It is when we are *playing*, not practicing, that technical work pays off and can be forgotten—not abandoned, but rather consigned to the subconscious to serve us from there, like a benevolent genie. Our technique becomes as secure, finally, as brushing our teeth. We no longer have to think how it's done. But just as we all get routine brushing and flossing reminders from our dentist, so even the simplest technique can be brought to the surface, re-examined, renewed, and deepened at any time. "Good technique" is a wonderful thing to have, but "wrong" or "bad" technique will not ruin you or keep you out of the midst of music. Don't put off music making or the acquisition of other skills because you fear your technique is insufficient. It is more important to *play music.*

Habit begins as a spider's thread and ends as a steel cable.

♪ Chinese proverb

READING MUSIC

The ability to read music never made a musician out of anyone. It's simply a way for musicians to share their music with each other. As a way of communicating, written music is actually crude and imprecise compared to the message it is intended to convey. Nevertheless, the ability to read gives us access to a great wealth of musical ideas and traditions. Learning to read is an absorbing endeavor and a thrilling accomplishment.

Why Is Learning to Read Music So Difficult?

Learning the *principles* of written music is not difficult or time-consuming. But learning to apply the principles as you play or sing takes consistent and dedicated practice. Musicians who learn to read as adults generally find it a slow process. It's slow for children, too, though that doesn't always seem so obvious. For example, a twelve-year-old who reads easily has probably been working at it for five or six years. Adults tend to feel frustrated after five or six weeks.

One source of difficulty is that new musicians are usually trying to learn how to play an instrument and how to read at the same time. Either one of those tasks is enough to swamp your powers of concentration. If you find yourself in this situation, it would be worth learning to play a few things by ear or by rote before you tackle written music. (That's the trick that gets all those Suzuki tots off to such a flying start.)

Another puzzling aspect about written music is that no matter what anyone tells you, it's not "just another written language." In a written language, every letter or letter combination has a fixed identity—a single sound or a small number of sounds that the letters always stand for. In music, no melodic symbol has any fixed identity. Each little oval takes its meaning relative to the others, determined by its location on a kind of ladder called a *staff.* Information about rhythm is layered over these melody-making ovals, while other systems of symbols and words are squeezed in, generally any place they will fit, to suggest phrasing and interpretation. Reading music is much more like reading a map than reading a language. (There's scientific evidence for the idea that music reading is not a linguistic skill. In *Art, Mind, and Brain,* Howard Gardner describes several cases of musicians who, following a stroke or a brain injury, could no longer read words but could still read music.)

Some new readers get puzzled trying to sort out what is significant information in written music from what is not. For example, the notes in carefully prepared music are "nicely spaced" horizontally to make reading easier, but the actual horizontal distance between notes is not meaningful. The vertical distance between notes, however, is always meaningful. On the other hand, the up-or-down direction of stems on notes is meaningful in some circumstances but not in others: sometimes stem direction is a matter of convenience, and sometimes it conveys essential information.

Another difficulty in music reading arises from multiple meanings assigned to a scant handful of letters and numbers. An ordinary *2* for example, like a magician's tired rabbit, can

I'm learning to read music and play the piano. And it is hard, excruciatingly hard, for me. I literally sweat with concentration, trying to figure out what those strange symbols are trying to tell me. But I love it. I love the struggle, and I love the reward.

♪ Denise Hodges, homemaker and amateur pianist

People should not learn to read music until they have a good repertoire of songs under their belt. When they know what kind of music they like and how they want to sing it, then they can learn to read. One wouldn't teach a child dance notation before the child could dance. One never teaches a baby to read before it can talk. Music notes can be a valuable aid later on, but they are a real danger too early. They tend to freeze the musician into thinking these notes are the way it must go.

♪ Pete Seeger

be hauled out time after time, describing a note lasting for two beats falling on the second beat of the second bar of the second ending played with the second finger on the second degree of the scale!

It would seem logical to learn music reading by studying familiar tunes—"Auld Lang Syne" or "Happy Birthday" or "Yankee Doodle." There are two big problems with this approach, though. First of all, anyone who can play by ear tends, usually unconsciously, to lean on ear skills and doesn't really develop reliable reading skills in this way. The other problem is that music often looks misleading on the page. Even experienced readers can fail to recognize a well-known tune until they begin to play it. (It's a bit like the little boy who burst into tears when he was told that *o-n-c-e* spells *once*.) Some things that are actually very easy to play look formidable when they're written down. Anyone, for example, can make interesting tunes by playing on the black keys of a piano, but any such tune written out would make a lot of pianists go pale.

That's the bad news. The good news is that if you take heart and have patience, *you can learn how to read music.* Your playing ability will likely surge ahead of your reading ability at first, but the day will come when the struggle stands on its head, when you look at a piece of music and realize that you can read it but you can't quite play it.

Reading Rhythm

Although the musical symbols for melody and rhythm are combined in written music, it is possible to separate them and learn each component independently. Most methods teach music reading this way to some extent. Of the two components, rhythm reading, or "learning to count," is the one to learn first and to learn best. Inaccurate melody is easy to forgive, but inaccurate rhythm makes musical trouble. Imagine a marching band. If the piccolo players play a lot of wrong notes, it might sound terrible, but the band can still keep marching. But if the piccolos start marching in an erratic rhythm—too slow or too fast, starting and stopping unpredictably—there will be a mighty big pileup in very little time. In the same way, any piece of music becomes confusing and finally "piled up" and incomprehensible if the rhythm is unclear.

Another reason for giving priority to rhythm reading comes up in the next section of this chapter: research has shown that rhythm-reading ability is the single best predictor of sight-reading ability. In other words, good sight readers are first of all good rhythm readers.

In written music, rhythm is represented by symbols that organize time as evenly spaced pulses or beats. Groups of beats or parts of beats are called by the same names we use for fractions—*eighth, quarter, half, whole*. This system is, in fact, *too accurate* for musical rhythm, which is always a free rhythm and not a clock rhythm. In the learning stages, though, the written rhythm is taken literally. (An exception: jazz and blues players will usually substitute a swing rhythm for even divisions of the beat fairly early in their rhythm reading.)

Many systems have been devised to help musicians understand rhythmic notation, and when you learn to read you will learn one or more of these systems. Some teachers and books have systems of their own; others use one of the more-or-less "standard" systems. We'll look at four systems here and give some brief examples so that you can evaluate and put into a context what you're learning.

1. The mathematical system. This system describes the mathematical principles of rhythm writing—four quarter notes equal a whole note, two quarter notes equal a half note, two eighth notes equal a quarter note, and so forth. Although this information is interesting for its own sake, it's not particularly useful because it doesn't give you any idea of what the rhythm actually sounds like. When the music begins, you literally "don't have time" to add and divide fractions as you play. All musicians rely on the mathematical system when they write music as a way of checking that every measure has the right number of beats in it. But for playing music a system of ongoing counting is more useful than a system of calculating.

2. The numerical counting system. This system has, in the past, been the most commonly taught in North America. Adults who studied music in childhood probably "learned to count" in this way. The system is based on counting the number of beats in a bar. For example, if a piece is in three-four time—waltz time—a numerical counter would count *1-2-3, 1-2-3, 1-2-3.* Di-

It was no coincidence that Einstein played the violin, for "time" as a fourth dimension is no mere abstraction to a musician, but rather an infinite living, pulsating continuum, varied and mobile, sometimes dense, sometimes weightless, sometimes eruptive, sometimes still, its laws identical with those interacting ones of gravity, speed and weight which govern spatial phenomena.

♪ Yehudi Menuhin, *Theme and Variations*

137

vided beats are counted with extra syllables—*ee*s and *and*s and *ah*s—squeezed in between the main beats. See Figure 9-1 for examples. An advantage of this system is that it is widely known—many ensemble musicians and music teachers learned this system as students and still use it to analyze rhythm. Numerical counting also helps delineate the patterns of strong and weak beats in each measure, since each beat is represented by a different number. The disadvantage, especially for a self-taught adult learner, is that the system is not self-correcting. It's possible to assign everything its proper count and still get the rhythm wrong if you inadvertently take extra time between beats or between divisions of beats.

3. The Kodály system. This system was developed by Zoltán Kodály (pronounced koh-DYE-ee; the *l* is silent), a Hungarian composer and music educator. Versions of this system are fairly common in current music education, especially in teaching vocal music. The Kodály system assigns a nonsense syllable that begins with the letter *t* to every common rhythmic value or pattern. So, a quarter note is called *tah* (written as *ta*), two eighth notes are called *tee-tee* (written as *ti-ti*), four sixteenths are called *tiri-tiri* or *tuka-tuka*, and so forth. The Kodály system tends to be more accurate and more self-correcting than the numerical counting system because common rhythmic patterns are expressed as a single unit. For example, when reading a group of repeating sixteenth notes, the Kodály *tuka-tuka tuka-tuka tuka-tuka* is easier, both to say and to remember, than the numerical *one-ee-and-ah two-ee-and-ah three-ee-and-ah*. The Kodály system has an additional benefit for wind players in that it prepares the way for natural tonguing. A disadvantage of Kodály is that it can be confusing to learn, especially on your own. Unless you have someone to imitate, it is hard at the beginning to keep *ta*s and *ti*s and *tiri*s straight and to keep the beat going as each unit is read off. With more complex rhythmic patterns—dotted notes, ties, syncopations—the method becomes less straightforward. Also, the Kodály system has no built-in way of calling attention to patterns of strong and weak beats.

4. The word cue system. This system has probably been used in an unorganized way since the dawn of musical time. Research in music education is beginning to indicate that this system is more efficient and reliable than others at the learning stage. The word cue system assigns a common English word to every common rhythmical unit. So, a quarter note is called by a one-syllable word such as *Ruth* or *Maine* or *grape*. A group of two eighths is assigned a two-syllable word such as *Linda* or *Kansas* or *partners*. Four sixteenths are called by a four-syllable word— *Alexander* or *Mississippi* or *alligator*. Other samples are shown in Figure 9-1. It's a system that's easy and fun to learn—it's a little bit silly, which helps keep the learning process low-key. Also, it seems to work better than other systems for "keeping the beat," for keeping rhythmic groups intact, and for putting rhythmic emphasis in the appropriate place. There is less likelihood of inappropriate pauses or accents, and this makes it especially useful to self-taught musicians. One disadvantage is that it's not a widely known system, at least among current adult musicians, and there is no commonly used set of words that are assigned as standard cues.

Rhythm Reading System	 ♩	 ♫	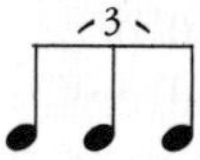 ³ ♫♪	 ♬♬	 ♬	 ♪♬
Mathematical	quarter	two eighths	triplet	four sixteenths	two sixteenths and one eighth	one eighth and two sixteenths
Numerical	1	1-and	1-triplet	1-ee-and-ah	1-ee-and	1-and-ah
Kodály	ta	ti-ti	triola *or* tirola *or* tripolet	tiri-tiri *or* tuka-tuka	tiri-ti *or* tuka-ti	ti-tira *or* ti-tuka
Word Cue	Maine *or* grape	Kansas *or* partners	Washington *or* pineapple	Mississippi *or* alligator	anyone *or* cantaloupe	run pony *or* dishwater

Figure 9–1

Whichever method you use, the result—the rhythm patterns that you produce from a given text—should be identical. For example, this pattern

Figure 9–2

sounds the same whether you read it as *1-and 2 3-ee-and-ah 4* or *ti-ti ta tuka-tuka ta* or *partners grape Mississippi grape.*

However you learn to read—with a teacher, a group, a self-help book, or a computer program—you'll probably be taught one or two of these systems. It's worth remembering, though, that other systems exist. If you run into problems, look for another book or ask around for another helper who might be able to approach counting in a different way.

Reading Melody

By "reading melody" here, we mean reading the pitches that you play or sing. The pitches may not make up a melody per se—they may be a harmony line or a series of chords. We're just using the term here as a shortcut to distinguish pitches from rhythm.

If you're just beginning to read melody, and you're utterly confused, be sure that you are clear about conventions for naming up and down, or high and low, on your instrument. There is no logical reason for calling a pitch that has many vibrations per second (such as a soprano would sing) a "high" note and one with few vibrations (such as a bass would sing) a "low" note. We just do it by mutual agreement. We could just as well call them "open and closed" or "thick and thin" or "light and dark." Most people have no problem with this part of it. The trouble begins when we apply these terms to an instrument. For example, on stringed instruments, notes get higher as you go towards the body of the instrument, which musicians call "up" the fingerboard. So on a violin, "up" is toward the musician's body; but on a guitar, "up" is to the right, and on a cello, "up" is towards the floor!

The systems in common use for teaching melody reading fall into two main categories—*note-naming* and *interval-recognition*. In a note-naming system, the student learns to identify notes on a staff by their alphabetical name (A, B, C, D, E, F, and G) and learns where each note is located on the instrument. Reading then becomes a process of identifying a note and playing the corresponding pitch. In interval-recognition, the student learns to identify the musical distance between notes, to think in such terms as "up a second, down a third, down a second, up a fifth," and to play the intervals rather than the note names. The note names are still learned, but sometimes this is postponed until interval reading is secure. Sometimes interval-recognition is taught by a method called *solfège* or *solmization*, assigning the syllables *do, re, mi, fa, sol, la,* and *ti* to the notes of the scale.

The system that works best for any student is the one that leads to the most musical playing, though ultimately a combination of the two systems has the greatest advantages for most people. The note-naming system is easier to learn and apply. Sometimes, though, it produces mechanical, unmusical results. Students who learn only note-naming sometimes tend to play note by note rather than in melodic patterns, and at some later time they must break the habit of naming each note as they play. Note-naming is an "eye-centered" method, whereas interval-recognition is "ear-centered."

Though interval-recognition may take longer to learn, it helps enormously in understanding musical structure. Interval-recognition requires direct listening, which, when it comes to learning music, is always a good thing. Anyone who wants to play by ear will benefit especially from this system. If your teacher or self-instruction method does not present interval-recognition, you might want to shop around for a helper or a self-teaching book that can get you started.

Helping Yourself Learn to Read

Here are some suggestions—some contributed by teachers and some by amateurs—to help you learn to read music:

1. Keep a pencil and some music manuscript paper handy. Reinforce what you learn by writing out examples for yourself. Even just copying out music from a book will attune you to all the components of written music.

2. If you are teaching yourself, choose a book intended for that purpose. As mentioned on page 50, many music-learning books in music stores are intended to be used with a teacher's help and often don't contain enough information for you to teach yourself. Be sure any book you buy specifies that it's for self-teaching. Howard Shanet's *Learn to Read Music* is a thorough and inexpensive introduction, and Homespun Tapes has a good audiotape series by Matt Glaser (see appendix 2). You might also check at a college or university bookstore in the music or education coursebook section. Most elementary education students are required to take a course in music, and many of them have to learn to read. You may find a workbook with cassette tapes aimed at that group. You can also watch for continuing education programs in music reading or basic music theory, which usually include reading principles.

3. Always be willing to ask. Your best ally in your learn-to-read campaign is someone, of any age, who can give clear and patient explanations and demonstrations. Keyboard demonstrations are especially useful for melody reading, even for players of nonkeyboard instruments, because you can see the interval relationships clearly.

4. Stay close to your body, your voice, and your instrument. You can only learn how to read music if you make music. Always work in here-and-now sound, no matter how simple. Sometimes learning to read involves us in activities that make us feel a bit silly. Push your way though your inhibitions! Clapping, tapping, marching, dancing, arm swinging, and interval singing will make your work more secure. Some teachers of adult students recommend that anyone with rhythm-reading difficulties take a class in dance or movement.

5. Remember that melody and rhythm are normal human actions, not abstractions. When it's cast in writing, music too easily lays down its life. It's the musician's responsibility to keep it vital. Melody is a flow, not a parade of separate events. Rhythm is movement, not mathematical symbol. Work to avoid the feeling that when you read music, you are doing something artificial. Relate the music you read to events and actions you know. When you "keep a steady beat," think of swinging in a playground swing, of how the movement drives on between the "beats." Musical rhythm is like that, not like the stilted gait of a bridesmaid processing down the aisle too slowly to keep her balance.

6. Be patient and forgiving with yourself. Don't beat up on yourself because you don't remember things from one day to the next. When you encounter problems, lighten up!

7. Try your hand at composing. As soon as you learn how to write one note and one rhythm, you can write a song! It doesn't matter how short or simple it is. Have fun making something new out of what you learn. As you turn up the need for more skills or more information, go after it. Anything you learn will mean much more if you use it actively.

8. Always think in patterns. Apply the principle of chunking. Take in and play back as much at one time as you can. If, at the beginning, that amounts to two notes, that's terrific! That's reading music, not just reading notes. Read in logical rhythmic and melodic groups as soon as possible. Learn to recognize common chord shapes rather than reading the names of each note in the chord.

9. Join a singing group. Many amateurs interviewed for this book mentioned that singing from music in a chorus or a choir had helped improve their reading substantially, especially the skills of interval recognition and rhythmic accuracy.

10. Learn to read in the style in which you would like to play, if at all possible. It's all the same system, and everyone gets to the same place in the end, but if you want to play rock and your reading material is classical, your motivation may flag. Browse in a music store for easy material written for children or adult beginners in your favorite style. You'll find simple music in almost every idiom—classical, pop, country, jazz, rock, folk, ragtime, gospel, blues, and contemporary art music. Most children's and beginners' reading material is printed in large notes, which is psychologically encouraging for some people.

11. Use any crutch that will help you, no matter how silly. You will discard your crutches eventually, but for as long as you need them, they are very handy. Here are some old standards to start your collection:

- *Every Good Boy Does fine* names the line notes from the bottom to the top of the treble clef staff, and the space notes spell *FACE.*
- *Good Boys Do fine Always* names the line notes from the bottom to the top of the bass clef staff. The spaces are *All Cows Eat Grass.*
- The order of the sharps for sharp key signatures is *Father*

Everything I know about reading music I learned as a boy in Friends Meeting. There would be singing before Meeting. We'd sit down in the meetinghouse by soprano, alto, tenor, and bass, and we'd sing hymns in four-part harmony.

♪ Dick Pollard, carpenter and amateur fiddler

Charles Goes Down And Ends Battle. The order of the flats is the same sentence backwards—*Battle Ends And Down Goes Charles's Father.*

SIGHT-READING

Sight-reading is the ability to play written music at sight, without having to "figure it out" or practice it first. Probably no other musical skill offers a greater return for a more modest investment of practice time. If you're learning how to read, you can start learning to sight-read. If you can already read but have always thought of yourself as a poor sight reader, you can get better. Sight-reading makes a good time-limited project. Over the course of a summer, for example, fifteen minutes a day spent sight-reading first thing in the morning will pay dividends by the time the band gets together again in September.

If sight-reading seems beyond the possible to you, there are probably some secrets that you haven't heard. The first is that you don't have to be able to sight-read everything. It's true of most musicians that the level of the music they can sight-read well is easier than the music they can play if they have a chance to practice. Nearly everyone has a limit—the place where the notes are going by too fast or in too many unexpected patterns. Good sight readers are also not too picky about playing all the right notes. They keep the tempo, follow the rhythm, play in the right key, and let the notes fall where they may. Daring counts for more than dexterity.

If you play a kind of music where reading is important, you'll be glad you learned to sight-read. It can be a source of immense pleasure to read your way through the literature for your instrument or to read on a regular basis with friends. Here are some guidelines for boosting your sight-reading skill:

1. **Read a lot of simple music.** Struggling once a week with a few bars of a major project won't help much. But playing easy tunes for ten minutes a day can make a big difference. You'll sight-read much better if you're confident and relaxed than if you're off balance and panicky. Start by working your way through *very* easy material—things you can already play at sight—lots and lots of it. Pick up beginners' books at yard sales, secondhand stores, or from families whose children are done with them. Buy some easy anthologies of the kind of music you

like best, whether it's simplified Baroque or big-note Beatles. Keyboard players can play very easy music with both hands and slightly harder music one hand at a time. Set goals and move yourself through as much music as you can, choosing harder material only when you feel completely ready for it.

2. Look before you play. Just as you take a moment when you drive an unfamiliar car to find the lights, the turn signals, and the parking brake, so you can take a moment with a piece you're about to sight-read to look at the time signature, the key signature, the location of any key or tempo changes, repeat signs, and other landmarks. Look for repeated rhythmic or melodic patterns. Run through a scale and an arpeggio in the key to get the key feeling into your body. Set a working tempo in your mind before you begin, and then . . .

3. Keep a steady tempo. Don't "give in" and slow down at the tricky parts. Just skim on over them and keep going. You can go back when you're done and polish if you want, but the whole point of sight-reading is *not to stop*, no matter what. Never go back to correct a mistake or to replay a phrase. Always choose a tempo that will allow you to keep going, even if it's slow. If you find it hard to keep yourself going, try playing with a metronome, or—what's more fun—play alongside someone else who is singing, clapping, or playing the melody or accompaniment with you. Your central goal is not speed but primarily an even tempo and secondarily as many accurate notes as possible.

4. Keep your eyes on the music. This is mostly for keyboard, string, and guitar players: don't watch your hands. Research has shown that fluent sight readers are those who "look down" the least. If you've already established the habit and it's hard to break, get someone to hold a music book or record jacket cover (because it's about the right size) over your hands as you play. Ignore the wrong notes and keep going.

5. Look ahead. Work on training your eyes to travel a little ahead of your playing in the same way they do when you read words aloud. If you have a partner who is a good reader, you can ask that person to help you practice by covering up the beat, the measure, or the group of notes you are playing at the moment so your eyes are forced to move ahead. You can also do this for yourself by glancing at a playable group of notes and then looking away or closing your eyes as you play them. (This isn't true sight-reading, but it's good exercise.)

Keep the tempo! *Then, even if there are mistakes, the music will still be alive!*

♪ Nadia Boulanger

6. Read in patterns. This is related to the last item. As your eyes travel ahead, take in a logical group of notes in each "eye-ful" and focus mainly on reproducing the rhythm. Watch for patterns that are familiar to you from your technique practice—scales, arpeggios, chromatic passages, root-position chords. Keep yourself from naming notes. If you work better sub-vocalizing, or talking to yourself as you play, then sing the lyrics or count out loud.

7. Keep track of your progress. You'll find some ideas about keeping practice records in chapters 3 and 7. If sight-reading is one of your goals, you can keep a record of your development. Make a list of the pieces you read, with notes about your playing—what's comfortable, what's hard, what scares you, what slows you down, what helps you, what gets in your way. Do you bog down at thick clusters of fast-looking notes, like groups of sixteenths? or on dotted rhythms? syncopations? block chords? accidentals? If you can find out what trips you up, you can find a way to get comfortable with that part of music by getting more familiar with it. Isolate the problem and go looking for material to help yourself.

8. Be fearless. Don't worry about mistakes. The only mistake you can make in sight-reading is to slow down or to hesitate. Listen to what you play, but withhold your judgments. It really doesn't matter if you get all the notes. What matters is that you keep doing it and keep getting better at it.

PLAYING BY EAR

There's no better way to get to know your instrument than playing by ear—a musical skill that deserves more esteem than is usually accorded it. On page 126 we discussed the idea of *chunking*—playing in meaningful patterns. Playing by ear is pure chunking, pure pattern playing. You hear a pattern in your head and you play it.

When you play by ear, your ear drives the music making instead of following it. The ear becomes a divining rod and not just a sponge. It's a wonderful exercise for stretching your powers of inner hearing and for developing fluidity, for following the musical line rather than hanging on each note.

All you need to play by ear are rudimentary skills on an instrument, a simple tune that you know, and a little bit of pluck. A song list is also a big help. Prop open your favorite songbook or fake book to the index and pick from the titles. Play nursery tunes, folk songs, camp songs, hymns, and Christmas carols—anything that you can hum or sing or hear in your head. Start with tunes that are short and that don't skip around too much.

The initial difficulty that you'll encounter is not finding the first note but finding the second one. Remember that there are only three possibilities: every "next note" will be higher than the previous note, lower than the previous note, or the same. If it's higher or lower, it will either be close by (a small interval) or far away (a large interval). Singing the phrase often helps you get a physical feeling for the shape of a tune.

The next difficulty you'll likely encounter will come from wading into a difficult key and getting tangled up in sharps or flats. You can avoid that by starting in a key that's easy to play on your instrument. Play a scale and an arpeggio in your easy key, not too fast, up and down, two or three times. Then sing the starting note of the tune you're going to play. Match that pitch on your instrument, and away you go. Although tunes are built on a scale, they don't always begin on the first note of that scale. "Jingle Bells," for instance, can be played in any key, but it always begins on the third note of the scale in that key. By playing a scale before you begin, you get a key feeling in your ear and are much more likely to pick a starting note that will keep you out of trouble later. If this strategy doesn't work—if you find yourself in a landscape bristling with sharps or flats—just start again a half step higher or lower. Eventually you'll hit a playable key, and eventually your ear will learn how to find good starting notes. Once you've had some success in easy keys, you can push on to the harder ones.

Once you begin to play, don't be timid. Have fun. It doesn't have to be perfect. As one amateur said, "If you can't play the right notes, then play the wrong notes, but play something." Amateur pianist Susan Price, of Vero Beach, Florida, abandoned caution with gratifying results:

> Last night I had some music on the stereo and decided to see
> if I could play along with it at all. I'd tried before at times and
> got very frustrated because I couldn't do it very well. I always

147

was left behind—by the time I'd find a right note to play, the music would be on to other notes. Well, last night I just started hitting keys in time with the music and kept on doing it until gradually I was getting a few of the right notes. I kept getting more and more until I knew which key it was in, and by the end of a couple of songs, I could play the melody line pretty well.

Donna Richoux, of Boston, Massachusetts, used her tape recorder to refine her playing-by-ear skills, but she didn't wait for a flawless take:

At one point I had what seemed like a promising way to arrange a particular song, so I taped it so I could hear better what it sounded like. Since I was just starting to bumble my way through that song, I had to accept the fact that there were lots of wrong notes, false starts, hesitations, etc., on the tape, but it really wasn't too hard to ignore them. I was listening for the overall effect, and I found it very encouraging. Over the next few days, I re-recorded the same tune a number of times, and each time I could hear it going faster and smoother.

The skills of *transposition* and *harmonization* mentioned in chapter 6 are just other varieties of playing by ear. To practice transposition, take a tune you know, either by ear or by reading music, and play it in different keys. (Select keys you feel comfortable with—run through a scale and an arpeggio first.) All the notes will be different, but all the intervals will be the same. Learning chordal harmonization—how to choose appropriate chords to fit a given melody—typically involves a good deal of trial and error. A knowledge of basic music theory is helpful. Many teach-yourself piano and guitar books contain ideas and practice materials for chordal harmonization.

Most people who play by ear or harmonize find it very helpful at some point to learn some theory about interval naming, scale construction, and chord progressions. It might also help to know some of the standard song openers that use common intervals. For instance, the interval of a major sixth (from note one to note six in a major scale) is what you hear when you sing the first two notes of "My Bonny Lies Over the Ocean." Here's a list of common melodic intervals matched to songs that use the interval in the opening notes. Start collecting your own interval crutches, and substitute freely others that you discover:

Ascending Intervals

Minor second	"Billy Boy"
Major second	"On the Street Where You Live"
Minor third	"Greensleeves"
Major third	"I Could Have Danced All Night"
	"Did You Ever See a Lassie?"
Perfect fourth	"Here Comes the Bride"
	"The Farmer in the Dell"
Perfect fifth	"Twinkle, Twinkle, Little Star"
	"God Rest You Merry Gentlemen"
Minor sixth	"Go Down, Moses"
Major sixth	"My Bonny Lies Over the Ocean"
	"It Came Upon a Midnight Clear"
Minor seventh	"Somewhere," from *West Side Story*
Perfect octave	"Somewhere Over the Rainbow"
	"Bali Hai"

Descending Intervals

Minor second	"Joshua Fought the Battle of Jericho"
Major second	"Mary Had a Little Lamb"
	"Three Blind Mice"
Minor third	"Oh Dear, What Can the Matter Be?"
	"Camptown Races"
Major third	"Swing Low, Sweet Chariot"
Perfect fourth	"Clementine"
	"I've Been Working on the Railroad"
Perfect fifth	"Bring a Torch, Jeannette, Isabella"
Minor sixth	"Love Story"
Major sixth	"Nobody Knows the Trouble I've Seen"

IMPROVISATION

Improvisation draws us directly to sound. We can read music and not listen to ourselves play because our attention is consumed by the business on the page. We can play from memory and not listen because our attention is consumed by the effort of remembering and the fear of forgetting. But we cannot improvise and not listen. Improvisation demands that we attend to our sound.

In the place we call Music, improvisation is that window off to the side—an irresistible view for some musicians, all they ever look at, really. But for others, it is the Unknown. Many musicians—even those who are totally at home with their instruments, who can memorize and perform fluently, who play with skill and confidence—believe that they cannot improvise.

The flaw is not in ourselves but in our history. Improvisation has had a bad reputation for the last century among classical musicians and music educators, which is a shame, since it had traditionally been the backbone of a musical education. Orchestral musicians of Bach's day were often given a mere sketch of a composition, a "chart" we might call it, which they were able confidently to fill in.

In recent generations, however, musical education hardened and set. Some kinds of music were crowned "proper music," and all else was dismissed until finally, when many of us were young, if we dared to improvise at all, we'd hear Mother from the kitchen: "Practice your lesson! I'm not paying two dollars a week to have you sit there and fool around." Those who survived the "talent weeding" at school found their musical impulses molded into "acceptable" forms by well-meaning teachers who had a very low tolerance for "mistakes." Classical training in particular often inhibited the improvisation impulse by the value it placed on written music and on "being right."

Improvising—for a musician who has not done it before—requires nothing more than relinquishing the rules and the attitudes that have kept us from improvising in the past. Mildred Portnoy Chase has written a wise and encouraging book called *Improvisation: Music from the Inside Out.* Chase says, "Simply giving ourselves permission to play what we seem to hear in our minds or what our fingers mindlessly find for us, intuitively led, is really all that is required to release our ability to improvise."

But what do you actually *do* when you begin to improvise? As a way of getting started, you could experiment with these different approaches and see which fits your impulses best, which takes you in a direction that opens outward:

If somebody says to me, "I can't improvise!"—and this could be somebody with the biggest chunk of classical training imaginable in their background—I would find that very inspiring. Because I know that within a very short time they will be doing it and saying, "Oh, is that it?" And then they will do it again. You see, it's the most natural thing in the world.

♪ John Stevens, professional drummer and improvisation teacher

The only thing that stands in the way of improvising is a reluctance to take the first steps.

♪ Mildred Portnoy Chase, *Improvisation*

The Unstructured Approach

This approach to improvisation is closest to a young child's impulsive behavior at an instrument or with her voice. What will this do? What sounds can I make? How high? How low? How long and how short? How loud and how soft? How fast and how slow? How many ways can I move up? Down? Up and down? Using the natural resources available on our instruments or in our voices, we can improvise music that would look downright impossible to play if it were written out. Unstructured improvisation often results in sounds that trained musicians spend years trying *not* to make, but for all that it can also reveal to us the potential of our expressive range. Before long we begin to hear sounds and ideas that we find pleasing or exciting or beckoning. Our unstructuredness loses some of its aimlessness and begins to attract to itself skills and knowledge. Amateur Flutist Lynelle Inwood used unstructured improvisation as a way to begin:

> When I started the flute, I didn't study normal technique. I just figured out a C scale and went from there by ear. I played with a jazz guitarist, and all we did was improvise. He'd say crazy things like, "Now here just play as fast as you can!" I started out, from the very beginning, doing "special effects." I experimented with things that most flute players who study a method don't get to until much later. Instead of working slowly up to the fun stuff, I started out with it, even though there wasn't much technique behind it at first.

The Structured Approach

This approach begins on the other side, with our current skills and knowledge. This is the kind of improvising that builds from what we already know, perhaps decorating a folk tune with fresh ideas or varying a technical exercise with new rhythms and dynamics or building a new melody over a familiar chord progression. Professional sax player John Payne, director of the John Payne Music Center in Brookline, Massachusetts, has drawn dozens of new musicians into improvisation. He teaches his students an easy scale on the sax, and when they know it well, going

To improvise means to have fun with something—to change it around and make it different.

♪ Willie Ruff,
jazz French horn and bass player,
Mitchell-Ruff Duo

151

Once a student has begun improvising, and once the barriers of self-doubt and self-consciousness have been broken down, the gap between the level of improvising and that of already acquired playing skills is easily bridged, regardless of the student's age or degree of experience.

♪ Mildred Portnoy Chase,
Improvisation

both up and down through one octave, he puts on a recording of a slow blues ballad accompaniment, one of the Jamey Aebersold backup records (see appendix 2 for details). "I just tell them to play the scale up and down to this blues back-up, and before they get to the bottom again, about 60 percent of them start improvising. Another 30 percent start after a few suggestions from me. Very few really need any direct teaching."

Patterns that you practice during technique building—scales, chromatics, arpeggios, licks, and progressions—are the raw material for structured improvisation. Building on what you know already in this way allows lots of room for genius without requiring that you enter an unmarked wilderness.

Another way to structure your improvisation is to work with a pedal tone or an ostinato. A *pedal tone* (also called a *drone*) is a sustained, unchanging tone or chord, usually below the melody. An *ostinato* is a simple, repeating pattern above or below the melody. An ostinato can be purely rhythmic—a steady drum beat or a simple, repeated rhythmic pattern. Or it can be melodic—a simple sequence of two or three notes repeated over and over. A partner—even a nonmusical one—can give you a pedal tone or an ostinato on a tambourine, a drum, a recorder, or a piano. So can most synthesizers. You can make your own ostinato on a cassette tape, and you can use an electronic tuner to produce a pedal tone. An ostinato or a pedal tone gives rhythmic focus and melodic organization to your improvising. It is something to bounce off of and return to, without offering any competition.

The Meditative Approach

This approach starts from silence, with deep listening to our inner experience. A melodic fragment, a rhythmic impulse, a single note moves our hand or voice to bring it into sound. This note or idea may extend itself, or it may stop at its own conclusion and return us to silence. We may repeat the motif, experiment with it, or wait quietly for a new one. This approach is unhurried and leads us to listen attentively and to trust deeply our own expressive powers.

A synthesis of these approaches is inevitable, of course. Unstructured improvisation reveals boundaries that can contain a structured improvisation. A structured improvisation can grow out of a meditative silence. The best mode to use at any moment is the one you feel called upon to use. Here are five additional ideas to help you grow in improvising:

1. **Make no judgments.** Say *yes*. Think in terms of opportunities, not mistakes. If you play something that doesn't sound like it fits, keep going—let it evolve.

2. **Keep it simple.** "One of the big problems people have when they begin to improvise," according to John Payne, "is that they start too heavy too soon." In improvisation it is always a good idea to give yourself some place to build to. When you start a structured improvisation, for example, you might decide to stay within the first five notes of a scale rather than trying to come up with a complex melody right away. Begin with a simple rhythmic scheme, perhaps the same rhythmic pattern repeated over and over. Most music is strongly repetitive. You don't have to work in continuously changing patterns. Some of the most beautiful and enduring tunes are very simple. Don't worry about being original.

3. **When you hear a direction inside your head, honor it.** Follow it no matter how small or how ordinary it seems at the moment. Look for the path on your instrument. If you miss it, that's OK. Just listen for the next one. Value the interplay between your mind's ideas and your instrument's ideas. If you don't feel an appropriate rhythm, then just allow the rhythm to grow in its own way from the improvisation. Don't try to fit notes into an arbitrary metric design. Improvisation is a beautiful example of feedback, where the information coming from one system changes the other.

4. **If you feel lost, repeat a motif several times until a clear or fresh direction opens.** Let your improvisation have a beginning and an end—try not to abandon it just because it wanders away. Call it gently back and continue until the thought has finished.

5. **Improvise often, even if it's just for a few minutes a day.** Improvisation is about fearlessness and freedom in your music, about feeling music from the inside out, and about letting music speak through you.

Appreciating and understanding how improvisation works is achieved through the failures and successes involved in attempting to do it.

♪ Derek Bailey, *Musical Improvisation*

Improvisation is a way of achieving identity.

♪ Alfred Nieman, composer

Do not get too fussy about how every part of the thing sounds. Go ahead. All processes are at first awkward and clumsy and "funny."

♪ Carl Whitmer, *The Art of Improvisation*

MEMORIZATION

Research has revealed how substantial and concrete human memory really is. We now know that memory is no ephemeral neural event but that it produces actual chemical and physical changes in brain tissue, mainly in the hippocampus region of the cerebral cortex. This news is cold comfort, of course, to the sweaty-palmed musician on the stage, scouring the hippocampean hills for a chord gone AWOL.

We can, though, take advantage of what is known about memory to give ourselves the best possible chance of retrieving musical information when we need it. We're going to take a moment to look at memory in general before we get back to musical memory in particular.

Understanding Memory

We know that there are two distinct kinds of memory. *Long-term memory—LTM* to the psychologists—stores information that we can retrieve later. *Short-term memory—STM*—stores information for only a few seconds, usually until our attention turns to new data or to a new sensation. For example, we use STM when we look up phone numbers or library call numbers. We usually remember these numbers only for as long as it takes us to dial the phone or to find the book. As soon as we've done that, or if something happens to interrupt us, we forget the number.

Now suppose that you don't want to forget. Someone gives you an important phone number—"Call me tomorrow at 276-8742"—but you have no way to write that number down at the moment. At this point you invoke your favorite strategy for activating your LTM. Maybe you repeat the number over and over. Maybe you visualize it written down, or you trace it with your finger in the air or on a table-top. Maybe you like to figure out words to match up with phone numbers—27-MUSIC. Maybe you analyze it mathematically or compare it to another number you know.

When we memorize a piece of music, we do the same kind of thing—we activate strategies for getting the music into our long-term memory. Musicians have found that the more strategies used, the more secure the memory. In practical terms, musicians rely mostly on four basic memory strategies:

1. Aural strategies. Think about how the music sounds. Sing it or hum it to yourself. Listen to yourself play it. Listen to recordings. Conduct the music as it plays on a recording or in your imagination.

2. Visual strategies. If you're working from printed music, notice how it looks on the page. Observe patterns, melody shapes, and landmarks. Copy out the music. See if you can write out tricky passages from memory. Notice how your hands look when they play.

3. Muscular or kinesthetic strategies. Observe how it feels to play the piece or to play certain passages. Play the music over many times until your fingers "know where to go." Play without your instrument, miming the movements. Play with a simultaneous competing stimulus, such as the radio or TV.

4. Conceptual or analytical strategies. Analyze the structure of the music. Look for melodic motifs, chord progressions, rhythmic variations, harmonic developments, and dynamic design. Play the piece at a very slow tempo. (This blocks your muscular memory and tests your conceptual understanding.) Notice ways in which this piece is similar to other music that you know. Discover standard historical or stylistic principles at work in the music. Sophisticated theoretical knowledge is not required for this strategy. Make your own original observations without worrying too much about theoretical correctness.

At the heart of all of these strategies is the principle of *chunking*, which we met on page 126. As efficient as our memory system is, it cannot consume a very large amount of data at one time. *For a short-term memory to become a long-term memory, the memory must be placed into a meaningful context and reinforced by regular review.*

It should be obvious that memory is not really a separate musical function but always treads on the toes of other mental processes, including perception and learning. When we're working by ear—picking up a tune from a recording, for example—it's obvious that learning and memorizing happen simultaneously. But even when we learn from written music, our memory starts to form as soon as we make acquaintance with the piece.

Helping Yourself to Memorize

Musicians who memorize face two lofty challenges. first, we frequently have to retrieve memories under intense stress. The anxiety we call *stagefright* tends to compete with and block conscious access to long-term memory. (There's more about stagefright in chapter 15.) Second, our ultimate goal is not to reproduce a sequence of data but to realize the spirit of the music. At some point we have to make a very large leap from technical details to an artistic whole. (For some additional ideas about this, read about the technique called *mapping* on page 178.) With these two challenges in mind, here are seven steps you can take to improve your long-term musical memory:

1. Use more than one memory strategy, and tailor the strategy to the material.   Most musicians depend on one strategy to the exclusion of the others. We usually pick the strategy that makes use of the musical skills we've developed. Children and new musicians tend to rely heavily on the muscular strategy—sometimes with disastrous results, since this kind of memory is very fragile under stress. The most reliable approach is to employ as many strategies as possible in order to gain the advantages that each offers and to make the strongest memory links.

2. Overlearn.   Go back frequently to review material recently memorized. Do your first review right away and your next one a few minutes later. If you can, try to schedule another review later the same day and another the very next day. Continue going over the material daily for several days and at least weekly after that. If you are using written music, go back and play from the music once in a while to consolidate your visual memory.

3. Set up "stations" in the music.   You've probably shared vicariously in the distress of a performer who had a memory lapse and had to start all over again (and sometimes had another memory lapse in exactly the same place). To beat your anxiety at this game, mark "stations" through your music at logical places—every eight bars or every time the theme returns or at every new verse—let the music suggest practical spots. Mark each station with a letter—*A, B, C, D*—and write each letter on a slip of paper. Draw a slip at every practice and start playing the piece from that station. In this way, if you have a memory lapse while performing, you can drop back or go ahead to the closest station rather than having to begin all over.

4. Know what is coming next.   During a performance it is never the note we are playing that gives us memory problems—it is the next note. As you study, learn, and memorize a piece, work from the idea that every note is a preparation for the next note. As you practice, stop playing from time to time, but let your mind keep going. Hear the next passage in your head. (For those who don't play by ear, this is a good way to activate your aural memory.)

5. Memorize backward.   This is a very old trick, used by both concert musicians and amateurs, as well as by dancers and actors. Start memorizing from the end. Take the very last logical chunk and memorize it. (Don't play the music backward! Just memorize the last chunk first.) When that feels secure, memorize the next-to-last chunk and play through to the end, and so on. The enormous advantage to this system is that when you play the complete piece, you will always be moving into areas of greater and greater familiarity and confidence. When we memorize from the beginning, we tend to play the beginning many, many more times than we ever play the end, and so we tend to grow increasingly insecure as we proceed. Another advantage of this trick is that it helps sustain your motivation to do a complete job of memorizing. It feels so good to get to the beginning!

6. Form an association with the surroundings or with a talisman.   If you are getting ready for a performance, it can help a surprising amount to practice your memory work in the place where you will perform. That's not always possible, of course, but as an alternative you can use a talisman—perhaps a

157

special necklace, a scarf, or a belt that you put on when you practice and plan to wear when you perform. Suzanne McGrath learned this trick from her teenage daughter:

> Kathryn always studies for exams wearing the same shoes that she's going to wear on exam day. I used to laugh at her for being superstitious, but she persuaded me to try it when I was getting ready for a recital. I kept my concert shoes next to my music stand and slipped them on when I worked on my recital number. (Kathryn absolutely *insisted* that I must never, *never* wear them for anything else, or the spell wouldn't work.) And you know what? It worked! I had this very eerie feeling while I was playing that if I forgot anything, it would be down there in my shoe somewhere! At one point I even started to giggle because this idea struck me funny. But I'll definitely do it again.

Practice with a talisman—a special necklace, scarf, or hat.

7. Concentrate on musical values. Don't just memorize fingering, intervals, chords, and melody lines. Memorize as well the feelings, impressions, moods, and energy levels that go with the notes.

MUSIC THEORY

The "laws" and "rules" of music theory are not at all like the laws of gravity or the rules of the road. There's very little that's inevitable about music theory. For the most part, it's a collection of observations about how musicians in Western cultures have made music in the past. Working within this framework, musicians have created both immortal art and insignificant drivel. Progress, change, and nearly all new musical developments come about by stretching or reconstructing a previous generation's framework.

Studying music theory is like looking at music's shop manual, examining its materials and understanding its joints and linkages. No matter what your other interests in music, it's very likely that knowing some theory can help you do your music better. Ensemble players who know basic harmony are less likely to get desperately lost. Improvisers benefit from learning the qualities and functions of their basic materials. People who play by ear find their work made easier by understanding musical structure and chord progressions. Technique makes more sense to everyone who understands principles of scale and chord construction. Reading goes better with a knowledge of key signatures and interval relationships. Retired librarian Ann MacNab came to theory late in her musical life, and she's glad she did:

> I had years of piano lessons as a child, but I had no theory. I started taking lessons again after I retired, and I'm now working my way through elementary, introductory, absolutely beginning level theory and finding out how much it helps me not only to play music but to listen to music.

Finally, knowing some theory makes it much easier to talk to other musicians. Music is not a language-based activity, but when it becomes necessary to discuss it, the dialects that musicians use are generally rooted in music theory.

This is one area where you'll find plenty of self-teaching materials. If you want a conventional textbook, visit the bookstore of a music conservatory, or a college or university that has a music department, and look over the texts sold for the first-year theory and harmony course. Any fair-sized music store will have a selection of self-teaching theory texts, including jazz theory. A high quality and widely used introductory work is the Norton *Scales, Intervals, Keys, Triads, Rhythm, and Meter,* by John Clough and Joyce Conley. Like many theory books, this is a "programmed learning text"—you read a bit, answer a question, and then immediately check your answer by uncovering it with a card. You can take theory in night school in many locations, and several universities offer it as a correspondence course.

The most important thing to know about learning music theory is this: To be of any use, music theory has to be studied with your instrument at hand. It's possible to "do" music theory as abstract exercises on paper, but it makes more sense much faster when you put your own sound to it. As you practice your everyday music making, be alert for opportunities to observe and to apply what you know.

Computer software developers were quick to see the application of the computer to self-taught theory. Software is substantially more expensive than a book (though less expensive than a private teacher). Probably the best use of theory software is for review and drill. The learning of principles is still best done by you on your own instrument. Don't let a computer come between the instrument and you!

If you are taking lessons, let your teacher know if you're interested in theory. You might agree to set aside a few minutes of each lesson for systematic theory study, or you might choose to explore theory points as they come up in your regular lesson materials.

SOLVING MUSICAL PROBLEMS

If we could play perfectly, we would not have to practice. For most amateurs—and even most professionals—any piece of music that is challenging enough to interest us has some parts in it we have to work on.

Nothing really worth having comes quickly and easily; if it did, I doubt that we would ever grow.

♪ Eknath Easwaran

The 80/20 rule seems to apply in music as well as anywhere else. We spend 80 percent of our practice time on 20 percent of the piece. Music has a way of being efficient, however. If you find one tricky bit, chances are very good that it's repeated elsewhere in the same piece, and your work will only have to be done once. Polishing only two measures may in fact polish eight.

The Sticky Bits and the Hard Parts

If you're confronting a tricky passage, first of all, *before* you start playing it over and over a hundred times a day, do two things:

1. Look at the rhythm. Surprisingly often, what appears as a technical problem is really a slight rhythmic inaccuracy. Once we're thrown off balance rhythmically, we tend to trip over anything that comes next.

Deal with a thing while it is still nothing; keep a thing in order before disorder sets in.

♪ Lao Tzu, *Tao Te Ching*

2. Look at the preparation. The preparation is the part that comes just before the hard part—the easy chord just before the complicated one, the sustained note just before the run, the melody notes just before the big leap. A high diver puts great attention into preparation; so does a musician. If you study your physical movements during the preparation and between the preparation and the hard part, you can sometimes clean up your problem with no further work. An unconventional fingering on a simple chord might put your hand in better position to take the notes of a difficult chord that follows it. Feeling the coming pulse of a run as you sustain the lead-in note can prevent you from rushing through the run in a panic and tripping. A conscious feeling of release through the low notes prior to a leap prepares you to *receive* the next tone rather than strain for it.

Once you've tidied up the rhythm and polished the preparation, it's time to look at the passage itself. Always remember that your purpose in practicing any passage is not to do it again but to know it better. It is useless to go over and over a difficult passage with no effort to change. You will only drive the problems in more deeply. As soon as you say, "That's not right," then ask immediately, "What's not right?" Stop. Analyze the problem. Is it fingering? breath control? wrong notes? tone quality? tempo? intonation? Decide on a goal and think creatively about how to get there. The time to begin playing a passage over and over is when you have it exactly the way you want it. If you play a passage ten times, the first nine times faulty and the tenth one correct, you've only been lucky. You haven't fixed the problem.

If you play an instrument that requires you to calculate fingering, breathing, or bowing, make these decisions very early in your practice and be sure your plan will work when you're playing up to tempo. Always think ahead. figure out what choice best prepares you for what's coming next. Think of every note as a preparation for the next note. If you're using written music, your edition may suggest some fingerings, breathings, or bowings. Give these a try, but realize that they're not written in stone. They may be awkward or unplayable. You are free to change them, though you should know why you have chosen the patterns you decide to use.

The cherished approach to perfecting a fast passage—the one some of us remember from childhood—is to start practicing it very slowly and repeat it over and over, getting faster and faster each time. There are two very big problems here, though. first, there's an inherent trap in repeating short bits of anything. Think of a sticky passage in music as being like a tongue twister. We only have to say a really good tongue twister (try "toy

It has been my experience that practicing with a strong sense of rhythmic involvement, no matter what the tempo, lends incredible excitement and meaning to the practice—that solutions to most problems one is attempting to overcome are to be found in it—that potential anxiety can be converted to excitement through it, in performance as well as in practice.

♪ Dale Reubart, *Anxiety and Musical Performance*

161

boats") three or four times before it's completely bent out of shape. Similarly, when we repeat a fast musical passage several times, it often gets more tangled, not less.

Repetition can be efficient if it's done with awareness. You can avoid the "toy boats" effect by putting a very short passage into a slightly longer context ("Ten toy boats on a shelf" is not a tongue twister) and by simply pausing between repetitions. Release your playing muscles after every repetition. Listen in your mind to what you just played. Release that sound and listen in your mind to how you want it to sound the next time. And then repeat. If you omit the release-and-listen between repetitions, you run the risk not only of "toy boating" and of playing mindlessly but also of teaching yourself to connect the end of a troubled passage with the beginning, thus setting the stage for memory and continuity problems later on. (Here's a verbal example of this: Say "cows and milk" over and over with no pauses. Before long, you will probably link the end of the phrase to the beginning and start saying—*and thinking*—"milk cows and milk cows.")

The second big problem with the idea of starting slowly and working up speed is that our bodies don't work that way. Playing slowly requires a different kind of muscular control than playing fast. A runner, for example, would not train for a race by running first in very slow motion and then gradually picking up speed. A runner works at near top speed and studies her form to see how to increase that speed even more. In the same way, a child learning to walk usually walks from the very start at near normal speed but goes only a short distance.

The efficient way to work through a long, fast passage is to break it into the smallest playable bits—two notes to begin with are fine—and play those up to tempo, or nearly so. Pause long enough to prepare the next group of two and play those. And then the next group and the next, and so on. When two-note groups feel comfortable and controlled up to tempo, expand the groups to three notes and then four and so on. Here's an example. Suppose you want to speed up this passage:

Figure 9–3a

162

Play it first up to tempo in groups of two with a clear pause between each group:

Figure 9–3b

When that's easy, then play in groups of three and then four and then six:

Figure 9–3c

Fast passages are best practiced lightly, even if you will be putting great energy into them in their final form. A light, soft practice lets you work efficiently. If you have anything to add, it will come naturally as you grow easy with the notes.

There is definitely a place for slow practice. It just doesn't belong to fast passages. Slow practice is a chance to savor the contours of the music, to find your singing tone, to explore nuance and interpretation, to feel the impulse of the music pull you ahead.

Mistakes

Sometimes we make the same mistake every time, and sometimes mistakes take us by surprise. The "surprise" mistakes are often lapses of attention or listening, or else they occur in sections that we haven't really prepared completely, perhaps because we didn't initially see any problems there. The most frustrating kind of mistake is the one that draws from the player a sigh and a comment like, "I *always* miss that note." Usually it is *always* missed because the player has thoroughly learned to play it that way.

The same approach applies to "learned mistakes" as to sticky bits. first study the rhythm and the preparation. Sing the passage, if you can, to check the accuracy of your rhythm and intervals. Next, analyze the passage itself. Many mistakes are actually completely logical, reasonable behaviors. Rather than despising yourself for making an error, assume that you've acted in a perfectly reasonable way and that there's a perfectly good reason for the mistake. find that reason! Finding the "why" behind the mistake usually puts you hot on the trail of a solution.

When you're ready to practice the passage, try this experiment with it: Take the passage at a manageable tempo and "play it right." Then do it again and "play it wrong"—make your famous mistake on purpose. Keep alternating back and forth between the new way and the old way of playing it until you definitely feel that you are in control and that *you can choose* which way to play it. (Don't worry that by playing it wrong you'll teach yourself to do so. If it's a "famous mistake," then you've already done that!) This procedure circumvents the tendency to make only a "muscular correction." By alternating the old and new ways of playing, you also make mental and musical corrections as well.

The time always comes when you need to reassemble the fragments you've been working on to make a complete piece once again, and sometimes that point comes before you've quite worked out all the bugs. Perhaps you have a rehearsal or a lesson coming up, or perhaps you're just plain eager to make music again. One approach to practicing an entire piece that still has sticky bits in it is to alternate two ways of playing it:

1. Play all the way through the piece up to or close to the final tempo, getting around the sticky bits any way you can—simplify, muddle through, or drop something out if necessary. But keep the tempo! Play as if this were a performance. If you make a mistake, don't flinch and don't fix it. Just go right on.
2. The next time through, play every note accurately, even

if that means playing the whole piece more slowly and playing the hard parts more slowly still. Don't worry about the tempo. Strive for accuracy.

If you continue alternating these two approaches, the day will come when you finish the piece up to tempo and completely clean, and you'll wonder, "Which version was that?—the tempo one or the accurate one?" And it will be both. Congratulations. You can do it.

Rhythmic Problems

The ongoing quality of musical rhythm is very much a foundation of confident playing. If we're unsure of the rhythm, or if it begins to waver because we're tense or nervous, a passage we might otherwise play with ease can fall outside our technique. Sorting out a rhythmic puzzle often means applying at close range and in painstaking detail the counting method you know best. (See pages 136–140 for information about counting methods.)

Rhythmic patterns often look more complicated on the page than they really are. For complex-looking rhythms, there's a useful trick that requires pencil, paper, and a bit of patient calculating. Just copy out the passage, but double the time values. For example, suppose you're puzzled by this bar:

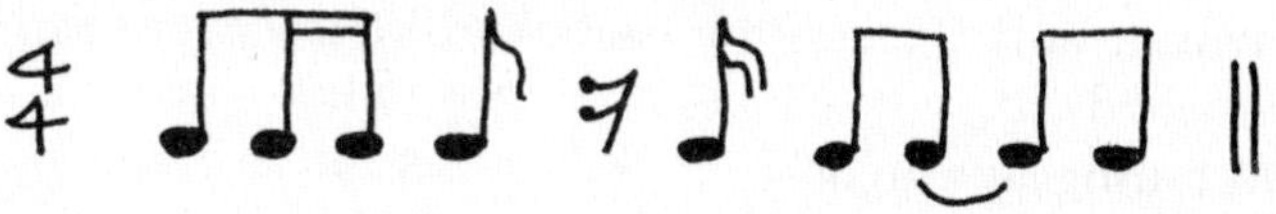

Figure 9–4a

If you double all the time values (write sixteenths as eighths, eighths as quarters, and quarters as halves) and put in a temporary bar line halfway through, it looks like this:

Figure 9–4b

As soon as you're able to translate a rhythm into a counting method, mark the main beats in the music with a long pencil line:

Figure 9–4c

Before you play it, feel the rhythm in your body—conduct it, clap it, tap it, dance it, play it on one note, sing it, or say it out loud. Make up some words that fit:

Figure 9–4d

Get the rhythm into your body.

This step—getting the rhythm into your body—is the crucial one and often the greatest challenge to musicians who play from written music. We've said elsewhere that musical time is not like clock time. It's not mechanical—it's alive, flexible, and meaningful. It has all of the distinct and contrasting qualities of life—reaching and withdrawing, statement and response, tension and relaxation, activity and repose. Rhythm organizes the meaning in music. Think about the word game that kids and actors love to play, accenting each word of a sentence in turn:

WILL you play with me?
Will YOU play with me?
Will you PLAY with me?
Will you play WITH me?
Will you play with ME?

It's possible to say each of these sentences in the same metrical pattern while giving each version a distinct meaning by changing the rhythmic stress. That's how musical rhythm works, too. Moving an abstract rhythm into your body helps you discover the "sense" of the rhythm so that you can make musical sense of the passage. It's hard to grasp a string of apparent nonsense: *Iw illar isea ndgon ow.* When you can make sense of it, when you see where meaningful groups begin and end, and where the stresses belong, it is immediately easier: *I will arise and go now.*

Some of us like to work on rhythmic problems with a metronome. We need to remember, though, that a metronome provides only a mechanical beat. It is still up to us to make the rhythm vital and meaningful. The best use of a metronome is to double-check the accuracy of your beat placement and the steadiness of your tempo *after you have figured out the rhythm for yourself.* Use a metronome sparingly and never as a crutch for insecure counting.

Playing with a metronome actually requires a bit of practice. When the thing is ticking, your awareness is divided; the rhythmic impulse is arriving from an external source. Always listen to at least a full bar of ticks before you begin to play. Feel the tempo inside you—don't just listen to it. If the tempo doesn't "settle," change the speed setting slightly until you find one that's comfortable. Once you start playing, it's surprisingly easy to ignore a metronome, to turn it off mentally. One trick for staying in contact (and in time!) is to imagine that *you* are making the metronome tick. It will not tick until you feel and play on the beat.

The worst rhythmic fault of inexperienced musicians is probably not miscounting but rather "clipping" notes—cutting them off too soon instead of holding them for their full value, especially in a passage that has longer note values mixed with very short ones—quarters and sixteenths, for example, or dotted rhythms. Clipping the long notes creates rhythmic insecurity, which, often beyond our awareness, undermines our best effort to express a passage.

Underneath many rhythmic problems is tension. Compare the uneven, staggering, and unbalanced gait of someone walking on ice and "trying not to fall" to the constant, loose, easy gait of a happy, relaxed person out for a stroll on level ground. Maddeningly, it is our intense desire to "do it right" that so often prevents us from giving rhythmic life to our music. Teachers report that of all the musical skills, rhythmic expression is the biggest dilemma for many adult amateurs. Other kinds of rhythmic experiences—especially dance and movement to music—can significantly enhance the development of musical rhythm in general. For specific pieces it's fun to work on the rhythm by humming, singing, or listening through headphones while walking, searching for exactly the right pace and the right gait to fit the sound.

Intonation Problems

Those of us who play instruments that demand intonation have our moments of longing for a piano, an accordion, anything where you just have to push down a key and the right note comes out. Playing in tune is so devilishly hard. String players, trombonists, singers, and wind players (especially in their extreme ranges) all have to give enormous attention to intonation because the smallest error can make an otherwise musically adequate performance sound so downright awful.

To play in tune we have to be able to imagine the pitch that we want to make. The best way to refine your mental intonation is by singing. A little vocal training never did any musician any harm, and for intonation instruments it's a definite asset. Reading by intervals will help, too (see page 141), as will some ear training. It's much more important to get notes in tune relative to one another than it is to tune them one by one using some external standard such as a piano or an electronic tuner.

It's crucial to know the peculiarities of your instrument. In the low register, for example, clarinets are likely to play sharp and flutes are likely to play flat. Strings tend to play sharp in flat keys, and winds tend to play flat in sharp keys.

The basic rule for intonation practice is to *play slowly and softly.* Loud tones are often distorted for intonation anyway, and they make hearing much more difficult. Surely the most delightful way to practice intonation is to play easy music, in unison or in parts, with other musicians in small ensembles. If you don't have a partner handy, you can do some valuable intonation practice with a tone-generating electronic tuner. Set the tuner to produce your instrument's tuning pitch and then experiment playing various intervals and slow scales in that key. Listen closely to match up the unisons and to produce full, clean-sounding intervals. If you can produce other tuning pitches, you can experiment in other keys.

The individual tone is not music until it is directly connected with other tones, and tonal relations are not operative until tones and tonal combinations are in motion.

♪ Paul Hindemith

ON PENCILS

Of all the accessories that can help a musician who uses written music, the pencil gets the prize. Music is *always* marked with a pencil, never, ever with a pen. The best kind of music pencil has soft lead and a large, working eraser. The next time you're in a stationery store, buy yourself a *box* of HB or softer pencils and also buy ten of those little, pink, pointed erasers. Keep two pencils in your case, keep two pencils on your stand, and hide all the others where your family will never find them.

Mark your music boldly. You may want to erase your marks later if you change your mind or if your music is rented or borrowed, but for now your markings are important. You shouldn't have to squint to see them. This is especially true if you are marking over something that's printed in the music, as when changing a fingering.

Develop your own way of marking music, and once you have a system stick with it so that you don't have to decide every time what to put down. Musicians already have a host of standard music-marking symbols, and you'll develop others for yourself. Be generous with your marking. If it doubt, write it in. One helpful symbol is a mark that means "this part needs work"—perhaps an *X* in a circle—something you can jot down on the fly at a lesson, at a rehearsal, or during your own practice. You can't always stop to work everything out as you come to it; this mark helps you remember what to work on later. There is a slight psychological difficulty with flagging trouble spots, however. Your mark can easily become an alarm—"Uh oh, here comes trouble!" The obvious way around this is to erase your marks as the spots get cleaned up. A better solution, though, is to let your mark be a strong signal that means "release"—a sign reminding you to let go of any extra tension and to begin listening.

ON RESISTANCE

Professional pianist and teacher Eric Stumacher defines talent as "the absence of resistance." This chapter and the one before it are really about talent in just that sense. When we let go of tension, let go of haste and expectations, let go of trying and of trying to please, then the way into music opens to us. Our intuition becomes a resource as valuable as any teacher or any book. We develop the openness to let the music itself teach us.

Many amateurs interviewed for this project remembered vivid "breakthroughs"—times when their practice bore fruit with unexpected abundance. A common thread through all their stories was the element of "no resistance." Breakthroughs seem to wait until the ego gives up, until our guards go to sleep and our judges retire. Some found their breakthroughs at the end of a long, weary plateau. Some, like computer programmer Robin Carswell, found it at the end of long, weary day:

> I will never forget the night a Mozart sonata *played itself* under my fingers. I'd worked most of the previous year on the *Sonata Facile*. The first movement is full of very fast runs. Kids love to show off with this piece, but I got very discouraged. I couldn't get it up to a decent speed, so I finally put it away and started something else.
>
> One night, I came home after working late, and I got out the *Sonata Facile*. I don't know why. I was dead tired, in a real stupor. I started to play the first movement, and suddenly music—this *beautiful music*—just poured through my hands. It felt as if the sonata were writing itself, right at that moment, and I was just hearing it unfold. It wasn't note-perfect but it wasn't a struggle. It was a *whole*, a living thing. I know that sounds corny, but I don't know how else to explain it.
>
> That night changed all my ideas about music. Before, it was always, "Can I play this faster? or louder? or all the way through without a mistake?" Now I'm in it not for what I can do but for what the music itself *is*.

CHAPTER 10

Beyond the Notes: Musicianship, Mapping, and the Music You Play

In the previous three chapters we looked at music making in its smallest details—the *where, when, why,* and *how* of playing and practicing. This chapter takes the long view. We'll look at music making as an experience, as a living thing. We'll talk about musicianship, interpretation, music selection, and an unusual technique called *mapping*—all steps on the way to making music for the joy of it.

FROM BREAKTHROUGHS TO MUSICIANSHIP

Musical breakthroughs usually take us by surprise. They have a curious way of happening when we're tired, discouraged, sick, or distracted. The common thread in all these situations is the element of "no resistance." Economist Eugene Dykema finds his vocal practice goes better, as he puts it, "when I feel almost disconnected from it, when it's as if there's no *I* that is actually singing. That's when I find capacities I have never used before."

Unfortunately, we can't schedule or predict breakthroughs.

171

Even virtuosos don't rely on them. "It isn't something you hit every night," according to jazz great Art Blakey. "It's only once or twice a month you really get to play, you really feel in your heart what you play." What that occasional breakthrough does for us is to demonstrate the nature of *musicianship*, how our technique and our spirit can merge, giving life to sound. It's a chance to know that our emotional energy can pour into the music rather than into self-consciousness and that our movements can be natural and spontaneous rather than controlled and mechanical.

As in any art, one purpose of our involvement in music—at whatever level—is to find this balance between our playing apparatus and our passions. If we're preoccupied by technical concerns, we may find our work dry. "Sometimes," said one oboe player, "the more I practice, the less I care. That's when I know I've lost the heart of the music and I need to rethink my approach." In contrast, a preference for passion over technique puts us in league with Oscar Wilde's Algernon: "I don't play accurately—anyone can play accurately—but I play with wonderful expression. As far as the piano is concerned, sentiment is my forte." In seeking a balance between technique and spirit, three concepts are especially helpful: making contact with music, making peace with our mistakes, and making honest musical decisions. We'll look at these topics one by one.

Making Contact with Music

Musicianship—this balance of feeling and technique—is not an "advanced" subject. It is not something you have to wait for until you have mastered everything else. Every time you *make contact with music*, every time you make a link between the technical act of making music and the personal act of enjoying music, using music, or responding to music, you are building your musicianship. It's easy to be so involved with "getting it right" that we forget that music is a normal human activity. It's perfectly natural to whistle while you work, dance cheek to cheek, sing in the shower, and make a joyful noise. Amateur cellist Shula Haveman put it this way:

> It was when my children were young that I started noticing how music really functioned in my life—and I mean capital *M*

Music is a swift weaver of deep feelings.

♪ Andrés Segovia

Music, not just the music I was practicing. I turned a very big corner when I realized how rich and valid my own musical impulses were, how basic and right it was for me to chant and drum and make up songs and clap and skip *and* play the cello. Maybe that's the only real advantage that children studying music have over us. They're still close to all that. I'd been taking lessons for six years previous to this, but it wasn't until I experienced music with my children that I really understood: I was *meant* to do this. I was *born* to do this.

Some of your best training in musicianship happens when you are not playing. Every movement that enters your awareness refines your understanding of rhythm; everything you see with awareness refines your understanding of shape and form. Sometimes the most valuable thing we can do for our musical development is to spend time doing something else—dance, creative writing, photography, drawing, or painting.

If you have been concentrating on technique and other individual skills of music making, you can feel confident that the moment will come when you engage your feelings, too. You may have to invite that moment. You may, for example, decide to stop paying attention to how you move your muscles when you make a *crescendo* (growing louder) or an *accelerando* (growing faster). Instead, you'll begin to *feel* the real importance of that crescendo or the meaning of that accelerando. It isn't the kind of "importance" or "meaning" that you express in words. *You feel the sense of the music, and you trust your body to express it.* That's the connection between feeling and technique. It's the difference between, on the one hand, running to catch a bus and, on the other hand, thinking about how to move your muscles if you wanted to run to catch a bus. When your attention is focused on a genuine motive, your actions follow naturally. As Eric Stumacher says, "When we feel an aesthetic impulse, our bodies find a way to get it done."

Making Peace with Mistakes

In seeking our own personal balance between technique and emotion, it's helpful to remember that something can be beautiful and also be imperfect. Perfection is a closed system to which nothing more can be added. Imperfection is a kind of

Music to have life, must be practiced; to have health, must not become ingrown. Music is not music's only soil.

♪ Ernst Bacon, *Notes on the Piano*

Something can be beautiful and also be imperfect.

openness that continues to seek and grow. Amateur pianist Donna Richoux discovered how her "mistakes" contribute to her musical growth:

> Often while I was recording I would be aware that I made a mistake, and I would think, "Oh, shoot." But when I played back the tape, several times those "mistakes" sounded *better* than I had expected—they broke the monotony, provided a change in rhythm or harmony or overall sound, and suggested a new idea that I could deliberately incorporate into the song! Talk about learning from mistakes! What a change from the usual music education attitude that a mistake is something wrong, painful, bad.

Mistakes in music are a bit like minor stumbles when we're walking. If we stumble a bit in real life, we just stay on our feet and carry on. But when we stumble musically, we sometimes act like cartoon characters. We fall on our face in the dust and lie there cursing and seeing stars. Don't overdramatize musical stumbles. Use your practice to correct mistakes, but when you play, just play. The music wants to keep going; it doesn't care if you make a mistake. One of the skills of really good musicianship is the ability to cover mistakes—to go right on as if nothing happened, without even missing a beat. Donald Payne, professor of music at Case Western Reserve University, says, "When the mind is occupied mainly with mistakes, what happens to music making, to the re-creation of an expressive sound structure? Should not the student aspire to something more meaningful than accuracy?" If we are feeling the music and trusting our technique, a mistake cannot stop us because the music will carry us on.

Making Musical Decisions: Interpretation

As you study and learn a piece of music, you are entitled to make it your own, to interpret the music in your own way. You don't have to play it the way you hear it on a record or the way suggested by an editor or even the way your teacher tells you to. Every good piece of music, like every good play or poem, welcomes the performer's contributions. The introduction to the Alfred Masterwork Edition of Bach's *Two Part Inventions* has an interesting chart showing the performance tempo of each *Invention* by eight distinguished keyboard artists and Bach editors. Czerny, for example, indicates a tempo of 120 M.M. (beats per minute) for *Invention No. 1,* and Rosalyn Tureck recorded it at 66. Glenn Gould played *Invention No. 2* at 40 M.M., and George Malcolm played it at 80. But Gould recorded *Invention No. 10* at 160 M.M., and Wanda Landowska recorded it at 96.

Admittedly, Bach is an unusual case. The structure of his music will carry a multitude of interpretations. Yet these drastic tempo variations by these caring artists are significant even for the most inexperienced musician of any style. We are entitled to allow our playing to grow out of our own exploration of the music, our own deeply personal experience of it. We need never play in the manner of a bored child reciting a half-understood poetry assignment.

Interpretation begins and ends, of course, with the music—the melody line, the rhythmic design, the lyrics, the style, the printed score if we have one. Like an actor interpreting a script, we first follow the directions we are given. We seek to be true to the composer's intentions as far as we can know them and to the music as it stands. Much interpretation is nothing more than a clear statement of what already exists in the music. It is not something laid on from the outside but rather something insisted on by the music itself.

Your interpretation may differ from someone else's. If you live with a piece of music for very long, you will likely change your own interpretation through time as your musical skills mature. But as long as you are guided by the music, by good taste, and by honesty, your interpretations are valid. The *how* of musical interpretation is a question that can occupy a lifetime. Here we can give only a few general guidelines:

Let your tone quality be expressive. Elsewhere in this book we've mentioned the importance of listening to, experimenting with, and developing your tone quality. It is in the act of interpretation that this work bears fruit. Tonal intensity (see page 131) is of special importance in expressive playing. Be careful not to let soft passages get flimsy.

Let your dynamic range and your tempo be expressive. *Dynamic range* refers here to sound levels, from loud to soft.

Many musicians acquire great technique, but taste is the final thing.

♪ Duke Ellington

Be sure it is you singing the song. Do not invent anyone to sing it for you. There is no hiding place in any song you will ever sing. How could there be? You are the song.

♪ David Craig, *On Singing Onstage*

175

For interpretive purposes, it may be more helpful to use the words *big* and *small*, thinking in terms of shape rather than effort. It's best to be careful whenever music tends to an extreme. For example, there is an upper limit to how fast a listener can perceive the notes in a fast passage. Played *too* fast, a passage becomes a blur. Played a bit more slowly, the passage sparkles. It's important to be in control of the extremes of dynamics and tempo so that your big sound is rich, your soft sound is delicate, your fast tempos glisten, and your slow tempos press on.

Changes in dynamics and tempo within a piece of music are often gradual, subtle changes. When we play by ear, we tend to handle such changes with more finesse than we sometimes do when we read. When we see something written down—a crescendo on the page, for example, or a ritard—we need to feel a meaningful change in the musical line, and to do this, it helps to *think the present level first.* For example, if you're playing softly and you see a crescendo coming up, think "small" and then grow. If you think "loud" you are likely to move too fast and so lose the musical character. Your body, remember, responds with exquisite precision to your musical ideas.

Resist thinking of accents, dynamics, and tempo as something to be stirred in after the piece is "done," like poppy seeds on top of bread. The interpretive content of music is the leavening in the loaf—it is what will make it rise—and it needs to be stirred in at the beginning.

Let your phrasing be expressive. In *The Dynamic Performance*, Donald Barra defines *phrasing* as "a sense of purposeful motion toward and away from specific points of reference." Musicians spend whole lifetimes studying and refining their phrasing. We can only touch lightly on this rich subject here, and we'll do that by comparing musical phrasing to language. A phrase in music is much like a sentence in speech or prose. If we neglect phrasing, in the musical sense, when we talk, our speech is flat, lifeless, a kind of robotlike imitation of human speech. If we neglect phrasing when we make music, our music is flat, lifeless, a kind of robotlike imitation of music.

For all musicians, skillful phrasing means careful attention to the relative importance of each note in a phrase. Our speech is full of musical-phrase-like qualities, patterns of stressed and unstressed syllables, of rising and falling intensities. Our musical phrasing can often be enhanced by making up words to a musical phrase, by improvising a movement that seems to express the phrase, by conducting the phrase, or by finding an image that seems to fit it. Heather Swope remembers the imagery she developed when she was learning Bach's *Two-Part Invention No. 1*: "The second half of this little piece has a melody that alternates between the left hand and the right hand. My teacher told me to 'go somewhere' with each phrase, to 'make it a conversation.' I thought about it during the week and—from where I don't know—this image popped into my mind of a mother looking for her lost child at a fair. The obvious words were an exact fit—

'Do you know where my daughter is?'
'I don't know where your daughter is.'
'Do you know where my daughter is?'
'I don't know where your daughter is.'

That image helped me build a sense of controlled, slowly rising intensity so that the passage wasn't dull or repetitious-sounding even though the notes themselves are repetitious."

Of all musicians, singers tend to have the best natural phrasing since their musical line is usually supported by words and since their tone comes entirely from within them, with no mechanical object to intervene. Among instrumentalists, wind, percussion, and bowed string players come closest to singers in natural opportunities to phrase—wind players because they coordinate their breath with the musical line, and percussion and bowed strings because their tone production is so closely tied to large gestures. Phrasing is the biggest challenge on keyboards and fretted (plucked or strummed) strings. For an instrumentalist, the experience of singing in a vocal group under a proficient conductor is usually a liberal education in phrasing. Amateur violinist Linda Baldwin said, "I've learned as much from choral directors about music in general—about phrasing, intonation, rhythm, projection—as from any piano or violin teacher or anyone else."

Let the rhythm guide your expression. Like time itself, musical rhythm is multilayered. Just as in clock and calendar time we have years, seasons, moon cycles, months, days, min-

In my playing I have always tried to "tell" my music as I might tell a story to a friend.

♪ Jean-Pierre Rampal,
Music, My Love

Singing is easier than playing because it comes more directly from you. There's nothing in the way. You don't have this piece of wood or metal or horsehair between you and what you're trying to get out.

♪ David Hobbie, university
student, singer, and violinist

utes, and seconds, so in music we have pieces, movements, sections, phrases, bars, beats, subdivisions, and frequencies. Each of these rhythmic entities provides clues for interpretation. A good place to begin is to feel the *quality* of the rhythmic pulse. Does the sound you're after want to sink down into the beat, as in a dirge or a slow ballad, or does it want to spring up and away from the beat, as in a jig or a scherzo?

Let your interpretation come from the inside out. If technique has been developed with care, interpretation can be accomplished in the mind and in the heart. We don't have to tell our fingers or our breath to make an accent or to play a smooth legato. If the technique for doing it is in hand, we need only *think* an accent or a legato, and our body will follow.

LEARNING NEW MUSIC: MAPPING

Conventional wisdom about learning a new piece of music suggests that the very first time we play the piece through, we should do two things: 1) play it close to the correct tempo (to get a good overall feeling for the piece as a whole) and 2) play all the right notes (to avoid teaching our muscles how to play wrong ones). For technically skillful musicians who read or play by ear fluently, this approach works well enough if the music is not too complicated.

Amateurs, however—at least those with limited technique or reading ability—find this advice hard to apply. Early attempts at a new piece are often far below tempo and full of hesitations and mistakes. The subsequent effort to learn consists of patiently weeding out errors while slowly gathering speed, and the result of this process is sometimes satisfying, sometimes not. After weeks of work, a much-loved piece may still be slow, hesitant, and error-ridden.

If we have learned from written music and we want to memorize the piece, we add a further step. After we've learned to play it as best we can, then we memorize it. This can add several more weeks to our learning, and the results, again, are sometimes satisfying and sometimes not. The flaw in this process shows up in the uneasy feeling that as we memorize, we are los-

Frequently sing in choruses, especially the middle parts. This will help to make you a real musician.

♪ Robert Schumann, *Advice to Young Musicians*

I pay more attention to conductors and singers than I do to pianists. There is more to learn from them.

♪ Alfred Brendel

ing something. The music we worked so hard to "get" is now literally being taken away.

It sounds as if the learning method we're using is working against us. One obvious flaw is that we are attempting to create a meaningful whole by building up from very small details. We don't use that procedure for other activities. If we want to build a house, we don't begin by laying the first brick; we begin with a plan, with an understanding of how long and how wide and how high this house will be and where the important features will go. If we want to drive from Seattle to Miami, we don't begin planning our trip with a neighborhood street map of Seattle; we get out a map of the whole United States and get some idea of the overall route and distance. If we want to draw a friend's portrait, we don't put in the freckles and the eyelashes first; we begin by sketching the overall shape of the head and marking out the placement of the main features.

Dr. Rebecca Shockley, a member of the piano faculty at the University of Minnesota, has developed a procedure for learning and memorizing music simultaneously. She calls it *mapping*. It is a method of learning music that begins with an understanding of the whole and adds the details as the musician needs or discovers them. Mapping is appropriate for any age or skill level, but it has some very special advantages for the amateur musician. According to Shockley,

> Mapping is a Gestalt approach to learning that starts from the basic structure and gradually fills in the details instead of starting with details and adding more until the whole structure is pieced together. It is in direct opposition to the one-measure-at-a-time approach many students take, where the accumulation of details without awareness of the whole results in a patchy performance that lacks unity, direction, and musical meaning.

Mapping relies on two principal activities—improvisation and the creation of a written map—to aid learning and memorizing. We'll describe how Shockley's technique could be used with a very short piece—one page or less—of written music, and we'll use as an example a piano piece called "Teeter-Totter" ("Tape-Cul" in French), by Joan Hansen, shown in Figure 10-1. You can follow these steps yourself with any short piece (or a short section of a longer piece) that you're working on or would

An artist should never lose sight of the thing as a whole. He who puts too much into details will find that the thread which holds the whole thing together will break.

♪ Frédéric Chopin

like to learn. Don't leave us now if you don't read music or if you play mostly by ear. You'll find things here that apply to you, too. This is just an example of one way that mapping can be used.

Mapping from Written Music

1. Study the music for one minute—sixty seconds—away from your instrument. *Get a general, overall idea about what this piece is like. Make as many observations as you can about any aspects of the music that interest you.* For example, you might observe things about mood, tempo, rhythm, dynamics, melodic shape, texture, pitch range, repeated motifs, interval patterns, harmony, and so forth. (You don't have to look at all those things. Look at what interests you. Make observations that are meaningful and important to you.) You could imagine that you are playing or singing the piece. (Don't worry about singing "the right notes"— just sing higher when the notes go up and lower when the notes go down.) You could clap the rhythm, or you could conduct the piece.

Figure 10–1

For example, in "Teeter-Totter" you might notice that the left hand plays a steady, unvarying rhythm of two pulses per bar through almost the entire piece. If you know something about intervals, you might notice that the left hand always plays a perfect fifth. You might notice that the right hand plays one note at a time, usually starts just after beat 1 in the bass line, and alternates a "busy" bar with a sustained bar. You might notice the time signature, the tempo marking, the pedaling, and the long slurs, all of which suggest that this piece is played very smoothly. You might notice that there are five "melody chunks" (two-bar units). You might notice that the first three melody chunks start on a D and the last two start on an E. You might notice that the first and last melody chunks stay near the middle of the keyboard whereas the middle three chunks are an octave higher. If you know something about scale construction, you might notice that, although there's no key signature to confirm this, the left hand looks like the key of E. You might notice that it begins mezzo forte, gets louder in the middle, and then gets much softer and a little bit slower at the very end.

2. Go to your instrument, without the music, and improvise your way straight through the piece, reasonably up to tempo. You probably won't know many notes at this point—you may not know any. That's all right. Just make something up that generally fits the overall design and the mood, something that more or less expresses the observations you have just made. Fake it. If you don't know how to improvise, fake that, too! Have fun with this step. No one is judging you. If it sounds crazy and very "modern" at this point, you're doing just fine. *Your goal is not to play the right notes but to capture the general musical idea, the overall shape, the sense or feeling of the piece as a whole.* Think of making a very rough, preliminary sketch in sound, catching only the very broad outlines. When you finish, take a moment to think about what parts of the piece seem clear and what parts are unclear. Decide what you would like to find out about next.

One amateur pianist tried mapping for the first time on a short waltz by Schubert, and after doing this step, she said, "I didn't get one single note right! I didn't even play it in the right key! But I know I had the *idea* right. It had that lilt that I've always loved Schubert for."

3. Return to the music (away from your instrument) and make a map of the entire piece. *Do this in one or two minutes, no* *more. Use a pencil and plain paper (not music paper).* Your map can be drawn or written in any kind of symbols, sketches, numbers, or notation that makes sense to you—curving lines, zigzags, dots, arrows, chord symbols, time lines, note names, rhythmic representations. Include only information that you want right now and that you think will be helpful to you. Since you're working fairly fast, just get down the main ideas. Think about the piece as a whole. Don't worry about details yet. Once again, you are just making a very rough sketch, but on paper this time.

Figures 10-2, 10-3, and 10-4 are maps for "Teeter-Totter" done by three different musicians. (Don't worry if your first map doesn't look this neat. These have been "prettied up" a bit for this book. The originals were sloppy!) The musician who mapped Figure 10-2 noticed the left-hand rhythm and the starting notes for each melody unit. She drew dots for each melody note and then connected them like a graph. She wrote "Key of C?" at the beginning and then circled every black note, beginning to answer her own question. We might guess that she is interested in the tonality and the movement of the melody.

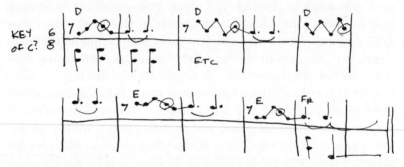

Figure 10–2

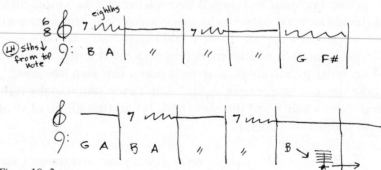

Figure 10–3

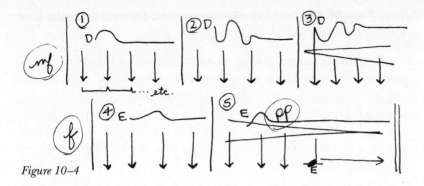

Figure 10–4

The musician who drew the map in Figure 10-3 noticed the pattern of fifths in the left hand and wrote down enough information so that he could reconstruct the entire bass line accurately from his map. (We might guess that this was an important feature to him—he wanted to know "how the bass went" or how to set the rhythm or what to do with his left hand.) He noticed the alternating "busy" and sustained right hand, indicating the busy measures with a wavy line and the sustained measures with a straight line.

Figure 10-4 was mapped by someone who noticed a lot of details about shape and interpretation. She copied the exact dynamic structure into her map, indicated the pedaling, and represented the right hand by smooth curves that follow the general melodic shape. She showed the left hand by downward–pointing arrows that seem to reflect the pulsing nature of this line. Rather than indicating measures, she indicated the five melodic chunks and found a way to note the one instance (at the beginning of the third chunk) when the hands enter together.

Each mapmaker captured valuable but different information. Each map is useful and valid. There is no right or wrong way to draw a map.

4. Return to your instrument with your map and play the piece again. Once again, if you don't know the exact notes, make up something that fits. Play what you have written on your map.

5. Continue alternating between making a map away from your instrument and playing your map. You can start a new map if you'd like, or you can fill in gaps on your old one. Let your own curiosity and needs guide you.

6. When it seems useful to do so, choose a short section, a phrase, or several measures to work on.   You could continue to apply the mapping technique, perhaps lengthening the time you spend mapping. Or you could take the music to your instrument and read through the piece from the music. Proceed in a way that answers your own questions and fills in what you need to know next.

Does this process seem daunting to you? It's an unusual way to learn music, but it's not an unusual way to learn in general. Think about the last time you picked up the lyrics of a favorite song from the radio or from a recording. At first you just had a vague feeling for how the song went: maybe you could hum a bit; maybe you knew a few words here and there or a line from the chorus. Every time you heard it again, if you were paying attention, you picked up a little more. Perhaps you finally got to the place where you knew quite a bit of the song and began to listen to fill in missing bits—the words at the beginning of the second verse or that special ending. The amateurs who volunteered to try mapping for this book were unanimously enthusiastic *after* they had done it once—even the ones who were very wary or perplexed at first. The very special thing about mapping is that it allows you to do your own perceiving, your own organizing, your own analysis. It lets you learn in your own style, relying on your strengths and natural curiosity.

Musicians who try mapping sometimes wonder about the time limits imposed. Even for a short piece of music, one minute is not very long to spend "learning" it before you play it! But it is the time limit that makes Shockley's system work so well, for several reasons. Most important, a brief exposure time prevents you from getting mired in details and encourages you to focus only on general outlines. It also helps improve your concentration and reduces your panic and expectations. If you had, say, thirty minutes for your initial study, you could easily feel that you are "supposed" to be able to learn it all. In one minute, of course you can't learn very much, so your expectations of your own performance are more relaxed. Finally, the short time limit creates the possibility of what Shockley calls "sudden flashes of insight"—instantaneous and surprising new perceptions of patterns and ideas.

Mapping offers some strong advantages over conventional music-learning techniques. For one thing, the improvisation at your instrument when you are at the "faking it" stage is wonderful preparation for a performance. Should you draw a blank in your memory, you at least know the overall structure, and you have experience playing "something like" the piece. Consequently, you are unlikely to freeze up.

Another memory-related advantage is that learning and memorizing usually happen simultaneously when you map. By the time you have actually learned the notes using mapping, you have memorized the piece, too, because you haven't had the music in front of you at your instrument very much. It's easier to memorize from your own map because the information on it is concise and tailored to your own needs.

Mapping draws you into the character and mood and meaning of the piece from the very first. There's no feeling that you're trying to wring meaning out of a disparate collection of bits and pieces picked up one at a time like confetti. The very first thing you look at, in the first sixty seconds of contact, is the piece as a whole. This is a tremendous advantage for musicians who learn from written music, where the tendency is to atomize the music into nearly meaningless details.

Finally, mapping puts you in the position of "needing to know" rather than "trying to remember." You are actively seeking answers to your own questions and meeting your own logical needs—a prime setting for good learning.

Mapping can be adapted to many musical situations. A longer piece can be broken down into logical sections and mapped a section at a time. A piece that's already learned just gets mapped from a different point of view than a new piece. You can map something you're learning by rote or from a recording by drawing a map as you listen to the entire piece. Shockley has found the process especially useful in group learning because members get the benefit of seeing one another's maps and sharing different perceptions. (For more information about mapping, see Rebecca Shockley's book, *A Practical Guide to Mapping: The New Way to Learn Music.*)

As amateur and student musicians, we are often working to learn music that we really cannot play very well *right now*—music that outruns our technical ability at the moment. The problem, as we discussed at the beginning of this chapter, is how to balance expression and technique, especially when the technical obstacles seem so large. One solution comes through understanding the music as a whole, as in the process of mapping. No matter how small the fragments we finally break the music into, if we understand where each fragment fits and how it contributes to the overall idea, our work will make sense to us and provide its own motivation.

CHOOSING MUSIC

What do you like to play? For a dedicated amateur, a long browse in a big sheet music store is a glorious treat. If there's a style you love, get the best music you can find in that style. Good music is no harder to play than shoddy music. In fact, it's easier in some ways because good music holds together and makes sense whereas mediocre music sometimes gives us very little "meat" to hang on our musical bones. "Teaching pieces" and "educational music" sometimes fall, unfortunately, in the category of the mediocre. The classics of any style—whether classical, ragtime, rock, jazz, hymns, or country—have stood the musical test of time.

Folk songs make excellent beginning material for a new musician. Their musical meaning is not flamboyant or obscure, and their musical structure is nearly always familiar-sounding. These simple tunes let us build musical skills and understanding while playing "real" music. Folk songs are also a good introduction to a variety of musical styles, since virtually every style has borrowed heavily from the folk tradition.

Composer to Editor to Performer

When you go music shopping, you will encounter several species of printed music, including Urtext, editions, arrangements, and transcriptions.

An *Urtext* is the closest possible thing to a composer's original work, with no markings, changes, or additions by anyone else. The word is generally applied only to art music. Many an Urtext is not, in fact, completely the work of the composer. The original composition may have been lost or left incomplete, may have existed in several versions, or may have contained omissions that an improvising performer of the day would have known how to fill. But to the best of any music scholar's ability to re-create it, an Urtext is faithful to the composer's intention.

An *edition* is the original version of a composition with technical and interpretive suggestions contributed by a music editor. In many cases it is impossible to tell which are the editor's marks and which were present in the original. Marks indicating fingering and breathing are almost certainly an editor's, but dynamics, phrase markings, tempo, and articulation could be original or could have been added. In a few editions the editor's notations are printed in smaller type or in a lighter shade of type than the original material. Any art music that is not an Urtext is an edition, and many musicians have their favorite (and not-so-favorite) editors.

An *arrangement* is a setting of a melody, with harmony and other notes or parts added by an arranger. Melodies or themes can be set in different arrangements just as a gem can be set into different pieces of jewelry. Folk songs and popular songs are commonly sold as arrangements. The melody defines the work; the arrangement can be changed to suit a particular instrument or ensemble or skill level. "Greensleeves" is an example of a work that has been arranged hundreds of times, for solo voice and for solo instrument, for small ensembles, for bands and orchestras, in traditional, contemporary, and jazz settings.

A transcription has been modified to make it playable by a different musical medium.

A *transcription* is a work in very nearly the same form as the composer wrote it, modified to make it playable in a different musical medium than called for by the original. For example, a solo song may be transcribed for flute, a string quartet transcribed for four saxophones, or a symphony transcribed for piano duet. (A work for a large group transcribed for a soloist or a small group may also be called a *reduction.*) As few changes as possible are made, although the final result, of course, sounds very different than the original. Composers sometimes transcribe their own works. Ravel wrote *Ma mère l'oye* (*Mother Goose Suite*) for piano duet and transcribed it for orchestra. Other transcriptions are the work of performers. The Myra Hess transcription of Bach's chorale "Jesu, Joy of Man's Desiring" is part of the standard solo piano repertoire. Be a little cautious about transcriptions. Some are considered by experienced musicians to be in questionable taste, as millwright Brian Swanson discovered the hard way:

> I made arrangements to begin piano lessons. He said to bring something that I could play, so I polished up a piece I still knew by heart from when I was a kid—the first movement of Beethoven's *Moonlight Sonata*. I wasn't scared when I started to play for him, but I was totally unnerved by his reaction. He was obviously trying to stifle a laugh. I started playing worse and worse and finally gave up. I was very angry. I thought I had been playing fairly well. I couldn't believe he was laughing at me. He apologized and then asked if I knew what key the piece was in. I told him it was in A minor and he said, "You're *playing* it in A minor, but Beethoven wrote it in *C-sharp* minor. You're playing a transcription!"
>
> We finally established a good relationship, but we sure got off to a terrible start. I'd never heard about this before. I didn't know then that it made any difference what key you played in. My old teacher had never mentioned it.

When we play a classical composition or an individual's particular arrangement, we do our very best to be true to the music on the page. But here's a heretical *however* for amateurs: If slight changes will render playable a piece that you love and that is within reach except for a few small difficulties, *make the changes.* Leave out the double-note trill, take a variation down an octave, write your own cadenza, play the whole piece more slowly than it's usually performed. It would be in poor taste to present a significantly altered composition to a paying audience (and in some cases it would be in violation of the copyright law). But if small changes make the music accessible to you in your own private playing sessions, there is nothing wrong with doing it.

PLAYING MUSIC THAT IS NEW TO YOU

It's fun to wander into new territory—for a classicist to take on the blues, for a jazz player to pick up Debussy, or for a gospel singer to learn some Purcell. Probably the most important attitude, if you're attempting a crossover, is to *believe in the music.*

Even if it's not apparent at the outset, trust that the composers or the artists who write or play this music work from honest musical impulses. Be observant and analytical. You already know a lot that will help you understand a new form. Think about the title, look at the rhythmic design, and study the patterns of intensity. Try to figure out where the greatest musical interest resides—in the melodic shape? in the rhythmic patterns? in the texture?

Pay close attention to intonation, especially in contemporary music. Intonation is always important, of course. Out-of-tune J. S. Bach sounds no better than out-of-tune Milton Babbitt. However, with contemporary and unconventional harmonies, some musicians have a tendency to shrug off intonation problems with, "Oh well, that's close enough." If you believe in the music and make an effort to tune your intervals, you will often be delighted to hear the sound move off the page in extraordinary ways—passages will shimmer and harmonies will "pop" into place.

AND SOMETIMES . . . JUST PLAY

Whatever kind of amateur you are—the four-hour-a-day practice-to-perfectionist or the twice-a-year party horn—remember to cherish your own love of music. Play as often as you can. It's all right—even after all the conventional wisdom about careful practicing—to go at it all out, to make glorious mistakes, to make a joyful noise. Margaret Hillis, conductor of the Chicago Symphony Chorus, sometimes tells her singers, just before they begin a number, that this music has been going on for all eternity, and it will continue for an eternity after they are done singing. When we play or sing, we only make audible, now and in this place, that eternal music. The music will go on, beyond us, as strengthened by our love as we are by it.

All the music that ever was still sounds; all the music that is to be still slumbers.

♪ Thomas Surette, *Music and Life*

189

Part Four

PLAYING AND PRACTICING WITH OTHERS

If there is a means of interesting, delighting, and elevating a large number of people at very small expense, by something which they can all do together and which brings them all into sympathy with one another, and if the result of this cooperation is to produce something beautiful, is it not worth doing?

Thomas Surette, *Music and Life*

CHAPTER 11

Inside Ensembles: The Musical View

I look at the people in the orchestra and I realize that we have almost nothing in common. The concertmaster is a novelist and the first cellist is a farmer. The first clarinet is an electrician and the guy in the very back of the second violin section—the one who's lost all the time—he's a neurologist. We don't talk about ourselves much. I don't even know everyone's name—I just call them Marion Oboe and Gail Viola. This is not my "social circle," yet I feel closer to these people than to anybody else on earth.

♪ Susan Willis, bartender and amateur percussionist

As a glue to bind a diverse group of people together, it is hard to find anything better than music. Members of a musical ensemble don't need very much in common—certainly not political affiliations, social background, financial status, age, or occupational interests. They simply come together for the joy of music. Singing or playing in a group gives a perspective on music that you just can't get when you're alone. Robert Schauffler knew that in 1911 when he asked, in *The Musical Amateur*:

Why is *ensemble* music the sole recreation definitely promised us in the future life? Obviously because it combines the most fun with the fewest drawbacks. Milton, indeed, goes so far as to give the angelic musicians "harps ever tuned," thereby reducing the drawbacks to zero.

Schauffler oversells the ease of it all just a bit, but even the drawbacks of ensemble playing are, for most musicians, easy to tolerate in light of the immense satisfaction that group music making offers. In this chapter we'll start with some ideas for finding ensembles to play in. Then we'll look at skills needed by all ensemble musicians—both general skills and skills specific to particular kinds of ensembles. We'll also have some encouraging words about surviving the personal turmoil that happens sometimes in ensemble work, and we'll close with a brief checklist.

FINDING OR FORMING AN ENSEMBLE

Unlike professional musicians, who may have to take any job that comes along, amateurs have the luxury of choosing the groups they play with. It may take some searching and some trial and error, but it's likely that you can find one or more welcoming groups to match your level, your style, your tastes, and your musical goals. It would be impossible to describe every kind of amateur ensemble, but we can at least start the process by recognizing two general categories: *conducted ensembles*, medium-size to large groups that play or sing under the direction of a conductor or musical leader, and *unconducted ensembles*, small groups that play without a conductor (though they may have a leader or a coach).

Members of a musical ensemble don't need very much in common.

Finding a Conducted Ensemble

Most cities and fair-sized towns have a variety of ongoing conducted ensembles—choruses, concert bands, stage bands, and orchestras large and small. Often these groups recruit new members in the fall, about the time school starts. Watch for announcements in papers. Also, many musical groups solicit new players a month or two before a "big event"—the Christmas production of the *Messiah*, for example. Ask people you know who play the kind of music you like if they know of any groups. Watch for notices posted in instrument repair shops, music stores, teaching studios, and college or university music departments. Also watch announcements in adult education bulletins.

Some large groups admit new members by audition, but many are open to all who would like to join. If you are uncertain about your skills, talk with the conductor in advance. If the group seems inappropriate, the conductor may be able to sug-

I often think that if more people in cities—young and old—could join choirs and choral societies, it would cure a lot of loneliness.

♪ Maureen Forrester, *Maureen Forrester: Out of Character*

193

When I began to study the cello, I thought I would have about seven years of drudgery before I began to have any fun. But not so. Before I had studied for even a year, I had my first chance to play with other people. One evening I went to a concert. . . . As we were leaving the hall, a pleasant-looking, dark-haired woman said to me, "You seemed to enjoy the music." I said I thought it was gorgeous. She asked if I was a musician. I said I had only just started to play the cello. She said, "The cello! We need cellos!" . . . and went on to ask me if I would like to play in a small chamber orchestra. I said I had just started to play and wasn't very good. She said, "Oh that doesn't make any difference. We don't play very hard music; come play with us."

♪ John Holt, *Never Too Late*

gest one more suitable. In a small town or rural area, it's sometimes especially hard to find a group that can take a beginning adult player. It's worth asking the local school district. Some school music programs open their bands and orchestras to community players. Senior citizen groups are also active in ensemble organizing and may welcome both senior and not-so-senior members to fill out the ranks.

Nearly all conducted groups—especially large ones—are performing ensembles. That is, their work is always directed toward a public concert—usually two or three a year. Groups that do not perform are called *reading groups*, and get together simply to explore the repertoire and to enjoy each other's musical company.

Finding or Forming an Unconducted Ensemble

An unconducted ensemble has no stand-up-in-front leader and so, by definition, is nearly always a small ensemble—under ten players. The range of musical styles represented by unconducted ensembles is enormous, ranging from ragtime bands to string quartets, from Renaissance madrigal groups to bluegrass banjo pickers.

Finding an unconducted group can take more sleuthing than finding the conducted sort. Word-of-mouth is the most powerful search tool. You can also organize your own group. Unconducted ensembles usually start with a small group of friends meeting casually at someone's house. To find groups or potential group members, contact other musicians, ask teachers, and post and read notices in likely places. Attending a weekend or summer workshop is an excellent way to make contacts. Some cities have newsletters sent out by organizations of jazz aficionados or early music devotees or gospel music followers.

It's usually easy to find musicians in a large group who are eager to join a small group. Every community band has a brass choir lurking inside it, and every choral society has a potential madrigal group or several barbershop quartets.

A duet is an ensemble, too, and is probably the gentlest possible introduction to playing with others. Easy duet music is available for nearly every imaginable combination of instruments. If you take lessons or take a group class, ask your teacher if she has other students who might be interested in duet work.

Some unconducted ensembles are performing groups; some are for reading or jamming only. Some meet only once, play for an evening, and make no future plans; others have a long-term ongoing commitment, like the Kokanee String Quartet of Nelson, British Columbia, which has played together for over fifteen years with the same members.

IF YOU ARE A NEWCOMER TO ENSEMBLE PLAYING

The first experience playing with a group is a bit daunting for almost everyone, and especially for beginning musicians. Suddenly there is a great deal going on and many, many distractions. If you'd like to join an ensemble but feel uncertain of your skills, see if you can arrange to sit in or to "shadow" an experienced player for few sessions in the kind of group you'd like to join. As a "shadow" you simply sit or stand as close as you can, watch what's going on, and join in whenever you're able. Ken McDougall started off as a shadow member of a local band:

> The band director told me to just sit in the section and listen until I felt ready to play. He gave me a folder with all the music. I'd show up for band practice, put my clarinet together, sit with the clarinets, and follow the music. It took some time before my mind was quick enough to keep up with what they were doing. During the first month I didn't play a single note.

Nothing will pull up your sight-reading or ear-playing skills more quickly than playing with a group. But until you can keep up, being a "shadow" can help you collect a lot of tips about how to find your place, when to come in, and what to listen for.

SKILLS FOR ENSEMBLE PLAYING

Most musicians who play both solo and with others say that playing in an ensemble is easier. You always have both the personal and the musical support of your colleagues. Even so, playing with others requires a number of special skills, most of which you can't "practice" anywhere but in a group. We'll look

I found every group I've ever played in by luck. I know enough to join the local orchestra when I move to a new area, and soon I find people with whom to play chamber music. CAMMAC has brought me several long-standing groups and untold numbers of friends. I get into choirs because my husband is a tenor. Tenors are always in demand and no director yet has had the heart to refuse entry to the wife of a tenor.

♪ Jane Wilson, nurse and amateur singer and string player

Lurking ostentatiously in a chair near the wings, I would wait until the notes E and F turned up in whatever they were rehearsing, leap on them with a vengeance, and then drop out until the chance returned again.

♪ Christian Williams, journalist and amateur cellist

195

first at four basic skills needed by all ensemble players, and then we'll look separately at skills required in conducted and unconducted ensembles.

Extended Awareness

An ensemble member's awareness must "move over" and make room for information coming from the outside. A soloist rarely hears the word *watch*, but ensemble players hear it endlessly. You can never keep your eyes and ears on your own musical line for very long.

Every member's extended awareness—watching and listening "out"—is what lets a group of any size play and feel the music together. This extended awareness also weaves a safety net for any member who runs into trouble. If you need help, you are in instant communication. Fiddler Dick Pollard explains the importance of another player's awareness: "I've played with accordionist Gail Bearham for ten years. When we play together, I never worry about the music falling apart if I drop a note because even though Gail's right into the tune, I know she's also listening to me. That's one of the things that makes somebody really nice to play with. You have to be sensitive and responsive but not dependent. There's a freedom there to dare, to try. You're like pillars holding up the roof of music."

When a group first reads or plays a new piece together, this extended awareness is usually at a low level. The first time through it's enough just to keep your place, find your notes, and get in and get out at something like the right moment. The next time through, however, even if individual parts aren't settled in yet, everyone begins playing *with* everyone, listening to see how the parts fit together. The group begins to think in dimensions—playing *under, over, through,* and *around* one another, leading, supporting, holding back, and drawing out. It is this multilayered, dimensional aspect of playing together that is both exhilarating and bewildering.

Balance of Sound

There's a story told about the time Brahms was accompanying one of his own cello sonatas. The cellist shouted out, "I can't hear myself!" and Brahms shouted back, "Lucky you!" Mr.

Brahms's opinion notwithstanding, the cellist had the right idea. The only way a group can play together is if they can hear themselves and one another.

This often means considerable adjustment to individual sound levels. An indication in the music to play *piano* (softly) may, if taken too literally, mean that a soft passage is not heard at all, while a too faithful *forte* may blot out everything else. Achieving good balance in an ensemble requires measuring your sound level in relative terms, not in absolute terms. If a part can't be heard, it is often a more musical solution to subdue the heavier parts than to "bring out" the faint part—to lighten one line rather than to force another.

The more types and ranges of instruments in a group, the more challenging good balance becomes. A quartet of recorders is easier to blend than a quartet of recorder, violin, guitar, and string bass. To achieve a thoughtful balance every player needs to appreciate to some degree what other players are up against. Very soft tones and extreme diminuendos are difficult, for example, for the brass, who have to keep a certain volume of air going through to make any tone at all. However, the brass owe it to their colleagues to refine their technique as much as possible so that they can offer a range of dynamics and not force everyone else to play at extremes all the time. Any group that commands a range of dynamics has, in fact, a splendid virtue that can be put to all kinds of tasteful musical ends. Any group can blow loud, but an intense ensemble *piano* is a great achievement.

Another part of being in balance is being in tune. When intervals are poorly tuned, the overall effect is blurry, and balance becomes elusive. When the intonation is accurate, vertical harmonies "pop" in an almost palpable way, and balance is easier to achieve. Sometimes clean ensemble intonation means playing or singing with a simpler tone than you would use if you were playing alone—with less vibrato or less individual coloring—while the group or the conductor seeks a tone quality that will serve the music's needs.

Contributing to effective balance means understanding your role in the ensemble, finding a balance in attitude between assertiveness and subordination. Both personally and musically, ensembles usually include individuals with "top-voice mentality"—the melody instruments, the ones who shine, who willingly

What good is to play piano if nobody hear the notes? Play mezzo forte. Must be clear.

♪ Arturo Toscanini

take the lead. Supporting and contrasting with these are the "oom-pah voices"—the steady, reliable bottom line—and the "middle voices"—the ones who blend, who close up gaps, who relate to all sides, who can be, both musically and personally, the mediators.

These are not hard-and-fast personality types, of course, though researchers Atarah Ben-Tovim and Douglas Boyd have found a steady consistency between personality and satisfaction with an instrument. What matters to an ensemble is that each player contributes to a total sound. Middle and bottom voices sometimes have to be ready to step smoothly into the limelight, and top voices have to be willing to relinquish it. June Ryder, a Vancouver geologist, finds genuine pleasure in the balanced sound of her recorder ensemble, T'Andernaken: "We all enjoy listening to the sound that we produce. We like the sound of recorders played well together. I enjoy fitting my particular line into the total fabric of sound, and I think the others do, too."

If there's a lead or principal player on a part like yours, or similar to it, musical protocol decrees that you take your cues for styling, volume, and technique from that person. If the lead sax plays the melody smoothly and quietly, other players who have a similar line follow suit, at least while the group is playing. You might discuss it later on and try it again some other way, but each time through the group has to adopt a common approach in order to check the effect of any decision about styling or interpretation.

Catching the Tempo, Sharing the Rhythm, and Making Entrances

Any group of musicians, from two to two thousand, from beginners to pros, must work uncommonly hard to find and settle into a tempo. But it is one of the magical moments of ensemble playing when "the beat goes on," when the rhythm takes wings on the players' collective spirit.

Your attitude about rhythm and tempo is significant. It's not helpful to think of "following" a beat or "keeping up." A tempo—the speed at which the music moves—is something you take, not something you find, something you catch, not something you chase. Beginning a piece of music or making an entry

The humblest member of a choral society, the shy beginner who takes his place at the back desk of the second violins in an amateur orchestra . . . if he sings or plays with understanding and purpose, is a creator.

♪ Ralph Vaughan Williams,
The Making of Music

There's Central Standard Time, Eastern Standard Time, and Newman Standard Time, which is always behind. I'm not used to playing with a band, so I have trouble with tempo.

♪ Randy Newman

in the middle is like stepping onto a moving escalator, not like a riding a loaded freight train that's slowly gathering speed.

Inexperienced or timid players have to be especially careful about staying inside the rhythm and not riding behind it. If you follow another player—that is, if you wait for someone else to play before you come in—you will be late. Players of low instruments—cello, bass, tuba, bassoon—have to anticipate the beat because of the extra time required to get these instruments to "speak" in their low registers.

Most conductors of amateur groups and most small group leaders are very careful about preparatory beats, about giving a clear tempo before the piece begins. This is a time when eye-to-eye contact is essential. In rehearsal, at least the first few times, a conductor or ensemble leader often counts out loud to establish the tempo. This step may be dropped after the piece is better known, but a conductor or leader will often continue to mouth the tempo or to give several very small preparatory beats. Eventually, the tempo may be set by only an upbeat—a single preparatory beat. It's at this point that some players get uneasy about catching the tempo. The most reliable procedure is to have your instrument ready, to have the character of the piece clearly in mind, and to relax as you watch the upbeat. Your body will usually know what to do. Even if you start off wrong, you can at least adjust quickly rather than fighting the established tempo in your panic to find it.

Your skill at picking up a beat can be exercised any time you listen to live or recorded music. Start tapping time or feeling the tempo internally. Is it in two? three? four? six? Where does a phrase end and the next one begin? If you read music, can you imagine what the music you're hearing might look like written out? Are there lots of long, sustained notes for everyone? faster groups of notes in the melody over a steady beat? layers of moving parts?

Rhythmically complicated passages sometimes touch off a kind of helpless panic in amateur ensemble players, especially ones who play from written music. Use your pencil freely in such a case, putting a vertical slash through the main beats, as shown in chapter 9, on page 166. Don't be distracted by the number of *notes* in any bar. The number of beats will always be the same (unless the time signature changes), so if you lose your way for a moment, just jump back in on the next main beat.

A common place to get lost is during a really thick passage at a fast tempo, when a lot of notes are flying by. Don't insist on playing every note if they're going by too fast for you to play them up to tempo. Pay the most attention to the first and last beat in every bar. If you stumble in the middle of a bar, just stop playing, prepare on the last beat, and join in again on "one" of the next bar. If you know you can't possibly play all the notes, just play the first note of every beat or the first note of every bar. A good exercise to use at home in preparation for such a situation is to choose a fairly hard piece of music, set a metronome, and practice playing only the first beat of each bar or the first note of each beat.

Another common place to get lost is during a very long rest, where your part has a number of silent bars. It can be hard to make the next entry, partly because it's so easy to miscount a long rest and partly because it takes a certain amount of nerve to barge in again—like trying to join an ongoing conversation. As you become more familiar with your part, it's less necessary to count long rests, as long as you have listened carefully to know the sounds that precede your entry. However, when you are just learning the music, you will have to count your way. As you count, stay in touch with the music. It's deadly to daydream and hope you'll "feel" the right place to come in (or worse, to follow someone else who might be lost, too). Equally dangerous is to count mindlessly, without listening to the sound around you.

The most reliable initial way to count through a long rest is to count measures, not beats, keeping track with your fingertips pressed against your instrument or some part of your body. Many musicians count beats as well as measures—a four-bar rest in three-four time would be counted 1-*2-3*, 2-*2-3*, 3-*2-3*, 4-*2-3*. However, in all but the slowest tempos you can trust your body to pick up the beats from the music around you while you actually count only measures. This strategy helps to make sure that your internal rhythm stays in step with the music rather than doggedly going its own way and perhaps straying off. When your entry is near, you may want to resume counting beats or even subdivided beats. For example, if you enter playing sixteenth notes after a six-bar rest, it helps to count your last bar as 6 *tuka-tuka tuka-tuka tuka-tuka*. (See page 138 for more about this counting system.)

Another common place to get lost is during a very long rest.

Ensembles tend to share certain rhythmic aberrations, including the tendency to rush (get faster) as they play louder, and to drag (get slower) as they play softer. Rushing also happens when rests and sustained notes are short-changed—not counted out to their full value. Musicians speak of "leaning" on a rest or a sustained note to be sure it gets its whole value. The biggest culprit is the note at the end of a phrase. One beat cannot end until the next one begins, so if a four-four phrase ends on beat four, the last note is not over until beat one of the next bar.

The percussion section, by the way, is not there to *lead* the rhythm but to *support* the rhythm. Even with a drummer, all the players must still carry the ongoing beat inside themselves, leaving the drummer free to *respond* to the group rather than to haul it forward or hold it back.

Foot tapping as a way of keeping the rhythm gets varied reviews depending on the style of music. It's accepted in jazz but taboo in classical ensembles, recorder consorts, most vocal groups, and any large ensemble (where it simply *looks* ridiculous). If foot tapping is necessary to keep the group together, it's best to assign one person to the job. Otherwise, the result can be several varieties of tempo and the problem grows worse. (In any ensemble where visible foot tapping is outlawed, it's perfectly all right to twitch your big toe inside your shoe.)

Finding Your Place

Everyone gets lost from time to time. The rule in an ensemble, if you think you're lost, is *stop playing but keep thinking.* If you keep going mentally with the music and don't panic, you have a very good chance of jumping back in again. If anyone else is playing or singing your line, glue your attention to their sound and try to find your place. If you've played the piece before, you may recognize a landmark coming up—a key change, a tempo change, the beginning of a phrase or a chorus. Don't jump too far ahead. Some players panic and begin searching the music far, far ahead of where the ensemble is. Just keep counting!

Look around. If someone can help you, they will, perhaps by calling out a rehearsal number or a chord name or a bit of the lyrics. If you have a conductor, a puzzled look in her direc-

I always have a moment of panic when I get lost. I start counting as soon as I know I'm lost, but I'm never quite sure of myself. Did I count through the moment of panic or not?

♪ Kathryn Chapman, mother, tree planter, and amateur cellist

201

tion will eventually catch her eye, and she will probably do what she can to cue you back in.

Sometimes, of course, it becomes pointless or impossible to continue. In a conducted ensemble, the conductor will usually stop the proceedings. In an unconducted ensemble, however, it is *your* responsibility (a responsibility to use discreetly) to call a halt. In all but the most contemporary music it will become apparent by the discordant sound that people are no longer together. Theo Wyatt gives this advice to recorder consorts:

> [I]f a new piece of old music starts to sound to you discordant, you may properly wait a measure or two to see whether it was the composer being extra daring. If that hypothesis becomes untenable, you may wait another measure or two to see whether the culprit can get himself back on the right track. And it goes without saying that all this while you will have been examining your own bar lines and cadences to see whether you have put a foot wrong. But if the music is then still discordant, you must cry "Stop!" You may be the youngest, smallest, poorest, shyest, ugliest of the party, but you have a duty to forget your inadequacy and to take the lead in bringing the music to a halt. . . . you will usually find that if the music stops, someone will admit to having been lost or at least to having been unsure of his whereabouts.

After an ensemble has stopped, the players have to find a place to start again. (Only rarely does an ensemble go back to the very beginning.) One of the most perplexing tasks for a newcomer in an ensemble that plays from printed music—according to the amateurs who contributed to this book—is finding the right place to begin playing when the group starts somewhere other than the beginning. When your conductor or colleague instructs you to begin at something such as *six before H, in two, one for nothing,* he means this:

Six before H. Music for ensembles is usually marked at regular intervals with *rehearsal numbers* or *rehearsal letters* placed above the line of music. If you start exactly at one of these rehearsal marks, you start "at 75" or "at B." But it's just as common to start a few measures before or after a rehearsal mark. If you're told to start *before* a rehearsal mark, *do not count the meas-*

ure *containing the rehearsal mark.* So, "six before H" is six full measures before H, not counting the measure in which H is found. However, if you start *after* a rehearsal mark, you *do count the measure containing the rehearsal mark.* So, "six after H" would count the measure of H as measure one. See Figure 11-1.

Figure 11–1

In two. A conductor does not always beat the number of beats in a bar shown by the time signature. If a piece has four beats to the bar, but the tempo is very fast, it makes for a lot of unhelpful and silly-looking arm waving if the conductor beats four times in each bar. He is more likely to say "in two" and beat only twice in each bar. Similarly, a fast 3/4 piece is often conducted "in one" or a 6/8 piece "in two" so the counting and the playing is light and smooth. However, a very slow piece in 3/4 time is sometimes counted "in six," and a slow 4/4 is sometimes counted "in eight."

One for nothing. This is called the *conductor's solo.* Before the ensemble begins to play, the conductor or ensemble leader who offers "one for nothing" will beat one full silent bar (called an empty bar), so that everyone feels the tempo. "*One* for nothing" is almost certainly one full bar. "*Two* for nothing" is a bit ambiguous—in a fast tempo it most likely means two full bars, but in a moderate or slow tempo it probably means only two beats. "*Three* for nothing" or any higher number almost always refers to *beats* for nothing and not to *bars* for nothing.

So, when you hear "six before H in two, one for nothing," you first find H, count back six full bars (not counting the bar of H), and get ready. The conductor or leader beats "one-two," and then you start playing (or counting if you don't have any notes) on the first beat of six before H.

Playing in a Conducted Ensemble

A conductor is more than a metronome in fancy dress. Much of a conductor's contribution to a group's musical life is given during rehearsals, as a coach and teacher. The conductor's central role is to unify and to vitalize the ensemble; beating time is only part of that job. If the conductor is to be effective in this role, the players have to give him their attention. This means, in a word, *watch*.

Watching a conductor is a learned skill and an absolutely essential one. A good conductor, it should be said, *earns* watchfulness by virtue of his skill, his knowledge, and his relatedness to the players and to the music. Here are some tips to help you watch:

1. Sit or stand where you can see.   If your line of sight is blocked by someone's head or music or instrument, then move. You are entitled to tell your colleagues that you can't see and to expect that they will do what they can to adjust. Note that you don't have to see the entire conductor—just the torso and head.

2. Watch out of the corner of your eye.   Except for beginnings and endings, not much conductor-watching is actually done eyeball-to-eyeball. You can take in almost everything you need with peripheral vision. This might mean raising your stand or lifting your music so that you can just see the conductor over the top.

3. Listen as you watch.   Watching does no good unless you act on the information you receive. Even a group that is watching can still come apart. Internalize the conductor's rhythmic pulse. Once in a while, try the same trick suggested for playing with a metronome on page 167—imagine that *you* are making the conductor move, that his arm will not come down for the beat until you sing or play.

4. Be especially watchful at musical landmarks.   Watch at the beginning and end of a number, at a tempo change, at a major dynamic change, or at an important entrance. A skillful conductor will cue most entrances—that is, give you some sig-

An orchestra which does not watch the conductor's baton has no conductor.

♪ Hector Berlioz

Gentlemen, I know very little about this work—I shall follow you.

♪ Sir Thomas Beecham

nal that helps you come in after a rest or when you have an exposed line. Most cues—again, from a skillful conductor—are subtle. You may get just a nod, a glance, or a small hand signal. However it arrives, a good cue is one that's ready for you slightly ahead of time. A florid gesture at the very moment of your entrance may look impressive to an audience, but it's too late to be of any use to a musician. You can ask your conductor for a cue wherever you need one—and once you've asked, be sure you are looking up to get it.

5. Learn how to read your conductor's pattern of beats. The most important to be able to find are the first beat ("one") and the last beat in every bar. These are the only ones that every player or singer can see unambiguously. In a large group that wraps around the conductor in a semicircle, the players on the sides have a very poor view of the other beats. Normally, "one" is on a downstroke, and the actual moment of "one" happens at the bottom of the stroke, the point called the ictus. But sometimes the ictus is obscure. On a slow downstroke, you can't predict where the baton will stop, while a very vigorous downstroke sometimes rebounds at the bottom, and you don't know which point is supposed to be "one." A lyrical conductor may reach the ictus and then sort of ooze past it, and a downright careless one will conduct into the stand so that the end of the downstroke falls out of everyone's line of sight. That brings us to the next point.

6. Don't be afraid to speak up. If you are puzzled by the conductor's intentions, if you can't find "one," if your cues are offered too late, or if you can't make the conducting pattern match up with what you see on the page, *ask*—politely and soon. If you are confused, it's very likely that others are, too.

The business of asking brings up a delicate issue. Most conductors are warm, encouraging, sympathetic people, but a few are unarguably long on ego. It comes with the job, really. A timid soul is no use to anyone up on a podium. Nevertheless, conductors can be touchy about what they consider to be criticism. When you do speak up, speak in questions and "I" statements and avoid the word "you" (unless you know your conductor well enough to know that you will not create hard feelings). Instead of saying, "You're dropping your stick below the stand," say in-

If the players are trained to expect and to respond to numerous cues, the conductor's control over his forces will be increased and the players will derive added confidence from the knowledge that they may depend on him in case of any lapses due to faulty counting or loss of place. Only by constant control of this sort can a player making a false entry be waved out or a player missing an entry be brought in.

♪ Malcolm H. Holmes, dean of the New England Conservatory of Music, 1945–1953

stead, "I can't see the end of the stick on the first beat. Is there a way to keep it a bit higher?"

Playing in an Unconducted Ensemble

Small ensembles, working perhaps with a leader or a coach but without an up-front conductor, are the most numerous, most flexible, and most versatile of all musical ensembles. Many amateurs agree that they're also the most rewarding. Ken Mah, of San Francisco, has played and sung with groups of all sizes: "When I'm one of a dozen tenors or one of twenty violins, I get a kind of corporate thrill. You can collect a lot of goose bumps doing something like the *Messiah* or *Elijah*. But I also know that if I slack off or don't show up, they'll go on without me and sound pretty much the same. It's different when I'm the only tenor in a quartet or the only fiddle in a band. Then my personal sound really matters. There's not many goose bumps but a lot more satisfaction. It's the difference between being part of something big and being part of something deep."

Many of the skills needed by a small ensemble player resemble the skills needed by a larger group's conductor. In many small ensembles the responsibility for the group's welfare is shared equally by the members; decision making, rehearsal management, problem solving, and the like fall on everyone.

Communication in a Small Ensemble

The rule in a conducted ensemble is "look up," but the rule in an unconducted ensemble is "look around." Make eye contact with the other players. Use eye contact as a way to start together, to stay together, to make entrances, to make decisions, and generally to pull each of you out of the self-contained world into which music making, in all its complexity, can sometimes drive you. You don't need complete eye contact all the time or with everyone. As with a conductor, peripheral vision is plenty, especially when the going is thick, although there are definitely times when your eyes will meet.

Setting the tempo and starting together, for example, is an "eyes up" moment. Experienced groups that play from music often memorize their opening bars so they can maintain eye contact not just during the downbeat but until everyone has settled into the tempo and mood.

I could hear and feel right away how my part fit into the music, how it helped. . . . Even more than in the orchestra I felt myself at the heart of the music. And once again I heard or felt, right down to my bones, a message that this was something I loved and was meant to do.

♪ John Holt, *Never Too Late*

If you have a leader—a lead guitarist or vocalist, for example—then everyone looks to that person at the beginning. If not, then the group as a whole usually agrees on a tempo and chooses one player to lead each particular opening.

It's best to derive the tempo from the fastest or slowest notes that must be played. If the number has a long series of rapid sixteenth notes for the trumpet, the top speed will be determined by how fast that player can tastefully handle the notes. To begin any faster is simply planning for a breakdown. In a slow number the tempo has to stay within the players' abilities to sustain their phrases—winds and vocalists need enough air to get through their phrases musically.

In a leaderless group the best choice for the tempo setter is usually the player facing the greatest "musical risks"—the one who has the trickiest passages. Let that player feel an internal tempo that she can handle musically, and then she can count the others in with a bar for nothing or lead with a gesture—a breath, a nod, a sniff, or an arm movement.

As you play, always listen first to any other part that is in unison with you or that is similar in rhythm. Also be aware, at the same time, of who is playing on the main beats. If you have a tricky rhythmic pattern, narrow your listening to the person playing on the beat. For the sake of security, this sometimes means you have to ignore other players. For example, with a rhythmic pattern such as the one shown in Figure 11-2, players A and B draw their rhythmic focus from player C. If A and B listen to each other, everyone will come unhinged very soon.

We'll often ask Dave [Soyer] to lead in pizzicato passages. A cellist's preparatory motion for pizzicato is larger and slower than that of a violinist. It's much easier for us to follow him than for him to follow us.

♪ John Dally, second violinist,
Guarneri Quartet

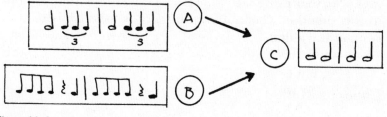

Figure 11–2

When you make an entrance at the same time as another player, look at each other before you come in. (It can save you an embarrassing mistake if you've miscounted.) If you have a difficult entry by yourself, it's likely that someone in the group can help you. Get the clarinet to mark in her music, "Look at Joe," the bar before your entry. There's nothing so reassuring in a doubtful moment as a friendly nod across the music stand.

Always look for natural "gathering points"—any spot where simply keeping a steady rhythm won't keep you together—a tempo change, a ritard, a fermata, a passage in free rhythm, a distracting cross-rhythm. Your eyes meet in space, you gather your musical selves in time, and you carry on together.

At the end of every piece, all eyes meet as they did at the beginning, and the leader or the player with the last moving part signals the cutoff by a gesture as triumphant or as slight, as decisive or as subtle, as the music bids.

Leading the Ensemble

Even as a novice player you may be called on to lead an entry. This is a good case for modeling—for watching how others who sing or who play your particular instrument signal entries. Practice at home in front of a mirror. Singers are relatively free to lead in any tasteful way, but instrumentalists always have some part of their anatomy glued to a *thing* and so have fewer choices. Flutes, violins, and violas can easily make an up-and-down motion in tempo; wind players can breathe visibly, nod, or shrug. Hardest of all to lead from is a keyboard. The instrument is immobile, a playing hand often can't make a large enough lead-off gesture and still enter with control, and the player is usually physically removed from the group by the bulk of the instrument. An expressive face will take a keyboard player a long way in this situation. Communication here is mostly by direct eye contact and a nod.

Choosing Music

One of the great advantages of small ensemble playing—especially for a group that gets together often—is that the music can be chosen to fit the tastes and skills of the members. Many amateurs have sheet music collections that they willingly share with ensemble partners. Most lead-line groups and others who play without printed scores draw on their collective experience.

A leader's role has to do with sight much more than with sound. You can lead with sound only if yours is the fastest moving part.

♪ Theo Wyatt, professional recorder player

Other ideas for music can come from browsing in a sheet music store or music library, from recommendations by teachers and other musicians, from workshops and camps, and from sheet music catalogues. Magazines and newsletters such as *American Recorder, Flute Talk,* and *Piano Quarterly* carry ads and reviews of ensemble music.

Amateur ensembles in the "scored" category—the ones who play from printed music—often enjoy and keep alive lesser-known works. For classical ensembles and recorder consorts there is a huge literature of chamber music that is rarely played by professional groups either because it's for odd combinations of instruments or because professionals tend to program the more virtuosic works. Much of this literature was written for the composer to play with a group of friends, and parts are often tailored for players with modest skills.

Assigning Parts

It's a rare ensemble that doesn't sometimes find itself with one flute too many, one cello too few, an extra drummer, or not enough tenors. Malcolm Holmes once wryly remarked, "One cannot help but wish that there were an orchestra 'major league' so that one might trade three flutes, two clarinets, and a sum of cash for a promising oboe or bassoon."

The great advantage of being an amateur, of being in it for the joy of it, is that all the obvious solutions will work. If you have extra players, they can take turns, this trumpet playing one number and the other trumpet the next—a possibility unheard of where the musicians' union has a say. Or you can double parts—put two or more players on a part intended for one. This will unbalance the group, of course, so the doubled players will have to hold back, but for reading or playing for your own enjoyment, that's a minor matter. Doubling is also very close to *shadowing*, mentioned on page 195, a wonderful way for an inexperienced or uncertain player to gain confidence.

If you're missing instruments, you can usually find a substitute. Any instruments that play approximately in the same range can substitute for one another, although it sounds better if you also try to match sound quality. For example, a violin is a better substitute for a flute than a trumpet.

Music just happens at one friend's house or another. We use regular instruments, jars of beans, anything that resonates. Sometimes it's just a song or two; sometimes it lasts a whole evening. These sessions lift us, emotionally and spirtually. They're clean and exuberant, removed from thought, just pure expression. That's their value.

♪ Daniel Fredgant, college
English instructor and
amateur guitarist

You may run into problems with transposition when you substitute. Most brass and some woodwinds are "transposing instruments," which means that their parts are not written in the same key as parts written for nontransposing instruments (called "C instruments"), although when they play their music as written, the sound comes out right. (The common transposing instruments are clarinet, sax, French horn, all of the brass except trombone, and alto, bass, and sopranino recorder. The viola is a C instrument, but music for viola is written in the alto clef and so presents basically the same problem.) Many players of transposing instruments can read a part for a C instrument, but the reverse is hardly ever true. Most flute players, for example, are never called on to transpose, so giving them a part written for B♭ clarinet will make big trouble. If you need to substitute a C instrument for a transposing instrument or a viola, you may have to write out a transposed part in advance.

Sometimes, if you don't have enough players to cover all the parts, you can just leave something out. If two parts are ba-sically alike, leave out the simplest-looking one. Or leave out the part that has the least to do. This will inevitably make holes, and you'll have to judge whether that renders the piece unplayable or not. You might be able to patch it up with a few bars of substitution.

Above all, don't call off the music because you don't have the "right" combination of instruments. It's much more important to make music than it is to wait for conditions to improve.

Rehearsing a Small Ensemble

The word *rehearsing* is used loosely here. You can select from this list of organizing suggestions whatever applies to your own group. The more informal and less performance-oriented your group, the fewer items will be pertinent.

Have the room ready. If you play in someone's home, this is the responsibility of your host. If you meet in a community hall, classroom, or other "outside" location, someone will have to see that the room is booked in advance, the door is unlocked, the lights and heat are turned on, and any needed equipment is set up. (One amateur chamber orchestra gathered one evening

Musicians practise alone but rehearse with others. One speaks of band practice but orchestra rehearsal. Church singers have choir practice, but cathedral, chamber and symphonic choirs rehearse. . . . Americans practice rationalized spelling.

♪ Fritz Spiegl, *Music Through the Looking Glass*

to find that its usual rehearsal hall had been specially booked for the night by a bagpipe band.)

Encourage people to arrive on time. Be willing nevertheless to start a little bit late but never go overtime, unless you're "hot" and everyone is eager to stay. If most people are eager to continue but one or two have to go, accept it gracefully. People do have other commitments, and players do get fatigued. Going overtime builds resentment quickly and creates real problems for members who have to catch a bus, get to work, or take a baby-sitter home.

Plan rehearsals to make the best use of your personnel. If you don't need all your available players for the entire rehearsal, plan ahead so you can use everyone's time judiciously. Begin a rehearsal with the largest possible group, and let people go as they are no longer needed. Try not to ask a section or a player to show up in mid-rehearsal if you can avoid it. Chances are good that you won't be ready for them when they get there. Professionals, who are paid to wait, tolerate this all the time, but for busy people donating their time, however enjoyable the activity is, it becomes irksome to be called for eight o'clock only to find that you're not needed for another forty-five minutes.

If your group includes both vocalists and instrumentalists, schedule separate vocal rehearsals to set the parts so that the players don't sit idle while the singers sort out their harmony lines.

Arrange the ensemble to facilitate hearing each other. Sit or stand as close together as your instruments and equipment will allow. Unless you're rehearsing for a staged performance, set up without an "audience" presence—face one another rather than facing "out there."

Set a loose agenda. A few minutes chatting together before you begin, selecting what to play and in what order, will let you devote the maximum time to making music and minimize paper shuffling and repeated petty decision making. Plan to rehearse your most challenging works early in the session.

Tune up! Tune before you begin, play something short

For twelve years I was violist in a string quartet. We had weekly meetings and rotated homes. The menu for the evening was decided simply: The host chose the warm-up, last week's host chose the sight reading, next week's host chose the movement to work together on, and the other one chose the "dessert," the piece to play at the end of the evening to top it off.

♪ Jane Wilson, nurse and amateur string player

211

and easy, and then check your tuning again. If you need to, tune each instrument separately, while the others are *quiet*. Woodwinds and strings are particularly sensitive after they are brought into heated rooms from cold weather. Ten minutes of careful tuning can ensure two hours of enjoyable playing.

Talk over each piece briefly before you begin. Reach some agreement about tempo, how many choruses you'll play, and whether or not to take repeats. In *At Home with Music*, Leonard Marsh, a social scientist and active string quartet player all his adult life, gently chides the kind of quartet that "makes no real decision at the beginning and [who] confuse each other by calling out 'go on' and 'repeat' simultaneously at the critical points, so that two go on, one repeats, and one usually stops—to be resented politely or otherwise by all the others for not understanding a simple instruction."

It's always worthwhile taking the time to put a consistent set of rehearsal letters or numbers in the music. Some music already has them, but sometimes players use different editions, which have different numbering systems, and the aggravating minutes pile up as everyone tries to find the point that is "about two bars before the crescendo, where the trombone comes in for the second time." The most useful kinds of rehearsal marks are measure numbers. Just start counting at the beginning and pencil in the measure number above the first bar of every line. Check with each other at obvious points to make sure your numbers match. Experienced players can give a hand to newcomers.

Keep your rehearsal volume in proportion to your rehearsal space. Brass, percussion, electronic instruments, and strong vocalists need to adjust their volume to suit the environment. It's just part of being a good musician. Experienced wind players and singers frequently rehearse below their top level. According to Sandy Lowenthal, a British session player, arranger, and producer,

Ears tire quickly when buffeted with volume, especially in a confined space; concentration goes, tempers fray, and timing is impaired. This is not to say that you should not have a good blow now and again, especially at the start of a rehearsal. Music is exciting and intoxicating, and you will probably arrive at a gig or rehearsal with a great deal of adrenaline, so it is good to let off some steam. When you get down to serious work, however, you will find that you have more staying power if you rehearse at reasonable volume.

Once you start playing, keep going unless there's a good reason to stop. Sometimes you have to stop because too many people get lost, you come unstuck, and the house of cards finally collapses. Everyone can have a good laugh and pick up again. But otherwise, keep going, making mental notes of places you need to go back to. Don't stop the rehearsal just for wrong notes or temporary rhythmic fumbles. Chances are good that the person who played a wrong note realizes it. If he can fix it, he will, and if not, it's something for him to work on at home.

Make sure everyone knows where to start when you begin in the middle. Give singers a word cue and a pitch. Give instrumentalists a rehearsal letter, a measure number, or a line and chord.

Isolate the difficult passages. If you want to polish a number, then go at it collectively as you would each treat a solo. Once you're familiar with the overall structure of the music, concentrate on cleaning up the sticky bits. Don't begin playing at the beginning every time. Identify the places where people get lost, where the rhythm goes astray, where the intonation is shaky, where the musical meaning is obscured by a technical shortcoming. Work together on those, with everyone contributing their best ideas. Susannah Coolidge Jones, a retired innkeeper and experienced amateur chamber musician, advises, "Don't be too heavy about your opinions and your advice. 'Let us try . . . ' is better than 'You shouldn't . . . '" Use any tactic that might help: play the passage slowly, simplify it, play only two or three parts together at a time, play chord by chord for intonation, play up to tempo in playable fragments. Never simply repeat a difficult passage over and over without attempting to locate and remedy the problem. Endless repetition of difficulties is a formula for resentment and diminishing musical returns. If necessary, mark the passage for individual attention at home and carry on.

I was popular as a player because I was good at accommodating the vagaries of other musicians. I could drop a beat or add a beat as needed, without making an issue of it. That's all about listening to what other people are doing. Of course, you develop a preference for playing with people who put the same number of beats in every bar, but it sure is good training.

♪ Dick Pollard, carpenter and amateur fiddler

213

Before you end the rehearsal, agree on what you'll do next. If you plan to meet again, set a specific time and place (and assign someone to make sure the place is available, if it has to be reserved). Discuss briefly what you'll do next time. If you're going to work on some pieces you're learning, encourage everyone to practice them at home. If you want to read or to try out some new numbers, draw up a list so that players can prepare, if possible. Distribute the music or charts in advance. Find out who has a recording that might be helpful. Schedule a vocal rehearsal, if needed, before the next whole ensemble rehearsal.

THE DOWNSIDE OF ENSEMBLE PLAYING

Just as your own private practice has plateaus and discouraging terrain, so ensemble playing, too, has its snares. The biggest one is inexperience. When you play on your own, you can choose your music and choose your tempo. But in an ensemble, those two matters are often out of your hands. Difficulties are likeliest when there are extreme skill differences in a group. A community ensemble that is open to all often attracts the vastly experienced as well as the near beginners. In a large choral group, if you find yourself in deep water musically, you can quietly do the next best thing to shadowing: stand near an experienced singer and monitor your volume so that you can hear him. It's fine to explain your situation to your nearest colleagues. They will usually do all they can to help you.

In bands and orchestras the situation is different, since players usually have more-or-less "assigned seats" from the first rehearsal. Unfortunately, the more experienced players are often seated near the front, where it's easiest to see and hear, while the new players cluster in the back. This plan is copied from professional and auditioned ensembles where competition for places can be fierce, but it's highly inappropriate in large, unselected amateur groups. An enlightened conductor will seat new players near experienced players and will frequently switch seats so that everyone gets a chance at every kind of part. If you find yourself segregated in a beginner's outback, and you get discouraged, it's worth speaking to the conductor, possibly in the company of any sympathetic experienced players you know. You may be able to influence the policy, at least for rehearsals.

I was not so much playing as constantly struggling just to find my place. At the end of a couple of hours of this, I was tense, sweaty, and exhausted, struggling against feelings of shame and discouragement. But it was good practice, if only at keeping cool under stress, and at training my eyes and my mind to move across the notes much faster than I had been used to.

♪ John Holt, *Never Too Late*

The situation is drastically different in a small ensemble, where you may be the only player on your part. Extreme skill differences in this setting can take everyone by surprise if you get together with people you've never played with before—as, for example, when you pick a name from a list, answer a note on a bulletin board, or enroll in a workshop. It would seem possible to forestall the situation—if you wanted to do that—by giving an honest assessment of your ability. But this curiously doesn't seem to help very often. Cellist John Holt ran into this phenomenon repeatedly:

> The trouble is, many amateurs say that they are much worse than they really are, to be "modest," to have their alibi in advance, to protect themselves against disappointment, and for the fun of hearing people say later, "But you're much better than you said you were." So amateurs tend to assume that most other amateurs are much better than they say they are. When I speak the literal truth, say that I am not a good player, or that I cannot play quick movements up to tempo, at least not without long practice, or that I am a very slow and uncertain sight reader, they say, "Oh, you're just being modest, I'm sure you'll do just fine." Sometimes I do "just fine." Sometimes I don't do "just fine" at all.

Nearly all players will tolerate gracefully one session with a much less skilled player, but only some will offer to repeat the experience. If you find yourself in this situation, don't take other players' responses personally. Through music making, people fulfill a variety of needs, not just musical ones. Some experienced players—including some professionals—love to play with less-skilled partners because they like to teach, they like to share, they like to initiate others. But some musicians are just not motivated in that way. They want, instead, to stretch themselves out, to take on very difficult musical challenges. It's extremely important to remember that this attitude is not meant to hurt anyone—it's just another way of relating to music.

Still, it can be embarrassing to find yourself in over your head, especially if you're a beginner. Rarely will a group of experienced musicians wait while an inexperienced player finds her place. Rarely will experienced players slow down very much so that a struggling player can keep up. It's a bit like going on a

I've been in groups where I'm the strongest player and in groups where I'm the weakest, and I enjoy both of them. In a situation where I'm a weaker player, I always grow a lot musically. When I'm a stronger player, I learn about group dynamics and the personal— rather than the technical—side of music.

♪ Lynelle Inwood, homemaker and amateur flutist

hike with enthusiastic but indifferent strangers who won't wait if you fall behind. None of this means that they are trying to ostracize you or humiliate you. It only means that these players are there more strongly with the music than with any individual in the room—as if this Other commands obedience, even if not everyone can come along.

If you're a novice in the midst of experts, you may feel intimidated and exhilarated at the same time. It will probably help everyone if you speak up early and briefly to explain that the music is too hard for you but that you'll give it your best. (Everyone has been in this situation at some time. Even if the other players won't wait for you, it's likely they understand what you're going through.) Play full out, listen your hardest, enjoy the experience for all it's worth, but don't persist in complaining or apologizing. It is universally true that an inexperienced player is pulled up by a strong group. If they will have you, the experience can be a concentrated musical education. Just monitor your own feelings, and don't let the idea that you're "no good" take hold.

If you find yourself in this situation repeatedly—perhaps because you are the only available player on your instrument, even though you're not up to the music—you can do a few things to help yourself. First of all, practice. Give the parts your best individual attention. Ask someone in the group who seems sympathetic to go over the parts with you. Take the parts to your teacher or set up a lesson or two with someone who can help. Consider simplifying your part in musically tasteful ways. If you have a solo or prominent line that you absolutely cannot handle, ask if another player can take it over or double it with you.

It's never bad to be the worst guy in the band because you learn more that way than any other way.

♪ Warren Bernhardt, professional jazz pianist

A CHECKLIST FOR ENSEMBLE PLAYERS

We've taken a long general look at the experience of playing in conducted and unconducted ensembles. Finally, very briefly, here's a summary of six basic ensemble-playing skills. First of all, watch and listen. And then . . .

1. Be bold. Or as musicians say, "play out." No matter how uncertain you feel, no matter how retiring you are in the rest of your life, as an ensemble player you must be intrepid. Cautious playing saps an ensemble of energy and, in a small group, is likely to confuse and aggravate the other players. Conductors often say and truly mean, "If you make a mistake, make a big one." That's the only way anyone can know where the problem is, and finding the problem is the first step in fixing it. (This doesn't mean, of course, that you thunder out every note heedlessly. If the music calls for soft, you play soft, but a soft that's loud enough to hear.)

The advice to play out is easy to give and hard to follow, especially when your line emerges from the mist and stands alone—when you have a solo, however short. (Musicians call it an *exposed* line, a canny choice of words.) But no one can ask you to do more than pay attention, give it your best, and play out. As Theo Wyatt says, "The actual playing of that note is in every case an act of faith, a leap in the dark, bread cast upon the musical waters with absolutely no way of guaranteeing in advance that it will coincide with what the other players are doing. We are to that extent alone, though together."

2. Prepare for every entry. Fill your lungs, get your instrument in place with your entering note under your fingers or in your mind, and look up. (You can easily pick out the inexperienced players in any band or orchestra. When the conductor's arms are raised for the downbeat, their instruments are still in their laps.)

3. Keep going. Unless the conductor stops you, or unless the whole ensemble comes to ruin, don't stop. Never stop playing just because you make a mistake. Play right over it and let it go.

4. Mark your music. Unlike borrowed books, no one will complain if you write in your music. *Always write in pencil, and always erase your marks afterward if the music is borrowed or rented.* Bold strokes with a soft pencil are the easiest to see. The next time you come to your mark, you won't have time to puzzle out what it says. Write in all dynamics, phrasing, fingering, repeats, cuts, pronunciation, and breathing places that the conductor asks for or the group agrees on. Don't trust your memory for this mass of details. Ensemble players are expected to write

> **A** *natural and becoming modesty in ordinary life can be a menace in the orchestra.*
>
> ♪ Malcolm H. Holmes, dean of the New England Conservatory of Music, 1945–1953

these things down the first time they're mentioned. If you come to a passage that needs your attention at home, put a mark next to it. At spots where you must remember to look up, write the word *WATCH* or—an equivalent symbol used by many, many musicians—draw a pair of glasses over the spot.

Figure 11–3

5. Practice. Practice your part if it will help the ensemble, but practice at home. Except for a brief warm-up while an ensemble sets up, it's poor form to practice your part individually during a rehearsal. It's important to mark the lines or passages that need work because it can be hard to find the sticky spots when you get home. The hard parts in ensemble music often don't stand out as clearly as they do on solo music.

When you analyze your difficulties, don't struggle against what is obviously impossible. Some passages are unplayable for anyone but a virtuoso, and some passages are even unplayable by many of them! A famous example is the cello and bass line from the Allegro movement—"The Storm"—of Beethoven's *Symphony No. 6.* The music looks like this

*P*ractice is getting your individual chops up; rehearsal is putting a song together with a band. If the members of a band each practice sufficiently, rehearsal time can be effective and kept reasonably short.

♪ Claudia Suzanne,
For Musicians Only

*E*ven a taskmaster such as Toscanini, in rehearsing Debussy's Fêtes with a renowned European orchestra, went on without fussing when he noticed that some bars were beyond the capacity of a certain player.

♪ Max Rudolf, conductor of the Cincinnati Symphony Orchestra

Figure 11–4

You may be sure that even the best players in the best orchestras are not playing all those notes. It's the overall feeling that has to come across. When you're in doubt about a particular passage, check with an experienced player. It's a rule of thumb that an amateur group should not forfeit the pleasure of a piece of music because of a handful of unapproachable notes.

6. Use common sense. Keep your instrument in good condition. Come to the rehearsals on time. Come to the rehearsals prepared. Bring a stand if you need one (if you don't know, assume you need it), *always* a pencil with an eraser, your music, and any accessories you need, such as mutes. Take care of your music. Keep it in a folder or in your case. If it's borrowed, return it promptly when you're finished with it. If you need to fix your music—to tape, to trim, to repair, to number bars, whatever—do it at home so that you don't keep everyone else waiting. Watch. Listen. Love what you do.

Of all the attractions of playing in a group, the one that amateurs value the most is the chance to create and communicate beyond themselves. Leslie Sonder, a geophysicist and amateur violist from Hanover, New Hampshire, says, "There's something really magical about playing with a group. What comes out is suddenly more than the sum of the parts—as if it's not you making the music. The music is just carried through you." Nurse and amateur chamber player Jane Wilson explains,

> What do I get out of these sessions? Life, sanity, camaraderie, richness, salvation, freedom from the troubles of an ordinary life. It is my opportunity to make contact with the greatest composers through their works, and with ordinary human beings as we try to do justice to these works. You make very close friends playing music; there is a oneness of purpose which bonds those lucky enough to have a chance to make music together.

I'd rather play chamber music than go to a party or a movie.

♪ Linda Hecker, teacher and amateur violinist

CHAPTER 12

Inside Ensembles: The Social View

"People who make music together," according to composer Paul Hindemith, "cannot be enemies, at least while the music lasts." However, like people in other intense relationships—marriage or business partners, for example—people in musical ensembles sometimes have problems, and those problems have to be solved.

In this chapter we'll look at what helps and what hampers ensembles in their quest for both musical and personal harmony. We'll begin by looking at common organizational and social patterns in amateur music making and at some of the benefits and potential problems associated with these patterns. Then we'll discuss tactics that individuals and groups can use both to prevent and to resolve the worst of these problems—those involving conflicts among group members.

THE STRUCTURE OF AN AMATEUR ENSEMBLE

The first step toward a smoothly functioning group is some understanding of the structure of that group. We can think about

the social structure of an amateur music group in three different ways: in terms of its management (who organizes or runs
the ensemble?), in terms of the level of commitment and involvement of group members (does the group divide into subgroups of more or less committed or involved members?), or in
terms of the goals of group members (does the group divide
into subgroups devoted to separate goals, or are there goals
shared by all members of the group that can serve as a foundation for creating a unified whole?).

Leadership and Management of the Ensemble

In terms of management and leadership, there are basically
three kinds of amateur ensembles—leader's groups, institutional groups, and players' groups.

1. Leader's groups. These groups arise from and are largely sustained by the efforts of one individual. (In a conducted
ensemble, the leader is usually, though not always, the conductor.) The musical community is blessed with many spirited,
sensitive, and generous leaders who work out of a deep love for
music and fellow musicians, and the musical quality of a
leader's group can be stellar. However, no matter how gifted
and energetic the leader, the future of such a group is always
precarious if the group is heavily dependent on this one person.
Similarly, if a leader is inflexible and unresponsive to the players' needs and resources, the ensemble may stagger and ultimately collapse because responsibility for the group's well-being has not been shared.

2. Institutional groups. These groups are a standing sideline operation of an organized body such as a church, college,
city, union, or corporation. Institutional backing lifts much of
the administrative detail from the leader and the musicians.
Music is purchased, rehearsal space provided, publicity organized, and a leader is sought and salaried. Thus many of the
issues that burden other groups are tidily managed by the
sponsoring institution and many possible sources of conflict
between individual members are generally eliminated. The
only thing that cannot be supplied through institutional chan-
nels is enthusiasm. In many communities, that already exists in

*One way to grow a band is to
get one strong musician who
rounds up some backup people.
The leader tells you what to
do. You do what the leader
says or you leave.*

♪ Dick Pollard, carpenter and
amateur fiddler

After a year I joined a small, nameless orchestra that gathered Sunday afternoons at a local college. Its conductor was a young graduate student, a Joan of Arc cut prematurely from her stake. . . . I had heard much about the camaraderie of orchestras, but this one had none. We came, we rehearsed, we went home.

♪ Christian Williams, journalist and amateur cellist

abundance. However, where it is scarce, an institutional group can run into the same difficulties as a leader's group, for the same reasons—responsibility for growth and development is not shared.

3. Players' groups. These groups are organized and run by the players or singers themselves. Management and administrative chores are shared. If the group needs a conductor or musical leader, that person is hired, invited, or recruited by the group. A players' group can make tremendous, sometimes exhausting, nonmusical demands on the players or singers. The musicians themselves must either do all of the nonmusical tasks or they must find willing nonmusicians to do them. (In the case of large ensembles, volunteers from the community are sometimes able to take over nonmusical chores such fund-raising, publicity, and the transportation and setup of stands and risers.) Among the most trying problems for players' groups—especially large ones—is the ever-present financial thin edge. Nonetheless, a players' group is potentially the most flexible and responsive of the three, tailored to the pool of ability and the community's needs and offering the satisfaction of building not just a musical but a human network.

Involvement and Commitment of Ensemble Members

A remarkable number of problems that arise in musical ensembles are related to the musicians' varying levels of individual *commitment* or *involvement*. In his book *Amateurs: On the Margin between Work and Leisure*, sociologist Robert Stebbins (himself an amateur musician) defines three levels or "circles" of participation in amateur activities. Although Stebbins's book does not address music making per se, his concept is completely applicable to amateur musical endeavors:

1. The inner circle. This circle includes musicians with substantial skills, a high level of commitment, the ability to give musical activities a high priority, and a high level of experience or seniority.

2. The middle circle. This circle includes musicians who resemble the inner circle in many ways except that their participation is limited by their skill level, by time, or by other circumstances of their nonmusical lives, such as health problems. This circle includes accomplished players and singers who cannot participate as fully as they might like because family or work commitments limit their availability.

3. The outer circle. This circle includes newcomers to music or to the local community.

The Goals of Ensemble Members

One way of viewing a group's structure is in terms of the goals of group members. If the group members are united behind a single goal or set of goals, the group forms a unified and harmonious whole. If, however, the group is divided into factions with competing or incompatible goals, problems can result.

We could devote a whole book to detailing the many different goals that amateur musicians bring to ensembles. However, a couple of generalizations can be made about the goals of most amateur group members:

1. Amateurs seek a balance between their time commitment to the ensemble and the benefits that they derive from ensemble membership. By definition, amateurs are donating their limited time to any ensemble in which they play or sing, but the significance of this fact is sometimes forgotten, particularly by professional musicians who teach or conduct amateurs. A professional musician who goes to an ensemble rehearsal is going to work. An amateur musician who goes to a rehearsal has already done a day's work, whether as an employee at a paid job, as a student in school, or as a parent caring for a family and a home. As rejuvenating as the music making might be, it is also true that the amateur may have had no rest, no supper, and no time that day between work and rehearsal to attend to personal details such as phoning the baby-sitter, filling the gas tank, or buying groceries. Such situations can be possible sources of conflict. For every amateur there is a point, perhaps never actually reached, at which a time commitment becomes excessive and begins to outweigh the benefits derived from membership in the ensemble. Amateurs differ considerably in their thresholds in this regard, and these differences can, again, be a source of conflict. Generally speaking, the leader(s) and members of the ensemble must simply recognize this as a reality, set mutually-agreed-upon criteria for minimal involvement, and be willing to make compromises, when necessary, to accommodate demands made upon individual members by other parts of their lives.

2. Amateurs make music to fill personal and social needs as well as musical needs. This statement applies to most professionals as well, but the balance of needs is truly different. Relationships in professional groups—especially large ones—are usually based on discipline and authority. The music is the focus, not the individual musician. Professionals in an ensemble are usually expected (and usually able) to give unquestioning compliance to the group leader, the conductor, or the principal player in the section. Amateur groups, in contrast, are typically more relaxed. Although music is the primary reason for coming together, and although musical values may be very high, there is usually also strong concern for the quality of the musicians' experience. There may be more socializing, more contributions from members to solving problems, and more willingness to adapt musical demands to the pool of musical ability. It is usually assumed in a professional ensemble that everyone comes completely prepared to handle the musical tasks. This is not always the case with amateurs. Amateur rehearsals frequently include a great deal of teaching (if there is a leader) or self-teaching. This automatically means that there is more concern for individual growth and personal satisfaction. Again, amateur ensembles must strike a balance—in this case between the group's need for commitment to the actual business of making music and individual members' nonmusical needs.

Differences in goals among members are generally less pronounced in institutional groups than in leader's groups or player's groups. This is because institutional groups tend to have specific goals set in advance—usually performance goals, such as playing in the Fourth of July parade or singing for the eleven o'clock service every Sunday. Anyone who joins the group accepts, tacitly, the group's goals. In leader's groups and players' groups, however, overall or long-term goals may not be so clear, and group members must be willing to discuss the group's goals openly and honestly.

STRATEGIES FOR CONFLICT PREVENTION

Not every ensemble pays attention to social dynamics. Not every ensemble really needs to. Many groups—especially small, informal ensembles—make music together amicably for years with no overt attention to organization, decision making, or conflict prevention. Most of these ensembles have simply discovered and applied intuitively the same attitudes and procedures that other groups have to think about and adopt deliberately.

It's helpful to realize from the very beginning that a musical ensemble is a group like any other and that the potential for conflict always exists. As one thoroughly experienced rock musician put it,

> Musicians seem to go into a group with a kind of naïveté that other groups just don't have. You know when you get married that you're going to have problems, and you know in a business that you're going to have problems. Even theatre groups know they're going to have problems. But musicians walk into a group as if the music is going to save them. They've got MUSIC, so they think they don't need anything else. They don't see the hard times coming.

If everyone knows that conflicts are possible, then efforts to prevent and resolve them can begin early, before resentment, misunderstanding, and bitterness collect too deeply and preclude a solution. To consider conflict prevention, we'll look at attitudes and strategies for individuals first and then at strategies for the group as a whole.

Individual Strategies for Conflict Prevention

The following four strategies are ones you can adopt yourself to prevent conflicts:

1. Have a sense of humor. Keep things in perspective. Take the music seriously, but take the moment lightly. Ensemble music is a bit like square dancing in this regard. There's enormous pleasure in executing a complicated pattern smoothly, but there's also enormous glee when the pattern breaks down and everyone ends in a great tangle. David Blum, biographer of one of classical music's great ensembles, the Guarneri Quartet, says of them, "A striking characteristic of these four musicians is their individual and collective sense of humor, which, given the difficulties inherent in two decades of touring and the presentation of over two thousand concerts, provides a blessed relief from stress. Jokes are traded around the clock—gentle or satiric, witty or corny."

My amateur experience was that players only improved by self-criticism and criticism of others, quite openly. This however is not done by professionals.

♪ Antony Pay, professional
clarinetist

2. Give and take criticism constructively. In general there is much more open criticism of individual players among amateurs than among professionals. Professional musicians with extensive training and thorough experience can usually hear what needs to be done and can draw on their own resources to work things out. The sound of an amateur group, however, often falls far short of what the players would wish, and sometimes there are very basic problems of rhythm, intonation, and interpretation to be sorted out.

If the group has a conductor or a leader, most of the suggestions will come from that person, and the members, by agreeing to play at all, also agree to be open to these suggestions. Many amateur groups are blessed with leaders who teach with tact, correct with compassion, and criticize in a supportive way. There is never any need for intimidation or humiliation with an amateur ensemble. It's OK to be tough, but not tyrannical. The players are there for growth and because of their own love for what they do. No one's reputation should ever be at stake.

Each man tried to make the other man sound better. . . . We found happiness in each other. . . . We did not realize how much of life we really had a hold of.

♪ Smokey Dacus, drummer with
Bob Wills and His Texas Playboys

In a small group, unless you know your colleagues extremely well, it's best to start your comments with the word *I* or *we* in order to avoid even the appearance of blame and disapproval.

- Instead of *You're too loud,* say *I can't hear all the parts.*
- Instead of *You're out of tune,* say *Can we improve the intonation?*
- Instead of *You're miscounting,* say *Let's figure out this rhythm.*

A good suggestion from James Van Horn, conductor of the Bremerton Symphony, in Washington State, is to give compliments and appreciation by name: "Way to go, Christine!" and

"Gorgeous solo, Don!" But give criticisms by instrument or section names: "Clarinets—do you all have an E♭ in that phrase?" and "Can the trumpet be a little softer at the end?" (If there are repeated errors in note playing, check the parts. It's not at all uncommon to find typographical errors in sheet music.)

It's a basic rule for every ensemble player that you *never* turn and look—in a rehearsal or a performance—at a player who has made a mistake. That's for the benefit of both the player and the audience. A group that knows each other well often has a good laugh when someone really louses up a passage, but that's different from the musician who turns with a scowl at a colleague who comes in at the wrong time or plays a wrong note.

3. Be willing to tolerate a certain level of inconvenience, confusion, and dissatisfaction. As with any group endeavor, some compromise is always necessary. Players who gripe and complain incessantly, who are impatient, and who have unrealistic expectations are often not asked back.

4. Speak up if you have a problem. The advice about compromise does not mean that you have to be the ensemble's doormat. If you are troubled about something, speak up. If your group has a leader, she may not know you are troubled, or she may know but may not know how to be helpful. In some situations—especially where musical skills are the issue—many amateurs prefer to keep quiet and be left alone. This is not always a good solution, however, if the player's self-confidence is being undermined or if the player undermines the group's morale with private complaining and faultfinding.

Group Strategies for Conflict Prevention

We can't prevent every conflict single-handedly. Ensembles have to work together, both musically and interpersonally, to make a group work. This "working together" doesn't always happen right away. Sometimes a group exists in a kind of ensemble limbo for a long time while it searches for an identity, for a steady roster of players, and for a direction. But once the group feels like a group, once personal commitments begin to gel, then the group must tackle some decisions.

The process of decision making itself is probably the first conflict-prevention strategy. Decision making doesn't have to be an explicit, committee-style process. T'Andernaken, a five-member recorder ensemble from Vancouver, has played together for five years, operating, as member June Ryder says, "on basic compatibility and respect." The group does not hold any formal discussions about goals or procedures, but, as Ryder explains,

> we're musically compatible. We all have about the same playing and sight-reading ability, and we enjoy the same kinds of music. We all have a serious commitment to make the group work. We give our weekly rehearsals priority: everyone is there at 7:30 every Tuesday evening unless someone is sick or out of town. We share instruments freely, assuming that the others will look after an instrument as if it were their own. And we have developed contributing roles—three of us find appropriate music, one keeps lists of repertoire and makes programs for performances, and I make the tea.

Whether decisions are made tacitly or are openly discussed, every member of an ongoing group needs to feel involved and responsible. Lynelle Inwood has been an active amateur musician for fifteen years, singing and playing flute and saxophone in a wide variety of ensembles, from duos to orchestras to *a cappella* choir, from Baroque to gospel to progressive jazz. Respected by her colleagues as a musical mediator, Inwood believes that the key to conflict prevention is shared communication and decision making.

> A small ensemble can work without a leader if the responsibility for leadership is really shared. But when too many demands start to come from one person, then problems come up. There's also a natural point where people stop communicating because the group gets too large. You have to know your limit as far as numbers go and be very, very careful about that. It can make or break a group. Problems happen when people don't feel comfortable about speaking out.
>
> If you decide to have a leader, that can work, too, as long as the goals and directions are agreed on by the group. But you

Compatibility sooner or later is a basic requirement, and there are many elements in a good quartet which are not unlike those of a good marriage: give-and-take, common interests, mutual respect.

♪ Leonard Marsh, social scientist and amateur cellist, *At Home with Music*

have to decide. Everybody has to take a certain amount of responsibility, even if that is just being willing to give over the responsibility to somebody else. People have to feel like they're part of the experience.

A group that has a way to make decisions has a way to meet changes and challenges. When attendance at concerts falls off, when a key player moves away, when several members drift toward a new sound, then the means for deciding what to do are in place. The group may face an uncertain path, but not a brick wall.

Every group, whatever its size or organizational structure, has to make a few very basic decisions, including all of these:

What is our purpose for making music?   Many groups meet simply to play for their own pleasure—to jam, to read through the literature, to experiment with new sounds, or to get a friendly workout. Other groups are only active when they are preparing for a performance. They may spend time reading or jamming to build a repertoire, but their basic goal is to polish the music and play it for others. For convenience, we can call the first kind of group a *reading group* and the second a *rehearsal group.*

The choice between reading and rehearsing is one issue that must be decided fairly soon—as soon as it's clear that the group will be ongoing. As Lynelle Inwood says, "When everybody has different expectations about what the group is for, when everybody has a different idea about why we're making music—that's when problems come up. The issue is very basic but very deep: *Why are we doing this?*"

The distinction between reading and rehearsing has different implications for the different "circles" of players discussed on page 222. Many players in the inner circle tend to be both available for and interested in rehearsal groups. Players in the middle and outer circles are often more comfortable (given their skill level) or more available (given their schedule) as reading group players. Rehearsal groups can make extremely stressful demands on these individuals. Middle and outer circle players often tolerate these stresses willingly, but it improves their experience and supports their morale if their skill or time

It's frustrating for me to play in a group that just reads. I want to learn and grow musically, and for me that means working on things, being coached, getting down to details.

♪ Raye Miller, community worker and amateur flutist

After a year and a half of lessons I joined a sight-reading orchestra in Philadelphia. When I started, I may have been playing one-third of the notes. I sat in the back and just counted like mad. By the end of the year I was playing maybe two-thirds of the notes. There were no performances, so I didn't have to worry about not being good enough. Now I like reading better than anything. I'd rather read than work.

♪ Linda Baldwin, secretary and amateur violinist

limitations are accepted graciously by group leaders and inner circle players.

A group's decision about its purpose usually needs to be reconsidered and renewed from time to time. Sometimes it happens, for example, that a group changes its goal as it develops musically. As fiddler Dick Pollard explains,

> Any time you get a bunch of live musicians together and you play together and work and practice, you're going to progress. Then comes that time when people start asking you to play and maybe paying you to play, and then you start to refine things. Now you have a *product*, and you usually have some musicians with a lot invested in that product. That's when people start to get impatient with the ones who don't have the skills, the people who are farthest back. And that's one of the risks. I don't think you can predict it.

What kind of music do we want to play? Some musicians are genuinely happy playing almost anything. Others have very strong preferences and become restless and dissatisfied if at least some of their choices are not considered. Some players prefer certain eras, certain composers, certain styles, certain roles in the ensemble. It's best to get these out on the table early and to honor as many requests as possible while still balancing the needs of the rest of group.

How do we choose new members? Every ensemble's policy about new members needs to reflect the ensemble's goals. You may decide that you're open to anyone who would like to join, and in that case you must be truly welcoming. The group with an open-door policy must be ready to make every player's path a growing one. An unselected or unauditioned group needs to select music and a performance quality that is suited to the group's pool of skills.

If an ensemble's goal is to read challenging music, then the experience can be attractive to almost any musician willing to take the plunge. If the group's goal is "quality performance"— perhaps a public performance of a challenging work for a paying audience—then it sounds very much like a case for an auditioned or selected membership, which then requires a decision about selection criteria.

Every time somebody new joins the band, they change it. The personalities change it.

♪ Miles Davis

230

STRATEGIES FOR CONFLICT RESOLUTION

In the midst of a conflict of any kind, a musical ensemble can apply the same principles of conflict resolution that work for a small business or a family. In fact, it would do no harm, if you are a regular ensemble player, to have on your musical bookshelf something on conflict resolution. There are lots of good titles available—*Getting to Yes* by Roger Fisher and William Ury is concise and applicable to any kind of situation.

One of the most important steps to take during a conflict is to *establish points of agreement*. Nearly any musical group can generate a rich collection of shared goals. The solution to the conflict becomes a matter (though rarely a "simple" matter) of finding the widest possible path to the goals held in common.

Problems that arise in ensembles usually seem to fall into one of three categories—problems with an individual, problems with a leader, or problems in the group as a whole. (We say "seem to fall" into these categories because, in fact, many problems and conflicts have multiple causes. In this brief discussion, though, we will group problems as they are perceived by ensemble members.)

Dealing with Difficult Individuals

Musicians are some of the nicest people we all know, but even musicians are sometimes hard to get along with. Maybe it has something to do with how close music lies to our personality and our being human and how easily ego spills over into musical activity. Most groups sooner or later encounter ego problems: the advanced player who is impatient with beginners, the inexperienced player who sulks, the soloist who is unwilling to give anyone else an opportunity. Lynelle Inwood has seen enough different situations to find a common thread:

> Every time egos step into the picture, there's trouble. Every time. If an ego problem causes the rest of the group to suffer, everyone just has to put forth as much positive energy as they can. Part of it is always the other people's responsibility—they're letting themselves be provoked. It never helps to say things like, "You're messing up. You're holding us back." It's more likely to help if you say, "People would feel better, or

I would feel better, or it would sound better, if we tried it this way."

The swiftest conclusion to a disruptive ego problem is the one that keeps communication open and support systems intact for everyone. If you decide to confront an individual about a problem (which is far preferable to griping about it behind his back), think carefully about who and how many of you need to be directly involved. There is never any reason to humiliate or embarrass anyone. Most likely to help is a nonblaming discussion in a nonmusical setting, although the problem is also likely to continue to surface. It usually requires an ongoing effort, not a one-time approach.

If an individual is having a musical problem—playing too loudly, not watching, not practicing—then probably the best person to tackle the job is the musical leader, the conductor, or the most experienced or respected musician. But even a respected member of the group must handle such a situation with tact and care.

Problems with Ensemble Leaders

The solutions to problems with musical leadership, like the solutions to problems with individual players or singers, are rarely simple or obvious. A great deal depends on the personalities involved and on the structure of the organization. The most common problems with leaders and conductors of amateur ensembles seem to fall into three categories:

1. The musical leadership is inadequate. Beats are irregular, cues are ambiguous, and directions are unclear. This problem is most common when the conductor is an amateur as well or when a professional musician untrained in conducting is dropped into a conductor's role as part of a job description or simply for lack of a better candidate. Be sympathetic. The conductor is probably doing his best but possibly never intended to be on a podium. Some conductors-by-default—especially if they're keyboard players—have never even played in a conducted ensemble themselves.

When faced with unclear messages from a conductor, you should speak up and ask for the help you need. If the conductor is open to suggestions, you might talk to her privately and explain how she can help you play better. If you encounter defensiveness or hostility, it may be best to approach the conductor as part of a small group so that you don't appear to be making a personal insult.

Unfortunately, there is no durable solution to inadequate conducting except to secure more training for the conductor. The American Symphony Orchestra League offers conducting workshops in the summer, as do many choral organizations; perhaps the ensemble could encourage and partially subsidize attendance.

2. The conductor or leader is hard to get along with. In an amateur group there is never any justification for surliness, tyranny, or insults. Hard work, *yes*. High standards, *yes*. But despotism and callousness, definitely *no*. The players come of their own free will, volunteering their time, often even paying a membership fee. It is for their own enjoyment and enrichment that they play, not for any conductor's reputation.

In a large, professional group, when a personality clash threatens the morale of the ensemble, a conductor's contract can be allowed to expire and a replacement sought. In amateur settings arrangements are rarely as clear-cut. Some conductors have tenure by tradition, some by default (there is simply no one else able or willing to do the job), and some are self-appointed. In an intolerable dilemma, amateurs usually vote with their feet. A steady decline in membership will sometimes turn around a deteriorating situation, but the cost is very high. Time is wasted, good players are lost, and the outcome is always uncertain.

Whatever the problem, it makes sense first of all to work together to repair a relationship rather than to let the group flounder. In a large group, repair work is best done by a delegation that has the support of most of the group. Endless grumbling, complaining, and faultfinding within the membership is damaging to morale. Tactful discussions in a relaxed, nonthreatening setting may be of some real value, first establishing

Duncan Martin's conducting is very explicit. He combines clear cuing with a good sense of humor as he tries to decrease our nervousness before an audience and make us have fun while we're performing. When we get too deep into an arrangement or worry about how we're sounding, he'll hold up signs that say, "SMILE," or, "I LOVE YOU," or "GET HIP!"

♪ Patrick Farenga, publisher and amateur saxophonist

Any asino can conduct—but to make music . . . eh? Is difficile.

♪ Arturo Toscanini

points of agreement and then sorting out goals and expectations. Some leaders who are or have been professional musicians may need to readjust their attitudes and approaches in an amateur setting. A neutral mediator can be helpful, especially if feelings are running very high.

3. The leader or conductor chooses music that is too difficult.   For a performing ensemble, an overambitious selection of music—especially combined with too few rehearsals or inadequate conducting—will almost guarantee a disaster, if not in performance at least in morale. The challenge of playing and learning difficult works is welcome and exhilarating in some circumstances. However, when committed to a performance, ensemble members sometimes feel helpless, resentful, or ashamed when they are faced with music they cannot possibly learn to play in the time available. This problem comes in two versions: the music may be too hard for you personally (or for several of you), or it may be too hard for the majority of the ensemble.

If you are inexperienced and you feel you're in too deep, talk with the leader before you withdraw from the group. Once you are admitted to an amateur ensemble, it becomes the leader's responsibility to make it possible for you to participate. Even if you can't play all the notes, your contribution is still valuable, and your own growth is still important. A conductor may be able to help you with a learning or practice strategy or to pair you up with another musician who can. If you feel certain that practice alone will not get you through, ask about altering your part—perhaps by doubling an exposed solo with another instrument or by rewriting a harmony line in a simpler way. It's the sort of thing that is rarely done in professional groups, but is accepted among amateurs. If you are told that it is impossible or inappropriate to accommodate your skill level, then there is something amiss with the organization's policy about accepting members and selecting music. This is a problem that has nothing to do with your own musicality or your own worth. It is not right for a group to admit members freely and then to program performance of works that some of the members cannot hope to play. It is the organization's problem. Do not take it personally.

If the music appears to be too difficult for the majority of

The concerts were attended by family members who shuffled in like impressed seamen called to witness the punishment of a well-liked man—in this case, Mozart. Burned in my ear forever is our Overture to The Magic Flute *as it taxis toward tempo, takes flight for one white-knuckled moment, then sinks beyond the runway to disintegrate in a welter of flaming pieces.*

♪ Christian Williams, journalist and amateur cellist

the group, then a delegation of tactful members should approach the conductor or music director as early as possible. It may be feasible to make a program change if the issue is tackled quickly. Or you may find that the conductor is aware of the difficulties and is confident that they are containable, that the group will be able to pull it off.

If parts have been rented and the program has been indelibly set—perhaps even soloists hired—all is not necessarily lost. Individual sections can rehearse separately from the whole group to work out problem passages. It may be possible to redistribute some parts—to assign an overly difficult tenor solo to a soprano or to move some of the first violins to the second violin section. If necessary, parts can be simplified, either by rewriting or by making judicious cuts. Some amateur ensembles bring in reinforcements in the form of paid professional or semiprofessional players or singers.

Where there is a very large difference in skill levels in a group or where the problem of overly difficult programs is a recurrent one, a need for reorganization is indicated. A separate reading orchestra, preparatory band, or choral ensemble might help less-experienced musicians get additional background in a low-pressure situation, whereas a madrigal group, chamber orchestra, or other small ensemble would allow advanced players to take on difficult works. Such a split group could still come together for some numbers and offer a public program full of both variety and confidence.

Group Problems: The Care and Feeding of Ensemble Morale

If music is an ensemble's soul, then morale is the face that the ensemble presents to the world (and to itself when it looks in its metaphorical group mirror). Morale is an expression of the group's confidence, enthusiasm, and well-being. All the problems and conflicts already mentioned can affect morale. So can a host of other difficulties. The morale-diminishing problems mentioned most often by amateurs interviewed for this book were inadequate leadership, large inequalities in skill level, too heavy a schedule of rehearsals and performances, too light a schedule (the group doesn't meet often enough to build positive morale), segregation of inexperienced players at the back or sides of a large ensemble, and nonmusical responsibilities either too concentrated on a few individuals or not looked after at all.

Almost every group will go through patterns of progress and plateaus, just as individual musicians do. Long plateaus tend to feel like times of low morale, though with confidence and mutual encouragement things will often improve with time. Genuine morale-threatening conditions require careful analysis and brainstorming by concerned members. Outside help can be valuable, perhaps in the form of contact with similar groups in other locales or in the form of a special workshop with a guest leader or coach. Some groups get a boost from collaborating with other musical groups or from using their talents to stage a benefit for a cause that the group as a whole would like to support.

Many amateurs value the social aspects of music making very highly, and this fact can give an amateur ensemble enormous leverage in coping with morale problems. However, the social milieu is itself a component of morale and needs careful tending. Large groups, in particular, are sometimes inclined to develop cliques. One singer interviewed for this book had looked forward to joining a choral society:

> I only sang with them for a year, though. I didn't get to know
> anyone in the chorus except the woman I drove with. We had
> a ten-minute break during the rehearsal, but people were not
> very friendly to new members. I loved the singing, but I never
> felt welcome.

Nonmusical social events can help cement relationships in ensembles—an annual picnic, pizza extravaganza, or family potluck. Nonmusical settings are also a good place to settle nonmusical business, which tends to accumulate as the group goes on. This doesn't mean that a musical group is automatically a social group as well, but a bit of socializing often improves overall morale and makes it easier to accomplish nonmusical tasks.

A modest but simple way to support morale is to maintain and distribute an updated membership list to all active members. (There's someone in nearly every group who has a nifty computer program that will keep track of this information.)

Large groups usually set up phone-tree-type communications. In a small group, one person can be in charge of phoning. If everyone has everyone else's home and work number, it becomes easy to set up rides, to change rehearsal times, to get copies of music, to send messages. A phone list also encourages non-group-related interaction between group members.

In every amateur ensemble, the ultimate principle to remember is that music is important, but people are important, too. The world of professional music making can sometimes be personally arduous and unforgiving, but such an environment is incompatible with amateur music making. Our common purpose as amateurs is to discover, nurture, and share our joy in music. The path through our conflicts is the path that leads most directly to that goal.

CHAPTER 13

Making Music with Your Family

May 17, 1661 *To the office and sat there all the afternoon till 9 at night. So home to my musique; and my wife and I sat singing in my chamber a good while together. And then to bed.*

♪ Samuel Pepys

Of all possible opportunities for music making, some of the best times can be had right in your own family. Whether you are accompanied by a toddler thumping a sauce pan or an adolescent whose technique passed yours some years ago, music and families just go together . . . well . . . harmoniously.

Making ensemble music with your partner and children is an extraordinary experience—perhaps one of the purest examples of making music for the joy of it. But before that moment arrives, there are—with children at least—the years of preparation and anticipation, the years of living with musicians in their most natural state. In this chapter we'll look at life with young musicians, at singing and playing instruments together, and we'll also share some ideas for creating a vital and lasting musical environment at home.

LIVING WITH MUSICAL CHILDREN

As amateur musicians ourselves, we know how our children might enjoy having some musical skills when they are adults. We have a hunch that it may be less frustrating for them to learn now than to wait until they are our age. We become impatient and uneasy if they don't seem "musical," if they do seem "musical" but don't "make progress," or if they do "make progress" but don't like it. We may worry and wonder how to introduce our children to music, when to begin the lessons, and how to get the practicing done.

But all this seems to go at it from the wrong side. Life with children presents literally dozens of musical occasions every day that have nothing at all to do with "music education" but everything to do with becoming a musician. Young children are irrepressibly musical. Rather than waiting for us to lead them, our children invite us, over and over, to embrace the world musically. They love rhythmic actions—swinging, whirling, skipping. They naturally offer, many times a day, chants, rhythmic and rhyming word games, snatches of song heard somewhere or completely made up. Given a drum, they will thwap it. Given a piano, they will bang on it. They eagerly will blow, bow, pluck, or strum almost anything put in their hands, and they need restraint in these explorations only for the protection of the instrument.

In the interest of quiet and order, however, many young children are told to "stop that racket" and to "sit down and be still." All the spoon banging, boot stomping, and drumming on the side of the house with sticks is called "annoying." Their chants and nonsense verse are dismissed as "silliness." And then they are chauffeured to their music lesson where their parents wonder why they are so awkward and confused.

Leading children to organized music is so like leading them to literature. The best single predictor of a child's reading ability is the amount she is read to at home. It would stand to reason that the best investment in a child's musical future is a warm, inclusive musical environment from the very beginning—one that honors the child's innate musicality and "sets a good example" as well.

If music is to be a natural, joyful part of a child's life, then it must be nurtured from the inside out, not just painted on. Music has to be a normal and shared part of every day—not just thirty lonely minutes each day at the piano. We can sing to celebrate every small event of life—not only birthdays and New Year's but also getting dressed ("This is the way we brush our

My father was dead keen on sight-reading. After dinner, he and I would sit down and bang through the four-hand versions of all the standard Symphonies, at the correct speed and damn the mistakes. I learned the Symphonies of Beethoven, Schubert, Mozart, Haydn and Brahms that way, and to this day I can remember what colours the bindings were, where the tricky page turns came, and that the Primo part of the second movement of the "Pastorale" had four bars torn off which I would have to fake. It was all inexact and exciting and sloppy and wonderful, and I wish that the custom of four-handed music at home were still as much in vogue as it was then. It's a hell of an education.

André Previn, *Orchestra*

. . . one of the purest examples of making music for the joy of it.

239

teeth"), going out ("Take me for a ride in the car, car"), shopping ("Oats peas beans and barley grow"), going to sleep ("Sleep my child and peace attend thee, all through the night"). Music can be drawn as large as the child's world.

If parents are alert, they will hear—even from older children like pre-adolescents—natural, child-led rhythmic and melodic activities. You don't have to plan this, pay anyone to teach it, send the children anywhere to get it, or buy any books about it. If it's all right with the child, you can join in, echo, make a new gesture, imitate and improvise until that moment's thread plays itself out.

In the natural acts of singing, clapping, chanting, spinning, swinging, and bouncing balls, children internalize a host of musical concepts—song structure, tonality, tempo, dynamics, and a deep, internal sense of rhythm and phrasing.

SINGING WITH CHILDREN

If you have children of elementary school age or younger, and if you're rusty on traditional children's songs, look in your public library for songbooks in the children's or juvenile collection under Dewey decimal number M786. Be sure that your children get to sing *real* children's songs. These are not an inferior or diminutive form of music but rather are part of a very rich heritage. (See appendix 2 for a list of songbooks.)

Different kinds of songs speak clearly to children of different ages. There's an age for counting-out songs, for cumulative verses, for finger plays. You need never feel bound by the words or the tunes of any song. "Eat, eat, eat your corn" fits just as well as "Row, row, row your boat," and if you forget the tune to "This Old Man," you are permitted to make up a new one.

Some wonderful songs to share as early as possible are the rounds—"Three Blind Mice," "Row, Row, Row Your Boat," "Frère Jacques," and all the rest. You don't have to treat a round as any special kind of song. Keep it a secret. Until the right moment comes, they're just songs, like any other. And then (if a sibling or playmate doesn't spill the beans), perhaps when the child is four or seven or ten, one day you start a favorite round tune, and when the child is singing strongly, you begin again, singing softly, maybe turning your head slightly away so you'll

As soon as I became personally involved in music, I found myself extremely interested in whatever ideas and advice our kids could give me about my own efforts. I learned quickly that they were capable of being understanding, sympathetic, and even wise, and that they had a great deal to teach me. Our common interest in music has done as much to nourish our rapport as anything else we have ever done as a family.

♪ Frank R. Wilson, neurologist and amateur pianist, *Tone Deaf and All Thumbs?*

We had music pumped into our blood just by having it in the house. That gives you music. Then it's a question of what you do with it.

♪ John Rubinstein, Arthur Rubinstein's son

The most musical communities are not those where all the music of the year is crowded into a festival of three or four days, but those where there is the most real music made at home.

♪ Thomas W. Surette, *Music and Life*

240

make a minimal distraction. You will have one very astonished child beside you, and from that day on, every song you know will be tried out as a round. And that's a wonderful discovery in itself—to find out that some songs "work" as rounds and that some don't and to begin to figure out why.

PLAYING TOGETHER

As our children grow older, some will begin to imitate us, perhaps deciding to play the instrument that we play. Or they may have a strong urge to play something entirely different. There is no room here to go into the turbulent question of practicing, except to say that you—whatever your own musical capacities— are always a model of the importance of music in life, of the way to do music and of the reasons for being a musician.

If your children develop even the slightest ability on an instrument, you can begin duets or family improvisations. Frans Brugger, a renowned recorder artist, grew up with more ensemble partners than he sometimes wished for: "We had a happy musical life at home. I remember that with the help of some uncles and aunts we could play the complete *Brandenburg Concertos.* I was often taken out of my bed by this older brother in the middle of the night. He'd whisper to me, 'Come on, you have to play something, you have to fill in a part.'"

Social worker Max Freeman was led to music by the example of another musical family: "A colleague from work asked my family to dinner. After dinner we were invited into the 'music room,' and they showed us their instruments. (Everyone in their family plays at least two.) At the slightest glimmer of interest, an instrument was thrust into our hands, and we were given a one-minute lesson. I got the string bass, my wife had a flute, Kari was at the piano, Les had a little violin, and Anna had a basket full of bells, rattles, a tambourine, sand blocks, and a triangle. We made the most glorious racket! Then we traded instruments and started in again. Our hostess would come in from time to time with wine, juice, coffee, another instrument. When I finally looked at my watch, we had been in that room for over two hours!

"Later I realized that that was the *only* time we had ever been visiting with the kids where we had all spent the whole evening

*(A*fter an improvised song)
Father: *Is that a round?*
Son: *Uh . . . well . . . it's straight.*

♪ Steve and Damian Lester

I started [my son] off on trumpet and he plays well and gets a good tone, but every teacher I sent him to would say, "Why don't you get your dad to teach you?"

♪ Clark Terry

241

doing something together. Usually the two older kids drift off to watch TV, and the little one whines and clings all evening. I had a long talk with my friend at work, and she told me that she, her husband, and their two kids make music together *every night*. They don't even *have* a TV!

"Well, about a week later, I went into a music store and I bought myself an alto sax. Just like that. We don't have a family music scene on the 'every night' level yet, but Kari has started taking piano lessons again and practices without being nagged about it. Sometimes she accompanies me, if the piano part isn't too hard, and she and her mother are learning a duet for her next recital. (Vivian hadn't touched a piano for twenty years.) It's a start."

CREATING A MUSICAL HOME

Finally I move back with my father. And because of him I become a musician. Every Sunday he used to take me to hear orchestras, and that's when I first become acquainted with a lot of Debussy and Ravel. I wanted to play something. And my father wanted to distract me and keep me a bit quiet. So he took me into a store on Rue Rochechouart and bought me a three-quarter violin. All the way home I hugged it so hard I almost broke it. . . . I still have that violin in my desk at home.

♪ Stéphane Grappelli

Family music begins with natural, child-led, spontaneous rhythms, and it continues on with lots of singing. In between these activities are other events and attitudes with which you can create a positive musical environment:

Listen to music. This does not mean listening to heavy classics, unless that is what you genuinely enjoy. Nor should it mean very loud music of any kind. Children's ears are extremely sensitive, and excessive volumes are painful. Nor does it mean an unremitting background of sound without letup. Music in that case becomes like wallpaper, without life or spirit. But listen, by all means, to music you really enjoy, to music that moves you.

Go to concerts. Take children to concerts that *you* enjoy, making any necessary contingency plans for younger folk whose attention may not last out the event.

Make music yourself. Do all you can to keep your own music going as your family grows. Enjoy your music making, at whatever level. Young children are not judgmental. They will absorb your attitudes and forgive your faults.

Make music welcoming, participatory, and noncompetitive. Be willing—maybe not every time you play, but often enough—

to be accompanied by a little percussionist. (Don't buy toy instruments, by the way. Real percussion instruments don't cost much more but do make a much more satisfying sound.) Don't assume that an apparent lack of attention or participation means a lack of interest. It could also mean that a great deal of learning is taking place through observation.

Provide gentle, caring, careful instruction.   When it is time for music lessons, choose a teacher carefully and monitor the relationship as you would with your own teacher. Value your child's opinions. Poor teaching is often worse than no teaching.

Talk about music.   Make *genuine* comments and ask *genuine* questions (especially as teenagers and "their music" begin to make an appearance). Ask for opinions. Discuss preferences. Keep an open mind.

Joane Sunahara, a medical research technician from Vancouver, is now reaping one of the richest rewards of a family life with music:

> Some of the greatest pleasures of my life have been playing music with my children. While my two daughters were still in high school, we had many enjoyable times playing recorder trios. Now my children are all grown up and on their own, although one of my daughters is living here in Vancouver. She has a very hectic life with her career and husband, but she still seems to have a need for music making and has joined our recorder group. My other daughter is in Ontario, but we keep in touch musically. Besides the recorder, she also plays keyboards, so she records the continuo part of recorder sonatas for me. When I play along with her tape, she is right here beside me.

Dick grew up with piano lessons, skipped to trumpet, taught himself how to play guitar, and now fiddles around with all kinds of instruments. He is our music initiator and has brought a lot of unity into our lives with family band night.

♪ Debbie Westheimer, mother and amateur singer

My wife, daughter, grandchildren, and I serenade each other when we visit. It is a touching experience, but one of my grandsons says I should learn something new. He is getting tired of the Chopin Prelude in A Major.

♪ Hilliard Bennett, retired commercial artist and amateur pianist

243

Part Five

PLAYING AND PERFORMING: MAKING MUSIC FOR OTHERS

We learn in performance ultimate requirements which no other experience can teach us. Perhaps the most important is the purification of our attitude, freeing ourselves of external concerns that are irrelevant to making music. We learn more about care and honesty in our work.

Mildred Portnoy Chase, *Just Being at the Piano*

CHAPTER 14

𝄞 *Preparing a Performance*

An impromptu living-room entertainment after Thanksgiving dinner. A concert in the park. A black-tie benefit in a glittering hall. It's a performance—an extraordinary setting for music making. Leonard Marsh, amateur cellist and veteran of hundreds of homestyle musical evenings, said a performance for him is when he's on a stage, clearly separated from an audience composed mostly of people he doesn't know. Other amateurs find that the presence of even one listener turns playing into performing.

However we define it, a performance brings us to our music in a fresh way. We become aware of details that we haven't noticed before, careful about technique that we might otherwise have let slip, involved in our interpretation as it will be heard through someone else's ears.

Giving a performance also plunges us into a host of nonmusical and extra-musical events and activities. In this chapter, we'll look at *performing* music for the joy of it: program planning, rehearsing, stage presence, and some of the nonmusical details. We'll close with some thoughts about special performing opportunities for amateurs.

PROGRAM PLANNING

The length of your program depends on the nature of the occasion. If you are one player in a teacher's annual recital, you and your teacher together will select your pieces. If you or your group are doing an entire program or several numbers as part of a show, then you need to devote some careful thought to program selection. Several issues will affect your decision:

1. The amount of rehearsal time available. You'll want sufficient time to bring every number to a high gloss. This time will have to include learning the numbers if they are new to you and memorizing them if you plan to play from memory.

2. Playing time. If you have been assigned a limited amount of time for your set or your portion of the program, you need to do your very best to come in under that time. If, however, you have the entire event to yourself or for your group, you will have to consider the players' stamina and the community's standards. In *The Recorder Book*, Kenneth Wollitz has advice for recorder ensembles that is useful to any group or soloist.

> It is far preferable to leave your audience wanting more than to have them wondering when the performance will be over. The more inexperienced the group, the more this applies. Forty to forty-five minutes is a good length for a concert without intermission, an hour and twenty minutes to an hour and a half with intermission. You should time your pieces. Figure twenty to twenty-five minutes of solid music if there is to be no intermission and forty to forty-five if there is one. The rest of the time will be filled with changing instruments, seatings, explanatory remarks to the audience or reading of texts (if you choose to do so), and, let us hope, applause.

3. Tastes of the audience and the nature of the event. Your selection will be guided, to some extent, by what your audience expects or is used to, with perhaps some "educational" function

I shall never forget being the co-author of a program performed by the Harvard Orchestra in the college chapel which, though it looked ample on paper, was over in just twenty-nine minutes. As it closed, latecomers were still arriving!

♪ Malcolm H. Holmes, Dean of the New England, Conservatory of Music, 1945–1953

247

on your part. At a party the crowd wants mostly familiar tunes, but introducing a new song helps to leave your special mark on the event. An audience that turns out for chamber orchestra concerts may be coming largely for Baroque, but a contemporary selection can demonstrate another facet of your group.

4. The overall shape of the program.   Seek both unity and contrast. Unity can be derived in several different ways. A single program performed, for example, by a dulcimer and guitar duo has unity in its texture, in its complete "dulcimer-and-guitarness." An entire program of hits from the fifties or Baroque sonatas or compositions by Beethoven also has unity. Contrast comes from variety in tempo, key, texture, instrumentation, style, and mood. If you have several very short pieces, arrange them in logical groups by composer, instrumentation, or theme.

5. The musicians' abilities and preferences.   Choose numbers that will enhance the confidence of your players. Aim for a musical and enjoyable experience for the musicians as well as for the audience. Simple music skillfully and beautifully played is preferable to a toweringly difficult work just barely survived. Showcase pieces are fine, but too many stress-laden numbers in one program will take a toll on the players. If there are several numbers, some should be ones that everyone can relax into. The first number on the program should be something all can do with gusto and flair.

REHEARSING FOR A PERFORMANCE

Rehearsing for a performance is practicing with a very special goal. As in any other practice, it is useless to go over and over your music, especially the troublesome bits, with no attempt to address problems. Especially if a part is giving someone a problem, nothing will be accomplished by repetition except to drive in more deeply the troubles that already exist. (See chapter 9 for general practice strategies.)

An individual's rehearsal work and a group's work are similar in many ways except that the group's time is more closely bound. An individual can rehearse at will, but a group must

I like my programs to have something soft, something energetic, something slow, something blue, something red, something burning.

♪ Stéphane Grappelli

work around everyone's schedule and may be hard-pressed to find time beyond the normal rehearsals. (Most amateur musicians are willing to make extra time available in the final week or two before a performance.) A group usually depends not on adding extra practice time but on starting early enough to get the work done. Each group will discover the right number of rehearsals needed for a concert or performance. Too few means a sloppy, insecure, demoralizing performance, but too many makes for boredom, resentment, and a loss of enthusiasm.

To keep up morale and use time efficiently, ensembles may need to schedule *sectionals* so that small groups of players or vocalists can go over their work. It's common for an orchestra to split up into strings, woodwinds, and brass for at least one rehearsal. A sectional can be led by an experienced player so that several sectionals can go on simultaneously without requiring the conductor or leader to be present. A lot can be accomplished in a good sectional in a very short time. It's valuable enough to deserve the first twenty minutes or so at the very beginning of a rehearsal. It's not usually a good idea to hold a sectional at the end of a rehearsal when attention is beginning to wane.

An unconducted ensemble or an individual working alone might consider using a coach at some point during performance rehearsals. A coach is ideally a very good teacher with a clear knowledge of the kind of music you're getting ready. It is not someone who instructs in basic technique but rather someone who will help you build dimension into your playing, to bring it off the stage and into the audience.

One good time to bring in a coach is fairly early in your preparation, after you've learned your parts and are ready to break the music down for detailed work. You can get some ideas about developing and doing your best work, getting over the hurdles with room to spare, and using your instrumental skills to best advantage. The other good time for a coach is when you are ready to put the pieces back together. The least productive time for coaching is at the very end, just days or hours before the show. At that point it can feel a bit too late to everyone, especially if the coach has very many basic suggestions to make.

You will naturally think about the acoustics of the performance space, but if you have a choice, think about the acoustics of

Distraction is a very powerful force when one is before an audience. If you have the security of careful preparation, and you keep your concentration, the stimulus of performance will make you play better than you ever have before. Ill-prepared spots will be fraught with anxiety and will probably go wrong. So prepare! If you cannot play something consistently well in rehearsal, don't attempt to perform it. Miracles don't happen.

♪ Kenneth Wollitz,
The Recorder Book

Consider using a coach.

your rehearsal space as well. Consider challenging yourself and rehearsing in a "dry" environment, one that lacks resonance, that is what musicians call "dead." A resonant space gives richness to your overall sound, but it also conceals your mistakes and makes you sound much better than you actually are. It can be downright dangerous to rehearse in a live hall and perform in a dead one.

Most of the issues discussed in chapter 9 about practicing also apply to preparing a performance. Mark your music liberally, especially at critical points where you must watch, change tempo, change keys, take a repeat, hold a rest, bring out or subdue your part, or remember an accidental or a fingering.

STAGE PRESENCE

Nearly everyone who sees Suzuki music students is impressed with their poise and confidence on stage. Every performance begins and ends with a dignified bow, and every child takes time to be in balance with the instrument and to be quiet for a moment before playing. No shuffling, no bashfulness, no rush. One reason these kids look so natural and so dignified is that they practice this poise *every time they play*. The very first lesson is a lesson in how to bow. Every subsequent lesson and practice begins and ends with a bow. A note is never played until the child is standing or seated with good posture and balance. These young kids are so accustomed to bowing and playing with poise that it becomes completely natural. They don't feel self-conscious or apologetic about it. We grown-ups could probably do just as well if we gave the issue as much care.

Stage Manners

As part of your general rehearsals, and definitely in your final and dress rehearsals, practice all of the nonmusical movements you'll be making. An act that includes theatrics and choreography will naturally give much attention to this, but it's often the case that other groups give too little. Don't wait for a panicky, whispered conference backstage to decide who walks on first, when you bow, how you leave, and what to do when the audience applauds. Exactly what you need to practice depends on

In the final bars of the Hallelujah Chorus there is a momentary silence expressly designed, it seems, for the over-enthusiastic singer to add that extra "hallelujah" of his own without which no amateur performance of Messiah is complete. The singer who adds it is immediately recognizable as being the only radish in full evening dress on the platform.

♪ Antony Miall, *Musical Bumps*

People only half listen to you when you play. The other half is watching.

♪ Itzhak Perlman

250

how formal the occasion will be, how large or varied the group is, and the nature of the program. An informal living-room concert for friends calls for an equal quality of stage presence but much less *quantity* than, for example, a formal, classical concert with several groupings of performers and ensembles. Scan this list and pick out the items you'll need to consider:

Bows. Bowing as general social behavior has been out of style for generations, with the exception of stage performers. It's a pity that we no longer get any regular practice at it, because most of us feel silly when we bow. That's a shame, because it can get your whole performance off to a poor start if the first thing you have to do is walk out and do something that makes you feel self-conscious.

If your performance logically will include a bow—and this applies to all soloists, unconducted small ensembles, and the leaders of conducted ensembles—it pays to learn how to do a good bow and to practice it so that, even if you don't feel at ease, at least you look decent. Become a connoisseur of bows. Watch other performers and see what looks natural.

One workable routine for bowing is to stand with your feet together, holding your instrument in whatever is your "rest" or carrying position. If it's a piano, you can rest one hand lightly on it. Look at the audience for a slow count of two. Bend at the waist and look at your shoes for a slow count of two. Come up again and look at the audience for a slow count of two. That's all. Just remember to keep your feet together and *look down at the floor* when you bow. If you keep your head up, it looks very awkward. (Ballet dancers take bows with their heads up, but they're skilled at making incredibly awkward movements appear graceful.)

Ordinarily, a soloist bows, but not the accompanist, unless the soloist gestures for the accompanist to take a bow. An unconducted small ensemble bows together, which needs practice. One player—anyone, as long as everyone else can see the person—leads the bow for a small ensemble. The leader or conductor of a larger group takes a bow on the group's behalf and then signals any seated musicians to stand. They rise together and look at the audience with a pleasant expression—no chatting, sorting music, or disassembling instruments. On a signal, usually from someone in the group, they sit again.

- *Downstage—toward the audience, to the front of the stage*
- *Upstage—away from the audience, to the back of the stage*
- *Stage left—to the performer's left, facing the audience*
- *Stage right—to the performer's right, facing the audience*

Walking onto the stage. What needs to be worked out here is the order. Large instrumental groups often drift onstage a few at a time well before the concert starts, which is fine, because otherwise it looks like a marching band going through an obstacle course as players wend their way around stands, chairs, risers, and bulky instruments. Choruses, however, usually enter in file, which makes sense, too, since their path is clear, and they are crowded together once they get on. An effective way to be sure that the chorus files on in the right order is to stand backstage in an arrangement identical to the stage arrangement and then file on a row at a time. This is usually safer than making one long, snaky line backstage. If someone is missing, the "remember-who-you're-next-to" system can break down in a line. (It's also possible to get a chorus onstage in reverse order with the "single line" system.)

A small ensemble usually enters all at once from the same side of the stage. You may have to map out a strategy for getting to your places with minimal awkwardness, and that's worth practicing, too.

Acknowledging applause. Do this with dignity and friendliness. Watch your favorite performers and see what they do. This is the place for your simple, dignified bow, but not for grandiose gestures or apologetic shrugs. Groups need to practice this. A leader or conductor can indicate when to stand and when to sit. Usually a soloist, a featured player, or a featured section will stand and acknowledge applause first, and then the rest of the group joins them. After acknowledging applause, it is customary to sit again until the applause dies down, even if the program is over.

Players on stage, by the way, applaud or not depending on the kind of music being made. The less formal the group and the occasion, the more open is the players' response to their soloing colleagues. In professional orchestras, wind players sometimes shuffle their feet, and string players tap their bows on their stands. Some amateur groups follow this model, but many applaud openly.

Leaving the stage. Large groups generally leave in reverse order to their entry—first the conductor and then the players. A soloist, though, would leave first, followed by the accompanist.

Groups need to prearrange a signal so they'll know when to leave, assigning one person to rise first. Leave stands, chairs, large instruments, and equipment on the stage when you go, and come back for them later. It looks rude if you start breaking down the stage set while the audience is still applauding.

At all times the audience should see warmth and communication among group members, but the stage is not the place for private discussions, whispering, or elaborate, mimed gestures. Rock and pop musicians often employ more theatrical movements, but these, too, should be well worked out and communicated in advance so that no player is left puzzled about what to do.

Concert Dress

As soon as more than one performer is involved, dress becomes an issue, and the larger the group, the bigger the issue simply because more uniformity is required to make a large group look unified. A group that is informal and low-key still needs to discuss dress so that everyone looks informal and low-key together. Remember that *everything worn on stage automatically becomes a costume.* A rock group needs to decide on T-shirts-and-jeans or leather-and-glitter just as much as a classical ensemble has to decide on suits or tuxes.

The all-time standard for large amateur ensembles—aside from those that wear matching outfits—is white above, black below. This has the advantage of fairly instant uniformity, though it may need to be refined by specifying long or short skirts, long or short sleeves, and ties or open necks. If you agree on ties, then you need to agree on bow ties or four-in-hand. (Remind everyone to wear dark or black shoes and men to wear dark socks.)

With a small ensemble, some nice variations are possible on the white-and-black standard. The Kokanee String Quartet, of British Columbia, has played for years in pastel turtlenecks and dark skirt or slacks. The overall effect is relaxed but neat and pulled together.

On a lighted stage, any shiny jewelry, including large earrings and cufflinks, are reflective and best avoided (unless your ensemble is making a statement with glitter and flash). Also, stage lights are hot. Remind people to forgo the perfume or scented aftershave and to be very, very light on scented deodorants and hair sprays. Some of your musical colleagues may get nauseous.

THE NONMUSICAL ASPECTS OF PERFORMING

Even the smallest communities usually include several individuals with expertise in the managerial aspects of performing events—ticket sales, promotion, and so forth. If you're planning a major performance, you don't have to go out and pay an exorbitant fee to an arts manager, but it might be well worth your time to seek out a competent volunteer or a modestly paid worker *who is not part of the performing group* to take on some of your nonmusical tasks and to provide general advice and encouragement. Ask other musical groups in your area (or small theatre groups) how they handle the nonartistic details of their performances. Some participating musicians enjoy this kind of work and will volunteer their efforts readily, but some of the tasks can be onerous for a performer (who should be practicing and rehearsing). Nonmusical details often extend right up to the last second before the downbeat. A nonperforming majordomo can, after consultation with you or your group, arrange promotion, tickets, photographs, equipment transport, piano tuning, backstage and door personnel, program printing, refreshments, bills, and correspondence. That still leaves some items for the musicians themselves to look after.

The Performing Space

Find out about the performing space well in advance. You want to know how large the space is and what kind of equipment is available to you (piano, music stands, risers, power, lights). Check especially the kind of chairs available, if you will need them. More than one string quartet has arrived at the concert hall to find the stage set with armchairs. Arrange to use the space for at least one rehearsal if at all possible.

Before you commit yourself to a date for a performance, ask what other events are scheduled just before, during, or after your event. Concurrent events can make havoc with the sound

Most any space can be used as a performance area if properly adapted.

254

or the stage area. A common example is the basketball game in a gym that adjoins an auditorium, or a high-school or town theatre that is being used for a concert on Friday night and a play on Saturday night. If the stage sets for the play must stay in place—which is usually the case—what you thought was a roomy stage turns out to be a broom closet. One amateur music workshop ran concurrently with a drama workshop and shared stage space for their final presentations. The small ensembles performed on the set of a gracious Victorian drawing room. The orchestra and stage band did not fare so well—they played in a graveyard.

Timing

Amateurs have the luxury of creative scheduling. The eight-o'clock-in-the-evening performance is the standard for many professional music events. But amateurs can realistically consider the habits of the community and the preference of the audience and the players. An earlier hour will often mean that children can attend more easily. Or you might consider noon-hour, brown-bag concerts in building lobbies, libraries, or schools. Other groups like Sunday morning brunch concerts, perhaps also creating an opportunity for another local organization to raise funds by selling muffins and croissants.

If you *must* schedule a concert on the last Sunday of October or the first Sunday of April, beware of time changes! The October date is not really that dangerous—anyone who forgets the time change will just have to wait around for an hour. But the spring changeover can invite disaster. Take no chances. Make sure *everyone* knows. Double-check. Set up a phone tree or a buddy system.

Before any concert in a school, be sure that all automatically timed bells and buzzers are manually turned off.

Programs and Announcements

A printed program is not necessary for every kind of event. A warm announcer can easily take the place of a program. Programs make nice souvenirs, though, and many audience members appreciate having them. Remember that the program will be the first event in your concert, since it's the first thing the

I think the best time to schedule [such] a concert is between four and six o'clock in the afternoon. Not only is my mind the best then, but audiences are more content to attend concerts at that time of day, and they are more alert and relaxed, too. I also find a certain magic in the afternoon, unexplainable, but nevertheless there.

♪ Vladimir Horowitz

255

The oboe volunteered her secretary to type up our program and it didn't get done until 5:00 on the day of the concert. No one even thought to look it over ahead of time. So that's how we ended up playing numbers by George Frederick Handle and Giovanni Sam Martini.

♪ Emily Renwick, librarian and amateur violinist

audience will see. This is a good job for a talented volunteer, but the musicians themselves must provide all the information. Double-check the spelling of *everything*, especially performers' names. Get your program proofread two or three times. Allow plenty of time for your program designer to get the program to printable stage. It often takes quite a bit of juggling to get all the titles and names to fit attractively and legibly on the page. If your group will be using programs often, start up an idea file of programs collected from other concerts and events so you'll have something to refer to when you need to see how to list the title, movements, composer, and soloist's names all in a limited space.

If, instead of or in addition to a program, you plan to talk to the audience, keep your remarks short. The audience has come to hear your music. Keep anecdotes, introductions, and expressions of gratitude very brief. Given this general policy, talking to your audience is a wonderful thing to do. It builds an immediate bond between musicians and listeners and cuts through the "invisible curtain" that hangs between someone on the stage and anyone in an audience seat.

Backstage Arrangements

Except in the most informal of settings, players will need a place to leave their coats and instrument cases, to warm up, and possibly to change clothes. Plan in advance for some kind of security if you need it, and advise the players about the arrangements. *If the backstage room is locked during the performance, be sure that it can be unlocked promptly whenever it is needed.* Don't let a maintenance person wander off with the key; you might have to go on a safari at intermission to find it. Either get the key yourself or give unmistakable instructions about your needs.

Sound and Amplification

Some kinds of music require amplification, and some abhor it. If you are putting on a concert for someone else, work out this question in advance. Most groups that work with amplification do best to provide their own, since you never know about the quality or availability of equipment elsewhere. If you don't want amplification, make that very clear ahead of time. Don't assume that the program organizer at the community center will know that a string trio doesn't want to be heard through a PA system.

Consider the Weather

In very cold weather allow extra warm-up time for instrumentalists. Find out about arrangements for heating the space you'll play in, and have it warm when the musicians arrive. For an outdoor performance, check with the musicians before you make final arrangements. String players may refuse to play in open sunshine—it's hard on the instruments. Wind players dislike outdoor concerts in cold weather because condensation builds up inside the instruments faster than the players can keep up with it.

Lighting and Set Pieces

Musicians need two kinds of lighting during a performance: one so they can see their music and the other so the audience can see them. When you play in a theatre, lighting is usually looked after by someone else—often someone with theatrical inclinations. You may have to negotiate with this person to turn up the overhead stage lights so you can read your music and to turn down spotlights so you're not blinded when you look up at the conductor or each other.

Many amateur performances, though, take place in untheatrical and sometimes downright unattractive, venues—community centers, church halls, and junior-high gymnasiums. In these places the lighting designer will have to be recruited from your own ranks. For a daytime performance, test the room without overhead lights. If sufficient natural light is available, leave overheads off—especially buzzing fluorescents. For an evening performance, use lights selectively. If overheads are in panels, controlled by separate switches, use only the lights over the performing area and leave the audience area unlit.

With a few borrowed furnishings, you can create an elegant and adequately lit performing area for a soloist or a small ensemble. Start with the handsomest rug you can find—an Oriental looks marvelous, but avoid busy designs. Arrange your ensemble seating on or around the rug. Put end tables on either side, slightly in front of your group. (Maybe you can find matching ones?) On each table put a lamp on the back and a basket of flowers or a healthy plant on the front. Stand two or three floor lamps behind your group and *voilà!*—an intimate, attractive stage setting, even in the visual vacuum of a basketball court.

If you try this, be prepared with armfuls of extension cords and warn your players to watch their step. Tape running cords to the floor and give the rug owner a pair of complimentary tickets.

Test this setting before the audience arrives to be sure you have enough of both kinds of light. The floor lamps behind you light your music. The lamps on the tables in front light the scene for the audience. Adjustable reading lamps or goose-necks work better in front than decorative table lamps. (That's what the flowers or the Boston ferns are for—to hide your son's Darth Vader desk lamp.) If the setting is too dim for musicians or audience, you can still use the rug and tables. Just turn off the lamps and revert to the regular room lighting.

AMATEUR PERFORMERS IN THE COMMUNITY

The amateurs who contributed to this book had experienced virtually every possible size and style of public performance. Some very special kinds of performances, however, created both for the amateur musicians and for their audience very deep feelings of satisfaction. These special performances were all—for lack of a better phrase—"community building" endeav-ors. They included playing at community events such as fairs and parades, playing at senior citizens homes, and playing in hospitals, schools, community centers, churches, and syna-gogues. Musicians also found great satisfaction playing for spe-cial family or community events such as weddings and funerals. One amateur madrigal group sang at the bedside of a dear friend who was dying of cancer. "She was so touched," said one group member. "We didn't sing for very long, but it was a very, very important thing for all of us. I will never forget it."

In none of these settings would a professional musician or a professional ensemble be quite right. Professionals, as wonder-ful and as accomplished as they are, have to be scheduled in advance and have to be paid. Professionals are also often strang-

It's always easier when you make music for a purpose. We just sang for a funeral this week. It was practical, it was useful, it was part of our community. It felt good and right and it made sense.

♪ Lynelle Inwood, homemaker and amateur flutist and singer

ers when they enter an event. Amateurs come as friends, as relatives, as part of the community. Amateurs in these settings serve a larger purpose than simply making music for an audience of listeners. The music itself serves a larger purpose. Neither the music nor the musicians are the focus; both become builders of the community that generated the music and the musicians in the first place—building on the past, building into the future with great love.

CHAPTER 15

🎵 Stagefright

I gave my first real concert in Barcelona when I was fourteen. It was a benefit performance at the Teatro de Novedades. . . . My father, who had come to Barcelona for the occasion, took me on the tramway. I was terribly nervous. When we got to the concert hall, I said, "Father, I've forgotten the beginning of the piece! I can't remember a note of it! What shall I do?" He calmed me down. That was eighty years ago, but I've never conquered that dreadful feeling of nervousness before a performance. It is always an ordeal. Before I go onstage, I have a pain in my chest. I'm tormented. The thought of a public performance is still a nightmare.

Pablo Casals, *Joys and Sorrows*

There are few activities in life which can produce tension and anxiety as rapidly and thoroughly as playing a musical instrument in public.

♪ Kato Havas, professional violinist and teacher

You and me and Pablo Casals. Everyone gets stagefright. For musicians, it's not the fear itself that's distressing—it's the way our fear disables us, as if some Bad Fairy visits each one on concert day and bestows the most aggravating symptoms possible: a trembling arm to the strings, a dry mouth to singers, clammy hands to pianists, scant wind to the winds, and a foundering memory to us all.

This is the "fight or flight" response, the body's reaction to hormones poured into the bloodstream when we're under stress. It's Nature's way of ensuring our survival in the jungle. The trouble is, Nature's plan is too drastic for our purpose. We're not going onstage to wrestle tigers but to play music.

The physical symptoms of stagefright are identical to any other state of heightened anxiety: increased heart rate, increased blood pressure, rapid breathing, a dry mouth, and an upset stomach. The blood vessels in the extremities constrict, which accounts for your cold hands and—literally—cold feet. Accompanying these standard mammalian symptoms are a host of other signals peculiar to *Homo sapiens*—the psychological symptoms: confusion, disorientation, panic, feelings of powerlessness and loneliness. There's a very real urge to run away, to cancel, to change your mind, to call in sick.

You *can* do something about stagefright, but you have to do your own thinking about it. What works for someone else will not necessarily work for you. In this chapter is a collection of tricks and techniques for coping with stagefright at three levels—physically (emergency measures), psychologically, and musically. Read these lists as you would a menu and try only those items that make sense to you.

You'll probably never get rid of stagefright completely, and you probably wouldn't want to. Skillfully channeled, an adrenaline rush can give a vibrant edge to a performance. So think of each technique here not as a cure but as a way to guide your energy.

I've got worse—terrible bad nerves all the time . . . I just can't stand sitting around, and I worry about playing badly. . . . Everybody in the band is the same, and each has some little thing they do before we go on, like pacing about or lighting a cigarette.

♪ John Bonham, drummer with Led Zeppelin

New ideas keep emerging out of my work with people who have stage fright problems. The clues that release them are different for each person, and impossible to predict in advance.

♪ Eloise Ristad, *A Soprano on Her Head*

EMERGENCY MEASURES

If you've turned to this chapter because you're playing onstage *tonight*, this is the place to start. If your performance is days or weeks away, test out these techniques in advance and find out what works best. Use them in any stressful situation—in a traffic jam, a dental chair, or an interview with your boss. All these techniques attempt to control the physical symptoms of anxiety by reducing or depleting your supply of adrenaline.

Exhale. Anxiety disrupts normal breathing patterns, producing either shallow breathing or air gulping in an attempt to conserve the body's supply of oxygen. The simplest immediate control measure is to *exhale*, blowing slowly and steadily through your lips until your lungs feel completely empty. Don't "breath deeply." It's too easy to hyperventilate and make yourself dizzy. As long as you make a slow, full exhale, the inhaling will look after itself. If you know a "calming breath" technique from yoga, meditation, or a similar practice, this is the perfect place to use it.

Do the "Sarnoff Squeeze." While she was appearing in *The King and I* on Broadway, Dorothy Sarnoff observed Yul Brynner backstage pushing a wall as if he were trying to push it over. He told her he did it to control his nervousness. She tried it, and it worked for her, too.

The wall pushing, Sarnoff discovered, contracts muscles that inhibit the production of adrenaline. She adapted the exercise for public speakers (who can't always push a wall discreetly before they go on). She describes the "Sarnoff Squeeze" in her book *Never Be Nervous Again*:

"Sit down in a straight-backed chair. Carry your rib cage high, but not so high you're in a ramrod straight military position. Incline slightly forward. Now put your hands together out in front of you, your elbows akimbo, your fingertips pointing upward, and push so that you feel an isometric opposing force in the heels of your palms and under your arms.

"Say *sssssssss*, like a hiss. As you're exhaling the *s*, contract those muscles in the vital triangle [below the ribs, where they begin to splay] as though you were rowing a boat against a current, pulling the oars back and up. . . . Relax the muscles at the end of your exhalation, then inhale gently. . . .

"While you're waiting to go on, sit with your vital triangle contracting, you lips slightly parted, releasing your breath over your lower teeth on a silent *sssss*."

Halve your anxiety. Paul Hirata of Seattle, a professional violinist and a black belt in aikido, teaches musicians a technique he calls *Half-Half-Half.* You know that you cannot simply will away your anxiety, but you could probably, by consciously relaxing, let go of *half* of it. Exhale, relax, loosen your tight muscles, and let go of half your tension, saying quietly to yourself, "Half." Immediately, very lightly and quickly, take another breath, relax a bit more, let go of half the tension that still remains, saying again, "Half." Continue relaxing and saying, "Half. Half. Half. . . ."

Confront your symptoms.   This tactic takes a bit of nerve, but everyone who tries it swears it works. When the physical symptoms begin to intensify, focus your attention on them very closely. Observe them. Study them. Hands clammy? How clammy? Is one clammier than the other? What's the clammiest part—wrist, palm, fingers? Are they warm and clammy or cold and clammy? Give your symptoms your total attention and your complete permission to happen. Eloise Ristad even tried to make her symptoms worse. "My body can only produce so much adrenaline," she said, "and when I find out exactly how much and what it will do to me, I lose some of my irrational fear of it. I don't go over the precipice after all."

When you've done a thorough job of paying attention to your symptoms, turn your focus to something else: playing through your music, getting dressed, listening to another performer. The symptoms themselves may be unchanged (though many people report they diminish dramatically), but they will no longer be snagging at the edges of your awareness, and you don't have to try to ignore them. If they build up again, just give them permission to happen again.

Laugh . . . or at least smile.   Researchers at the University of Maryland have found that watching a funny film lowers the level of stress hormones in the bloodstream. So on recital day, check out some video comedies or read a funny novel. This technique will not help you backstage (though you can still keep your sense of humor), but it could ease you through the day if you're the sort who wakes up on the morning of the concert with a full-blown case of nerves.

Anxiety affects levels of muscle tension all over the body, and this is nowhere more obvious than in the face. Smiling disrupts this pattern of tension and can actually redirect your emotional state somewhat. You don't need a wide grin—a gentle, soft smile will do, or even just a pleasant expression.

Take a pill?   Propranolol is one of a group of drugs, called *beta-blockers*, used to treat high blood pressure, heart conditions,

The man I take lessons from has a recital every year. I had my lesson the night before, and I came without my cello. "Bob," I said, "I'm not here to play. I'm here to talk." I just told him I couldn't do it, and that was that. He was very nice. He said, "That's okay. You don't have to if you don't want to. Come and listen to everybody else, and bring your cello if you feel like it."

So I did. The lady who was on before me had the shakiest arm. I felt so sorry for her. And I decided that if she could do it, I could. So I said, "Bob, I think I'll play after all," and he said, "Fine." I sailed through it.

♪ Lucy Melzack, special education teacher and amateur cellist

and migraine. Sold under the trade name *Inderal,* this compound and several similar ones work by competing with stress hormones for receptor sites. They have been found extremely effective in subduing stagefright. Performers who use beta-blockers report that they still feel nervous, but it doesn't affect their performance—that is, no dry mouth, constricted chest, or wobbly knees.

In the last few years beta-blockers have become the street drug of the musical world, in fairly common use among professionals and even some amateurs. Presently their use for controlling stagefright is not strictly legal, since they are approved by governmental regulations only for hypertension, heart problems, migraine, and similar medical conditions. However, many musicians take propranolol anyway for a "legal" condition, and others unwisely "borrow" it from cooperative friends or relatives.

A common attitude among medical personnel who have investigated propranolol for stagefright is that the drug is appropriate for short-term relief in cases where the performance anxiety is so debilitating that a career is jeopardized, but that it is a temporary measure and should be supplemented by nondrug therapies while the propranolol is gradually withdrawn.

"Borrowing" a beta-blocker from another person's prescription is hazardous. The side effects on otherwise healthy individuals are not completely known. Some users report unpleasant physical sensations and a kind of distant and detached feeling. (It would seem reasonable that a drug that blocks undesirable physical signals may also block desirable ones as well—that is, it may interfere with the performer's physical responses to his or her own music.) Although other side effects are uncommon, they can be serious, especially in the presence of diabetes, asthma, or unusually low blood pressure. *Propranolol and similar drugs should be used only under medical supervision.*

PSYCHOLOGICAL APPROACHES

We react with anxiety when we perceive danger. Where is the danger in a musical performance? Every musician answers this a little differently, and in a candid answer lie the clues for self-treatment. We may fear memory failure or that our technique is unreliable under stress or that we won't meet our own standards or that the audience will ridicule us or that we'll let down our teacher or our friends or that we'll be revealed as a charlatan. Tobias Matthay, a great piano pedagogue of the early 1900s, considered fear of failure to be pure selfishness, putting our own reputation and aggrandizement ahead of the music itself. In a more affirming attitude, contemporary teachers often point out the positive value of fear—how it measures your depth of caring, your hopes, your desires, your sense of responsibility.

If you are anticipating a performance, two constructive steps you can take in advance are, first, to analyze your own pattern of anxiety in order to plan an appropriate coping strategy, and second, to lower your overall level of stress. If your life is already filled with worry and tension, the stress of a performance may well be the proverbial last straw. Lowering your daily level of stress will help to some extent in controlling your stagefright.

Here is another menu of stress-reducing strategies, this time in the psychological realm. First analyze your needs (fears of musical inadequacy will be treated on page 269), and then select any methods here that seem appropriate.

The Inner Game

W. Timothy Gallwey coined the phrase "inner game" to describe the way our inner experience affects our outer performance. He spoke first to athletes in *The Inner Game of Tennis* and *Inner Skiing.* Later, Barry Green, principal bassist with the Cincinnati Symphony, collaborated with Gallwey and wrote *The Inner Game of Music.* The Inner Game seeks to block self-critical, judgmental, berating attitudes by focusing your awareness on your immediate experience: What do you hear? What do you see? What does it feel like? With your attention gathered in this way, you silence the voice in your head that shouts at you, "Look out!" and "What if?" and "You can't."

Inner Game techniques—and there are endless variations —reduce performance anxiety by getting your attention out of your head and into your body and your music. Although specific techniques could be considered "emergency measures," the Inner Game is not really a cure for stagefright per se. It's a process and an attitude, and it will be most effective on concert day if it's been part of your routine practice. You can incorporate as much or as little as you want. It can't do you any harm, and the techniques are unlikely to conflict with anything your teacher might tell you. If Green's book seems too prescriptive, Eloise Ristad's *A Soprano on Her Head* is a freewheeling and anecdotal approach to similar ideas.

Personal Growth Techniques and Therapies

The current mind/body and growth/therapy landscape is ripe with methods that can be applied to performance anxiety with good results, especially where there's a history of debilitating stagefright. Musicians have reported success with hypnosis, yoga, meditation, t'ai chi, rebalancing, biofeedback, and visualization, among others. Concert flutist Robert Aitken learned self-hypnosis from a medical hypnotist: "It is a very useful thing. . . . I think many of the great musicians always used it, maybe without knowing it. It can be used for very specific uses—even speeding up a trill." He confines his practice of self-hypnosis to these "specific uses," however, and doesn't perform in a hypnotic trance. "I tried it," he says, "and found that I wasn't really there, and therefore it wasn't successful."

One great advantage of many of these approaches is that they benefit all of the practitioner's life, not just musical performance, and therefore result in an advantageous lowering of overall stress.

A reliable favorite among musicians is Alexander Technique—a system of body alignment and balance developed by F. Matthias Alexander. The method uses simple exercises learned in a student-teacher setting to promote efficient use of the body and to reduce overall tension. Alexander Technique instructors usually work with clients on an individual basis. Look in the phone book white pages under Alexander Technique.

Blocking Negative Thoughts

Our minds can drive our bodies crazy. Eavesdrop on your own conversations and internal monologues to see if recurring negative thoughts are fueling your anxiety: "I'm going to mess up, I

I was treated for stagefright on a stage, in front of fifty people. The therapist was a Neurolinguistic Programming (NLP) practitioner, doing a demonstration for a group of students. The improvement was immediate and it has lasted. On a scale of 10, my nervousness has gone from a paralyzing 9.9 to an acceptably anxious 3, though I still have to work at it. I learned from that session that the audience is not coming to take anything from me—I am giving them something, of my own free will.

♪ Stephanie Judy

know it. I just can't get those high notes." Since we can't think two thoughts simultaneously, it's possible to block a negative thought with a neutral or positive one.

A *mantra* is one kind of thought pattern you can use to block negative thoughts. Often taught in conjunction with a meditation technique, a mantra is a word or short phrase that is simply repeated quietly, over and over, aloud or in thought. *Peace* can be a mantra, as well as *one* or *love*. *Om* and *Shanti* are Sanskrit mantras. The former is a universal word of affirmation or assent; the latter might be translated as, "The peace that passeth understanding." If you are religious, you can adopt a short prayer or the name of a saint or holy figure as a mantra. Used over time, in any situation when the mind is "free to roam," a mantra builds a kind of quiet, confident peacefulness.

A personal affirmation is another way to block a negative thought. The most powerful kind of affirmation takes the anxious thought itself and transforms it. "I'm going to lose control in the scherzo" can become "I can handle the scherzo." An affirmation can be repeated like a mantra, written down twenty times a day, posted on a mirror, or put onto a cassette tape. It doesn't matter if you don't believe it. It matters only that your affirmation be positive, in the present tense, and specific to your situation. "I won't miss the high note" is a weak affirmation. It's better to say, "The high note is clear and ringing." Telling yourself, "I will play in tune," is placing your action forever in the future. If you want to play in tune *now*, tell yourself, "I play in tune."

Avoiding Avoidance

Some musicians seek to control their anxiety by resisting any thought or any behavior that reminds them of the upcoming event. This sometimes, unfortunately, results in poor preparation as serious practice is postponed and practical activities such as marking the date on the calendar and getting gas for the car are neglected. The unhappy result is often an excruciating level of panic at the very last minute, which simply reinforces the behavior.

If you recognize this pattern, make a date with yourself to start worrying. According to psychologist and amateur violinist Paul Lehrer, "Worrying about things in advance may help re-

Imagine the worst that could happen.

duce anxiety about them when they occur." This doesn't mean to pay constant and obsessive attention to your fear. That, too, would increase your ultimate anxiety. But it's healthy to acknowledge your fear, to let it point you to action and sensitize you to musical values and practical behaviors. Have a mental rehearsal of the entire event to pinpoint things that could go wrong—in either musical or practical terms—and begin to plan your coping strategies. What if you forget to take your music? How could you prevent that? What if you break a string? What can you do about that possibility now? What if you start off playing too fast? What would you do then?

Constructive Catastrophizing

This technique, in a way, is the reverse of the previous one. It's meant for the "What if?" artists, those of us who worry relentlessly about all the really terrible things that could go wrong. Psychologists call this behavior *catastrophizing*, and it can be put to surprisingly good use in anxiety control if you're willing to be a little silly.

Make a date with yourself to do some constructive catastrophizing. Don't do a lot of it—just enough to get a good strong result once or twice and have a good laugh at yourself. Imagine the very worst thing that could happen . . . and then keep asking, "What then?" You'll play wrong notes? What then? The audience will think you're stupid. What then? You'll blush. What then? The audience will laugh at you. What then? You'll cry. What then? They'll hate you forever. What then? You'll have to change your name and move to New Zealand. What then? And so forth, until your worst-case scenario becomes absurd.

At some point during your constructive catastrophizing, you might remember seeing someone who actually went through what you're fearing. Did you ever hear anyone play wrong notes? How did the audience really react? Did you ever see anyone panic so completely that he or she utterly fell apart or froze onstage and couldn't perform at all? What did the audience do? Usually everyone's heart goes out to this person who is living through their own worst fears.

Amateur violinist Debra Tompkins had a chance to find out firsthand what her audience was *really* thinking:

When I played in the student recital, I was absolutely petrified. A lot of it was all the adults in the audience—other parents and people I knew. I kept imagining what they were thinking. "What is she doing this for? What is she trying to prove?" I had the idea that people would think I was crazy, especially to choose the violin, of all things.

Afterwards, when people came up to me, do you know what they said? They said, "I wish that had been me up there."

MUSICAL PREPARATION

The most significant musical preparation you can make is to expand your hearing, your understanding, and your attitude to encompass *all the aspects of music, and not just "the right notes."* Often we are so fearful of making a mistake that we neglect to appreciate all the other things that we do well and that make music a sublime art. A mistake played with a beautiful tone in a well-shaped line is just as musical—more musical, really—than an accurate handful of dead notes.

In Part Three of this book, you found the idea that "how we practice is how we play." This is never more true than at a performance. The aspects of music making that have been in your awareness, the techniques that you have been able to make automatic, the benevolent genies that you have invited in— these will stand by you. But aspects that have been left to look after themselves—fingering, perhaps, or maybe intonation or breath control or phrasing—will offer up a foothold to your brand of nerves. Your final performance begins at your first practice.

Practice with Awareness

Conscientious practice will not ward off stagefright, but it will almost certainly prevent a downright bad performance. If you practice well, you will be able to say with President Roosevelt that "the only thing we have to fear is fear itself."

Consider the alternative. If you don't practice, you may have every reason to be afraid. When you are indecisive about fingering, hazy about tempo, unsure when to come in, "any mistake

The pianist is in trouble who believes that only perfection can represent quality.

♪ Dale Reubart, *Anxiety and Musical Performance*

No psychological technique can substitute for proper artistic preparation.

♪ Paul Lehrer

Working hard at practice is also the best defense I know against pre-concert nervousness, which can never be entirely eliminated but can be psychologically prepared for by convincing oneself that one has done all the homework necessary for a solid performance and everything will work out all right.

♪ Vladimir Ashkenazy

can begin a landslide—one thing leads to another, you lose concentration, and pretty soon you're fighting just to maintain sanity." (That's from the flute-playing experience of Al Zalon, an ad agency art director in New Rochelle, New York.)

As part of your practice, try the technique called *mapping* explained on pages 178–186. You can use it even with a piece you already know; it's not just a learning technique. Through the experience of mapping, you develop the confidence to stay with the music, even if the exact notes escape you momentarily.

Rehearse

When the performance is a week or ten days away, it's time to bridge the mental gap between practicing and performing. (If there's a footwear gap, cross that one now, too. If you usually practice in flat shoes, and your concert garb includes heels, rehearse accordingly.) Here are four specific rehearsal techniques:

1. Play your program "cold" at least once a day. Just after you get up, or when the kids leave for school, play your music through with minimal warm-up. If you have a problem, don't stop to fix it. Just observe it calmly and nonjudgmentally. If you find consistent trouble spots or memory lapses, work on those during your regular practice time.

2. Arrange some "dry runs" that simulate, as nearly as possible, the performance milieu. Do at least one of these alone and at least one in front of a small audience (neighbors, musical colleagues, or friends who owe you a favor). Set the performance for a specific time and put on your concert clothes. Teacher and concert pianist Seymour Bernstein has a charming personal routine for his dry runs, described in his book *With Your Own Two Hands.* He begins by inviting his "fantasy audience,"

> all those respected and admired figures who have contributed so much to my musical life. Their imagined presence can in itself induce nervousness in me, my desire to please them being that great. Instantly, my studio becomes a concert hall. I then repair "offstage," to the kitchen, my "artists' room" for

the occasion, where I wait for a signal to walk "on stage." I bow to the "audience" and sit quietly at the piano listening for a hush to descend on the "house." The moment has come, I tell myself—*one chance only* to play through the works that have taken months to master. That thought is enough to make my breathing difficult. Sit erect, I command myself; rest your hands easily in your lap. Now, place your feet on the pedals and ground your heels to the floor. Breathe deeply and, for goodness' sake, stop clenching your jaw! Move your shoulders and head just a little to get rid of tension. Concentrate now on the first note—let it sound in your mind. With this flash of familiarity, the transition from silence to sound is eased. My fingers reach for the keys and as my mind focuses on each passing phrase, I hear in retrospect exactly what I would if I were myself a member of my fantasy audience.

If you can gather a small and sympathetic audience who will sit through your program more than once, you have a matchless opportunity to defuse your stagefright. Veteran performers agree that nervousness decreases with repeated performances *of the same piece.* At work, no doubt, is the same principle that sends a horseback rider into the saddle again after a spill or a diver back to the board after a belly flop. The first time through, let yourself be distracted by nervousness. If your program is short, play it, exit, enter again right away, and play once more, and you will almost certainly find that the worst of your anxiety has spent itself and that your consciousness is now available to the music. Performance workshops are an ideal setting for this experiment. If your program is too long for this treatment, try to arrange "two shows," perhaps a matinee and an evening.

3. If possible, rehearse at least once in the hall where you will perform. When you rehearse in the hall, the purpose is not to get used to the acoustics. Playing in an empty hall is completely misleading in this respect. It's simply so that you get used to the space, used to walking from backstage to the performing area, used to the height of the stage, the distance from the audience, the general feel of the place. Dr. Frank Wilson, amateur pianist and author of *Tone Deaf and All Thumbs*? missed the run-through that was scheduled before his student recital:

I had a real insight this spring. We did the St. John Passion—this was the second time I'd played it—and we rehearsed the heck out of it. We rehearsed almost every day for several weeks. I was so immersed in that music and so well rehearsed that I loved the performance. It was such a high for me and I thought, this is what it feels like to be confident and to really get a kick out of what you do.

A week later, a friend asked me to play some diddly-squat stuff for a choir concert. I came in at the last minute—no rehearsals—and it was terrible. It went so badly and I was so nervous and embarrassed. I thought, this is a lesson to me. I really need to rehearse in order to feel confident.

♪ Joann Alexander, arts administrator and amateur cellist

Arrange a dry run in front of a small audience.

I walked onto a stage which was formally set and found myself illuminated by a spotlight. This arrangement had a startling impact on my feelings about the occasion, since it signaled the recital to be considerably more stately and important than I had imagined it would be. . . .

When I did sit down at the piano, which was a nine-foot grand (I had never sat at the keyboard of such an enormous instrument before), it seemed to me that I was at the controls of a locomotive, a machine completely beyond my comprehension and highly unlikely to submit to my directions. At that moment my mind went blank, and I have absolutely no recall of anything that happened from that moment on while I was onstage. . . . Later I learned that some of the more sophisticated listeners had recognized what I was supposed to play.

4. If you are using an accompanist, rehearse until YOU are satisfied. It's not enough for the accompanist to feel at ease. You're the one in the spotlight. During your rehearsals, work out your procedure for setting the tempo. Be clear about which repeats you will take. Decide how to arrange yourselves so that you have unobstructed eye contact. Ask for anything that will help you play your best, and be sure the accompanist marks the part with your requests.

Know Your Music

When you learn to play the notes, you acquire muscular knowledge—an essential kind of knowing, but fragile in the face of adrenaline overload. Knowing the piece on other, nonmuscular levels makes it likelier that you'll stay in contact even at a stressful moment. You will not let go easily of something that is really yours. Explore, as part of your practice, every relevant approach:

The analytical approach. Understand, in your own terms, the harmonic and melodic design and the overall structure. You don't need years of music theory to do this. Make your own observations, put things in your own words, apply the mapping technique. Nothing anyone tells you will stick nearly as well as what you discover for yourself.

The historical approach. Read a good book about the composer or the style. Find out where your music fits in musical life in general.

The emotional approach. Let the music speak to you. Know it "by heart"—not in an overdramatic way but so that it resonates with feelings familiar to you. Experiment. Play the piece wistfully, charmingly, impatiently. Be silly. Be bored. Be sorrowful. Don't "settle in" on this level, but keep the channel open in both directions—you affect the music, and the music affects you.

The narrative approach. Not every piece of music "tells a story," but if you're the sort of person who thinks easily in images, feel free to invent your own private bit of cinema or choreography. Titles often suggest storylines: *Ballade, Nocturne, Fantasia.* If structural analysis of music leaves you cold, or if it's not part of your vocabulary, a little story can lead you safely through a memorized piece, especially one that has repeats, variations, or—the ultimate test of nerves—a rondo.

And what if you're a beginner and your recital piece is "Donkey Riding" or "London Bridge"? The fact is, folk songs and nursery tunes are fine music, but we have to let go of our "adultism" to see that sometimes. Find your way into "Donkey Riding" through the heart and ears and enthusiasm of a child. Learn the words. Sing them in the shower. Let yourself be pleased. It's like the old Shaker song—" 'Tis the gift to be simple, 'tis the gift to be free." You don't have to go at "Yankee Doodle" with high passion and overbaked theatrics, but intelligence and joy are always appropriate. (Don't overlook the historical here, either. Lots of nursery lore is another generation's thinly veiled political discontent.)

ADVANCE PLANNING: A CHECKLIST OF PRACTICAL MEASURES

A week or two in advance, look after the practical details so you eliminate unnecessary sources of panic:

1. Double-check the time, date, and address of the con-

273

I looked down at my feet and realized I was in big trouble. I'd been wearing white athletic socks with my running shoes and hadn't brought any black socks with me. That's a disaster! I play my bass on a high stool at the very edge of the stage, and my whiter than white socks would be extremely visible. . . .

I burst through the double doors and noticed a closed toolbox next to the boilers. My inner feelings told me to open the box—and voilà, eureka, and lo and behold: three-inch black duct tape.

As I heard the orchestra tuning to the A, I taped my ankles, ran to the stage entrance, walked casually onstage, and took my place in the nick of time.

♪ Barry Green, *The Inner Game of Music*

cert. Find out when you're expected to be there, calculate your travel time, and plan accordingly.

2. Arrange for babysitters and transportation. Phone ahead for weekend or evening schedules for your bus, train, or subway.

3. Check over your instrument carefully. Clean it, polish it, and fix anything needing attention. Replace dead or fraying strings. Check your own sound equipment—pickup, cables, and connections.

4. Check your extra supplies—strings, reeds, picks—and replenish anything that's low. Make up a musical first-aid kit with tape, glue, scissors, clothespins (for keeping music on a stand in a draft), needle and thread, pencil, eraser—anything that might be handy to you or to your colleagues in a pinch.

5. Make a list of everything—*everything*—that you have to take with you. Then post it where you'll see it on your way out the door. If you have a pre- or postconcert clothing change, include on your list *every single item* you'll need. Don't forget your music stand, glasses, shoes, socks, necktie, undergarments, deodorant, hairpins, and makeup.

6. Collect your concert clothes, including shoes, and try everything on. Choose your clothes with an eye to comfort and confidence. Fashion is nice, but secondary. If you feel good, you'll look good.

PERFORMANCE DAY: FINAL STRATEGIES

Five simple steps will help to make your performance day go smoothly:

1. Keep this day as clear as possible. Rest, eat, exercise, and practice when you need to. No one else's regime will be exactly right for you. Avoid, if you can, anyone who will undermine you. ("What's the big deal? It's just a stupid little violin recital.") But if you have allies, welcome their support and be willing to let them help you.

2. Eat lightly. Anxiety interrupts the body's digestive functions. A steak or a big dish of pasta could give you a lump in your stomach to go with the one in your throat. Minimize your sugar intake, but stick to your customary level of caffeine. Avoid fats—butter, mayonnaise, sauces, dips, fatty meats, chocolate—since they'll make your digestion even more sluggish. If the concert schedule means an unusually long time between meals, take along a light snack. A low-fat protein, eaten by itself, will tend to energize you and sharpen your responses—try cold chicken or shrimp or low-fat cottage cheese, yogurt, or milk. Carbohydrates alone (without fats) are calming—crackers, plain toast, a muffin, some dry cereal. (For more detailed eating strategies, see *Managing Your Mind and Mood Through Food*, by Judith Wurtman.)

3. Don't fight your anxiety. You don't have to cover it up, repress it, apologize, or feel guilty. Some of your nervousness is pure excitement. (Do you remember how you felt when you were a kid just before the guests arrived for your birthday party? Fluttery stomach? Wobbly knees? Breathless? That's excitement—the physical symptoms are identical to preconcert nerves.)

When you become aware of your own constellation of symptoms gaining hold—they might accumulate hours ahead of time, or they might not hit until you hear the applause for the person before you—go to work on any emergency measures that you have in your repertoire. (See pages 261–263.)

4. While you wait your turn backstage. . . . Remember to exhale. Release tension with loose, gentle movements. Short-circuit some of the effects of adrenaline by aligning your body—bend your knees very slightly, open your chest, lengthen your spine. Feel, from the waist down, grounded and solid, and from the waist up, buoyant and released.

If you can play without being heard, and you think it will calm you, go over entrances and rough passages but a little under tempo and very lightly. Don't push—be easy. If you're taking music on stage, check, just once, that it's organized—pieces in the right order, pages right-side up.

5. Enjoy your talismans and superstitions. Ignace Paderewski always wore the same socks to every performance, and

*M*y husband doesn't play an instrument, but he supports me because he knows it's important to me. He's always there at my recitals. He's not critical. He's only there to hope that I will do my best. He checks off each performer as they play. Otherwise, I wouldn't know when to go up. He just says, "It's your turn. Go." I walk up feeling as if my legs won't carry me. But I know that Peter is there, just for me.

♪ Anna Hamel, teacher and amateur pianist

I never eat anything before a performance because I believe that every fiber of your body has to serve the performance and you cannot burden your stomach by making your digestive juices work. If you do, you function too much in the stomach and not enough in the spirit and the brain.

♪ Lili Kraus

Luciano Pavarotti will not go on until he's found a bent nail on the floor backstage.

YOU'RE ON!

Your entrance onto the stage contributes a surprising amount to your overall composure. If you don't actually *feel* confident and glad as you walk on, then just pretend. The effect is basically the same. Your nervousness shows much, much less than you think it does. You'll eventually evolve an entrance routine that suits your personality. Here's an example from Andrea Bodo, a nurse in Boston, an amateur pianist, and a veteran performer who appears frequently with chamber ensembles:

"When I walk out, I acknowledge the audience in some way. I look around a little bit and notice who's there. I want to thank people with my expression. I'm so glad that they're willing to come and listen.

"Then I focus on the piano. I look at the eighty-eight keys like smiling teeth. The piano is my friend. It's my ally. I always touch the piano as I sit down. Then I look at the other players so we all relax together and have eye contact.

"And then there's that moment when I'm sitting out there, and I just let everything float away. I have an image that I'm on a pool with water lilies. I think of myself in a Monet painting. I do it very quickly, but I do it.

"Then I start to think of the tune, and I try to think of it a little bit slower, because the adrenaline is always going. I just allow myself that extra minute to pull everything together, to look relaxed, to savor the moment."

If you trace Andrea Bodo's process, you can pick out five steps that bring her to a confident performance:

1. Acknowledge your audience.
2. Make contact with your instrument.
3. Make contact with the other musicians.
4. Think of a calming image.
5. Think about the music.

The last step here is especially important if your piece is very short. In a long program, anxiety tends to diminish naturally,

I used to take my pulse rate just before a concert out of scientific curiosity, and it was always very fast. So there was obviously a kind of unnatural excitement. But it wasn't the sort that paralyzed me with fear.

♪ Glenn Gould

I'm nervous my first five or ten minutes. My hands are clammy and shaky and my adrenaline is way up. But after that I love it.

♪ Leslie Sonder, geophysicist and amateur violist

There are no heroes a moment before a recital.

♪ Gregor Piatigorsky

Sometimes when I come on stage I find myself saying "Hello" under my breath as I bow. It may seem silly and ridiculous, but that's how I feel.

♪ André Watts

but if you're to occupy the stage only briefly, there's no time for preperformance nerves to fade while you play. When you take a moment to hear the opening phrase in your head—when you let the music begin before you play—then it's as if you open a door and the audience follows you through it.

. . . AND YOU'RE PLAYING

Guiding Your Consciousness as You Play

Once you begin to play, you give up the striving and the fears. The time to calm yourself down or psych yourself up has passed. Your only task is to be present, where music happens. If your mind reels back, cursing a mistake you just made, or strains forward, dreading the next rough passage, you leave the *now* up to chance. If you've practiced well, the odds are in your favor, but even so, you lose the vitality of the moment.

This is easy to say, but how does it translate into action? What do you really *do* when the music starts? How do you sustain concentration while you play? What do you think about? Where do you put your awareness and your intention?

Part of what you do has already been conditioned by what you have done before—by the way you have practiced and rehearsed, by the way you have thought about yourself and your music. Under the stress of performance, your basic, ingrained habits will spring up to serve you (or undermine you) and everything else will fall away. This does not normally mean that you will play like an automaton, although that happens. Many musicians have had the experience of "blanking out," of playing (usually accurately) but having no recollection later that they did so. Among inexperienced performers the best explanation seems to be uncontrolled panic, although seasoned professionals sometimes "blank out" as well.

The goal—and it's a hard one—is to stay in contact, to be aware and to be with the music—not with the audience, or your anxiety, or your self-judgments.

For a listener the performance drives the ear, but for the musician the ear must drive the performance. Your first level of awareness—the very base of your awareness—is in listening to the music. Your entire self comes to dwell at that point where

Make contact with your instrument.

M*aurice Chevalier once told me:* "You must start very well, finish very well and in the middle it's nobody's business." *But me, I try to do the business in the middle, too.*

♪ Stéphane Grappelli

E*very so often a strange thing happens when I sing. I do a song, but I am not conscious of it. After we leave the stage, I ask my musicians,* "Did I sing such-and-such a song?"

"Oh, yes," *they tell me. But I have no memory of it.*

♪ Miriam Makeba,
Makeba: My Story

277

the music happens, and it is a place that has no room for ego. Not self, but sound.

In his book *Anxiety and Musical Performance*, concert pianist and teacher Dale Reubart identifies two appropriate focal points for a performer's attention: musical values and musical gestalt. By *musical values*, he means the "auditory experience," the sound itself—its mood, its texture, its quality. *Musical gestalt* he explains as the here-and-now location in the whole musical structure—where you are on the map. Inappropriate focal points, according to Reubart, are detail—what we might call the submusical components of performance such as fingering, intonation, counting, and note names.

In compiling his book, Reubart asked distinguished performers what they concentrated on during their *best* performances. Anton Kuerti replied that his best playing happened when his mind was free of detail:

> I like to imagine the music as being alive during the performance, as displaying a will of its own, so that the precise lengths of notes, the relative dynamics and tensions and shapes are creating themselves at the instant they are heard, rather than being churned out in a preordained way. . . .
>
> I will try to think, during a difficult passage, not of the individual notes or motions, but of the effect I want from the entire passage; if there is a difficult leap, I think of the sound of the notes I am leaping to, not of the location or any mechanical detail; in fact I leap to the sound, not the spot, *I imagine the result, not the cause.*

A Leash on Your Awareness

Excessive anxiety precludes well-focused attention; poorly focused attention may result in uncontrollable anxiety.

♪ Dale Reubart, *Anxiety and Musical Performance*

Even the best-trained hound does better in a distracting environment if it's on a leash. If you experience the performing milieu as full of distractions or if anxiety competes too successfully with the music for your attention, that's all right. Centering your awareness is a learning process. You will get better at it. In the meantime it can help to choose ahead of time some braking techniques in the event that your attention begins to run away:

1. Direct your attention to something physical. Feel the shape of the mouthpiece against your lips, the texture of the keys under your fingers, the amount of air between your sides and your elbows. Where in your body can you feel vibrations? Where can you feel pressure and where weightlessness? If you start to give yourself orders—"Sustain those half notes"—speak to your senses instead—"Listen to the long tones."

2. Use imagery as you play, if it helps you. If you have an image or a narrative developed for your music, bring that to mind. Or you can apply imagery to the environment. Instead of a hall full of concertgoers, transform the setting into a wooded hillside or a grand ballroom or a New Orleans street festival. Most players who use "environmental imagery" of this sort agree that it works by far the best if the image complements the music. Imagining that the audience is naked or that their heads are rows of cabbages—"tricks" that some of us have been encouraged to use—adds extraneous and irrelevant ideas through which the music still has to speak.

3. Find things to enjoy in the performance. Rather than dreading the hard parts, anticipate the good parts. If you love the melody you're playing, you're entitled to love it in performance. Anticipate that lush chord. Look forward to the surprise tempo change. Richard Wagner's advice is to "experience first with the heart and then allow the brain to control the performance."

4. Listen with special care to the phrase endings. Let each phrase be a thread that draws your awareness along to the very end.

5. Listen to your instrument. Instruments and voices vary from day to day, depending on weather, acoustics, and how they've been played lately. Feel your instrument's strengths and play to them. Think of playing *with* and not *on* your instrument. Instrumentalists who have to use unfamiliar instruments—pianists, organists, and percussionists—can move even more deeply into using the performance as a way of "meeting" this new instrument. There is indeed an enormous challenge in playing well on a strange instrument—like doing something very intense with a complete stranger.

I get into trouble if I think about the next rough passage. If I do that, I miss it every time. You have to be prepared for it but you don't think about it. There's a fine line between knowing it's coming and thinking about it ahead of time.

♪ Don Mitchell, biologist and amateur violinist

When a difficult passage is coming, I take a deep breath and I get closer to the keys and embrace the piano, because the piano will help me. I try to get closer to the core of what I'm doing.

♪ Andrea Bodo, nurse and amateur pianist

6. Don't send your mind ahead to meet the hard parts. Keep a sense of proportion about the sticky bits in your music. They most likely account for only a few seconds of time in a much longer context. It's natural to feel fearful, but that natural reaction is almost certain to work against you. If you're afraid of an approaching passage, and your attempts to stay in contact with the moment are ineffective, then block your negative thoughts with something like a mantra or an affirmation—even something as simple as "Easy does it" or "I'm doing fine."

7. Let go of your errors. Maybe you'll make some mistakes. More about that in the next section, but most errors can just wash over you and be forgotten. Keep your ear and your mind on the present moment.

8. Don't think too much about your own personal responsibility. Music simply is, without regard for who plays it or how well. When you play or practice or perform, you are dipping into an inexhaustible reservoir of energy and intention. You have the power to add to it, but you cannot detract from it, no matter how you play. Arnold Steinhardt, first violinist of the Guarneri Quartet, says, "If we're well enough prepared instrumentally and open to the experience, we are, in a very true sense, only vessels through which the music passes; we have to acknowledge a force greater than ourselves."

Usually the things I've really worked on seem to go all right in a concert, but I often make some other mistake I've never made before in a rehearsal. I miscount some phrase or flub some easy thing.

♪ Jim Whipple, lawyer and amateur French horn player

THE ULTIMATE STRATEGY

Keep smiling, enjoy yourself, and—are you ready to hear this?—play with abandon. Artur Schnabel used to tell his students, "Safety last." The balance between care and abandon is fragile, but when you find it, your adrenaline will give you an edge, a special depth. Before her first solo performance, violist Lyn Rodger, a potter from Harvard, Massachusetts, had to force herself to walk out on stage and not run away. "But when I stood up to play," she says, "I felt like Alice in Wonderland stepping through the looking glass, only I was stepping through the music, and something wonderful happened."

Finally, through it all, remember your purpose. Stay in touch with *why* you're making music. In *The Inner Game of Music,*

Barry Green relates the words of a French horn player who got off to a bad start in a concert:

> I was a nervous wreck. I asked myself why I was feeling like such a jerk, and what the point of it all was. And then I began to think about music, and remembered why I had become a musician in the first place. I began to listen to the grand sweep of the music, and by the time my next entrance came around, I knew why I loved Brahms so much. I played with all the feeling and skill I'm capable of—and it was marvelous.

In your own darkest moments, take a global view of your situation. In the scope of geological time, what you're doing doesn't really matter very much in one way. Yet in another way you're handing out exactly the kind of energy and love that keeps this whole show on the road. We can't order it up in bulk. It has to come, impulse by impulse, from people like you.

WHEN THINGS GO WRONG

All musicians who perform accumulate a pocketful of it-wasn't-funny-at-the-time stories, which most of them can laugh at and enjoy later. You might as well know now that things *will* go wrong. Soloists leave out bars, gusts of wind scatter parts across the audience, music stands collapse, essential players show up late, nervous players come in early, strings break, keys stick, and electricity fails.

Everyone who was at the CAMMAC Music Camp at Lake MacDonald, Quebec, in July of 1988 remembers the lights going out in the middle of the Mozart *Requiem.* The choir had just sung "Et lux perpetua." The orchestra continued bravely on for another bar or two, the chorus for two or three more, but finally the whole crew gave up. That's an example of what we'll call a "Type 3" problem—a show stopper. We can arbitrarily think of three kinds of problems, classified by how the musicians cope:

Type 1 is the fluff, the small mistake. It might be a wrong note, a lost beat quickly recovered, a mistimed entrance, a phrase of mangled lyrics, a mute clattering to the floor, or a conductor's baton sailing into the percussion section—any little

I always lose a little confidence when I get out onstage. I suppose it's because I'm such a sensitive and emotional person. It's very hard for me to give a great performance; I tend to freeze up. But, at the same time, I think it is that quality that helps me get a lot of feeling. I can always play with feeling, and only my technique is hampered when I freeze up. I make mistakes.

♪ Chet Atkins, *Country Gentleman*

thing that can be passed over easily. Which is exactly what to do. Go on and forget it. Don't make a wry face or shake your head or look mournfully at the audience. As in rehearsal, never turn and look at a player who's made a mistake unless you're offering assistance. Stay inside the music and carry on. In many instances the audience will not notice the problem. If they do—well, they're people, too, and have all made their share of mistakes.

Sometimes one member of an ensemble gets lost, forgets a repeat, plays the wrong line, has the wrong music up. The rest of the ensemble should carry on and trust the lost sheep to catch up. If you're sitting nearby, you can offer assistance. A whispered "One, two, three," might help locate the beat. Some note names or chord names, if they're not going by too fast, can help: "E7 . . . low A . . . A7 . . . hold the D . . . here's G." Or you can prepare for a rehearsal letter: "Four bars to C . . . three . . . two . . . one . . . C." If you've rehearsed well, not stopping for every mistake but giving everyone practice in jumping back in, it's nearly always possible to stick things together again on the fly.

Jean-Pierre Rampal tells a wonderful "Type 1" story in his autobiography, *Music, My Love.* He was giving a solo recital at Ravinia with his accompanist, John Steele Ritter. The stage—open at one end with the audience on the lawn—was suddenly invaded by a swarm of large insects. Halfway through the final movement of a sonata, as Rampal remembers,

John suddenly found himself playing solo. He looked up to find out what had happened to me. I had opened my mouth to take a breath, and one of the enormous insects had flown into it. I could barely breathe, let alone play. But, as they say, the show must go on. Very stoically and with what I felt was considerable courage, I swallowed my insect and rejoined John some ten measures later.

Type 2 is the slightly bigger problem—the one that calls for a brief pause and a gracious recovery. The soloist who draws a total blank can quietly walk over to the accompanist, point out a starting place, and stroll back to center stage. The ensemble that comes completely unstuck—perhaps because several members are lost—can stop, agree quickly on a starting place, and

I make mistakes—I make mistakes on the bandstand, and the guys crack up. When I make a booboo I make a loud one, but that's the fun in playing music. You learn.

♪ Art Blakey

Years ago, during the middle of a recital at Boston's Jordan Hall, the British tenor Sir Peter Pears had a memory lapse in the middle of a little Haydn sailor's song. He stopped, threw his head back and mockingly pounded it with his fist, then smiled and sauntered over to his nonplussed accompanist, Murray Perahia. With his hands on Perahia's shoulders for support, Pears leaned over and read from the pianist's score—to the absolute delight of his audience.

♪ Anthony Tommasini

carry on. A drastically slipped peg on a stringed or fretted instrument is cause to stop and retune. Any musician or group who makes a false start can just stop, pause a moment, and begin again. It happens often with a conductor who is swept up in a concerto and starts the orchestra off—usually on a second or third movement—before the soloist is ready. Sometimes a quiet "Excuse me" or a reassuring smile to the audience feels right, especially if the pause is more than a few seconds. They will be sharing your distress.

When you begin again, you'll have to make a very quick decision about where to start. If you've had a memory lapse, you can go back to a "station" as described on page 156. If the pause is only a second or two, you can probably pick up where you left off. But the longer the break, the farther back you need to go. If you must completely stop to readjust your instrument or reassemble your music, it's best to go back to the beginning or to the start of a major section. The most important thing is to stay relaxed and calm and realize, as vulnerable as you feel, that the audience is sympathetic and won't mind waiting. Anna Hamel, of Toronto, Canada, remembers her first piano recital as an adult student:

The person before me was playing Chopin, too, and as I listened, I said to myself, "Don't get this one in your head. You're next." But as this piece went on, I couldn't help listening. I felt as if I were being sucked right into it.

When that piece was finished, sure enough—I didn't have my own music in my head any more. I had that other Chopin. But I thought, "Don't be stupid. You know your piece backwards and forwards. You know where the first chord is. When you hear the first chord, you'll be away." So I walked up to the front, sat down at the piano, played the first chord . . . and there was nothing there. And I thought, "You poor people in the audience. You will be in agony for me, but you're not leaving until I play my piece! If I have to sit here for five minutes, I'll sit here, because I'm going to play this."

So I sat there, and I played the chord again, and I still had nothing. I played several chords. I just went around the piano playing chords. It never occurred to me to ask for my music. I just played chords until I hit one that got the thing going, and it was in the second or third bar. I didn't even start at the

It's not important how other people feel about your playing. It's how you feel. I have changed my thinking. I don't think about the audience—how they're going to react to me and what's going to happen. I don't try to really prove anything. I want to go out there and share my passion, my love for music. I want to play as musically as possible. The correct notes are secondary. Yes, it would be wonderful to do both, but I think it is more important to play beautifully than to go out there and play all technically correct.

♪ Andrea Bodo, nurse and amateur pianist

283

beginning! As soon as I played a bar or two, I remember thinking, "I've got it. Peter (he's my husband), it's all right, you can relax, I've got it. Richard (he was my teacher), don't have a fit, I've got it. You're all right. I'm all right. Everybody's all right."

And then I completely forgot about everyone and I just *played*. When I was done, I gave a great big grin because I thought it was so funny. A man came up to me afterwards—he was walking out the door, and he turned around and came back to me, and he said, "I just wanted to tell you that you did play beautifully." And I said, "You mean after I got started I played beautifully." And he said, "No, I don't. I mean you played beautifully."

Type 3 is the show-stopper. This is the kind of problem that makes it literally impossible to carry on, at least for the moment: the soloist taken suddenly ill, the stack of music left at home, the totally unplayable instrument, the blackout that shuts down amps, the key to the piano lid that can't be located. In the great tradition of show business, the show should go on, perhaps by substituting something else, until, if at all possible, the problem is remedied. No matter what happens, stay calm and supportive. No matter how another musician plays or behaves, keep your head. Once again, the audience will be on your side. If the problem is apparent before the concert begins and can be fixed in a reasonable length of time, it's OK to make an announcement that the program will be delayed a few minutes.

Coping with the problem is one thing. Coping with your feelings about it is another. The key, as hard as it is to apply, is *never look back.* Tying your awareness to an error you've already made robs the present moment. If you go out there realizing that errors are possible and the music will go on in spite of them, you are already miles ahead. In *A Soprano on Her Head,* Eloise Ristad talks about the amount of "plain old hard work" that leads up to a good performance. "Somewhere along with the hard work," she says, "must be the permission to blow it. With that permission we can afford to be a little more reckless in what we dare. As we become more reckless, we also become more committed, for we know we are stretching ourselves."

That battle against fear and shame is never completely or finally won; it will always take some will power, some courage, to perform before others, and that is part of the excitement and pleasure.

♪ John Holt, *Never Too Late*

When a performance takes flight I feel as if all four personalities meet somewhere in the air—maybe two and a half feet above the quartet.

♪ Arnold Steinhardt, first violinist, Guarneri Quartet

284

Your feelings during a performance can run a grand gamut
—from anxiety to exhilaration to embarrassment to elation—
and all within the same performance or even the same piece!
For every breakdown, there will also be some rapture, those as-
tonishingly gathered moments when you fly.

♪♪ Postlude

Nowhere on that scale of "no fun" to "fun" can I find any of the emotions that I feel when I am working with my cello. These range from arduous effort to intense concentration, great frustration and exasperation to something that can only be called exaltation. There are feelings so deep that one can barely play the music. You can't use the word fun to describe that range of feelings.

♪ John Holt, *Learning All the Time*

When I interviewed amateurs for this book, I asked very different questions of different people. I naturally wasn't seeking the same kind of information from adult beginners and from those who had played since childhood, from soloists and from ensemble players, from those who took lessons and from those who taught themselves. But one question I did ask everyone: What would your life be like without music? This is, of course, an indirect way of asking, "Why?" Why do you make music?

This question almost never failed to touch something heartfelt, something earnest, something that spoke with an eloquent voice. No amateur musician that I interviewed plays music to pass the time of day, to while away idle hours, to have fun, or to amuse themselves or anyone else. Those things may happen in the course of music making, but that is not why.

Anna Hamel went back to music at the age of forty-five, in the midst of a busy life in Toronto with her husband and three teenage sons:

286

In my "former life"—before I went back to making music—I was a very stable, steady, plodding kind of person, doing for everyone else whatever I could to support them. And then suddenly, I had this thing which made me demanding because it made demands on me that nothing has ever made before.

People would say to me, "Gosh, it must be relaxing for you. It must be lovely for you to sit down at the piano and play." But it wasn't relaxing at all! It was amazing and incredible, and it was hell at the same time. I wasn't doing it as relaxation. So I began thinking, Why am I doing this? What is keeping me going? And I found it was a compulsion to play, to reflect what I suddenly discovered I had inside. I desperately wanted to produce a little of what I had found within me.

Just as music draws out Anna Hamel's strength and artistic energy, so it also draws Lynelle Inwood toward those gifts in others. Inwood lives in rural British Columbia where she is a quiet but constant advocate of people making music together. Even with a new baby in arms, she continues to seek, to form, and—when necessary—to mend amateur ensembles, keeping music alive in her community:

> I play music for that heart-to-heart communication that happens when you play together. It's so deep and so intimate. I can't think of too many other ways that you can experience that closeness. You're not using ordinary ways of communication, and so it draws you in and puts you in touch with the whole spirit. If I didn't have music, I'd look for another way to find that.

Leonard Marsh's professional reputation was built as a social scientist. In his case I think it's fair to talk about his "amateur reputation" as well, which grew from his tireless devotion to chamber music and good string playing. I was never privileged to meet him (how I wish I'd had the chance to attend a musical evening at his house!), but he left for all of us to enjoy an open-hearted little book called *At Home with Music*:

> [M]usic has been the source of unbounded solace to me in a difficult world, the source of ever-expanding, easily-made,

Music gives voice to feelings floating around within me. Making music allows these feelings to resonate, to be audible and tangible. Soft pieces, slow pieces, romantic pieces, fiery pieces—making that music is the most direct way I know of to be in touch with those parts of myself.

♪ Daniel Fredgant, college
English teacher and amateur
guitar player

well-tended and reciprocated friendships, an avocation which has continually opened up new branches of interest and enjoyment and enthusiasm. It wears well: it was fun when I was young; it is even more solidly satisfying in my middle years as I add layers of experience to what I hear, new and old; it will, I know, sustain me buoyantly if I am lucky enough to attain old age. . . . To be as much at home with music as I have gradually found myself becoming is to be a very full man, and a very grateful man.

Many amateurs spoke about the refreshing, revitalizing aspect of music. It's possible to discuss business on the golf course, mull over family problems in the garden, or carry on an argument as you cook or carve or knit, but when you make music, you only make music. It demands your whole body and your whole mind and often reaches out to claim your whole spirit, too. As one amateur put it, "Music is like doin' the Hokey-Pokey—you put your whole self in." One of England's famous amateurs, former prime minister Edward Heath, reported that not only he benefited from his musical interludes but his staff did, too: "Whenever they could hear the Steinway at No. 10, they all heaved a sigh of relief, knowing that for a brief time at least the demands made upon them would slacken."

Music draws us into the present moment because it exists only in the present moment. When we can let go, not only of our outside cares but even of our very resistance to the music itself, we sometimes find ourselves suddenly opened, in the midst of what is called a "peak experience" or a "flow state," a place of no ego, no anxiety, no preoccupation with technique, no judgments, and no expectations. As amateurs we have every right to treasure—never to belittle or disparage—our own triumphs, our own moments of musical ecstasy. They are real, however modest their source.

I remember one of my own musical "flow states," which happened during the final concert at a summer music camp. First I have to confess how much I sometimes admire and sometimes loathe my friends who jog, run marathons, lift weights, swim laps, "go for the burn." I thought I couldn't do that. I couldn't push my body that way. I always gave up at the first sign of discomfort, even though I felt like a lout.

The purpose of art is the gradual, lifelong construction of a state of wonder and serenity.

♪ Glenn Gould

I redeemed myself, in my own eyes anyway, during this particular concert. We were playing Mendelssohn's *Octet* for strings. It is a long, difficult piece of music, and it came at the end of a long program on a muggy day in July. I was drenched—my fingers were sticking to the fingerboard and my shirt was sticking to my back. My shoulder was throbbing, I had a terrible cramp in my thumb, and I was exhausted.

And then we started the final movement, the Presto, too fast. I felt a rush of panic and then exhilaration. We all did. We looked up at each other and this jolt, this tangible current, swept through all eight of us. The look on everyone's face said, "Go for it!"

Suddenly, I just broke through the pain, the sweat, the fatigue. I flew through that movement, making my entrances somehow, pulling those notes out of somewhere in long ribbons of sound, and at one point I realized—*this is it. This* is what *I* do.

One of the things we hunger for in life is the experience of crossing boundaries, and many musicians recognize music as a vehicle for that journey. Virtually every culture has recognized it, too, as a link to the spiritual realm. Few religious rites or significant rituals, anywhere in the world, anywhere in time, have not included singing, playing, drumming, chanting, or dance. Ralph Vaughan Williams talks of the power of music to "open the magic casements and enable us to understand what is beyond the appearances of life."

Of all the responses amateurs gave to my question of "Why?" by far the largest number mentioned this spiritual face of music. And it was not only in a transcendent sense that spiritual values were apparent but also in the dailiness of music, the commitment, the routine that becomes ritual. From Heather Swope, a college student and amateur pianist:

> The religious dilettante goes to services once a week to hear someone preach, but the person who's "got religion" gets in there every day and *prays.* You don't expect to be a saint, but if religion means anything, it's because it's something you do yourself, every day. Music is like that for me. I don't expect to be Rubinstein or Horowitz. But if music means anything to me, it's because I do it myself.

M*y general outlook about spiritual things has changed through the years, but music has remained at the center of it.*

♪ Linda Hecker, teacher and amateur violinist

289

No art lover can be an agnostic when the chips are down. If you love music, you are a believer.

♪ Leonard Bernstein,
The Joy of Music

Even the difficulties of music, the slow and patient approach it requires, connect us to the spiritual realm. Eric Stumacher, professional pianist, thoughtful teacher of adults, and executive coordinator of the Apple Hill Center for Chamber Music, considers his own students:

> I think what people are after is a sense of ceremony and an awareness of the spiritual side of human beings, a way of connecting themselves to things that are somehow outside the world. Generally, old kinds of religions have some kind of gradual course of study and a process of becoming. And that's exactly what music is all about.

More than one amateur pointed out the significant contribution that music can make to world peace and to understanding between people. As a means of communication beyond words, as a means of reaching across centuries and continents to bring the fullness of humanity into the present moment, it is hard to find a better channel than music.

Music, to me, is the highest of the arts; and art, along with religion, is the way in which people express the best that is in them. Expressing the best that is in us brings a spiritual reward more potent and more permanent than worldly goods.

♪ Sydney J. Harris

Music as discovery, as communication, as renewal, as ecstasy, as liturgy, as initiation, as a celebration of the best in ourselves—we come to music open-hearted, and our hearts are filled.

It hasn't been possible in this book to say everything that could be said about amateur music making. However, as Canadian writer R. D. Cumming said, a good book has no ending. The rest is up to you. If you go on making music for the joy of it, then this book has been good enough.

Teaching a Not-Yet-Singer to Match Pitches

To the learner: If you would like to overcome "tone deafness" and learn to sing, find a helper who fits the description given on page 292 and make an appointment to begin. Plan on about three half-hour sessions in some private place—your home, your helper's home, a music studio, a church or synagogue music room, or a classroom. If you have a piano available, that will be an advantage, but it's not necessary. It will also be easiest if men find a male helper and women find a female helper, so that you and your helper are singing in the same range. Your helper could be a music teacher, a music student, a choir director, an amateur or professional singer or instrumentalist, or any other musically confident person who's interested in helping you become a musician, too.

You might be feeling a little self-conscious. The process of learning to match pitches and learning to sing may involve doing some things that make you feel silly or inhibited. Have a sense of humor about this and push your way past it in any way you can. If your helper has had any musical training, he or she will understand what you're going through. Every new skill we learn feels awkward at first. This will pass.

If you're not sure whether you have any natural musical ability, please read pages 3–6 in this book. The method outlined below was developed by Dale Topp of the Calvin College Department of Music and according to him, "It is demonstrable that everyone who can make talking sounds can also learn to sing."

If you're interested in working on your own, or if you want some additional ideas about pitch-matching and singing technique, singer Penny Nichols has a videotape, *Singing for "Tin Ears,"* available from Homespun Tapes, at the address given on page 304.

Good luck! Enjoy singing!

To the helper: Given below is a method for helping a not-yet-singer learn to match pitches and to begin singing for enjoyment. You do not have to be a voice teacher or a highly accomplished musician to be the helper in this process. You do need to be able to sing in tune yourself, and it would be useful to know something about intervals and scale construction. It's a little easier to demonstrate the process on a piano, but it's not essential. It would also help if you know a little about voice production, especially about the difference between chest tones and head tones. Again, you can get started without this, and you or your not-yet-singer can seek further help later. This process will work best if you are the same sex as the not-yet-singer so that you are matching tones in the same octave. But if you have a piano to demonstrate with, you can work around this one, too.

The single most important qualification for the helper is a willingness to be supportive—never impatient or judgmental. You must be genuinely reassuring, positive, loving, and ready to accept and acknowledge the smallest effort and the smallest step forward with sincere enthusiasm. You must create an environment of total safety, and you must honestly believe that the not-yet-singer is able to sing.

Most not-yet-singers "break through the barrier," as Dale Topp puts it, in about three half-hour sessions, and many do it much faster. It is not unusual to undo years of "tone deafness" in five or ten minutes. However, you should plan to work at a relaxed, unpressured pace, allowing for at least three sessions over a span of one or two weeks.

PROCEDURE FOR TEACHING PITCH-MATCHING SKILLS

Preparation

Before each session, spend a few minutes chatting together. Respond to the not-yet-singer's reservations or self-consciousness with accepting reassurance. (Do you remember your own music learning experiences? You probably felt nervous and inhibited some of the time, too.) Begin the session with some brief physical and vocal warm-ups. Physical warm-ups can include easy stretching, shoulder shrugging, and gentle neck rolls to loosen the muscles in the chest and throat. Do three kinds of vocal warm-ups for three different purposes:

1. Help the not-yet-singer feel comfortable making non-speech sounds. Start with nonvocalized sounds—hisses, clicks, pops, huffing, sighing—asking the person to copy you. Be light and humorous about this. Go on to vocalized sounds—grunts, roars, squeaks, bleats, and so forth. Barnyard sounds are perfect. An especially useful imitation to introduce here is a "cuckoo clock."

2. Show the not-yet-singer how to "siren." Imitate a siren on the vowel *oo*, starting as low as possible, progressing up smoothly to the highest possible range, and sirening back down. Accompany the sirens with hand motions demonstrating low to high. Use the siren to be sure the not-yet-singer comprehends "high-low" and "up-down" in musical terms. Some not-yet-singers understandably confuse pitch with volume, since we normally say things such as, "Turn the radio up" or "Lower the sound." (On her videotape *Singing for "Tin Ears,"* singer Penny Nichols teaches the siren with hand motions from side to side, emphasizing tonal movement without creating anxiety about high notes. If you prefer this approach, you can use barnyard sounds to explain range—a chick makes a high sound, and a bull makes a low sound.)

3. Get the not-yet-singer to make nasal sounds. Wrinkle up your nose and do the old schoolyard taunt—*nyah, nyah-nyah, nyah nyah.* Talk through your nose. Whine. Pinch your nose

293

closed and talk in a high voice. Then let go of your nose but keep talking with the same nasal quality. This bit of silliness is to help the not-yet-singer experience the sensation of nasal and head tones, which will be used near the end of the pitch-matching process.

Go through these warm-ups quickly and lightly. They should take only a few minutes and will give you some opportunities to relax and laugh a bit.

To Teach Pitch-Matching

The steps outlined below are based on a method developed by Dale Topp and are given here with his kind permission. The process has six steps:

1. Ask the not-yet-singer to sing one tone, any tone. (If he cannot do this, ask him to say a word and stretch out the vowel —*to-da-a-a-a-ay* or *slee-e-e-e-eep*.) Match his pitch on the piano or with your own voice. Explain that these pitches match, that they are the same. Reinforce this idea with a physical gesture, such as pressing your palms together or intertwining your fingers. Move your own pitch—by voice or piano—away from the selected pitch and then back again until it matches. Explain in words and show with hand gestures that the pitches now match (hands together), now don't match (hands apart), and now match again (hands together).

Spend a little time singing your matching pitches together if the learner is willing. Support this with the piano if you have one, especially if you are singing in a different octave. Gently reinforce the sensation of singing matched pitches.

If you are matching the pitch with your own voice, and if the learner seems confused or insists that your pitch and his are not the same, try matching your *voice quality* to his. Sing at about the same volume as the learner and eliminate any vibrato from your own voice. Some not-yet-singers confuse differences in pitch with other musical qualities. You might want to explain that every voice has its own unique characteristics that aren't affected by pitch. (As one new singer put it, "Voices are like faces—they're all different.") You could demonstrate how pitch can stay the same while other qualities change—soft, loud, breathy, clear, with and without vibrato, tone in chest, throat, nose, and head.

2. Ask the singer to move to a new pitch. (She has already produced one musical tone, so we can call her a singer now.) Say something like, "You move your voice to a new place, and I'll find it." You're only looking for a small change here. A semitone is fine. Accept any tone produced, and praise the singer's effort. Find this tone and compare it to the pitch in Step 1 by labeling it "higher," "lower," or "the same." (If you haven't already done so during a warm-up, you might need to explain the convention for labeling frequencies as "high" and "low." You can demonstrate with your own voice or on the piano.) Continue this sort of matching a few more times until the singer's voice has moved through an interval of about a third. You might need to help this along by suggesting, very gently, to "sing a bit higher this time" or "sing a bit lower." Once again, spend enough time here to reinforce the sensation of singing matched pitches.

3. Ask the singer to match a pitch that you produce. Choose one within the range that the singer has already offered. If the singer's match is not accurate, move quickly and with no concern to the pitch he produces. If it seems appropriate, you might mention that the singer's pitch was "a little low" or "a little high." Toronto piano teacher Margaret Grant talks about "focusing" the voice like a camera—an image that may be helpful at this point. Keep working gently at this until the singer can match your pitches most of the time. Go at a leisurely pace, reinforcing new sensations with a little repetition.

4. Introduce a fragment of a song in the range the singer prefers. Match the opening pitch carefully and then ask the singer to sing the song fragment back to you. A song that begins with a descending minor third is the most natural to sing. (This is when the "cuckoo" imitation during the warm-up comes in handy.) The first phrase of "This Old Man, He Had One" is a good choice. "Rain, Rain, Go Away," "Pease Porridge Hot," or simply the person's name or "Hello" sung on a descending mi-

nor third will also work. Be sure the singer has the starting pitch confidently matched before she begins singing.

5. When the singer can produce a song fragment on a descending minor third in tune, begin moving the starting pitch of the fragment up the scale. Going up by semitones, begin on progressively higher and higher notes. (Rarely will a not-yet-singer offer pitches in Steps 1 and 2 that are in too high a range. They are almost universally very low—out of the individual's best vocal range and fully in the chest register.) The singer may need much encouragement, guidance, and support to extend into a higher range. Your goal here is to help the singer produce head tones—to open up the entire vocal range, including the clear head register.

If the singer reaches a point where the voice cracks and he is uncertain about going further, you can try several things:

- If the singer is not inhibited, press him to go on "even if it squeaks."
- Ask the singer to imitate a great opera star hitting his or her high note.
- Siren up and down, as far in each direction as you both can go, accompanying this by sweeping hand gestures. Then ask the singer to hold the top note of the siren.
- If the singer's tone seems "stuck in the throat," ask for softer, lighter sound. Try an oo vowel on a soft "cuckoo" call. Suggest that he "sing through his eyes."
- Sing the minor third interval on a nonsense syllable that begins with the letter *m* or *n*—*nee nee nee* or *ma ma ma*— singing completely through the nose. Remind the singer of the nasal warm-ups if you did those. Although a highly nasal sound is not the desired end product, a nasal tone will automatically push the voice into the head.
- Ask the singer to put his fingers on his face and skull to feel the vibrations as he sings.

During your quest for head tones, continue to respect the singer's personal limits—she may still be feeling very self-conscious. However, if you have any leverage at all, this is the place to push. With good humor and loving support, use any tactic you can think of to push the singer into the head range. When you get the first clear head tone, react to this accomplishment as if, according to Dale Topp, you had just discovered gold in your backyard.

6. When the singer has a feel for head tones, return to Steps 1, 2, and 3 and match pitches in the new range. When the singer can do this fairly reliably, congratulations to both of you! You can welcome a new singer to the musical community.

When you and your colleague finish Step 6, talk over what to do next. Most new singers need continued nurturing and encouragement. Seek an opportunity that will keep the newfound skills alive in a nonthreatening environment. As Dale Topp says, "If bad singing experiences can cause such personal harm, think what affirmation of the human spirit can be achieved by good singing experiences!"

Some new singers may be eager and able to participate in a vocal group right away, especially standing next to a strong singer. Others might find a group, especially a part-singing ensemble, confusing. These singers will prefer to gain confidence from some gentle one-to-one singing experiences. Simple rounds are a good introduction to part-singing. Some new singers—especially those who are uncomfortable with their own voice quality—might be interested in taking a few lessons from a warm, supportive voice teacher. For new singers working alone, you might recommend Penny Nichols's audiotape series, *Basic Vocal Technique*, available from Homespun Tapes.

Resources for Amateur Musicians

This list includes books, organizations, magazines, accessories, mail-order sources, and other products of special interest to amateur musicians. Given the many fine publications and products on the market, it is impossible to put together a comprehensive and up-to-date list of resources. The items here are examples of "best buys" for the adult amateur.

BOOKS AND RECORDINGS

A Basic Bookshelf

Bamberger, Carl, ed. *The Conductor's Art*. New York: McGraw-Hill, 1965.

Benade, Arthur H. *Horns, Strings, and Harmony*. Science Study Series. Garden City: Anchor Books, 1960.

Brodnitz, Friedrich S. *Keep Your Voice Healthy*. Boston: College-Hill, 1988.

Dunn, Thomas. *How to Shake the Money Tree: Creative Fund Raising for Today's Non-Profit Organizations*. New York: Penguin, 1988.

Green, Barry, and W. Timothy Gallwey. *The Inner Game of Music*. Garden City: Doubleday, 1986.

Hewitt, Graham. *How to Sing*. New York: Taplinger, 1978.

Holt, John. *Never Too Late: My Musical Life Story*. New York: Delta/Seymour Lawrence, 1978.

Kagen, Sergius. *On Studying Singing*. New York: Dover, 1950.

Linklater, Kristin. *Freeing the Natural Voice*. New York: Drama Book Specialists, 1976.

Menuhin, Yehudi, ed. *Yehudi Menuhin Music Guides*—a series of books by outstanding instrumentalists with basic information on history, repertoire, technique, and instrument maintenance. Titles include *Cello,* by William Pleeth (1983); *Clarinet,* by Jack Brymer (1977); *Flute,* by James Galway (1983); *Horn,* by Barry Tuckwell (1983); *Piano,* by Louis Kentner (1976); and *Violin and Viola,* by Yehudi Menuhin and William Primrose (1976) (all New York: Schirmer).

Randel, Don Michael, comp. *Harvard Concise Dictionary of Music*. Cambridge, MA: Belknap, 1978.

Ristad, Eloise. *A Soprano on Her Head: Right-Side-Up Reflections on Life and Other Performances*. Moab, UT: Real People, 1982.

Shockley, Rebecca. *A Practical Guide to Mapping: The New Way to Learn Music*. White Plains, NY: Pro-Am Music Resources, 1990.

Suzanne, Claudia; Thomas Stein; and Michael Niehaus. *For Musicians Only*. New York: Billboard, 1988.

Toff, Nancy. *The Flute Book*. New York: Scribner's, 1985.

Van Horn, James. *The Community Orchestra: A Handbook for Conductors, Managers, and Boards*. Westport: Greenwood, 1979.

Vaughan Williams, Ralph. *The Making of Music*. Ithaca: Cornell University Press, 1965.

Wilson, Frank R. *Tone Deaf and All Thumbs? An Invitation to Music-Making for Late Bloomers and Non-Prodigies*. New York: Viking, 1986.

Wollitz, Kenneth. *The Recorder Book*. New York: Knopf, 1982.

Music Reading, Ear Training, Theory, and Composition

Abrams, Daniel. *Understanding the Language of Music: A Beginner's Guide to Music History, Theory, and Structure*. Audiotape. Homespun Tapes, 1988. (See address under "Mail-Order Sources.")

Burge, David. *Perfect Pitch Ear Training Course*. Audiotape. American Educational Music Publications, Music Resources Building, Fairfield, IA 52556, 1983.

Clough, John, and Joyce Conley. *Scales, Intervals, Keys, Triads, Rhythm, and Meter*. New York: Norton, 1983. A programmed course in basic theory, followed by *Basic Harmonic Progressions* by the same authors.

Glaser, Matt. *Ear Training for Instrumentalists.* Audiotape. Woodstock, NY: Homespun Tapes, 1984.

Harder, Paul O. *Basic Materials in Music Theory.* Boston: Allyn and Bacon, 1977. A programmed course in basic theory followed by two other volumes by the same author—*Harmonic Materials in Tonal Music, Part One and Part Two.*

Piston, Walter. *Harmony.* New York: Norton, 1969.

Russo, William. *Composing Music: A New Approach.* Chicago: University of Chicago Press, 1983.

Shanet, Howard. *Learn to Read Music.* New York: Simon & Schuster, 1956.

Zucherkandl, Victor. *The Sense of Music.* Princeton: Princeton University Press, 1959.

Improvisation

Aebersold, Jamey. Various recordings and instructional books available comprising a self-teaching improvisation method for any instrument; mainly jazz, blues, and rock styles. Available in music stores or from Jamey Aebersold, 1211 Aebersold Drive, New Albany, IN 47150.

Bailey, Derek. *Musical Improvisation: Its Nature and Practice in Music.* Englewood Cliffs: Prentice-Hall, 1980.

Chase, Mildred Portnoy. *Improvisation: Music from the Inside Out.* Berkeley: Creative Arts, 1988.

Nachmanovitch, Stephen. *Free Play: Improvisation in Life and Art.* Los Angeles: Jeremy P. Tarcher, Inc., 1990.

Performance and Stagefright

Craig, David. *On Singing Onstage.* New York: Schirmer, 1978.

Reubart, Dale. *Anxiety and Musical Performance: On Playing the Piano from Memory.* New York: Da Capo Press, 1985.

ORGANIZATIONS AND PERIODICALS

Amateur Chamber Music Players, Inc., 545 Eighth Ave., New York, NY 10018 —Maintains a directory of members listed by instrument and skill level.

American Symphony Orchestra League, 777 74th Street. NW, Washington, DC 20005.

Amateur Organists and Keyboard Association International, 6436 Penn Avenue So., Minneapolis, MN 55423—Primarily for electronic and chord organ players; publishes *Hurdy Gurdy.*

American Recorder Society, 13 East 16th Street, New York, NY 10003—Publishes *American Recorder.*

American String Teachers Association, UGA Station Box 2066, Athens, GA 30612—Although this is primarily a professional teachers association, the ASTA sponsors numerous string playing workshops around the United States each year, which nearly always include activities for adult players, including those at the beginning level.

CAMMAC (Canadian Amateur Musicians/Musiciens amateurs du Canada), P.O. Box 353, Westmount, PQ H3Z 2T5.

Cello News, Carey Cheney, ed., 5001 Holston Drive, Knoxville, TN 37914.

Chamber Music America, 545 Eighth Avenue, New York, NY 10018—Publishes the *Directory of Summer Chamber Music Workshops, Schools, and Festivals,* which includes some jazz, contemporary, and electronic events as well as classical.

Clavier, 200 Northfield Road, Northfield, IL 60093—For pianists and organists.

Flute Talk, 1418 Lake Street, Evanston, IL 60201.

Guitar Review, 40 West 25th St., New York, NY 10010—A quarterly for classical guitarists.

International Clarinet Society/ClariNetwork International, P.O. Box 450622, Atlanta, GA 30345-0622—Publishes *The Clarinet.*

International Double Reed Society, Lowry Riggins, Executive Secretary-Treasurer, 626 Lakeshore Drive, Monroe, LA 71203-4032—Publishes *The Double Reed.*

International Horn Society, c/o Ellen Powley, 2220 North 1400 E., Provo, UT 84604—Publishes *Horn Call.*

International Society of Bassists, School of Music, Regenstein Hall, Northwestern University, Evanston, IL 60208—Publishes *ISB Magazine.*

International Trombone Association and Journal, c/o Vern Kagarice, School of Music, University of North Texas, Denton, TX 76203.

International Trumpet Guild, School of Music, Florida State University, Tallahassee, FL 32306-2098—Publishes *ITG Journal.*

Keyboard, GPI Corporation, 20085 Stevens Creek, Cupertino, CA 95014.

Keys: Piano Music Magazine, 200 Northfield Road, Northfield, IL 60093—For adult beginning to intermediate pianists.

Music for the Love of It, 67 Parkside Drive, Berkeley, CA 94705—A newsletter for amateur musicians; mainly classical and small ensemble styles.

301

Piano Quarterly, Box 815, Wilmington, VT 05363.

The Piano Stylist and Jazz Workshop, 352 Evelyn St., Paramus, NJ 07652.

Saxophone Journal, P.O. Box 206, Medfield, MA 02052.

Society for the Preservation of Barber Shop Quartet Singing in America (SPBSQSA), 6315 3rd Avenue, Kenosha, WI 53140-5199—Men's vocal organization; publishes *The Harmonizer.*

Suzuki Association of the Americas, P.O. Box 354, Muscatine, IA 52761-0345—Promotes Suzuki Method of music instruction; publishes *American Suzuki Journal.*

Sweet Adelines, 5334 East 46th Street, Tulsa, OK 74135—Women's vocal organizations specializing in four-part barbershop harmony; publishes *The Pitch Pipe.*

Tubists Universal Brotherhood Association and Journal, c/o David Lewis, School of Music, University of North Carolina at Greensboro, Greensboro, NC 27412-0001.

The Violoncello Society, Inc., 340 West 55th Street/5D, New York, NY 10019.

West Coast Amateur Musicians, c/o Jack Downs, 943 Clements Ave., North Vancouver, B.C. V7R 2K8.

ACCESSORIES

Ed's Cases, Box 743, Norristown, PA 19404-0743—Huge selection of cases, standard combination cases, and accessories at discount prices.

Gamble Hinged Music Co., 312 Wabash Ave., Chicago, IL 60604—Storage boxes for sheet music.

Music Book Covers, Charisma Enterprises, P.O. Box 702, Holmdel, NJ 07733—Heavy, flexible plastic covers sized to fit standard editions of classical and popular music.

Music Study Recorder by Marantz (available by mail from Homespun Tapes, Shar Products, and Workshop Records)—A variable-pitch tape recorder (you can tune the recorder to match your instrument) with a half-speed playback feature.

Olathe Instrument, 13260 Lakeshore Drive, Olathe, KS 66061—Makes Woodwind Carry-Alls—soft-sided shoulder bags to carry standard combinations of woodwinds plus music and accessories.

Reunion Blues, 2525-16th Street, San Francisco, CA 94103—Soft cases with shoulder straps for brass, woodwinds, percussion, synthesizers, low strings, and fretted strings, including many standard combination cases.

Teachers Discount Music, P.O. 390T, New Market, VA 22844—Metronomes at discount prices.

Tempo Tutor, Electronic Innovation Corporation, 3301 Aldwyche Drive, Austin, TX 78704—Program in any rhythmic sequence of up to forty notes, select a speed, and Tempo Tutor beeps out the rhythm. If you are puzzled by dotted notes, ties, and subdivided beats, this could be a valuable gadget; battery operated; also works as a regular metronome and electronic tuner.

RESOURCES FOR FAMILY AND COMMUNITY MUSIC MAKING

Glazer, Tom. *Tom Glazer's Treasury of Songs for Children*. Garden City: Doubleday, 1964.

Heritage Music Press Publications, The Lorenz Corporation, 501 East Third St., P.O. Box 802, Dayton, OH 45401-0802—Publishes a series of patriotic, sacred, and Christmas music arranged for *any combination of instruments*. For example, if you have a French horn, a guitar, a tenor sax, two flutes, and a viola (or any other unmanageable combination), you can play Christmas carols together! Available in music stores or by mail from Lorenz.

Marxner, Marcy and Cathy Fink. *Making and Playing Homemade Instruments*. Videotape. Homespun Tapes, 1989. (See address under "Mail-Order Sources.")

Rhythm Band Inc., P.O. Box 126, Fort Worth, TX 76101—Rhythm instruments and simple melody instruments such as resonator bells, recorders, flutophones, and ukuleles.

Rise Up Singing, Sing Out, P.O. Box 5253, Bethlehem, PA 18015—Probably the best lyrics-only songbook ever published.

Seeger, Ruth Crawford. *American Folk Songs for Children*. New York: Doubleday, 1948.

Traditional Rounds, Canons, and Harmonies by the Incredible Luminous Universal Musical Family (New Moon Records, P.O. Box 203, Joshua Tree, CA 92252)—The perfect sing-along tape for family car trips; a collection of rounds sung by the Lester family—Mom, Dad, and *five boys*! Other tapes available from the same source demonstrate spontaneous homestyle family music making: *The Incredible Luminous Universal Musical Family* and *My School*.

Wilder, Alec and William Engvick. *Lullabies and Night Songs*. Illus. Maurice Sendak. New York: Harper, 1965.

World Around Songs, Inc., 5790 Highway 80 S., Burnsville, NC 28714—Some of the best and lowest-priced songbooks anywhere. Good family titles include *Very Favorites of the Very Young, Bright Morning Stars, Songs to Sing and Sing Again,* and *101 Rounds for Singing.* They also have international songbooks—songs from Hawaii, South and Central America, Germany, Denmark, Guiana, Czechoslovakia, India, Japan, and many more.

303

MAIL-ORDER SOURCES

Most of these places publish a catalog. Some have a nominal charge for their catalogs, and some of the really big outfits listed here have more than one kind of catalog. Give them some idea of what you're looking for so they'll know what to send you.

Boston Music Company, 116 Boylston Street, Boston, MA 02116—A total mail order source for musicians; music from virtually any domestic or foreign publisher, as well as instruments, accessories, metronomes, calendars, stationery, gifts, and toys.

DCI Music Video, 541 Avenue of the Americas, New York, NY 10011—Instructional videos by outstanding performers in rock, jazz, blues, funk, and Latin styles.

The Drum/Keyboard/Guitar Shop, 5626 Southwest Freeway, Houston, TX 77057—No catalog; it's all done by phone. Get more information and place orders by calling 1-800-624-2347.

Duane Shinn's Keyboard Workshop, Box 700, Medford, OR 97501—Over 500 self-teaching tapes aimed at very specific keyboard skills; to sample the wares, phone (503) 664-6751 at any hour for a three-minute taped piano lesson.

Greg Baker Publications, P.O. Box 12230, Portland, OR 97212-0230—Publishes *The Fiddle Series* by Greg Baker, a set of eight self-instruction book and tape sets on fiddling.

Heartleaf, Box 40, Slocan Park, BC V0G 2E0—Books, music, and tapes for amateurs, children, families, and teachers in the performing arts.

Homespun Tapes, Box 694, Woodstock, NY, 12498—Outstanding self-instruction audio- and videotapes for keyboards, voice, and folk/blues/jazz instruments and styles.

Joseph Wood Music Co., 148 East Main Street, Norton, MA 02766—Woodwind music and supplies.

Legacy Books, P.O. Box 494, Hatboro, PA 19040—Publications about folk traditions; music, as well as literature, dance, art, and scholarly materials.

Mandolin Bros., 629 Forest Ave., Staten Island, NY 10310-2576—Contemporary and vintage guitars, banjos, Dobros, mandolins, dulcimers, ukuleles, and accessories.

Musical Design, Inc., Box 375 Green Street, Waltham, VT 05491—A series of keyboard teaching materials for the complete beginner written by Susan Gallagher and Deborah Harte Felmeth; can be used for self-instruction or with a teacher.

The Robbie Music Company, P.O. Box 506, Wayne, NJ 07470—Complete stock of both foreign and domestic sheet music and instructional materials; specify instrument and areas of interest when requesting information.

Robert King Music Sales, 28 Main Street, North Easton, MA 02356-1499—Sheet music for brass; instructional, solo, and ensemble.

Sampson-Ayers House of Music, West 1325 First Ave., Spokane, WA 99204—Mail-order service for sheet music specializing in educational, ensemble, and standard instrumental and vocal repertoire.

Shar Products Company, 2465 South Industrial, P.O. Box 1411, Ann Arbor, MI 48106—Everything for string players, including instruments, bows, cases, strings, accessories, educational materials, and sheet music.

Southwestern Stringed Instruments, 1228 E. Prince Road, Tucson, AZ 85719—Instruments, accessories, and supplies for strings.

Sylvia Woods Harp Center, P.O. Box 29521, Los Angeles, CA 90029—Complete mail-order source for harpists, especially folk harp.

Teacher's Pet Productions Inc., P.O. Box 3783, Spokane, WA 99202-3783—Video teaching materials for keyboards including *Videano: Beginning Keyboard for Real People* by Yvonne Kovacevich.

Workshop Records, P.O. Box 49507, Austin, TX 78765—Audio- and video-tapes for folk, blues, jazz, and rock; self-instruction tapes for guitar, Dobro, banjo, mandolin, and other folk instruments; home studio recording equipment.

MISCELLANEOUS

Great Composer Calendar, Bellerophon Books, 36 Anacapa Street, Santa Barbara, CA 93101.

The Music-Lover's Birthday Book. New York: Metropolitan Museum of Art, 1987.

Sazer, Victor. *Musical Puzzles of Note,* Ofnote Publishing, P.O. Box 66760, Los Angeles, CA 90066.

Bibliography

Abrams, Daniel. *Put Your Hands on the Piano and Play! A Beginner's Guide to Piano and Musicianship.* Audiotape. Woodstock, NY: Homespun Tapes, 1988.

Ampolsk, Alan G. "An Interview with Rosalyn Tureck." *Piano Quarterly* Fall 1988: 18–25.

Atkins, Chet, and Bill Neely. *Country Gentleman.* Chicago: Regnery, 1974.

Bacon, Ernst. *Notes on the Piano.* Syracuse: Syracuse University Press, 1963.

Bailey, Derek. *Musical Improvisation: Its Nature and Practice in Music.* Englewood Cliffs, NJ: Prentice-Hall, 1980.

Bamberger, Carl, ed. *The Conductor's Art.* New York: McGraw-Hill, 1965.

Barnett, David. *Living with Music.* New York: George W. Stewart, 1944.

Barra, Donald. *The Dynamic Performance: A Performer's Guide to Musical Expression and Interpretation.* Englewood Cliffs, NJ: Prentice-Hall, 1983.

Barzun, Jacques. "The Indispensable Amateur." *Juilliard Review* 1 (1954): 19–25.

Bebeau, Muriel J. "Effects of Traditional and Simplified Methods of Rhythm-Reading Instruction." *Journal of Research in Music Education* 30 (1982): 107–119.

Bennett, Hilliard T. "An Adult Student Strikes Back." *Clavier* May-June 1989.

Ben–Tovim, Atarah, and Douglas Boyd. *The Right Instrument for Your Child.* New York: Morrow, 1985.

Bernhardt, Warren. *You Can Play Jazz Piano.* Videocassette. Woodstock, NY: Homespun Tapes, 1988.

Bernstein, Leonard. *The Joy of Music.* New York: Simon & Schuster, 1959.

Bernstein, Seymour. *With Your Own Two Hands: Self-Discovery Through Music.* New York: Schirmer, 1981.

Blum, David. *The Art of Quartet Playing: The Guarneri Quartet in Conversation with David Blum.* New York: Knopf, 1986.

Camp, Max. "Rhythmic Control and Musical Understanding." *Piano Quarterly* Summer 1988: 41–47.

Campbell, Don G. *Introduction to the Musical Brain.* St. Louis: Magnamusic–Baton, 1983.

——*Master Teacher: Nadia Boulanger.* Washington, DC: Pastoral Press, 1984.

Cannel, Ward, and Fred Marx. *How to Play the Piano Despite Years of Lessons: What Music Is and How to Make It at Home.* Paterson, NJ: Crown and Bridge, 1976.

Casals, Pablo, and Albert E. Kahn. *Joys and Sorrows: Reflections by Pablo Casals.* New York: Simon and Schuster, 1970.

Chase, Mildred Portnoy. *Improvisation: Music from the Inside Out.* Berkeley: Creative Arts, 1988.

——*Just Being at the Piano.* Berkeley: Creative Arts, 1985.

Colgrass, Ulla. "Aitken on Flute: By Popular Demand." *Music Magazine* Sept.-Oct. 1981: 6–11.

Collier, Graham. *Cleo and John: A Biography of the Dankworths.* London: Quartet Books, 1976.

Cott, Jonathan. *Forever Young.* New York: Random House/Rolling Stone, 1977.

Craig, David. *On Performing: A Handbook for Actors, Dancers, Singers on the Musical Stage.* New York: McGraw-Hill, 1987.

——*On Singing Onstage.* New York: Schirmer, 1978.

Dance, Stanley. *The World of Duke Ellington.* New York: Scribner's, 1970.

Daniels, Robin. *Conversations with Menuhin.* New York: St. Martin's Press, 1980.

Davies, John Booth. *The Psychology of Music.* London: Hutchinson, 1978.

Dennis, Allan. "The Effect of Three Methods of Supporting the Double Bass on Muscle Tension." *Journal of Research in Music Education* 32 (1984): 95–103.

Doerschuk, Bob. "Randy Newman: Dreams of the Piano Player." *Keyboard* Feb. 1989: 58ff.

Duckham, Henry. "A Conversation with Buddy de Franco." *The Clarinet* Spring 1983: 14–19.

Edwards, Ruth. *The Compleat Music Teacher.* Los Angeles: Geron–X, 1970.

Elliott, Charles A. "The Relationships among Instrumental Sight–Reading Ability and Seven Selected Predictor Variables." *Journal of Research in Music Education* 30 (1982): 5–14.

Elson, Margaret. "Breathing Life into Practicing." *Music for the Love of It* June 1988: 1–2.

Farenga, Patrick. "Pat Plays in Public." *Growing Without Schooling* 38 (1984): 22.

——"Pat Plays the Blues." *Growing Without Schooling* 37 (1984): 22–25.

——"Saxophone Lessons with John Payne." *Growing Without Schooling* 34 (1983): 17–19.

Fiore, Neil. *The Now Habit.* Los Angeles: Jeremy P. Tarcher, Inc., 1989.

Forrester, Maureen. *Maureen Forrester: Out of Character.* Toronto: McClelland and Stewart, 1986.

Freff. "Tell Me Again about the Rabbits, George." *Keyboard* Nov. 1986: 32ff.

Galway, James. *Flute.* Yehudi Menuhin Music Guides. New York: Schirmer, 1982.

Gardner, Howard. *Art, Mind, and Brain: A Cognitive Approach to Creativity.* New York: Basic Books, 1982.

Gibbons, Alicia Clair. "Music Aptitude Profile Scores in a Noninstitutionalized, Elderly Population." *Journal of Research in Music Education* 30 (1982): 23–29.

Grant, Margaret. *Your Child and the Piano: How to Enrich and Share in Your Child's Musical Experience.* Don Mills, ONT: General Publishing, 1980.

Green, Barry, and W. Timothy Gallwey. *The Inner Game of Music.* Garden City: Anchor-Doubleday, 1986.

Green, Elizabeth A. H. *The Dynamic Orchestra: Principles of Orchestral Performance for Instrumentalists, Conductors, and Audiences.* Englewood Cliffs, NJ: Prentice-Hall, 1987.

Grindea, Carol, ed. *Tensions in the Performance of Music.* London: Kahn and Averill, 1978.

Gross, Ronald. *The Lifelong Learner.* New York: Simon and Schuster, 1977.

Hanson, Peter G. *The Joy of Stress: How to Make Stress Work for You.* Islington, ONT: Hanson Stress Management Organization, 1985.

Havas, Kato. *Stage Fright.* London: Bosworth, 1973.

Heath, Edward. *Music: A Joy for Life.* London: Sidgwick and Jackson, 1976.

Hodges, Denise. "Family at the Piano." *Growing Without Schooling* 43 (1985): 23–24.

Holmes, Malcolm H. *Conducting an Amateur Orchestra.* Cambridge, MA: Harvard University Press, 1951.

Holt, John. *John Holt and Cello at Home.* Audiotape. Boston: Holt Associates, n.d.

——*Learning All the Time.* Reading, MA: Addison-Wesley, 1989.

——*Never Too Late: My Musical Life Story.* New York: Delta/Seymour Lawrence, 1978.

——"Violin Update." *Growing Without Schooling* 37 (1984): 25–26.

Hopkins, Antony. *Music All Around Me: A Personal Choice from the Literature of Music.* London: Leslie Frewin, 1967.

Kahn, Barry. "Another Teacher." *Growing Without Schooling* 16 (1980): 8–9.

Kelly–Rosenberg, Andrea. "Mom Shares Love of Music." *Growing Without Schooling* 50 (1986): 28–29.

Kenyon, Nicholas. "An Interview with Frans Brugger." *The American Recorder* Nov. 1983: 150–153.

Lange, Art. "Ornette Coleman and Pat Metheny: Songs of Innocence and Experience." *Downbeat* June 1986: 16ff.

Lehrer, Paul. "Performance Anxiety and How to Control It: A Psychologist's Perspective." *Tensions in the Performance of Music*. Ed. Carol Grindea. London: Kahn and Averill, 1978: 134–52.

London, Peter. *No More Secondhand Art: Awakening the Artist Within*. Boston: Shambhala, 1989.

McGreevy, John, ed. *Glenn Gould: By Himself and His Friends*. Toronto: Doubleday, 1983.

Mackinnon, Lilias. *Music by Heart*. London: Oxford University Press, 1938.

McPartland, Marian, and Robert J. Silverman. "The Lady Swings: A Talk with Marian McPartland." *Piano Quarterly* Spring 1988: 27–31.

Mach, Elyse. *Great Pianists Speak for Themselves*. New York: Dodd, Mead and Co., 1980.

Makeba, Miriam, and James Hall. *Makeba: My Story*. New York: New American Library, 1987.

Malitz, Nancy. "Domingo Diversifies." *Ovation* Mar. 1985: 8ff.

———"Wynton Marsalis: Crossover Trumpeter at the Crossroads." *Ovation* Oct. 1985: 10–14.

Marsh, Leonard. *At Home with Music: The Recollections and Reflections of an Unabashed Amateur*. Vancouver: Versatile Publishing, 1972.

Martin, George, ed. *Making Music: The Guide to Writing, Performing, and Recording*. London: Frederick Muller, 1983.

Matthay, Tobias. *Musical Interpretation: Its Laws and Principles*. London: John Williams, 1913.

Max, Peter, and Dominic Milano. "Peter Max: Zen and the Creative Process." *Keyboard* July 1989: 90–95.

Menuhin, Yehudi. *The Compleat Violinist: Thoughts, Exercises, Reflections of an Itinerant Violinist*. New York: Summit Books, 1986.

———*Theme and Variations*. London: Heinemann, 1972.

Miall, Antony. *Musical Bumps*. London: J. M. Dent and Sons, 1981.

Montparker, Carol. "John Rubinstein: Life with Father." *Clavier* Jan. 1987: 12–17.

Morgenstern, Sam, ed. *Composers on Music: An Anthology of Composers' Writings from Palestrina to Copland*. New York: Pantheon, 1956.

Nachmanovitch, Stephen. *Free Play: Improvisation in Life and Art*. Los Angeles: Jeremy P. Tarcher, Inc., 1990.

Newman, William S. *The Pianist's Problems: A Modern Approach to Efficient Practice and Musicianly Performance*. 3rd ed. New York: Harper and Row, 1974.

Nichols, Penny. *Singing for "Tin Ears."* Videotape. Woodstock, NY: Homespun Tapes, 1987.

Ortmann, Otto. *The Physiological Mechanics of Piano Technique.* New York: E. P. Dutton, 1962.

Pavarotti, Luciano, and William Wright. *Pavarotti: My Own Story.* Garden City: Doubleday, 1981.

Payne, Donald. "Teaching Students to Practice." *Piano Quarterly* Winter 1985–86: 27–32.

Payne, John. "Hanging Out a Shingle." *Growing Without Schooling* 28 (1982): 18–19.

Perry, John, and Robert J. Silverman. "John Perry." *Piano Quarterly* Winter 1987–88: 24–27.

Pickard, Bonni–Belle. "Left-Handers Are Different!" *Clavier* Oct. 1986: 24–29.

Pino, David. *The Clarinet and Clarinet Playing.* New York: Scribner's, 1980.

Pleeth, William. *Cello.* Yehudi Menuhin Music Guides. New York: Schirmer, 1983.

Previn, André, ed. *Orchestra.* New York: Doubleday, 1979.

Price, Susan. "Playing by Ear." *Growing Without Schooling* 25 (1982): 18–19.

Raccoli, Susan. "Why Do Piano Lessons Fail?" *American Music Teacher* Feb.–Mar. 1983: 40–41.

Rampal, Jean-Pierre. *Music, My Love.* New York: Random House, 1989.

Reubart, Dale. *Anxiety and Musical Performance: On Playing the Piano from Memory.* New York: Da Capo, 1985.

Richoux, Donna. "Using a Tape Recorder." *Growing Without Schooling* 25 (1982): 19.

Ristad, Eloise. *A Soprano on Her Head: Right–side–up Reflections on Life and Other Performances.* Moab, UT: Real People, 1982.

Roberson, Steven. "Lili Kraus: An Interview." *Piano Quarterly* Winter 1986–87: 29–31.

Rosenberg, Bernard, and Deena Rosenberg. *The Music Makers.* New York: Columbia University Press, 1979.

Rosenthal, Roseanne Kelly. "The Relative Effects of Guided Model, Model Only, Guide Only, and Practice Only Treatments on the Accuracy of Advanced Instrumentalists' Musical Performance." *Journal of Research in Music Education* 32 (1984): 265–273.

Rossman, Michael. "Music Lessons." *New American Review* 18 (1973).

Sachs, Harvey. *Virtuoso.* New York: Thames and Hudson, 1982.

Sarnoff, Dorothy. *Never Be Nervous Again.* New York: Crown, 1987.

Schaffer, James. "Carlos Santana: An Inner View." *Downbeat* Feb. 1988: 16–19.

Schauffler, Robert Haven. *The Musical Amateur: A Book on the Human Side of Music.* Boston: Houghton Mifflin, 1911.

Schleuter, Stanley L. "Effects of Certain Lateral Dominance Traits, Music Aptitude, and Sex Differences with Instrumental Music Achievement." *Journal of Research in Music Education* 26 (1978): 22–31.

Schmid, Will. "Reflections on the Folk Movement: An Interview with Pete Seeger." *Music Educators Journal* Feb. 1980: 42ff.

Schonberg, Harold. *The Glorious Ones: Classical Music's Legendary Performers.* New York: Times, 1985.

Schumann, Robert. *Advice to Young Musicians.* Trans. Henry Hugo Pierson. New York: Schuberth, 1860.

Seay, Albert. "The Rise of the Amateur." *American Recorder* May 1982: 51–53.

Seeger, Pete. *Henscratches and Flyspecks: How to Read Melodies from Songbooks in Twelve Confusing Lessons.* New York: Putnam's, 1973.

Segovia, Andrés. *Segovia: An Autobiography of the Years 1893–1920.* Trans. W. F. O'Brien. New York: Macmillan, 1976.

Shanet, Howard. *Learn to Read Music.* New York: Fireside-Simon and Schuster, 1956.

Sherer, Lon. "Practicing: A Liturgy of Self-Learning." *American Music Teacher* Jan. 1987: 37–39.

Shockley, Rebecca. "An Experimental Approach to the Memorization of Piano Music with Implications for Music Reading." Diss. University of Colorado, 1980.

———"A New Approach to Memorization." *Clavier* July–Aug. 1986: 20–23.

———*A Practical Guide to Mapping: The New Way to Learn Music.* White Plains: Pro-Am Music Resources, 1990.

Shuter–Dyson, Rosamund, and Clive Gabriel. *The Psychology of Musical Ability.* 2nd ed. London: Methuen, 1981.

Sloboda, John A. *The Musical Mind: The Cognitive Psychology of Music.* Oxford Psychology Series No. 5. Oxford: Clarendon Press, 1985.

Smith, Frank. *Insult to Intelligence: The Bureaucratic Invasion of Our Classrooms.* New York: Arbor House, 1986.

Spiegl, Fritz. *Music Through the Looking Glass.* London: Routledge and Kegan Paul, 1984.

Spock, Benjamin and Michael B. Rothenberg. *Dr. Spock's Baby and Child Care.* New York: Simon and Schuster, 1985.

Stebbins, Robert A. *Amateurs: On the Margin between Work and Leisure.* Newbury Park, CA.: Sage Publications, 1979.

Street, Eric. "Consider the Adult Piano Student." *Piano Quarterly* Fall 1987: 66–67.

Sudnow, David. *Ways of the Hand: The Organization of Improvised Conduct.* Cambridge, MA: Harvard University Press, 1978.

Surette, Thomas W. *Music and Life: A Study of the Relations Between Ourselves and Music.* Boston: Houghton Mifflin, 1917.

Suzanne, Claudia, et al. *For Musicians Only.* New York: Billboard, 1988.

Terhardt, Ernst, and Manfred Seewann. "Aural Key Identification and Its Relationship to Absolute Pitch." *Music Perception* 1 (1983): 63–83.

Toff, Nancy. *The Flute Book: A Complete Guide for Students and Performers.* New York: Scribner's, 1985.

Tommasini, Anthony. "Knowing the Score." *Piano Quarterly* Summer 1988: 48–53.

Topp, Dale. "It's Never Too Late to Sing!" *Music Educator's Journal* Oct. 1987: 49–52.

———*Music in the Christian Community.* Grand Rapids, MI: William B. Eerdmans, 1976.

Townsend, Charles P. *San Antonio Rose: The Life and Music of Bob Wills.* Urbana, IL: University of Illinois Press, 1976.

Tuckwell, Barry. *Horn.* Yehudi Menuhin Music Guides. New York: Schirmer, 1983.

Van Horn, James. *The Community Orchestra: A Handbook for Conductors, Managers, and Boards.* Westport, CN: Greenwood, 1979.

Vaughan Williams, Ralph. *The Making of Music.* Ithaca, NY: Cornell University Press, 1955.

Watrous, Peter. "Miles Davis: Rebel Without a Pause." *Musician* May 1989: 49ff.

Watts, Alan. *This Is It.* New York: Random House, 1973.

Whitehead, Kevin. "Art Blakey: Class Action." *Downbeat* Dec. 1988: 16–19.

Wibberly, Leonard. *Ah Julian: Memoir of Julian Brodetsky.* New York: Ives Washburn, 1963.

Williams, Christian. "Mid-life and the Cello." *Esquire* Sept. 1983: 88–92.

Wills, Geoff, and Cary L. Cooper. *Pressure Sensitive: Popular Musicians under Stress.* London: Sage Publications, 1988.

Wilson, Frank R. *Tone Deaf and All Thumbs? An Invitation to Music-Making for Late Bloomers and Non-Prodigies.* New York: Viking, 1986.

Wolff, Konrad. "Dorothy Taubman: The Pianist's Medicine Woman." *Piano Quarterly* Spring 1986: 25–32.

Wollitz, Kenneth. *The Recorder Book.* New York: Knopf, 1982.

Woodard, Josef. "The Herbie Hancock Interview." *Downbeat* June 1988: 16–19.

Wurtman, Judith. *Managing Your Mind and Mood Through Food.* New York: Harper and Row, 1988.

Wyatt, Theo. "Techniques of Consort Playing." *American Recorder* Feb. 1983: 3-6.

Zinsser, William. *Willie and Dwike: An American Profile.* New York: Harper and Row, 1984.

Zuckerkandl, Victor. *The Sense of Music.* Princeton: Princeton University Press, 1971.

———*Sound and Symbol.* 2 vols. Princeton: Princeton University Press, 1973.

Index

Index of Proper Names

THE ARCHITECTURE READER

THE ARCHITECTURE READER

ESSENTIAL WRITINGS FROM VITRUVIUS TO THE PRESENT

Edited By A. Krista Sykes

George Braziller Publishers
New York

For information, please address the publisher:

George Braziller, Inc.

171 Madison Avenue

New York, New York 10016

www.georgebraziller.com

Library of Congress Cataloging-in-Publication Data
The Architecture reader : essential writings from Vitruvius to the present / edited by
A. Krista Sykes. p. cm.
Includes bibliographical references.
ISBN 978-0-8076-1579-9 (hardback) -- ISBN 978-0-8076-1580-5 (pbk.)
1. Architecture. 2. Architectural criticism. I. Sykes, A. Krista. II. Title.
NA2560.A71 2007
720--dc22   2006034835

Designed by Saira Kathpalia
Printed and bound in Singapore
First edition

TABLE OF CONTENTS

ACKNOWLEDGMENTS

Throughout the process of planning, compiling, and writing this text, I received assistance from many individuals who deserve recognition. I thank George Braziller for approaching me with the idea for this reader and for giving me the opportunity to undertake this project; Jessica Benko and Elizabeth Monroe for providing wonderful editorial commentary, much-needed advice, and overall guidance; Amy Finstein, Michael Hays, Robert Mark, John McMorrough, Brendan Moran, Mark Morris, Vincent Scully, and Julia Sluzenski for their insightful and valuable critiques of the manuscript; Lee Gray for his perceptive thoughts, indispensable counsel, and constant willingness to talk through the project; my parents and siblings for their never-failing support and assurance; and my cats for the entertainment and companionship. Finally, I am grateful to my husband, Joshua, for his patience, help, and encouragement throughout this and all other endeavors.

PREFACE

The writings that comprise this reader span more than two thousand years, include authors of many nationalities, and cover topics from primitive huts through, in the words
of Shumon Basar, "poisonous mixtures." Additionally, the documents do not represent
a single genre; they include journal articles, editorials, book chapters, lectures, interviews, and manifestos. Yet, among these excerpts, unifying characteristics exist. In
these works, the authors—primarily architects—concern themselves with their own
specific moment in time. They ponder, critique, and occasionally attack architectural
norms and, in many cases, pose alternative methods of architectural thought and practice. As products of individuals active during different eras, these works demonstrate
a broad array of attitudes toward architecture as both subject and discipline. Taken
together, these texts provide a general overview of significant concepts encompassed
by the field of architecture.

Regarding the selection of excerpts, it was crucial that the writings confront basic issues that endure throughout the history of architecture to our own era. For example,
since the age of Vitruvius, architects have been concerned with the role that architecture plays in society. Thus, the social nature of the discipline, while subject to
numerous interpretations, can be understood as a fundamental and recurring topic
of architectural discourse. This leads to another aspect of the texts included in this
reader. The discipline of architecture is inundated with specialized terminology that
can render writings on architecture difficult to interpret. As an introductory collection of writings aimed toward non-architects, I attempted to include excerpts that
would be accessible and of interest to those outside the field and that represent different approaches to architecture. It was not my intent, nor would it be possible, to
present a comprehensive compilation of such approaches. Rather, I hoped to assemble
noteworthy writings that, in most circumstances, have influenced the perception and
creation of architecture through to our present day. Adolf Loos's essay "Ornament and

Crime" (1908) and Robert Venturi's text "Complexity and Contradiction in Architecture" (1966) are examples of such works. I also included a handful of excerpts that may not have had an immediately discernable effect within the discipline, but that nevertheless offer interesting and fruitful ideas for consideration. Daniel Libeskind's speech "Proof of Things Invisible" (1997) and Shumon Basar's article "The Poisonous Mixture" (2004) fall into this latter category.

The majority of the excerpts stem from the twentieth and twenty-first centuries. I made an effort to represent each decade within those eras, with the greatest concentration of texts falling in the last fifteen years. This emphasis reflects the proliferation of writing architects as well as my desire to convey the diversity that characterizes contemporary views of architecture. It also reveals my interest in the history and theory of twentieth-century architecture, particularly from the 1960s to the present.

However, I also strongly believe that our present is inevitably, if not consciously, informed by the past. Thus I included a number of significant texts predating the twentieth century, beginning with Vitruvius, the author of *The Ten Books on Architecture* (circa 25 B.C.E.), the only complete architectural treatise to survive intact from antiquity. As such, this work established the standard for all later architects who set out to write about architecture. The next excerpt, from Abbot Suger's account of the renovation of the Abbey Church of St.-Denis, dates from the Middle Ages. A selection from the Leon Battista Alberti architectural treatise of the mid-1400s, "On the Art of Building in Ten Books," follows Suger. The subsequent texts by Andrea Palladio (*The Four Books on Architecture*, 1570); Claude Perrault (*Ordonnance for the Five Kinds of Columns after the Method of the Ancients*, 1683); Etienne-Louis Boullée (*Architecture, Essay on Art*, 1770–1784); and Eugène-Emmanuel Viollet-le-Duc (*Dictionnaire raisonné*, 1854–1869) lead us toward the twentieth century. The exclusion of other architects is not meant to imply that they were insignificant or have left no lasting impression. For the purposes of this collection, however, I feel that the selections by Vitruvius, Suger, Alberti, Palladio,

Perrault, Boullée, and Viollet-le-Duc provide the most suitable foundation to prepare the reader for the contemporary excerpts, since each of these texts introduce or address issues that reappear throughout architectural discourse in general.

One other issue worthy of mention involves the decision to focus this collection on architecture without directly engaging issues of urbanism. In practice, architecture is inextricably intertwined with urbanism and attempting to divorce the two is somewhat artificial. For this book, however, I chose to deal almost exclusively with architecture in order to limit the size and scope of the collection. To include significant texts on urbanism would have proved impossible in the space allowed, while the incorporation of only a few writings would have done the topic an injustice, providing only a cursory glimpse into the complex and multifaceted subject. Hopefully the issues raised throughout this collection will prompt the reader to independently explore ideas of architecture and urbanism.

Indeed, we may conceive of the built environment in a multitude of ways if we take the time to think of it at all. The need for architectural and urban awareness is great, as is the need for wide-spread discussion. I hope that the issues broached in this book will inspire readers to thoughtfully consider what exists, what was before, and what may be in the coming years.

INTRODUCTION

The notion of architecture is quite complex. Two thousand years ago, the architect Vitruvius identified three branches of the discipline: "the art of building, the making of time-pieces, and the construction of machinery"[1]—everything from houses and roads to hydraulics and clocks. While the contemporary field of architecture is far more specialized, we still lack a consensus on what architecture encompasses; even the meaning of the term "architecture" can vary widely. Nevertheless, the basic concept of "architecture" generally relates to the design and fabrication of structures. Yet problems still arise when attempting to determine what structures today qualify as architecture. Is a bridge an architectural structure? An aqueduct? A fountain? Or does the term "architecture" apply only to buildings proper?

Another question appears with respect to buildings: what types of buildings qualify as architecture? Is there a difference between a work of architecture and a building? Some would say that the two are equivalent terms, interchangeable. Often, however, architects and scholars of architecture draw a distinction between architecture and building. The architectural historian Nikolas Pevsner opens his text *An Outline of European Architecture* with such a distinction, declaring: "A bicycle shed is a building; Lincoln Cathedral is a piece of architecture." Pevsner then qualifies this statement by explaining that, "Nearly everything that encloses space on a scale sufficient for a human being to move in is a building; the term architecture applies only to buildings designed with a view to aesthetic appeal."[2] So according to Pevsner, only certain buildings, those designed to be aesthetically appealing, can be considered architecture. Yet, this definition may raise a few objections. For example, Pevsner's idea of aesthetic appeal may differ quite dramatically from what I or you find aesthetically appealing. What about buildings Pevsner finds appealing and we do not? Are they still architecture? Or what about a bicycle shed that is "designed with a view to aesthetic appeal"? Does this bicycle shed ascend to the realm of architecture or does its utilitarian function preclude it from achieving the status of architecture?

A similar question arises regarding "anonymous" built environments. In 1964, the Austrian architect Bernard Rudofsky coordinated an exhibition at the Museum of Modern Art in New York entitled Architecture Without Architects. Featuring photographs of subterranean Chinese villages, African tree dwellings, and terraced Mediterranean housing, this show focused attention on a previously neglected aspect of the built environment: the "world of nonpedigreed architecture." While these creations were often appreciated for their ingenuity and functionality, historians had commonly excluded them from accounts of the architectural past, relegating such "primitive" structures "to the pages of geographic and anthropological magazines." Rudofsky's exhibition and accompanying publication, however, helped to extend the realm of architecture beyond the established "formal" canon to include indigenous and vernacular construction.[3] Indeed, architecture can exist without architects.

The "architecture without architects" concept raises a larger issue concerning the position of the architect, both past and present. What is an architect? What are the responsibilities of the architect? What should an architect's education entail? What skills must the architect possess? Elusive and ever changing, the answers to these questions mirror the shifting role of the architect and, in turn, influence our understanding of architecture as an object and as a discipline. Thus, a study of architecture necessitates a reflection upon the idea of the architect.

The Architect

Throughout time, people have defined the architect in different ways, alternately and sometimes simultaneously as designer, tradesman, artist, intellectual, and professional. Vitruvius, the author of *The Ten Books on Architecture* (written circa 25 B.C.E) presented the architect as an amalgam of all these traits. He believed that the architect's education should involve not only the study of drawing and geometry, but also history, medicine, astronomy, and law. In addition to this vast array of knowledge, Vitruvius's architect also needed the manual skill to construct his designs. Thus, according to Vitruvius, a successful architect was both a scholar and a craftsman.

During the Middle Ages, Vitruvius's notion of the architect was overshadowed by the concept of the master mason. As the name implies, the master mason was a trained craftsman, a member of a guild who rose to the top of his field through apprenticeship and experience, not scholarly study. Often a master mason served as a designer and on-site construction coordinator, procuring materials and directing workmen. Yet, it is somewhat problematic to speak of the medieval master mason as Vitruvius does of his architect, in part because few written records from this time period exist. Those documents that have survived tend to focus on financial and practical matters rather than theoretical and design issues. Furthermore, construction of large projects frequently spanned decades, if not centuries, making a succession of master masons necessary. Even when construction was completed rather quickly, the projects most often were associated with the architectural patron, not the designers or builders. Indeed, patrons frequently played a significant role in the final manifestation of a commissioned work, as did Abbot Suger in the renovation of the Church of St.-Denis (1140–1144). Such heavy patronal involvement further complicate considerations of the medieval architect.

A few centuries later, a different concept of the architect emerged in the writings of Leon Battista Alberti. Vitruvius's ghost clearly haunted Alberti, who in the mid-fifteenth century composed his own treatise, *On the Art of Building in Ten Books*. Alberti did not reproduce the work of Vitruvius, but rather used a humanist impulse to revise and update the material for his Renaissance audience. Like Vitruvius, Alberti also envisioned the architect as a man privileged with a classical education. However, Alberti felt that the arts, philosophy, and mathematics should be the primary emphases for schooling. He believed that more pragmatic concerns, such as legal and environmental issues, rest in the domain of the builder, who learns through experience, not formal study. This difference in prescribed education underlies an important distinction between Alberti's and Vitruvius's notions of the architect. Unlike Vitruvius's architect—not to mention the medieval master mason—Alberti's architect was not a craftsman. Rather, Alberti presented the Renaissance architect as a learned individual who designs but does not personally take part in construction. This separation of the architect and the building process—the notion of the gentleman architect posited by Alberti—has colored the perception of the architect to the present day. While this idea of the gentleman architect has had the effect of raising the status of the architect above that of the workman, it also has imposed limitations on the architect's accepted range of activity.

The breach between the architect and the process of production is somewhat analogous to the division of labor that arose during industrialization. The emergence of engineering as a distinct field sparked debates over the very nature of architecture and raised concerns regarding the future of the architect. Would the architect be surpassed or perhaps even replaced by the engineer? In the early 1920s, the Swiss architect Le Corbusier proposed an alternative: the architect must learn from the engineer who was in tune with the demands of contemporary existence. According to Le Corbusier, the architect, burdened by centuries of architectural convention, created traditional works neither relevant to nor appropriate for the conditions of twentieth-century life. Rather, Le Corbusier announced, the architect must rely not on historical decrees but, like the engineer, must state the problem to be solved and then devise a solution based on ideas of economy and propriety. In this way, the architect—in Le Corbusier's mind, the ultimate artist—could create beautiful architecture suitable for modern needs.

The great American architect Frank Lloyd Wright was also concerned with the creation of an appropriate architecture for his time. Wright believed the integrity of architecture, and of the architect, to be threatened by blind adherence to tradition and the growth of commercialization. As early as 1900, Wright expressed disgust with fellow architects who "[had] been caught in the commercial rush and whirl and hypnotized into trying to be commercial [themselves]."[4] Instead of designing works for early twentieth-century America, his colleagues, Wright felt, were, for the sake of profit and popularity, peddling architectural styles from foreign lands and past eras. As an alternative, Wright devised an original and unique architectural language that responded to the democratic intent and geographical particularities of the American Midwest. He viewed this "Prairie Style" architecture, perhaps best characterized by the Robie House (Chicago, 1909), as an artistic, practical, and dignified creation, not as a money-making tool. In this way, Wright felt he differed greatly from other architects of his day for whom success hinged on quantity instead of quality and on profit instead of propriety. For Wright, architecture was not a mere commodity, but a means of elevating humanity.

While Wright lamented the impact of commercialism on the architect, others such as Denise Scott Brown have found inspiration in commodification. Scott Brown feels that architects should learn from the commercial interests of the average person, that architects must examine what people buy in order to understand what they want. Such beliefs have led Scott Brown, along with her husband and business partner Robert Venturi, to study "everyday" environments—including New York subway stations, Las Vegas, and the suburb of Levittown, New Jersey—to further understand popular taste and the ways in which people inhabit and modify their surroundings. According to Scott Brown, such explorations are imperative for the socially conscious designer. It is the responsibility of the architect, she has asserted, to create an architecture that resonates with the common man, not one that caters to the elite members of society. Scott Brown's thoughts have signaled a shift from an attitude of superiority held by some modern architects toward the increasingly permissive pluralist and populist attitudes of the past few decades.

The architect Samuel Mockbee also was interested in the creation of architecture for the common man. With the founding of the Rural Studio in 1993, Mockbee initiated a program through Auburn University in which students designed and built housing for a poor community in Alabama. In an interview in 2001, Mockbee stated that the architect's greatest contemporary struggle involves remembering, in the midst of our corporate world, that it is people, not capital, who really matter. For Mockbee, the Rural Studio was not only a way to house economically deprived members of Hale County; it was also a way to cultivate a generation of socially sensitive architects who, as students, were provided with invaluable experience in both design and construction. The Rural Studio, based on Mockbee's philosophy, has thus helped to prompt a reconceptualization of the architect as a professional who, unlike Alberti's architect, can and perhaps even should take an active part in the construction process. In addition, Mockbee's sentiment regarding the social responsibilities of the profession echoes Frank Lloyd Wright's earlier call for a dignifying architecture of quality. The Rural Studio demonstrated that an architecture of quality need not be an architecture of expense. Working with a minimal budget, Mockbee and his students often employed non-traditional materials such as dirt-filled, stucco-covered tires, old street signs, and salvaged car windows to make what Mockbee called a "warm, dry, and noble" architecture.

While some architects aspire to a warm, dry, noble architecture, others aim to evoke the excitement born of the instability and apparent chaos of contemporary existence. For example, in the 1970s, Rem Koolhaas identified new opportunities for human activity that arose in New York City as a result of urban congestion. He continued this line of thought in his design for the Student Center at the Illinois Institute of

Technology in the late 1990s. In this project, Koolhaas and the Office for Metropolitan Architecture (OMA) interwove various and often conflicting zones of activity, allowing the "L" train to literally invade part of the building. Such designs simultaneously highlight and exacerbate the commotion of everyday life.

Disorder is not just accepted; it is embraced. This is Koolhaas's message to the contemporary architect, eloquently announced by the architect Shumon Basar in his article, "The Poisonous Mixture." The title of Basar's essay stems from a comment made by Koolhaas in a lecture at Columbia University in 1989. "Architecture," Koolhaas declared, "is a poisonous mixture of power and impotence."[5] Perhaps this concept provides a clue to the shifting definition of the architect throughout time. Could it be that the architect simply has been attempting to stave off feelings of helplessness in a world, and in a discipline, constantly in flux? This idea implies that different definitions of the architect—the architect as designer and tradesman; the architect as artist, intellectual, and professional—may not be so different after all.

Architecture and Nature

Nature plays a significant and multifaceted role in the architectural realm. At its most basic, nature, considered as the environment as a whole, provides a setting for architecture. Even in urban areas where the original landscape ceases to exist, architecture still interacts with the earth, the sky, the sun, and other natural elements. To assure the comfort of the occupants, responsible architects take into consideration such topographical and geographical information. The orientation of a building on its site, for example, can maximize the amount of natural light an interior receives, shelter the structure from prevalent winds, or provide visually appealing views of the surrounding environs. These concepts are nothing new; Vitruvius addressed issues concerning a building's placement within the environment, demonstrating that even two thousand years ago, architects were aware of the potential benefits to be derived from attention to the land.

In recent years, interest in a building's impact on the environment has grown considerably. Ideally, the creation and existence of any given structure would have no negative repercussions on the earth. Yet, through the processes of construction, daily operation, and demolition, buildings consume an astounding amount of the earth's energy and natural resources. As architects become increasingly aware of this problem, many have responded by adapting ideas of sustainability to inform their designs. For example, the Australian architect Glen Murcutt works with the specifics of the site and employs traditional Aboriginal techniques in his house designs. While Murcutt turns to local building customs to decrease the ecological impact of his work, the British architect Norman Foster utilizes advanced modern technology to create buildings that strive for self-sustainability. The architect William McDonough, in conjunction with the chemist Michael Braungart, has taken his concern for the environment beyond the realm of architecture proper, extending his efforts to all aspects of industrial production. These two men advocate a "cradle to cradle" paradigm that investigates and develops materials that can be used, recycled, and reused without producing tangible waste. Thus in the work of Murcutt, Foster, and McDonough and Braungart, we witness different methodologies derived from the same source: concern for the earth as a whole.

In a theoretical sense, nature and natural creations have long provided a model for architecture. In his treatise, Vitruvius cited the proportion and symmetry of the human body as an inspiration for architectural elements. His account of the Greek classical orders serves as one example of this tendency. He stated that the Doric, the most robust and massive of the orders, derived from the measurements of a man. The Ionic's more attenuated proportions and delicate features were modeled on a woman. The most slender of the orders, the Corinthian, echoed the lithe physique of a young maiden. Thus, the Greek classical orders as described by Vitruvius reflect both physical characteristics and symbolic meaning from nature via the study of the human body.

Centuries later, Alberti elaborated upon the relationship between architecture and nature in his discussion of *concinnitas*. This term concerns beauty as achieved through the harmonious correspondence among the parts of a composition and their relationship to the whole. *Concinnitas* is perhaps best described in the following passage from *On The Art of Building in Ten Books*: "Beauty is a form of sympathy and consonance of the parts within a body, according to definite number, outline, and position, as dictated by *concinnitas*, the absolute and fundamental rule in Nature. This is the main object of the art of building, and the source of her dignity, charm, authority, and worth."[6] According to Alberti, then, architecture—not to mention music and other arts—is governed by *concinnitas*, an underlying principle of nature. From similar natural inspiration, the American architect Frank Lloyd Wright later developed his idea of organic architecture, which strove, among other things, for the integration of the parts with the whole, as well as the building with the site.

For Viollet-le-Duc, natural organisms provided a structural model for architecture. From his studies of plants and animals, Viollet-le-Duc determined that the form and structure of each part of a creature was directly related to the function that part performed. For example, the shape of a bat's wing derives from its function. Nature has crafted the wing to facilitate the bat's flight, and each section of the wing contributes to the function of the whole; nothing is extraneous. Thus Viollet-le-Duc's understanding of appropriate architectural structure corresponds to nature's expression of structure. The ideas of structural clarity and rationality were continued in the work of the American architect Louis Sullivan, who also turned to nature as a model for design. These investigations led Sullivan to famously declared that "form ever follows function,"[7] a dictum that, somewhat modified, became a guiding principle of numerous modern architects.

The British social and architectural commentator John Ruskin adopted a different approach, finding in nature the perfect model for architectural ornament. Patterns extracted from actual flora and fauna could be rendered in stone by the skilled hands of craftsmen. Ruskin also appreciated the effects of nature's actions on a building. The weathering of the façade, the vegetation creeping through the cracks, the alterations made over the years—these aspects marked the passage of time. Regarding buildings from an older age, Ruskin declared, "*We have no right whatever to touch them*. They are not ours. They belong partly to those who built them, and partly to all the generations of mankind who are to follow us."[8] For Ruskin, architecture provided a record of the past to be interpreted in the present.

Architecture and the Past, Architecture and the Present

Architecture's relationship to the past and present raises a number of points for consideration. On the most basic level, we learn from studying history, from what has come before us. Alberti learned from Vitruvius, as did Palladio, Perrault, Boullée, and Viollet-le-Duc. We, in turn, learn from them all. We learn what works, what building types may be suitable for certain activities. We also learn what does not work, what materials fail under certain situations. History, however, can be a great constraint. Robert Venturi alludes to this dilemma in his book *Complexity and Contradiction in Architecture* when he discusses the growing complexities of twentieth-century life and the resulting demands on contemporary architecture.[9] It is not enough to abide by the rules of our fathers—in Venturi's case, the outmoded and simplistic notion that "form follows function." Venturi suggests that, at its best, architecture responds to present needs and conditions as well as information inherited from the past.

What information should we take from the past? How can this information shape an appropriate architecture in the present? What *is* an appropriate architecture for the present? Such inquiries rest at the center of architectural debates characterized by a wide range of responses. The Italian architect Antonio Sant'Elia, author of the "Manifesto of Futurist Architecture" (1914), sought to eradicate all traces of the past. Only an architecture based on the principles of speed, mechanization, and technological progress was fitting for the present. Such an environment would both cultivate and respond to a new futuristic society. However, John Ruskin was so discouraged by the negative effects of industrialization that he attempted to almost entirely discount the present. His nostalgic appreciation for the perceived social values of the medieval era prompted his call for an architecture modeled on that of fourteenth-century Venice.

Sant'Elia and Ruskin's positions represent extremes in the continuum of feelings about past and present aesthetics, skills, and ideologies. More commonly, architects rest somewhere in between, adopting both traditional and progressive aspects of architectural inspiration. For example, the German architect Bruno Taut, like Ruskin, yearned for a revived traditional notion of community, yet he relied on new materials such as glass and steel to create an architecture of social cohesiveness. Walter Gropius, a German architect recognized as the founder and original leader of the Bauhaus, turned to the medieval craft guild as a model for a cooperative artistic workshop. Gropius's new workshop, however, chose to interact with industry, to design and generate prototypes for factory production. Likewise, Le Corbusier drew upon both the past and the present. Interested in ideas of standardization, Le Corbusier identified a similar logic—the refinement of essential compositional elements—underlying both the classical Greek temple and the early twentieth-century automobile. This logic served in part as a foundation for Le Corbusier's reconceptualization of a house conducive to modern life. Thus, in the thought of Taut, Gropius, Le Corbusier, and many others, we find a marriage of the old and the new, the traditional and the progressive, the past and the present.

The past to which an architect looks may be quite distant. Indeed, in his search for a meaningful architecture, an architecture of harmony and strength in a world of chaos and instability, the twentieth-century architect Louis Kahn employed the visual mass and permanence manifested in the ruins of antiquity. Others architects such as Daniel Libeskind have discovered inspiration in the more recent past. Two of his most famous works, the Jewish Museum in Berlin and the Master Plan for the World Trade Center, draw upon the rich and tragic histories associated with the Holocaust and September 11th. In Libeskind's designs, the glaring absences left by these horrible events translate into physical reminders that simultaneously evoke the loss of the past and the hope of the present.

Another use of the past involves the adoption of historic stylistic elements in contemporary architecture. This technique of appropriating classical forms is often associated with postmodernism, an architectural movement spanning the 1960s through the 1980s.[10] First theorized by Charles Jencks in the 1970s, the resurgence of classical elements was characterized in part as a backlash against modern architecture's perceived rejection of history and ornament. In defiance of the mandate "form follows function," architects such as Robert A. M. Stern, Michael Graves, and Philip Johnson turned to the past for inspiration, incorporating Doric columns, classical swags, and broken pediments into their present designs. Controversy abounded; admirers praised this work as ironic and witty while critics defamed it as superficial and simplistic. Regardless of various opinions, the postmodernist use of the past nevertheless focused attention on the difficult relationship between architecture and history, a theme that has persisted—and will no doubt continue to persist—throughout time.

Architecture as Science, Architecture as Art

Another frequent discussion surrounding architecture involves the categorization of the discipline and its product as *either* science *or* art. Even teaching institutions differ on their interpretations of architecture's "place"; in some schools, architectural instruction is allied with the studio arts, while in others it appears alongside engineering and technological studies. Yet in reality, it is extremely difficult—if not impossible—to separate the two, as architecture by its very nature incorporates elements of both science and art. This was clear to Vitruvius when he wrote that the architect must be versed not only in drawing and handcraft, but also in what we would now consider more scientific realms such as astronomy, geology, and medicine. In the subsequent centuries, architects have stressed to varying degrees the "scientific" or the "artistic" within the discipline. In general, the distinction depends on the architect's personal views and predilections. Consequently, discussion about whether architecture is a science or an art is somewhat futile. It is more helpful to examine various ways in which architects have positioned their work with respect to the scientific and artistic realms.

Because the term "science" can refer to a broad domain, for the purposes of this discussion I will focus on a specific scientific area that has had a tremendous impact on architecture and design: technological and industrial development. During the late 1700s and early 1800s, industrialization and the availability of new materials, such as iron, glass, and steel, presented many opportunities for the creation of innovative architectural forms and new methods of production. The Crystal Palace, created by the greenhouse designer Joseph Paxton to accommodate England's Great Exhibition of 1851, incorporated a system of prefabrication and modular construction in order to erect the immense structure of cast iron and glass. Almost forty years later, new materials featured prominently in the Paris Exhibition of 1889 thanks to the iron Eiffel Tower, soaring 300 meters high, and the Galerie des Machines, a large, barrel-vaulted display hall composed of steel and glass. Another thirty years later, Le Corbusier relied on steel-reinforced concrete to create the Maison Domino (1915), a prototype for a factory-produced housing frame composed of thin vertical piers supporting concrete floor slabs. This experimentation with reinforced concrete became the foundation of Le Corbusier's "Five Points towards a New Architecture" (1926), developed in conjunction with his cousin Pierre Jeanneret, and ultimately contributed to Le Corbusier's concept of the house as "a machine for living in."

The machine has served both as a model for architecture and a tool for architectural production. Especially during the twentieth century, architecture has been based on or conceived as a machine, as a specialized and efficacious creation for a specific purpose. This was the case with R. Buckminster Fuller, whose quest to revolutionize the housing industry resulted in a one piece, lightweight, inexpensive aluminum home. Not only did he design his house to operate with mechanical efficiency, but he also intended for the house to be produced by factories that formerly made World War II supplies. Thus, Fuller's house was to be machinelike in its conception, function, and fabrication.

Such concepts of machinelike efficiency and production also pervaded the thoughts of the British architectural group Archigram, whose members in the 1960s devised a series of projects reliant on mechanical operation and technological innovation. For example, Peter Cook's Plug-in City of 1964 consisted of a basic urban infrastructure that would support "plug-in" or interchangeable parts. This scheme included prefabricated housing pods that could be moved via crane and inserted into various service outlets throughout the city. As elements of the pod became obsolete, they could be replaced with newer, more progressive parts that would better fit the owner's needs. Archigram's ideas could be described as hi-tech fantasies, many of which remain unbuildable to this day. Yet, the group's futuristic projects sparked the imagination of other architects. Archigram, as did Fuller, drew on the potential offered by mechanization and machine production to question traditional notions of architecture as stable, fixed, and permanent.

In more recent years, the machine in the form of the computer has emerged onto the architectural scene with dramatic results. In many cases, the computer has functioned as an addendum to conventional means of architectural creation; after designing on paper, architects could use various software programs to digitally model their work. Yet, architects such as Greg Lynn now use the computer as a design tool, not merely a presentation device. Lynn assimilates concepts from aeronautic and automobile design to create dynamic architectural forms that move beyond the rectilinear realm. He appears not to think in terms of line and plane, but of flow and force. The resulting structures—bulging, rippling, and asymmetrical—advertise this difference in Lynn's conception and formulation of architecture. Thus in both working method and final product, Lynn's architecture challenges conventional expectations. The Korean Presbyterian Church of New York, completed in 1999, serves as an example. Along with the firms of Garofalo Architects and Michael McInturf Architects, Lynn transformed a 1931 laundry factory into a visually and spatially unique church complex. Industrial materials such as aluminum panels wrap around and rise above the original masonry structure, creating a series of screens and reflective surfaces through which light filters into the building. The result is a progressive and almost otherworldly atmosphere that enlivens a formerly bleak site in Queens.

The American architect Frank Gehry also utilizes advanced software programs to design and construct his equally unique, and increasingly popular, structures. These twisting, turning, unfurling forms derive in part from the use of digital technology, but they are perhaps guided more by a creative act, by an artistic sense, by Gehry's "intuition." As an architect, Gehry acknowledges the importance and relevance of technology, as each of his complex buildings attests. Yet, Gehry feels that architecture is most certainly an art, and the architect is most certainly an artist. He clearly conveyed this message in his acceptance speech for the Pritzker Architecture Prize in 1989:

> Architecture must solve complex problems. We must understand and use technology, we must create buildings which are safe and dry, respectful of context and neighbors, and face all the myriad of issues of social responsibility, and even please the client.

> But then what? The moment of truth, the composition of elements, the selection of forms, scale, materials, color, finally, all the same issues facing the painter and the sculptor.[11]

The painter, the sculptor, the architect . . . for Gehry, these individuals are siblings, if not the same person. Indeed, throughout history, they have at times been the same individual. Michelangelo is perhaps the exemplar of the artist-architect. Another example of such a figure is Le Corbusier, an architect who reportedly split his day between painting and design. Michelangelo and Le Corbusier serve as prominent illustrations of the crossover between architecture and other artistic ventures, yet the phenomenon is hardly unique; contemporary examples of the artist-architect include Samuel Mockbee, a painter, Daniel Libeskind, a poet and musician, and Frank Gehry, often considered a sculptor.

Architects also derive inspiration from other artistic media. For example, Bernard Tschumi drew on cinematography, photography, and choreography to produce his "Manhattan Transcripts" (1976–1981), a series of images that probed the architectural relationships among space, movement, and events—considerations that would inform his design for the Parisian Parc de la Villette in the early 1980s. Similarly, Denise Scott Brown and Robert Venturi credit works of Pop Art, including Edward Ruscha's images of gas stations and Jasper Johns's superimposed American flags, with directing the pair's attention to the ordinary and the everyday, concerns that continue to condition their work forty years later. Gehry, too, cites artistic influences for his architectural creations ranging from Renaissance and Baroque painters to more contemporary artists. This includes his friends Claus Oldenberg and Coosje van Bruggen, with whom Gehry collaborated to create the Giant Binoculars that contain conference rooms and serve as an entrance to the Chiat/Day Building in Venice, CA (1985–1991). This inhabitable gateway serves as a clear reminder that, in many ways, art and architecture are inextricably intertwined.

Many architects believe that the relationship between architecture and art extends beyond compatibility or influence. Just as architecture inevitably incorporates elements of science—at the very least, gravity is an issue that affects built works—architecture, as an act of creativity and design, also encompasses aspects of art. This conceptual act stems from the will of the architect who is, in Gehry's opinion, fundamentally an artist. "Architecture," he declares, "is surely an art, and those who practice the art of architecture are surely architects."[12]

As I hope this introduction suggests, the relationship between architecture and art, and the relationships between architecture and nature, history, and science are neither clear nor direct. What makes these issues more complex is the human element that underlies all architectural production. Our interactions with our environment—man-made and natural—as well as our interactions with each other unavoidably factor into considerations of architecture, and into architecture's associations with society, politics, economics, psychology, and other aspects of life. With this in mind, my introductory discussion is necessarily brief and incomplete. My intention is not to provide an exhaustive account of architectural themes and influences. Rather I offer an overview of topics that weave throughout the following excerpts, our past and our present, and the entirety of architectural discourse.

---

[1] Vitruvius, "The Departments of Architecture," in *The Ten Books on Architecture*, vol.1, trans. Morris Hickey Morgan (New York: Dover Publications, Inc., 1960), 16.

[2] Nikolas Pevsner, *An Outline of European Architecture*, 7th ed. (London: Pelican Books, 1974), 15.

[3] Bernard Rudofsky, preface in *Architecture Without Architects: A Short Introduction to Non-Pedigreed Architecture* (Albuquerque: University of New Mexico Press, 2002).

[4] Frank Lloyd Wright, "The Architect," in *Collected Writings*, vol. 1, ed. Bruce Brooks Pfeiffer (New York: Rizzoli, 1992), 46.

[5] Rem Koolhaas, in Shumon Basar, "The Poisonous Mixture," in *Content,* ed. Rem Koolhaas and Brendan McGetrick (Cologne: Taschen GmbH, 2004), 67.

[6] Leon Battista Alberti, *On the Art of Building in Ten Books*, trans. Joseph Rykwert, Neil Leach, and Robert Tavernor (Cambridge: MIT Press, 1988), 303.

[7] Louis Sullivan, "The Tall Office Building Artistically Considered" in *America Builds: Source Documents in American Architecture and Planning*, ed. Leland M. Roth (New York: HarperCollins/Icon Editions, 1983), 345.

[8] John Ruskin, *The Seven Lamps of Architecture* (New York: Dover Publications, Inc., 1989), 197. Ruskin's emphasis.

[9] Robert Venturi, *Complexity and Contradiction in Architecture* (New York: Museum of Modern Art, 1966), 19.

[10] Postmodernism is understood as a cultural movement, not solely architectural. Jencks is credited with popularizing the preexisting term "postmodernism" with regard to architecture.

[11] Frank Gehry, "Frank Gehry's Acceptance Speech," The Pritzker Architecture Prize web site, http://www.pritzkerprize.com/gehry.htm

[12] Ibid.

Vitruvius, 1ˢᵗ Century b.c.e.

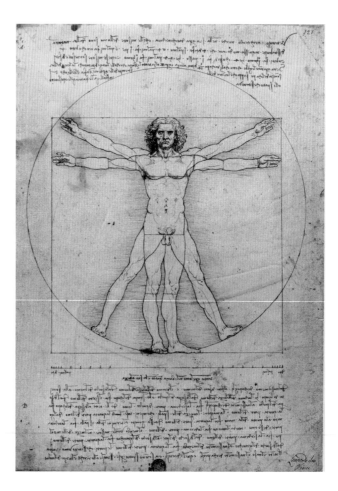

Leonardo da Vinci, *Vitruvian Man*, ca. 1492
Drawing of ideal proportions of the human figure
according to Vitruvius's treatise. Photo Credit: Alinari/Art Resource, NY

Little is known about the Roman architect and writer Vitruvius, including his full name (possibly Marcus Vitruvius Pollio) and his date of birth (approximately 80 B.C.E.). His treatise, *De aedeficatora* (translated as *On Architecture* and now known as *The Ten Books on Architecture*), is the only ancient text of its kind to survive intact. Written circa 25 B.C.E., this work disappeared for hundreds of years; its rediscovery in 1414 at the Swiss Monastery of St. Gall contributed to the renewed interest in classicism and humanism associated with the Renaissance as it took hold in Italy. Vitruvius's work drew primarily on the architecture of his Greek predecessors and addressed all aspects of the discipline from the training of architects through the construction of fortifications. According to Vitruvius, built architecture must encompass three requirements: *firmitas* (durability), *utilitas* (usefulness) and *venustas* (beauty). With this declaration, Vitruvius established the standards by which most subsequent architecture would be judged.

Another significant aspect of *The Ten Books on Architecture* involved the relationship between architecture and nature, and, by extension, architecture and man. Vitruvius positioned nature as the model for architecture; in particular, the proportion and symmetry of the human body inspired architectural designs. The perfection of the human body as discussed by Vitruvius was embodied in a late-fifteenth-century work by Leonardo da Vinci. The drawing—a man inscribed within a circle and square—referenced the harmonic proportions of the body while the title of the work—*Vitruvian Man*—memorialized Vitruvius and extended his influence beyond the realm of architecture.

The Ten Books on Architecture (ca. 25 B.C.E.)

Book I.

Chapter 1. The Education of the Architect

1. The architect should be equipped with knowledge of many branches of study and varied kinds of learning, for it is by his judgment that all work done by the other arts is put to test. This knowledge is the child of practice and theory. Practice is the continuous and regular exercise of employment where manual work is done with any necessary material according to the design of a drawing. Theory, on the other hand, is the ability to demonstrate and explain the productions of dexterity on the principles of proportion.

2. It follows, therefore, that architects who have aimed at acquiring manual skill without scholarship have never been able to reach a position of authority to correspond to their pains, while those who relied only upon theories and scholarship were obviously hunting the shadow, not the substance. But those who have a thorough knowledge of both, like men armed at all points, have the sooner attained their object and carried authority with them.

3. In all matters, but particularly in architecture, there are these two points—the thing signified, and that which gives it its significance. That which is signified is the subject of which we may be speaking; and that which gives significance is a demonstration on

Vitruvius, *The Ten Books on Architecture*, trans. Morris Hicky Morgan (New York: Dover Publications, Inc., 1960). Reprinted with permission of the publisher. For the Greek terms provided throughout Vitruvius's treatise, see Morris Hicky Morgan's translation from which this excerpt is derived.

scientific principles. It appears, then, that one who professes himself an architect should be well versed in both directions. He ought, therefore, to be both naturally gifted and amenable to instruction. Neither natural ability without instruction nor instruction without natural ability can make the perfect artist. Let him be educated, skilful [*sic*] with the pencil, instructed in geometry, know much history, have followed the philosophers with attention, understand music, have some knowledge of medicine, know the opinions of the jurists, and be acquainted with astronomy and the theory of the heavens.

4. The reasons for all this are as follows. An architect ought to be an educated man so as to leave a more lasting remembrance in his treatises. Secondly, he must have a knowledge of drawing so that he can readily make sketches to show the appearance of the work which he proposes. Geometry, also, is of much assistance in architecture, and in particular it teaches us the use of the rule and compasses, by which especially we acquire readiness in making plans for buildings in their grounds, and rightly apply the square, the level, and the plummet. By means of optics, again, the light in buildings can be drawn from fixed quarters of the sky. It is true that it is by arithmetic that the total cost of buildings is calculated and measurements are computed, but difficult questions involving symmetry are solved by means of geometrical theories and methods.

5. A wide knowledge of history is requisite because, among the ornamental parts of an architect's design for a work, there are many the underlying idea of whose employment he should be able to explain to inquirer. . . .

7. As for philosophy, it makes an architect high-minded and not self-assuming, but rather renders him courteous, just, and honest without avariciousness. This is very important, for no work can be rightly done without honesty and incorruptibility. . . .

8. Music, also, the architect ought to understand so that he may have knowledge of the canonical and mathematical theory. . . .

10. The architect should also have a knowledge of the study of medicine on account of the questions of climates, air, the healthiness and unhealthiness of sites, and the use of different waters. For without these considerations, the healthiness of a dwelling cannot be assured. And as for principles of law, he should know those which are necessary in the case of buildings having party walls, with regard to water dripping from the eaves, and also the laws about drains, windows, and water supply. And other things of this sort should be known to architects, so that, before they begin upon buildings, they may be careful not to leave disputed points for the householders to settle after the works are finished, and so that in drawing up contracts the interests of both employer and contractor may be wisely safe-guarded. For if a contract is skillfully drawn, each may obtain a release from the other without disadvantage. From astronomy we find the east, west, south, and north, as well as the theory of the heavens, the equinox, solstice, and courses of the stars. If one has no knowledge of these matters, he will not be able to have any comprehension of the theory of sundials.

11. Consequently, since this study is so vast in extent, embellished and enriched as it is with many different kinds of learning, I think that men have no right to profess themselves architects hastily, without having climbed from boyhood the steps of these studies and thus, nursed by the knowledge of many arts and sciences, having reached the heights of the holy ground of architecture. . . .

Chapter II. The Fundamental Principles of Architecture

1. ARCHITECTURE depends on Order, Arrangement, Eurythmy, Symmetry, Propriety, and Economy.

2. Order gives due measure to the members of a work considered separately, and sym-

metrical agreement to the proportions of the whole. It is an adjustment according to quantity. By this I mean the selection of modules from the members of the work itself and, starting from these individual parts of members, constructing the whole work to correspond. Arrangement includes the putting of things in their proper places and the elegance of effect which is due to adjustments appropriate to the character of the work. . . .

3. Eurythmy is beauty and fitness in the adjustments of the members. This is found when the members of a work are of a height suited to their breadth, of a breadth suited to their length, and, in a word, when they all correspond symmetrically.

4. Symmetry is a proper agreement between the members of the work itself, and relation between the different parts and the whole general scheme, in accordance with a certain part selected as standard. Thus in the human body there is a kind of symmetrical harmony between forearm, foot, palm, finger, and other small parts; and so it is with perfect buildings. . . .

5. Propriety is that perfection of style which comes when a work is authoritatively constructed on approved principles. It arises from prescription, from usage, or from nature. From prescription, in the case of hypaethral edifices, open to the sky, in honour of Jupiter Lightning, the Heaven, the Sun, or the Moon: for these are gods whose semblances and manifestations we behold before our very eyes in the sky when it is cloudless and bright. The temples of Minerva, Mars, and Hercules, will be Doric, since the virile strength of these gods makes daintiness entirely inappropriate to their houses. In temples to Venus, Flora, Proserpine, Spring-Water, and the Nymphs, the Corinthian order will be found to have peculiar significance, because these are delicate divinities and so its rather slender outlines, its flowers, leaves, and ornamental volutes will lend propriety where it is due. The construction of temples of the Ionic order to Juno, Diana, Father Bacchus, and the other gods of that kind, will be in keeping with

the middle position which they hold; for the building of such will be an appropriate combination of the severity of the Doric and the delicacy of the Corinthian.

6. Propriety arises from usage when buildings having magnificent interiors are provided with elegant entrance-courts to correspond; for there will be no propriety in the spectacle of an elegant interior approached by a low, mean entrance. Or, if dentils be carved in the cornice of the Doric entablature or triglyphs represented in the Ionic entablature over the cushion-shaped capitals of the columns, the effect will be spoilt by the transfer of the peculiarities of the one order of building to the other, the usage in each class having been fixed long ago.

7. Finally, propriety will be due to natural causes if, for example, in the case of all sacred precincts we select very healthy neighbourhoods with suitable springs of water in the places where the fanes are to be built, particularly in the case of those to Aesculapius and to Health, gods by whose healing powers great numbers of the sick are apparently cured. For when their diseased bodies are transferred from an unhealthy to a healthy spot, and treated with waters from health-giving springs, they will the more speedily grow well. The result will be that the divinity will stand in higher esteem and find his dignity increased, all owing to the nature of his site. There will also be natural propriety in using an eastern light for bedrooms and libraries, a western light in winter for baths and winter apartments, and a northern light for picture galleries and other places in which a steady light is needed; for that quarter of the sky grows neither light nor dark with the course of the sun, but remains steady and unshifting all day long.

8. Economy denotes the proper management of materials and of site, as well as a thrifty balancing of cost and common sense in the construction of works. This will be observed if, in the first place, the architect does not demand things which cannot be found or made ready without great expense. . . .

9. A second stage in Economy is reached when we have to plan the different kinds of dwellings suitable for ordinary householders, for great wealth, or for the high position of the statesman. A house in town obviously calls for one form of construction; that into which stream the products of country estates requires another; this will not be the same in the case of money-lenders and still different for the opulent and luxurious; for the powers under whose deliberations the commonwealth is guided dwellings are to be provided according to their special needs: and, in a word, the proper form of economy must be observed in building houses for each and every class.

Chapter III. The Departments of Architecture

. . . 2. All [structures] must be built with due reference to durability, convenience, and beauty. Durability will be assured when foundations are carried down to the solid ground and materials wisely and liberally selected; convenience, when the arrangement of the apartments is faultless and presents no hindrance to use, and when each class of building is assigned to its suitable and appropriate exposure; and beauty, when the appearance of the work is pleasing and in good taste, and when its members are in due proportion according to correct principles of symmetry. . . .

Book III.
Chapter I. On Symmetry: In Temples and in the Human Body

1. The design of a temple depends on symmetry, the principles of which must be most carefully observed by the architect. They are due to proportion. Proportion is a correspondence among the measures of the members of an entire work, and of the whole to a certain part selected as standard. From this result the principles of symmetry. Without symmetry and proportion there can be no principles in the design of any temple; that is, if there is no precise relation between its members, as in the case of those of a well shaped man.

2. For the human body is so designed by nature that the face, from the chin to the top

of the forehead and the lowest roots of the hair, is a tenth part of the whole height; the open hand from the wrist to the tip of the middle finger is just the same; the head from the chin to the crown is an eighth, and with the neck and shoulder from the top of the breast to the lowest roots of the hair is a sixth; from the middle of the breast to the summit of the crown is a fourth. If we take the height of the face itself, the distance from the bottom of the chin to the under side of the nostrils is one third of it; the nose from the under side of the nostrils to a line between the eyebrows is the same; from there to the lowest roots of the hair is also a third, comprising the forehead. The length of the foot is one sixth of the height of the body; of the forearm, one fourth; and the breadth of the breast is also one fourth. The other members, too, have their own symmetrical proportions, and it was by employing them that the famous painters and sculptors of antiquity attained to great and endless renown.

3. Similarly, in the members of a temple there ought to be the greatest harmony in the symmetrical relations of the different parts to the general magnitude of the whole. Then again, in the human body the central point is naturally the navel. For if a man be placed flat on his back, with his hands and feet extended, and a pair of compasses centered at his navel, the fingers and toes of his two hands and feet will touch the circumference of a circle described therefrom. And just as the human body yields a circular outline, so too a square figure may be found from it. For if we measure the distance from the soles of the feet to the top of the head, and then apply that measure to the outstretched arms, the breadth will be found to be the same as the height, as in the case of plane surfaces which are perfectly square.

4. Therefore, since nature has designed the human body so that its members are duly proportioned to the frame as a whole, it appears that the ancients had good reason for their rule, that in perfect buildings the different members must be in exact symmetrical relations to the whole general scheme. Hence, while transmitting to us the

proper arrangements for buildings of all kinds, they were particularly careful to do so in the case of temples of the gods, buildings in which merits and faults usually last forever.

2 ABBOT SUGER, 1081–1151

Ambulatory and chapels, Abbey Church, St.-Denis, France, 1140–44
Photo Credit: Foto Marburg/Art Resource, NY

In 1122, Suger was appointed the head of the Abbey Church of St.-Denis, an institution that for many centuries had been associated with the sovereigns of France. As the original ninth-century church was in need of enlargement and repair, Suger set out to create a magnificent and lavish religious building to surpass all others. Indeed, the new St.-Denis, as conceived by Suger but completed after his death, contained a number of structural, spatial, and aesthetic innovations. For example, exterior buttressing allowed the mass of the walls to dematerialize and be largely replaced by colorful stained glass. This was especially apparent in the newly devised double ambulatory (located at the far end of the church behind the altar and choir), an area replete with dazzling colored light that filtered in through stained glass windows. The increased transparency, brightly colored light, and novel planning configurations, as well as other specialized developments, caused many architectural historians to acknowledge the renovated St.-Denis, begun largely at Suger's behest, as the first truly Gothic structure. Suger's documentation of St.-Denis's reconstruction, excerpted below, provides a rare glimpse into a significant work of medieval architecture.

The Book of Sugar, Abbot of St.-Denis, On What Was Done Under His Adminis-tration (1144–49)

XXV. Of the First Addition to the Church

. . . I found myself, under the inspiration of the Divine will and because of that inadequacy which we often saw and felt on feast days . . . (for the narrowness of the place forced the women to run toward the altar upon the heads of the men as upon a pavement with much anguish and noisy confusion), encouraged by the counsel of wise men and by the prayers of many monks . . . to enlarge and amplify the noble church consecrated by the Hand Divine; and I set out at once to begin this very thing. . . . Thus we began work at the former entrance with the doors. We tore down a certain addition asserted to have been made by Charlemagne on a very honorable occasion . . . and we set our hand to this part. As is evident we exerted ourselves incessantly with the enlargement of the body of the church as well as with the trebling of the entrance and the doors, and with the erection of high and noble towers. . . .

The Other Little Book on the Consecration of the Church of St.-Denis (1144–46/47)

II. . . . Since in the front part, toward the north, at the main entrance with the main doors, the narrow hall was squeezed in on either side by twin towers neither high nor very sturdy but threatening ruin, we began, with the help of God, strenuously to work

Abbot Suger of St.-Denis, "On What Was Done Under His Administration" and "The Other Little Book on the Consecration of the Church of St.-Denis, 1144–1149," in *The Book of Suger, Abbot of St.-Denis*, trans. and ed. Erwin Panofsky (Princeton: Princeton University Press, 1946) 43–51, 89–91. 2nd ed. Gerda Panofsky-Soergel (Princeton: Princeton University Press, 1979). Originally titled *Liber de rebus in administratione sua gestis* (1144–1149) and *Libellus alter de consecratione ecclesiae Sancti Dionysii* (1144–1146/47), respectively. Reprinted with permission of the publisher.

on this part, having laid very strong material foundations for a straight nave and twin towers, and most strong spiritual ones of which it is said: *For other foundation can no man lay than that is laid, which is Jesus Christ.* Leaning upon God's inestimable counsel and irrefragable aid, we proceeded with this so great and so sumptuous work to such an extent that, while at first, expending little, we lacked much, afterwards, expending much, we lacked nothing at all and even confessed in our abundance: *Our sufficiency is of God.* Through a gift of God a new quarry, yielding very strong stone, was discovered such as in quality and quantity had never been found in these regions. There arrived a skillful crowd of masons, stonecutters, sculptors and other workmen, so that—thus and otherwise—Divinity relieved us of our fears and favored us with Its goodwill by comforting us and by providing us with unexpected [resources]. . . .

In carrying out such plans my first thought was for the concordance and harmony of the ancient and the new work. . . .

[from *On What Was Done Under His Administration*]
XXVII. Of the Cast and Gilded Doors

Bronze casters having been summoned and sculptors chosen, we set up the Main doors on which are represented the Passion of the Savior and His Resurrection, or rather Ascension, with great cost and much expenditure for their gilding as was fitting for the noble porch. Also [we set up] others, new ones on the right side and the old ones on the left beneath the mosaic which, though contrary to modern custom, we ordered to be executed there and to be affixed to the tympanum of the portal. We also committed ourselves richly to elaborate the tower[s] and the upper crenelations of the front, both for the beauty of the church and, should circumstances require it, for practical purposes. Further we ordered the year of the consecration, lest it be forgotten, to be inscribed in copper-gilt letters in the following manner:

> For the splendor of the church that has fostered and exalted him.
> Suger has labored for the splendor of the church.

Giving thee a share of what is thine, O Martyr Denis,

He prays to thee to pray that he may obtain a share of Paradise.

The year was the One Thousand, One Hundred, and Fortieth

Year of the Word when [this structure] was consecrated.

The verses on the door, further, are these:

Whoever thou art, if thou seekest to extol the glory of these doors,

Marvel not at the gold and the expense but at the craftsmanship of the work.

Bright is the noble work; but, being nobly bright, the work

Should brighten the minds, so that they may travel, through the true lights,

To the True Light where Christ is the true door.

In what manner it be inherent in this world the golden door defines:

The dull mind rises in truth through that which is material

And, in seeing this light, is resurrected from its former submersion.

. . .

XXVIII. Of the Enlargement of the Upper Choir

In the same year, cheered by so holy and so auspicious a work, we hurried to begin the chamber of the divine atonement in the upper choir. . . . How much the Hand Divine Which operates in such matters has protected this glorious work is also surely proven by the fact that it allowed that whole magnificent building [to be completed] in three years and three months, from the crypt below to the summits of the vaults above, elaborated with the variety of so many arches and columns, including even the consummation of the roof. Therefore the inscription of the earlier consecration also defines, with only one word eliminated, the year of completion of this one, thus:

The year was One Thousand, One Hundred, Forty and Fourth of the Word when [this structure] was consecrated.

To these verses of the inscription we choose the following ones to be added:

Once the new rear part is jointed to the part in front,

The church shines with its middle part brightened.

For bright is that which is brightly coupled with the bright,

And bright is the noble edifice which is pervaded by the new light;

Which stands enlarged in our time,

I, who was Suger, being the leader while it was being accomplished.

Eager to press on my success, since I wished nothing more under heaven than to seek the honor of my mother church which with maternal affection had suckled me as a child . . . we devoted ourselves to the completion of the work and strove to raise and to enlarge the transept wings of the church [so as to correspond] to the form of the earlier and latter work that had to be joined by them.

3   Leon Battista Alberti, 1407–1476

While the Italian humanist Leon Battista Alberti excelled in multiple disciplines including art, music, mathematics, cryptography, and literature, his most renowned printed work, *De re aedificatoria*, belongs to the realm of architecture. Translated as *On the Art of Building in Ten Books*, this text (composed around 1450) is commonly recognized as the first modern treatise on architecture and the first encyclopedic architectural text since that of Vitruvius. Yet, as Joseph Rykwert points out, Vitruvius essentially compiled information about existing architecture; he wrote of "how the buildings . . . *were* built." In contrast, Alberti extrapolated from a number of sources, including the ruins of ancient Rome and Vitruvius's rediscovered text, to formulate principles for architectural production; he "[prescribed] how the buildings of the future [*were*] *to be* built."* Drawing upon ideas of harmony, variety and beauty as found in nature, Alberti redefined and introduced the classical orders for contemporary use. Upon its printing in 1486, *On the Art of Building in Ten Books* became a highly influential text for subsequent generations of architects.

As an architect, Alberti is credited with relatively few constructed works. Perhaps the most recognized are the façade of Santa Maria Novella in Florence (1456–70) and the Church of San Andrea in Mantua (1470–76). The former incorporates classical elements into medieval remnants of the preexisting façade, while the latter merges the flowing barrel-vaulted interior of the ancient Roman basilica, the tripartite motif of the triumphal arch, and the pediment of the temple to create a Renaissance interpretation of older building elements.

---

* Joseph Rykwert, "Introduction," in Leon Battista Alberti, *On the Art of Building in Ten Books*, trans. J. Rykwert, R. Tavernor, and N. Leach (Cambridge, MA: MIT Press, 1999), x. Rykwert's italics.

On the Art of Building in Ten Books (ca.1450, published 1486)

Prologue

Many and various arts, which help to make the course of our life more agreeable and cheerful, were handed down to us by our ancestors, who had acquired them by much effort and care. All of them seem to compete toward the one end, to be of the greatest possible use to humanity, yet we realize that each has some integral property, which shows it has a different advantage to offer from the others. For we are forced to practice some of these arts by necessity, while others commend themselves to us for their utility, and still others we appreciate because they deal with matters that are pleasant to know. I need not specify these arts: it is obvious which they are. Yet, if you reflect on it, you would not find one among all the most important arts that did not seek and consider its own particular ends, excluding anything else. If, however, you were eventually to find any that proved wholly indispensable and yet were capable of uniting use with pleasure as well as honor, I think you could not omit architecture from that category: architecture, if you think the matter over carefully, gives comfort and the greatest pleasure to mankind, to individual and community alike; nor does she rank last among the most honorable of the arts.

Before I go any farther, however, I should explain exactly whom I mean by an architect; for it is no carpenter that I would have you compare to the greatest exponents of other disciplines: the carpenter is but an instrument in the hands of the architect.

From Leon Battista Alberti, *On the Art of Building in Ten Books*, trans. Joseph Rykwert, Robert Tavernor, and Neil Leach (Cambridge, MA: MIT Press, 1999), 2–5, 23–24, 301–303, 315–317. © 1988 Joseph Rykwert, Robert Tavernor, and Neil Leach. Reprinted with permission of the publisher. Translators' commentary omitted from this reprinting.

Him I consider the architect, who by sure and wonderful reason and method, knows both how to devise through his own mind and energy, and to realize by construction, whatever can be most beautifully fitted out for the noble needs of man, by the movement of weights and the joining and massing of bodies. To do this he must have an understanding and knowledge of all the highest and most noble disciplines. This then is the architect. But to return to the discussion.

Some have said that it was fire and water which were initially responsible for bringing men together into communities, but we, considering how useful, even indispensable, a roof and walls are for men, are convinced that it was they that drew and kept men together. We are indebted to the architect not only for providing that safe and welcome refuge from the heat of the sun and the frosts of winter (that of itself is no small benefit), but also for his many other innovations, useful to both individuals and the public, which time and time again have so happily satisfied daily needs.

How many respected families both in our own city and in others throughout the world would have totally disappeared, brought down by some temporary adversity, had not their family hearth harbored them, welcoming them, as it were, into the very bosom of their ancestors? Daedalus received much praise from his contemporaries for having constructed a vault in Selinunte where a cloud of vapor emanated so warm and gentle that it induced a most agreeable sweat, and cured the body in an extremely pleasant manner. What of others? How could I list the devices—walks, swimming pools, baths, and so forth—that help to keep us healthy? Or even vehicles, mills, timepieces, and other smaller inventions, which nonetheless play so vital a role in our everyday lives? What of the methods of drawing up vast quantities of water from hidden depths for so many different and essential purposes? And of memorials, shrines, sanctuaries, temples, and the like, designed by the architect for divine worship and for the benefit of posterity? Finally, need I stress how, by cutting through rock, by tunneling through mountains or filling in valleys, by restraining the waters of the sea and lakes, and by draining marshes, through the building of ships, by altering the course and dredging the mouths of rivers, and through the construction of harbors and bridges, the architect has not only met the temporary needs of man, but also opened up new gateways to all the provinces of the world? As a result nations have been able to serve each other by exchanging fruit, spices, jewels, experience and knowledge, indeed anything that might improve our health and standard of living.

Nor should you forget ballistic engines and machines of war, fortresses and whatever else may have served to protect and strengthen the liberty of our country, and the good and honor of the state, to extend and confirm its dominion. It is my view moreover that, should you question all the various cities which within human memory have fallen into enemy hands by siege, and inquire who defeated and conquered them, they would not deny that it was the architect; and that they could easily have scorned an enemy armed with weapons alone but could no longer have resisted the power of invention, the bulk of war machines and the force of ballistic engines, with which the architect had harassed, oppressed, and overwhelmed them. On the other hand, those besieged would consider no protection better than the ingenuity and skill of the architect. Should you examine the various military campaigns undertaken, you would perhaps discover that the skill and ability of the architect have been responsible for more victories than have the command and foresight of any general; and that the enemy were more often overcome by the ingenuity of the first without the other's weapons, than by the latter's sword without the former's good counsel. And what is more important, the architect achieves his victory with but a handful of men and without loss of life. So much for the use of architecture.

But how congenial and instinctive the desire and thought for building may be to our minds is evident—if only because you will never find anyone who is not eager to build something, as soon as he has the means to do so; nor is there anyone who, on making some discovery in the art of building, would not gladly and willingly offer and broadcast his advice for general use, as if compelled to do so by nature. It often happens that we ourselves, although busy with completely different things, cannot prevent our minds and imagination from projecting some building or other. Or again, when we see some other person's building, we immediately look over and compare the individual dimensions, and to the best of our ability consider what might be taken away, added, or altered, to make it more elegant, and willingly we lend our advice. But if it has been well designed and properly executed, who would not look at it with great pleasure and joy? Need I mention here not only the satisfaction, the delight, but even the honor that architecture has brought to citizens at home or abroad? Who would not boast of having built something? We even pride ourselves if the houses we live in have been constructed with a little more care and attention than usual. When you erect a wall or portico of great elegance and adorn it with a door, columns, or roof, good citizens approve and express joy for their own sake, as well as for yours, because they realize that you have used your wealth to increase greatly not only your own honor and glory, but also that of your family, your descendants, and the whole city. . . .

To conclude, then, let it be said that the security, dignity, and honor of the republic depend greatly on the architect: it is he who is responsible for our delight, entertainment, and health while at leisure, and our profit and advantage while at work, and in short, that we live in a dignified manner, free from any danger. In view then of the delight and wonderful grace of his works, and of how indispensable they have proved, and in view of the benefit and convenience of his inventions, and their service to posterity, he should no doubt be accorded praise and respect, and be counted among those most deserving of mankind's honor and recognition. . . .

Book I. Chapter IX
All the power of invention, all the skill and experience in the art of building, are called upon in compartition; compartition alone divides up the whole building into the parts

by which it is articulated, and integrates its every part by composing all the lines and angles into a single, harmonious work that respects utility, dignity, and delight. If (as the philosophers maintain) the city is like some large house, and the house is in turn like some small city, cannot the various parts of the house—atria, *xysti*, dining rooms, porticoes, and so on—be considered miniature buildings? Could anything be omitted from any of these, through inattention and neglect, without detracting from the dignity and worth of the work? The greatest care and attention, then, should be paid to studying these elements, which contribute to the whole work, so as to ensure that even the most insignificant parts appear to have been formed according to the rules of art. . . .

The parts ought to be so composed that their overall harmony contributes to the honor and grace of the whole work, and that effort is not expended in adorning one part at the expense of all the rest, but that the harmony is such that the building appears a single, integral, and well-composed body, rather than a collection of extraneous and unrelated parts.

Moreover, in fashioning the members, the moderation shown by nature ought to be followed; and here, as elsewhere, we should not so much praise sobriety as condemn unruly passion for building: each part should be appropriate, and suit its purpose. For every aspect of building, if you think of it rightly, is born of necessity, nourished by convenience, dignified by use; and only in the end is pleasure provided for, while pleasure itself never fails to shun every excess. Let the building then be such that its members want no more than they already have, and what they have can in no way be faulted.

Then again, I would not wish all the members to have the same shape and size, so that there is no difference between them: it will be agreeable to make some parts large, and good to have some small, while some are valuable for their very mediocrity. It will be equally pleasing to have some members defined by straight lines, others by curved ones, and still others by a combination of the two, provided, of course, that the advice on which I insist is obeyed and the mistake is avoided of making the building appear like some monster with uneven shoulders and sides. Variety is always a most pleasing spice, where distant objects agree and conform with one another; but when it causes discord and difference between them, it is extremely disagreeable. Just as in music, where deep voices answer high ones, and intermediate ones are pitched between them, so they ring out in harmony, a wonderfully sonorous balance of proportioned results, which increases the pleasure of the audience and captivates them; so it happens in everything else that serves to enchant and move the mind.

This whole process should respect the demands of use and convenience, and follow the methods sanctioned by those who are experienced: to contravene established customs often detracts from the general elegance, while conforming to them is considered advantageous and leads to the best results. Although other famous architects seem to recommend by their work either the Doric, or the Ionic, or the Corinthian, or the Tuscan division as being the most convenient, there is no reason why we should follow their design in our work, as though legally obliged; but rather, inspired by their example, we should strive to produce our own inventions, to rival, or, if possible, to surpass the glory of theirs. . . .

Book IX. Chapter V

. . . The great experts of antiquity . . . have instructed us that a building is very like an animal, and that Nature must be imitated when we delineate it. Let us investigate, then, why some bodies that Nature produces may be called beautiful, others less beautiful, and even ugly. . . .

When you make judgments on beauty, you do not follow mere fancy, but the workings of a reasoning faculty that is inborn in the mind. It is clearly so, since no one can look at anything shameful, deformed, or disgusting without immediate displeasure and aversion. What arouses and provokes such a sensation in the mind we shall not inquire in detail, but shall limit our consideration to whatever evidence presents itself that is relevant to our argument. For within the form and figure of a building there resides some natural excellence and perfection that excites the mind and its immediately recognized by it. I myself believe that form, dignity, grace, and other such qualities depend on it, and as soon as anything is removed or altered, these qualities are themselves weakened and perish. Once we are convinced of this, it will not take long to discuss what may be removed, enlarged, or altered, in the form and figure. For every body consists entirely of parts that are fixed and individual; if these are removed, enlarged, reduced, or transferred somewhere inappropriate, the very composition will be spoiled that gives the body its seemly appearance.

From this we may conclude, without my pursuing such questions any longer, that the three principle components of that whole theory into which we inquire are number, what we might call outline, and position. But arising from the composition and connection of these three is a further quality in which beauty shines full face: our term for this is *concinnitas;* which we say is nourished with every grace and splendor. It is the task and aim of *concinnitas* to compose parts that are quite separate from each other by their nature, according to some precise rule, so that they correspond to one another in appearance.

That is why when the mind is reached by way of sight or sound, or any other means, *concinnitas* is instantly recognized. It is our nature to desire the best, and to cling to it with pleasure. Neither in the whole body nor in its parts does *concinnitas* flourish as much as it does in Nature herself; thus I might call it the spouse of the soul and of reason. It has a vast range in which to exercise itself and bloom—it runs through man's entire life and government, it molds the whole of Nature. Everything that Nature produces is regulated by the law of *concinnitas*, and her chief concern is that whatever she produces should be absolutely perfect. Without *concinnitas* this could hardly be achieved, for the critical sympathy of the parts would be lost. So much for this.

If this is accepted, let us conclude as follows. Beauty is a form of sympathy and consonance of the parts within a body, according to definite number, outline, and position, as dictated by *concinnitas*, the absolute and fundamental rule in Nature. This is the main object of the art of building, and the source of her dignity, charm, authority, and worth.

All that has been said our ancestors learned through observation of Nature herself; so they had no doubt that if they neglected these things, they would be unable to attain all that contributes to the praise and honor of the work; not without reason they declared that Nature, as the perfect generator of forms, should be their model. And so, with the utmost industry, they searched out the rules that she employed in producing things, and translated them into methods of building. By studying in Nature the patterns both for whole bodies and for their individual parts, they understood that at their very origins bodies do not consist of equal portions, with the result that some are slender, some fat, and others in between; and observing the great difference in purpose and intention between one building and another, . . . they concluded that, by the same token, each should be treated differently.

Following Nature's own example, they also invented three different ways of ornamenting a house, their names taken from the nations who favored one above the others, or even invented each, as it is said. One kind was fuller, more practical and enduring: this they called Doric. Another was slender and full of charm: this they named Corinthian. The one that lay in between, as though composed of both, they called the Ionic; they devised these for the body as a whole. When they observed the particular contribution of each of the three factors mentioned above, number, outline, and position, in the production of beauty, they established how to employ them, having studied nature's works. . . .

Book IX. Chapter X

. . . A great matter is architecture, nor can everyone undertake it. He must be of the greatest ability, the keenest enthusiasm, the highest learning, the widest experience, and, above all, serious, of sound judgment and counsel, who would presume to call himself an architect. The greatest glory in the art of building is to have a good sense of what is appropriate. For to build is a matter of necessity; to build conveniently is the product of both necessity and utility; but to build something praised by the magnificent, yet not rejected by the frugal, is the province only of an artist of experience, wisdom, and thorough deliberation.

Moreover, to make something that appears to be convenient for use, and that can without doubt be afforded and built as projected, is the job not of the architect so much as the workman. But to preconceive and to determine in the mind and with judgment something that will be perfect and complete in its every part is the achievement of such a mind as we seek. Through his intellect he must invent, through experience recognize, through judgment select, through deliberation compose, and through skill effect whatever he undertakes. I maintain that each is based on prudence and mature reflection. But as for other virtues, in him I expect no more humanity, good nature, modesty, honesty, than in any other person given to any form of vocation; for anyone who lacks these qualities, in my opinion, does not deserve to be called a man. But above all he must avoid any frivolity, obstinacy, ostentation, or presumption, and anything that might lose him good will or provoke enmity among his fellow citizens.

Finally, I would have him take the same approach as one might toward the study of letters, where no one would be satisfied until he had read and examined every author, good and bad, who had written anything on the subject in which he was interested. Likewise, wherever there is a work that has received general approval, he should inspect it with great care, record it in drawing, note its numbers, and construct models and examples of it; he should examine and study the order, position, type, and number of the individual parts, especially those employed by the architects of the biggest and most important buildings, who, it might be conjectured, were exceptional men, in that they were given control of so great an expenditure. . . .

The architect should strive constantly to exercise and improve his ability through keen and animated interest in the noble arts; in this way he should gather and store in his mind anything of note, either dispersed and scattered abroad, or hidden in the remotest recesses of Nature, that might lend his works remarkable praise and glory. . . .

[The architect] should therefore develop his ability through practice and experience in any matter that might make some commendable contribution to his knowledge; and he should not think it his only duty to possess that skill without which he could not be what he professes to be, but he should apply himself to gain understanding and appreciation of all the noble arts so far as they are relevant, which understanding should be so ready and so serviceable that he will have no need of any further learning in this field; and he must not abandon his study, nor cool his application, until he feels that he is very close to those who are awarded the highest praise. He should not consider himself satisfied until he has employed every faculty with which art and talent have endowed him, and assimilated everything to the best of his ability so that he attains the highest degree of praise for it.

Of the arts the ones that are useful, even vital, to the architect are painting and mathematics. I am not concerned whether he is versed in any others. I will not hear those who say that an architect ought to be an expert in law, because he must deal with the rules for containing water, establishing boundaries, and proclaiming the intention to build, and with the many other legal constraints encountered during the course of building. Nor do I demand that he should have an exact understanding of the stars, simply because it is best to make libraries face Boreas, and baths the setting sun. Nor do I say that he ought to be a musician, because he must place sounding vases in a theater; nor an orator, to instruct his client on what he proposes to do. Let him have insight, experience, wisdom, and diligence in the matters to be discussed, and he will give an articulate, accurate, and informed account of them, which is the most important thing in oratory.

Yet he should not be inarticulate, nor insensitive to the sound of harmony; and it is enough that he does not build on public land, or on another person's property; that he does not obstruct the light; that he does not transgress the servitudes on rain dripping from the eaves, on watercourses, and on rights of way, except where there is provision; and that he has a sound knowledge of the winds, their direction, and their names; still, I would not criticize him for being better educated. But he should forsake painting and mathematics no more than the poet should ignore tone and meter. Nor do I imagine that a limited knowledge of them is enough.

But I can say this of myself: I have often conceived of projects in the mind that seemed quite commendable at the time; but when I translated them into drawings, I found several errors in the very parts that delighted me most, and quite serious ones; again, when I return to drawings, and measure the dimensions, I recognize and lament my carelessness; finally, when I pass from the drawings to the model, I sometimes notice further mistakes in the individual parts, even over the numbers. For all this I would not expect him to be a Zeuxis in his painting, or a Nichomachus in arithmetic, or an Archimedes in geometry. Let it be enough that he has a grasp of those elements of painting of which we have written; that he has sufficient knowledge of mathematics for the practical and considered application of angles, numbers, and lines, such as that discussed under the topic of weights and the measurements of surfaces and bodies, which some called *podismata* and *embata*. If he combines enthusiasm and diligence with a knowledge of these arts, the architect will achieve favor, wealth, fame for posterity, and glory.

4 ANDREA PALLADIO, 1508–1580

Andrea Palladio, Villa Rotonda, Vicenza, Italy, 1550s
Photo Credit: Cameraphoto Arte, Venice/Art Resource, NY

Andrea Palladio, originally named Andrea di Pietro della Gondola, first established himself as a stonemason in Vicenza. In the mid-1530s, he came under the patronage of the amateur architect Giangiorgio Trissino, a wealthy Renaissance scholar who bestowed the name Palladio upon Andrea and encouraged him undertake a classical education in the arts and mathematics. With Trissino as a mentor, Palladio immersed himself in the writings of Vitruvius and traveled to Rome to study the great architectural works of Roman antiquity. Through his illustrations of ancient structures and his own architectural designs—first country villas, the most famous of which may be the Villa Capra (1566–71), also known as the Villa Rotunda) and later larger religious buildings such as the Church of San Giorgio Maggiore (1564–80)—Palladio became well known throughout the Venetian region. Yet, perhaps his greatest architectural contribution is *I Quattro Libri dell'Architettura*, a text Palladio began in the 1550s and finally published in 1570. In this treatise, known in English as *The Four Books on Architecture*, Palladio discussed his architectural philosophy and offered practical guidance for builders, thoroughly illustrated with woodcuts of his works. Unlike Alberti's architectural writings, Palladio's text was intended for a nonacademic audience, for anyone involved in construction. This lack of pretension no doubt contributed to the work's popularity; within the next century, portions of *I Quattri Libri* had been translated into multiple languages. In eighteenth-century England, Palladio's work was extremely admired, generating numerous classical designs in a style often referred to as "Palladian," thus memorializing one of the most influential architects of the Italian Renaissance.

The Four Books on Architecture (ca. mid-1550s, published 1570)

The First Book on Architecture: Foreword to the Readers

Guided by a natural inclination, I dedicated myself to the study of architecture in my youth, and since I always held the opinion that the ancient Romans, as in many other things, had also greatly surpassed all those who came after them in building well, I elected as my master and guide Vitruvius, who is the only ancient writer on this art. I set myself the task of investigating the remains of the ancient buildings that have survived despite the ravages of time and the cruelty of the barbarians, and finding them much worthier of study than I had first thought, I began to measure all their parts minutely and with the greatest care. I became so assiduous an investigator of such things that, being unable to find anything that was not made with fine judgment and beautiful proportions, I repeatedly visited various parts of Italy and abroad in order to understand the totality of buildings from their parts and commit them to drawings. Accordingly, seeing how different the usual manner of building is from the things that I had observed in those structures and had read about in Vitruvius and Leon Battista Alberti and the other excellent writers who came after Vitruvius, and also from those which I myself built recently, which have been greatly appreciated and praised by those who employed me, I considered it worthy of man, who is not born for himself alone but also to be of use to others, to make public the designs of those buildings that I have collected over such a long period and at such personal risk, and to expound briefly what it is about them that seemed to me to be most worthy of consideration, and also the rules that I have followed and still follow when building; so that those who read my books may benefit from what is useful in them and supply themselves

Andrea Palladio, *The Four Books on Architecture*, trans. Robert Tavernor and Richard Schofield (Cambridge, MA: MIT Press, 1997), 5–7. © 1997 Massachusetts Institute of Technology. Reprinted with permission of the publisher. Translators' commentary omitted from this reprinting.

those things (of which perhaps there will be many) which I will have overlooked; so that, little by little, one may learn to set aside those strange abuses, barbarous inventions, and pointless expenses and (most importantly) avoid the common failures of various kinds that have been seen in many buildings. . . . I hope therefore that this manner of building will, to the benefit of all, soon achieve that level so desirable in all the arts. . . . [Since] I must publish the results of those labors which, since my youth, I have devoted to studying and measuring the ancient buildings that I knew about with as much care as I was capable of, and take this occasion to discuss architecture as briefly, methodically, and clearly as I could, I thought it would be most appropriate to begin with private houses; for it is plausible that they supplied the models [ragione] for public buildings, since it is very likely that man previously lived by himself, and then, seeing that he needed the help of other men in providing those things which would make him happy (if happiness is to be found down here), he quite naturally longed for and loved the company of other men: so they formed settlements from a number of houses and from settlements cities in which there were public places and buildings; and also because, of all the branches of architecture, none is more essential to man nor more often built than this. I shall discuss, therefore, private houses, and will then proceed to public buildings. I shall deal briefly with roads, bridges, squares, prisons, basilicas (that is, places of judgment), xysti, palaestrae, which were places where men took exercise, temples, theaters and amphitheaters, arches, baths, aqueducts, and finally I shall deal with the fortification of cities, and with harbors. In all these books I shall avoid being long-winded and will simply provide the advice [avertenza] that seems essential to me, and will make use of those terms widely used nowadays by craftsmen. For my part, I can promise no more than long labor, great diligence, and the devotion which I put into understanding and practicing what I offer; if it pleases God that I have not worked in vain I shall give thanks for his goodness, with all my heart, while still remaining greatly indebted to those who, through their own ingenious inventions and the experience they gained, have bequeathed us the rules of this art, for they opened up an easier and more direct route to the study of new things, and (thanks to them) we know of many things that would perhaps have remained hidden. This first part will be divided into two books; the first will be concerned with the preparation of materials and, once prepared, how and in what form they are to be used from the foundations up to the roof; and where those universal rules, which should be followed in all public as well as private structures, should be applied. The second will be concerned with the types [qualità] of buildings suitable to various classes of men; first I will discuss buildings in the city and then well-chosen and convenient sites required for buildings in the country [villa] and how they are to be laid out [compartire]. And, as we have very few ancient examples to refer to in this part, I will include plans and elevations [impiede] of many buildings which I designed [ordinare] for various gentlemen, and the designs of houses of the ancients with the most noteworthy parts of them following Vitruvius' teachings about how they were to be made.

Chapter I. On What Must Be Considered and Prepared Before Building Can Start
One must consider carefully every aspect of the plan [pianta] and elevations [impiede] of a building before starting to build. There are three things in every building (as Vitruvius says) that have to be considered, without which none deserve credit; these are usefulness or convenience [commodità], durability, and beauty. For one could not describe as perfect a building which was useful, but only briefly, or one which was inconvenient for a long time, or, being both durable and useful, was not beautiful. Convenience will be provided for when each member [membro] is given its appropriate position, well situated, no less than dignity requires nor more than utility demands; each member will be correctly positioned when the loggias [loggia], halls, rooms, cellars, and granaries are located in their appropriate places. Durability will be guaranteed when all the walls are plumb vertical, thicker below than above, and have sound and strong foundations; and further, when the columns above stand vertically over those below and all the solid openings, such as doors and windows, are one above the other: so that solid is above solid and void above void. Beauty will derive from a graceful shape and the relationship of the whole to the parts, and of the parts among themselves and to the whole, because buildings must appear to be like complete and well-defined

bodies, of which one member [membro] matches another and all the members are necessary for what is required. Having weighed up these things by mean of drawings and the model, one must carefully calculate the entire cost involved, making provision for the money in good time and preparing the materials that are likely needed, so that, when building, nothing is missing or hinders the completion of the work; for the patron [edificatore] will get great credit and the whole building will be at a great advantage if it is built at the appropriate pace, and all its walls, having been built up at the same height together, settle to the same extent, for then they will not develop those cracks seen so often in buildings which were constructed at different times and brought to their conclusion haphazardly. Then, once the most skillful craftsmen available have been chosen, so that the work may be carried out in the best possible manner according to their advice, provision should be made for timber, stone, sand, lime, and metals; on the subject of these materials one should heed the following rule [avertenza] that, for instance, to make the woodwork of the ceilings [travamenta, solaro] of halls and rooms, a sufficient quantity of beams should be provided so that, when putting them all in place, there is a space as wide as a beam and a half between them. Similarly, with stone, bear in mind that the jambs [erta] of the doors and windows do not require pieces of stone thicker than one fifth of the width of the opening nor less than one sixth. And if the ornament of a building is to be supplied by columns or pilasters [pilastri], their bases, capitals, and architraves should be stone, and the other parts of brick [pietro cotta]. As to walls, take care to make them thinner as they rise; such a rule should ensure the cost is reasonable and cut expenses considerably. Since I will talk in detail about all these subjects in their proper place, it is enough for now to have mentioned these general considerations here and to have made, as it were, a sketch of the whole building. But because, as well as the quantity one must also consider the type [qualità] and quality when choosing the best material, much will be gained from having experienced the buildings of others, because, having learned from them, we can already decide what is appropriate and suited to our own needs.

5 CLAUDE PERRAULT, 1613–1688

Claude Perrault, east front of the Louvre, Paris, 1666–70
View along the Quai du Louvre
Photo Credit: Réunion des Musées Nationaux/Art Resource, NY

Claude Perrault began his career as a physician interested in the study of anatomy, natural history, and physics. He received no formal architectural training, but nevertheless was involved in a number of architectural endeavors. His design for the East Façade of the Louvre (1665–80), at that time the Parisian royal residence, is his most well known. In combination, the East Façade's distinctive paired colonnade, raised basement level, and central crowning pediment inspired a number of works built throughout Europe and the United States, including Charles Garnier's Paris Opera (1857–74) and Charles Bulfinch's State House in Boston (1795–98). Perrault's notoriety also stemmed from his 1673 French translation of Vitruvius's *Ten Books on Architecture* as well as Perrault's 1683 publication, *Ordonnance des cinq espèces de colonnes selon la méthode des Anciens*, or *Ordonnance for the Five Kinds of Columns after the Method of the Ancients*. In the latter treatise, excerpted below, Perrault argued against the existence of universally fixed proportions arising from nature that, when changed, destroy architectural beauty. Disagreeing with this notion of absolute beauty based upon proportion, Perrault identified two types of beauty: positive and arbitrary. Positive beauty, according to Perrault, results from an inherent quality that is pleasing to everyone, such as rich materials or the precise execution of a work. Arbitrary beauty, however, stems not from innate qualities but from culturally conditioned preferences. With this distinction between positive and arbitrary beauty, Perrault provided an alternate framework through which architecture, and popular taste, could be viewed.

Ordonnance for the Five Kinds of Columns after the Method of the Ancients (1683)

Preface

The ancients rightly believed that the proportional rules that give buildings their beauty were based on the proportions of the human body and that just as nature has suited a massive build to bodies made for physical labor while giving a slighter one to those requiring adroitness and agility, so in the art of building, different rules are determined by the different intentions to make a building more massive or more delicate. Now these different proportions together with their appropriate ornaments are what give rise to the different architectural orders, whose characters, defined by variations in ornament, are what distinguish them most visibly but whose most essential differences consist in the relative size of their constituent parts.

These differences between the orders that are based, with little exactitude or precision, on their proportions and characters are the only well-established matters in architecture. Everything else pertaining to the precise measurement of their members or the exact outline of their profiles still has no rule on which all architects agree; each architect has attempted to bring these elements to their perfection chiefly through the things that proportion determines. As a result, in the opinion of those who are knowledgeable, a number of architects have approached an equal degree of perfection in different ways. This shows that the beauty of a building, like that of the human body, lies less in the exactitude of unvarying proportion and the relative size of constituent

Claude Perrault, *Ordonnance for the Five Kinds of Columns after the Method of the Ancients*, trans. Indra Kagis McEwen (Los Angeles: The Getty Center for the History of Art and the Humanities, 1993) 47–48, 50–51, 53–54. © 1993 The Getty Center for the History of Art and the Humanities, the J. Paul Getty Trust, Los Angeles. Reprinted with permission of the publisher.

parts than in the grace of its form, wherein nothing other than a pleasing variation can sometimes give rise to a perfect and matchless beauty without strict adherence to any proportional rule. A face can be both ugly and beautiful without any change in proportions, so that an alteration of the features—for example, the contraction of the eyes and the enlargement of the mouth—can be the same when one laughs or weeps, with a result that can be pleasing in one case and repugnant in the other; whereas, the dissimilar proportions of two different faces can be equally beautiful. Likewise, in architecture, we see works whose differing proportions nevertheless have the grace to elicit equal approval from those who are knowledgeable and possessed of good taste in architectural matters.

One must agree, however, that although no single proportion is indispensable to the beauty of a face, there still remains a standard from which its proportion cannot stray too far without destroying its perfection. Similarly, in architecture, there are not only general rules of proportion, such as those that, as we have said, distinguish one order from anther, but also detailed rules from which one cannot deviate without robbing an edifice of much of its grace and elegance. Yet these proportions have enough latitude to leave architects free to increase or decrease the dimensions of different elements according to the requirements occasioned by varying circumstances. . . . It is . . . also for this very reason that all those who have written about architecture contradict one another, with the result that in the ruins of ancient buildings and among the great number of architects who have dealt with the proportions of the orders, one can find agreement neither between any two buildings nor between any two authors, since none has followed the same rules.

This shows just how ill-founded is the opinion of people who believe that the proportions supposed to be preserved in architecture are as certain and invariable as the proportions that give musical harmony its beauty and appeal, proportions that do not depend on us but that nature has established with absolutely immutable precision and that cannot be changed without immediately offending even the least sensitive ear. For if this were so, those works of architecture that do not have the true and natural proportions that people claim they can have would necessarily be condemned by common consensus, at least by those whom extensive knowledge has made most capable of discernment. . . .

Now, even though we often like proportions that follow the rules of architecture without knowing why, it is nevertheless true that there must be some reason for this liking. The only difficulty is to know if this reason is always something positive, as in the case of musical harmonies, of it, more usually, it is simply founded on custom and whether that which makes the proportions of a building pleasing is not the same as that which makes the proportions of a fashionable costume pleasing. For the latter have nothing positively beautiful or inherently likable, since when there is a change in custom or in any other of the nonpositive reasons that make us like them, we like them no longer, even though the proportions themselves remain the same.

In order to judge rightly in this case, one must suppose two kinds of beauty in architecture and know which beauties are based on convincing reasons and which depend only on prejudice. I call beauties based on convincing reasons those whose presence in works is bound to please everyone, so easily apprehended are their value and quality. They include the richness of materials, the size and magnificence of the building, the precision and cleanness of the execution, and symmetry, which in French signifies the kind of proportion that produces an unmistakable and striking beauty. For there are two kinds of proportions. One, difficult to discern, consists in the proportional relationship between the parts, such as that between the size of various elements, either with respect to one another or to the whole, of which an element may be, for instance, a seventh, fifteenth, or twentieth part. The other kind of proportion, called symmetry, is very apparent and consists in the relationship the parts have collectively as a result of the balanced correspondence of their size, number, disposition, and order. . . .

Against the beauties I call positive and convincing, I set those I call arbitrary, because they are determined by our wish to give a definite proportion, shape, or form to things that might well have a different form without being misshapen and that appear agreeable not by reasons within everyone's grasp but merely by custom and the association the mind makes between two things of a different nature. By this association the esteem that inclines the mind to things whose worth it knows also inclines it to those things whose worth it does not know and little by little induces it to value both equally. This principle is the natural basis for belief, which is nothing but the result of a predisposition not to doubt the truth of something we do not know if it is accompanied by our knowledge and good opinion of the person who assures us of it. It is also prejudice that makes us like the fashions and the patterns of speech that custom has established at court, for the regard we have or the worthiness and patronage of people in the court makes us like their clothing and their way of speaking, although these things in themselves have nothing positively likable, since after a time they offend us without their having undergone any inherent change.

It is the same in architecture, where there are things such as the usual proportions between capitals and their columns that custom alone makes so agreeable that we could not bear their being otherwise, even though in themselves they have no beauty that must infallibly please us or necessarily elicit our approval. . . .

. . . [Neither] imitation of nature, nor reason, nor good sense in any way constitutes the basis for the beauty people claim to see in proportion and in the orderly disposition of the parts [of a work of architecture]; indeed, it is impossible to find any source other than custom for the pleasure they impart. Since those who first invented these proportions had no rule other than their fancy (*fantaisie*) to guide them, as their fancy changed they introduced new proportions, which in turn were found pleasing. . . .

The first works of architecture manifested richness of materials; grandeur, opulence, and precision of workmanship; symmetry (which is a balanced and fitting correspondence of parts that maintain the same arrangement and position); good sense in matters where it is called for; and other obvious reasons for beauty. As a result, these works seemed so beautiful and were so admired and revered that people decided they should serve as the criteria for all others. And inasmuch as they believed it impossible to add to or to change anything in all these positive beauties without diminishing the beauty of the whole, they found it unimaginable that the proportions of these works could be altered without ill effect; whereas, they could, in fact, have been otherwise without injury to the other beauties. In the same way, when a person passionately loves a face whose only perfect beauty lies in its complexion, he also believes its proportions could not be improved upon, for just as the great beauty of one part makes him love the whole, so the love of the whole entails the love of its parts.

It is therefore true that in architecture there is positive beauty and beauty that is only arbitrary, even though it appears to be positive due to prejudice, against which one guards oneself with great difficulty. It is also true that even though good taste is founded on a knowledge of both kinds of beauty, a knowledge of arbitrary beauty is usually more apt to form what we call taste and is that which distinguishes true architects from the rest.

Etienne-Louis Boullée, 1728–1799

6

Born and raised in Paris, Etienne-Louis Boullée initially pursued painting before turning to architecture. He trained and practiced in a neoclassical idiom, but relatively little of his work was actually constructed. Rather, Boullée's reputation rests largely on his work as a teacher, theorist, and designer of visionary projects. In his treatise *Architecture, Essai sur l'art* (*Architecture, Essay on Art*), written in the 1790s but unpublished until the mid-1950s, Boullée espoused his view of architecture as a highly poetic and psychological art grounded in nature. He believed the sphere, a naturally occuring form and Boullee's "image of perfection," supported this assertion. According to Boullée, the sphere's appealing qualities—symmetry, regularity, and variety—have an "immeasurable hold over our senses"; these immutable qualities, in Boullée's estimation, derive from nature.

Boullée's visionary projects employed a stripped neoclassical vocabulary that has come to be associated with French revolutionary architecture. His designs relied heavily on geometric forms and the ways in which they would be modeled by light and shadow; they also drew on the permanence and emotive power of ancient Egyptian monuments. For example, Boullée's project for Newton's Cenotaph (1784), a funerary monument to the British scientist and mathematician, involves a gigantic sphere 500 feet in diameter embedded within a cylindrical base. At its center, this sphere would contain the tomb of Newton, as well as a suspended globe representing both the sun and moon. Boullée intended the Cenotaph to symbolize the universe and communicate with those experiencing the structure. This idea of *architecture parlante*, or "speaking architecture," discussed by Boullée's contemporary, Claude Nicolas Ledoux, gained renewed interest in the latter half of the twentieth century after the 1953 publication of Boullée's *Architecture, Essay on Art*.

Architecture, Essay on Art (1770–84)

Introduction

What is architecture? Shall I join Vitruvius in defining it as the art of building? In-deed, no, for there is a flagrant error in this definition. Vitruvius mistakes the effect for the cause.

In order to execute, it is first necessary to conceive. Our earliest ancestors built their huts only when they had a picture of them in their minds. It is this product of the mind, this process of creation, that constitutes architecture and what can consequently be defined as the art of designing and bringing to perfection any building whatsoever. Thus, the art of construction is merely an auxiliary art which, in our opinion, could appropriately be called the scientific side of architecture.

Art, in the true sense of the word, and science, these we believe have their place in architecture.

The majority of authors writing on this subject confine themselves to discussing the technical side. That is natural if we think about it a little. It was necessary to study safe building methods before attempting to build attractively. And since the technical side is of paramount importance and consequently the most essential, it was natural that this aspect should be dealt with first.

Etienne-Louis Boullée, *Architecture, Essay on Art*, in Helen Rosenau, *Boullée & Visionary Architecture* (London: Academy Editions; New York: Harmony Books, 1976), 83, 85–87.

Moreover, it must be admitted that the beauty of art cannot be demonstrated like a mathematical truth; although this beauty is derived from nature, to sense it and apply it fruitfully certain qualities are necessary and nature is not very generous with them.

What do we find in books on architecture? Ruins of ancient temples that we know were excavated in Greece. However perfect these examples may be, they are not sufficient to provide a complete treatise on art. . . .

And now Reader, let me ask you, "Am I not to some extent justified in maintaining that architecture is still in its infancy, for we have no clear notion of its basic principles?"

In common with all education me, I admit that tact and sensibility can result in excellent work. I admit that even artists who have not acquired sufficient knowledge to search out the basic principles at the root of their art will nevertheless be competent, provided they are guided by that gift of Nature that permits men to choose wisely.

But it is nonetheless true that there are few authors who have considered architecture from the artistic point of view; what I mean is that few authors have attempted to study in depth that side of architecture that I term art, in the strict sense of the word. We have some precepts based on good examples but these are few and far between. . . .

The Present Problem
Is architecture merely fantastic art belonging to the realm of pure invention or are its basic principles derived from Nature?

Allow me first of all to challenge the existence of any art form that is pure invention.

If by the strength of his mind and the techniques it devises, a man could arouse in us with his art those sensations we experience when we look at nature, such art would be far superior to anything we possess, for we are limited to more or less imperfect [imitations]. But there is no art that we can create alone, for if such an art existed it would mean that the Divine Being, the creator of Nature, had endowed us with a quality that is part of His own essential being.

What, therefore, could Perrault have meant by a purely inventive art? Don't we derive all our ideas from nature? And does not genius for us lie in the forceful manner in which our senses are reminded of nature?. . .

Let us listen to a modern Philosopher [John Locke] who tells us, "All our ideas, all our perceptions come to us via external objects. External objects make different impressions on us according to whether they are more or less analogous with the human organism." I should add that we consider "*beautiful*" those objects that most resemble the human organism and that we reject those which, lacking this resemblance, do not correspond to the human condition.

On the Essential Quality of Volumes. On Their Properties. On Their Analogy with the Human Organism

. . . [A] sphere is, in all respects, the image of perfection. It combines strict symmetry with the most perfect regularity and the greatest possible variety; its form is developed to the fullest extent and is the simplest that exists; its shape is outlined by the most agreeable contour and, finally, the light effects that it produces are so beautifully graduated that they could not possibly be softer, more agreeable or more varied. These unique advantages, which the sphere derives from nature, have an immeasurable hold over our senses.

A great man (Montesquieu) once said, "Symmetry is pleasing because it is the image of clarity and because the mind, which is always seeking understanding, easily accepts and grasps all that is symmetrical."[1] I would add that symmetry is pleasing because it is the image of order and perfection.

Variety is pleasing because it satisfied a spiritual need which, by its very nature, likes to be stimulated and sustained by what is new. And it is variety that makes things appear new to us. It therefore follows that variety puts new life into our faculties by offering us new pleasures and it is as pleasing to us in the objects that are part of any given volume, as it is in the light effects so produced.

Grandeur, too, always pleases us whatever form it takes for we are ever eager to increase our pleasure and would like to embrace the Universe.

Finally, the image of Grace is one which, deep in our hearts, is the most pleasing of all. . . .

Consideration of How We Can with Certitude Define the Basic Principles of an Art and of Architecture in Particular

What constitute to perfection the principles of any given art are those principles from which no deviation is possible. . . .

---

[1] Here Boullée refers to the article "Goût" on page 764 of Montesquieu's *Encyclopédie* (1757).

What . . . is the primary law on which architectural principles are based?

Let us consider an example of architecture that has been imperfectly observed and lacks proportion. This will certainly be a defect but the defect will not necessarily be such an eyesore that we cannot bear to look at the building. . . .

In architecture a lack of proportion is not generally very obvious except to the eye of the connoisseur. It is thus evident that although proportion is one of the most important elements constituting beauty in architecture, it is not the primary law from which its basic principles derive. Let us try, therefore, to discover what it is impossible not to admit in architecture, and that from which there can be no deviation without creating a real eyesore.

Let us imagine a man with a nose that is not in the middle of his face, with eyes that are not equidistant, one being higher than the other, and whose limbs are also ill-matched. It is certain that we would consider such a man hideous. Here we have an example that can readily be applied to the subject under discussion. If we imagine a Palace with an off-centre front projection, with no symmetry and with windows set at varying intervals and different heights, the overall impression would be one of confusion and it is certain that to our eyes such a building would be both hideous and intolerable.

It is easy for the reader to surmise that the basic rule and the one that governs the principles of architecture, originates in regularity. . . .

. . . Symmetrical compositions are true and pure. The slightest disorder, the slightest confusion becomes intolerable. Order must be in evidence and paramount in any composition based on symmetry. In short, the wheel of reason should never desert an architect's genius for he should always make a rule of the excellent maxim, "Nothing is beautiful if all is not judicious."

West façade of Notre-Dame, Paris, France, ca. 1200–50
Photo Credit: Scala/Art Resource, NY

The French architect Eugène-Emmanuel Viollet-le-Duc is well known for his restoration work on Gothic monuments such as Sainte-Chappelle and Notre Dame in Paris. Yet, his legacy rests on his theoretical writings. Deeply influenced by buildings of the Middle Ages, Viollet-le-Duc championed Gothic architecture as a model for the designers of his day. However, he did not call for a Gothic revival, but rather emphasized the governing logic behind medieval architecture. In particular, Viollet-le-Duc identified the direct correlation between the form and structure of the Gothic cathedral. Ultimately, Gothic builders aspired to construct the lightest, tallest, most graceful works possible. This meant a dematerialization of the building itself, a reduction of the building's mass in favor of vast amounts of glass. Every feature of the Gothic cathedral, from the elongated compound piers to its ribbed groin vaults, needed to function structurally. All forms, even seemingly ornamental elements, were direct manifestations of the building's structure. According to Viollet-le-Duc, the underlying principles of this structure stem from the logic and rationality of nature, the harmony of parts, proportion, and use, evident in natural creations. Viollet-le-Duc discussed this universal principle of structural rationalism as well as other architectural theories in his ten-volume *Dictionnaire raisonné de l'architecture française du XI au XVI siècle* (literally, the *Reasoned Dictionary of French Architecture of the 11th to the 16th Centuries*, but often called the *Dictionnaire raisonné*) of 1854–69 and his two volume *Entretiens sur l'architecture* (*Discourses on Architecture*) of 1858–72. Viollet-le-Duc's notion of structural rationalism was particularly influential for modern architects of the late-nineteenth and early-twentieth centuries.

Dictionnaire raisonné (1854–68)

STYLE, s.m. There is *style*; then there are the *styles*. Styles enable us to distinguish different schools and epochs from one another. The styles of Greek, Roman, Byzantine, Romanesque, and Gothic architecture differ from each other in ways that make it easy to classify the monuments produced by these various types of art. . . .

We will speak here of *style* only as it belongs to art understood as a conception of the human mind. Just as there is only *Art* in this sense, so there is only one *Style*. What, then, is style in this sense? It is, in a work of art, the manifestation of an ideal based on a principle.

Style can also be understood as mode; that is, to make the form of an art appropriate to its objective. In art, then, there is *absolute style*; there is also *relative style*. The first dominates the entire artistic conception of an object; the second can be modified depending upon the purpose of the object. The style appropriate for a church would not be appropriate for a private dwelling; this is relative style. Yet a house can reveal the imprint of an artistic expression (just as can a temple or a barracks) that is independent of the object itself, an imprint belonging to the artist or, more precisely, to the principle that he took as a starting point: this is *style*. . . .

Style is for a work of art what blood is for the human body: it develops the work, nourishes it, gives it strength, health, and duration; it gives it, as the saying goes, the real blood that is common to all humans. Although each individual has very different

Eugène-Emmanuel Viollet-le-Duc, "Style," in *Dictionnaire raisonné*, trans. Kenneth D. Whitehead (New York: George Braziller, Inc., 1990). Reprinted with permission from the publisher.

physical and moral qualities, we must nevertheless speak of style when it is a question of the artist's power to give body and life to works of art, even when each work of art still has its own proper character. . . .

. . . Architecture as an art is a human creation. Such is our inferiority that, in order to achieve this type of creation, we are obliged to proceed as nature proceeds in the things she creates. We are obliged to employ the same elements and the same logical method as nature; we are obliged to observe the same submission to certain natural laws and to observe the same transitions. When the first man traced in the sand with a stick a circle pivoting upon its axis, he in no way *invented* the circle; he merely discovered a figure already existing. All discoveries in geometry have resulted from observations, not creations. The angles opposite the vertex of a triangle did not have to wait to be discovered by somebody in order to be equal to each other.

Architecture, this most human of creations, is but an application of principles that are born outside us—principles that we appropriate by observation. Gravitational force existed before we did; we merely deduced the statics of it. Geometry, too, was already existent in the universal order; we merely took note of its laws, and applied them. The same thing is true of all aspects of the architectural art; proportions—indeed, even decoration—must arise out of the great natural order whose principles we must appropriate in the measure that human intelligence permits us to do so. It was not without reason that Vitruvius said that the architect had to be in possession of most of the knowledge of his time, and for his part he put philosophy at the head of all knowledge. Among the ancients, of course, philosophy included all of the sciences of "observation," whether in the moral order or in the physical order.

If, therefore, we succeed in acquiring some little knowledge of the great principles of the universal natural order, we will quickly realize that all creation is developed in a very logical way and, very probably, is subject to laws anterior to any creative idea.

So much is this the case that we might well claim: "In the beginning, numbers and geometry existed!" Certainly the Egyptians and, after them, the Greeks understood things that way; for them, numbers and geometric figures were sacred. We believe that the style the Egyptians and Greeks achieved—for style is never lacking in their artistic productions—was due to the religious respect they had for the principles to which universal creation itself was the first to be subject, that universal creation which itself is style *par excellence*.

In questions of this order, however, we need to bring forward some simple and obvious demonstration. We are not here concerned with philosophy; we are concerned with bringing some great and fundamental principles within our grasp—simple principles, in fact. Style is able to enter into architectural work only when it operates in accordance with these fundamental principles.

There are those who appear to be persuaded that artists are simply born with the faculty to produce works with style and that all they have to do is to open themselves to a sort of inspiration of which they are not the masters. This idea would appear to be too broadly general in its sweep; it is, nevertheless, favored by the fuzzy-minded. It is not an idea, however, that ever seems to have been favored or, indeed, even admitted in those epochs that knew best how to produce the works of art that have been most noted for their style. On the contrary, in those times it was believed that the most perfect kind of artistic creation was the consequence of a profound observation of the principles on which art can and must be based. (It was, of course, also granted that artists did possess artistic faculties.)

We will leave it open to poets and painters to decide whether what we call inspiration can or cannot get along without a long and profound observation of nature. As far as architecture is concerned, however, this particular pursuit is compelled on its scientific side to observe the imperatives that rule it; it is obliged from the very first to seek the elements and the principles on which it will be based, and then to deduce from them with an utterly rigorous logic all the consequences that follow. It happens to be the truth that we cannot pretend to proceed with a power greater than that possessed by universal creation itself, for we act at all only by the virtue of our observation of the laws of that creation. Once we have recognized that nature (however we suppose nature herself to have been inspired) has never so much as joined two single atoms together without being subject to a completely logical rule; once we have recognized that nature always proceeds with mathematical exactitude from the simple to the complex, without ever abandoning its first principles—once we have recognized these things, we will surely have to be allowed to smile broadly if we then find an architect waiting for an *inspiration* without first having some recourse to his reason. . . .

. . . If we were to follow through and examine all the phases of creation in our world, both organic and inorganic, we would quickly find it to be the case that, in all of nature's various works, however different they may be in appearance, the same logical order proceeding from a fundamental principle is followed; this is an *a priori* law, and nature never deviates from it. And it is to this natural method that is owing the "style" with which all of nature's works are imbued. From the largest mountain down to the finest crystal, from the lichen to the oaks of our forests, from the polyp to human beings, everything in terrestrial creation does indeed possess style—that is to say, a perfect harmony between the results obtained and the means employed to achieve them.

This is the example that nature has provided for us, the example we must follow when, with the help of our intelligence, we presume to create anything ourselves.

What we call imagination is in reality only one aspect of our human mind. It is the part of the mind that is alive even while the body is asleep; it is through that same part of the mind that, in dreams, we see spread out before us bizarre scenes consisting of impossible facts and events that have no connection one with the other. This part of ourselves that is imagination still does not sleep when we are awake; but we generally regulate it by means of our reason. We are not the masters of our imagination; it distracts us unceasingly and turns us away from whatever is occupying us, although it seems to escape entirely and float freely only during sleep. However, we are the masters of our reason. Our reason truly belongs to us; we nourish it and develop it. With constant exercise, we are able to make out of it an attentive "operator" for ourselves, able to regulate our actions and ensure that our accomplishments are both lively and lasting.

Thus, even while we recognize that a work of art may exist in an embryonic state in the imagination, we must also recognize that it will not develop into a true and viable work of art without the intervention of reason. It is reason that will provide the embryonic work with the necessary organs to survive, with the proper relationships between its various parts, and also with what in architecture we call its proper proportions. Style is the visible sign of the unity and harmony of all the parts that make up the whole work of art. Style originates, therefore, in an intervention of reason.

The architecture of the Egyptians, like that of the Greeks, possessed style because both architectures were derived by means of an inflexible logical progression from the principle of stability on which both were based. One cannot say the same of all the constructions of the Romans during the Roman Empire. As for the architecture of the Middle Ages, it, too, possessed style once it had abandoned the debased traditions of antiquity—that is, in the period from the twelfth to the fifteenth centuries. It possessed style because it proceeded according to the same kind of logical order that we have observed at work in nature. Thus, just as in viewing a single leaf it is possible to reconstruct the entire plant, and in viewing an animal bone, the animal itself, it is also possible to deduce the members of an architecture from the view of an architectural profile . . . Similarly, the nature of the finished construction can be derived from an architectural member. . . .

. . . [Style] as well as the beautiful, we must insist, resides not merely in forms, but in the harmony of a form with reference to an end in view, to a result to be achieved. If a form clearly delineates an object and makes understandable the purpose for which that object was produced, then it is a beautiful form. It is for this reason that the creations of nature are always beautiful in the eyes of the observer. The correct application of a form to its object and to its use or function, and the harmony that necessarily always accompanies such a correct application, can only evoke our admiration, whether we observe it in a stately oak tree or in the smallest of insects. We will discover style in the mechanisms of the wings of a bird of prey, just as we will discover style in the curves of a body of a fish; in these cases style clearly results from mechanisms or curves so aptly designed that flight results in one case and swimming in the other. It hardly concerns us if someone points out that a bird has wings in order to be able to fly or that this bird is able to fly only because of its wings; the fact is that the wings are a perfect machine, which produces flight. This machine represents a precise expression of the function that it fulfills. We other artists need go no further than this. . . .

. . . Now, style is inherent in an architectural art when that art is practiced in accordance with a logical and harmonious order, whether in its details or as a whole, whether in its principles or in its form; nothing in such an architectural art is ever left to chance or fantasy. It is, however, nothing but fantasy that guides an artist if, for example, he provides a wall that has no need of it with an architectural order; or if he provides with a buttress a column already erected with a view toward carrying a load. It is fantasy that includes in the same building concave bays along with square bays terminating with horizontal beam members; or that inserts projecting cornices or ledges between the floors of a building where there are no roof drains; or that raises up pediments over bays opening on a wall; or that cuts into an upper story in order to make a door opening for the people or vehicles that must pass through the door; and so on. If it is not fantasy that leads to the construction of such things, so contrary to reason, then it must be what is commonly called *taste*. But is it a proof of good taste in architecture not to proceed in accordance with reason? Architecture, after all, is an art that is destined to satisfy, before everything else, material needs that are perfectly well defined; and architecture is obliged to make use of materials whose qualities result from laws to which we must necessarily submit.

It is an illusion to imagine that there can be style in architectural works whose features are unexplained and unexplainable; or that there can be style where the form is nothing but the product of memory crammed with a number of different motifs taken from here or from there. It would be equally valid to say that there could be style in a literary work of which the chapters or, indeed, even the sentences were nothing but a loose collection of words borrowed from ten different authors, all writing on different subjects. . . .

Style is the consequence of a principle pursued methodically; it is a kind of emanation from the form of the work that is not consciously sought after. Style that is sought after is really nothing else but *manner*. Manner becomes dated; style never does.

When an entire population of artists and artisans is strongly imbued with logical principles in accordance with which form is the consequence of the object as well as its purpose, then style will be present in the works that issue from their hands, from the most ordinary vase to the most monumental building, from the simplest household utensil to the costliest piece of furniture. We admire this unity in the best of Greek antiquity, and we find the same kind of thing again in the best of what the Middle Ages produced, though the two types of art are different because the two civilizations that produced them were different. We cannot appropriate to ourselves the style of the Greeks, because we are not Athenians. Nor can we re-create the style of our predecessors in the Middle Ages, for the simple reason that time has moved on. We can only affect the manner of the Greeks or of the artists of the Middle Ages; that is to say, we can only produce pastiches. If we cannot accomplish what they did, we can at least proceed as they did by allowing ourselves to become penetrated with principles that are true and natural principles—just as they were imbued with true and natural principles. If we succeed in doing this, our works will possess style without our having to seek after it.

8 LOUIS SULLIVAN, 1856–1924

During the late-nineteenth century, Louis Sullivan played a central role in the development of an American architecture that rejected the use of historicist styles. As discussed in the excerpt below, Sullivan felt that architecture should draw on a principle he discerned in nature, namely, that "form ever follows function." At its most basic, this dictum implies that a building's form, like an eagle's wing, must reflect its function or use. For example, Sullivan's Wainwright Building in St. Louis, Missouri (1890) has three distinct zones that correspond to the presumed interior activities. The ground floor, dedicated to commercial purposes, features large windows for product display. The smaller, regular windows of the middle floors relate to the individual offices housed within, while the uppermost floor, occupied by mechanical equipment for the building, has no need for daylight and thus is marked by small round voids surrounded by vegetal-like ornament. Indeed, Sullivan's designs often included ornamental motifs derived from nature, as function for Sullivan involved not only the practical use of the building by its occupants, but also their psychological and aesthetic experience of the building. Furthermore, function encompassed the efficiency and durability of the building itself. It is not surprising, then, that Sullivan embraced modern technology, in particular steel frame construction, which allowed for increased floor space, flexible arrangement of the interiors, and a maximum amount of light due to amplified fenestration. Thus, Sullivan combined ideas of nature and technology in his search for a unique American architecture, a philosophy that set him apart from his contemporary architects and would inspire the work of Frank Lloyd Wright.

"The Tall Office Building Artistically Considered" (1896)

. . . All things in nature have a shape, that is to say, a form, an outward semblance, that tells us what they are, that distinguishes them from ourselves and from each other.

Unfailingly in nature these shapes express the inner life, the native quality of the animal, tree, bird, fish, that they present to us; they are so characteristic, so recognizable, that we say, simply, it is "natural" it should be so. Yet the moment we peer beneath this surface of things, the moment we look through the tranquil reflection of ourselves and the clouds above us, down into the clear, fluent, unfathomable depth of nature, how startling is the silence of it, how amazing the flow of life, how absorbing the mystery. Unceasingly the essence of things is taking shape in the matter of things, and this unspeakable process we call birth and growth. Awhile the spirit and the matter fade away together, and it is this that we call decadence, death. These two happenings seem jointed and interdependent, blended into one like a bubble and its iridescence, and they seem borne along upon a slowly moving air. This air is wonderful past all understanding.

Yet to the steadfast eye of one standing upon the shore of things, looking chiefly and most lovingly upon that side on which the sun shines and that we feel joyously to be life, the heart is ever gladdened by the beauty, the exquisite spontaneity, with which life seeks and takes on its forms in an accord perfectly responsive to its needs. It seems ever as though the life and the form were absolutely one and inseparable so adequate is the sense of fulfillment.

Louis Sullivan, "The Tall Office Building Artistically Considered," in *America Builds*, ed. Leland Roth (New York: Icon/Harper and Row, 1983), 344–46. © Leland M. Roth. Reprinted with permission from the publisher.

Whether it be the sweeping eagle in his flight or the open apple-blossom, the toiling work-horse, the blithe swan, the branching oak, the winding stream at its base, the drifting clouds, over all the coursing sun, form ever follows function, and this is the law. Where function does not change form does not change. The granite rocks, the ever-brooding hills, remain for ages; the lightning lives, comes into shape, and dies in a twinkling.

It is the pervading law of all things organic, and inorganic, of all things physical and metaphysical, of all things human and all things superhuman, of all true manifestations of the head, of the heart, of the soul, that the life is recognizable in its expression, that form ever follows function. This is the law.

Shall we, then, daily violate this law in our art? Are we so decadent, so imbecile, so utterly weak of eyesight, that we cannot perceive this truth so simple, so very simple? It is indeed a truth so transparent that we see through it but do not see it? Is it really then, a very marvelous thing, or is it rather so commonplace, so everyday, so near a thing to us, that we cannot perceive that the shape, form, outward expression, design or whatever we may choose, of the tall office building should in the very nature of things follow the functions of the building, and that where the function does not change, the form is not to change?

Does this not readily, clearly, and conclusively show that the lower one or two stories will take on a special character suited to the special needs, that the tiers of typical offices, having the same unchanging function, shall continue in the same unchanging form, and that as to the attic, specific and conclusive as it is in its very nature, its function shall equally be so in force, in significance, in continuity, in conclusiveness of outward expression? From this results, naturally, spontaneously, unwittingly, a three-part division, not from any theory, symbol, or fancied logic.

And thus the design of the tall office building takes its place with all other architectural types made when architecture, as has happened once in many years, was a living art. Witness the Greek temple, the Gothic cathedral, the medieval fortress.

And thus, when native instinct and sensibility shall govern the exercise of our beloved art; when the known law, the respected law, shall be that form ever follows function; when our architects shall cease struggling and prattling handcuffed and vainglorious in the asylum of a foreign school; when it is truly felt, cheerfully accepted, that this law opens up the airy sunshine of green fields, and gives to us a freedom that the very beauty and sumptuousness of the outworking of the law itself as exhibited in nature will deter any sane, any sensitive man from changing into license, when it becomes evidence that we are merely speaking a foreign language with a noticeable American accent, whereas each and every architect in the land might, under the benign influence of this law, express in the simplest, most modest, most natural way that which it is in him to say; that he might really and would surely develop his own characteristic individuality, and that the architectural art with him would certainly become a living form of speech, a natural form of utterance, giving surcease to him and adding treasures small and great to the growing art of his land; when we know and feel that Nature is our friend, not our implacable enemy—that an afternoon in the country, an hour by the sea, a full open view of one single day, through dawn, high noon, and twilight, will suggest to us so much that is rhythmical, deep, and eternal in the vast art of architecture, something so deep, so true, that all the narrow formalities, hard-and-fast rules, and strangling bonds of the schools cannot stifle it in us—then it may be proclaimed that we are on the high-road to a natural and satisfying art, and architecture that will soon become a fine art in the true, the best sense of the word, an art that will live because it will be of the people, for the people, and by the people.

9 FRANK LLOYD WRIGHT, 1867–1959

Frank Lloyd Wright, Robie House, Chicago, IL, 1908–10
Photo from *The Early Work of Frank Lloyd Wright: The "Ausgeführte Bauten" of 1911*
(NY: Dover Publications, 1982), 122

The American architect Frank Lloyd Wright began his career as a draughtsman in the office of Louis Sullivan and his partner, Dankmar Adler (1844–1900). During this time, Wright absorbed many lessons from Sullivan, including the older architect's appreciation for nature and his rejection of historicist styles. Wright developed very specific ideas about architecture, and he communicated them through numerous designs, lectures, and publications. Wright's architectural activity spanned more than six decades, during which time he developed a highly unique architecture inspired by varied sources such as the nineteenth-century American Shingle Style and the art and architecture of Japan. Wright produced masterpieces such as the Dana-Thomas House in Springfield, Illinois (1902–04); the Kauffman House, otherwise known as Fallingwater, in Bear Run, Pennsylvania (1936–37); and the Guggenheim Museum in New York City (1946–59). Each of these works represents a different phase of Wright's practice, but all demonstrate his desire for an organic architecture in which all parts contribute to a unified whole.

Wright began to express this natural philosophy quite early in his career with the development of his Prairie Style homes. Exemplified by the Robie House in Chicago, Illinois (1908–10), Wright's Prairie Style works are generally characterized by long, low, horizontal roofs that echo the flat landscape of American Midwest. A vertical chimney often anchors the building to its site, establishing the hearth as the symbolic, if not the literal, center of the family dwelling. As Wright discussed in the article excerpted below, other features such as a raised foundation, screen windows, built-in furniture, and interior flowing spaces contribute to the Prairie Style. Furthermore, Wright embraced new materials and technology, viewing the machine not as a threat to the architect's creativity but rather as a tool to assist him in his task of creating harmonious, integrated, and original works. Throughout his life, Wright maintained this philosophy as he consistently sought to develop an architecture reflective of American democracy and individuality, inspired by the integrity of the artist and of the land.

"In the Cause of Architecture" (1908)

. . . Primarily, Nature furnished the materials for architectural motifs out of which the architectural forms as we know them to-day have been developed, and, although our practice for centuries has been for the most part to turn from her, seeking inspiration in books and adhering slavishly to dead formulae, her wealth of suggestion is inexhaustible; her riches greater than any man's desire. I know with what suspicion the man is regarded who refers matters of fine art back to Nature. I know that it is usually an ill-advised return that is attempted, for Nature in external, obvious aspect is the usually accepted sense of the term and the nature that is reached. But given inherent vision there is no source so fertile, so suggestive, so helpful aesthetically for the architect as a comprehension of natural law. As Nature is never right for a picture so is she never right for the architect—that is, not ready-made. Nevertheless, she has a practical school beneath her more obvious forms in which a sense of proportion may be cultivated, when Vignola and Vitruvius fail as they must always fail. It is there that he may develop that sense of reality that translated to his own field in terms of his own work will lift him far above the realistic in his art; there he will be inspired by sentiment that will never degenerate to sentimentality and he will learn to draw with a surer hand the every-perplexing line between the curious and the beautiful.

A sense of the organic is indispensable to an architect; where can he develop it so surely as in this school? A knowledge of the relations of form and function lies at the root of his practice; where else can he find the pertinent object lessons Nature so readily fur-

Frank Lloyd Wright, "In the Cause of Architecture," in *Architectural Record* 23, no. 3 (1908). Reprinted in *The Origins of Modern Architecture: Selected Essays from Architectural Record*, ed. Eric Uhlfelder (New York: Dover Publications, Inc., 1998), 50–53, 57–58, 60. Reprinted with permission from the publisher.

nishes? Where can he study the differentiations of form that go to determine character as he can study them in the trees? Where can that sense of inevitableness characteristic of a work of art be quickened as it may be by intercourse with nature in this sense?

Japanese art knows this school more intimately than that of any people. In common use in their language there are many words like the word "edaburi," which, translated as near as may be, means the formative arrangement of the branches of a tree. We have no such word in English, we are not yet sufficiently civilized to think in such terms, but the architect must not only learn to think in such terms but he must learn in this school to fashion his vocabulary for himself and furnish it in a comprehensive way with useful words as significant as this one. . . .

In 1894, with this text from Carlyle at the top of the page—"The Ideal is within thyself, thy condition is but the stuff thou art to shape that same Ideal out of"—I formulated the following "propositions." I set them down here much as they were written then, although in the light of experience they might be stated more completely and succinctly.

I. Simplicity and Repose are qualities that measure the true value of any work of art. But simplicity is not in itself an end nor is it a matter of the side of a barn but rather an entity with a graceful beauty in its integrity from which discord, and all that is meaningless, has been eliminated. A wild flower is truly simple. Therefore:

> 1. A building should contain as few rooms as will meet the conditions which give it rise and under which we live, and which the architect should strive continually to simplify; then the ensemble of the rooms should be carefully considered that comfort and utility may go hand in hand with beauty. Beside the entry and necessary work rooms there need be but three rooms on the ground floor of any house, living room, dining room and kitchen, with the

possible addition of a "social office"; really there need be but one room, the living room with requirements otherwise sequestered from it or screened within it by means or architectural contrivances.

2. Openings should occur as integral features of the structure and form, if possible, its natural ornamentation.

3. An excessive love of detail has ruined more fine things from the standpoint of fine art or fine living than any one human shortcoming—it is hopelessly vulgar. Too many houses, when they are not little stage settings or scene paintings, are mere notion stores, bazaars or junk-shops. Decoration is dangerous unless you understand it thoroughly and are satisfied that it means something good in the scheme as a whole, for the present you are usually better off without it. Merely that it "looks rich" is no justification for the use of ornament.

4. Appliances or fixtures as such are undesirable. Assimilate them together with all appurtenances into the design of the structure.

5. Pictures deface walls oftener than they decorate them. Pictures should be decorative and incorporated in the general scheme as decoration.

6. The most truly satisfactory apartments are those in which most or all of the furniture is built in as a part of the original scheme considering the whole as an integral unit.

II. There should be as many kinds (styles) of houses as there are kinds (styles) of people and as many differentiations as there are different individuals. A man who has individuality (and what man lacks it?) has a right to its expression in his own environment.

III. A building should appear to grow easily from its site and be shaped to harmonize with its surroundings if Nature is manifest there, and if not try to make it as quiet, substantial and organic as She would have been were the opportunity Hers.[1]

We of the Middle West are living on the prairie. The prairie has a beauty of its own and we should recognize and accentuate this natural beauty, its quiet level. Hence, gently sloping roofs, low proportions, quiet sky lines, suppressed heavy-set chimneys and sheltering overhangs, low terraces and out-reaching walls sequestering private gardens.

IV. Colors require the same conventionalizing process to make them fit to live with that natural forms do; so go to the woods and fields for color schemes. Use the soft, warm, optimistic tones of earths and autumn leaves in preference to the pessimistic blues, purples or cold greens and grays of the ribbon counter; they are more wholesome and better adapted in most cases to good decoration.

V. Bring out the nature of the materials, let their nature intimately into your scheme. Strip the wood of varnish and let it alone—stain it. Develop the natural texture of the plastering and stain it. Reveal the nature of the wood, plaster, brick or stone in your designs; they are all by nature friendly and beautiful. No treatment can be really a matter of fine art when these natural characteristics are, or their nature is, outraged or neglected.

VI. A house that has character stands a good chance of growing more valuable as it grows older while a house in the prevailing mode, whatever that mode may be, is soon out of fashion, stale and unprofitable.

---

[1] In this I had in mind the barren town lots devoid of tree or natural incident, town houses and board walks only in evidence.

Buildings like people must first be sincere, must be true and then withal as gracious and lovable as may be.

Above all, integrity. The machine is the normal tool of our civilization, give it work that it can do well—nothing is of greater importance. To do this will be to formulate new industrial ideals, sadly needed. . . .

In the hope that some day America may live her own life in her own buildings, in her own way, that is, that we may make the best of what we have for what it honestly is or may become, I have endeavored in this work to establish a harmonious relationship between ground plan and elevation of these buildings, considering the one as a solution and the other an expression of the conditions of a problem of which the whole is a project. I have tried to establish an organic integrity to begin with, forming the basis for the subsequent working out of a significant grammatical expression and making the whole, as nearly as I could, consistent.

What quality of style the buildings may possess is due to the artistry with which the conventionalization as a solution and an artistic expression of a specific problem within these limitations has been handled. The types are largely a matter of personal taste and may have much or little to do with the American architecture for which we hope.

From the beginning of my practice the question uppermost in my mind has been not "what style" but "what is style?" and it is my belief that the chief value of the work illustrated here will be found in the fact that if in the face of our present day conditions any given type may be treated independently and imbued with the quality of style, then a truly noble architecture is a definite possibility, so soon as Americans really demand it of the architects of the rising generation.

I do not believe we will ever again have the uniformity of type which has characterized the so-called great "styles." Conditions have changed; our ideal is Democracy, the highest possible expression of the individual as a unit not inconsistent with a harmonious whole. The average of human intelligence rises steadily, and as the individual unit grows more and more to be trusted we will have an architecture with richer variety in unity than has ever arisen before; but the forms must be born out of our changed conditions, they must be *true* forms, otherwise the best that tradition has to offer is only an inglorious masquerade, devoid of vital significance or true spiritual value. . . .

The present industrial condition is constantly studied in the practical application of these architectural ideals and the treatment simplified and arranged to fit modern processes and to utilize to the best advantage the work of the machine. The furniture takes the clean cut, straight-line forms that the machine can render far better than would be possible by hand. Certain facilities, too, of the machine, which it would be interesting to enlarge upon, are taken advantage of and the nature of the materials is usually revealed in the process.

Nor is the atmosphere of the result in it completeness new and hard. In most of the interiors there will be found a quiet, a simple dignity that we imagine is only to be found in the "old" and it is due to the underlying organic harmony, to the each in all and the all in each throughout. This is the modern opportunity—to make a building, together with its equipment, appurtenances and environment, an entity which shall constitute a complete work of art, and a work of art more valuable to society as a whole than has before existed because discordant conditions endured for centuries are smoothed away; everyday life here finds a expression germane to its daily existence; an idealization of the common need sure to be uplifting and helpful in the same sense that pure air to breathe is better than air poisoned with noxious gases.

An artist's limitations are his best friends. The machine is here to stay. It is the forerunner of the democracy that is our dearest hope. There is no more important work before the architect now [than] to use this normal tool of civilization to the best advantage instead of prostituting it as he has hitherto done in reproducing with murderous ubiquity forms born of other times and other conditions and which it can only serve to destroy. . . .

As for the future—the work shall grow more truly simple; more expressive with fewer lines, fewer forms; more articulate with less labor; more plastic; more fluent, although more coherent; more organic. It shall grow not only to fit more perfectly the methods and processes that are called upon to produce it, but shall further find whatever is lovely or of good repute in method or process, and idealize it with the cleanest, most virile stroke I can imagine. As understanding and appreciation of life matures and deepens, this work shall prophesy and idealize the character of the individual it is fashioned to serve more intimately, no matter how inexpensive the result must finally be. It shall become in its atmosphere as pure and elevating in its humble way as the trees and flowers are in their perfectly appointed way, for only so can architecture be worthy [of] its high rank as a fine art, or the architect discharge the obligation he assumes to the public—imposed upon him by the nature of his own profession.

Although the architect Adolf Loos was born in Brno, Moravia, he spent the majority of his career in Vienna. He built relatively little but gained notoriety through his impassioned and often sarcastic writings on architecture and society. For example, in his essay "Ornament and Crime" (1908), excerpted below, Loos criticized the use of ornament on moral grounds. He believed "the evolution of culture [to be] synonymous with the removal of ornamentation from objects of everyday use." According to this theory of societal development, the application of decoration to utilitarian objects such as jackets, bicycles, or buildings was an affront to human progress. Yet, this "degenerate" behavior registered as criminal when modern people wasted time, money, and effort to create unnecessary and inappropriate ornament. Related to this concept was Loos's assertion that architecture was fundamentally shelter—a useful object—and thus was not art. While architects such as Walter Gropius sought to merge art and life, to infuse everyday objects with an aesthetic beauty, Loos argued for the strict separation of art and life. For Loos, architecture belonged to life.

"Ornament and Crime" (1908)

In the womb the human embryo goes through all phases of development the animal kingdom has passed through. And when a human being is born, his sense impressions are like a new-born dog's. In childhood he goes through all changes corresponding to the stages in the development of humanity. At two he sees with the eyes of a Papuan, at four with those of a Germanic tribesman, at six of Socrates, at eight of Voltaire. At eight he becomes aware of violet, the color discovered by the eighteenth century; before that, violets were blue and the purple snail was red, Even today physicists can point to colors in the solar spectrum which have been given a name, but which it will be left to future generations to discern.

A child is amoral. A Papuan too, for us. The Papuan slaughters his enemies and devours them. He is not a criminal. But if a modern person slaughters someone and devours him, he is a criminal or a degenerate. The Papuan covers his skin with tattoos, his boat, his oars, in short everything he can lay his hands on. He is no criminal. The modern person who tattoos himself is either a criminal or a degenerate. There are prisons in which eighty percent of the inmates have tattoos. People with tattoos not in prison are either latent criminals or degenerate aristocrats.

The urge to decorate one's face and anything else within reach is the origin of the fine arts. It is the childish babble of painting. But all art is erotic.

A person of our times who gives way to the urge to daub the walls with erotic symbols is a

---

Adolf Loos, *Ornament and Crime, Selected Essays*, trans. Michael Mitchell (Riverside, CA: Ariadne Press, 1998), 167–75. Reprinted with permission from the publisher.

criminal or a degenerate. What is natural in the Papuan or the child is a sign of degeneracy in a modern adult. I made the following discovery, which I passed on to the world: *the evolution of culture is synonymous with the removal of ornamentation from objects of everyday use. . . .*

. . . I do not accept the objection that ornament is a source of increased pleasure in life for cultured people, the objection expressed in the exclamation, "But if the ornament is beautiful!" For me, and with me for all people of culture, ornament is not a source of increased pleasure in life. When I want to eat a piece of gingerbread, I choose a piece that is plain, not a piece shaped like a heart, or a baby, or a cavalryman, covered over and over with decoration, A fifteenth-century man would not have understood me, but all modern people will. The supporters of ornament think my hunger for simplicity is some kind of mortification of the flesh. No, my dear Professor of Applied Arts, I am not mortifying the flesh at all. I find the gingerbread tastes better like that.

It is easy to reconcile ourselves to the great damage and depredations the revival of ornament had done to our aesthetic development, since no one and nothing, not even the power of the state, can hold up the evolution of mankind. It can only be slowed down. We can afford to wait. But in economic respects it is a crime, in that it leads to the waste of human labor, money, and materials. That is damage time cannot repair. . . .

Ornament means wasted labor and therefore wasted health. That was always the case. Today, however, it also means wasted material, and both mean wasted capital.

As there is no longer any organic connection between ornament and our culture, ornament is no longer an expression of our culture. The ornament being created now bears no relationship to us, nor to any human being, or to the system governing the world today. It has no potential for development. . . . In the past the artist was a healthy, vigorous figure, always at the head of humanity. The modern ornamental artist, however, lags behind or is a pathological case. After three years even he himself disowns his own products. Cultured people find them intolerable straight away, others become aware of it only after a number of years. . . . Modern ornament has no parents and no offspring, no past and no future. Uncultivated people, for whom the greatness of our age is a closed book, greet it rapturously and then disown it after a short time.

Humanity as a whole is healthy, only a few are sick. But these few tyrannize the worker, who is so healthy he is incapable of inventing ornaments. They compel him to execute the ornaments they have invented, in a wide variety of different materials.

The changing fashion in ornament results in a premature devaluation of the product of the worker's labor; his time and the materials used are wasted capital. I have formulated the following principle: *The form of an object should last, that is, we should find it tolerable as long as the object itself lasts.* I will explain: A suit will change its style more often than a valuable fur. A woman's ball outfit, intended for one night alone, will change its style more quickly than a desk. Woe betide us, however, if we have to change a desk as quickly as a ball outfit because we can no longer stand the old style. Then we will have wasted the money we paid for the desk.

Ornamental artists and craftsmen are well aware of this, and in Austria they try to show this deficiency in a positive light. They say, "A consumer who has furnishings he cannot stand after ten years, and thus is forced to refurnish his apartment every ten years, is better than one who buys something only when the old one becomes worn out with use. Industry needs that. The rapid changes in fashion provide employment for millions."

This seems to be the secret of the Austrian economy. When a fire breaks out, how often does one hear someone say, "Thank God! Now there is work for people again." Just set a house on fire, set the Empire on fire, and everyone will be rolling in money! Just keep on making furniture we chop up for firewood after three years, mountings we have to melt down after four, because even at auction they will not fetch a tenth of the cost of labor and materials, and we will get richer and richer!

Not only the consumer bears the loss, it is above all the producer. Nowadays, putting decoration on objects which, thanks to progress, no longer need to be decorated, means a waste of labor and an abuse of material. If all objects would last as long in aesthetic terms as they last physically, the consumer would be able to pay a price for them that would allow the worker to earn more money and work shorter hours. For an object from which I am convinced I will get full use until it is worn out I am quite happy to pay four times the price of another I could buy. I am happy to pay forty crowns for my shoes, even though there are shoes for ten in another shop. But in those trades that languish under the yoke of the ornamental artist, no value is put on good or bad workmanship. Work suffers because no one is willing to pay for it at its true value.

And that is a good thing too, since these ornamented objects are bearable only when they are shoddily produced. I find it easier to accept a fire when I hear it is only worthless rubbish that is being destroyed. I can enjoy the trumpery in the *Künstlerhaus* [The Association of Viennese Artists] because I know it takes a few days to put it up and one day to tear it down. But throwing coins instead of stones, lighting a cigar with a bank note, crushing up and drinking a pearl, I find unaesthetic. . . .

A modern person, who regards ornament as a symptom of the artistic superfluity of previous ages and for that reason holds it sacred, will immediately recognize the unhealthy, the forced—painfully forced—nature of modern ornament. Ornament can no longer be produced by someone living on the cultural level of today. It is different for individuals and people who have not yet reached that level.

The ideal I preach is the aristocrat. What I mean by that is the person at the peak of humanity, who yet has a profound understanding of the problems and aspirations of those at the bottom. One who well understands the way the African works patterns into his cloth according to a certain rhythm, so the design appears only when the fabric is taken off the loom; likewise the Persian weaving his rug, the Slovak peasant woman making her lace, the old woman making marvelous needlework from silk and glass beads. The aristocrat lets them carry on in their own accustomed way, he knows the time they spend on their work is sacred to them. The revolutionary would go and tell them it was all pointless, just as he would drag an old woman away from the wayside shrine, telling her there is no God. But the atheist among the aristocrats still raises his hat when he passes a church.

My shoes are covered with decoration formed by sawtooth patterns and holes. Work done by the shoemaker, work he has not been paid for. Imagine I go to the shoemaker and say, "You charge thirty crowns for a pair of shoes. I will pay you forty-eight." It will raise the man to such a transport of delight he will thank me through his workmanship and the material used, making them of a quality that will far outweigh my extra payment. He is happy, and happiness is a rare commodity in his house. He has found someone who understands him, who respects his work, and does not doubt his honesty. He can already see the finished shoes in his mind's eye. He knows where the best leather is to be found at the moment, he knows which of his workers he will entrust with the task, and the shoes will have all the sawtooth patterns and holes an elegant pair of shoes can take. And then I say, "But there is one condition. The shoes must be completely plain." I will drag him down from the heights of bliss to the depths of hell. He will have less work, and I have taken away all his pleasure in it.

The ideal I preach is the aristocrat. I can accept decoration on my own person if it brings pleasure to my fellow men. It brings pleasure to me, too. I can accept the African's ornament, the Persian's, the Slovak peasant woman's, my shoemaker's, for it provides the high point of their existence, which they have no other means of achieving. *We* have the art that has superseded ornament. After all the toil and tribulations of the day, we can go to hear Beethoven or *Tristan*. My shoemaker cannot. I must not take his religion away from him, for I have nothing to put in its place. But anyone who goes to the *Ninth* and then sits down to design a wallpaper pattern is either a fraud or a degenerate.

The disappearance of ornament has brought about an undreamed-of blossoming in the other arts. Beethoven's symphonies would never have been written by a man who had to dress in silk, velvet, and lace. Those who go around in velvet jackets today are not artists, but clowns or house painters. We have become more refined, more subtle. When men followed the herd they had to differentiate themselves through color, modern man uses his dress as a disguise. His sense of his own individuality is so immensely strong it can no longer be expressed in dress. Lack of ornamentation is a sign of intellectual strength. Modern man uses the ornaments of earlier or foreign cultures as he likes and as he sees fit. He concentrates his own inventive power on other things.

11 Antonio Sant'Elia, 1888–1916

The Italian architect Antonio Sant'Elia is best known for the "Manifesto of Futurist Architecture" (1914) and the associated sketches of the *Città Nuova*, his visionary metropolis of the future. As a member of the Italian Futurist movement founded by Filippo Tommaso Marinetti, Sant'Elia called for the renunciation of tradition and convention, a divorce from all things of the past. He and his fellow Futurists advocated an entirely new way of life based on technology, progress, and speed. Sant'Elia's drawings of the *Città Nuova* depict a multilevel city of colossal, terraced towers in which transmission antennas, electric wires, external elevators, skywalks, and a sense of modernity abound. Sant'Elia's crusade for the future far exceeded his contemporaries' conceptions of modernity, making the proclamations of Le Corbusier and Gropius appear conservative in comparison. A glorification of battle and violence, viewed as the necessary means of eradicating the past, accompanied the Futurist cries for progress. Unfortunately, Sant'Elia became a victim of this philosophy, perishing on the fields of World War I. Nevertheless, despite the brevity of his life and his few built works, Sant'Elia's visions of the future as discussed in his manifesto and embodied in the *Città Nuova* influenced subsequent generations of architects.

"Manifesto of Futurist Architecture" (1914)

No architecture has existed since 1700. A moronic mixture of the most various stylistic elements used to mask the skeletons of modern houses is called modern architecture. The new beauty of cement and iron are profaned by the superimposition of
motley decorative incrustations that cannot be justified either by constructive necessity or by our (modern) taste, and whose origins are in Egyptian, Indian or Byzantine
antiquity and in that idiotic flowering of stupidity and impotence that took the name
of NEOCLASSICISM.

These architectonic prostitutions are welcomed in Italy, and rapacious alien ineptitude
is passed off as talented invention and as extremely up-to-date architecture. Young
Italian architects (those who borrow originality from clandestine and compulsive de-
vouring of art journals) flaunt their talents in the new quarters of our towns, where a
hilarious salad of little ogival columns, seventeenth-century foliation, Gothic pointed
arches, Egyptian pilasters, rococo scrolls, fifteen-century cherubs, swollen caryatids,
take the place of style in all seriousness, and presumptuously put on monumental
airs. The kaleidoscopic appearance and reappearance of forms, the multiplying of
machinery, the daily increasing needs imposed by the speed of communications, by
the concentration of population, by hygiene, and by a hundred other phenomena of
modern life, never cause these self-styled renovators of architecture a moment's perplexity or hesitation. They persevere obstinately with the rules of Vitruvius, Vignola

---

Antonio Sant'Elia, "Manifesto of Futurist Architecture," trans. Caroline Tisdall, in Umberto Apollonio,
ed., *Futurist Manifestos*, trans. R. Brain, R. W. Flint, J. C. Higgitt, C. Tisdall (London: Thames & Hudson,
Ltd., 1973), 160, 169–172. Original © 1970 by Verlag M. Dumont Schauberg and Gabriele Mazzotta
editore. Reprinted with permission of Viking Penguin, a division of the Penguin Group, Inc.

and Sansovino plus gleanings from any published scrap of information on German architecture that happens to be at hand. Using these, they continue to stamp the image of imbecility on our cities, our cities which should be the immediate and faithful projection of ourselves.

And so this expressive and synthetic art has become in their hands a vacuous stylistic exercise, a jumble of ill-mixed formulae to disguise a run-of-the-mill traditionalist box of bricks and stone as a modern building. As if we who are accumulators and generators of movement, with all our added mechanical limbs, with all the noise and speed of our life, could live in streets built for the needs of men four, five or six centuries ago.

This is the supreme imbecility of modern architecture, perpetuated by the venal complicity of the academies, the internment camps of the intelligentsia, where the young are forced into the onanistic recopying of classical models instead of throwing their minds open in the search for new frontiers and in the solution of the new and pressing problem: THE FUTURIST HOUSE AND CITY. The house and the city that are ours both spiritually and materially, in which our tumult can rage without seeming a grotesque anachronism.

The problem posed in *Futurist* architecture is not one of linear rearrangement. It is not a question of finding new mouldings and frames for windows and doors, of replacing columns, pilasters and corbels with caryatids, flies and frogs. Neither has it anything to do with leaving a façade in bare brick, or plastering it, or facing it with stone or in determining formal differences between the new building and the old one. It is a question of tending the healthy growth of the Futurist house, of constructing it with all the resources of technology and science, satisfying magisterially all the demands of our habits and our spirit, trampling down all that is grotesque and antithetical (tradition, style, aesthetics, proportion), determining new forms, new lines, a new harmony of profiles and volumes, an architecture whose reason for existence can be found solely in the unique conditions of modern life, and in its correspondence with the aesthetic values of our sensibilities. This architecture cannot be subjected to any law of historical continuity. It must be new, just as our state of mind is new.

The art of construction has been able to evolve with time, and to pass from one style to another, while maintaining unaltered the general characteristics of architecture, because in the course of history changes of fashion are frequent and are determined by the alternations of religious conviction and political disposition. But profound changes in the state of the environment are extremely rare, changes that unhinge and renew, such as the discovery of natural laws, the perfecting of mechanical means, the rational and scientific use of material. In modern life the process of stylistic development in architecture has been brought to a halt. ARCHITECTURE NOW MAKES A BREAK WITH TRADITION. IT MUST PERFORCE MAKE A FRESH START.

Calculations based on the resistance of materials, on the use of reinforced concrete and steel, exclude 'architecture' in the classical and traditional sense. Modern constructional materials and scientific concepts are absolutely incompatible with the disciplines of historical styles, and are the principal cause of the grotesque appearance of 'fashionable' buildings in which attempts are made to employ the lightness, the superb grace of the steel beam, the delicacy of reinforced concrete, in order to obtain the heavy curve of the arch and the bulkiness of marble.

The utter antithesis between the modern world and the old is determined by all those things that formerly did not exist. Our lives have been enriched by elements the possibility of whose existence the ancients did not even suspect. Men have identified material contingencies, and revealed spiritual attitudes, whose repercussions are felt in a thousand ways. Principal among these is the formation of a new ideal of beauty that is still obscure and embryonic, but whose fascination is already felt even by the masses. We have lost our predilection for the monumental, the heavy, the static, and we have enriched our sensibility with a *taste for the light, the practical, the ephemeral and the swift*. We no longer feel ourselves to be the men of the cathedrals, the palaces and the podiums. We are the men of the great hotels, the railway stations, the immense streets, colossal ports, covered markets, luminous arcades, straight roads and beneficial demolitions.

We must invent and rebuild the Futurist city like an immense and tumultuous shipyard, agile, mobile and dynamic in every detail; and the Futurist house must be like a gigantic machine. The lifts must no longer be hidden away like tapeworms in the niches of stairwells; the stairwells themselves, rendered useless, must be abolished, and the lifts must scale the lengths of the façades like serpents of steel and glass. The house of concrete, glass and steel, stripped of paintings and sculpture, rich only in the innate beauty of its lines and relief, extraordinarily 'ugly' in its mechanical simplicity, higher and wider according to need rather than the specifications of municipal laws. It must soar up on the brink of a tumultuous abyss: the street will no longer lie like a doormat at ground level, but will plunge many storeys down into the earth, embracing the metropolitan traffic, and will be linked up for necessary interconnections by metal gangways and swift-moving pavements.

THE DECORATIVE MUST BE ABOLISHED. The problem of Futurist architecture must be resolved, not by continuing to pilfer from Chinese, Persian or Japanese photographs or fooling around with the rules of Vitruvius, but through flashes of genius and through scientific and technical expertise. Everything must be revolutionized. Roofs and underground spaces must be used; the importance of the façade must be diminished; issues of taste must be transplanted from the field of fussy moulding, finicky capitals and flimsy doorways to the broader concerns of BOLD GROUPINGS AND MASSES, AND LARGE SCALE DISPOSITION OF PLANES. Let us make an end of monumental, funereal and commemorative architecture. Let us overturn monuments, pavements, arcades and flights of steps; let us sink the streets and squares; let us raise the level of the city.

I COMBAT AND DESPISE:

1. All the pseudo-architecture of the avant-garde, Austrian, Hungarian, German and American;

2. All classical architecture, solemn, hieratic, scenographic, decorative, monumental, pretty and pleasing;

3. The embalming, reconstruction and reproduction of ancient monuments and palaces;

4. Perpendicular and horizontal lines, cubical and pyramidical forms that are static, solemn, aggressive and absolutely excluded from our utterly new sensibility;

5. The use of massive, voluminous, durable, antiquated and costly materials.

AND PROCLAIM:

1. That Futurist architecture is the architecture of calculation, of audacious temerity and of simplicity; the architecture of reinforced concrete, of steel, glass, cardboard, textile fibre, and of all those substitutes for wood, stone and brick that enable us to obtain maximum elasticity and lightness;

2. That Futurist architecture is not because of this an arid combination of practicality and usefulness, but remains art, i.e., synthesis and expression;

3. That oblique and elliptic lines are dynamic, and by their very nature possess an emotive power a thousand times stronger than perpendiculars and horizontal; and that no integral, dynamic architecture can exist that does not include these;

4. That decoration as an element superimposed on architecture is absurd, and that THE DECORATIVE VALUE OF FUTURIST ARCHITECTURE DEPENDS SOLELY ON THE USE AND ORIGINAL ARRANGEMENT OF RAW OR BARE OR VIOLENTLY COLOURED MATERIALS;

5. That, just as the ancients drew inspiration for their art from the elements of nature, we—who are materially and spiritually artificial—must find that inspiration in the elements of the utterly new mechanical world we have created, and of which architecture must be the most beautiful expression, the most complete synthesis, the most efficacious integration;

6. That architecture as the art of arranging forms according to pre-established criteria is finished;

7. That by the term architecture is meant the endeavour to harmonize the environment with Man with freedom and great audacity, that is to transform the world of things into a direct projection of the world of the spirit;

8. From an architecture conceived in this way no formal or linear habit can grow, since the fundamental characteristics of Futurist architecture will be its impermanence and transience. THINGS WILL ENDURE LESS THAN US. EVERY GENERATION MUST BUILD ITS OWN CITY. This constant renewal of the architectonic environment will contribute to the victory of Futurism which has already been affirmed by WORDS-IN-FREEDOM, PLASTIC DYNAMISM, MUSIC WITHOUT QUADRATURE AND THE ART OF NOISES, and for which we fight without respite against traditionalist cowardice.

12

In 1907, the English scholar and writer Geoffrey Scott moved to Florence, Italy, where he became part of the literary circle surrounding the American Mary Berenson and her husband Bernard, an art historian and critic. Alongside the British landscape architect Cecil Pinsent, Scott took part in the garden design for the Berenson's villa, I Tatti. Scott would be involved in a few other minor design projects throughout his life, but his fame stems from his writing, particularly his 1914 text, *The Architecture of Humanism: A Study in the History of Taste*. In this work, Scott addressed the declining appreciation for humanist principles established by Renaissance architecture. He traced the perceived shift from humanist values to five underlying "fallacies"—the natural, picturesque, mechanical, ethical, and biological—prevalent in nineteenth- and early twentieth-century thought, principles that supplanted humanism as the basis for architecture. Scott felt that the concepts governing architecture should derive from the human body and human experience, not scientific, functional, or moral concerns. Drawing on the aesthetic theory of empathy, Scott declared *"We have transcribed ourselves into terms of architecture . . . {and} architecture into terms of ourselves."* This "dual transcription," he concluded, "is the humanism of architecture." Scott's understanding of humanism and its role in architecture is particularly striking when considered alongside the more functionalist approaches to architecture that gained currency in the years surrounding World War I.

The Architecture of Humanism (1914)

Chapter VIII. Humanist Values

I. Architecture, simply and immediately perceived, is a combination, revealed through light and shade, of spaces, of masses, and of lines. These few elements make the core of architectural experience. . . .

The spaces, masses and lines of architecture, as perceived, are appearances. We may infer from them further facts about a building which are not perceived; facts about construction, facts about history or society. But the art of architecture is concerned with their immediate aspect; it is concerned with them as appearances.

And these appearances are related to human functions. Through these spaces we can conceive ourselves to move; these masses are capable, like ourselves, of pressure and resistance; these lines, should we follow or describe them, might be our path and our gesture.

Conceive for a moment a 'top-heavy' building or an 'ill-proportioned' space. No doubt the degree to which these qualities will be found offensive will vary with the spectator's sensibility to architecture; but sooner or later, if the top-heaviness or the disproportion is sufficiently pronounced, every spectator will judge that the building or the space is ugly, and experience a certain discomfort from their presence. So much will be conceded.

Geoffrey Scott, *The Architecture of Humanism: A Study in the History of Taste* (London: Constable and Co., Ltd., 1924) 157–63. Reprinted with permission of W.W. Norton & Company, Inc. Scott's footnotes have been omitted from this excerpt; the italics are his.

Now what is the cause of this discomfort? It is often suggested that the top-heavy building and the cramped space are ugly because they suggest the idea of instability, the idea of collapse, the idea of restriction, and so forth. But these ideas are not in themselves disagreeable. . . .

. . . [Our] discomfort in the presence of such architecture cannot spring merely from the idea of restriction or instability.

But neither does it derive from an actual weakness or restriction in our immediate experience. It is disagreeable to have our movements thwarted, to lose strength or to collapse; but a room fifty feet square and seven feet high does not restrict our actual movements, and the sight of a granite building raised (apparently) on a glass shop-front does not cause us to collapse.

There is instability—or the appearance of it; but it is in the building. There is discomfort, but it is in ourselves. What then has occurred? The conclusion seems evident. The concrete spectacle has done what the mere idea could not: it has stirred our physical memory. It has awakened in us, not indeed an actual state of instability or of being overloaded, but that condition of spirit which in the past has belonged to our actual experiences of weakness, of thwarted effort or incipient collapse. We have looked at the building and identified ourselves with its apparent state. *We have transcribed ourselves into terms of architecture.*

But the 'states' in architecture with which we thus identify ourselves need not be actual. The actual pressures of a spire are downward, yet no one speaks of a 'sinking' spire. A spire, when well designed, appears—as common language testifies—to soar. We identify ourselves, not with its actual downward pressure, but its apparent upward impulse. So, too, by the same excellent—because unconscious—testimony of speech, arches 'spring,' vistas 'stretch,' domes 'swell,' Greek temples are 'calm,' and baroque façades 'restless.' The whole of architecture is, in fact, unconsciously invested by us with human movement and human moods. Here, then, is a principle complementary to the one just stated. We *transcribe architecture into terms of ourselves.*

This is the humanism of architecture. The tendency to project the image of our functions into concrete forms is the basis, for architecture, of creative design. The tendency to recognize, in concrete forms, the image of those functions is the true basis, in its turn, of critical appreciation.

II. . . . This 'rising' of towers and 'springing' of arches, it will be said—these different movements which animate architecture—are mere metaphors of speech. . . .

. . . But a metaphor, when it is so obvious as to be universally employed and immediately understood, presupposes a true and reliable experience to which it can refer. . .

. . . [When] we speak of a tower as 'standing' or 'leaning' or 'rising,' or say of a curve that it is 'cramped' or 'flowing,' the words are the simplest and most direct description we can give of our impression. . . . [Art] addresses us through immediate impressions rather than through the process of reflection, and this universal metaphor of the body, a language profoundly felt and universally understood, is its largest opportunity. A metaphor is, by definition, the transcription of one thing into terms of another, and this in fact is what the theory under discussion claims. It claims that architectural art is the transcription of the body's states into forms of building.

. . . The processes of which we are least conscious are precisely the most deep-seated and universal and continuous, as, for example, the process of breathing. And this habit of projecting the image of our own functions upon the outside world, of reading the outside world in our own terms, is certainly ancient, common, and profound. It is, in fact, the *natural* way of perceiving and interpreting what we see. It is the way of the child in whom perpetual pretence and 'endless imitation' are a spontaneous method of envisaging the world. It is the way of the savage, who believes in 'animism,' and conceives every object to be invested with powers like his own. It is the way of the primitive peoples, who in the elaborate business of the dance give a bodily rendering to their beliefs and desires long before thought has accurately expressed them. It is the way of a superbly gifted race like the Greeks, whose mythology is one vast monument to just this instinct. It is the way of the poetic mind at all times and places, which [humanizes] the external world, not in a series of artificial conceits, but simply so perceiving it. To perceive and interpret the world scientifically, as it actually is, is a later, a less 'natural,' a more sophisticated process, and one from which we still relapse even when we say the sun is rising. The scientific perception of the world is forced upon us; the humanist perception of it is ours by right. The scientific method is intellectually and practically useful, but the naïve, the anthropomorphic way which [humanizes] the world and interprets it by analogy with our own bodies and our own wills, is still the aesthetic way; it is the basis of poetry, and it is the foundation of architecture.

13 LE CORBUSIER, 1887–1966

Le Corbusier, Villa Savoye, Poissy, France, 1928–29
© 2007 Artist Rights Society (ARS), New York/ADAGP, Paris/FLC
Photo Credit: Anthony Scibilia/Art Resource, NY

Le Corbusier, born Charles-Edouard Jeanneret in the Swiss town of Le Chaux-de-Fonds, forced a reconsideration of functional and aesthetic expectations in architecture; he is thus recognized as one of the most brilliant and influential architects of the twentieth century. Particularly intrigued by the possibilities of standardization and industrial production, in 1915 Le Corbusier devised the Maison Domino, an inexpensive, mass-producible housing frame composed of reinforced-concrete slab floors and vertical point supports. Two years later, he moved to Paris where he adopted the name Le Corbusier and began writing articles he would later publish together as *Vers une Architecture* (1923, translated as *Towards a New Architecture*). In this text, Le Corbusier urged architects to reconsider the accepted notion of the house and with it, the possibilities of twentieth-century life. Much as engineers devised the airplane to allow man to fly, Le Corbusier felt that architects must recreate the house for man to live in modern terms, with updated social ideals of space, hygiene, and technology; like the machine, the house should efficiently function in the service of its occupants. To support his argument Le Corbusier highlighted mechanized objects such as the airplane as models for contemporary architectural thought.

During the early 1920s, Le Corbusier collaborated with his cousin, **Pierre Jeanneret** (1896–1967). Together they expanded Le Corbusier's ideas concerning mass production and mechanization to formulate "Five Points towards a New Architecture" (1926). In place of conventional construction methods that relied on a buried foundation, load-bearing walls, and a pitched roof, Le Corbusier and Jeanneret proposed a new building system that incorporated structural *pilotis* (stilts of reinforced concrete), an open interior plan, an enclosing but non-load-bearing façade, strip or ribbon windows, and a flat rooftop garden. This set of revolutionary principles challenged traditional notions of structure and aesthetics, and established a new approach to architectural design.

Towards a New Architecture (1923)

Eyes Which Do Not See
II. Airplanes

> *There is a new spirit: it is a spirit of construction and of synthesis guided by a clear conception.*
> *Whatever may be thought of it, it animates to-day the greater part of human activity.*
> A GREAT EPOCH HAS BEGUN
>
> Programme of l'Espirit Nouveau
No. 1, October, 1920.

There is one profession and one only, namely architecture, in which progress is not considered necessary, where laziness is enthroned, and in which the reference is always to yesterday.

Everywhere else, taking thought for the morrow is almost a fever and brings its inevitable solution: if a man does not move forward he becomes bankrupt.

But in architecture no one ever becomes bankrupt. A privileged profession, alas!

*   *   *

The airplane is indubitably one of the products of the most intense selection in the range of modern industry.

Le Corbusier, *Towards a New Architecture*, trans. Frederick Etchells (New York: Dover Publications, Inc., 1986), 109–27. Reprinted with permission from the publisher.

The War was an insatiable "client," never satisfied, always demanding better. The orders were to succeed at all costs and death followed a mistake remorselessly. We may then affirm that the airplane mobilized invention, intelligence and daring: *imagination* and *cold reason*. It is the same spirit that built the Parthenon.

Let us look at things from the point of view of architecture, but in the state of mind of the inventor of airplanes.

The lesson of the airplane is not primarily in the forms it has created, and above all we must learn to see in an airplane not a bird or a dragon-fly, but a machine for flying; the lesson of the airplane lies in the logic which governed the enunciation of the problem and which led to its successful realization. When a problem is properly stated, in our epoch, it inevitably finds its solution.

The problem of the house has not yet been stated.

One commonplace among Architects (the younger ones): *the construction must be shown.*

Another commonplace amongst them: *when a thing responds to a need, it is beautiful.*

But . . . To show the construction is all very well for an Arts and Crafts student who is anxious to prove his ability. The Almighty has clearly shown our wrists and our ankles, but there remains all the rest!

When a thing responds to a need, it is not beautiful; it satisfies all one part of our mind, the primary part, without which there is no possibility of richer satisfactions; let us recover the right order of events.

Architecture has another meaning and other ends to pursue than showing construction and responding to needs (and by "needs" I mean utility, comfort and practical arrangement).

ARCHITECTURE is the art above all others which achieves a state of platonic grandeur, mathematical order, speculation, the perception of the harmony which lies in emotional relationships. This is the AIM of architecture.

But let us return to our chronology.

If we feel the need of a new architecture, a clear and settled organism, it is because, as things are, the sensation of mathematical order cannot touch us since *things no longer respond to a need*, and because there is no longer real construction in architecture. An extreme confusion reigns. Architecture as practiced provides no solution to the present-day problem of the dwelling-house and has no comprehension of the structure of things. It does not fulfill the very first conditions and so it is not possible that the higher factors of harmony and beauty should enter in.

The architecture of to-day does not fulfill the necessary and sufficient conditions of the problem.

The reason is that the problem has not been stated as regards architecture. There has been no salutary war as in the case of the airplane.

But you will say, the Peace has set the problem in the reconstruction of the North of France. But then, we are totally disarmed, we do not know how to build in a modern way—materials, systems of construction, THE CONCEPTION OF THE DWELLING, all are lacking. Engineers have been busy with barrages, with bridges, with Atlantic liners, with mines, with railways. Architects have been asleep.

The airplane shows us that a problem well stated finds its solution. To wish to fly like a bird is to state the problem badly, and Ader's "Bat" never left the ground. To invent a flying machine having in mind nothing alien to pure mechanics, that is to say, to search for a means of suspension in the air and a means of propulsion, was to put the problem properly: in less than ten years the whole world could fly.

LET US STATE THE PROBLEM

Let us shut our eyes to what exists.

A house: a shelter against heat, cold, rain, thieves and the inquisitive. A receptacle for light and sun. A certain number of cells appropriated to cooking, work and personal life.

A room: a surface over which one can walk at ease, a bed on which to stretch yourself, a chair in which to rest or work, a work-table, receptacles in which each thing can be put at once in its right place.

The number of rooms: one for cooking and one for eating. One for work, one to wash yourself in and one for sleep.

Such are the standards of the dwelling.

Then why do we have the enormous and useless roofs on pretty suburban villas? Why the scanty windows with their little panes; why large houses with so many rooms locked up? Why the mirrored wardrobes, the washstands, the commodes? And then, why the elaborate bookcases? The consoles, the china cabinets, the dressers, the sideboards? Why the enormous glass chandeliers? The mantelpieces? Why the draped curtains? Why the damasked wall-papers thick with colour, with their motley design?

Daylight hardly enters your homes. Your windows are difficult to open. There are no ventilators for changing the air such as we get in any dining-car. Your chandeliers hurt the eyes. Your imitation stone stucco and your wall-papers are an impertinence, and no good modern picture could ever be hung on your walls, for it would be lost in the welter of your furnishings.

Why do you not demand from your landlord:

1. Fittings to take underclothing, suits and dresses in our bedroom, all of one depth, of a comfortable height and as practical as an "Innovation" trunk;

2. In your dining-room fittings to take china, silver and glass, shutting tightly and with a sufficiency of drawers in orders that "clearing away" can be done in an instant, and all these fittings "built in" so that round your chairs and table you have room enough to move and that feeling of space which will give you the calm necessary to good digestion;

3. In your living-room *fittings to hold your books and protect them from dust and to hold your collection of paintings and works of art.* And in such a way that the walls of your room are unencumbered. You could then bring out your pictures one at a time when you want them.

As for your dressers, and your mirrored wardrobes, you can sell all these to one of those young nations which have lately appeared on the map. There *Progress* rages, and they are dropping the traditional home (with its fittings, etc.) to live in an up-to-date house *à l'européenne* with its imitation stone stucco and its mantelpieces.

Let us repeat some fundamental axioms:

(a) *Chairs are made to sit in.* There are rush-seated church chairs at 5s., luxuriously upholstered arm-chairs at £20 and adjustable chairs with a movable reading-desk, a shelf for your coffee cup, an extending foot rest, a back that raises and lowers with a handle, and gives you the very best position either for work or a nap, in a healthy, comfortable and right way. Your *bergères*, your Louis XVI *canseuses*, bulging through their tapestry covers, are these machines for sitting in? Between ourselves, you are more comfortable at your club, your bank or in your office.

(b) *Electricity gives light*. We can have concealed lighting, or we can have diffused and projected lighting. One can see as clearly as in broad daylight without ever hurting one's eyes.

A hundred-candle-power lamp weighs less than two ounces, but there are chandeliers weighing nearly two hundredweight with elaborations in bronze or wood, and so huge that they fill up all the middle of the room; the upkeep of these horrors is a terrible task because of the flies. These chandeliers are also very bad for the eyes at night.

(c) *Windows serve to admit light, "a little, much or not at all," and to see outside.* There are windows in sleeping-cars which close hermetically or can be opened at will; there are the great windows of modern cafés which close hermetically or can be entirely opened by means of a handle which causes them to disappear below ground; there are the windows in dining cars which have little louvres opening to admit air "a little, much, or not at all," there is modern plate glass which has replaced bottle-glass and small panes; there are roll shutters which can be lowered gradually and will keep out the light at will according to the spacing of their slats. But architects still use only windows like those at Versailes or Compiègne, Louis X, Y or Z which shut badly, have tiny panes, are difficult to open and have their shutters outside; if it rains in the evening one gets wet through in trying to close them.

(d) *Pictures are made to be looked at and meditated on.* In order to see a picture to advantage, it must be hung suitably and in the proper atmosphere. The true collector of pictures arranges them in a cabinet and hangs on the wall the particular painting he wants to look at; but your walls are a riot of all manner of things.

(e) *A house is made for living in.*—"No!"—"But of course!"—"Then you are a Utopian!"

Truth to tell, the modern man is bored to tears in his home; so he goes to his club. The modern woman is bored outside her boudoir; she goes to tea-parties. The modern man and woman are bored at home; they go to night-clubs. But lesser folk who have no clubs gather together in the evening under the chandelier and hardly dare to walk through the labyrinth of their furniture which takes up the whole room and is all their fortune and their pride.

The existing plan of the dwelling-house takes no account of man and is conceived as a furniture store. This scheme of things, favourable enough so the trade of Tottenham Court Road, is of ill omen for society. It kills the spirit of the family, of the home; there are no homes, no families and no children, for living is much too difficult a business.

The temperance societies and the anti-Malthusians should address an urgent appeal to architects; they should have the MANUAL OF THE DWELLING printed and distributed to mothers of families and should demand the resignation of all the professors in the architectural schools.

THE MANUAL OF THE DWELLING
Demand a bathroom looking south, one of the largest rooms in the house or flat, the old drawing-room for instance. One wall to be entirely glazed, opening if possible on to a balcony for sun baths; the most up-to-date fittings with a shower-bath and gymnastic appliances.

An adjoining room to be a dressing-room in which you can dress and undress. Never undress in your bedroom. It is not a clean thing to do and makes the room horribly untidy. In this room demand fitments for your linen and clothing, not more than 5 feet in height, with drawers, hangers, etc.

Demand one really large living room instead of a number of small ones.

Demand bare walls in your bedroom, your living room and your dining-room. Built-in fittings to take the place of much of the furniture, which is expensive to buy, takes up too much room and needs looking after.

If you can, put the kitchen at the top of the house to avoid smells.

Demand concealed or diffused lighting.

Demand a vacuum cleaner.

Buy only practical furniture and never buy decorative "pieces." If you want to see bad taste, go into the houses of the rich. Put only a few pictures on your walls and none but good ones.

Keep your odds and ends in drawers or cabinets.

The gramophone or the pianola or wireless will give you exact interpretations of first-rate music, and you will avoid catching cold in the concert hall, and the frenzy of the virtuoso.

Demand ventilating panes to the windows in every room.

Teach your children that a house is only habitable when it is full of light and air, and when the floors and walls are clear. To keep your floors in order eliminate heavy furniture and thick carpets.

Demand a separate garage to your dwelling.

Demand the maid's room should not be an attic. Do not park your servants under the roof.

Take a flat which is one size smaller than what your parents accustomed you to. Bear in mind economy in your actions, your household management and in your thoughts.

Conclusion. Every modern man has the mechanical sense. The feeling for mechanics exists and is justified by our daily activities. This feeling in regard to machinery is one of respect, gratitude and esteem.

Machinery includes economy as an essential factor leading to minute selection. There is a moral sentiment in the feeling for mechanics.

The man who is intelligent, cold and calm has grown wings to himself.

Men—intelligent, cold and calm—are needed to build the house and to lay out the town.

"Five Points Towards a New Architecture" (1926)

The theoretical considerations set out below are based on many years of practical experience on building sites.

Theory demands concise formulation.

The following points in no way relate to aesthetic fantasies or a striving for fashionable effects, but concern architectural facts that imply an entirely new kind of building, from dwelling house to palatial edifices.

1. **The supports**. To solve a problem scientifically means in the first place to distinguish between its elements. Hence in the case of a building a distinction can immediately be made between the supporting and the non-supporting elements. The earlier foundations, on which the building rested without a mathematical check, are replaced by individual foundations and the walls by individual supports. Both supports and support foundations are precisely calculated according to the burdens they are called upon to carry. These supports are spaced out at specific, equal intervals, with no thought for the interior arrangement of the building. They rise directly from the floor to 3, 4, 6, etc. metres and elevate the ground floor. The rooms are thereby removed from the dampness of the soil; they have light and air; the building plot is left to the garden, which consequently passes under the house. The same area is also gained on the flat roof.

Le Corbusier and Pierre Jeanneret, "Five Points Towards a New Architecture," from Ulrich Conrads, ed., *Programs and Maifestoes on 20ᵗʰ Century Architecture*, trans. M. Bullock (Cambridge, MA: MIT Press, 1970) 99–101. Text in Conrads quoted from *Towards a New Architecture* (London, 1927). English translation © 1970 Lund Humphries, London, and the Massachusetts Institute of Technology, Cambridge, Massachusetts. Reprinted with permission from the MIT Press.

2. The roof gardens. The flat roof demands in the first place systematic utilization for domestic purposes: roof terrace, roof garden. On the other hand, the reinforced concrete demands protection against changing temperatures. Over-activity on the part of the reinforced concrete is prevented by the maintenance of a constant humidity on the roof concrete. The roof terrace satisfies both demands (a rain-dampened layer of sand covered with concrete slabs with lawns in the interstices; the earth of the flowerbeds in direct contact with the layer of sand). In this way the rain water will flow off extremely slowly. Waste pipes in the interior of the building. Thus a latent humidity will remain continually on the roof skin. The roof gardens will display highly luxuriant vegetation. Shrubs and even small trees up to 3 or 4 metres tall can be planted. In this way the roof garden will becomes the most favored place in the building. In general, roof gardens mean to a city the recovery of all the built-up area.

3. The free designing of the ground-plan. The support system carries the intermediate ceilings and rises up to the roof. The interior walls may be placed wherever required, each floor being entirely independent of the rest. There are no longer any supporting walls but only membranes of any thickness required. The result of this is absolute freedom in designing the ground-plan; that is to say, free utilization of the available means, which makes it easy to offset the rather high cost of reinforced concrete construction.

4. The horizontal window. Together with the intermediate ceilings the supports form rectangular openings in the façade through which light and air enter copiously. The window extends from support to support and thus becomes a horizontal window. Stilted vertical windows consequently disappear, as do unpleasant mullions. In this way, rooms are equably lit from wall to wall. Experiments have shown that a room thus lit has an eight times stronger illumination than the same room lit by vertical windows with the same window area.

The whole history of architecture revolves exclusively around the wall apertures.

Through use of the horizontal window reinforced concrete suddenly provides the possibility of maximum illumination.

5. Free design of the façade. By projecting the floor beyond the supporting pillars, like a balcony all round the building, the whole façade is extended beyond the supporting construction. It thereby loses its supportive quality and the windows may be extended to any length at will, without any direct relationship to the interior division. . . . The façade may thus be designed freely.

The five essential points set out above represent a fundamentally new aesthetic. Nothing is left to us of the architecture of past epochs, just as we can no longer derive benefit from the literary and historical teaching given in schools.

Constructional Considerations

Building construction is the purposeful and consistent combination of building elements.

Industries and technological undertakings are being established to deal with the production of these elements.

Serial manufacture enables these elements to be made precise, cheap and good. They can be produced in advance in any number required.

Industries will see to the completion and uninterrupted perfecting of the elements.

Thus the architect has at his disposal a box of building units. His architectural talent can operate freely. It alone, through the building programme, determines his architecture.

The age of the architects is coming.

14 WALTER GROPIUS, 1883–1969

Throughout his life, the German architect Walter Gropius promoted collaboration between artists and industry. As a member of the Deutsche Werkbund, an organization dedicated to the qualitative improvement of German manufactured goods, Gropius recognized that standardization and factory production could lead to the availability of inexpensive, everyday items for public consumption. The promise for architecture was equally great; modular construction, made possible by creative design and the industrial production of building materials, could grant the common man access to affordable quality housing. These thoughts contributed to Gropius's 1919 founding of the Bauhaus, a school that sought to unify the arts under the rubric of design. Student training was based on an apprentice-like system that emphasized an understanding of craft and materials, as well as functionalism, composition, and aesthetics. Another focus concerned the reality of mechanical reproduction. Indeed, the Bauhaus eventually served as a workshop geared toward the creation of prototypes for industrial production, a concept Gropius discussed in "Principles of Bauhaus Production," reproduced below. Under Gropius's leadership, the Bauhaus fostered an alliance between the artist and industry, a relationship that helped raise the standards for machine-made goods and thus provide society with inexpensive, high-quality products. Gropius later carried these social and cooperative interests to the United States where he established the design firm aptly named The Architects' Collaborative.

"Principles of Bauhaus Production" (1926)

The Bauhaus wants to serve in the development of present-day housing, from the simplest household appliances to the finished dwelling.

In the conviction that household appliances and furnishings must be rationally related to each other, the Bauhaus is seeking—by systematic practical and theoretical research into formal, technical, and economic fields—to derive the design of an object from its natural functions and relationships.

Modern man, who no longer dresses in historical garments but wears modern clothes, also needs a modern home appropriate to him and his time, equipped with all the modern devices of daily use.

An object is defined by its nature. In order, then, to design it to function correctly—a container, a chair, or a house—one must first of all study its nature; for it must serve its purpose perfectly, that is, it must fulfill its function usefully, be durable, economical, and 'beautiful.' This research into the nature of objects leads to the conclusion that by resolute consideration of modern production methods, constructions, and materials, forms will evolve that are often unusual and surprising, since they deviate from the conventional (consider, for example, the changes in the design of heating and lighting fixtures).

Walter Gropius, "Principles of Bahaus Production," from H. Wingler, *The Bauhaus: Weimar, Dessau, Berlin, Chicago*, trans. Wolfgang and Basil Gilbert (Cambridge, MA: MIT Press, 1969), 109–10. © 1969 by the Massachusetts Institute of Technology. Reprinted with permission from the publisher.

It is only through constant contact with newly evolving techniques, with the discovery of new materials, and with new ways of putting things together, that the creative individual can learn to bring the design of objects into a living relationship with tradition and from that point to develop a new attitude toward design, which is:

> a resolute affirmation of the living environment of machines and vehicles;
> the organic design of things based on their own present-day laws, without romantic gloss and wasteful frivolity;
> the limitation to characteristic, primary forms and colors, readily accessible to everyone;
> simplicity in multiplicity, economical utilization of space, material, time, and money.

The creation of standard types for all practical commodities of everyday use is a social necessity.

On the whole, the necessities of life are the same for the majority of people. The home and its furnishings are mass consumer goods and their design is more a matter of reason than a matter of passion. The machine—capable of producing standardized products—is an effective device which, by means of mechanical aids—steam and electricity—can free the individual from working manually for the satisfaction of his daily needs and can provide him with mass-produced products that are cheaper and better than those manufactured by hand. There is no danger that standardization will force a choice upon the individual, since due to natural competition the number of available types of each object will always be ample to provide the individual with a choice of design that suits him best.

The Bauhaus workshops are essentially laboratories in which prototypes of products suitable for mass production and typical of our time are carefully developed and constantly improved.

In these laboratories, the Bauhaus wants to train a new kind of collaborator for industry and the crafts, who has an equal command of both technology and form.

To reach the object of creating a set of standard prototypes which meet all the demands of economy, technology, and form requires the selection of the best, most versatile, and most thoroughly educated men who are well grounded in the workshop experience and who are imbued with an exact knowledge of the design elements of form and mechanics and their underlying laws.

The Bauhaus represents the opinion that the contrast between industry and the crafts is much less marked by the difference in the tools they use than by the division of labor in industry and unity of the work in the crafts. But the two are constantly getting closer to each other. The crafts of the past have changed, and the future crafts will be merged in a new productive unity in which they will carry out the experimental work for industrial production. Speculative experiments in laboratory workshops will yield models and prototypes for productive implementation in factories.

The prototypes that have been completed in the Bauhaus workshops are being reproduced by outside firms with whom the workshops are closely related.

The production of the Bauhaus thus does not represent any kind of competition for either industry or crafts but rather provides them with impetus for their development. The Bauhaus does this by bringing creatively talented people with ample practical experience into the actual course of production, to take over the preparatory work for production, from industry and the crafts. The products reproduced from prototypes that have been developed by the Bauhaus can be offered at a reasonable price only by utilization of all the modern, economical methods of standardization (mass production by industry) and by large-scale sales. The dangers of a decline in the quality of the product by comparison to the prototype, in regard to quality of material and workmanship, as a result of mechanical reproduction will be countered by all available means. The Bauhaus fights against the cheap substitute, inferior workmanship, and the dilettantism of the handicrafts, for a new standard of quality work.

15 | HENRY-RUSSELL HITCHCOCK, 1903–1987, AND PHILIP JOHNSON, 1906–2005

Ludwig Mies van der Rohe, Barcelona Pavilion, International Exposition, Barcelona, 1929
© 2007 Artist Rights Society (ARS), New York/VG Bild-Kunst, Bonn
Photo Credit: Digital Image © The Museum of Modern Art/Licensed by SCALA/Art Resource, NY

In 1932, the Museum of Modern Art (MOMA) in New York staged Modern Architecture—International Exhibition. Using models, photographs, and the occasional plan, this show presented a new architectural aesthetic that, during the past few decades, had been developed largely by European practitioners such as Le Corbusier, Mies van der Rohe, Walter Gropius, and J. J. P. Oud. With Philip Johnson, who had recently earned his undergraduate degree in philosophy from Harvard University, the architectural historian Henry-Russell Hitchcock organized the exhibition. Together Hitchcock and Johnson prepared an accompanying catalog—*The International Style: Architecture since 1922*—that further defined the work on display. In their text, excerpted below, Hitchcock and Johnson listed three characteristics of this new "International Style" architecture: an emphasis on volume instead of mass, an organization based on regularity instead of classical axial symmetry, and a prohibition of applied ornament. Significantly, this summary focused on formal characteristics and made no mention of the desired social improvements that led to the development of this new architectural language.

The majority of the work included in the MOMA exhibition was dominated by European architects, but the designs of a few Americans, including Frank Lloyd Wright, did appear. However, the show and catalog emphasized the sleek and novel appearance of the International Style, featuring buildings executed in steel, glass, and concrete. Presented as a coherent and fashionable body of work, the International Style, along with the accompanying formal principles enunciated by Hitchcock and Johnson, had a tremendous impact on American architecture through the mid-twentieth century, strongly influencing commercial, civic, and residential design.

The International Style: Architecture since 1922 (1932)

Introduction

The Idea of Style

The light and airy systems of construction of the Gothic cathedrals, the freedom and slenderness of their supporting skeleton, afford, as it were, a presage of a style that began to develop in the nineteenth century, that of metallic architecture. With the use of metal, and of concrete reinforced by metal bars, modern builders could equal the most daring feats of Gothic architects without endangering the solidity of the structure. In the conflict that obtains between the two elements of construction, solidity and open space, everything seems to show that the principle of free spaces will prevail, that the palaces and houses of the future will be flooded with air and light. Thus the formula popularized by Gothic architecture has a great future before it. Following on the revival of Græco-Roman architecture which prevailed from the sixteenth century to our own day, we shall see, with the full application of different materials, a yet more enduring rebirth of the Gothic style.

Salomon Reinach, Apollo, *1904*

Since the middle of the eighteenth century there have been recurrent attempts to achieve and to impose a controlling style in architecture such as existed in the earlier epochs of the past. The two chief of these attempts were the Classical Revival and the Mediæval Revival. Out of the compromises between these two opposing schools and difficulties of reconciling either sort of revivalism with the new needs and the new methods of construction of the day grew the stylistic confusion of the last hundred years.

Henry-Russell Hitchcock and Philip Johnson, *The International Style: Architecture Since 1922* (New York: W. W. Norton & Company, Inc., 1995), 33–37 and 44–49. © 1932 by W. W. Norton & Company, Inc.; renewed © 1960 by Henry-Russell Hitchcock and Philip Johnson. Reprinted with permission of the publisher.

The nineteenth century failed to create a style of architecture because it was unable to achieve a general discipline of structure and of design in the terms of the day. The revived "styles" were but a decorative garment to architecture, not the interior principles according to which it lived and grew. On the whole the development of engineering in building went on regardless of the Classical or Mediæval architectural forms which were borrowed from the past. Thus the chaos of eclecticism served to give the very idea of style a bad name in the estimation of the first modern architects of the end of the nineteenth and the beginning of the twentieth century.

In the nineteenth century there was always not one style, but "styles," and the idea of "styles" implied a choice. The individualistic revolt of the first modern architects destroyed the prestige of the "styles," but it did not remove the implication that there was a possibility of choice between one aesthetic conception of design and another. In their reaction against revivalism these men sought rather to explore a great variety of free possibilities.

The result, on the whole, added to the confusion of continuing eclecticism, although the new work possessed a general vitality which the later revivalists had quite lost. The revolt from stylistic discipline to extreme individualism at the beginning of the twentieth century was justified as the surest issue from an impasse of imitation and sterility. The individualists decried submission to fixed aesthetic principles as the imposition of a dead hand upon the living material of architecture, holding up the failure of the revivals as a proof that the very idea of style was an unhealthy delusion.

Today the strict issue of reviving the styles of the distant past is no longer one of serious consequence. But the peculiar traditions of imitation and modification of the styles of the past, which eclecticism inherited from the earlier Classical and Mediæval Revivals, have not been easily forgotten. The influence of the past still most to be feared is that of the nineteenth century with its cheapening of the very idea of style. Modern architecture has nothing but the healthiest lessons to learn from the art of the further past, if that art be studied scientifically and not in a spirit of imitation. Now that it is possible to emulate the great styles of the past in their essence without imitating their surface, the problem of establishing one dominant style, which the nineteenth century set itself in terms of alternative revivals, is coming to a solution.

The idea of style, which began to degenerate when the revivals destroyed the disciplines of the Baroque, has become real and fertile again. Today a single new style has come into existence. The aesthetic conceptions on which its disciplines are based derive from the experimentation of the individualists. They and not the revivalists were the immediate masters of those who have created the new style. This contemporary style, which exists throughout the world, is unified and inclusive, not fragmentary and contradictory like so much of the production of the first generation of modern architects. In the last decade it has produced sufficient monuments of distinction to display its validity and its vitality. It may fairly be compared in significance with the styles of the past. In the handling of the problems of structure it is related to the Gothic, in the handling of the problems of design it is more akin to the Classical. In the preeminence given to the handling of function it is distinguished from both.

The unconscious and halting architectural developments of the nineteenth century, the confused and contradictory experimentation of the beginning of the twentieth, have been succeeded by a directed evolution. There is now a single body of discipline, fixed enough to permit individual interpretation and to encourage general growth.

The idea of style as the frame of potential growth, rather than as a fixed and crushing mould, has developed with the recognition of underlying principles such as archaeologists discern in the great styles of the past. The principles are few and broad. They are not mere formulas of proportion such as distinguish the Doric from the Ionic order, they are fundamental, like the organic verticality of the Gothic or the rhythmical symmetry of the Baroque. There is, first, a new conception of architecture as volume rather than as mass. Secondly, regularity rather than axial symmetry serves as the chief means of ordering design. These two principles, with a third proscribing arbitrary applied decoration, mark the productions of the international style. This new style is not international in the sense that the production of one country is just like that of another. Nor is it so rigid that the work of various leaders is not clearly distinguishable. The international style has become evident and definable only gradually as different innovators throughout the world have successfully carried out parallel experiments.

In stating the general principles of the contemporary style, in analyzing their derivation from structure and their modification by function, the appearance of a certain dogmatism can hardly be avoided. In opposition to those who claim that a new style of architecture is impossible or undesirable, it is necessary to stress the coherence of the results obtained within the range of possibilities thus far explored. For the international style already exists in the present; it is not merely something the future may hold in store. Architecture is always a set of actual monuments, not a vague corpus of theory. . . .

It is particularly in the early work of three men, Walter Gropius in Germany, Oud in Holland, and Le Corbusier in France, that the various steps in the inception of the new style must be sought. These three with Mies van der Rohe in Germany remain the great leaders of modern architecture.

Gropius' factory at Alfeld, built just before the War, came nearer to an integration of the new style than any other edifice built before 1922. In industrial architecture the tradition of the styles of the past was not repressive, as many factories of the nineteenth century well illustrate. The need for using modern construction throughout and for serving function directly was peculiarly evident. Hence it was easier for Gropius to advance in this field beyond his master, Behrens, than it would have been in any other. The walls of the Alfeld factory are screens of glass with spandrels of metal at the floor levels. The crowning band of brickwork does not project beyond these screens. The purely mechanical elements are frankly handled and give interest to a design fundamentally so regular as to approach monotony. There is no applied ornamental decoration except the lettering. The organization of the parts of the complex structure is ordered by logic and consistency rather than by axial symmetry.

Yet there are traces still of the conceptions of traditional architecture. The glass screens are treated like projecting bays between the visible supports. These supports are sheathed with brick so that they appear like the last fragments of the solid masonry wall of the past. The entrance is symmetrical and heavy. For all its simplicity it is treated with a decorative emphasis. Gropius was not destined to achieve again so fine and so coherent a production in the contemporary style before the Bauhaus in 1926. There he profited from the intervening aesthetic experimentation of the Dutch Neoplasticists. The Bauhaus is something more than a mere development from the technical triumph of the Alfeld factory.

During the years of the War, Oud in Holland came into contact with the group of Dutch cubist painters led by Mondriaan and Van Doesburg, who called themselves Neoplasticists. Their positive influence on his work at first was negligible. Oud remained for a time still a disciple of Berlage, whose half-modern manner he had previously followed rather closely. He profited also by his study of the innovation of Wright, whose work was already better known in Europe than in America. Then he sought consciously to achieve a Neoplasticist architecture and, from 1917 on, the influence of Berlage and Wright began to diminish. At the same time he found in concrete an adequate material for the expression of new conceptions of form. Oud's projects were increasingly simple, vigorous and geometrical. On the analogy of abstract painting he came to realize the aesthetic potentialities of planes in three dimensions with which Wright had already experimented. He reacted sharply against the picturesqueness of the other followers of Berlage and sought with almost Greek fervor to arrive at a scheme of proportions ever purer and more regular.

In his first housing projects carried out for the city of Rotterdam in 1918 and 1919 he did not advance as far as in his unexecuted projects. But at Oud-Mathenesse in 1921–

22, although he was required to build the whole village in traditional materials and to continue the use of conventional roofs, the new style promised in his projects came into being. The avoidance of picturesqueness, the severe horizontality of the composition, the perfect simplicity and consistency which he achieved in executing a very complex project, all announced the conscious creation of a body of aesthetic disciplines.

Oud-Mathenesse exceeded Gropius' Alfeld factory in significance if not in impressiveness. Gropius made his innovations primarily in technics, Oud in design. He undoubtedly owed the initial impetus to the Neoplasticists, but his personal manner had freed itself from dependence on painting. The models Van Doesburg made of houses in the early twenties, in collaboration with other Neoplasticists, with their abstract play of volumes and bright colors, had their own direct influence in Germany.

But the man who first made the world aware that a new style was being born was Le Corbusier. As late as 1916, well after his technical and sociological theorizing had begun, his conceptions of design were still strongly marked by the Classical symmetry of his master Perret. His plans, however, were even more open than those of Wright. In his housing projects of the next few years he passed rapidly beyond his master Perret and beyond Behrens and Loos, with whom he had also come in contact. His *Citrohan* house model of 1921 was the thorough expression of a conception of architecture as radical technically as Gropius' factory and as novel aesthetically as Oud's village. The enormous window area and the terraces made possible by the use of ferroconcrete, together with the asymmetry of the composition, undoubtedly produced a design more thoroughly infused with a new spirit, more completely freed from the conventions of the past than any thus far projected.

The influence of Le Corbusier was the greater, the appearance of a new style the more remarked, because of the vehement propaganda which he contributed to the magazine *L'Esprit Nouveau*, 1920–1925. Since then, moreover, he has written a series of books effectively propagandizing his technical and aesthetic theories. In this way his name has become almost synonymous with the new architecture and it has been praised or condemned very largely in his person. But he was not, as we have seen, the only innovator nor was the style as it came generally into being after 1922 peculiarly his. He crystallized; he dramatized; but he was not alone in creating.

When in 1922 he built at Vaucresson his first house in the new style, he failed to equal the purity of design and the boldness of construction of the *Citrohan* project. But the houses that immediately followed this, one for the painter Ozenfant, and another for his parents outside Vevey, passed further beyond the transitional stage than anything that Oud or Gropius were to build for several more years. Ozenfant's sort of cubism, called Purism, had perhaps inspired Le Corbusier in his search for sources of formal inspiration for a new architecture. But on the whole Le Corbusier in these early years turned for precedent rather to steamships than to painting. Some of his early houses, such as that for the sculptor Miestchaninoff at Boulogne-sur-Seine, were definitely naval in feeling. But this marine phase was soon over like Oud's strictly Neoplasticist phase, or the Expressionist period in the work of the young architects of Germany. Various external influences helped to free architecture from the last remnants of a lingering traditionalism. The new style displayed its force in the rapidity with which it transmuted them beyond recognition.

Mies van der Rohe advanced toward the new style less rapidly at first than Gropius. Before the War he had simplified, clarified, and lightened the domestic style of Behrens to a point that suggests conscious inspiration from Schinkel and Persius. After the War in two projects for skyscrapers entirely of metal and glass he carried technical innovation even further than Gropius, further indeed than anyone has yet gone in practice. These buildings would have been pure volume, glazed cages supported from within, on a scale such as not even Paxton in the nineteenth century would have dreamed possible. However, in their form, with plans based on clustered circles or sharp angles, they were extravagantly Romantic and strongly marked by the contemporary wave of Expressionism in Germany.

It was in Mies' projects of 1922 that his true significance as an aesthetic innovator first appeared. In a design for a country house he broke with the conception of the wall as a continuous plane surrounding the plan and built up his composition of sections of intersecting planes. Thus he achieved, still with the use of supporting walls, a greater openness even than Le Corbusier with his ferroconcrete skeleton construction. Mies' sense of proportions remained as serene as before the War and even more pure. This project and the constructions of Oud and Le Corbusier in this year emphasize that it is just a decade ago that the new style came into existence.

The four leaders of modern architecture are Le Corbusier, Oud, Gropius and Mies van der Rohe. But others as well as they, Rietveld in Holland, Lureat in France, even Mendelsohn in Germany, for all his lingering dalliance with Expressionism, took parallel steps of nearly equal importance in the years just after the War. The style did not spring from a single source but came into being generally. The writing of Oud and Gropius, and to a greater degree that of Le Corbusier, with the frequent publication of their projects of these years, carried the principles of the new style abroad. These projects have indeed become more famous than many executed buildings.

From the first there were also critics, who were not architects, to serve as publicists. Everyone who was interested in the creation of a modern architecture had to come to terms with the nascent style. The principles of the style that appeared already plainly by 1922 in the projects and the executed buildings of the leaders, still control today an ever increasing group of architects throughout the world.

16 R. Buckminster Fuller, 1895–1983

R. Buckminster Fuller, Dymaxion House, Wichita, KS, 1946
Courtesy of the Estate of R. Buckminster Fuller

Buckminster Fuller has been described as an inventor, architect, scientist, mathematician, and poet. Indeed, he practiced in all of these fields and appears to have viewed them not as separate disciplines but as parts of a larger universal realm. After losing his first child to polio, Fuller dedicated himself to improving mankind's quality of life through technology. His efforts focused on doing more with less—designing structures and vehicles that required a minimum of energy, money, and material to construct and operate. The geodesic dome, a strong, lightweight enclosure composed of multiple self-bracing triangles, was perhaps Fuller's most famous invention. It was designed with the "more-with-less" philosophy in mind, as was his airframe dwelling, the Dymaxion House: an inexpensive, efficient, durable home to be factory produced and either delivered via airlift in one piece or assembled on site. The aluminum house used natural means for temperature control, required little external maintenance, and contained systems to recycle waste. The interior could be reconfigured easily to accommodate the occupants' needs. With the end of World War II in sight, Fuller proposed that factories previously used for wartime production manufacture his Dymaxion homes. This could preserve jobs for factory employees and provide low-cost housing for returning soldiers and their families. Fuller elaborated on these ideas in a lecture in 1946, excerpted below, given to the engineers charged with making Fuller's vision a reality. Although his Dymaxion homes never achieved a full run of production, Fuller, for the remainder of his life, continued his quest for innovative and progressive ways to raise the standard of living.

"Designing a New Industry" (1946)

. . . We have now actually met the theoretical requirements of the physical problem. We have gotten down to the proper weight. We are down, not including the bathroom and partitions, to 5,400 pounds. The copper bathroom now in the house weights 430 pounds—but in aluminum with plastic finish, as we are going to manufacture it, the bathroom will weigh around 250 pounds. The partitions, two bathrooms, kitchen, laundry, and energy unit will probably come to not more than 2,000 pounds. We will be right on our curve of the size of things man can mass produce in 1946. In other words, due to the development of the airplane industry, the house has become an extremely practical and now very real affair.

Overnight [there was] the necessity of democracy for a great number of planes to accommodate the increasing mobility of man brought about by war because man had not provided ways of developing that air technology expansion through peaceful means. This was because man was not living in a preventive pathology . . . but in a curative pathology, which has to have war to bring about the inevitable and major economic changes. *Industry* as preoccupied with the airplane overnight became *four time*s as large as *industry* preoccupied with the automobile. People do not seem to realize it but that is what happened.

You must now realize this evolution was simply the *principle* which we have defined earlier this evening as constituting *industry* itself being comprehensively tuned up

Excerpt from Buckminster Fuller's Writings © The Estate of Buckminster Fuller. Originally appeared in *Designing a New Industry: A Composite of a Series of Talks by R. Buckminster Fuller, 1945–1946* (Wichita: Fuller Research Institute, 1946), 38–42. Reprinted with permission.

through its inherent self-improving advantages, which had been accumulating incre-ment for a generation, to demonstrate dramatically a new range and degree of ability. Therefore the *airplane* industry should not be thought of as a species of industry apart, for instance, from the *automobile* industry or the *hat* industry. It should be thought of as the phenomenon industry itself, simply mobilized to its best ability or to its most recent record high in *standards of performance.*

In *industry,* as preoccupied with aircraft manufacture and maintenance during World War II, the standards and tolerances of precision that could be maintained, the size of units, the relative strength, the degree of complexity control all represent a sum total of somewhere around a ten-to-one magnitude increase in technical advantages over *industry* as we know it before this war idling along on 1917 standards.

For us now as composite proprietors, workers, and consumers, to give up the standards of industry as recently preoccupied with the technical necessities of worldwide flight of man in order to assist him to establish ultimate world-wide democracy, and to go back instead to the phase of industry as we knew it in its earlier preoccupation with exploitation of man's innate tendency to *mobilize for security* by tentative adaptation of the automobile to his paralyzed domiciling, would be to actually deflate our whole economic ability by 90%. To deflate our economic ability 90% is to decrease our potential ability 90%, which, as viewed from old-fashioned static economics simply means a 900% inflation of prices, relative to wage-hour dollars. It is an unthinkable thing. I don't think it is going to happen.

I think our house is going to have an important part in helping us to keep on upward instead of downward in historical degree of technical advantage that was developed during World War II. I don't have to talk to you much about that. You have heard about the possibility of using the aircraft plants. Last year the president of your com-pany delivered an excellent address to the National Convention of the International

Association of Machinists. . . . It [covered] the subject of the aircraft industry's inclusion of the manufacture of *airframe dwellings*, the name we have given to that portion of dwelling machines to be manufactured by the airframe industry. Wright Field calls our dwelling machines "stationary airplanes." The power plant and electrical manufacturing and many other areas of the older industry's component parts manufacturers will provide the organic apparatus of our dwelling service.

The big fact that confronts us is that you of the aircraft industry have suddenly developed a whole new world which has recently been operating four times as much technology as was ever operated before—which happened to represent precisely the level of technology for which I had been waiting to get my house realized. We had suddenly broken through into a world where young architects who didn't have building design jobs and who couldn't find building design jobs because building technology had stalemated suddenly found the aircraft world a very good place to go. In this welcoming world of aircraft they matriculated rapidly into the performance per-pound language. They now think that way irrevocably. Everybody, throughout the whole aircraft industry thinks that way. It is no longer a *hard mental* job for us to sit down and talk, as we have talked tonight, *about how much housing weighs*, too.

Here is one more thing on the economics side I would like you to think about. Housing, as you have known it up to now, used the wood or stone or clay which was at hand. These component materials were not understood scientifically to any important degree. Wood might be considered *pretty* as oak, or pretty as maple. One was a little harder or softer to work and suited a man better than another. But it was little understood what a tree was. Despite academic study, man's understanding of trees was popularly vague. Then trees began to be used industrially by the chemical industry. It began to develop wood pulps and other by-products of wood. To some extent this began to affect the "scarcity" or "quantity" of wood relative to its availability for house building. These new industries, particularly newsprint pulp, exhausted a lot of it. Builders had to take greener and greener lumber as stock piling dwindled.

During World War II one of the most extraordinary things that happened, in its broad effects on technology and on economics, is what the Germans were forced to accomplish in wood chemistry in order to plan on how to survive during this extraordinary industrial warfare which they introduced and in which energy played such an important role. The Germans had to plan in advance on being bombed out of their oil fields. It was obvious that they could plan to use oil to a certain extent but that eventually their most vulnerable position was their oil supply. This was an "oil warfare" in a big way. Therefore the Germans set about finding other important sources of energy. They went to wood technology. The chemistry of wood developed in many directions in Germany. They suddenly discovered that here was Nature's most important trick in impounding sun energy—and in a most useful way, for therefrom you could release energy in many useful directions. They immediately brought it to the one great "Grand Central Station" of energy, in its most storable form, which was alcohol. From alcohol of various kinds you could make foods first for cattle, then for people. You could make high octane gas or synthetic rubber or plastics. The chemistry of wood began playing such an important part that the scientists in Washington were talking about it constantly. . . .

Wood technology has advanced the basic economic case for wood to such an important position in the advancing technical world that we no longer can afford to use wood in the careless way we have in the past to put it in houses for termites to eat up, or a possible fire to consume. Even if we could, world-wide technology forces our technical hand as it never has before, the rest of the world is now industrializing and is starting at the most advanced World War II levels of technology and not at our 1861 or 1890 or 1917 level. Industrial technology is born of latent knowledge and is not an inventory of obsolete machinery, so wood is in a very new historical position. How does that affect the historical wood house picture?

As children of the pioneers also came along to build a house—or their grandchildren wanted to—there was no longer much wood on the farm. They had to go increasing distances for it. Finally they went out of the state for it. Today they have to send 1,000 to 5,000 miles for most of their building wood.

They were using it simply by habit because it was originally handy and suddenly they had exhausted that supply. Long ago wood boxes disappeared from our cellars. In the war's great motion packing cases went all over the world. That broke the wood supply equilibrium altogether. World increased paper needs and the new chemistry of wood-energy conversion makes it unthinkable that wood will ever again be available in any large way for building it into houses, even into prefabs which average 70% wood. Wood is suddenly going from 'for free' as it sat stacked on the farm because it had to be cleared away, to a rapidly inflating price structure—owing not so much to its scarcity, as to its newly recognized inherent wealth.

On the other hand, there are now the many *by-products of the soil* and *by-products of the wood* which chemistry is developing, whether it is cellulose as plastics, or the metals developed from the clay, etc., which were just kicking around unrecognized on the early farm. These by-products, however, were very expensive to extract in the beginning and called for a large energy expenditure and fancy and complicated mammoth plants with giant stills and ovens such as required millions of dollars to install and develop. Few industries could afford to buy the original specialty by-products of high performance characteristic.

However in developing the aircraft industry we had to have *high performance per pound*, so for a military plane the federal government could afford to pay for special alloys of aluminum and steel. Then we suddenly called for an enormous wartime application of industry to produce those same materials and they were brought into relatively low cost brackets. They could be extremely low for they came from sands, clay, coal, air, water, etc. Producers however held up their prices during the war because of the enormous amount of inspection necessary. In order to amplify industry to the ability to mass produce planes, which meant withstanding terrific stresses with minimum of weight and bulk, it was necessary to be supercareful of the quality of the materials. So the cost of inspection, pyramided upon inspection all along the line, was reflected in the high price structure of those materials, despite quantity production.

We now have enough 24ST aluminum in war surplus and scrap to make it worthwhile to segregate 24ST scrap so that the aluminum company will say, "We will give you 24ST because we can now recirculate the scrap, and it is better scrap, actually having a little higher alloy content and preferable qualities at a much lower price than you have been paying." Just within a couple of postwar months I am beginning to see price structure of aircraft metals and other high performance materials on the way down. As you study the basic economics of the plastics or aluminum industry, you find the price structure has got to go down as we employ their mass production by our less stringent standards and large mass outlet. Why?—Because we have alternate materials for every part's design.

In the materials we are dealing with in our new airframe houses, we are in a deflating price structure, while wood of the conventional house is in a very rapidly inflating price structure.

Those are some of the really outstanding trend data for you. If you would like to have in mind before you go away some of the absolutes in the old building world, so you can see where you are situated as you enter our endeavor with us, I will read these figures. I gave you the all-time high in housing which was in 1925, when 827,000 dwelling units were built, of which 572,000 were single-family dwellings, of which 270,00 had some interior plumbing. The top wartime total of dwelling units in one year was 575,000. That was 300,000 less than 1925, despite very much larger population and despite very much increased technology in all other directions. That was 1943 and was in all classes of dwellings.

We find that during the war a lot of other kinds of dwellings or shelters were developed, in which Quonsets were among those with which to reckon. In case authorities determine that "Our standard of living will have to go down during the 1946–47–48 housing emergency, and two million G.I.s who have made the mistake of getting married and are looking for some place to live will have to live in Quonsets and prefabs," what would be the projected production of Quonset huts and other prefabs? Sixty thousand Quonsets in one year is that industry's reported top capacity. The prefabricated house industry indicated in a recent government survey that it hoped to double its production from the best prediction year during the war to a new total of 142,950 units. That is the capacity they dreamed about. Their best war capacity rate, which was never sustained, amounted to a potential 71,475 houses per year. That doesn't come anywhere near your need this coming year just for two million homeless G.I.s and their brides, paying no attention at all to the rest of the housing shortage, which is somewhere about twelve million in the United States. Those are important figures for you to have in mind to know whether you are on the right track in joining up with us here in the airframe dwelling machine industry.

I must caution you that you will be confronted constantly by the statement that mass production of houses eliminates the aspect of individuality which is so cherished by humans and without which they are afraid they will lose the identity of their personality; therefore, mass production of houses will never gain popular acceptance.

My answer to that is that reproduction or regeneration of form is a fundamental of nature and that it is neither good nor bad in itself. However, reproduction of originally inadequate or awkward forms, or poor mechanics or wasteful structures, either by the hand of man or by the regeneration of the biological species, tends to amplify the original characteristic. If the original is annoying, reproductions become increasingly annoying; if the original is highly adequate to its designed purpose, reproductions become increasingly pleasing in that confirmation of adequacy. In the latter light, we continuously admire a fine species of cultivated rose or nature's wildflowers—the more frequently repeated, the more beautiful. Conversely, the more frequently we see a maimed soldier, the more disheartening becomes the repetition. There would be even less virtue of the so-called individuality in discovery of soldiers' sons born with half a face blown away, or with three legs.

Individuality goes far deeper than these surface manifestations with which people have sought to deceive one another as to the relative importance of their status in the bitter struggle to validate one's right to live. Those who were powerful but ugly and lazy paid for fine clothes and fine surface architecture and a superstition has persisted that people who could afford to pay must be superior individuals. The powerful have whipped the weak for centuries on end to instill that superstition. As long as *might excelled over right* that superstition had to continue. Now that we propose housing to be produced by an industry in which *right makes might* at less than a pound per horsepower the superstition is obsolete.

There is no individuality in conventional houses. They are all four-square boxes with varying lengths of rotting wood Greek column nailed onto the front, every house so similar that without signboards the stranger cannot tell the difference between one American town and another, let alone detect individuality in the separate and pathetic homes.

On the other hand, it has been discovered that the more uniform and simple the surfaces with which the individual is graced, the more does the individuality, which is the abstract life, come through. Trained nurses in uniform working in a hospital are notoriously more attractive as individuals than the same girls in their street clothes when off duty.

To somebody who says, "what are your houses going to cost?" we are not yet able to say very accurately but the indications are the cost will be relatively low. "That," we say, "is very unimportant." My argument and I hope yours is going to be that costs are entirely relative. Your wage structure is going up fairly fast. If your wage structure is different your price will be different. Houses that cost $5,000 before the war are now costing $8,000. Houses reflect relative prices. Suppose we are somewhere around or below the $5,000 mark—I think that is pretty good.

What is more important, however, I think is for us all to realize the actual picture of production potential of our houses in terms of the capacity of the metals produced for the aircraft industry during this war. Not going outside of the aircraft capacity—not infringing at all on the old building world, leaving it to build as best it can we can get set up in the aircraft plants and be producing two million houses a year just as fast as we can get ready. Just as fast as you boys can get out good production drawings and complete your calculations and get this house tooled up, we can produce two million houses a year.

That is talking entirely new figures and we can amplify the aluminum capacity and amplify the aircraft capacity and get up to five million houses and approach the automobile figures. That is perfectly reasonable. There is nothing fantastic about that number of units. We are talking about something we know is really practical.

As it is practical and we really need two million houses right now for G.I.s, and need twelve million for people in substandard and crowded houses in the United States, and need thirty million houses for 100% bombed-out families in the war-torn countries, I say the cost of *not* having our houses is not only enormous, it is history's tragedy. It leads rapidly into lawlessness and ill health, to an enormous cost to society. I would ask a senatorial committee or a congressional committee asking me what houses cost, *"How much is it going to cost not to have our houses?"* That is what is important and I really look at the accumulating national debt as the accumulation of the cost of maintaining curative pathology instead of investing a few billions in establishing a preventive pathology through a scientific worldwide housing service industry. We have already come a long way downhill from the industrial peak in the face of an enormous ability to create wealth and put our environment under control. The initial cost is very important. If we can get the thing rolling we can make houses available to everyone who wants houses, and very rapidly obsolete all old standards of living. We will set up a new industry that promises to go on to rehouse the whole world and employ the whole world in the continuous wealth-making of improving living advantages.

That is clear enough as a simple a picture to the building trades. Some of the building trades people I talk to understand this, and it is very clear to mechanics that we are talking about starting up a new industry and not a new house. They are not going to be so concerned about whether the building trades are employed in erecting those houses. The building trades men tell me they have participated in the building of less than 4% of single-family dwellings. It is not a very important item to them. When you talk to them about giving them a new industry, the new industry, like the telephone, would cause a great deal of bricklaying of the individual plants, the power stations, etc. Therefore, you want to say, all of you, that you are designing an additional industry which is going to get everybody busy. Your labor man doesn't mind the idea of short man-hours, or better working conditions or steady year-round work.

Beech figures show way less than 100 man-hours per house to manufacture. Our indications are that in the field we will start with 100 man-hours and before we get through with developing the boom jig upon which we are going to hang the house as we assemble it and feed the parts off the tailboard to give a very fast assembly, we will be down to relatively few man-hours—40 man-hours or something like that—in the field. (That of course is not what we are going to do out here in the early days.)

I will prophesy however than within two years we will be down to somewhere under 100 man-hours from raw materials as delivered to the aircraft industry (that is, as sheet aluminum in rolls, steel in rods and tubes, etc.) to finished house—under 100 man-hours. So your living cost is going to be low and your standards high and rapidly rising.

Obviously, boys, the thing is now reasonably good enough to dare to put it out on the world, and the world will be reasonably tolerant enough with it to "take" all the bugs that are still in it. It is full of them. But we have harnessed out there now in our prototypes the right principles within the right weight and the right dimensions, so that's where you boys have to take over.

Thank you very much.

PHILIP JOHNSON, 1906–2005 17

As co-curator with H. R. Hitchcock, Johnson participated in his first great architectural endeavor, the exhibition of Modern International Style Architecture at the New York Museum of Modern Art, before he began his formal architectural studies. Over the next few decades, Johnson established himself as a prominent figure in the field, working with a simplified, reductive architectural vocabulary of glass and steel derived from the works of Mies van der Rohe. A clear example is Johnson's own residence, the Glass House in New Canaan, Connecticut (1949), which draws upon Mies's Farnsworth House in Plano, Illinois (1946–50). From 1954 through 1958, Johnson worked with Mies on the design of the Seagram Building in New York. In the following text, originally a talk given in 1954 to students at Harvard University's Graduate School of Design, Johnson irreverently questioned the architect's reliance on certain modernist principles, or "crutches." Ultimately, he insisted that the act of creation is intensely personal and relies not on preconceived tenets, but on the architect's agency. Johnson's declaration coincided with his own architectural shift toward the postmodern playfulness expressed in his AT&T Building (New York, 1980–84).

"The Seven Crutches of Modern Architecture" (1955)

Art has nothing to do with intellectual pursuit—it shouldn't be in a university at all. Art should be practiced in the gutters—pardon me, in attics.

You can't learn architecture any more than you can learn a sense of music or of painting. You shouldn't talk about art, you should do it.

If I seem to go into words it's because there's no other way to communicate. We have to descend to the world around us if we are to battle it. We have to use words to put the "word" people back where they belong.

So I'm going to attack the seven crutches of architecture. Some of us rejoice in the crutches and pretend that we're walking and that poor other people with two feet are slightly handicapped. But we all use them at times, and especially in the schools where you have to use language. It's only natural to use language when you're teaching, because how are teachers to mark you? "Bad entrance" or "Bathrooms not backed up" or "Stairway too narrow" or "Where's head room?" "Chimney won't draw," "Kitchen too far from dining room." It is so much easier for the faculty to set up a set of rules that you can be marked against. They can't say, "That's ugly." For you can answer that for you it is good-looking, and *de gustibus non est disputandum*. Schools therefore are especially prone to using these crutches. I would certainly use them if I were teaching, because I couldn't criticize extra-aesthetic props any better than any other teacher.

Philip Johnson, "The Seven Crutches of Modern Architecture," in *Philip Johnson: Writings* (London: Oxford University Press, Inc., 2005), 136–40. © Oxford University Press. Reprinted with permission from the publisher.

The most important crutch in recent times is not valid now: the *Crutch of History*. In the old days you could always rely on books. You could say, "What do you mean you don't like my tower? There it is in Wren." Or, "They did that on the Subtreasury Building—why can't I do it?" History doesn't bother us very much now.

But the next one is still with us today although, here again, the *Crutch of Pretty Drawing* is pretty well gone. There are those of us—I am one—who have made a sort of cult of the pretty plan. It's a wonderful crutch because you can give yourself the illusion that you are creating architecture while you're making pretty drawings. Fundamentally, architecture is something you build and put together, and people walk in and they like it. But that's too hard. Pretty pictures are easier.

The next one, the third one, is the *Crutch of Utility*, of usefulness. This is where I was brought up, and I've used it myself; it was an old Harvard habit.

They say a building is good architecture if it works. This building works perfectly— if I talk loud enough. The Parthenon probably worked perfectly well for the ceremonies they used it for. In other words, merely that a building works is not sufficient. You expect that it works. You expect a kitchen hot-water faucet to run hot water these days. You expect any architect, a graduate of Harvard or not, to be able to put the kitchen in the right place. But when it's used as a crutch it impedes. It lulls you into thinking that that is architecture. The rules that we've all been brought up on—"The coat closet should be near the front door in a house," "Cross-ventilation is a necessity"—these rules are not very important for architecture. That we should have a front door to come in and a back door to carry the garbage out—pretty good, but in my house I noticed to my horror the other day that I carried the garbage out the front door. If the business of getting the house to run well takes precedence over your artistic invention the result won't be architecture at all; merely an assemblage of useful parts. You will recognize it next time you're doing a building; you'll be so satisfied when you get the banks of elevators to come out at the right floor you'll think your skyscraper is finished. I know. I'm just working on one.

That's not as bad, though as the next one: the *Crutch of Comfort*. That's a habit that we come by, the same as utility. We are all descended from John Stuart Mill in our thinking. After all, what is architecture for but the comforts of the people who live there? But when that is made into a crutch for doing architecture, environmental control starts to replace architecture. Pretty soon you'll be doing controlled environmental houses which aren't hard to do except that you may have a window on the west and you can't control the sun. There isn't an overhang in the world, there isn't a sun chart in Harvard University that will help. Because, of course, the sun is absolutely everywhere. You know what they mean by controlled environment; it is the study of "microclimatology," which is the science that tells you how to recreate a climate so that you will be comfortable. But are you? The fireplace, for example, is out of place in the controlled environment of a house. It heats up and throws off thermostats. But I like the beauty of a fireplace so I keep my thermostat way down to sixty, and then I light a big roaring fire so I can move back and forth. Now that's not controlled environment. I control the environment. It's a lot more fun.

Some people say that chairs are good-looking that are comfortable. Are they? I think that comfort is a function of whether you think the chair is good-looking or not. Just test it yourself. (Except I know you won't be honest with me.) I have had Mies van der Rohe chairs now for twenty-five years in my home wherever I go. They're not very comfortable chairs, but, if people like the looks of them they say, "Aren't these beautiful chairs," which indeed they are. Then they'll sit in them and say, "My, aren't they comfortable." If, however, they're the kind of people who think curving steel legs are an ugly way to hold up a chair they'll say, "My, what uncomfortable chairs."

The *Crutch of Cheapness*. That is one that you haven't run into as students because no one's told you to cut $10,000 off the budget, because you haven't built anything.

But that'll be your first lesson. The cheapness boys will say, "Anybody can build an expensive house. Ah, but see, my house only cost $25,000." Anybody that can build a $25,000 house has indeed reason to be proud, but is he talking about architecture or his economic ability? Is it the crutch you're talking about, or is it architecture? That economic motive, for instance, goes in New York so far that the real-estate-minded people consider it un-American to build a Lever House with no rentals on the ground floor. They find that it's an architectural sin not to fill the envelope.

Then there's another very bad crutch that you will get much later in your career. Please, please, watch out for this one: the *Crutch of Serving the Client*. You can escape all criticism if you can say, "Well, the client wanted it that way." Mr. Hood, one of our really great architects, talked exactly that way. He would put a Gothic door on a skyscraper and say, "Why shouldn't I? The client wanted a Gothic door on the modern skyscraper, and I put it on. Because what is my business? Am I not here to please my client?" As one of the boys asked me during the dinner before the lecture, where do you draw the line? When do the client's demands permit you to shoot him and when do you give in gracefully? It's got to be clear, back in your own mind, that serving the client is one thing and the art of architecture another.

Perhaps the most trouble of all is the *Crutch of Structure*. That gets awfully near home because, of course, I use it all the time myself. I'm going to go on using it. You have to use something. Like Bucky Fuller, who's going around from school to school— it's like a hurricane, you can't miss it if it's coming: he talks, you know, for five or six hours, and he ends up that all architecture is nonsense, and you have to build something like discontinuous domes. The arguments are beautiful. I have nothing against discontinuous domes, but for goodness sake, let's not call it architecture. Have you ever seen Bucky trying to put a door into one of his domed buildings? He's never succeeded, and wisely, when he does them, he doesn't put any covering on them, so they are magnificent pieces of pure sculpture. Sculpture also cannot result in architecture because architecture has problems that Bucky Fuller has not faced, like how do you get in and out. Structure is a very dangerous thing to cling to. You can be led to believe that clear structure clearly expressed will end up being architecture by itself. You say, "I don't have to design any more. All I have to do is make a clean structural order." I have believed this off and on myself. It's a very nice crutch, you see, because after all, you can't mess up a building too badly if the bays are all equal and all the windows are the same size.

Now why should we at this stage be that crutch-conscious? Why should we not step right up to it and face it: the act of creation. The act of creation, like birth and death, you have to face yourself. There aren't any rules; there is no one to tell you whether your one choice out of, say, six billion for the proportion of a window is going to be right. No one can go with you into that room where you make the final decision. You can't escape it anyhow; why fight it? Why not realize that architecture is the sum of inescapable artistic decisions that you have to make. If you're strong you can make them.

I like the thought that what we are to do on this earth is to embellish it for its greater beauty, so that oncoming generations can look back to the shapes we leave here and get the same thrill that I get in looking back at theirs—at the Parthenon, at Chartres Cathedral. That is the duty—I doubt if I get around to it in my generation—the difficulties are too many, but you can. You can if you're strong enough not to bother with the crutches, and face the fact that to create something is a direct experience.

I like Corbusier's definition of architecture. He expressed it the way I wish I could have: "L'architecture, c'est le jeu savant, correct et magnifique des formes sous la lumière"—"Architecture is the play of forms under the light, the play of forms correct, wise, and magnificent." The play of forms under the light. And, my friends, that's all it is. You can embellish architecture by putting toilets in. But there was great architecture long before the toilet was invented. I like Nietzsche's definition—that much misunderstood European—he said, "In architectural works, man's pride, man's triumph over gravitation, man's will to power assume visible form. Architecture is a veritable oratory of power made by form."

Now my position in all this is obviously not as solipsistic, not as directly intuitional as all that sounds. To get back to earth, what do we do next if we don't hang on to any of these crutches? I am a traditionalist. I believe in history. I mean by tradition the carrying out, in freedom, the development of a certain basic approach to architecture which we find upon beginning our work here. I do not believe in perpetual revolution in architecture. I do not strive for originality. As Mies once told me, "Philip, it is much better to be good than to be original." I believe that. We have very fortunately the work of our spiritual fathers to build on. We hate them, of course, as all spiritual sons hate all spiritual fathers, but we can't ignore them, nor can we deny their greatness. The men, of course, that I refer to: Walter Gropius, Le Corbusier, and Mies van der Rohe. Frank Lloyd Wright I should include—the greatest architect of the nineteenth century. Isn't it wonderful to have behind us the tradition, the work that these men have done? Can you imagine being alive at a more wonderful time? Never in history was the tradition so clearly demarked, never were the great men so great, never could we learn so much from them and go our own way, without feeling constricted by any style, and knowing that what we do is going to be the architecture of the future, and not be afraid that we wander into some little bypath, like today's romanticists where nothing can possibly evolve. In that sense I am a traditionalist.

18 Louis I. Kahn, 1901–1974

As an architect, educator, and writer, Louis Kahn occupied a unique role in the architectural realm, bridging the dogmatism of modern architecture and the introspective posmodern era that followed. Born in Estonia, Kahn emigrated to the United States with his family in 1905 and settled in Philadelphia. He proved to be a talented musician and artist and, in 1924, he graduated with a degree in architecture from the University of Pennsylvania, a program then based on the traditional Beaux-Arts model. Kahn's mature work combined this classical training with modernist concepts of social improvement and the seemingly eternal qualities of ancient ruins to create a monumental architecture characterized by solidity, mass, and the use of platonic forms. These qualities are apparent in all of his major works including the Yale University Art Gallery in New Haven, Connecticut (1951–55); the Salk Institute for Biological Sciences in La Jolla, California (1959–65); and the Kimbell Art Museum in Fort Worth, Texas (1962–72). Kahn paid particular attention to the inherent nature of the materials—often brick and concrete—with which he worked, and spoke about architecture in almost mystical terms: Thought and Feeling, the measurable and the unmeasurable, the "existence will" of architectural spaces, and the realization of "what a thing wants to be." The comments below, originally titled "Structure and Form," were first presented as a radio broadcast in the Voices of America series on architecture. Through such lectures and as an educator at various institutions, primarily Yale and the University of Pennsylvania, Kahn influenced numerous architects with his humane and spiritual approach to design.

"Form and Design" (1961)

A young architect came to ask a question. "I dream of spaces full of wonder. Spaces that rise and envelop flowingly without beginning, without end, of a jointless material white and gold. When I place the first line on paper to capture the dream, the dream becomes less."

This is a good question. I once learned that a good question is greater than the most brilliant answer.

This is a question of the unmeasurable and the measurable. Nature, physical nature, is measurable.

Feeling and dream has no measure, has no language, and everyone's dream is singular.

Everything that is made however obeys the laws of nature. The man is always greater than his works because he can never fully express his aspirations. For to express oneself in music or architecture is by the measurable means of composition or design. The first line on paper is already a measure of what cannot be expressed fully. The first line on paper is less.

"Then," said the young architect, "what should be the discipline, what should be the

---

Louis I. Kahn, "Form and Design," in Vincent Scully, *Louis I. Kahn* (New York: George Braziller, Inc., 1962), 114–21. Reprinted with permission from the Louis I. Kahn Archive at the University of Pennsylvania. After the radio broadcast, the lecture was published as "A Statement by Louis Kahn" in *Arts and Architecture* (February 1961), and as "Form and Design" in *Architectural Design* (April 1961).

ritual that brings one closer to the psyche. For in the aura of no material and no language, I feel man truly is."

Turn to Feeling and away from Thought. In Feeling is the Psyche. Thought is Feeling and presence of Order. Order, the maker of all existence, has No Existence Will. I choose the word Order instead of knowledge because personal knowledge is too little to express Thought abstractly. This Will is the Psyche.

All that we desire to create has its beginning in feeling alone. This is true for the scientist. It is true for the artist. But I warned that to remain in Feeling away from Thought means to make nothing.

Said the young architect: "To live and make nothing is intolerable. The dream has in it already the *will to be* and the desire to express this *will*. Thought is inseparable from Feeling. In what way then can Thought enter creation so that this psychic will can be more closely expressed? This is my next question."

When personal feeling transcends into Religion (not a religion but the essence religion) and Thought leads to Philosophy, the mind opens to realizations. Realization of what may be the *existence will* of, let us say, particular architectural spaces. Realization is the merging of Thought and Feeling at the closest rapport of the mind with the Psyche, the source of *what a thing wants to be*.

It is the beginning of Form. Form encompasses a harmony of systems, a sense of Order and that which characterizes one existence from another. Form has no shape or dimension. For example, in the differentiation of a spoon from spoon, spoon characterizes a form having two inseparable parts, the handle and the bowl. A spoon implies a specific design made of silver or wood, big or little, shallow or deep, Form is "what." Design is "how." Form is impersonal, Design belongs to the designer. Design is a circumstantial act, how much money there is available, the site, the client, the extent of knowledge. Form has nothing to do with circumstantial conditions. In architecture, it characterizes a harmony of spaces good for a certain activity of man.

Reflect then on what characterizes abstractly House, a house, home. House is the abstract characteristic of spaces good to live in. House is the form, in the mind of wonder it should be there without shape or dimension. *A house is a conditional interpretation of these spaces.* This is design. In my opinion the greatness of the architect depends on his powers of realization of that which is House, rather than his design of *a* house which is a circumstantial act. Home is the house and the occupants. Home becomes different with each occupant.

The client for whom a house is designed states the areas he needs. The architect creates spaces out of those required areas. It may also be said that this house created for the particular family must have the character of being good for another. The design in this way reflects its trueness to Form. . . .

I want to talk about the difference between form and design, about realization, about the measurable and the unmeasurable aspects of our work and about the limits of our work.

Giotto was a great painter because he painted the skies black for the daytime and he painted birds that couldn't fly and dogs that couldn't run and he made men bigger than doorways because he was a painter. A painter has this prerogative. He doesn't have to answer to the problems of gravity, nor to the images as we know them in real life. As a painter he expresses a reaction to nature and he teaches us through his eyes and his reactions to the nature of man. A sculptor is one who modifies space with the objects expressive again of his reactions to nature. He does not create space. He modifies space. An architect creates space.

Architecture has limits.

When we touch the invisible walls of its limits then we know more about what is contained in them. A painter can paint square wheels on a cannon to express the futility of war. A sculptor can carve the same square wheels. But an architect must use round wheels. Though painting and sculpture play a beautiful role in the realm of architecture as architecture plays a beautiful role in the realms of painting and sculpture, one does not have the same discipline as the other.

One may say that architecture is the thoughtful making of spaces. It is, note, the filling of areas prescribed by the client. It is the creating of spaces that evoke a feeling of appropriate use.

To the musician a sheet of music is seeing from what he hears. A plan of a building should reach like a harmony of spaces in light.

Even a space intended to be dark should have just enough light from some mysterious opening to tell us how dark it really is. Each space must be defined by its structure and the character of its natural light. Of course I am not speaking about minor areas which serve the major spaces. An architectural space must reveal the evidence of its making by the space itself. It cannot be a space when carved out of a greater structure meant for a greater space because the choice of a structure is synonymous with the light and which gives image to that space. Artificial light is a single tiny static moment in light and is the light of night and never can equal the nuances of mood created by the time of day and the wonder of the seasons.

A great building, in my opinion, must begin with the unmeasurable, must go through measurable means when it is being designed and in the end must be unmeasurable. The design, the making of things is a measurable act. In fact at that point, you are like physical nature itself because in physical nature everything is measurable, even that which is yet unmeasured, like the most distant stars which we can assume will be eventually measured.

But what is unmeasurable is the psychic spirit. The psyche is expressed by feeling and also thought and I believe will always be unmeasurable. I sense that the psychic Existence Will calls on nature to make what it wants to be. I think a rose wants to be a rose. Existence Will, *man*, becomes existence, through nature's law and evolution. The results are always less than the spirit of existence.

In the same way a building has to start in the unmeasurable aura and go through the measurable to be accomplished. It is the only way you can build, the only way you can get it into being is through the measurable. You must follow the laws but in the end when the building becomes part of living it evokes unmeasurable qualities. The design involving quantities of brick, method of construction, engineering is over and the spirit of its existence takes over. . . .

From all I have said I do not mean to imply a system of thought and work leading to realization from Form to Design.

Designs could just as well lead to realizations in Form.

This interplay is the constant excitement of Architecture.

19 ALDO VAN EYCK, 1918–1999

In his role as a designer, educator, and editor, the Dutch architect Aldo van Eyck campaigned against the notion of functionalism entrenched in the practice of modern architecture. In Van Eyck's opinion, the preoccupation with functional principles produced homogenous, vacuous spaces that failed to address humanist concerns such as man's desire for variety, specificity, and comfort. Van Eyck cited the need for "place and occasion" over "space and time"; the latter are abstract and theoretical, as opposed to "place and occasion," which imply an identifiable locale and a memorable experience. Van Eyck designed with these principles in mind, as is evident in his Amsterdam Orphanage of 1955–60. He organized this large building as he would a city, with spacious areas for communal interaction and smaller nodes tailored to the specific occupants. The children of the orphanage, both male and female, ranged in age, so Van Eyck crafted each place accordingly. The following comments address both architecture and urbanism, and were written shortly after the completion of the orphanage. They express Van Eyck's sentiments as a member of Team 10, a group of architects opposed to modernist functionalism and dedicated to the creation of a more humane built environment based on the physical, social, and psychological needs of man.

Untitled Thoughts on Place and Occasion (1962)

Space has no room, time not a moment for man. He is excluded.

In order to "include" him—help his homecoming—he must be gathered into their meaning. (Man is the subject as well as the object of architecture).

Whatever space and time mean, place and occasion mean more.

For space in the image of man is place, and time in the image of man is occasion.

Today, space and what it should coincide with in order to become "space"—man at home with himself—are lost. Both search for the same place, but cannot find it.

Provide that space, articulate the inbetween.

Is man able to penetrate the material he organizes into hard shape between one man and another, between what is here and what is there, between this and a following moment? Is he able to find the right place for the right occasion?

Aldo van Eyck, Untitled Thoughts on Place and Occasion, in *Team 10 Primer*, ed. Alison Smithson (Cambridge, MA: MIT Press, 1968), 101. Reprinted with permission from the publisher.

No—So start with this: make a welcome of each door and a countenance of each window.

Make of each place, a bunch of places of each house and each city, for a house is a tiny city, a city a huge house. Get closer to the shifting centre of human reality and build its counterform—for each man and all men, since they no longer do it themselves.

Whoever attempts to solve the riddle of space in the abstract, will construct the outline of emptiness and call it space.

Whoever attempts to meet man in the abstract will speak with his echo and call this a dialogue.

Man still breathes both in and out. When is architecture going to do the same?

Peter Cook, b. 1936, and Warren Chalk, 1927–1987

20

The term "Archigram"—an amalgamation of "architecture" and "telegram"—refers to both an irreverent, experimental magazine and the group of six young British architects associated with that publication. From 1961 through 1974, *Archigram* featured a collage of thoughts, cartoons, projects, and fantastic proposals by Peter Cook, Warren Chalk, and the four other members of the group. Their basic message involved issues of change and obsolescence. Archigram embraced new possibilities afforded by technology that modern architecture failed to make a reality. Impermanence, expendability, flexibility, growth—these qualities informed their projects to varying degrees. Peter Cook's Plug-in City (1964), for example, was a new expandable urban development comprised of building components, movable by crane and replaceable when outdated, that would plug into the larger infrastructural framework of the city. The group's Instant City (late 1960s) was a "traveling metropolis" conceived to jumpstart the cultural growth of nonurban areas. The city would descend on a small town by balloon and, over the course of a few days, expose the inhabitants to cosmopolitan excitement and vitality. In general, Archigram's designs extended beyond available technology and thus were not then possible to construct. Nevertheless, through their projects, publications, and exhibitions, Archigram had a considerable impact on the architectural community in England and elsewhere. They challenged the true modernity of modern architecture and the accepted notions of buildings as fixed and permanent. Archigram thus prompted a reconsideration of architecture as both an object and a discipline.

Editorial from *Archigram* 3 (1963)

Peter Cook

More and more

Almost without realizing it, we have absorbed into our lives the first generation of expendables . . . foodbags, paper tissue, polythene wrappers, ballpens, E.P.s . . . so many things about which we don't have to think. We throw them away almost as soon as we acquire them.

Also with us are the items that are bigger and last longer, but are nevertheless planned for obsolescence . . . the motor car . . . and its unit-built garage.

Now the second generation is upon us—paper furniture is a reality in the States, paper sheets are a reality in British hospital beds, the Greater London Council is putting up limited life-span houses.

Through and through

With every level of society and with every level of commodity, the unchanging scene is being replaced by the increase in change of our user-habits—and thereby, eventually, our user-habitats.

We are becoming much more used to the idea of changing a piece of clothing year by year, rather than expecting to hang on to it for several years. Similarly, the idea

Peter Cook and Warren Chalk, "Editorial from *Archigram* 3," in *Archigram*, ed. Peter Cook et al. (New York: Princeton Architectural Press,1999), 16–17. Reprinted with permission.

of keeping a piece of furniture long enough to be able to hand it on to our children is becoming increasingly ridiculous. In this situation we should not be surprised if such articles wear out within their 'welcome-life' span, rather than their traditional life span.

The attitude of mind that accepts such a situation is creeping into our society at about the rate that expendable goods become available. We must recognize this as a healthy and altogether positive sign. It is the product of a sophisticated consumer society, rather than a stagnant (and in the end, declining) society.

Our collective mental blockage occurs between the land of the small-scale consumer-products and the objects which make our environment. Perhaps it will not be until such things as housing, amenity-place and workplace become recognized as consumer products that can be 'bought off the peg'—with all that this implies in terms of ex-pendability (foremost), industrialization, up-to-date-ness, customer choice, and basic product-design—that we can begin to make an environment that is really part of a developing human culture.

Why is there an indefinable resistance to planned obsolescence for a kitchen, which in twelve years will be highly inefficient (by the standards of the day) and in twenty years will be intolerable, yet there are no qualms about four-year obsolescence for cars?

This idea of an expendable environment is still somehow regarded as akin to anarchy . . . as if, in order to make it work, we would bulldoze Westminster Abbey. . . .

We shall not bulldoze Westminster Abbey
Added to this, the idea of a non-permanent building has overtones of economy, auster-

ity, economy. Architects are the first to deny the great potential of expendability as the built reflection of the second half of the twentieth century. Most of the buildings that exist that are technically expendable have the fact skillfully hidden . . . they masquerade as permanent buildings—monuments to the past.

Housing as a consumer product
Warren Chalk

One of the most flagrant misconceptions held about us is that we are not ultimately concerned with people. This probably arises directly from the type of imagery we use. A section through, say, something like City Interchange, appears to predict some automated wasteland inhabited only by computers and robots. How much this is justified is difficult to assess, but if our work is studied closely there will be found traces of a very real concern for people and the way in which they might be liberated from the restrictions imposed on them by the existing chaotic situation, in the home, at work and in the total built environment.

Human situations are as concerned with environmental changes and activity within the city, as with the definition of places. Important in this is the precept of situation as an ideas generator in creating a truly living city. Cities should generate, reflect and activate life, their structure organized to precipitate life and movement. Situation, the happenings within spaces in the city, the transient throwaway world of people, the passing presence of cars, etc., are as important, possibly more important than the built environment, the built demarcation of space. Situation can be caused by a single individual, by groups or a crowd, their particular purpose, occupation, movement and direction.

This is in fact a follow-on from thinking related to the South Bank scheme where the original basic concept was to produce an anonymous pile, subservient to a series of pedestrian walkways, a sort of Mappin Terrace for people instead of goats.

So once again the pedestrian, the gregarious nature of people and their movement is upper-most in our minds and the built demarcation of space used to channel and direct pedestrian patterns of movement.

In an attempt to get closer to the general public, to study their attitudes and behavior, we have extended ourselves beyond the narrow boundaries of conventional architectural thought, causing the misconceptions about what we are trying to do. We must extend the conventional barriers and find people without any formal architectural training, producing concepts showing a marked intuitive grasp of current attitudes related to city images and the rest. In the world of science fiction we dig out prophetic information regarding geodesic nets, pneumatic tubes and plastic domes and bubbles.

If we turn to the back pages of the popular press we find ads for do-it-yourself living-room extensions, or instant garage kits. Let's face it, we can no longer turn away from the hard fact that everyone in the community has latent creative instincts and that our role will eventually be to direct these into some tangible and acceptable form. The present gulf between people, between the community and the designer may well be eventually bridged by the do-it-yourself interchangeable kit of parts.

In a technological society more people will play an active part in determining their own individual environment, in self-determining a way of life. We cannot expect to take this fundamental right out of their hands and go on treating them as cultural and creative morons. We must tackle it from the other end in a positive way. The inherent qualities of mass-production for a consumer orientated society and those of repetition and standardization, but parts can be changeable or interchangeable depending on individual needs and preferences and, given a world market, could also be economically feasible.

In the States one can select a car consisting of a whole series of interchangeable options, as Reyner Banham has pointed out (in his article on Clip-on Architecture). Chevrolet {produces} a choice of seventeen bodies and five different engines.

The current success of pop music is to an extent due to the importance of audience participation; the 'Frug' and the 'Jerk' are self-expressive and free-forming. The pop groups themselves are closer in dress and habits, including musical dexterity, to the audience. Despite pop music becoming a vast industry its success depends on its ability to keep up with the pace of its consumer taste.

Of course the idea of mass-produced expendable component dwellings is not new. We are all familiar with Le Corbusier's efforts in collaboration with Prouvé and with Prouvé's own bits and pieces, with Buckminister Fuller's Dymaxion house, the Phelps Dodge Dymaxion bathroom and the Dymaxion deployment unit, Alison and Peter Smithson's House of the Future at the Ideal Home Exhibition of 1955, Ionel Schien's pre-fabricated hotel units and the Monsanto Plastic House in Disneyland; there has also been work done by the Metabolist Group in Japan and Arthur Quarmby in England.

The Plug-in Capsule Home is an attempt to sustain the idea in the hope that some brave soul might eventually be persuaded to finance research and development.

The techniques of mass-production and automation are a reality, yet we see the research that goes into, and the products that come out of today's building and are dismayed.

The Plug-in Capsule attempts to set new standards and find an appropriate image for an assembly-line product. The order of its design criteria are in correct order to consumer requirements. First, a better consumer product, offering something better than, and different from, traditional housing, more closely related to the design of cars and refrigerators, than placing itself in direct competition with tradition.

21 | ROBERT VENTURI, B. 1925

Robert Venturi with John Rauch, Vanna Venturi House, Chestnut Hill, PA, 1962
Photo from R. Venturi and Denise Scott Brown, *A View from the Campidoglio: Selected Essays 1953–1984*
ed. P. Arnell, T. Bickford and C. Bergart (New York: Harper & Row, Publishers, 1984), 75
Photograph by Rollin R. La France
Courtesy of Venturi, Scott Brown and Associates, Inc.

Despite a number of constructed works, Venturi is perhaps best known as the author of *Complexity and Contradiction in Architecture*. This text appeared in 1966 as a challenge to the position held by many modern architects in which form—and hence meaning—theoretically derived from function, not from other sources such as history, tradition, or culture. In contrast, Venturi advocated an inclusive approach toward design that embraced multiplicity of meaning and form. To support this argument and to counter the perceived rift between modern and historical architecture, Venturi cited works from antiquity through the present. This view of architectural continuity placed the architecture of the past on a par with that of the present.

Demonstrating the ways in which revered modern architects learned from the past, Venturi encouraged his colleagues to accept both historical architecture and the "messy vitality" of contemporary life as valid sources of inspiration. This concept appears in Venturi's own architecture as well; for example, the design for his mother's house (the Vanna Venturi House, 1962) incorporates abstracted elements from classical architecture (the applied arch over the front door); modern architecture (the strip or ribbon window of Le Corbusier); and traditional and vernacular homes (the square window with mullions, the pitched roof, and the prominent chimney). To Venturi's dismay, many interpreted his message as a call for a revived classicism or stylistic eclecticism, practices which led in part to postmodernism, an architectural movement often characterized by irony and pastiche.

In 1967, Venturi married architect and urban planner Denise Scott Brown. Since then, they have been partners in design, have cotaught architectural studios, and have coauthored several texts including *Learning from Las Vegas* (1972), written in conjunction with Steven Izenour.

Complexity and Contradiction in Architecture (1966)

1. Nonstraightforward Architecture: A Gentle Manifesto

I like complexity and contradiction in architecture. I do not like the incoherence or arbitrariness of incompetent architecture nor the precious intricacies of picturesqueness or expressionism. Instead, I speak of a complex and contradictory architecture based on the riches and ambiguity of modern experience, including that experience which is inherent in art. Everywhere, except in architecture, complexity and contradiction have been acknowledged, from Gödel's proof of ultimate inconsistency in mathematics to T. S. Eliot's analysis of "difficult" poetry and Joseph Albers' definition of the paradoxical quality of painting.

But architecture is necessarily complex and contradictory in its very inclusion of the traditional Vitruvian elements of commodity, firmness, and delight. And today the wants of program, structure, mechanical equipment, and expression, even in single buildings in simple contexts, are diverse and conflicting in ways previously unimaginable. The increasing dimension and scale of architecture in urban and regional planning add to the difficulties. I welcome the problems and exploit the uncertainties. By embracing contradiction as well as complexity, I aim for vitality as well as validity.

Architects can no longer afford to be intimidated by the puritanically moral language of orthodox Modern architecture. I like elements which are hybrid rather than "pure,"

Robert Venturi, *Complexity and Contradiction in Architecture,* 2nd ed. (1966; New York: Museum of Modern Art, 1977, 16–19. © The Museum of Modern Art, New York, 1966, 1977). Reprinted with permission from the publisher.

compromising rather than "clean," distorted rather than "straightforward," ambiguous rather than "articulated," perverse as well as impersonal, boring as well as "interesting," conventional rather than "designed," accommodating rather than excluding, redundant rather than simple, vestigial as well as innovating, inconsistent and equivocal rather than direct and clear. I am for messy vitality over obvious unity. I include the non sequitur and proclaim the duality.

I am for richness of meaning rather than clarity of meaning; for the implicit function as well as the explicit function. I prefer "both-and" to "either-or," black and white, and sometimes gray, to black or white. A valid architecture evokes many levels of meaning and combinations of focus; its space and its elements become readable and workable in several ways at once.

But an architecture of complexity and contradiction has a special obligation toward the whole: its truth must be in its totality or its implications of totality. It must embody the difficult unity of inclusion rather than the easy unity of exclusion. More is not less.

2. Complexity and Contradiction vs. Simplification or Picturesqueness

Orthodox Modern architects have tended to recognize complexity insufficiently or inconsistently. In their attempt to break with tradition and start all over again, they idealized the primitive and elementary at the expense of the diverse and the sophisticated. As participants in a revolutionary movement, they acclaimed the newness of modern functions, ignoring their complications. In their role as reformers, they puritanically advocated the separation and exclusion of elements, rather than the inclusion of various requirements and their juxtapositions. As a forerunner of the Modern movement, Frank Lloyd Wright, who grew up with the motto "Truth against the World," wrote: "Visions of simplicity so broad and far-reaching would open to me and such building harmonies appear that . . . would change and deepen the thinking and culture of the modern world. So I believed."[1] And Le Corbusier, co-founder of Purism, spoke of the "great primary forms" which, he proclaimed, were "distinct . . . and without ambiguity."[2] Modern architects with few exceptions eschewed ambiguity.

But now our position is different: "At the same time that the problems increase in quantity, complexity, and difficulty they also change faster than before,"[3] and require an attitude more like that described by August Heckscher: "The movement from a view of life as essentially simple and orderly to a view of life as complex and ironic is what every individual passes through in becoming mature. But certain epochs encourage this development; in them the paradoxical or dramatic outlook colors the whole intellectual scene. . . . Amid simplicity and order rationalism is born, but rationalism proves inadequate in any period of upheaval. Then equilibrium must be created out of opposites. Such inner peace as men gain must represent a tension among contradictions and uncertainties. . . . A feeling for paradox allows seemingly dissimilar things to exist side by side, their very incongruity suggesting a kind of truth."[4]

Rationalizations for simplification are still current, however, though subtler than the early arguments. They are expansions of Mies van der Rohe's magnificent paradox, "less is more." Paul Rudolph has clearly stated the implications of Mies' point of view: "All problems can never be solved. . . . Indeed it is a characteristic of the twen-

---

[1] Frank Lloyd Wright, in *An American Architecture,* ed. Edgar Kaufmann (New York: Horizon Press, 1955), 207.

[2] Le Corbusier, *Towards a New Architecture* (London: The Architectural Press, 1927), 31.

[3] Christopher Alexander, *Notes on the Synthesis of Form* (Cambridge, MA: Harvard University Press, 1964), 4.

[4] August Heckscher, *The Public Happiness* (New York: Atheneum Publishers, 1962), 102.

tieth century that architects are highly selective in determining which problems they want to solve. Mies, for instance makes wonderful buildings only because he ignores many aspects of a building. If he solved more problems, his buildings would be far less potent."[5]

The doctrine "less is more" bemoans complexity and justifies exclusion for expressive purposes. It does, indeed, permit the architect to be "highly selective in determining which problems [he wants] to solve." But if the architect must be "committed to his particular way of seeing the universe,"[6] such a commitment surely means that the architect determines how problems should be solved, not that he can determine which of the problems he will solve. He can exclude important considerations only at the risk of separating architecture from the experience of life and the needs of society. If some problems prove insoluble, he can express this: in an inclusive rather than exclusive kind of architecture there is room for the fragment, for contradiction, for improvisation, and for the tensions these produce. Mies' exquisite pavilions have had valuable implications for architecture, but their selectiveness of content and language is their limitation as well as their strength.

I question the relevance of analogies between Japanese pavilions and recent domestic architecture. They ignore the real complexity and contradiction inherent in the domestic program—the spatial and technological possibilities as well as the need for variety in visual experience. Forced simplicity results in oversimplification. In the Wiley House, for instance, in contrast to his glass house, Philip Johnson attempted to go beyond the simplicities of the elegant pavilion. He explicitly separated and

---

[5] Paul Rudolph, in *Perspecta 7, The Yale Architectural Journal* (New Haven: Yale University Press, 1961), 51.
[6] Kenneth Burke, *Permanence and Change* (Los Altos, CA: Hermes Publications, 1954), 107.

articulated the enclosed "private functions" of living on a ground floor pedestal, thus separating them from the open social functions in the modular pavilion above. But even here the building becomes a diagram of an oversimplified program for living—an abstract theory of either-or. Where simplicity cannot work, simpleness results. Blatant simplification means bland architecture. Less is a bore.

The recognition of complexity in architecture does not negate what Louis Kahn has called "the desire for simplicity." But aesthetic simplicity which is a satisfaction to the mind derives, when valid and profound, from inner complexity. The Doric temple's simplicity to the eye is achieved through the famous subtleties and precision of its distorted geometry and the contradictions and tensions inherent in its order. The Doric temple could achieve apparent simplicity through real complexity. When complexity disappeared, as in the late temples, blandness replaced simplicity.

Nor does complexity deny the valid simplification which is part of the process of analysis, and even a method of achieving complex architecture itself. "We oversimplify a given event when we characterize it from the standpoint of a given interest."[7] But this kind of simplification is a method in the analytical process of achieving a complex art. It should not be mistaken for a goal.

An architecture of complexity and contradiction, however, does not mean picturesqueness or subjective expressionism. A false complexity has recently countered the false simplicity of an earlier Modern architecture. It promotes an architecture of symmetrical picturesqueness—which Minoru Yamasaki calls "serene"—but it represents a new

---

[7] T.S. Eliot, *Selected Essays, 1917–1932* (New York: Harcourt, Brace and Co., 1932), 96.

formalism as unconnected with experience as the former cult of simplicity. Its intricate forms do not reflect genuinely complex programs, and its intricate ornament, though dependent on industrial techniques for execution, is dryly reminiscent of forms originally created by handicraft techniques. Gothic tracery and Rococo rocaille were not only expressively valid in relation to the whole, but came from a valid showing-off of hand skills and expressed a vitality derived from the immediacy and individuality of the method. This kind of complexity through exuberance, perhaps impossible today, is the antithesis of "serene" architecture, despite the superficial resemblance between them. But if exuberance is not characteristic of our art, it is tension, rather than "serenity" that would appear to be so.

The best twentieth-century architects have usually rejected simplification—that is, simplicity through reduction—in order to promote complexity within the whole. The works of Alvar Aalto and Le Corbusier (who often disregards his polemical writings) are examples. But the characteristics of complexity and contradiction in their work are often ignored or misunderstood. Critics of Aalto, for instances, have liked him mostly for his sensitivity to natural materials and his fine detailing, and have considered his whole composition willful picturesqueness. I do not consider Aalto's Imatra church picturesque. By repeating in the massing the genuine complexity of the triple-divided plan and the acoustical ceiling pattern, this church represents a justifiable expressionism different from the willful picturesqueness of the haphazard structure and spaces of Giovanni Michelucci's recent church for the Autostrada.[8] Aalto's complexity is part of the program and structure of the whole rather than a

---

[8] *Venturi added the following note in the 2nd edition (1977):* "I have visited Giovanni Michelucci's Church of the Autostrada since writing these words, and I now realize it is an extremely beautiful and effective building. I am therefore sorry I made this unsympathetic comparison."

device justified only by the desire for expression. Though we no longer argue over the primacy of form or function (which follows which?), we cannot ignore their interdependence.

The desire for a complex architecture, with its attendant contradictions, is not only a reaction to the banality or prettiness of current architecture. It is an attitude common in the Mannerist periods: the sixteenth century in Italy or the Hellenistic period in Classical art, and is also a continuous strain seen in such diverse architects as Michelangelo, Palladio, Borromini, Vanbrugh, Hawksmoor, Soane, Ledoux, Butterfield, some architects of the Shingle Style, Furness, Sullivan, Lutyens, and recently, Le Corbusier, Aalto, Kahn, and others.

Today this attitude is again relevant to both the medium of architecture and the problem in architecture.

First, the medium of architecture must be re-examined if the increased scope of our architecture as well as the complexity of its goals is to be expressed. Simplified or superficially complex forms will not work. Instead the variety inherent in the ambiguity of visual perception must once more be acknowledged and exploited.

Second, the growing complexities of our functional problems must be acknowledged. I refer, of course, to those programs, unique in our time, which are complex because of their scope, such as research laboratories, hospitals, and particularly the enormous projects at the scale of city and regional planning. But even the house, simple in scope, is complex in purpose if the ambiguities of contemporary experience are expressed. This contrast between the means and the goals of a program is significant. Although the means involved in the program of a rocket to get to the moon, for instance, are almost infinitely complex, the goal is simple and contains few contradictions; although the means involved in the program and structure of buildings are far simpler and less sophisticated technologically than almost any engineering project, the purpose is more complex and often inherently ambiguous.

22   ALDO ROSSI, 1931–1997

Aldo Rossi, *La Fabbrica della Città*, 1978
Photo Credit: Digital Image © The Museum of Modern Art
Licensed by SCALA/Art Resource
NY Courtesy of the Foundazione Aldo Rossi

In 1966, the Italian architect and educator Aldo Rossi published *L'architettura della città*, or *The Architecture of the City*, which examined the European city as a source of architectural knowledge. Within the fabric of the city, Rossi identified "urban artifacts" that, while changing function as the city evolved, retained their basic forms. This concept posed a challenge to the modernist dictum that "form follows function,"—that a building's particular form should derive from its intended purpose—because Rossi showed that, over time, multiple functions had indeed been accommodated within a single form. He thus shifted focus from function to a quasi-scientific investigation of type, as he believed type to be the essence of architectural and urban elements. His architectural analysis reflected the work of sociologists concerned with the relationship between personal recollection and collective memory.

Rossi's own architecture incorporated aspects of his theoretical discoveries; for example, his vocabulary included forms that he recognized as recurrent and timeless, such as the square window and linear housing block. He found support in Boullée's recognition of immutable architectural principles; yet, where Boullée's point of reference was nature, Rossi's was architecture, as manifest in the historical city. In Italy, Rossi's architecture and theoretical work were seen as related enterprises, often associated with the development of the Tendenza—a group of like-minded architects who viewed the European city as a source of architectural inspiration—and a new Rational Architecture that found a basis for architecture within architecture itself. This was not the case in the United States, where Rossi's haunting, De Chirico-esque drawings appeared in the mid-1970s, essentially without his critical writings. These enigmatic images proved quite influential, but the American understanding of Rossi was largely incomplete until the arrival of his theoretical texts in the early 1980s.

The Architecture of the City (1966)

Introduction: Urban Artifacts and a Theory of the City

The city, which is the subject of this book, is to be understood here as architecture. By architecture I mean not only the visible image of the city and the sum of its different architectures, but architecture as construction, the construction of the city over time. I believe that this point of view, objectively speaking, constitutes the most comprehensive way of analyzing the city; it addresses the ultimate and definitive fact in the life of the collective, the creation of the environment in which it lives.

I use the term architecture in a positive and pragmatic sense, as a creation inseparable from civilized life and the society in which it is manifested. By nature it is collective. As the first men built houses to provide more favorable surroundings for their life, fashioning an artificial climate for themselves, so they built with aesthetic intention. Architecture came into being along with the first traces of the city; it is deeply rooted in the formation of civilization and is a permanent, universal, and necessary artifact.

Aesthetic intention and the creation of better surroundings for life are the two permanent characteristics of architecture. These aspects emerge from any significant attempt to explain the city as a human creation. But because architecture gives concrete form to society and is intimately connected with it and with nature, it differs fundamentally from every other art and science. This is the basis for an empirical study of the city as it has evolved from the earliest settlements. With time, the city grows upon itself;

Aldo Rossi, *The Architecture of the City*, trans. Joan Ockman and Diane Ghirardo (Cambridge, MA: MIT Press, 1982) 21, 35, 40–41. © 1982 by the Institute for Architecture and Urban Studies and the Massachusetts Institute of Technology. Reprinted with permission from the publisher. [*The Architecture of the City* appeared in 1982 in English, following the 1981 publication of *A Scientific Autobiography*, essentially Rossi's collected notes from the previous ten years.]

it acquires a consciousness and memory. In the course of its construction, its original themes persist, but at the same time it modifies and renders these themes of its own development more specific. Thus, while Florence is a real city, its memory and form come to have values that also are true and representative of other experiences. At the same time, the universality of these experiences is not sufficient to explain the precise form, the type of object which is Florence.

The contrast between particular and universal, between individual and collective, emerges from the city and from its construction, its architecture. This contrast is one of the principal viewpoints from which the city will be studied in this book. It manifests itself in different ways: in the relationship between the public and private sphere, between public and private buildings, between the rational design of urban architecture and the values of *locus* or place. . . .

Chapter 1. The Structure of Urban Artifacts

. . .

The Urban Artifact as a Work of Art

. . . We believe . . . that the whole is more important than the single parts, and that only the urban artifact in its totality, from street system and urban topography down to the things that can be perceived in strolling up and down a street, constitutes this totality. Naturally we must examine this total architecture in terms of its parts. . . .

Typological Questions

The city as above all else a human thing is constituted of its architecture and of all those works that constitute the true means of transforming nature. Bronze Age men adapted the landscape to social needs by constructing artificial islands of brick, by digging wells, drainage canals, and watercourses. The first houses sheltered their inhabitants from the external environment and furnished a climate that man could begin to control; the development of an urban nucleus expanded this type of control to the creation and extension of a microclimate. Neolithic villages already offered the first transformations of the world according to man's needs. The "artificial homeland" is as old as man.

In precisely this sense of transformation the first forms and types of habitation, as well as temples and more complex buildings, were constituted. The *type* developed according to both needs and aspirations to beauty; a particular type was associated with a form and a way of life, although its specific shape varied widely from society to society. The concept of type thus became the basis of architecture, a fact attested to both by practice and by the treatises.

It therefore seems clear that typological questions are important. They have always entered into the history of architecture, and arise naturally whenever urban problems are confronted. Theoreticians such as Francesco Milizia never defined type as such, but statements like the following seem to be anticipatory: "The comfort of any building consists of three principal items: its site, its form, "and the organization of its parts."[1] I would define the concept of type as something that is permanent and complex, a logical principle that is prior to form and that constitutes it.

One of the major theoreticians of architecture, Quatremère de Quincy, understood the importance of these problems and gave a masterly definition of type and model: "The word 'type' represents not so much the image of a thing to be copied or perfectly imitated as the idea of an element that must itself serve as a rule for the model. . . . The model, understood in terms of the practical execution of art, is an object that must be repeated such as it is; type, on the contrary, is an object according to which one

---

[1] Francesco Milizia, *Principi di Architettura Civile*, ed. Giovanni Antolini (Milan, 1832); 2nd ed., ed. L. Masieri, S. Majocchi (Milan: 1847); reprinted with "Riproduzione anastatica conforme all'originale" (Milan: Gabrielle Mazzotta, 1972). The phrase quoted is from the beginning of the second part, "Della comodità," 221.

can conceive works that do not resemble one another at all. Everything is precise and given in the model; everything is more or less vague in the type. Thus we see that the imitation of types involves nothing that feelings or spirit cannot recognize. . . .

"We also see that all inventions, notwithstanding subsequent changes, always retain their elementary principle in a way that is clear and manifest to the senses and to reason. It is similar to a kind of nucleus around which the developments and variations of forms to which the object was susceptible gather and mesh. Therefore a thousand things of every kind have come down to us, and one of the principal tasks of science and philosophy is to seek their origins and primary causes so as to grasp their purposes. Here is what must be called 'type' in architecture, as in every other branch of human inventions and institutions. . . . We have engaged in this discussion in order to render the value of the word *type*—taken metaphorically in a great number of works—clearly comprehensible, and to show the error of those who either disregard it because it is not a model, or misrepresent it by imposing on it the rigor of a model that would imply the conditions of an identical copy."[2]

In the first part of this passage, the author rejects the possibility of type as something to be imitated or copied because in this case there would be, as he asserts in the second part, no "creation of the model"—that is, there would be no making of architecture. The second part states that in architecture (whether model or form) there is an element that plays its own role, not something to which the architectonic object conforms but something that is nevertheless present in the model. This is the *rule*, the structuring principle of architecture.

---

[2] Antoine Chrysostôme Quatremère de Quincy, *Dictionnaire historique d'architecture comprenant dans son plan les notions historiques, descriptives, archaeologiques, biographiques, théoriques, didactiques et pratiques de cet art*, 2 vols. (Paris, 1832). The passage quoted is from volume 2, the section on "Type". . . . [Note: For more information on this concept, see note 11 on page 182 of Ockman and Ghirardo's translation of Rossi.]

In fact, it can be said that this principle is a constant. Such an argument presupposes that the architectural artifact is conceived as a structure and that this structure is revealed and can be recognized in the artifact itself. As a constant, this principle, which we can call the typical element, or simply the type, is to be found in all architectural artifacts. It is also then a cultural element and as such can be investigated in different architectural artifacts; typology becomes in this way the analytical moment of architecture, and it becomes readily identifiable at the level of urban artifacts.

Thus typology presents itself as the study of types of elements that cannot be further reduced, elements of a city as well as of an architecture. The question of monocentric cities or of buildings that are or are not centralized, for example, is specifically typological; no type can be identified with only one form, even if all architectural forms are reducible to types. The process of reduction is a necessary, logical operation, and it is impossible to talk about problems of form without this presupposition. In this sense all architectural theories are also theories of typology, and in an actual design it is difficult to distinguish the two moments.

Type is thus a constant and manifests itself with a character of necessity; but even though it is predetermined, it reacts dialectically with technique, function, and style, as well as with both the collective character and the individual moment of the architectural artifact. It is clear, for example, that the central plan is a fixed and constant type in religious architecture; but even so, each time a central plan is chosen, dialectical themes are put into play with the architecture of the church, with its functions, with its constructional technique, and with the collective that participates in the life of that church. I tend to believe that housing types have not changed from antiquity up to today, but this is not to say that the actual way of living has not changed, nor that new ways of living are not always possible. The house with a loggia is an old scheme; a corridor that gives access to rooms is necessary in plan and present in any number of urban houses. But there are a great many variations on this theme among individual houses at different times.

Ultimately, we can say that type is the very idea of architecture, that which is closest to its essence. In spite of changes, it has always imposed itself on the "feelings and reason" as the principle of architecture and of the city.

While the problem of typology has never been treated in a systematic way and with the necessary breadth, today its study is beginning to emerge in architecture schools and seems quite promising. I am convinced that architects themselves, if they wish to enlarge and establish their own work, must again be concerned with arguments of this nature.[3] Typology is an element that plays its own role in constituting form; it is a constant. The problem is to discern the modalities within which it operates and, moreover, its effective value.

Certainly, of the many past studies in this field, with a few exceptions and save for some honest attempts to redress the omission, few have addressed this problem with much attention. They have always avoided or displaced it, suddenly pursuing something else—namely *function*. Since this problem of function is of absolutely primary importance in the domain of our inquiry, I will try to see how it emerges in studies of the city and urban artifacts in general and how it has evolved. Let us say immediately that the problem can be addressed only when we have first considered the related problems of description and classification. For the most part, existing classifications have failed to go beyond the problem of function.

---

[3] Among the new aspects of the research by architects on the problems of typology, the lectures given by Carlo Aymonino at the Istituto di Architettura di Venezia are particularly interesting. . . . Aymonino's lectures are found in two volumes published by the Istituto Universaitario di Architettura di Venezia, *Aspetti e problemi della tipologia edilizia. Documenti del corso di caratteri distributivi degli edifici. Anno accademico 1963–1964* (Venice, 1964); and *La formazione del concetto di tipologia edilizia. Atti corso di caratteri distributivo degli edifici. Anno accademico 1964–1965* (Venice, 1965). Some of these lectures are also republished with revisions in *Carlo Aymonino, Il significato della città* (Bari: Editori Laterza, 1975).

23 DENISE SCOTT BROWN, B. 1931

Las Vegas Strip, Nevada, ca. 1968. Photograph from R. Venturi, D. Scott Brown, and S. Izenour,
Learning from Las Vegas, rev. ed. (Cambridge, MA: MIT Press, 1977), 126
Photograph by Denise Scott Brown. Courtesy of Venturi, Scott Brown and Associates, Inc.

An architect and an urban planner, Denise Scott Brown asserts that architects have
the responsibility to learn from the existing, often "unarchitected" environment, be it
Main Street or the Las Vegas Strip. She does not advocate the wholesale acceptance of
these environments; rather, she urges architects to learn what appeals to the public, to
understand "what people want." This has been a central theme in Scott Brown's career,
a message she has disseminated as a practitioner, educator, and author of writings such
as *Learning from Las Vegas* (1972), coauthored with Steven Izenour and her husband
Robert Venturi.

Robert Venturi, Duck and Decorated Shed, from R. Venturi, D. Scott Brown, and S. Izenour,
Learning from Las Vegas, rev. ed. (Cambridge, MA: MIT Press, 1977), 88–89.
Courtesy of Venturi, Scott Brown and Associates, Inc.

Learning from Las Vegas grew from a 1968 Yale studio held by Venturi, Scott Brown,
and Izenour with the intent of analyzing the form and symbolism of a unique popular
environment that appealed to common, working class people. Both versions convey
Venturi, Scott Brown, and Izenour's intent—to analyze the form and symbolism of
a unique popular environment that appealed to common, working class people. The
subsequent publication documented this process and proposed a controversial assessment: in the contemporary era, the authors declared, architecture was increasingly
concerned with the *communication across* space as opposed to the *creation of* space. This
concept linked to Scott Brown's and Venturi's notion of the "decorated shed."   In
place of the modernist "duck," a building whose external form reflects its purpose,
Scott Brown and Venturi proposed the "decorated shed," a boxlike structure accompanied by a sign that communicates its purpose. The essential argument was that, as
a building's use changed, it was far easier to replace the external decoration or sign
than to alter the form. Not surprisingly, the "decorated shed" theory as well as *Learning from Las Vegas* drew heavy criticism. The debates hinged on issues of populism,
social responsibility, and the role of the architect—themes that pervade architectural
discourse to the current day.

The article reprinted below, "Learning from Pop" (1971), addresses more concisely the
issues that characterize *Learning from Las Vegas*. These two writings, along with numerous others by Scott Brown, helped direct the attention of practitioners and theorists
toward a previously ignored aspect of the American environment and forged a path for
the reconsideration of the everyday landscape.

"Learning From Pop" (1971)

Las Vegas, Los Angeles, Levittown, the swinging singles on the Westheimer Strip, golf resorts, boating communities, Co-op City, the residential backgrounds to soap operas, TV commercials and mass mag ads, billboards, and Route 66 are sources for a changing architectural sensibility. New sources are sought when the old forms go stale and the way out is not clear; then a Classical heritage, an art movement, or industrial engineers' and primitives' "architecture without architects" may help to sweep out the flowery remains of the old revolution as practiced by its originators' conservative descendants. In America in the sixties an extra ingredient was added to this recipe for artistic change: social revolution. Urban renewal, supplier of work for architects for two decades and major focus of the soft remains of the Modern movement, was not merely artistically stale, it was socially harmful. The urgency of the social situation, and the social critique of urban renewal and of the architect as server of a rich narrow spectrum of the population—in particular the criticism of Herbert Gans—have been as important as the Pop artists in steering us toward the existing American city and its builders. If high-style architects are not producing what people want or need, who is, and what can we learn from them?

Needs, plural

Sensitivity to needs is a first reason for going to the existing city. Once there, the first lesson for architects is the pluralism of need. No builder-developer in his right mind would announce: I am building for Man. He is building for a market, for a group of people defined by income range, age, family composition, and life style. Levittowns,

---

Denise Scott Brown, "Learning from Pop," *Casabella*, 359/60 (December 1971), 15–23. Reprinted with permission of the author.

Leisureworlds, Georgian-styled town houses grow from someone's estimation of the needs of the groups who will be their markets. The city can be seen as the built artifacts of a set of subcultures. At the moment, those subcultures which willingly resort to architects are few.

Of course learning from what's there is subject to the caveats and limitations of all behavioristic analysis—one is surveying behavior which is constrained, it is not what people might do in other conditions. The poor do not willingly live in tenements and maybe the middle classes don't willingly live in Levittowns; perhaps the Georgian-styling is less pertinent to the townhouse resident than is the rent. In times of housing shortage this is a particularly forceful argument against architectural behaviorism since people can't vote against a particular offering by staying away if there is no alternative. To counteract this danger one must search for comparison environments where for some reason the constraints do not hold. There are environments which suggest what economically constrained groups' tastes might be if they were less constrained. They are the nouveau riche environments: Hollywood for a former era, Las Vegas for today, and the homes of film stars, sportsmen, and other groups where upward mobility may resemble vertical takeoff, yet where maintenance of previous value systems is encouraged.

Another source is physical backgrounds in the mass media, movies, soap operas, pickle and furniture polish ads. Here the aim is not to sell houses but something else, and the background represents someone's (Madison Avenue's?) idea of what pickle buyers or soap opera watchers want in a house. Now the Madison Avenue observer's view may be as biased as the architect's, and it should be studied in the light of what it is trying to sell—must pickle architecture look homey like my house or elegant like yours if it is to sell me pickles? But at least it's another bias, an alternative to the architectural navel contemplation we so often do for research, i.e., ask: What did Le Corbusier do? Both Madison Avenue and the builder, although they can tell us little of the needs of the very poor, cover a broader range of the population and pass a stiffer market test than does the architect in urban renewal or public housing, and if we learn no more from these sources than that architecture must differ for different groups, that is a great deal. But an alternative to both is to examine what people do to buildings—in Levittowns, Society Hills, gray areas and slums—once they are in them. Here, costs and availability are less constraining forces since the enterprise is smaller. Also, changes tend often to be symbolic rather than structural, and aspirations can perhaps be more easily inferred from symbols than from structures.

Attention to built sources for information on need does not imply that asking people what they want is not extremely necessary as well. This is an important topic, as is the relation between the two types of survey, asking and looking; but it is not the subject of this enquiry, which is on what can be learned from the artifacts of pop culture.

Formal analysis as design research

A second reason for looking to pop culture is to find formal vocabularies for today which are more relevant to people's diverse needs and more tolerant of the untidiness of urban life than the "rationalist," Cartesian formal orders of latter-day Modern architecture. How much low-income housing and nineteenth-century architecture has been cleared so some tidy purist architect or planner could start with a clean slate?

Modern architects can now admit that whatever forces, processes, and technologies determine architectural form, ideas about form determine it as well; that a formal vocabulary is as much a part of architecture as are bricks and mortar (plastics and systems, for futurists); that form does not, cannot, arise from function alone, newborn and innocent as Venus from her shell, but rather that form follows, *inter alia*, function, forces, and form. Formal biases, if they are consciously recognized, need not tyrannize as they have done in urban renewal; and formal vocabularies, given their place in architecture, can be studied and improved to suit functional requirements, rather than accepted unconsciously and unsuitably—an old hand-me-down from some irrelevant master. The forms of the pop landscape are as relevant to us now as were the forms of antique Rome to the Beaux-Arts, Cubism and Machine Architecture to the early Moderns, and the industrial midlands and the Dogon to Team 10, which is to say extremely relevant, and more so than the latest bathysphere, launch pad, or systems hospital (or even, *pace* Banham, the Santa Monica pier). Unlike these, they speak to our condition not only aesthetically, but on many levels of necessity, from the social necessity to rehouse the poor without destroying them to the architectural necessity to produce buildings and environments that others will need and like. The pop landscape differs from the earlier models in that it is also the place where we build; it is our context. And it is one of the few contemporary sources of data on the symbolic and communicative aspects of architecture, since it was untouched by the Modern movement's purist reduction of architecture to space and structure only. But formal analysis presents a problem. First, since form has for so long been an illegitimate topic, we have lost the tradition of analyzing it, and second, the forms we are dealing with are new and don't relate easily to traditional architectural or planning techniques of analysis and communications. Orthographic projection hardly conveys the essence of the Stardust sign, and, although this sign is a block long and has an overpowering visual impact "in situ," it doesn't show well on a land use map. Suburban space, being automobile space, is not defined by enclosing walls and floors and is therefore difficult to portray graphically using systems devised for the description of buildings. In fact, space is not the most important constituent of suburban form. Communication across space is more important, and it requires a symbolic and a time element in its descriptive systems which are only slowly being devised.

New analytic techniques must use film and videotape to convey the dynamism of sign architecture and the sequential experience of vast landscapes; and computers are needed to aggregate mass repeated data into comprehensible patterns. Valuable traditional techniques should also be resuscitated by their application to new phenomena;

for example, when Nolli's mid-eighteenth-century technique for mapping Rome is adapted to include parking lots, it throws considerable light on Las Vegas. It could also lend itself fairly easily to computer techniques.

Formal analysis should be comparative, linking the new forms, by comparison, to the rest of the formal tradition of architecture thereby incorporating them into the architectural discipline and helping us to understand our new experience in light of our formal training. By suggesting that form should be analyzed, I do not imply that function (the program), technologies, or forces (urban social processes or land economics) are not vital to architecture, nor indeed, that they too can't serve as sources of artistic inspiration to the architect. All are necessary and they work in combination. The others are merely not the subject of this particular enquiry.

The soup can and the establishment

There is an irony in the fact that the "popular" culture and the "popular" landscape are not popular with those who make the decisions to renew the city and rehouse the poor. Here is John Kenneth Galbraith, an important and influential liberal, quoted in *Life* magazine:

> For the average citizen there are some simple tests which will tell him when we have passed from incantation to practical action on the environment. Restriction of auto use in the large cities will be one. Another will be when the billboards, the worst and most nearly useless excrescence of industrial civilization, are removed from the highways. Yet another will be when telephone and electric wires everywhere in the cities go underground and we accept the added charge on our bills.
>
> My own personal test, for what it may be worth, concerns the gasoline service station. This is the most repellent piece of architecture of the past two thou-

sand years. There are far more of them than are needed. Usually they are filthy. Their merchandise is hideously packaged and garishly displayed. They are uncontrollably addicted to great strings of ragged little flags. Protecting them is an ominous coalition of small businessmen and large. The stations should be excluded entirely from most streets and highways. Where allowed, they should be franchised to limit the number, and there should be stern requirements as to architecture, appearance and general reticence. When we begin on this (and similar roadside commerce), I will think that we are serious.[1]

He does not even mention the need for low-income housing as an urgent environmental problem, and in my opinion he should stick to economics. But the conventional wisdom which Galbraith expounds is shared by his colleagues, the elderly architectural radicals who man American's fine arts commissions, the "design" departments of HUD and the planning and redevelopment agencies, who plan and build for the larger public and private corporations and have the ear of the city markers. If the public is to be well served by their decisions, these members of the architectural establishment must learn to separate out for a different type of scrutiny their aesthetic preoccupations from other concerns with "environmental pollution." Fouled water and billboards are not of the same magnitude or order of problem. The first cannot be done well, but the second can; particularly if we are given the opportunity to study them for a while, nonjudgmentally.

When "blighted" neighborhoods are swept away together with billboards and gasoline stations in the name of avoidance of "visual pollution," the social harm can be irreparable. However, an old aesthetic formula, even though it is shown to be obstructive,

---

[1]John Kenneth Galbraith, "To my new friends in the affluent society—greetings," *Life*, 27 Mar. 1970

will not be relinquished until it is replaced by a new one, since, as we have seen, form depends on form for its making. And, for the architectural establishment, the new vocabulary must have a respectable lineage. Hence, if the popular environment is to provide that vocabulary, it must be filtered through the proper processes for its acceptance. It must become a part of the high-art tradition; it must be last year's avant-garde. This is another reason to submit the new landscape to traditional architectural analysis: for the sake of its acceptance by the establishment. They can't learn from pop until Pop hangs in the academy.

Hop on pop

I have recommended an investigation of the forms of the new, existing city on both social and aesthetic grounds for architects who hope to hone their skills to a sharp new edge. High art has followed low art before and vice versa; in fact, where did the McDonald's parabola and the split-level rancher come from in the first place?

In the movement from low art to high art lies an element of the deferral of judgment. Judgment is withheld in the interest of understanding and receptivity. This is an exciting heuristic technique but also a dangerous one since liking the whole of pop culture is as irrational as hating the whole of it, and it calls forth the vision of a general and indiscriminate hopping on the pop bandwagon, where everything is good and judgment is abandoned rather than deferred. Yet artists, architects, actors, must judge, albeit, one hopes, with a sigh. After a decent interval, suitable criteria must grow out of the new source. Judgment is merely deferred to make subsequent judgment more sensitive.

The Egyptian architect, educator, and writer Hassan Fathy sought to improve rural living conditions in developing countries through an emphasis on vernacular architecture and building techniques. Fathy recognized the problematic nature of many housing proposals for these poorer regions; too often those in charge neglected the specifics of climate and topography in favor of modernist concepts that relied on materials too expensive and training too specialized. Aside from the practical issue of cost, Fathy believed that modernist tendencies threatened local building flavor and traditions that, in many cases, had persisted for centuries. These thoughts conditioned Fathy's approach to his most emblematic project, the design for New Gourna (1945–53), a village near Luxor intended to accommodate seven thousand Egyptian peasants displaced by archaeological excavations. Under Fathy's leadership, the plan for New Gourna incorporated time-honored architectural forms, such as domes, vaults, and the courtyard house, particularly suited to hot, arid climates. The village's primary method of construction involved mud brick, an infinitely available sun-baked mixture of straw and clay that was easily fabricated and worked by villagers. As is chronicled in *Architecture for the Poor* (first published in an abbreviated form in 1969 and then in its current form in 1973), Fathy's design for New Gourna was both an architectural and social experiment that, due to difficulties ranging from the sponsoring government to the villagers' resistance to change, did not turn out as planned. Nevertheless, Fathy's interest in the vernacular presented an alternative to universalizing modernist inclinations of the mid-twentieth century.

Architecture for the Poor (1973)

2. Chorale: Man, Society, And Technology
Architectural Character

Every people that has produced architecture has evolved its own favorite forms, as peculiar to that people as its language, its dress, or its folklore. Until the collapse of cultural frontiers in the last century, there were all over the world distinctive local shapes and details in architecture, and the buildings of any locality were the beautiful children of a happy marriage between the imagination of the people and the demands of their countryside. I do not propose to speculate upon the real springs of national idiosyncrasy, nor could I with any authority. I like to suppose simply that certain shapes take a people's fancy, and that they make use of them in a great variety of contexts, perhaps rejecting the unsuitable applications, but evolving a colorful and emphatic visual language of their own that suits perfectly their character and their homeland. No one could mistake the curve of a Persian dome and arch for the curve of a Syrian one, or a Moorish one, or an Egyptian one. No one can fail to recognize the same curve, the same signature, in dome and jar and turban from the same district. It follows, too, that no one can look with complacency upon buildings transplanted to an alien environment.

Yet in modern Egypt there is no indigenous style. The signature is missing; the houses of rich and poor alike are without character, without an Egyptian accent. The tradition is lost, and we have been cut off from our past even since Mohammed Ali cut the throat of the last Mameluke. This gap in continuity of Egyptian tradition has been

Hassan Fathy, *Architecture for the Poor* (New York and London: University of Chicago Press, 1973), 19–20, 23–26. © 1973 by The University of Chicago. Reprinted with permission from the publisher.

felt by many people, and all sorts of remedies have been proposed. There was, in fact, a kind of jealousy between those who regarded the Copts as the true lineal descendants of the Ancient Egyptians, and those who believed that the Arab style should provide the pattern for a new Egyptian architecture. Indeed, there was one statesmanlike attempt to reconcile these two factions, when Osman Moharam Pasha, the Minister of Public Works, suggested that Egypt be divided into two, rather as Solomon suggested dividing the baby, and that Upper Egypt be delivered to the Copts, where a traditional Pharaonic style could be developed, while Lower Egypt should go to the Moslems, who would make its architecture truly Arab!

This story goes to show two things. One is the encouraging fact that people do recognize and wish to remedy the cultural confusion in our architecture. The other—not so encouraging—is that this confusion is seen as a problem of style, and style is looked upon as some sort of surface finish that can be applied to any building and even scraped off and changed if necessary. The modern Egyptian architect believes that Ancient Egyptian architecture is represented by the temple with its pylons and cavetto cornice, and Arab by clustered stalactites, whereas Ancient Egyptian domestic architecture was quite unlike temple architecture, and Arab domestic architecture quite different from mosque architecture. Ancient Egyptian secular buildings like houses were light constructions, simple, with the clean lines of the best modern houses. But in the architectural schools they make no study of the history of domestic buildings, and learn architectural periods by the accidents of style, the obvious features like the pylon and the stalactite. Thus the graduate architect believes this to be all there is in "style," and imagines a building can change its style as a man changes clothes. It was thinking like this that led some architect to ruin the entrance to the classrooms at Gourna school by transforming the original archway into an Ancient Egyptian-style temple doorway complete with cavetto cornice. It is not yet understood that real architecture cannot exist except in a living tradition. . . .

The Process of Decision Making

... The world at any moment is a blank page awaiting our pencil; an open space may hold a cathedral or a slagheap.

Because no two men make the same decisions in similar circumstances, we say that men's characters differ. Decision making, choosing, is another word for self-expression—or, perhaps better, is the necessary prelude to all self-expression.

A conscious decision may be reached either by consulting tradition or by logical reasoning and scientific analysis. Both processes should yield the same result, for tradition embodies the conclusions of many generations' practical experiment with the same problem, while scientific analysis is simply the organized observation of the phenomena of the problem. ...

Tradition's Role

It may be that what we call modern is nothing but what is not worthy of remaining to become old.

Dante Alighieri

Tradition is the social analogy of personal habit, and in art has the same effect, of releasing the artist from distracting and inessential decisions so that he can give his whole attention to the vital ones. Once an artistic decision has been made, no matter when or by whom, it cannot profitably be made again; better that it should pass into the common store of habit and not bother us further.

Tradition is not necessarily old-fashioned and is not synonymous with stagnation. Furthermore, a tradition need not date from long ago but may have begun quite recently. As soon as a workman meets a new problem and decides how to overcome it, the first step has been taken in the establishment of a tradition. When another workman has decided to adopt the same solution, the tradition is moving, and by the time a third man has followed the first two and added his contribution, the tradition is fairly established. Some problems are easy to solve; a man may decide in a few minutes what to do. Others need time, perhaps a day, perhaps a year, perhaps a whole lifetime; in each case the solution may be the work of one man.

Yet other solutions may not be worked out fully before many generations have passed, and this is where tradition has a creative role to play, for it is only by tradition, by respecting and building on the work of earlier generations, that each new generation may make some positive progress toward the solution of the problem. When tradition has solved its problem and ceased developing, we may say that a cycle has been completed. However, in architecture as in other human activities and in natural processes, there are cycles just beginning, others that have been completed, and others at all stages of development in between, that exist simultaneously in the same society. There are, too, traditions that go back to the beginning of human society, yet which are still living and which will exist perhaps as long as human society does: in bread making for example, and in brick making.

There are, on the other hand, traditions which, although they have appeared only recently and ought to be in an early phase of their cycle, were in fact born dead. Modernity does not necessarily mean liveliness, and change is not always for the better. On the other hand there are situations that call for innovation. My point is that innovation must be a completely thought-out response to a change in circumstances, and not indulged in for its own sake. Nobody asks that an airport control tower be built in some peasant idiom, and an industrial structure like a nuclear power station may force a new tradition upon the designer.

Once a particular tradition is established and accepted, the individual artist's duty is to keep this tradition going, with his own invention and insight to give it that additional momentum that will save it from coming to a standstill, until it will have reached the end of its cycle and completed its full development. He will be relieved of many decisions by the tradition, but will be obliged to make others equally demanding to stop the tradition dying on his hands. In fact, the further a tradition has developed, the more effort the artist must expend to make each step forward in it. . . .

Architecture is still one of the most traditional arts. A work of architecture is meant to be used, its form is largely determined by precedent, and it is set before the public where they must look at it every day. The architect should respect the work of his predecessors and the public sensibility by not using his architecture as a medium of personal advertisement. Indeed, no architect can avoid using the work of earlier architects; however hard he strains after originality, by far the larger part of his work will be in some tradition or other. Why then should he despise the tradition of his own country or district, why should he drag alien traditions into an artificial and uncomfortable synthesis, why should he be so rude to earlier architects as to distort and misapply their ideas? This happens when an architectural element, evolved over many years to a perfect size, shape, and function, is used upside down or enlarged beyond recognition till it no longer even works properly, simply to gratify the architect's own selfish appetite for fame.

For example, it has taken men very many years to arrive at the right size for a window in various architectural traditions; if an architect now commits the gross error of enlarging the window till it takes up a whole wall, he is at once confronted with a problem: his glass wall lets in ten times a much radiation as did the solid wall. If now to shade the window he adds a brise-soleil, which is nothing more than an enlarged Venetian blind, the room will still receive 300 percent more radiation than one with a solid wall. Furthermore, when the architect enlarges the width of the slats of the Venetian blind from 4 centimeters to 40, so as not to upset the scale of the glass wall, what is the result? Instead of admitting a gentle diffused light, as a shutter or Venetian blind does, it dazzles the eye of anyone in the room with a pattern of broad black bars against a brilliant glare of light.

Not only that, but the view, the securing of which was the initial object of the glass wall, is permanently spoiled by these large bars cutting it up; the brise-soleil has not even the virtue of folding away, as have the shutter and the Venetian blind. Even in a cool climate like that of Paris, the glass wall can prove to be an unmanageable extravagance; during the hot summer of 1959 the temperature inside the UNESCO building, due to the "greenhouse effect" of its glass walls, and despite the labors of the air conditioning machinery, rose so high that many of the employees fainted. Superfluous then, to comment on the introduction of glass walls and brise-soleils in tropical countries; yet it is hard to find an example of modern tropical architecture that does not employ these features.

If the architect walks soberly in the tradition of his culture, then he must not suppose that his artistry will be stifled. Far from it; it will express itself in relevant contributions to the tradition and contribute to the advance of his society's culture.

25 PETER EISENMAN, B. 1932

Peter Eisenman, House II (Falk House), Hardwick, VT, 1969–70. © Norman McGrath

Since the 1967 formation of the Institute of Architecture and Urban Studies (IAUS) in New York, an architectural think tank largely responsible for introducing European philosophical thought into the American architectural realm, Peter Eisenman has earned a reputation as an intensely theoretical practitioner. Eisenman's early work was dedicated to the establishment of an autonomous or purely self-referential architecture. The abstracted forms of his Cardboard House series directly reflected this search; through a sequence of moves—superimposing, shifting, shearing, rotating the basic cubic volumes with which he began—Eisenman attempted to remove all normative meaning from architectural elements, an ambitious and ultimately impossible goal. He continued this line of thought in "Post-Functionalism," an editorial that appeared in *Oppositions*, the journal affiliated with the IAUS. Eisenman asserted that the path to true autonomy, already achieved by the other modern arts, demanded the displacement of man as the focus of these disciplines. Yet, due to modern architecture's fixation on anthropocentric functionalism, architecture had failed to become autonomous and thus truly modern. Eisenman's position was controversial for many reasons. Perhaps the most disturbing aspect of his postfunctionalist concept was that it countered accepted notions of architecture's purpose, questioning the fundamental nature of architecture as a creation of and for man. In the past few decades, initially in connection with theories of deconstruction, Eisenman has continued to challenge conventional architectural expectations concerning the realms of form, structure, and meaning.

"Post-Functionalism" (1976)

The critical establishment within architecture has told us that we have entered the era of "post-modernism." The tone with which this news is delivered is invariably one of relief, similar to that which accompanies the advice that one is no longer an adolescent. Two indices of this supposed change are the quite different manifestations of the "Architettura Razionale" exhibition at the Milan Triennale of 1973, and the "Ecole Des Beaux Arts" exhibition at The Museum of Modern Art in 1975. The former, going on the assumption that modern architecture was an outmoded functionalism, declared that architecture can be generated only through a return to itself as an autonomous or pure discipline. The latter, seeing modern architecture as an obsessional formalism, made itself into an implicit statement that the future lies paradoxically in the past, within the peculiar response to function that characterized the nineteenth century's eclectic command of historical styles.

What is interesting is not the mutually exclusive character of these two diagnoses and hence of their solutions, but rather the fact that both of these views enclose the very project of architecture within the same definition: one by which the terms continue to be function (or program) and form (or type). In so doing, an attitude toward architecture is maintained that differs in no significant way from the 500-year-old tradition of humanism.

The various theories of architecture which properly can be called "humanist" are characterized by a dialectical opposition: an oscillation between a concern for internal

---

Peter Eisenman, "Post-Functionalism," originally in *Oppositions* 6 (1976); reprinted in Peter Eisenman, *Eisenman Inside Out, Selected Writings, 1963–1988* (New Haven: Yale University Press, 2004), 83–87. © 2004 by Yale University. Reprinted with permission from the publisher.

accommodation—the program and the way it is materialized—and a concern for articulation of ideal themes in form—for example, as manifested in the configurational significance of the plan. These concerns were understood as two poles of a single, continuous experience. Within pre-industrial, humanist practice, a balance between them could be maintained because both type and function were invested with idealist views of man's relationship to his object world. In a comparison first suggested by Colin Rowe, of a French Parisian hotel and an English country house, both buildings from the early-nineteenth century, one sees this opposition manifested in the interplay between a concern for expression of an ideal type and a concern for programmatic statement, although the concerns in each case are differently weighted. The French hotel displays rooms of an elaborate sequence and a spatial variety born of internal necessity, masked by a rigorous, well-proportioned external facade. The English country house has a formal internal arrangement of rooms which gives way to a picturesque external massing of elements. The former bows to program on the interior and type on the façade; the latter reverses these considerations.

With the rise of industrialization, this balance seems to have been fundamentally disrupted. In that it had of necessity to come to terms with problems of a more complex functional nature, particularly with respect to the accommodation of a mass client, architecture became increasingly a social or programmatic art. And as the functions became more complex, the ability to manifest the pure type-form eroded. One has only to compare William Kent's competition entry for the houses of Parliament, where the form of a Palladian Villa does not sustain the intricate program, with Charles Barry's solution where the type-form defers to program and where one sees an early example of what was to become known as the *promenade architecturale*. Thus, in the nineteenth century, and continuing on into the twentieth, as the program grew in complexity, the type-form became diminished as a realizable concern, and the balance thought to be fundamental to all theory was weakened. (Perhaps only Le Corbusier in recent history has successfully combined an ideal grid with the architectural promenade as an embodiment of the original interaction.)

This shift in balance has produced a situation whereby, for the past fifty years, architects have understood design as the product of some oversimplified form-follows-function formula. This situation even persisted during the years immediately following World War II, when one might have expected it would be radically altered. And as late as the end of the 1960s, it was still thought that the polemics and theories of the early Modern Movement could sustain architecture. The major thesis of this attitude was articulated in what could be called the English Revisionist Functionalism of Reyner Banham, Cedric Price, and Archigram. This neo-functionalist attitude, with its idealization of technology, was invested with the same ethical positivism and aesthetic neutrality of the prewar polemic. However, the continued substitution of moral criteria for those of a more formal nature produced a situation which now can be seen to have created a functionalist predicament, precisely because the primary theoretical justification given to formal arrangements was a *moral* imperative that is no longer operative within contemporary experience. This sense of displaced positivism characterizes certain current perceptions of the failure of humanism within a broader cultural context.

There is also another, more complex, aspect to this predicament. Not only can functionalism indeed be recognized as a species of positivism, but like positivism, it now can be seen to issue from within the terms of an idealist view of reality. For functionalism, no matter what its pretense, continued the idealist ambition of creating architecture as a kind of ethically constituted form-giving. But because it clothed this idealist ambition in the radically stripped forms of technological production, it has seemed to represent a break with the pre-industrial past. But, in fact, functionalism is really no more than a late phase of humanism, rather than an alternative to it. And in this sense, it cannot continue to be taken as a direct manifestation of that which has been called "the modernist sensibility."

Both the Triennale and the Beaux Arts exhibitions suggest, however, that the problem is thought to be somewhere else—not so much with functionalism *per se*, as with the nature of this so-called modernist sensibility. Hence, the implied revival of neo-classicism and Beaux Arts academicism as replacements for a continuing, if poorly understood, modernism. It is true that sometime in the nineteenth century, there was indeed a crucial shift within Western consciousness: one which can be characterized as a shift from humanism to modernism. But, for the most part, architecture, in its dogged adherence to the principles of function, did not participate in or understand the fundamental aspects of that change. It is the potential difference in the nature of modernist and humanist theory that seems to have gone unnoticed by those people who today speak of eclecticism, post-modernism, or neo-functionalism. And they have failed to notice it precisely because they conceive of modernism as merely a stylistic manifestation of functionalism, and functionalism itself as a basic theoretical proposition in architecture. In fact, the idea of modernism has driven a wedge into these attitudes. It has revealed that the dialectic form and function is culturally based.

In brief, the modernist sensibility has to do with a changed mental attitude toward the artifacts of the physical world. This change has not only been manifested aesthetically, but also socially, philosophically, and technologically—in sum, it has been manifested in a new cultural attitude. This shift away from the dominant attitudes of humanism, that were pervasive in Western societies for some four hundred years, took place at various times in the nineteenth century in such disparate disciplines as mathematics, music, painting, literature, film, and photography. It is displayed in the non-objective abstract painting of Malevich and Mondrian; in the non-narrative, atemporal writing of Joyce and Apollinaire; the atonal and polytonal compositions of Schönberg and Webern; in the non-narrative films of Richter and Eggeling.

Abstraction, atonality, and atemporality, however, are merely stylistic manifestations of modernism, not its essential nature. Although this is not the place to elaborate a theory of modernism, or indeed to represent those aspects of such a theory which have already found their way into the literature of the other humanist disciplines, it can simply be said that the symptoms to which one has just pointed suggest a displacement of man away from the center of his world. He is no longer viewed as an *originating agent*. Objects are seen as ideas independent of man. In this context, man is a discursive function among complex and already-formed systems of language, which he witnesses but does not constitute. As Levi-Strauss has said, "Language, an unreflecting totalization, is human reason which has its reason and of which man knows nothing." It is this condition of displacement which gives rise to design in which authorship can no longer either account for a linear development which has a 'beginning' and an 'end'—hence the rise of the atemporal—or account for the invention of form—hence the abstract as a mediation between pre-existent sign systems.

Modernism, as a sensibility based on the fundamental displacement of man, represents what Michel Foucault would specify as a new *épistème*. Deriving from a non-humanistic attitude toward the relationship of an individual to his physical environment, it breaks with the historical past, both with the ways of viewing man as subject and, as we have said, with the ethical positivism of form and function. Thus, it cannot be related to functionalism. It is probably for this reason that modernism has not up to now been elaborated in architecture.

But there is clearly a present need for a theoretical investigation of the basic implications of modernism (as opposed to modern style) in architecture. In his editorial "Neo-Functionalism," in *Oppositions* 5, Mario Gandelsonas acknowledges such a need. However, he says merely that the "complex contradictions" inherent in functionalism—such as neo-realism and neo-rationalism—make a form of neo-functionalism necessary to any new theoretical dialectic. This proposition continues to refuse to recognize that the form/function opposition is not necessarily inherent to any architectural theory and so fails to recognize the crucial difference between modernism and humanism. In contrast, what is being called post-functionalism begins as an attitude which recognizes modernism as a new and distinct sensibility. It can best be understood in architecture in terms of a theoretical base that is concerned with what might be called a modernist *dialectic*, as opposed to the old humanist (i.e., functionalist) opposition of form and function.

This new theoretical base changes the humanist balance of form/function to a dialectical relationship within the evolution of form itself. The dialectic can best be described as the potential co-existence within any form of two non-corroborating and non-sequential tendencies. One tendency is to presume architectural form to be a recognizable transformation from some pre-existent geometric or platonic solid. In this case, form is usually understood through a series of registrations designed to recall a more simple geometric condition. This tendency is certainly a relic of humanist theory. However, to this is added a second tendency that sees architectural form in an atemporal, decompositional mode, as something simplified from some pre-existent set of non-specific spatial entities. Here, form is understood as a series of fragments—signs without meaning dependent upon, and without reference to, a more basic condition. The former tendency, when taken by itself, is a reductivist attitude and assumes some primary unity as both an ethical and an aesthetic basis for all creation. The latter, by itself, assumes a basic condition of fragmentation and multiplicity from which the resultant form is a state of simplification. Both tendencies, however, when taken together, constitute the essence of this new, modern dialectic. They begin to define the inherent nature of the object in and of itself and its capacity to be represented. They begin to suggest that the theoretical assumptions of functionalism are in fact cultural rather than universal.

Post-functionalism, thus, is a term of absence. In its negation of functionalism it suggests certain positive theoretical alternatives—existing fragments of thought which, when examined, might serve as a framework for the development of a larger theoretical structure—but it does not, in and of itself, propose to supply a label for such a new consciousness in architecture which I believe is potentially upon us.

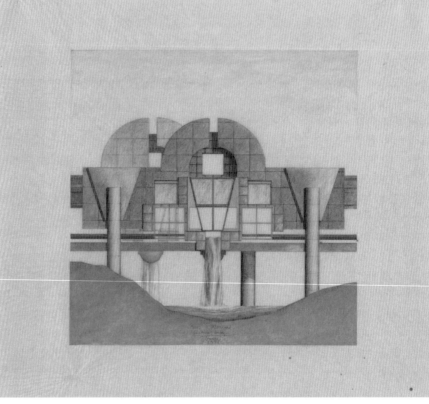

Michael Graves, Fargo-Moorhead Cultural Center Bridge project
Fargo, North Dakota and Moorhead, Minnesota, 1978. Drawing of south elevation
Photo Credit: Digital Image © The Museum of Modern Art/Licensed by SCALA/Art Resource, NY
Image courtesy of Michael Graves and Associates

While trained as an architect, the American architectural historian Charles Jencks is best known for his critical writings on postmodern architecture. He did not invent the term "Post-Modernism," but is generally credited with its introduction to architecture through his 1977 publication, *The Language of Post-Modern Architecture.*[*] In this text, Jencks theorized architecture of the 1960s and 70s that deviated from modernist tendencies of the time. As the main point of departure for postmodern architecture he identified "dual-coding," the ability to communicate on at least two levels simultaneously. Jencks suggested that double-coded architecture contains differing and sometimes contradictory meanings that exist in tension with one another; this plurality of meaning stood in marked opposition to doctrinaire modern architecture that sought to convey messages based on function. In theory, multiple meanings rendered postmodern architecture accessible to both architects and laymen. Some praised the eclecticism, historical quotation, and playfulness of works such as Graves's project for the Fargo-Moorhead Bridge (Fargo, North Dakota, and Moorhead, Minnesota, 1978) as witty and ironic while others criticized them as kitschy and superficial. Yet, despite their dichotomous views, both positions generally situated postmodern architecture as a response to and an expression of the complexity of contemporary life.

---

[*] Throughout the 1980s, Jencks frequently updated *The Language of Post-Modern Architecture*, first published in 1977 in London by Academy Editions and in New York by Rizzoli International Publications. The text is currently in its sixth edition (John Wiley & Sons and Academy Editions, 1991).

"Why Post-Modernism?" (1978)

The notion of Post-Modernism has had an unusual history which requires a little explanation. A situation has been developing over the past 20 years which is now in the process of focusing very quickly into a new style and approach. It has grown out of Modern architecture in much the way Mannerist architecture grew out of the High Renaissance—as a partial inversion and modification of the former language of architecture. This development is now generally being called Post-Modern architecture because the term is wide enough to encompass the variety of departures, and yet still indicate its derivation from Modernism. Like its progenitor the movement is committed to engaging current issues, to changing the present, but unlike the avant-garde it does away with the notion of continual innovation or incessant revolution.

A Post-Modern building is, if a short definition is needed, one which speaks on at least two levels at once: to other architects and a concerned minority who care about specifically architectural meanings, and to the public at large, or the local inhabitants, who care about other issues concerned with comfort, traditional building and a way of life. Thus Post-Modern architecture looks hybrid and, if visual definition is needed, rather like the front of a Classical Greek temple. The latter is a pure white architecture of elegantly fluted columns below, and a riotous billboard of struggling giants above, a pediment painted in deep reds and blues. The architects can read the subtle metaphors and subtle meanings of the column drums, whereas the public can respond to the explicit metaphors and messages of the sculptors. Of course everyone responds somewhat to both codes of meaning, as they do in a Post-Modern building,

---

Charles Jencks, "Why Post-Modernism?" *Architectural Design* 48, no. 1 (1978), 13–14. © John Wiley & Sons Limited. Reproduced with permission.

but certainly with different intensity and understanding, and it is this discontinuity in taste and cultures which creates both the theoretical base and 'dual coding' of Post-Modernism. The dual image of the Classical temple is a helpful visual formula to keep in mind as the unifying factor while different departures from Modernism are presented here. The buildings most characteristic of Post-Modernism show a marked duality, a conscious schizophrenia.

. . . [The] term 'Post-Modern' has to be clarified and used . . . precisely to cover, in general, only those designers who are aware of architecture as a *language*—hence one part of the title of my book: *The Language of Post-Modern Architecture.* Paul Goldberger and a few American critics have used the term this way and focused on other important qualities, its attention to historical memory and local context. These aspects are significant, but as history shows, they are only part of the story. For Post-Modern architecture also takes a positive approach toward metaphorical buildings, the vernacular, and a new, ambiguous kind of space. Hence only a plural definition will capture its many heads, something I have tried to clarify with the evolutionary chart. . . . For the same reason, there is no one architect who altogether combines these various strands, or one building which summarizes them. If forced to point at an entirely convincing Post-Modernist I would instance Antonio Gaudi, obviously not a possibility, as reviewers of my book have been quick to point out, because he was a Pre-Modernist. I still regard Gaudi as *the* touchstone for Post-Modernism, a model with which to compare any recent buildings to see if they are really metaphorical, 'contextual' and rich in a precise way, but I have confined my examples to the present.

The ambiguity of the prefix 'Post' has its amusing and powerful aspects, which partly explain why it has become current. People are naturally exhilarated at the prospect of being 'Post-Present.' In the middle 60s Daniel Bell wrote on the Post-Industrial Society, with the implication that some fortunate Westerners could escape laborious toil altogether. There was the short-lived 'Post-Painterly Abstraction,' a movement of

opposition as it states, and more recently President Carter has come out in favor of a new foreign policy based on the 'Post-War' world. Very convenient this slippery word, it simply states where you've left, not arrived.

But the mind rebels at all this linguistic paradox: how can we be beyond the modern age if we are still alive? Have we banished the present tense like the Futurists and located Elysium in a perpetual state of tomorrow (or yesterday)? If so we might look forward to a 'Post-Natal,' or is it 'Post-Coital' depression, as we reap the benefits of evading the present.

Such thoughts made me consider Post-Modern architecture as a temporary label when I first used it in 1975, but now I've changed my mind. Partly this is due to overtones of 'modern' which are still kept in the hybrid title; its power and contemporaneity. Architects, artists, people in general want to keep up to date, even if they don't want to relinquish their cultural past as the avant-garde has often done. We can see in the Renaissance an instructive parallel when the word 'modern' was first put into currency.

At that time they had debates, and confusions, similar and relevant to our own. Filarete, for instance, claimed he "used to like modern ([namely] Gothic) buildings" until the time "when I began to appreciate classical ones, I came to be disgusted with the former. . . ." But then as the renaissance of antiquity proceeded, the Gothic style became old-fashioned and, finally, with Vasari, the equation was reversed: the older, classical style was perfected, that is to say *improved* (or so they thought) as the new 'good modern style" (*buona maniera moderna*). Thus Renaissance writers were confused over the use of this term, *moderna* was applied to the Gothic, the classical Roman and its revival—three different modes. No matter how committed to the past the architects were they still called it 'modern' as if the term had (and still has?) an unchallengeable hold on the present tense—on being 'now.' Only after Giorgio Vasari systematically and consciously used *moderna* to mean revival style did his usage become common and accepted.

The battle of the 'Ancients and the Moderns' has been fought many times since then with equal confusion over usage, and in a sense we are again in such a predicament with the adversaries not only disagreeing, but also using their basic words differently. This is not the place to analyze the differing versions of 'the modern,' an analysis which I am sure will occur as the attacks and counter-attacks mount in vehemence. But it is the point to emphasize that the word 'modern' still has an ambiguous power, as it did for Vasari, because it refers to a contemporaneous, growing climate of opinion, and it has this power even for those who would deny, refute, or criticize it. Post-*Modernism* thus gains some of these overtones even while it attacks the concept of the avant-garde and the *Zeitgeist*.

Secondly, and more importantly, the label describes the *duality* of the present situation quite well. Most, if not all, the architects of the movement have been trained in Modernism yet have moved beyond or counter to this training. They have not yet arrived at a new synthetic goal, nor have they given up entirely their Modernist sensibility, but rather they are at a half-way house, half Modern, half Post. If we look at Venturi, Stern, or Moore's work—three of the hard-core PMs—we can see all the quotes from Le Corbusier, Kahn, the 20s *and* all the references to Palladio, Lutyens, and Route 66. There is no doubt such work is schizophrenically coded, something you'd expect *after* a movement has broken down and the architects have moved on. For we are talking here of an evolution out of or away from a shared position, not a revolutionary schism with the immediate past, and so one of the really surprising, even defining, characteristics of Post-Modernism emerges: it includes Modernist style and iconography as a potential approach, to be used where this is appropriate (on factories, hospitals, and a few offices). Whereas Modernism like Mies van der Rohe was exclusivist, PM is so totally inclusive as to allow even its purist opposite a place when this is justifiable. Put another way, Post-Modernism is finding a rationale for 20s revivalism, in an era when all revivals are possible and each depends on an argument from *plausibility*, since it certainly can't be proved as necessity.

27   Demetri Porphyrios, b. 1949

The Greek architect and educator Demetri Porphyrios studied architectural design, history, and theory at Princeton University, earning his Master of Architecture degree in 1974 and his doctorate in 1980. Since then, Porphyrios has become one of the foremost proponents of a traditional architectural vocabulary. In the following passage from the 1982 essay "Classicism Is Not a Style," Porphyrios posited classical architecture as a model for contemporary practice, arguing that classicism should not be viewed as a mere dressing or style, but as a theoretical system that describes the nature of architecture through reference to both the practical and representational aspects of building. He explained that classicism derives from basic universal tenets of construction that were first manifest in regional or vernacular architecture and then adopted by classical architecture. In his opinion, these constructional principles—the need for load-bearing, enclosing, and demarcating elements—give rise to architectural forms that convey pragmatic and symbolic information about structural and mythical functions. Porphyrios asserted that a contemporary architecture based on this classical system offers a meaningful alternative to the perceived architectural poverty of consumer culture.

As the principal of the London-based firm Porphyrios Associates, Porphyrios has continued to cultivate a present-day role for the classicism by which his work abides. His recent design of Princeton University's Whitman Residential College (fall 2007) in a collegiate Gothic idiom supports his belief that classicism is indeed not a style. Rather, as Porphyrios has emphasized, the principles of classicism offer a foundation for all architectural design.

"Classicism Is Not a Style" (1983)

The predicament of contemporary architecture . . . stems from our twofold inheritance: on the one hand, the symbolically mute elements of industrial production inherited from Modernism, and on the other the expendable historicist and high-tech signs of industrial kitsch inherited from Modern Eclecticism. This raises, in my opinion, the crucial problem we face today: if there is an opposition between the economic priorities of mass industrial society and the yearning for an authentic culture that would sustain individual freedom in public life, under what qualifications is it possible to practise architecture at all? Paradoxically, the only possible critical stance for architecture today is to build an alliance between building construction and symbolic representation. To construct, that is, a tectonic discourse which, while addressing the pragmatics of shelter, could at the same time represent its own tectonics in a symbolic way.

It is from such a perspective that classicism should be re-evaluated today: not as a borrowed stylistic finery but as an ontology of building. Classicism is not a style. Its lesson lies in the way by which it raises construction and shelter to the realm of the symbol.

The Constructional Logic of Vernacular

Despite the superficial associations with rusticity and nature that the word 'vernacular' brings to mind its essential meaning is different. The idea of vernacular has nothing to

---

Demetri Porphyrios, "Classicism Is Not a Style," *Demetri Porphyrios: Selected Buildings and Writings*, Architectural Monograph no. 25 (London: Academy Editions, 1993) 125–27. © John Wiley & Sons Limited. Reproduced with permission. A version of this essay first appeared in *Architecural Design* 5–6 (1982), 51–57

do with stylistics. It rather points to the universal ethos of constructing shelter under the conditions of scarcity of materials and operative constructional techniques.

By involving vernacular, one does not seek the primitivism of pre-industrial cultures. The temptation to turn one's back on contemporary industrial society in order to return to the security and institutions of some pre-industrial order, when pursued, leaves us suspended amid the reverberations of Plato's ghost: 'what then?' Instead, the essential meaning of vernacular refers to straightforward construction, to the rudimentary building of shelter, an activity that exhibits reason, efficiency, economy, durability and pleasure. Certainly, varying materials and techniques attribute regionalist characteristics to vernacular. But beyond appearances, all vernacular is marked by a number of constructional *a prioris* which are universal and essentially phenomenological.

To begin with, building—by its very nature—involves the experiences of load-bearing and load-borne, the primary manifestations of which are the column and the lintel. Secondly, it involves the experience of horizontal and vertical enclosure, the primary manifestations of which are the roof and the wall. The floor, since it repeats the original ground, is flat for it is meant to be walked upon; whereas the roof is inclined since, in addition to its shedding off water, it marks the terminus and should appear as such. Finally, since all construction is construction by means of finite elements, the act of building involves necessarily the experience of demarcating, the primary manifestations of which are the beginning and ending.

When applied to the making of shelter, these constructional a *prioris* give rise to a set of constructional forms: as for example the gable which marks the sectional termination of the roof and thus points to the primary experience of entry; or the engaged pilaster, which manifests the confluent experiences of load-bearing and enclosure; or the window and door, which manifest the experience of suspending enclosure locally for purposes of passage; or the colonnade, which demarcates the experience of boundary; and so on.

Classicism: The Symbolic Elaboration of Vernacular

Such constructional *a prioris* and their ensuing constructional corollaries can be identified—it would appear—beyond fear of interpretative dispute and could serve as the core of a common architectural knowledge.

Yet architecture cannot remain at this 'starting point.' Its vocation is to lift itself above the contingencies of building by commemorating those very contingencies from which it sprung in the first place. What distinguishes a shed from a temple is the mythopoeic power the temple possesses: it is a power that transgresses the boundaries of contingent reality and raises construction and shelter to the realm of the symbol.

This is the sense in which we can say that classicism is not a style. The classical naturalises the constructional *a prioris* of shelter by turning them into myth: the demarcations of beginning and ending are commemorated as base and capital; the experience of load-bearing is made perceptible through the entasis in the shaft of the column; the chief beam, binding the columns together and imposing on them a common load, becomes the architrave; the syncopation of the transversal beams resting on the architrave is rendered visible in the figures of the triglyphs and metopes of the frieze; the projecting rafters of the roof, supported by the frieze, appear in the form of the cornice; finally—and most significantly—the whole tectonic assemblage of column, architrave, frieze and cornice become the ultimate object of classical contemplation in the ideal of the Order.

The Order sets form over the necessities of shelter; it sets the myth of the tectonic over the contingencies of construction. The power of mythical fiction presides. It is the possibility of such an act of mythical fiction that constitutes the prime aesthetic subject-matter of classical thought. Classical architecture constructs a tectonic fiction out of the productive level of building. The artifice of constructing this fictitious world is seen as analogous to the artifice of constructing the human world. In its turn, myth allows for a convergence of the real and the fictive so that the real is redeemed. By rendering construction mythically fictive, classical thought posits reality in a contemplative state, wins over the depredations of petty life and, in a moment of rare disinterestedness, rejoices in the power it has over contingent life and nature.

Mythical thinking, of course, is not necessarily primitive or prelogical as common opinion might maintain today. It is true thinking for it reduces the world to order. Its truth is no less than that experimentally verified by science. Today, if it appears that the mythopoeic mind cannot achieve objectivity (and should therefore be doomed as an irrationality that can never attain consensus) this is not because it is incapable of dealing with the world, but rather because contemporary industrial life is dominated by vulgar positivism. That is why architecture today is systematically denied its mythopoeic power. The vulgarity lies not in the search for objectivity but in the immanence with which consumer culture boasts of being the mere extension of production.

Juhani Pallasmaa, b. 1936

In *The Architecture of Humanism* (1914), Geoffrey Scott discussed the power of architecture to elicit an emotional response from its occupants. Relying on the concept of empathy, he declared that "[we transcribe] ourselves into terms of architecture . . . [and] . . . transcribe architecture into terms of ourselves."* Seventy-one years later, the Finnish architect Juhani Pallasmaa addressed a similar line of thought in "The Geometry of Feeling: The Phenomenology of Architecture," an exegesis on the human experience of architectural form. Yet, while Scott countered what he perceived to be the progressive decline in taste since the fifteenth century, Pallasmaa described his contemporaries as obsessed with formal manipulation at the expense of "the artistic essence of architecture," namely, "the experiential and mental dimensions of architecture." Pallasmaa argued that architectural form derives meaning only from the images with which the form is connected. Form alone means nothing; it is the human interaction with and interpretation of that form that gives a form meaning.

Pallasmaa's humanism stems from the Finnish legacy exemplified by Alvar Aalto, an architect known for his careful attention to the tactile and material qualities of his design and concern for the ways in which his works would be inhabited. As an architect, professor, and author, Pallasmaa continues these phenomenological interests, offering a model of thought and design grounded in the realities of human experience and emotive possibility.

---

* Geoffrey Scott, *The Architecture of Humanism*, p. 119–20 in this collection.

"Geometry of Feeling: The Phenomenology of Architecture" (1985)

Why do so few modern buildings appeal to our emotions, when an anonymous house in an old town, or an unpretentious farm building, will give us a sense of familiarity and pleasure? Why is it that the stone foundations we discover in an overgrown meadow, or a dilapidated barn, or an abandoned boathouse can arouse our imagination, while our own houses seem to stifle and smother our day dreams? The buildings of our own time may arouse our curiosity with their daring or inventiveness, but they give us little sense of the meaning of our world or our own existence.

Efforts are being made to revitalize the debilitated language of architecture, through both a richer idiom and by reviving historical themes. But despite their effusive diversity, such avant-garde works are just as bereft of meaning as the coldly technical approach to building against which they rebel.

Architecture's impoverished inner meaning has also been considered in numerous recent writings on architectural theory. Some writers think our architecture is too poor in terms of form, others contend that its form is too abstract or intellectual. Philosophically, our culture of hedonistic materialism seems to be losing any meaningful dimension that might in general be worthy of perpetuation in stone. As Ludwig Wittgenstein argues, "Architecture glorifies and eternalizes something. When there is nothing to glorify there is no architecture."[1]

Juhani Pallasmaa, "The Geometry of Feeling: The Phenomenology of Architecture," *Encounters, Architectural Essays*, ed. Peter MacKeith (Helsinki: Rakennustieto Oy, 2005), 87–91, 93–96. Initially published in *Arkkitehti, The Finnish Review* 3 (Mar. 1985). Reprinted with permission of the author and publisher.

[1] Ludwig Wittgenstein, *Culture and Value*, ed. George Henrik von Wright, in collaboration with Heikki Nyman (Oxford: Blackwell, 1998), 74e.

Architecture as Play with Form

. . . [Proof] exits to demonstrate architecture's detachment from its proper background and purpose. I consider one viewpoint here: the relationship between architectural form and how architecture is experienced. Design has become so intensively a kind of game with form that the reality of how a building is experienced has been overlooked. We make the mistake of thinking of, and assessing, a building as a formal composition, no longer understanding that it is a metaphor, let alone experiencing the other reality that lies behind the metaphor. . . .

The Architecture of Imagery

The artistic dimension of a work of art does not lie in the actual physical thing; it exists only in the consciousness of the person experiencing that object. The analysis of a work of art is, at its most genuine level, an introspection by the consciousness subjected to it. The work of art's meaning lies not in its forms, but in the images transmitted by the forms and the emotional force that they carry. Form only affects our feelings through what it represents.

As long as teaching and criticism do not strive to clarify the experiential and mental dimensions of architecture, they will have little to do with the artistic essence of architecture. Current efforts to restore the richness of the architectural idiom through a greater diversity of form are based on a lack of understanding of the essence of art. The richness of a work of art lies in the vitality of the images it arouses, and—paradoxically—the simplest, most archetypal forms arouse the images open to the most interpretations. Post-Modernism's (superficial) return to ancient themes lacks emotive power precisely because these collages of architectural motifs are no longer linked with phenomenologically authentic feelings true to architecture. . . .

The Eidos of Architecture

As architects, we do not design buildings primarily as physical objects: we design with regard to the images and emotions of the people who live in them. . . . [The] effect of architecture stems from more or less shared images and basic emotions connected with building.

Phenomenology analyzes such basic responses, and its method has become a more common means of examining architecture, too, in the last few years. A philosophical approach initially attached most closely to the names of philosophers in nature, in contrast to the postivist's standpoint's desire for objectivity. Phenomenology strives to depict phenomena appealing directly to the consciousness as such, without any theories and categories taken from the natural sciences or psychology. Phenomenology thus means examining a phenomenon of the consciousness in its own dimension of consciousness. That, using Husserl's concept, means a "pure looking at" the phenomenon, or "viewing its essence."[2] Phenomenology is a purely theoretical approach to research in the original sense of the Greek word *theoria*, which means precisely "a looking at."

The phenomenology of architecture is thus "looking at" architecture from within the consciousness experiencing it, through architectural feeling, in contrast to the analysis of the physical proportions and properties of the building or a stylistic frame of reference. The phenomenology of architecture seeks the inner language of building. . . .

The Primary Emotions of Architecture
I have said that architecture cannot be a mere play with form. This view does not spring from the self-evident fact that architecture is tied to its practical purpose and many other external conditions. But if a building does not fulfill its basic phenomenological

---

[2] Edmund Husserl, *The Crisis of European Sciences and Transcendental Phenomenology* (Evanston, IL: Northwestern University Press, 1970); Edmund Husserl, *Phenomenology and the Crisis of Philosophy* (New York: Harper & Row, 1965).

conditions as a metaphor of human existence, it is unable to influence the emotions linked in our souls with the images a building creates. An architectural effect is based on a number of what we could call primary emotions. These emotions form the genuine "basic vocabulary" of architecture and it is by working through them that a work becomes architecture and not, for instance, a large-scale sculpture or scenography.

Architecture is a direct expression of existence, of human presence in the world, in the sense that architecture is largely based on a language of the body—of which neither the creator of the work nor the person experiencing the work is aware. . . .

Architecture exists in another reality from our everyday life and pursuits. The emotional force of the ruins of an abandoned house or of rejected objects, stems from the fact that these artifacts make us imagine and share the fate of their owners. They seduce our imagination into wandering away from the world of everyday realities. The quality of architecture does not lie in the sense of reality that it expresses, but in quite the reverse, in architecture's capacity for awakening our imagination.

Architecture is always inhabited by spirits. People known to us may well live in the building, but they are only understudy actors in a waking dream. In reality, architecture is always the home of spirits, the dwelling place of metaphysical beings. . . .

28 BERNARD TSCHUMI, B. 1944

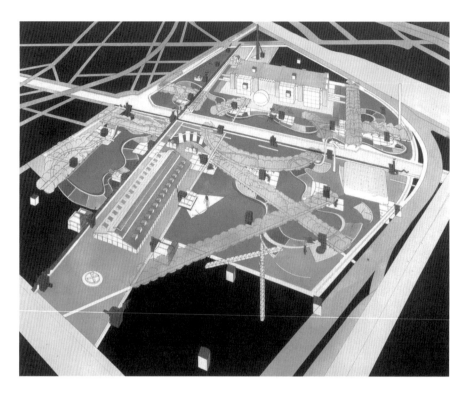

Bernard Tschumi, Parc de la Villette Paris, 1982, axonometric site plan
Courtesy of Bernard Tschumi Architects

Since the 1970s, the work of the Swiss architect, educator, and theorist Bernard Tschumi has challenged accepted ideas of space and program. Through text and design, Tschumi has proposed a novel view of architecture that embraces the "disjunction between use, form and social values." Space, Tschumi has contended, is neutral; the events that take place in a space, the use to which a space is put, are what generate meaning. One implication of this concept is that the correlation between form and function is neither exclusive nor direct, if it exists at all. Tschumi explored this idea in his *folies*, a series of small buildings based on variations of the cube. The *folies* appear at regular intervals throughout the Parisian Parc de la Villette (1982), Tschumi's first major public work, and are designed for no specific purpose. Rather, they can hold whatever programmatic event is deemed appropriate. These *folies* respond to the notion that the architect can never foresee what events actually will occur in a given space, for example, "pole vaulting in the chapel."[*] Variability and unpredictability give rise to unexpected and perhaps unprecedented meanings, interactions, and events. Another version of this idea appears in the text below, "De-, Dis-, Ex-," originally a lecture Tschumi presented in 1987 in which he discussed the de-regulated, dis-integrated, ex-centric nature of late-twentieth-century society.

---

[*] Bernard Tschumi, "Spaces and Events," in *Architecture and Disjunction* (Cambridge, MA: MIT Press, 1996), 146.

"De-, Dis-, Ex-" (1989)

Cities today have no visible limits. In America, they never had. In Europe, however, the concepts of "city" once implied a closed and finite entity. The old city had walls and gates. But these have long ceased to function. Are there other types of gates, new gates to replace the gates of the past? Are the new gates those electronic warning systems installed in airports, screening passengers for weapons? Have electronics and, more generally, technology replaced the boundaries, the guarded borders of the past? The walls surrounding the city have disappeared and, with them, the rules that made the distinction between inside and outside, despite politicians' and planners' guidelines, despite geographical and administrative boundaries. In *"L'Espace Critique,"* Paul Virilio develops a challenging argument for anyone concerned with the making of urban society: Cities have become *deregulated*. This deregulation is reinforced by the fact that much of the city does not belong to the realm of the visible anymore. What was once called urban design has been replaced by a composite of invisible systems. Why should architects still talk about monuments? Monuments are invisible now. They are *disproportionate*—so large (at the scale of the world) that they cannot be seen. Or so small (at the scale of computer chips) that they cannot be seen either.

Remember: architecture was first the art of measure, of proportions. It once allowed whole civilizations to measure time and space. But speed and the telecommunications of images have altered that old role of architecture. *Speed* expands time by contracting space; it negates the notion of physical dimension.

Bernard Tschumi, "De-, Dis-, Ex-," in *Architecture and Disjunction* (Cambridge, MA: MIT Press, 1996) 215–226. First published in Barbara Kruger and Phil Mariani, eds., *Remaking History* (Seattle: Bay Press, 1989). Originally delivered as a lecture at the Dia Foundation (New York, fall 1987). Reprinted with permission of the author and MIT Press.

Of course, physical environment still exists. But, as Virilio suggests, the appearance of permanence (buildings as solid, made of steel, concrete, glass) is constantly challenged by the immaterial representation of abstract systems, from television to electronic surveillance, and so on. Architecture is constantly subject to reinterpretation. In no way can architecture today claim permanence of meaning. Churches are turned into movie houses, banks into yuppie restaurants, hat factories into artists' studios, subway terminals into nightclubs, and sometimes nightclubs into churches. The supposed cause-and-effect relationship between function and form ("form follows function") is forever condemned the day function becomes almost as transient as those magazines and mass media images in which architecture now appears as such a fashionable object.

History, memory, and tradition, once called to the rescue by architectural ideologists, become nothing but modes of disguise, fake regulations, so as to avoid the question of transience and temporality.

When the philosopher Jean-Francois Lyotard speaks about the crisis of the grand narratives of modernity ("progress," the "liberation of humanity," etc.), it only prefigures the crisis of any narrative, any discourse, any mode of representation. The crisis of these grand narratives, their coherent totality, is also the crisis of limits. As with the contemporary city, there are no more boundaries delineating a coherent and homogenous whole. On the contrary, we inhabit a fractured space, made of accidents, where figures are disintegrated, *dis*-integrated. From a sensibility developed during centuries around the "appearance of a stable image" ("balance," "equilibrium," "harmony"), today we favor a sensibility of the disappearance of unstable images: first movies (twenty-four images per second), then television, then computer-generated images, and recently (among a few architects) disjunctions, dislocations, deconstructions. Virilio argues that the abolition of permanence—through the collapse of the notion of distance as a time factor—confuses reality. First deregulation of airlines, then deregulation of Wall

Street, finally deregulation of appearances: it all belongs to the same inexorable logic. Some unexpected consequences, some interesting distortions of long-celebrated icons are to be foreseen. The city and its architecture lose their symbols—no more monuments, no more axes, no more anthropomorphic symmetries, but instead fragmentation, parcellization, atomization, as well as the random superimposition of images that bear no relationship to one another, except through their collision. No wonder that some architectural projects sublimate the idea of *explosion*. A few architects do it in the form of drawings in which floor plans, beams, and walls seem to disintegrate in the darkness of outer space. Some even succeed in building those explosions and other accidents (by giving them the appearance of control—clients want control—but it's only a "simulation").

Hence the fascination for cinematic analogies: on the one hand, moving cranes and expressways and, on the other, montage techniques borrowed from film and video—frames and sequences, lap dissolves, fade-ins and fade-outs, jump cuts, and so forth. One must remember that, initially, the sciences were about substance, about foundation: geology, physiology, physics, and gravity. And architecture was very much part of that concern, with its focus on solidity, firmness, structure, and hierarchy. Those foundations began to crumble in the twentieth century. Relativity, quantum theory, the uncertainty principle: this shakeup occurred not only in physics, as we know, but also in philosophy, the social sciences, and economics.

How then can architecture maintain some solidity, some degree of certainty? It seems impossible today—unless one decides that the accident or the explosion is to be called the rule, the new regulation, through a sort of philosophical inversion that considers the accident the norm and the continuity the exception.

No more certainties, no more continuities. We hear that energy, as well as matter, is a discontinuous structure of points: punctum, quantum. Question: could the only certainty be the *point*?

The crises of determinism, or cause-and-effect relationships, and of continuity completely challenge recent architectural thought. Here, bear with me if I go through a rather tedious but quick recapitulation of "meaning" in architecture—without entering into a detailed discussion of Ferdinand de Saussure or Émile Benveniste. Ethnologists tell us that, in traditional symbolic relations, things have meanings. Quite often the symbolic value is separated from the utilitarian one. The Bauhaus attempted to institute a "universal semanticization of the environment in which everything became the object of function and of signification" (Jean Baudrillard). This functionality, this synthesis of form and function, tried to turn the whole world into a homogenous signifier, objectified as an element of signification: for every form, every signifier, there is an objective signified, a function. By focusing on denotation, it eliminated connotation.

Of course, this dominant discourse of rationality was bound to be attacked. At that time, it was by the surrealists, whose transgressions often relied on the ethics of functionalism, *a contrario*. In fact, some fixed, almost functionalist expectations were necessary to surrealists, for they could only be unsettled through confrontation: the surreal set combining "the sewing machine and the umbrella on the dissecting table" only works because each of these objects represents a precise and unequivocal function.

The transgressed order of functionality that resulted reintroduced the order of the symbolic, now distorted and turned into a poetic phantasm. It liberated the object from its function, denounced the gap between subject and object, and encouraged free association. But such transgressions generally acted upon singular objects, while the world was becoming an environment of ever-increasing complex and abstract systems.

The abstraction of the following years—whether expressionist or geometric—had its architectural equivalent. The endlessly repeated grids of skyscrapers were associated with a new zero-degree of meaning: perfect functionalism.

Fashion upset all that. It had always addressed issues of connotation: against fashion's unstable and ever-disappearing image, the stable and universal denotation of functionalism appeared particular and restrictive.

Partly fascinated by such connotation, partly longing for some long-lost traditional forms, architectural postmodernism in the seventies attempted to combine—to quote Charles Jencks—"modern techniques with traditional building, in order to communicate both with the public *and* with an elite" (hence "double-coding"). It was above all concerned with *codes*, with communicating some *message*, some *signifier* (perhaps characterized by irony, parody, eclecticism). Architectural postmodernism was totally in line with the mission of architecture according to dominant history, which has been to invest shelter with a given meaning.

Ten years later, the illusion was already vanishing. The Doric orders made of painted plywood had begun to warp and peel. The instability, the ephemerality of both signifier and signified, form and function, form and meaning, could only stress the obvious, what Jacques Lacan had pointed out years before: that there is no cause-and-effect relationship between signifier and signified, between word and intended concept. The signifier does not have to answer for its existence in the name of some hypothetical signification. As in literature and psychoanalysis, the architectural signifier does not represent the signified. Doric columns and neon pediments suggest too many interpretations to justify any single one. Again, there is no cause-and-effect relationship between an architectural sign and its possible interpretation. Between signifier and signified stands a barrier: the barrier of actual use. Never mind if this very room was once a fire station, then a furniture storage room, then a ritualistic dance hall, and now a lecture hall (it has been all of these). Each time, these uses distorted both signifier and signified. Not only are linguistic signs arbitrary (as de Saussure showed us long ago), but interpretation is itself open to constant questioning. Every interpretation can be the object of interpretation, and that new interpretation can in turn be interpreted, until every interpretation erases the previous one. The dominant history of architecture, which is a history of the signified, has to be revised, at a time when there is no longer a normative rule, a cause-and-effect relationship between a form and a function, between a signifier and its signified: only a deregulation of meaning.

The deregulation of architecture began long ago, at the end of the nineteenth century, with the world fairs of London and Paris, where light metallic structures radically changed the appearance of architectural solids. Suddenly, architecture was merely scaffolding supporting glass, and it was discredited as the "solid," symbolic character of masonry and stone. Human scale ceased to be an issue, as the logic of industrial construction took over. Human proportions from the ages of classicism and humanism were rapidly replaced by grids and modular systems, a superimposition of light and materials that were becoming increasingly immaterial—another form of deconstruction.

In the mid-seventies, nostalgic architects, longing for meaning and tradition, applied sheetrock and plywood cutouts to those scaffoldings, but the images they were trying to provide were weak in comparison to the new scaffoldings of our time: the mediatized images of ephemeral representations.

"To represent construction or to construct representation" (Virilio): this is the new question of our time. As Albert Einstein said, "There is no scientific truth, only temporary representations, ever-accelerating sequences of representation." In fact, we are forced to go through a complete reconsideration of all concepts of figuration and representation: the constant storm of images (whether drawings, graphs, photographs, films, television, or computer-generated images) increasingly negates any attempt to restore the Renaissance ideal of the unity of reality and its representation. The concept of double-coding was the last and futile attempt to keep some of that ideal intact by establishing a new relation between communication and tradition. It is the word "tradition" that misled much of the architectural scene in the late seventies and made some aspects of architectural postmodernism what I think will soon appear as a short-lived avatar of history: a form of contextual eclecticism that has been recurrent throughout architectural history, with and without irony, allegory, and other parodies.

In any case, the problem is not a problem of images: gables and classical orders, however silly, are free to be consumed by whoever wishes to do so. But to pretend that these images could suggest new rules and regulations in architecture and urbanism by transcending modernism is simply misplaced.

There are no more rules and regulations. The current metropolitan deregulation caused by the dis-industrialization of European and American cities, by the collapse of zoning strategies, contradicts any attempt to develop new sets of regulating forces, however desirable it may be for some. The 1987 Wall Street "crash" and its relation to the economic deregulation that immediately preceded it is another illustration that an important change has taken place. Let me go back to Virilio's argument. In the Middle Ages, society was self-regulated, auto-regulated. Regulation took place at its center. The prince of the city was the ruler; there was a direct cause-and-effect relationship between rules and everyday life, between the weight of masonry and the way that buildings were built.

In the industrial era, societies became artificially regulated. The power of economic and industrial forces took over by establishing a coherent structure throughout the whole territory: control was defined at the limits, at the edges of society. The relation between rules and everyday life ceased to be clear, and so large bureaucracies and administrators took over. Regulation was not at the center anymore but at the periphery. Abstract architecture used grids on its sheds International-style, before it discovered that one could decorate the same shed Multinational-style—regardless of what happened in them. Function, form, and meaning ceased to have any relationship to one another.

Today we have entered the age of deregulation, where control takes place *outside* of society, as in those computer programs that feed on one another endlessly in a form of autonomy, recalling the autonomy of language described by Michel Foucault. We witness the separation of people and language, the decentering of the subject. Or, we might say, the complete *decentering of society*.

Ex-centric, dis-integrated, dis-located, dis-juncted, deconstructed, dismantled, disassociated, discontinuous, deregulated . . . de-, dis-, ex-. These are the prefixes of today. Not post-, neo-, or pre-.

29 Rem Koolhaas, b. 1944

Office for Metropolitan Architects and LMN Architects, Seattle Central Library, Seattle, WA, 1999–2004
View from the corner of Madison Street and Fourth Avenue
Photo courtesy of the Seattle Public Library

In 1978, a Dutch journalist/screenwriter-turned-architect published *Delirious New York*. This engrossing book analyzed what the author termed the "culture of congestion" that characterized densely populated lower Manhattan. The author, Rem Koolhaas, welcomed the chaos of this metropolitan realm in which the skyscraper, with wildly disparate programs on each floor, was the ultimate "Social Condenser: a machine to generate and intensify desirable forms of human intercourse."[*] Where else could one discover the promise of new interactions and experiences such as "Eating oysters with boxing gloves, naked on the *n*th floor?"[†] Embedded in this explication of the skyscraper was a related yet distinct topic Koolhaas would later address: Bigness. Aptly, Koolhaas's meditations on this subject, "Bigness, or the Problem of the Large," appeared in *S, M, L, XL*, a hefty publication of 1995. In a discipline so fond of theorizing, Bigness, Koolhaas announced, has yet to be theorized. This "absence," he continued, "is architecture's most debilitating weakness," precisely because "only Bigness instigates the *regime of complexity* that mobilizes the full intelligence of architecture and its related fields." With this in mind, Koolhaas discussed the particular architectural qualities engendered by Bigness, issues he has no doubt encountered in his many design projects. Thus "Bigness, or the Problem of the Large" can be understood both as Koolhaas's attempt to conceptualize this neglected subject and to set forth thoughts conceived in the process of Big design.

---

[*] Rem Koolhaas, *Delirious New York* (1978; New York: Monacelli Press, 1994), 152.

[†] Ibid., 155.

"Bigness, or the Problem of Large" (1993)

Species

Beyond a certain scale, architecture acquires the properties of BIGNESS. The best reason to broach BIGNESS is the one given by climbers of Mount Everest: "because it is there." BIGNESS is the ultimate architecture.

It seems incredible that the size of a building alone embodies an ideological problem, independent of the will of its architects.

Of all possible categories, BIGNESS does not seem to deserve a manifesto; discredited as an intellectual problem, it is apparently on its way to extinction—like the dinosaur—through clumsiness, slowness, inflexibility, difficulty. But in fact, only BIGNESS instigates the *regime of complexity* that mobilizes the full intelligence of architecture and its related fields.

One hundred years ago, a generation of conceptual breakthroughs and supporting technologies unleashed an architectural BIG BANG. By randomizing circulation, short-circuiting distance, artificializing interiors, reducing mass, stretching dimensions, and accelerating construction, the elevator, electricity, air-conditioning, steel, and finally, the new infrastructures formed a cluster of mutations that induced another *species* of architecture. The combined effects of these inventions were structures taller and deeper—BIGGER—than ever before conceived, with a parallel potential for the reorganization of the social world—a vastly richer programmation.

Rem Koolhaas, "Bigness, or the Problem of the Large," OMA, Rem Koolhaas, and Bruce Man, *S, M, L, XL* (New York: Monacelli Press, 1995), 494–516. © 1994 by Rem Koolhaas and the Monacelli Press, Inc. Reprinted with permission of author and publisher.

Theorems

Fuelled initially by the thoughtless energy of the purely quantitative, BIGNESS has been, for nearly a century, a condition almost without thinkers, a revolution without program.

Delirious New York implied a latent "Theory of BIGNESS" based on five theorems:

1. Beyond a certain critical mass, a building becomes a BIG Building. Such a mass can no longer be controlled by a singular architectural gesture, or even by any combination of architectural gestures. The impossibility triggers the autonomy of its parts, which is different from fragmentation: the parts remain committed to the whole.

2. The elevator—with its potential to establish mechanical rather than architectural connections—and its family of related inventions render null and void the classical repertoire of architecture. Issues of composition, scale, proportion, detail are now moot. The 'art' of architecture is useless in BIGNESS.

3. In BIGNESS, the distance between core and envelope increases to the point where the façade can no longer reveal what happens inside. The humanist expectation of 'honesty' is doomed; interior and exterior architectures become separate projects, one dealing with the instability of programmatic and iconographic needs, the other—agent of disinformation—offering the city the apparent stability of an object. Where architecture reveals, BIGNESS perplexes; BIGNESS transforms the city from a summation of certainties into an accumulation of mysteries. What you see is no longer what you get.

4. Through size alone, such buildings enter an amoral domain, beyond good and bad. Their impact is independent of their quality.

5. Together, all these breaks—with scale, with architectural composition, with tradi-

tion, with transparency, with ethics—imply the final, most radical break: BIGNESS is no longer part of any tissue. It exists; at most, it coexists. Its subtext is *fuck* context.

Maximum

. . . The absence of a theory of BIGNESS—what is the maximum architecture can do?—is architecture's most debilitating weakness. Without a theory of BIGNESS, architects are in the position of Frankenstein's creators: instigators of a partly successful experiment whose results are running amok and are therefore discredited.

Because there is no theory of BIGNESS, we don't know what to do with it, we don't know where to put it, we don't know when to use it, we don't know how to plan it.

Big mistakes are our only connection to BIGNESS. But in spite of its dumb name, BIGNESS is a theoretical domain at this fin de siècle: in a landscape of disarray, disassembly, dissociation, disclamation, the attraction of BIGNESS is its potential to reconstruct the whole, resurrect the real, reinvent the collective, reclaim maximum possibility.

Only through BIGNESS can architecture dissociate itself from the exhausted ideological and artistic movements of modernism and formalism to regain its instrumentality as a vehicle of modernization.

BIGNESS recognizes that architecture as we know it is in difficulty, but it does not overcompensate through regurgitations of even more architecture. It proposes a new economy in which "all is architecture" no longer, but in which a strategic position is regained through retreat and concentration, yielding the rest of a contested territory to enemy forces.

Beginning

BIGNESS destroys, but it is also a new beginning. It can reassemble what it breaks.

A paradox of BIGNESS is that in spite of the calculation that goes into its planning—in fact, through its very rigidities—it is the one architecture that engineers the unpredictable. Instead of enforcing coexistence, BIGNESS depends on regimes of freedoms, the assembly of maximum difference.

Only BIGNESS can sustain a promiscuous proliferation of events in a single container. It develops strategies to organize both their independence and interdependence within the larger entity in a symbiosis that exacerbates rather than compromises specificity.

Through contamination rather than purity and quantity rather than quality, only BIGNESS can support genuinely new relationships between functional entities that expand rather than limit their identities. The artificiality and complexity of BIGNESS release function from its defensive armor to allow a kind of liquefaction; programmatic elements react with each other to create new events—BIGNESS returns to a model of programmatic alchemy.

At first sight, the activities amassed in the structure of BIGNESS *demand* to interact, but BIGNESS also keeps them apart. Like plutonium rods that, more or less immersed, dampen or promote nuclear reaction, BIGNESS regulates the intensities of programmatic coexistence.

Although BIGNESS is a blueprint for a perpetual performance, it also offers degrees of serenity and even blandness. It is simply impossible to animate its entire mass with intention. Its vastness exhausts architecture's compulsion to decide and determine. Zones will be left out, free from architecture.

Team
BIGNESS is where architecture becomes both most and least architectural: most because of the enormity of the object; least through the loss of autonomy—it becomes

instrument of other forces, it *depends*. BIGNESS is impersonal: the architect is no longer condemned to stardom.

Beyond signature, BIGNESS means surrender to technologies; to engineers, contractors, manufacturers; to others. It promises architecture a kind of post-heroic status—a re-alignment with neutrality.

Even as BIGNESS enters the stratosphere of architectural ambition—the pure chill of megalomania—it can be achieved only at the price of giving up control, of transmog-rification. It implies a web of umbilical cords to other disciplines whose performance is at critical as the architect's: like mountain climbers tied together by life-saving ropes, the makers of BIGNESS are a team (a word not mentioned in the last forty years of architectural polemic).

Bastion
If BIGNESS transforms architecture, its accumulation generates a new kind of city.

The exterior of the city is no longer a collective theater where 'it' happens; there's no collective 'it' left. The street has become residue, organizational device, mere segment of the continuous metropolitan plane where the remnants of the past face the equip-ments of the new in an uneasy standoff. BIGNESS can exist *anywhere* in that plane.

Not only is BIGNESS incapable of establishing relationships with the classical city—*at most, it coexists*—but in the quantity and complexity of the facilities it offers, it is it-self urban. BIGNESS no longer needs the city: it competes with the city; it preempts the city; or better still, it *is* the city. If urbanism generated potential and architecture exploits it, BIGNESS enlists the generosity of urbanism against the meanness of archi-tecture. BIGNESS = urbanism vs. architecture.

BIGNESS, through its very independence of context, is the one architecture than can survive, even exploit, the now-global condition of the tabula rasa: it does not take its inspiration from givens too often squeezed for the last drop of meaning; it gravitates opportunistically to locations of maximum infrastructural promise; it is, finally, its own *raison d'être*.

In spite of its size, it is modest. Not all architecture, not all program, not all events will be swallowed by BIGNESS. There are many 'needs' too unfocused, too weak, too unrespectable, too defiant, too secret, too subversive, too weak, too 'nothing' to be part of the constellations of BIGNESS.

BIGNESS is the last bastion of architecture—a contraction, a hyperarchitecture. The containers of BIGNESS will be landmarks in a postarchitectural landscape—a world scraped of architecture in the way Richter's paintings are scraped of paint: inflexible, immutable, definitive, forever there, generated through superhuman effort. BIGNESS surrenders the field to after-architecture.

30 DANIEL LIBESKIND, B. 1946

In the 1988 Deconstructivist Architecture exhibition at the New York Museum of Modern Art, the work of the Polish-American architect Daniel Libeskind was featured alongside those of Rem Koolhaas, Frank Gehry, Bernard Tschumi, Peter Eisenman, Zaha Hadid, and Coop-Himmelblau. What united these architects, according to the show's cocurator Mark Wigley, was their "ability to disturb our thinking about form."* Indeed, their works in general are characterized by fractured, skewed, abstracted elements. But that is where the similarities end; indeed, the divergence between their design philosophies is striking. Libeskind speaks most openly of the spiritual nature of architecture—spiritual in an emotive, experiential, and humanistic sense. This approach is conveyed in his architecture, whether it be his first large public commission, the Jewish Museum in Berlin (1989–99, opened 2001), or his most famous recent project, the Master Plan for the World Trade Center in New York (awarded 2003). The mystical nature of things present but not seen and the potential strength of architecture as a communicative device come through quite clearly in Libeskind's writings, including the comments below, originally issued in 1997 as his acceptance speech for an honorary degree from Humboldt University in Berlin.

---

* Mark Wigley, *Deconstructivist Architecture* (New York: Museum of Modern Art, 1988). Wigley curated the exhibition with Philip Johnson.

"Proof of Things Invisible" (1997)

As I was thinking about what to say today I realized how difficult it is for an architect to speak about his work without the usual paraphernalia of slide projectors and images. Architecture, which is evoked only by words, makes one almost feel 'at home' in language. By surrounding oneself with language one almost comes to believe that one has escaped from the opacity of space and that what remains 'out there' is only an empty stage set. That is perhaps why most intelligent people apply their intelligence and analytic powers to everything but architecture; why architecture is given over to technicians and specialists, and why one is resigned to it as an inevitable and anonymous force which will shape the cities without one's personal participation.

The experience of alienation from architecture, as a dimension of culture, should be contrasted with the stark and astonished encounter with IT—crowned-out, spewed-out into night—resistant to theorization. For then, one might see that architecture—something static and unfeeling, as all that's turned into a coming—can be interpreted, but itself continues to remain oblivious to the interpretation. It continues to live its own existence whether we share it or not.

Perhaps language and its meaning [are] grounded in the spaces of architecture, and not vice-versa. Consider the functions of foundation, circumcision, territorialization, openness and closure. These are all experiences of space—and of a certain kind of architecture—which provide a symbolic model and understanding of life itself. Is archi-

Daniel Libeskind, "Proof of Things Invisible," http://www.daniel-libeskind.com/words. Acceptance speech for an honorary doctorate awarded by Humbolt University, Berlin, in 1997. Reprinted with permission from the author.

tecture not the quintessential 'taken for granted,' the unthinkable, the monstrous, the gender-less, the repressed, the other? Perhaps this is the point of its madness, perhaps it is your conscience: the knot of life in which what is recognized is untied. And what thinking person does not want a fire-place, a home, a Utopia, 'the way it is,' 'the way it was'? What thoughtful person is not grateful for the beams of clear lines directed by this silent ray?

What ineffable—immeasurable power of building in the city! The epiphany of the constructible is the strange sucking of the earth's axis. In the realm of architecture, ideas having stared at Medusa turn to stone. Here it is matter which carries the aura of ideas—ideas which metastasize into crystalline sleep-shapes assumed in the language shadow. Wasps, buildings, antennae sting the air, driving the sting to pass through the world of dream and death in order to sense this axis: The Earth's Axis.

All this is accomplished through technique such as drawing wherein an exiled line falls to the ground. Two parallel lines signify a wall; precisely the wall which is between the lines and is not a line. Whether this wall imprisons and releases depends on whether one is a saint or a prisoner. It is doubly illegible; twice over. In attempting to surmount the inner poles of this contradiction, architecture becomes like the plow, turning time up, revealing its invisible layers on the surface.

The power of building is certainly more than meets the eye. It is the non-thematized, the twilight, the marginal, event. But architecture forming this background is a surplus beyond obvious need: that which itself has no legitimacy in a proper foundation. This has led some to ask whether the true and the real need to be embodied at all. Whether one needs architecture or just a simulation mechanism. Whether architecture can flutter nearby like a spirit, the bell or the Internet. It cannot.

In its opacity and resistance, architecture rebels and communicates that only the superfluous, the transcendent, the ineffable is allied to us: the sky, the stars, the gods. I would like to confess my fascination for this strange activity, quite distant from the obsessive technologism, globalized marketing and withered modernism progressively eradicating spiritual life.

I would like to share with you something about the nature of the approach to architecture which I am following, through buildings which not only house exhibitions within them but as architectural works 'exhibit' the world; are indeed the 'production' of the earth. Together they delineate a trajectory which musters the letters, mortal-immortal; show the Aleph as coming after the Beit; the alphabet after the House. Henry Adams considered the Virgin as the mobilizing form of medieval times and compared her to the dynamo, the mechanism of industrialization. Were he to write today, he would perhaps add to the Virgin and the dynamo—the Museum—as the catalyst and conveyor of reality, since this institution is seen today as a force able to regenerate areas of experience, revive histories, transform images and create a new identity.

Throughout my projects I have followed a certain path which one could name as the search for the Irreplaceable, that which was known by the pagans as the genus loci. I am interested in the unique portrayal of architecture and space of provinces, mountains, maps, ships, horoscopes, fish, instruments, rooms, stars, horses, texts, people. In this labyrinth of places, one can discover the uniqueness of a human face and of a particular hand as a figure of architecture and of the city.

Lines of history and of events; lines of experience and of the look; lines of drawing and of construction. These vectors form a patterned course towards 'the unsubsided' which paradoxically grows more heavy as it becomes more light. I think of it as that which cannot be buried: that which cannot be extinguished: Call it Architecture if you want. . . .

Architecture's reality is as old as the substance of the things hoped for. It is the proof of things invisible. Contrary to public opinion the flesh of architecture is not cladding, insulation and structure, but the substance of the individual in society and history; a figuration of the inorganic and organic, the body and the soul, and that which is visible beyond.

Some would deny this substance and as a result might themselves vanish into the emptiness of "facts" which as indices of power are only the illusory ghosts of a virtual world. One must reject the emptiness of ideologies, the nihilistic obsession with the return of the same, the vacuity of systems which base the whole on its part. The road to authentic construction, just like a smile, cannot be faked for it remains insubordinate, not slave. . . .

The Spiritual in architecture is urgent, though it seems to have become an embarrassment, a rumor on the street. The spiritual, appropriated by the fundamentalist right, has been expropriated from culture and history, eliminated from discourse through which it should be reclaimed. One should attempt to retrieve the spirit of architecture, to recall its Humanity, even within a situation in which the goal and the way have been eclipsed. The erasure of history and its carriers, the obliviousness of the market economy to the degradation and ongoing genocide of human beings must be countered with a deeper awareness and action.

Architecture is and remains the ethical, the true, the good and the beautiful, no matter what those who know the price of everything and the value of nothing may say.

Contemporary architecture is split bitterness/sweetness, strictly, the ends of its smile go off into the anarchy of life, opening a paradoxical freedom.

Greg Lynn's meditations and architectural projects have stimulated and contributed to the discipline's growing interest in computer-aided design. As an architect and philosopher, Lynn has reconceptualized the traditional practice of architecture, challenging the notion of the architectural object as static and fixed and the accepted method of "paper" design. Relying on the computer as a design tool, not solely a representational device, Lynn incorporates environmental and programmatic factors into the formation of his structures, creating an architecture that, in its form and organization, reflects the conditions of its site and intended use. The resulting work, rarely rectilinear, conveys a sense of fluidity and motion that suggest the forces that act on it. A former member of Peter Eisenman's architectural firm, Lynn's abstraction stems not from an attempt to strip architecture of external meaning, but rather reflects his desire to integrate an array of information into the process of architectural production.

Animate Form (1999)

Animation is a term which differs from, but is often confused with, motion. While motion implies movement and action, animation implies evolution of a form and its shaping forces; it suggests animalism, animism, growth, actuation, vitality and virtuality.[1] In its manifold implications, animation touches on many of architecture's most deeply embedded assumptions about its structure. What makes animation so problematic for architects is that they have maintained an ethics of statics in their discipline. Because of its dedication to permanence, architecture is one of the last modes of thought based on the inert. More than even its traditional role of providing shelter, architects are expected to provide culture with stasis. This desire for timelessness is intimately linked with interest in formal purity and autonomy. Challenging these assumptions by introducing architecture to models of organization that are not inert will not threaten the essence of the discipline, but will advance it. Just as the development of calculus drew upon the historical mathematical developments that preceded it, so too will an animate approach to architecture subsume traditional models of statics into a more advanced system of dynamic organizations. Traditionally, in architecture, the abstract space of design is conceived as an environment of force and motion rather than as a neutral vacuum. In naval design, for example, the abstract space of design is imbued with the properties of flow, turbulence, viscosity, and drag so that the form of

Greg Lynn, *Animate Form* (New York: Princeton Architectural Press, 1999), 9–11, 13–16, 41. Reproduced with permission from the publisher. All terms in bold face were treated as such by Lynn in his original text.

[1] For varied and rigorous discussions of the animal as the surrogate, model and metaphor for architecture in history, theory and design, see the chapter "Donkey Urbanism" in Catherine Ingraham's book *Architecture and the Burdens of Linearity* (New Haven: Yale University Press, 1998), as well as her essay, "Animals 2: The Problem of Distinction (Insects, For Example)" in *Assemblage* 14 (Cambridge, MA: MIT Press, 1991),25–29.

a hull can be conceived in motion through water. Although the form of a boat hull is designed to anticipate motion, there is no expectation that its shape will change. An ethics of motion neither implies nor precludes literal motion. Form can be shaped by the collaboration between an envelope and the active context in which it is situated. While physical form can be defined in terms of static coordinates, the visual force of the environment in which it is designed contributes to its shape. The particular form of a hull stores multiple vectors of motion and flow from the space in which it was designed. A sailboat hull, for example, is designed as a planing surface. For sailing into the wind, the hull is designed to heal, presenting a greater surface area to the water. A boat hull does not change its shape when it changes direction, obviously, but variable points of sail are incorporated into its surface. In this way, topology allows for not just the incorporation of a single moment but rather a multiplicity of vectors, and therefore, a multiplicity of times, in a single continuous surface.

Likewise, the forms of a dynamically conceived architecture may be shaped in association with virtual motion and force, but again, this does not mandate that the architecture change its shape. Actual movement often involves a mechanical paradigm of multiple discrete positions,whereas virtual movement allows form to occupy a multiplicity of possible positions continuously with the same form.

The term **virtual** has recently been so debased that it often simply refers to the digital space of computer-aided design. It is often used interchangeably with the term simulation. Simulation, unlike virtuality, is not intended as a diagram for future possible concrete assemblage but is instead a visual substitute. "Virtual reality" might describe architectural design but as it is used to describe a simulated environment it would be better replaced by "simulated reality" or "substitute reality." Thus, use of the term virtual here refers to an abstract scheme that has the possibility of becoming actualized, often in a variety of possible configurations. Since architects produce drawings of buildings and not buildings themselves, architecture, more than any other discipline, is involved with the production of virtual descriptions.

There is one aspect of virtuality that architects have neglected, however, and that is the principle of virtual force and the differential variation it implies. Architectural form is conventionally conceived in a dimensional space of idealized stasis, defined by Cartesian fixed-point coordinates. An object defined as a vector whose trajectory is relative to other objects, forces, fields and flows, defines form within an active space of force and motion. This shift from a passive space of static coordinates to an active space of interactions implies a move from autonomous purity to contextual specificity.[2]

Contemporary animation and special-effects software are just now being introduced as tools for design rather than as devices for rendering, visualization and imaging.[3]

The dominant mode for discussing architecture has been the cinematic model, where the multiplication and sequencing of static snap-shots simulates movement. The problem with the motion-picture analogy is that architecture occupies the role of static frame through which motion progresses. Force and motion are eliminated from form only to be reintroduced, after the fact of design, through concepts and techniques of optical procession.

---

[2] It is important to any discussion of parameter-based design that there be both the unfolding of an internal system and the unfolding of contextual information fields. This issue of contextualism is discussed more extensively in my essay "Architectural Curvilinearity: The Folded, the Pliant and the Supple," in *Architectural Design* 102, *Folding in Architecture* (London, 1993) where in the same volume it is also criticized by Jeffrey Kipnis in his essay "Towards a New Architecture."

[3] There are two instances of architectural theorists and designers crossing over from models of cinema to models of animation. The first is Brian Boigon's "The Cartoon Regulators" in *Assemblage* 19 (Cambridge, MA: MIT Press, 1992), 66–71. The second is Mark Rakatansky's discussions of the writing and animation of Chuck Jones regarding theories of mobility, action, and gesture in *Any Magazine* 23 (New York, 1998).

In contrast, animate design is defined by the co-presence of motion and force at the moment of formal conception. Force is an initial condition, the cause of both motion and the particular inflections of a form. For example, in what is called *"inverse kinematic"* animation, the motion and shape of a form is defined by multiple interacting vectors that unfold in time perpetually and openly. With these techniques, entities are given vectorial properties before they are released into a space differentiated by gradients of force. Instead of a neutral, abstract space for design, the context for design becomes an active abstract space that directs form within a current of forces that can be stored as information in the shape of the form. Rather than as a frame through which time and space pass, architecture can be modeled as a participant immersed within dynamic flows. In addition to the special-effects and animation industries, many other disciplines such as aeronautical design, naval design, and automobile design employ this animate approach to modeling form in a space that is a medium of movement and force. . . .

Stasis is a concept which has been intimately linked with architecture in at least five important ways, including 1) permanence, 2) usefulness, 3) typology, 4) procession, and 5) verticality. However, statics does not hold an essential grip on architectural thinking as much as it is a lazy habit or default that architects either choose to reinforce or contradict for lack of a better model. Each of these assumptions can be transformed once the virtual space in which architecture is conceptualized is mobilized with both time and force. With the example of permanence, the dominant cultural expectation is that buildings must be built for eternity when in fact most buildings are built to persist for only a short time. Rather than designing for permanence, techniques for obsolescence, dismantling, ruination, recycling and abandonment through time warrant exploration. Another characteristic of static models is that of functional fixity. Buildings are often assumed to have a particular and fixed relationship to their programs, whether they are intersected, combined or even flexibly programmed. Typological fixity, of the kind promoted by Colin Rowe for instance, depends on a closed static order to underlie a family of continuous variations. This concept of a discrete, ideal, and fixed prototype can be subsumed by the model of the numerically controlled multi-type that is flexible, mutable, and differential. This multi-type, or **performance envelope**, does not privilege a fixed type but instead models a series of relationships or expressions between a range of potentials. Similarly, independent interacting variables can be linked to influence one another through logical expressions defining the size, position, rotation, direction, or speed of an object by looking to other objects for their characteristics. This concept of an envelope of potential from which either a single or a series of **instances** can be taken, is radically different from the idea of a fixed prototype that can be varied.

Finally, static models underwrite the retrograde understanding of gravity as a simple, unchanging, vertical force. Architecture remains as the last refuge for members of the flat-earth society. The relationships of structure to force and gravity are by definition multiple and interrelated, yet architects tend to reduce these issues to what is still held as a central truth: that buildings stand up vertically. In fact, there are multiple interacting structural pressures exerted on buildings from many directions, including lateral wind loads, uplift, shear, and earthquakes, to name a few of the non-vertical conditions. Any one of these **live** loads could easily exceed the relative weight of the building and its vertical **dead** loads. The naive understanding of structure as primarily a problem of the vertical transfer of dead gravity loads to the ground excludes, for instance, the fact that lighter buildings have a tendency to uplift; the main structural concern in these cases is how to tether the roof. Of course architects and structural engineers do not ignore these other structural factors, but the primary perception of structure has always been that it should be vertical. A reconceptualization of ground and verticality in light of complex vectors and movements might not change the expediency and need for level floors, but it would open up possibilities for structure and support that take into account orientations other than the simply vertical.

These concerns are not merely technical as architecture presently expresses also the cultural diagrams of stasis. Despite the popular conception among architects that gravity is a fact, the contemporary debates about theories of gravity could inform present discussions of architecture in the same spirit that they have done in the past. The history of theories of gravity are extremely nuanced, fascinating and unresolved. Since the time of Sir Isaac Newton, gravity has been accepted as the mutual relative attraction of masses in space. Given a constant mass, stability is achieved through orbits rather than stasis. This distinction between stasis and orbital or dynamic stability is important. In the case of a single, simple gravity, **stasis** is the ordering system through the unchanging constant force of a ground point. In the case of a more complex concept of gravity, mutual attraction generates motion; **stability** is the ordering of motion into rhythmic phases. In the simple, static model of gravity, motion is eliminated at the beginning. In the complex, stable model of gravity, motion is an ordering principle. Likewise, discreteness, timelessness, and fixity are characteristics of stasis; multiplicity, change, and development are characteristics of stability. . . .

If architecture is to approach this more complex concept of gravity, its design technologies should also incorporate factors of time and motion. Throughout the history of architecture, descriptive techniques have impacted the way in which architectural design and construction has been practiced. . . . Events such as the advent of perspective, stereometric projection, and other geometric techniques have extended the descriptive repertoire of architectural designers. In our present age, the virtual space within which architecture is conceived is now being rethought by the introduction of advanced motion tools and a constellation of new diagrams based on the computer. . . .

The availability and rapid colonization of architecture design by computer-aided techniques presents the discipline with yet another opportunity to both retool and rethink itself as it did with the advent of stereometric projection and perspective. If there is a single concept that must be engaged due to the proliferation of topological shapes and computer-aided tools, it is that in their structure as abstract machines, these technologies are animate.

32 NORMAN FOSTER, B. 1935

Foster and Partners, Hearst Tower, New York City, NY, 2000–06
Photo courtesy of Nigel Young and Foster and Partners

Throughout his career, the British architect Norman Foster has relied on technological experimentation to create user-friendly and environmentally sensitive architecture. His relationship with Buckminster Fuller, with whom he collaborated on various projects during the 1970s and early 1980s, contributed to Foster's focus on his buildings' occupants and ecological concerns. Foster's first major work, the Willis Faber Dumas Building (1975) in Ipswich, England, took both issues into account. To provide a pleasant atmosphere for the company's workers, Foster's design incorporated amenities such as an open-air rooftop garden and restaurant and an indoor swimming pool. Innovative structural and mechanical systems allowed for flowing, flexible interior space infused with natural light. This hi-tech, glass-sheathed edifice was a precursor for many of Foster's later works, including the recently completed Hearst Tower in New York City (2000–06). This office tower utilizes recycled building materials, innovative steel structural bracing, a rainwater collection and rehabilitation system, and sensors to regulate energy use. A percentage of the harnessed rainwater contributes to a three-story "Icefall," a sculptural installation that helps cool, humidify, and animate the atrium of the Hearst Tower. Workers also benefit from maximum natural illumination afforded by the building's extensive glass skin. These inventive technological features attest to Foster's interest in user comfort and environmentally responsible design. As Foster conveys in the essay below, such issues will continue to guide his work.

"The Architecture of the Future" (1999)

The architecture of the future will, by necessity, be one that addresses the world's increasing ecological crisis. Architecture can contribute to dealing with the crisis to a degree that few other activities can. Buildings use half of the energy consumed in the developed world, yet virtually every building could be designed to run on a fraction of current energy levels.

Why do we rely so heavily upon artificial lighting when we can easily design buildings that are filled with daylight? Why do we continue to rely upon wasteful air-conditioning systems in locations where we could simply open a window? A holistic approach to architecture—one that sees buildings as the sum of all the systems at work within them—is the start of the solution to our problems. Structure, form and materials each have their part to play in this. Natural lighting and ventilation, recycled rainwater, and heat recycled from lights, computers and people, for example, can all contribute to reducing a building's energy demands.

Applying these methods in the Reichstag, in Berlin, we were able to reduce the building's energy requirements to such an extent that it creates more energy than it consumes. Our integrated energy strategy has also allowed us to reduce pollution; the Reichstag burns renewable vegetable oil, rather than dwindling fossil fuels, which has led to a dramatic reduction in the building's carbon dioxide emissions. If a nineteenth-century building can be transformed from an energy guzzler into a building so efficient that it is now a net provider of energy—literally a power station for its neighborhood—how much

Norman Foster, "The Architecture of the Future," in *On Foster, Foster On* (Munich: Prestel Publishing, 2000). © 2000, Foster and Partners, London and Prestel Verlag, Munich-London-New York. Reprinted with permission from the author and publisher.

easier is it to design new buildings that make responsible use of precious resources?

However, individual buildings cannot be viewed in isolation. They must be seen in the context of our ever expanding cities and their infrastructures. Unchecked urban sprawl is one of the chief problems facing the world today. One example will serve to illustrate this phenomenon. In the period 1970–1990 the population of greater Chicago increased by a mere 4 percent, yet its physical area grew by 50 percent. Moreover, the peripheral growth of cities is rarely accompanied by integrated public transport networks or other services. Instead, people are forced to travel greater distances by car, creating congestion and pollution.

Higher urban densities provide one solution to this problem—it is surprising to discover that the world's two most densely populated areas, Monaco and Macao, are at opposite ends of the economic spectrum. High density—or high rise—does not automatically mean overcrowding or economic hardship; it can also lead to an improved quality of life, where housing, work and leisure facilities are all close by.

The Millennium Tower that we have proposed in Tokyo takes a traditional horizontal city quarter—housing, shops, restaurants, cinemas, museums, sporting facilities, green spaces and public transport networks—and turns it on its side to create a super-tall building with a multiplicity of uses. It would be over 800 metres high with 170 storeys—twice the height of anything so far built—and would house a community of up to 60,000 people. This is 20,000 more than the population of Monaco and yet the building would occupy only 0.013 square kilometres of land in comparison to Monaco's 1.95 square kilometres. It would create a virtually self-sufficient, fully self-sustaining community in the sky.

This sounds like future fantasy. But we now have all the means at our disposal to create such buildings. There are no technological barriers to a sustainable architecture, only ones of political will. The architecture of the future could be the architecture of today.

33 SAMUEL MOCKBEE, 1944–2001

In the early 1990s, Samuel Mockbee left his well-established private practice and dedicated his attention to the creation of a socially responsible architecture. Mockbee's mission was two-fold: to create dignified, low-budget architecture for the impoverished and to cultivate a new generation of culturally aware architects. He accomplished these goals with the Rural Studio, a philanthropic initiative run through Auburn University. After immersing themselves in the community and determining the clients' needs, students under Mockbee's leadership designed and constructed small-scale sustainable structures such as housing and recreational centers for the underprivileged inhabitants of Hale Country, Alabama. The works often utilized unconventional materials such as hay bales, discarded license plates, and salvaged items to devise inexpensive contemporary structures based on local vernacular forms. Since Mockbee's death in 2001, the Rural Studio has continued to thrive, existing as a model for an innovative, socially conscious alternative to traditional methods of architectural practice.

"The Hero of Hale County" (2001)

This is the eighth year that Samuel Mockbee and his architecture students at Auburn University have been designing and building striking houses and community buildings for impoverished residents of Alabama's Hale County. In some ways, the place has changed little since James Agee and Walker Evans went there in 1936 to document the lives of poor white sharecroppers. The 1990 Census shows per capita income still averaging no more than $8,164 and 1,700 families still living in substandard houses. Most of the Rural Studio's clients are African-Americans, "left behind by Reconstruction," as Mockbee says. Many live in unheated, leaky shacks without plumbing in Masons Bend, a little settlement of about 150 people tucked into a bend of Black Warrior River at the end of a winding dirt road about 10 miles from Greensboro, the county seat.

In addition to being a social welfare venture, the Rural Studio—Taliesin South, it's been called—it also an education experiment and a prod to the architectural profession to act on its finest instincts. In June, Mockbee learned he had been awarded a MacArthur "genius grant." Not long afterward, speaking in the deep drawl of his region, the burly, bearded sixth-generation Mississippian had the following conversation with contributing editor Andrea Oppenheimer Dean:

ARCHITECTURAL RECORD: *What Will You Do With $500,000?*
SAM MOCKBEE: It'll allow me to take care of my family and get way out on the edge in my work and maybe do something that most people would think I was crazy to do, follow my instincts, let a project evolve, and concentrate on it. More than likely it'll be for the Rural Studio.

Samuel Mockbee, "The Hero of Hale County," interview by Andrea Oppenheimer Dean, *Architectural Record* 189, n. 2, (February 2001) 76–82. Reprinted with permission from the publisher, McGraw-Hill.

AR: *Any ideas what the project might be?*

SM: You know the profession's IDP internship development program? It is a well-intended program, but most interns dread it. I would like to offer architecture graduates an opportunity to come down to the Rural Studio as intern architects, under my stamp.

One idea is to also ask something of the premier architects in America, the Frank Gehrys, the I. M. Peis, the Richard Meiers, and Michael Rotondis. I'd like to ask each to design a cottage for a family that's living down here in a cardboard shack. I'd take their sketch and get four intern architects to build the house. Masons Bend, Alabama, would become like Seaside, Florida, but I'd be doing this for the poorest one percent of Americans.

I'd find the money to build these houses—we build them for $30,000—and make sure the workmanship is up to par. That's the sort of thing I'm thinking about.

AR: *You've stayed close to your Southern roots. Can you get an appropriate design from an architect who isn't rooted in place?*

SM: I'm not going to say that someone like Frank Gehry can't build something beautiful in a culture and place he doesn't know well. For the rest of us mere mortals, the best way to make real architecture is by letting a building evolve out of the culture and place.

I don't want to be pigeonholed as a regionalist, yet I am, and I certainly don't want to get marked as a local colorist. I pay attention to my region; I keep my eyes open. Then I see how I can take that and, using modern technology, reinterpret certain principles that are going to be true 200 years from now. I want the work to be looked at as contemporary American architecture, and in that sense, it has to have a certain honesty to it. That's what's wonderful about the really great American architecture, its honesty.

AR: *What do you mean by dishonesty in architecture?*

SM: There's a gluttonous affluence around, stage-set design that's way beyond the appropriateness for the client, the program, and it's all because a client or a developer has the money to build it. Alberti talked about choosing between fortune and virtue. The profession is becoming more a part of the corporate world while corporations (citizens of no place or anyplace) are more and more resembling nation-states. Every piece of architecture should express some moral. If it has moral merit, it deserves the title of 'architecture.' For me, the professional challenge, whether I am an architect in the rural American South or the American West, is how to avoid becoming so stunned by the power of modern technology and economic affluence that I lose focus on the fact that people and place matter.

These small projects designed by students at the Rural Studio remind us of what it means to have an American architecture without pretense. They remind us that we can be awed by the simple as much as by the complex, and if we pay attention, they will offer us a simple glimpse into what is essential to the future of American architecture . . . its honesty.

AR: *You say you've been cursed and blessed to be a Southerner. How so?*

SM: I grew up in a segregated South, in a very humanly warm environment, and had a wonderful education. But looking back on it, I know it was probably at the expense of the black community. I realize some of the things I'd been taught are wrong. The blessed part is that as an artist or an architect I have the opportunity to address wrongs and try to correct them.

AR: *So the Rural Studio is your way to redress wrongs?*

SM: We're excluding a whole army of people who've been excluded forever. These people down here are left over from Reconstruction; we need to reinstitute Reconstruction. W. E. B. Dubois said it 100 years ago: Reconstruction was prematurely stopped. He said that would be the big challenge of the 20th century; now we're in the 21st and we still have the problem and we're still ignoring it and they're still invisible.

AR: *What about the profession? What's happened to its social conscience?*
SM: Everyone's too busy trying to make a living. We have to be more than a house pet to the rich; we need to get out of that role.

AR: *Have your students had any problems learning to work with poor clients?*
SM: No. However, most of our students come from affluent families. For the most part, they haven't experienced this sort of poverty. They've seen it, but they haven't crossed over into that world, smelled it, felt it, experienced it. They come with abstract opinions that are fairly quickly reconsidered once they meet the families and realize that they're really no different from other American families. It's good to see these white middle-class students working hard all day trying to win the respect of people they wouldn't even acknowledge on the street before.

AR: *How important is the building process as an education tool?*
SM: It's valuable but not totally necessary. What's important is that students understand the process. It's the same regardless of whether they're building a little bitty studio for a basket weaver or a large building. We do preliminary sketches, schematic designs and foundation designs and then we go out and start digging the foundations. Everything then happens on-site. It's how architects worked 100 years ago.

What's important is that for young architects this experience takes it out of the theoretical and makes it real. They start to understand the power that architecture has and the responsibility they have to the creative process and how that manifests itself in something physical. That's what architecture is. It's not paper architecture. No one loves to draw and paint more than I do. But it's important that students learn that drawing on paper and building models is not architecture.

AR: *This is the Rural Studio's eighth year, and it has built more than 13 projects. Why haven't other schools adapted the model for their own use?*

SM: I don't think the 100-plus architecture schools across the country realize how alike each program is, how interchangeable their curricula and faculty are. I've spoken at most of them. The faculty are usually all dressed in black. They all seem to say the same things. It's all become redundant and very stale, unimaginative. What's ironic is that you hear professors talk about how out of the box we need to be, how risk-taking is part of being an architect, yet the faculty is often guilty of sitting on their hands. If architecture is going to nudge, cajole, and inspire a community or to challenge the status quo into making responsible environmental and social-structural changes now and in the future, it will take the "subversive leadership" of academics and practitioners to keep reminding the students of architecture that theory and practice are not only interwoven with one's culture but have a responsibility for shaping the environment, breaking up social complacency, and challenging the power of the status quo.

The Rural Studio is not an easy curriculum to run. It's a 24/7 obligation. During the week, I'm in Newbern living with students in a house built in 1890. If you're going to do this you gotta pack your bags, kiss your wife good-bye, and go to war. If you're not willing to do that, at least get out of the way and let the rest of us march on through.

AR: *It's unusual to really integrate teaching with practice as you've done.*

SM: I'm not an academician, but I am an educator. I'm an architect and I'm also a painter. It's all part of the creative act. That is my passion—to be responsible to the creative process. I enjoy certain technical ability, natural ability, and I get to use it. It's what all architects have and want to use. We're living the myth. I was willing to take the jump in the dark, as I like to say, and it's not going to be fatal.

34 WILLIAM McDONOUGH, B. 1951, AND MICHAEL BRAUNGART, 1958

Over the past three decades, the American architect William McDonough has dedicated his attention to the development of sustainable and environmentally friendly architecture. Early in his career, he discovered that such architecture depended on more than sensitive design; it required ecologically sound construction materials that simply did not exist. He later began collaboration with the German chemist Michael Braungart, eventually founding the firm MBDC (McDonough Braungart Design Chemistry, 1995) and issuing their manifesto, *Cradle to Cradle: Remaking the Way We Make Things* (2002). The phrase "cradle to cradle" describes a system or material that, throughout its lifecycle, produces no waste and can ultimately become "nutrients" for other processes. The inorganic "paper" of McDonough and Braungart's text, composed of plastic resins and synthetic fibers, is one such product.

Architecturally, McDonough relies on manmade and organic materials to create structures beneficial to both the environment and the client. McDonough's design for the Ford Rouge Truck Plant in Dearborn, Michigan (completed in 2004) is an example of such a work. This low-rise industrial structure is crowned by a 10-acre "living" grass roof that helps insulate the building and collects rainwater to be used in manufacturing processes. These aspects are intended to reduce heating, cooling, and production costs. In addition, the living roof provides a home for insects and birds displaced by the complex. Such innovative and considerate design corresponds to McDonough's broader interest in sustainability that encompasses, yet extends beyond, architectural production.

"This Book Is Not a Tree" (2002)

At last. You have finally found the time to sink into your favorite armchair, relax, and pick up a book. Your daughter uses a computer in the next room while the baby crawls on the carpet and plays with a pile of colorful plastic toys. It certainly feels, at this moment, as if all is well. Could there be a more compelling picture of peace, comfort and safety?

Let's take a closer look. First, that comfortable chair you are sitting on. Did you know that the fabric contains mutagenic materials, heavy metals, dangerous chemicals, and dyes that are often labeled hazardous by regulators—except when they are presented and sold to a customer? As you shift in your seat, particles of the fabric abrade and are taken up by your nose, mouth and lungs, hazardous materials and all. Were they on the menu when you ordered that chair?

That computer your child is using—did you know that it contains more than a thousand different kinds of materials, including toxic gases, toxic metals (such as cadmium, lead, and mercury), acids, plastics, chlorinated and brominated substances, and other additives? The dust from some printer toner cartridges has been found to contain nickel, cobalt, and mercury, substances harmful to humans that your child may be inhaling as you read. Is this sensible? Is it necessary? Obviously, some of those thousand materials are essential to the functioning of the computer itself. What will happen to them when your family outgrows the computer in a few years? You will have little other choice but to dispose of it, and both its valuable and its hazardous

---

William McDonough and Michael Braungart, "This Book Is Not a Tree," *Cradle to Cradle* (New York: North Point Press, 2002), 3–7, 13–16. Reprinted with permission from the author and publisher.

materials will be thrown "away." You wanted to use a computer, but somehow you have unwittingly become party to a process of waste and destruction.

But wait a minute—you care about the environment. In fact, when you went shopping for a carpet recently, you deliberately chose one made from recycled polyester soda bottles. Recycled? Perhaps it would be more accurate to say *downcycled*. Good intentions aside, your rug is made of things that were never designed with this further use in mind, and wrestling them into this form has required as much energy—and generated as much waste—as producing a new carpet. And all that effort has only succeeded in postponing the usual fate of products by a life cycle or two. The rug is still on its way to a landfill; it's just stopping off in your house en route. Moreover, the recycling process may have introduced even more harmful additives than a conventional product contains, and it might be off-gassing and abrading them into your home at an even higher rate.

The shoes you've kicked off on that carpet look innocuous enough. But chances are, they were manufactured in a developing country where occupational health standards—regulations that determine how much workers can be exposed to certain chemicals—are probably less stringent than in Western Europe or the United States, perhaps even nonexistent. The workers who made them wear masks that provide insufficient protection against the dangerous fumes. How did you end up bringing home social inequity and feelings of guilt when all you wanted was new footwear?

That plastic rattle the baby is playing with—should she be putting it in her mouth? If it's made of PVC plastic, there's a good chance it contains phthalates, known to cause liver cancer in animals (and suspected to cause endocrine disruption), along with toxic dyes, lubricants, antioxidants, and ultraviolet-light stabilizers. Why? What were the designers at the toy company thinking?

So much for trying to maintain a healthy environment, or even a healthy home. So much for peace, comfort, and safety. Something seems to be terribly wrong with this picture.

Now look at and feel the book in your hands.

This book is not a tree.

It is printed on a synthetic "paper" and bound into a book format developed by innovative book packager Charles Melcher of Melcher Media. Unlike the paper with which we are familiar, it does not use any wood pulp or cotton fiber but is made from plastic resins and inorganic fillers. This material is not only waterproof, extremely durable, and (in many localities) recyclable by convention means; it is also a prototype for the book as a "technical nutrient," that is, as a product that can be broken down and circulated infinitely in industrial cycles—made and remade as "paper" or other products.

The tree, among the finest of nature's creations, plays a crucial and multifaceted role in our interdependent ecosystem. As such, it has been an important model and metaphor for our thinking, as you will discover. But also as such, it is not a fitting resource to use in producing so humble and transient a substance as paper. The use of an alternative material expresses our intention to evolve away from the use of wood fibers for paper as we seek more effective solutions. It represents one step toward a radically different approach to designing and producing the objects we use and enjoy, an emerging movement we see as the next industrial revolution. This revolution is founded on nature's surprisingly effective design principles, on human creativity and prosperity, and on respect, fair play, and goodwill. It has the power to transform both industry and environmentalism as we know them.

Toward a New Industrial Revolution

We are accustomed to thinking of industry and the environment as being at odds with each other, because conventional methods of extraction, manufacture, and disposal are destructive to the natural world. Environmentalists often characterize business as bad and industry itself (and the growth it demands) as inevitably destructive.

On the other hand, industrialists often view environmentalism as an obstacle to production and growth. For the environment to be healthy, the conventional attitude goes, industries must be regulated and restrained. For industries to fatten, nature cannot take precedence. It appears that these two systems cannot thrive in the same world.

The environmental message that "consumers" take from all this can be strident and depressing: Stop being so bad, so materialistic, so greedy. Do whatever you can, no matter how inconvenient, to limit your "consumption." Buy less, spend less, drive less, have fewer children—or none. Aren't the major environmental problems today—global warming, deforestation, pollution, waste-products of your decadent Western way of life? If you are going to help save the planet, you will have to make some sacrifices, share some resources, perhaps even go without. And fairly soon you must face a world of limits. There is only so much the Earth can take.

Sound like fun?

We have worked with both nature and commerce, and we don't think so.

One of us (Bill) is an architect, the other (Michael) is a chemist. . . . [You] might say we came from opposite ends of the environmental spectrum. . . .

We met in 1991, when the EPEA [Environmental Protection Encouragement Agency] held a reception at a rooftop garden in New York City to celebrate the opening of its first American offices. (The invitations were printed on biodegradable diapers, to highlight the fact that conventional disposable diapers were one of the largest single sources of solid waste in landfills.) We began talking about toxicity and design. Michael explained his idea of creating a biodegradable soda bottle with a seed implanted in it, which could be grown on the ground after use to safely decompose and allow the seed to take root in the soil. There was music and dancing, and our discussion turned to another object of modern manufacture: the shoe. Michael joked that his guests were wearing "hazardous waste" on their feet, waste that was abrading as they spun on the rough surface of the roof, creating dust that people could inhale. He told how he had visited the largest chromium extraction factory in Europe—chromium is a heavy metal used in large-scale leather tanning processes—and noticed that only older men were working there, all of them in gas masks. The supervisor had explained that it took on average about twenty years for workers to develop cancer from chromium exposure, so the company had made the decision to allow only workers older than fifty to work with the dangerous substance.

There were other negative consequences associated with the conventional design of shoes, Michael pointed out. "Leather" shoes are actually a mixture of biological materials (the leather, which is biodegradable) and technical materials (the chromium and other substances, which have value for industries). According to current methods of manufacture and disposal, neither could be successfully retrieved after the shoe was discarded. From a material and ecological standpoint, the design of the average shoe could be much more intelligent. We discussed the idea of a sole coated with biodegradable materials, which could be detached after use. The rest of the shoe could be made of plastics and polymers that were not harmful, and which could be truly recycled into new shoes.

Incinerator smoke drifted from nearby rooftops as we discussed the fact that typical garbage, with its mixture of industrial and biological materials, was not designed for safe burning. Instead of banning burning, we wondered why not manufacture certain products and packaging that could be safely burned after a customer is finished with them? We imagined a world of industry that made children the standard for safety. What about designs that, as Bill put it, "loved all the children, of all species, for all time"?

Traffic was increasing on the streets below, a true New York traffic jam, with blaring horns, angry drivers, and increasing disruption. In the early evening light, we imagined a silent car that could run without burning fossil fuels or emitting noxious fumes, and a city like a forest, cool and quiet. Everywhere we turned, we could see products, packaging, buildings, transportation, even whole cities that were poorly designed. And we could see that the conventional environmental approaches—even the most well-intended and progressive ones—just didn't get it.

That initial meeting sparked an immediate interest in working together, and in 1991 we coauthored *The Hannover Principles,* design guidelines for the 2000 World's Fair that were issued at the World Urban Forum of the Earth Summit in 1992. Foremost among them was "Eliminate the concept of waste"—not reduce, minimize, avoid waste, as environmentalists were then propounding, but eliminate the very concept, by design. We met in Brazil to see an early version of this principle in practice: a waste-processing garden that was in essence a giant intestine for its community, turning waste into food.

Three years later, we founded McDonough Braungart Design Chemistry. Bill maintained his architectural practice and Michael continued to head the EPEA in Europe, and both of us started teaching at universities. But now we had a focused way to begin to put our ideas into practice, to turn our work in chemical research, architecture, urban design, and industrial product and process design to the project of transforming industry itself. Since then, our design firms have worked with a wide range of corporate and institutional clients, including the Ford Motor Company, Herman Miller, Nike, and SC Johnson, and with a number of municipalities and research and educational institutions to implement the design principles we have evolved.

We see a world of abundance, not limits. In the midst of a great deal of talk about reducing the human ecological footprint, we offer a different vision. What if humans designed products and systems that celebrate an abundance of human creativity, culture, and productivity? That are so intelligent and safe, our species leaves an ecological footprint to delight in, not lament?

Consider this: all the ants on the planet, taken together, have a biomass greater than that of humans. Ants have been incredibly industrious for millions of years. Yet their productiveness nourishes plants, animals, and soil. Human industry has been in full swing for little over a century, yet it has brought about a decline in almost every ecosystem on the planet. Nature doesn't have a design problem. People do.

35 ANDRÉS DUANY, B. 1949

Duany Plater-Zyberk & Company, Plan of Seaside, FL, 1978
Courtesy of Duany Plater-Zyberk & Company

American architect and urban planner Andrés Duany is intimately connected with the formation of New Urbanism, a design movement intended to address a variety of urban ills including congestion, sprawl, and the lack of affordable housing. Applicable on regional and local scales, its principles promote the creation of walkable and socially diverse neighborhoods that include homes, workplaces, and public amenities. Implementation of relevant zoning codes and ordinances to guide and regulate an area's growth is of paramount importance in the New Urbanist quest for what the architectural historian Vincent Scully has termed "The Architecture of Community."*

The town of Seaside, on Florida's Gulf coast, is the paradigmatic New Urbanist development. In the late 1970s, Duany and his partner/wife Elizabeth Plater-Zyberk designed the master plan of Seaside, modeled on a typical pre-1940s southern American town. A commercial and civic center forms the settlement's core, surrounded on three sides by residences and on the fourth by the ocean. Buildings display variety, however, Duany and Plater-Zyberk devised design codes to regulate formal and material vocabulary, street width and adornment, and building placement. Thus the visual diversity of Seaside is dependant on an overall aesthetic harmony.

Since Seaside's creation, the town has been a source of debate. Financially, it is successful and has almost reached built capacity, demonstrating that there is a public appreciation for the ordered community atmosphere Seaside provides. However, the town has been criticized as a traditional and nostalgic theme park for the privileged. Other charges have been leveled at New Urbanism as a planning and design strategy, yet the movement continues to grow. The comments below provide insight into the principles that generated New Urbanism, which, under the leadership of Duany, Plater-Zyberk and others, now flourishes both nationally and abroad.

---

* Vincent Scully, "The Architecture of Community," in Peter Katz, *The New Urbanism: Toward an Architecture of Community* (New York: McGraw-Hill, 1994).

"General Agreement on Architecture and Related Matters" (2003)

In response to an age rife with social stress, driven by economies so powerful that the entirety of the natural world is decisively affected by the pattern of human dwelling; for a design profession confused by the esoteric and the transient, we set forth these principles.

We are in agreement that:

The discipline of architecture should take substance from its own tradition and not be subjected to artistic or intellectual fashions. Architecture is not a consumer item.

The language of architecture should be in continual evolution but . . . not fall under the thrall of short fashion cycles.

Architecture should interact with the imperatives of economics and marketing but not be consumed by them. It is a role of the art of architecture to tame the savagery of commerce.

Architecture should engage the supporting disciplines of engineering and sociology but not be enslaved by them.

Certain critics—those who do not possess the craft and experience of building—should not be granted undue influence on the reputation of architecture and architects. Ar-

---

Andrés Duany, "General Agreement on Architecture and Related Matters," http://www.dpz.com/literature_andres_writings.htm. Courtesy of Duany Plater-Zyberk & Company. Reprinted with permission from the author.

chitects should develop an unmediated voice in the press, to explain their work themselves. (Architects should affect this demand by canceling their subscriptions to those publications that do not comply.)

Participation in a permanent avant-garde is an untenable position that consumes those who do. Architects at the peak of their abilities must not be marginalized merely because their time of fame has passed.

It is essential to eliminate the humiliation of architects performing for the opinion of an absurdly small number of critics. Such critics are empowered only because they are recognized as such by the architects themselves. This problem does not apply to architectural historians, who earn their standing through research and documentation rather than through personal preference. Historians support the knowledge base on which architecture stands and from which it evolves.

Buildings should be durable and mutable in balanced measure. This is crucial to the longevity required of urbanism.

The design schools should accept the responsibility of teaching a body of knowledge, and not attempt to incite individualism. Students should be exposed to the general vernacular and not just to the very few geniuses produced by each generation. Emulation of the exceptional does not provide an adequate model for professional training.

The architectural schools should be liberated from the thrall of sociologists, linguists and philosophers. Those who are primarily dedicated to other disciplines should depart to their own departments from which they can continue to educate architects in proper measure.

The wall between history and the design studio should be eliminated. History is to be a living continuum. The achievements of our predecessors [are] the basis of all human progress. Architecture cannot be the sole exception.

Students should be exposed to the apprenticeship system. There has been no more effective method of learning architecture. Most of the finest buildings of all time were the result of apprenticeship.

It is essential to our communities that architecture be practiced as a collective endeavor and not as a means of brand differentiation in pursuit of the attentions of the media.

Architects should retake responsibility for an urbanism that is currently abandoned to the statistical concerns of zoning, building codes, traffic and financing.

Architectural expression should assimilate the cultural and climatic context, no less than the will to form of the architect.

Architects honor the human scale in their designs, remembering that it is human beings whom we serve and whose environment we are creating. Buildings and spaces that alienate or intimidate the people who live or work in them, or the pedestrians who pass among them, are inhuman.

Buildings should acknowledge the character of a place. It is also necessary to acknowledge the opposite: that architectural influence can travel along cultural and climatic belts to positive effect.

Architecture should not become a pawn in the culture wars. It is a falsification of history to consider a style representative of this or that hegemony or liberation.

Architectural style should be independent of politics. The most cursory observation will reveal that buildings and cities are neither democratic nor fascist; that they easily transcend the ideology of their creators to become useful and beloved to other times. Buildings should incorporate authentic progress in material and production methods, but not for the sake of innovation alone.

Architects should harness those systems of production that make the best design available to the greatest number. Only those artifacts that are reproduced in quantity are consequential to present needs—we have the challenge of large numbers.

The techniques of mass production should affect the process of building, but it is not necessary that they determine the form of the building, or the urbanism.

It is essential to engage the mobile home industry, the prefabrication industry, and the house plan industry. These are efficient methods to provide housing. The current low quality of their production is the fault of non-participation by architects.

Architects should endeavor to publish their work in popular periodicals. How else will the people learn?

The techniques of graphic depiction should not determine the design of the buildings. Computer-aided design must remain an instrument for the liberation of labor and not become a determinant of form. Because a shape can be easily depicted does not necessarily mean that it should be constructed.

It is essential to recognize that each building should be coherently composed. A building cannot be the simulacra of an absent urbanism. Authentic variety can only result from a multiplicity of buildings. True urbanism is the result of many designers working in sequence.

Traditional and contemporary architectural styles should have equal standing, as they represent parallel, persistent realities. They may be used badly or well, but their evaluation should be on the basis of their appropriateness to context, and their quality, not to fashion.

It is essential to deny contemporary buildings dispensation for having been created in the so-called modernist era. They must be held to a standard as high as their predecessors'. After all, the means available to us are not less than theirs.

It is essential to acknowledge a preference for controls by known rules and properly constituted laws, rather than be subjected to the whims and opinions of review boards.

Architects should work concurrently with landscape architects in the process of design. Landscape architects must in turn abdicate their preference for autonomous layouts. The ground is not a canvas and nature is not material suitable for an installation piece.

Architects, like attorneys, should dedicate a portion of their time without compensation to those who do not otherwise have access to professional design.

Architects should participate in the political arena so as to affect the built environment at the largest scale. It is disastrous to create policy without the participation of those with an adequate design education.

Architects should debate those who through relativist argument undermine architecture's potential as a social and ecological instrument for the good. The academic imperative of weakening architecture and architects harms society.

We should not impose untested or experimental designs on the poor. The likelihood of failure in such cases has proven to be very great; and they are powerless to escape its consequences. Architects should experiment, if at all, with those wealthy enough to be patrons. They can afford to move out of their buildings if necessary.

It is essential to understand the difference between creativity, which we accept as necessary, and originality, which when pursued at all costs is destructive to architecture. The pursuit of originality condemns our cities to incoherence and the architect's life's work to unwarranted obsolescence.

Because so much of the craft of building has been lost, it is essential that architects allocate a portion of their time to its research and recovery; and to the sharing of the fruits of this endeavor by teaching and writing.

The architectural vernaculars of the world be the subjects of systematic study and that they be models for the design process. Good, plain, normative buildings must again be available everywhere and to all.

The analysis of everyday building should not result in the conclusion that the people will accept only mediocrity. It is pandering to give them only what they already know.

Buildings should incorporate passive environmentalism in siting, materials and the performance of their mechanical elements. Economic analysis alone will not reach this conclusion.

Architectural history should include not just the form-givers, but the masters of policy. Talented students who are not seduced by form making should be exposed to these role models. Municipal policy and administration is sorely in need of their abilities.

Architects should respond to context. If the context is not suitable, then the proper response is to inaugurate one that is so. Not until this is common practice will the proliferation of architectural review committees cease to bedevil both good and bad designers.

Architects must honor the human scale in their designs, remembering that it is human beings whom we serve and whose environment we are creating. Buildings and spaces that alienate or intimidate the people who live or work in them, or the pedestrians who pass among them, are inhumane.

36 FRANK GEHRY, B. 1929

Gehry Partners, The Stata Center for Computer, Information and Intelligence Sciences
Massachusetts Institute of Technology, Cambridge, MA, completed 2004
Photo by author

After studying architecture at the University of Southern California and urban planning at Harvard's Graduate School of Design, Frank Gehry worked in Los Angeles and Paris before opening his own practice in 1962. Since then, the Canadian-born architect has steadily earned a reputation for his unique and experimental designs. In the past decade, Gehry has gained international notoriety for his highly expressionistic, unconventional works, such as the titanium-clad surfaces of the Guggenheim Museum in Bilbao, Spain (completed in 1997) and the skewed, intersecting elements of the Stata Center at Massachusetts Institute of Technology (1998–2004). In addition to unexpected forms, Gehry has also used unusual materials; for the renovation of his own house in Santa Monica, California, Gehry juxtaposed common, inexpensive materials such as plywood, corrugated metal, and chain-link. Yet, in more recent years, he has incorporated advanced technologies into the design and fabrication of his works. Ultimately, Gehry's architecture is a product of personal decisions, of an "intuition" he likens to that of the artist. The resulting aesthetic, informed by the realities of materials and construction, is always one of transformation, of constant flux, of excitement and novelty. Some critics question the functionality of Gehry's buildings, feeling that his emphasis on form neglects both the user and the existing context. Others, however, are enthralled by his works; as Gehry's designs often read as both architecture and sculpture, he has found tremendous approval in both architectural and popular circles.

"Architecture and Intuition" (2003)

I was trained as a modernist. I came to school after the Beaux-Arts movement, and all my teachers said enough with that historic shit. Let's get on with it. I thought that historicism was a dead end. The painters and sculptors were doing stuff that was much more exciting; they were playing with ideas, forms, textures, and feelings that were infinitely more interesting to me. I wanted to discover how to make a building that had what I call juice—that is, feeling or a spirit. If you look at history, you find that over the centuries, numerous artists, sculptors, and architects have struggled to represent movement with inert materials. That was interesting to me. When I looked at sculpture, especially statues of the Indian goddess Shiva, I sensed the movement inside them. Then I thought to myself, cars have movement, planes have movement; there is movement all around us. How do you bring that into architecture? I started messing with those ideas.

Years ago, I did a trellis for Norton Smith. I wanted it to look like frozen motion, but I didn't know how to do it. I could draw and model it, but I didn't know how to build it, exactly, so I convinced Norton to let me construct it in sections. I built the first layer, and that was fine. I built the second layer and half of the third, and I was starting to get somewhere. Then he stopped me. He said he didn't want to spend any more money on my fancy ideas, and that it was going to be my unfinished symphony.

When some people started doing temples again—postmodern stuff—I reacted against it because of the way I was trained. If you're going to go back in history, you might as well go back millions of years—to fish—and I started drawing fish-like things. It was

Frank Gehry, "Architecture and Intuition," *The State of Architecture at the Beginning of the 21ˢᵗ Century*, ed. Bernard Tschumi and Irene Cheng (New York: Monacelli Press and the Trustees of Columbia University, 2003). © 2003 by the Monacelli Press Inc., and the Trustees of Columbia University in the City of New York. Reprinted with permission from the author and publishers.

intuitive. I started drawing, and I let it go to see where it would lead. I started making things. I made a thirty-five-foot-long fish sculpture for an exhibition, and I realized that when I stood next to it, I felt the movement. Other people sensed it, too. Even though it was an ugly piece of kitsch, it worked somehow. At thirty-five feet long, it was starting to approach an architectural scale. From there, I cut off the head and tail, and I made a fish room for the Walker Center in Minneapolis, at the request of Mildred Friedman, then curator of design. And it worked. We stripped it of some of the kitsch; we were making it more abstract and it started to work. After I learned how to build that, I took the next step and moved to a larger scale. It wasn't something I sat down and planned. If I knew what I was going to do, I wouldn't bother to do it—it would have been done already in my head.

When I was a kid, I studied the Talmud with my grandfather. The essence of the Talmud is the golden rule: "Do unto others as you would have others do unto you." That's the logic. It's not much more complicated than that. There was another saying when I was growing up: "If you step on a crack, you break your mother's back." So, when you're a kid, you don't step on a crack, because you don't want to break your mother's back. It's a childlike notion of power. I think we carry something of that sensibility into our adult lives; you think that if you stand on a certain place near a fulcrum you can move the universe. But if you go at things that way, your actions become so important and powerful that you can't do anything. You go into gridlock. For instance, I hired a kid who had studied with Peter Eisenman. He was talented, but his experience with Peter had caused him to view each line as so precious that he couldn't draw a line or make a wall. He strove for a perfection that he could never reach, and it paralyzed him. It's wonderful to search your psyche and to comb your life for meaning—for the meaning of the universe. But you're asking more than is humanly possibly of yourself. You are a product of nature. If you just follow your intuitions, you won't get out of line because gravity will hold you down. The culture around you, the building department, the economy, and the client will keep you in line, so in all likelihood, you will never destroy the world. You won't break your mother's back if you step on a crack. You can, however, do things that have an effect on the world. You just have to free yourself to let those things happen.

37 SARAH WHITING, B. 1964

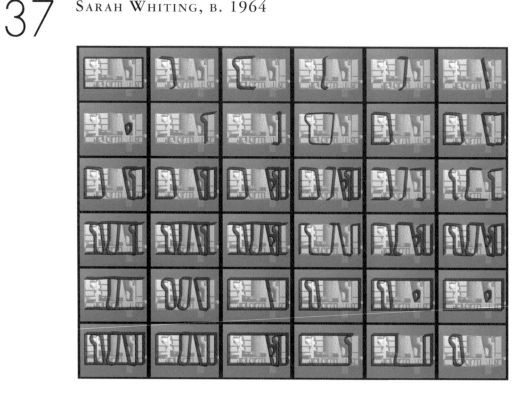

WW Architects, IntraCenter, Lexington, KY, 1997.
Diagram of spatial "parentheses" that weave between form and program in a community center project.
Courtesy of WW Architects

As an assistant professor of history and theory at Princeton University's School of Architecture and cofounder, with Ron Witte, of the design firm WW in 1990, Sarah Whiting merges the academic and professional realms of architecture. In her essay "Going Public," Whiting draws on this personal experience to provide a firm yet encouraging directive for contemporary architects. She begins by taking architects to task for what she perceives to be their recent inability to advance the field of architecture. Specifically, Whiting addresses architecture's reliance on past conceptual strategies that, once radical, are today merely repetitious and ineffective. In the early twenty-first century, she asserts that an acknowledgement of public heterogeneity lacks the impact it had thirty years ago—then it was novel; today it is a given. Whiting argues that, due to the rich architectural and intellectual legacy bequeathed by our forerunners, architects are now in a position to do more than recycle the past; they "must engage, lead, catalyze—*act*" to "contour tomorrow's cultural landscape." Architects must work toward the future.

The primary focus of this article is contemporary, encouraging the establishment of a "projective" or "postcritical" practice in architecture (as opposed to the "critical" practice of the previous few decades). However, Whiting also invokes a historical point of reference, namely the Vitruvian standards by which we, in large part, continue to measure architecture; she asks, "are we really so far removed from commodity, firmness, and delight?" Regardless of the answer, such a question reminds us that, even while looking forward, we cannot escape our past.

"Going Public" (2003)

Public Inquiry

Architects have a fondness for things public. Discussions about the rebuilding of the World Trade Center have revolved primarily around the public nature of the site, students want their thesis projects to "explore public space," and the duality of public and private life has become the binary of choice for academic as well as journalistic inquiry. Increasingly, however, architecture faces a public problem. Our public interest has become schizophrenic of late: *theory's* investment in publicness tends toward pluralization, while *practice's* public is increasingly marked by an interest in singular consensus. Perhaps most problematic for those of us with egos (and just try to find an architect without one) is that neither pole encourages, or even allows for, architectural assertion. As an instrument of progress, our commitment to a collective *civitas* risks becoming a posture (instead of a stance). Our altruism may well have become the enemy of architecture's forward motion, even at the very moment when our understanding of the public has entered a vastly more sophisticated era.

Public Opinion

Unlike "hegemony," the public sphere is less on the side of rule, more open to opposing views. Unlike "culture," it is more obviously a site of intersections with other classes and cultures. . . . Public sphere invokes "identity," but does so with more emphasis on actions and their consequences than on the nature or characteristics of the actors.[1]

Sarah Whiting, "Going Public," *Hunch* 6/7 (Rotterdam: Berlage Institute, 2003). © Sarah Whiting and the Berlage Insitute. Reproduced with the permission of the author and *Hunch*.

....

[1] Bruce Robbins, "Introduction: The Public as Phantom," *The Phantom Public Sphere* (Minneapolis:University of Minnesota Press, 1993), xvii.

By 1993, when Bruce Robbins penned the words above as part of his introduction to *The Phantom Public Sphere*, critical theorists were already fully immersed in unpacking what *public* might mean. Decades of important writing have profoundly advanced our understanding of the multifaceted nature of this term. We are now acutely attentive to the dangers of oversimplification, homogenization, and marginalization. We know a great deal more today about the tricky terrain of politics, agency, and action. For better or worse, we even know enough to state unequivocally that we frankly don't know much at all. This writing has had an enormously positive influence upon schools of architecture, including a resurgence of interest in the work of Henri Lefebvre, Michel de Certeau and Michel Foucault, and a production of sophisticated analyses of buildings and cities across broad historic and geographic spans. An inadvertent parallel to this public labor, however, has been the emergent role of the architect as public crossing guard: a generator of and mediator among multiple publics. While mediation has been rendered a productive strategy by theorists like Fredric Jameson and K. Michael Hays or practitioners like Peter Eisenman and Rem Koolhaas, who already long ago understood mediation as an *active between* (that is, an engaged interaction that itself generates new possibilities rather than compromise), more often than not, mediation has been misunderstood within architecture to mean a *passive between*—a simple conciliation between two sides.[2]

---

[2] Mediation as an *active between* engages and shapes the two forces that it is negotiating rather than merely reacting to them. For examples of such strategies in writing as well as design please see (among other works by these authors) Fredric Jameson, *The Political Unconscious: Narrative as a Socially Symbolic Act* (Ithaca, NY: Cornell University Press, 1981); K. Michael Hays, "Between Culture and Form," *Perspecta* 21 (Cambridge, MA: MIT Press, 1984): 14–29; Peter Eisenman, "Architecture as a Second Language: The Texts of Between," *Threshold: Restructuring Architectural Theory,* Marco Diani and Catherine Ingraham (Evanston, IL: Northwestern University Press, 1989), 69–73; Rem Koolhaas, *Delirious New York* (New York: Oxford University Press, 1978).

Public Safety

We represent a broad-based citizenry, composed of public and private sector leaders, community activists, and multidisciplinary professionals. We are committed to reestablishing the relationship between the art of building and the making of community, through citizen-based participatory planning and design.[3]

The public design charrette, where residents, practitioners and local politicians work together to generate design solutions, epitomizes what has become a numbing drive for consensus or conciliation within an increasing majority of architectural and development projects. Lower Manhattan, for example, is now under the watch of millions of eyes. Will this hyper-supervision guarantee that the outcome of the WTC rebuilding project will be less banal than the harrowingly dull six schemes initially proposed? Probably not. The implication that the broadest of publics needs to approve the WTC proposition—or that it ever could reach consensus—is an assumption that should raise a red flag for architecture today. This assumption is precisely where architecture's public crisis lies and where architects, schools, and clients should take notice.

Ideologies of inclusiveness and accommodation have unknowingly become the progenitors of such forms of compromise. The neutralities that (don't) steer architectural actions in today's compromise urbanism find a strange resonance in the DNA of our intellectual upbringing. Could it be that *The Critical*, in its contemporary guise, has placed us into a Novocain-laced stupor where we can't recognize the simultaneous di-

---

[3] Charter of the New Urbanism, 1996, 1 [note: a pdf of the Charter is available on the CNU website: www. cnu.org. An expanded version of the Charter was recently issued in book form, the Charter of the New Urbanism, Michael Leccese (New York: McGraw Hill, 2000)].

lution and desiccation of what were once potent critical strategies?[4] Recognizing and exposing options, differences, and similarities should not become an end in itself. The richness of alternatives has become an opiate whose ingestion satisfies our desire for the extraordinary, while drawing us ever deeper into a public coma.

Public Image

In the Downtown Athletic Club each "plan" is an abstract composition of activities that describes, on each of the synthetic platforms, a different "performance that is only a fragment of the larger spectacle of the Metropolis. . . . Such an architecture is an aleatory form of "planning" life itself: in the fantastic juxtaposition of its activities, each of the Club's floors is a separate installment of an infinitely unpredictable intrigue that extols the complete surrender to the definitive instability of life in the Metropolis.[5]

When Rem Koolhaas defined the "Culture of Congestion" in *Delirious New York*, he looked back to look ahead: he exposed the often unconscious strategy of radical hybridity present in the psychological explorations of Surrealism but also in the normative modernism of American mid-century corporate architecture. In his own projects (La Villette, Euralille, Congrexpo, ZKM, Jussieu, etc.), Koolhaas developed, accelerated, and refined the hybrid ethos, breathing life into this strategy through an aggressive urban and architectural research program. The aura that Koolhaas's work legitimately produced has become something altogether different in its contemporary proliferation

---

[4] For more on *The Critical* as a specific movement in architectural theory, see Sarah Whiting, "Critical Reflections"; Peter Eisenman, "Autonomy and the Will to the Critical"; and R.E. Somol, "In the Wake of Assemblage," *Assemblage* 41 (Cambridge, MA: MIT Press, 2000), 88–93.

[5] Rem Koolhaas, "Definitive Instability: The Downtown Athletic Club," *Delirious New York* (1978; rpt. New York: Monacelli, 1994), 157.

as a generalized architectural strategy of our time, however. Radical programmatic juxtaposition has become a mere sign, an accepted stand-in for a radicalized public realm. In its propagation, hybridity has endlessly reproduced the *image* of a pluralized and invigorated public, but its effects have returned once again to the unconscious, repeating *ad nauseum* the cross-programming strategies that were once radical but which are now only facile. Such strategies, which only twenty or thirty years ago created new worlds through the alchemy of juxtaposed conclusion, have become familiar in the hands of the less imaginative, and have only produced the repetitive inconclusiveness of hybridity as a *technique* rather than a *proposition*. The image of radicality in these derivative projects is not enough to veil their overwhelming nostalgia for a remembrance of radicality recently past.

Public Nature

I would rather look at a cultural landscape that is as desiccated as it is in actuality, rather than one that is falsely comforting.[6]

Of course, it is hard *not* to be nostalgic for the radicality of the late 1960s, 70s and 80s. And those working during that period were in turn nostalgic for the radicality of the 1910s, 20s and 30s. Juxtaposition, collage, rotation, dissection, assemblage, and other strategies were the "something borrowed, something new" for the second generation or neo-avant-garde—a new beginning that digested history as it decidedly stepped into the future. Rather than render repetition redundant,[7] which is what the superfi-

---

[6] Benjamin Buchloh, "Round Table: The Present Conditions of Art Criticism," *October* 100 (Cambridge, MA: MIT Press, 2002), 224.

[7] For more on the strategy of repetition, see R.E. Somol, "Dummy Text, or The Diagrammatic Basis of Contemporary Architecture," in Peter Eisenman, *Diagram Diaries* (New York: Universe, 1999), 6–25.

cial borrowing of these strategies does today, it is time to recognize them as a means embedded in a historical moment, not a timeless endpoint. Furthermore, while there is no doubt that we are fortunate to have inherited the ideologies of the neo-avant-garde, we don't need to treat them with kid gloves. As the *avant*³ (avant *x* avant *x* avant or neo-neo-avant-garde), we stand face to face with this historical pattern. In order to advance rather than recycle, we should revel in the conscious *manipulation* of borrowed techniques—in addition to forging new ones—in order to reflect our agendas. Our architectural ambitions can be honed through the exploitation of expanded architectural strategies. We are well equipped to identify today's architectural constituency (architecture's public) and to articulate architecture's commitments (are we really so far removed from commodity, firmness, and delight?). Architectural excellency is repeatedly defined according to criteria that are often out of date; the critical project is falsely comforting precisely because it was so important in advancing the discipline. The historical significance of the critical project is diluted, however, when we pretend that it can automatically impart architectural importance, as if criticality were simply a sprinkling of MSG. Today's cultural landscape *is* desiccated, but rather than burying our heads in the sand by trying to maintain a pretense of a landscape that has past, we need to exploit architecture today in order to contour tomorrow's cultural landscape.

Going Public

*"In this kind of world," Peterson said, "absurd, if you will, possibilities nevertheless proliferate and escalate all around us and there are opportunities for beginning again.*⁸

Wake up. Architects, students and theorists ought to sit up for a moment and take a look around. Thanks to decades of intellectual effort—the acumen of certain archi-

---

⁸ Donald Barthelme, "A Shower of Gold," *60 Stories* (New York: Penguin, 1982), 22.

tects, theorists, curators, schools, and publications such as *Oppositions* and *Assemblage*—we are surrounded by a remarkably fertile field of *stuff*. Our disciplinary ambitions—formal, technological, material, and intellectual—are poised to flourish. We would do well to shed at least a good part of our Obedience Complex. Lesson learned (really); let's move on. We know now that the public realm is a heterogeneous field; let's exploit the possibilities of our own architectural expertise. Rather than lose ourselves among its heterogeneity, we should aspire to change this field's topography. In order to do so, architects must engage, lead, catalyze—*act*, rather than only *react*. Our expertise lies in defining forms, spaces, and materialities; we should not be afraid of the results and subjectivities (read: *biases*) that such definition implies. Unlike other disciplines in the liberal arts, architecture's relationship to critical theory is not entirely concentric. Rather than bemoan this fact or conclude that theory has no bearing on architecture—two options that guarantee architecture's intellectual suicide—architects interested in the progressive project have no choice but to take advantage of our ability to slip in and out of critical theory's rule. After all, hasn't critical theory itself defined the rule-zone as, at best, a fuzzy entity? New spatial orders for the public realm thrive in the oxygen of expectant uncertainty. Architecture's ability to skip across, float on top of, or choose to obey critical theory's frameworks gives us an exhilarating vantage point. Damn the torpedoes. Full steam ahead.

Shumon Basar's article, "The Poisonous Mixture," an entertaining and enlightening meditation on the architect's position in the early twenty-first century, serves as a fitting conclusion for this collection. Previously employed in the office of Zaha Hadid and an educator at the Architectural Association in London, Basar no doubt has seen many professionals grapple with the various forms of "impotence" that may afflict the contemporary architect. Cultural, political, economic, technological, and other changes prompt (often unforeseen) transformations in the architectural discipline, issuing a constant challenge to the architect's abilities and adaptive skills. Indeed, Basar writes from experience, noting the young architect's devastating acknowledgement of powerlessness and the subsequent freedom to be earned by relinquishing the idealistic and ultimately unrealistic desire to "achieve everything." This message, passed on through Basar's text and his related activities as an editor, author, lecturer, critic, and curator, may prove particularly relevant to architects who today struggle to find their place in our ever-changing world.

"The Poisonous Mixture" (2004)

The Deal

A dopey-looking architect is happily married to an improbably beautiful woman when a sudden recession strikes. In a fit of panic, they go to Las Vegas to try to save themselves. In a casino, the wife duly declines the advances of a suave, smoldering magnate. He persists, finally making an offer to the financially desperate couple: One million dollars to spend one night with the beautiful wife. After dismissing the outrageous proposal, the architect and his wife lie back in bed and, from the righteous silence hovering between them, the possibility of agreeing to the million dollars begins to seem not so obscene after all. What's "one night," they think, compared to the thousands of nights that their fortified, water tight marriage will indubitably contain. But once the deal is consumed, the very edifice of the marriage begins to fall apart, brick by brick, as the architect-husband becomes distraught with anxieties that his wife might actually have enjoyed the night she spent with "the client." Nothing, the architect realizes, will ever be the same.

The Detail

Woody Harrelson's character in the film *Indecent Proposal* suffers an ignoble fate because he didn't focus on the detail. He didn't understand how the torrid part—Robert Redford's plea for "just one night"—would relate to the fragile whole of his marriage. The good parable should teach us that one must not underestimate the latent dangers of imperfect detailing—that vigilance to detail should be second only to breathing for

---

Shumon Basar, "The Poisonous Mixture," in *Content*, ed. Rem Koolhaas et al. (Cologne: Taschen, 2004). © 2004 Taschen GmbH and Office for Metropolitan Architecture. Reprinted with permission from the author and publisher.

any self-respecting architect. "God is in the details," pronounced Germany's very own architectural St. Augustine, Mies van der Rohe, which probably came as a surprise to those who thought God had died and gone to heaven. Amen.

The Virtuous

Indecent Proposal was released the year I started my education in architecture. Very quickly, I felt the need to become au fait with the rules governing what is considered virtuous and what is sinful. Ever since Mies's unique brand of fastidious, materially terse architecture proliferated to become the DNA of the neutered world that surrounds us, architects have valorized, with religious ferment, the absolute gravitas of "detailing": that is, a strange fetishization of screws, joints, gaps, and junctions. In a further twist of obsessive perversity, the construction of the detail should be almost imperceptible and, above all, it should not show evidence of having been made by human hands. Along with wearing one's shirt with the top button closed (without a tie) and listening to freeform jazz while drafting, the (male) architect's pursuit of the controlled finish is a wayward, contagious infliction peculiarly at odds with the true unwieldy scale of architecture and the manifold, abstract dimensions in which it is situated.

The Battle

"Architecture is a poisonous mixture of power and impotence."[*] When I read this statement as a student, my idealism was violated in the way a child's world is slowly dismantled with the successive abduction of Santa Claus, Superman, and the Man in the Moon. "But surely," I protested, "if our concepts are bold enough, if our passion is hi-octane fueled, can't we achieve anything? Shouldn't we be able to achieve everything?" It's only when one begins to try to build something that one understands the

---

[1] Rem Koolhaas, lecture at Columbia University, 1989.

second half of architecture's dialectical recipe. Like Hercules, or Bruce Willis in *Die Hard*, the architect must fight a veritable battle against ever-embittered combatants who seem to want to see him fail. There are building regulations, bored bureaucrats, economic vicissitudes, nefarious political climates, unspoken histories, indifferent construction industries and the "public." And often, above all of these harbingers of impotence, the architect faces The Client in a relationship that can be as infernal or beautiful as any marriage. This litany is sometimes referred to as "external forces," implying that the nature of practice is the reciprocity between this "outer realm" and the "inner realm"—the seat of the architect's creativity and will. Understanding the character of architecture's "impotence" might, I thought a few years later, be the key to liberation: how to unlock idealist delusion and give way to practicable strategy.

The Schism
There are two piles of images on my desk. The first includes a series of diagrams and flowcharts showing how a firm, OMA, has recently been extending its operations and presence by affiliating itself with diverse companies and experts. The other pile is a series of close-up photographs of three buildings in Holland, revealing how various joints, gaps, surfaces, and apertures have held out over time.[2] Cracks, oxidation, deterioration, patination, a panel falling off here, dead flies: a mesmerizing smear of decay in color. Leafing through the two sets of images is like looking at two possible future outcomes of a single decisive present.

The Inevitable
The pictures of aging buildings are a Dorian Gray-like reminder of the inevitable perishability of everything. It might sound portentous to claim that it is the fear of

---

[2] Netherlands Dance Theater, The Hague; Kunsthal, Rotterdam; Educatorium, Utrecht.

death that both plagues and motivates architects. This would assume that buildings are physical personifications of their authors, estranged metonyms, or abandoned look-alikes. Any building is however marked by the mortality of its material assemblage. It can go wrong at any time, and might do so in public. The author is unable to hide from the unforeseen problems—the imperfections—of the creation. This may be why James Stirling never revisited his finished buildings: he claimed it was too much like visiting ex-loves. Perhaps going back is so terrifying because, if the building is the architect, any tectonic failures are tantamount to corporeal failures. It's like staring at your own expiry, and realizing that there is nothing you can do to stop it.

The Tactical

"The important thing is to be aware one exists."[3]

I organize the diagrams into a matrix of my table and behold a spray of acronyms—OMA, AMO, VPRO, 2x4, IDEO; proper names—Prada, Harvard, Ove Arup; and a miscellany of individuals, some of whose names I recognize and others I don't. In relation to the photos of decay, these diagrams seem to outline an exploratory search for external, abstract organization—abstract not in the sense of "not-there," but in the way that freedom is abstract. The various permutations of letters and names look like a desire to discover tactics—tactics of ensuring one's freedom. Having been taught that the only way architects can generate the conditions of their freedom is by building more and better, getting bigger commissions and ending up with a fat cigar and a helipad, the spidery networks of interlaced diversification that orbit OMA look insane, and therefore the right thing to be doing. I can't help but think that the inward-looking species of architect—frozen by its love for frozen things—seems doomed to D-list subjugation.

---

[3] Jean-Luc Godard, *Pierrot Le Fou* (London: Lorimar, 1969).

These bubble diagrams on the other hand, linking Chinese TV broadcasting with notions of rethinking Europe, attest to an unbridled locomotive where Surrealistic juxtapositions begin to operate at the level of culture, economics, and language.

The Cure

It isn't just a question of accepting that there are waves, and agreeing to surf them. Imagine, like Leonardo da Vinci, that you can create weather, and with weather, the mother of all waves. It could strike anywhere (New York, China, Las Vegas, the Ruhr Valley, Portugal . . .) so one has to appear as though one can and will be everywhere at once. Make friends with culture (that's where the money is), hang out with fashion (it works for Christina Aguilera), celebrate superficiality (it's today's depth), be brutal and soft (we want it both ways), see the treasure in Junk (there is no such thing as obsolescence), spawn tribute clones (it's the true measure of fame), ditch piety and ennoble promiscuity (when have the youth ever been wrong?) and most of all, realize that power isn't something worth believing in, you have to live it. From architecture's funeral pyre, a new Andrew Lloyd Webber musical could be born. The project of architecture, if it is to survive intact and potent, must transcend its former self: it has to wake up and realize that the true and only important task is the vigilant corruption of the chain of causality that begins with "client" and ends in "building." Appear self-aggrandizing? Accept Machiavellian tendencies? Dance like John Travolta? Sure. Just don't look inwards, look out. The most powerful effect of impotence is the desire to find the cure.

SUGGESTIONS FOR FURTHER READING

The following is a selected list of additional readings pertaining to the authors featured in this collection. I have included works that provide a general overview of their respective subjects and that are, on the whole, intelligible to a non-architectural audience.

Dictionaries

Ching, Francis D.K. *A Visual Dictionary of Architecture*. New York: John Wiley & Sons, 1996.

Curl, James Steve. *A Dictionary of Architecture and Landscape Architecture*. 2nd ed. New York: Oxford University Press, 2006.

Fleming, John, Hugh Honour, and Nikolaus Pevsner. *The Penguin Dictionary of Architecture and Landscape Architecture*. 5th ed. New York: Penguin, 2000.

Surveys of the History and Theory of Architecture from Prehistory to the Present

Ching, Francis D.K., Mark M. Jarzombek, and Vikramaditya Prakash. *A Global History of Architecture*. New York: John Wiley & Sons, 2006.

Kostof, Spiro. *A History of Architecture: Settings and Rituals*. 2nd ed. New York: Oxford University Press, 1995.

Kruft, Hanno Walter. *A History of Architectural Theory from Vitruvius to the Present*. New York: Princeton Architectural Press, 1996.

Moffett, Marian, Michael Fazio, and Lawrence Wodehouse. *Buildings Across Time*. 2nd ed. New York: McGraw-Hill, 2004. Includes CD-Rom.

Trachtenburg, Marvin and Isabelle Hyman. *Architecture: From Pre-History to Postmodernism*. 2nd ed. New York: Prentice Hall, 2003.

Surveys of the History and Theory of Modern Architecture

Colquhoun, Alan. *Modern Architecture*. New York: Oxford University Press, 2002. Focuses on the history and theory of twentieth-century European architecture.

Curtis, William J. *Modern Architecture Since 1900*. 3rd ed. New York: Prentice Hall, 1996.

Frampton, Kenneth. *Modern Architecture: A Critical History*. 3rd ed. New York: Thames and Hudson, 1992. Suitable for those already possessing basic knowledge of twentieth-century architecture.

Mallgrave, Harry. *Modern Architectural Theory: A Historical Survey, 1673–1968.* New York: Cambridge University Press, 2005.

Architectural Anthologies and Readers

Benson, Tim and Charlotte, eds. *Architecture and Design 1890–1939.* New York: Whitney Library of Design/Watson Guptil Publications, 1975. Organized thematically, texts address the history, theory, and development of architecture.

Conrads, Ulrich, ed. *Programs and Manifestoes of 20th Century Architecture.* Cambridge, MA: MIT Press, 1975. Primary documents from 1903 through 1960 by prominent figures of modern architecture.

Gilmore, Elizabeth, ed. *From the Classicists to the Impressionists: Art and Architecture in the Nineteenth Century.* Vol. 3 of *A Documentary History of Art.* Garden City, NY: Anchor Books, 1966. Essays arranged thematically and preceded by brief biographical/contextual essays about the authors.

Harrison-Moore, Abigail, and Dorothy Rowe, eds. *Architecture and Design in Europe and America, 1750–2000.* Malden, MA and Oxford: Blackwell Publishing, 2006. Historical and contemporary essays that address the history and theory of architecture and design.

Hayes, K. Michael, ed. *Architecture Theory Since 1968.* Cambridge, MA: MIT Press, 1998. Advanced theoretical essays by key practitioners and thinkers; includes editor's commentary in form of general introduction and brief essays preceding entries.

Lefaivre, Liane, and Alexander Tzonis, eds. *The Emergence of Modern Architecture: A Documentary History from 1000 to 1810.* New York and London: Routledge, 2004. Excerpts by architects and architectural commentators; synthesizing introduction by Tzonis and helpful keyword cross-references.

Mallgrave, Harry Francis, ed. *An Anthology from Vitruvius to 1870.* Vol. 1. of *Architectural Theory.* Malden, MA and Oxford: Blackwell Publishing, 2006. Over 200 excerpts by architects and architectural thinkers from Vitruvius through Semper, along with general introduction and contextualizing introductory essays. Volume II (addressing 1870 through 2000) expected in winter 2007.

Nesbitt, Kate, ed. *Theorizing a New Agenda for Architecture, 1965–1995.* New York: Princeton Architectural Press, 1996. Essays by architectural figures, arranged thematically.

Ockman, Joan, ed. *Architecture Culture 1943–1968.* New York: Rizzoli Press, 1993. Excerpts by architects and architectural commentators; contains introductory essay and helpful briefs preceding each excerpt.

Roth, Leland M., ed. *America Builds: Source Documents in American Architecture and Planning.* New York:

HarperCollins/Icon Editions, 1983. Texts on the development of American architecture and urbanism from 1624 though 1980; contains contextual introductions for each excerpt.

Vitruvius and Roman Architecture

MacDonald, William. *An Introductory Study. The Architecture of the Roman Empire*. Vol. 1. Revised ed. New Haven: Yale University Press, 1982. A detailed examination of the form, construction, and symbolic meaning of major Roman monuments as they relate to culture and society.

Smith, Thomas Gordon. *Vitruvius on Architecture*. New York: Monacelli, 2004. A recent translation of five of the ten Vitruvian books; includes hypothetical recreations of Vitruvius's lost sketches.

Ward-Perkins, John B. *History of World Architecture: Roman Architecture*. New York: Phaidon Press, 2004.

Abbot Suger and Medieval Architecture

Coldstream, Nicola. *Medieval Architecture*. Oxford and New York: Oxford University Press, 2002. Addresses European architecture from 1150 to 1550.

Saalman, Howard. *Medieval Architecture*. New York: George Braziller, 1962. A concise survey.

Leon Battista Alberti and Italian Renaissance Architecture

Grafton, Anthony. *Leon Battista Alberti: Master Builder of the Italian Renaissance*. Cambridge, MA: Harvard University Press, 2002.

Murray, Peter. *The Architecture of the Italian Renaissance*. London: Batsford, 1963. Reprinted by Schocken Press, 1997. A popular and well-received survey of Renaissance architecture.

Wittkower, Rudolf. *Architectural Principles in the Age of Humanism*. London: Warburg Institute and University of London, 1949. 5th ed. New York: Academy Press, 1998. Addresses architects of the Renaissance, emphasizing relationship between architecture and culture. Considered a classic text on Renaissance architecture.

Andrea Palladio

Burns, Howard. *Andrea Palladio: The Complete Illustrated Works*. New York: Universe, 2001.

Palladio, Andrea, Vaughn Hart, and Peter Hicks. *Palladio's Rome*. New Haven: Yale University Press, 2006. First compilation and English translation of Palladio's illustrated guidebooks to Rome, originally published in 1554.

Summerson, John. *Inigo Jones*. London: Oxford University Press, 1964. New Haven: Paul Mellon Centre for Studies in British Art and Yale University, 2000. Discusses life and work of British architect Inigo Jones (1573–1652), often recognized as the foremost practitioner of Palladian architecture in England.

Claude Perrault

Herrmann, Wolfgang. *The Theory of Claude Perrault*. London: A. Zwemmer, 1973.

Pérez-Gómez, Alberto. *Architecture and the Crisis of Modern Science*. Cambridge, MA: MIT Press, 1983. Reprint 1985. Addresses shifts in architectural thought and design resulting from the scientific revolution.

Etienne-Louis Boullée and Eighteenth-Century Architecture

Bergdoll, Barry. *European Architecture 1750–1890*. New York: Oxford University Press, 2000. Considers social and contextual ideas in relationship to the historical and theoretical development of the period.

Laugier, Marc-Antoine. *An Essay on Architecture*. Translated by Wolfgang and Anni Herrmann. Los Angeles: Hennessy & Ingalls, Inc., 1977. Includes brief biographical essay on Laugier.

Middleton, Robin, and David Watkins, eds. *Architecture of the Nineteenth Century*. Milan: Electra, 2003. Detailed survey of architecture from the Enlightenment through the 1800s; Part I covers the eighteenth century.

Rosenau, Helen. *Boullée & Visionary Architecture*. London: Academy Editions; New York: Harmony Books, 1976. Addresses Boullée's life and work; contains an English translation of his *Architecture, Essay on Art*.

Eugène-Emmanuel Viollet-le-Duc and Nineteenth-Century Architecture

Bergdoll, Barry. "The *Dictionnaire raisonné*: Viollet-le-Duc's Encyclopedic Structure for Architecture." In *The Foundations of Architecture: Selections from the Dictionnaire raisonné,* by Eugène-Emmanuel Viollet-le-Duc. Translated by Kenneth D. Whitehead. New York: George Braziller, Inc., 1990. Discusses biographical information of Viollet-le-Duc, his concept of structural rationalism, and places him within a cultural and theoretical context. Also see Bergdoll's *European Architecture 1750–1890* listed above.

Middleton, Robin, and David Watkins, eds. *Architecture of the Nineteenth Century*. Milan: Electra, 2003. Detailed survey of architecture from the Enlightenment through the 1800s; Part II addresses the nineteenth century.

Viollet-le-Duc, Eugène-Emmanuel, and M.F. Hearn (ed). *The Architectural Theory of Viollet-le-Duc: Readings and Commentaries*. Cambridge, MA: MIT Press, 1990. Selections from Viollet-le-Duc's works, with contextual essays and commentary by the editor.

Viollet-le-Duc, Eugène-Emmanuel. *Lectures on Architecture*. 2 volumes. Translated by Benjamin Bucknall. New York: Dover Publications, 1987. Transcriptions of lectures on topics of architecture from history through construction and ornament.

Louis Sullivan

Frazier, Nancy. *Louis Sullivan and the Chicago School.* New York: Knickerbocker Press, 1999. Examines work of Sullivan and his contemporary Chicago architects.

Morrison, Hugh. *Louis Sullivan: Prophet of Modern Architecture*, revised ed. New York: W.W. Norton & Company, 2001. An introduction to the life and work of Sullivan; includes bibliography of Sullivan's writings and a list of his buildings.

Sullivan, Louis. *Kindergarten Chats and Other Writings.* New York: Dover Publications, 1980. Collected texts by Sullivan; reprint of 1918 edition.

Frank Lloyd Wright

Levine, Neil. *The Architecture of Frank Lloyd Wright.* New York: Princeton Architectural Press, 1996. A thorough survey and evaluation of Wright's work; takes into account his writings, philosophies, and personal life.

Wright, Frank Lloyd. *Frank Lloyd Wright: An Autobiography.* Petaluma, CA: Pomegranate Communications, 2005. First published in 1932.

Adolf Loos

Gravagnuolo, Benedetto, Aldo Rossi, and Roberto Schezen. *Adolf Loos: Theory and Works.* Translated by Marguerite McGoldrick. 4th ed. London: Art Data, 1995. Biographical overview, contextualization, and commentary precede extensive documentation of Loos's architectural works.

Tournikiotis, Panayotis. *Adolf Loos.* Translated by Marguerite McGoldrick. New York: Princeton Architectural Press, 2002. Monograph on Loos addressing his life, architectural designs, and writings.

Antonio Sant'Elia

Caramel, Luciano, and Alberto Longatti. *Antonio Sant'Elia, The Complete Works.* New York: Rizzoli, 1988. Commentary on Sant'Elia's sketches and designs.

Da Costa Meyer, Esther. *The Work of Antonio Sant'Elia: Retreat into the Future.* New Haven: Yale University Press, 1995. Comprehensive examination and analysis of Sant'Elia's life and work.

Geoffrey Scott

Dunn, Richard M. *Geoffrey Scott and the Berenson Circle: Literary and Aesthetic Life in the Early 20th Century.* Lewiston, NY: Edwin Mellen Press, 1998. Biography and contextualization of Scott.

Reed, Henry Hope. Foreword to *The Architecture of Humanism: A Study in Taste*, by Geoffrey Scott. New York: W.W. Norton & Company, Inc., 1974. Contextualizes and discusses importance of Scott's text.

Ruskin, John. *The Seven Lamps of Architecture*. New York: Dover Publications, 1989. British social and architectural critic associated with the ethical and naturalism "fallacies" discussed by Scott; originally published in 1849.

Le Corbusier

Boesiger, Willy. *Le Corbusier: Oeuvre complete* (or *Complete Works in Eight Volumes*), 11ᵗʰ ed. Boston: Birkhäuser Press, 1995.

Jenger, Jean. *Discoveries: Le Corbusier*. New York: Harry N. Abrams, 1996. Concise overview of Le Corbusier's life and work.

Le Corbusier. *Le Modulor*. Translated by Peter de Francia and Anna Bostock. Boston: Birkhäuser, 2000. Details Le Corbusier's universal measuring system based on the proportions of the human body; contains English translations of volumes 1 and 2, originally published in French in 1950 and 1955 respectively.

Walter Gropius and the Bauhaus

Fitch, James Marston. *Walter Gropius*. New York: George Braziller, Inc., 1960. A concise monograph.

Giedion, Sigfried. *Walter Gropius*. New York: Dover Publishing, 1992. Extensive discussion and analysis of Gropius's oeuvre; first published in 1954.

Gropius, Walter. *The New Architecture and the Bauhaus*. Cambridge, MA: MIT Press, 1965. Details Gropius's notion of the Bauhaus as a meeting ground for art and industrial production; originally published in 1935.

Whitford, Frank. *Bauhaus*. New York: Thames & Hudson, 1984. Historical overview of the Bauhaus's development as an institution and an artistic culture.

Henry-Russell Hitchcock and Modern Architecture—International Exhibition, 1932

Hitchcock, Henry-Russell. *Modern Architecture: Romanticism and Reintegration*. New York: Da Capo Press, Inc., 1993. First attempt to analyze and contextualize modern architecture within the trajectory of architectural history; first published in 1929, three years before the Museum of Modern Art exhibition.

———. "The International Style Twenty Years After." *Architectural Record* (Aug. 1951): 89–97. Reprinted in *Architecture Culture*, edited by Joan Ockman (see Anthologies section above). An evaluation, reconsideration, and partial repudiation of the formulaic principles concerning modern architecture presented in the exhibition and accompanying publication twenty years earlier.

Riley, Terence. *The International Style: Exhibition 15 and the Museum of Modern Art*. New York: Rizzoli and the Trustees of Columbia University, 1992. Catalogueue published for exhibition honoring the sixtieth anniversary of the MOMA International Style exhibition; examines formation, format and content of the original show.

R. Buckminster Fuller

Fuller, R. Buckminster. *Critical Path*. New York: St. Martin's Press, 1982. Appraisal of humanity's problematic situation during the late twentieth century and suggestions for continued survival; posed by many as the culmination of Fuller's thoughts.

———. *Operating Manual for Spaceship Earth*. New York: Princeton Architectural Press, 2000. Discussion and suggested corrections for the dangers facing our planet; originally published in 1969.

Sieden, Lloyd Steven. *Buckminster Fuller's Universe: His Life and Work*. New York: Perseus Books Group, 2000. Explanation of Fuller's life, philosophies, and projects.

Philip Johnson

Johnson, Philip. *The Architecture of Philip Johnson*. New York: Bulfinch Press, 2002.

———. *Philip Johnson: Writings*. New York: Oxford University Press, 1979. Collected essays by Johnson through the 1970s.

Schulze, Franz. *Philip Johnson: Life and Work*. Chicago: University of Chicago Press, 1996. Comprehensive biography of Philip Johnson.

Louis Kahn

Brownlee, David B., and David G. DeLong. *Louis I. Kahn: In the Realm of Architecture*. New York: Universe Publishing, 1991. Addresses Kahn's life, philosophies, and work.

Leslie, Thomas. *Louis I. Kahn: Building Art, Building Science*. New York: George Braziller, Inc., 2005. Uses cases studies to examine Kahn's innovative engineering and technological achievements.

Kahn, Nathaniel, dir. *My Architect*. DVD. New York: New Yorker Video, 2005. Film documenting Louis Kahn's son's search to learn about his father.

Scully, Vincent. *Louis I. Kahn*. New York: George Braziller, Inc., 1962. First monograph on Kahn.

Twombly, Robert, ed. *Louis Kahn: Essential Texts*. New York: W.W. Norton & Company, Inc., 2003. Kahn's most influential essays from 1944 through 1973; includes introductory essay by the editor and suggestions for further readings.

Aldo van Eyck

Ligtelijn, Vincent, ed. *Aldo van Eyck, Works*. Translated by Gregory Ball. Boston: Birkhäuser, 1999. Documentation and analysis of Van Eyck's work; prepared in commemoration of his eightieth birthday.

Strauven, Francis. *Aldo van Eyck: The Shape of Relativity*. Revised and updated English edition. Amsterdam: Architectura & Natura, 1998. Monograph, originally published in Dutch.

Archigram

Archigram, eds. *Archigram: Magazine for New Ideas in Architecture*. Vols. 1–9 (1961–1970). Issues of *Archigram*, containing work, thoughts, and commentary of contributors.

Sadler, Simon. *Archigram: Architecture without Architecture*. Cambridge, MA: MIT Press, 2005. Contextualizes and discusses Archigram's formation, development, and reception.

Robert Venturi and Denise Scott Brown

Brownlee, David B., David G. Delong, and Kathryn B. Hiesinger, eds. *Out of the Ordinary: Robert Venturi, Denise Scott Brown and Associates: Architecture, Urbanism, Design*. Philadelphia: Philadelphia Museum of Art, 2001. Accompanying text for an exhibition on Venturi, Scott Brown and Associates; includes analytical and contextualizing essays on the architects and their work.

Venturi, Robert, and Denise Scott Brown. *A View from the Campidoglio: Selected Essays 1953–1984*. Edited by Peter Arnell, Ted Bickford, and Catherine Bergart. New York: Icon Editions/Harper & Row Publishers, 1985. Collection of essays on Venturi and Scott Brown's architectural ideas and influences.

Von Moos, Stanislaus. *Venturi, Rauch, & Scott Brown: Buildings and Projects*. New York: Rizzoli, 1987. Extensive analysis and commentary by author, documentation of projects from the mid-1960s to mid-1980s.

————. *Venturi, Scott Brown, and Associates: Buildings and Projects, 1986–1997*. New York: Rizzoli, 1999. Analysis and commentary by author, documentation of projects from the mid-1980s to the 1990s, and an interview with Venturi and Scott Brown.

Aldo Rossi

Ferlenga, Alberto, ed. *Aldo Rossi: The Life and Works of an Architect*. Germany: Konemann Press, 2002. Builds upon 1999 exhibition on Rossi's oeuvre curated by Ferlenga; discusses biographical information in conjunction with architectural production.

Moneo, José Rafael. *Theoretical Anxiety and Design Strategies in the Work of Eight Contemporary Architects*. Cambridge, MA: MIT Press, in association with Harvard University, Graduate School of Design, 2004.

Considers Rossi alongside seven other contemporary architects, including Venturi, Scott Brown, Eisenman, Gehry, and Koolhaas.

Rossi, Aldo. *A Scientific Autobiography*. Translated by Lawrence Venuti. Cambridge, MA: MIT Press, 1981. Based on Rossi's notebooks from the ten years between 1971 and 1981, the original date of publication.

Hassan Fathy

Fathy, Hassan. *Natural Energy and Vernacular Architecture: Principles and Examples with Reference to Hot Arid Climates*. Chicago: United Nations University and University of Chicago Press, 1986.

Richards, James M. *Hassan Fathy*. Singapore: Concept Media; London: Architectural Press, 1985. Criticism and interpretation of Fathy's work and architectural approach in Egypt.

Steele, James. *An Architecture for the People: The Complete Works of Hassan Fathy*. London: Thames and Hudson, 1997.

Peter Eisenman

Eisenman, Peter, et al. *Five Architects*. New York: Wittenborn & Company, 1972. Reprint, New York: Oxford University Press, 1975. Projects by and commentary on the work of five New York architects later characterized as the "Whites"—Eisenman, Graves, Gwathmey, Meier, and Hejduk—as opposed to the "Grays"—Stern, Moore, and others. Originally published in 1972.

Frank, Suzanne Shulof, and Peter Eisenman. *Peter Eisenman's House VI: The Client's Response*. New York: Watson-Guptill Publications, 1994. Owners of Eisenman's House VI discuss the joys and difficulties of construction, occupation, and renovation.

Galofaro, Luca. *Digital Eisenman: An Office of the Electronic Era*. Architecture and Informatics Series. Translated by Lucinda Byatt. Boston: Birkhauser Press, 1999. Explores the ways in which Eisenman now uses digital technologies to assist design.

Oppositions Reader: Selected Readings from a Journal for Ideas and Criticism in Architecture, 1973–1984. Edited by K. Michael Hays. New York: Princeton Architectural Press, 1998. Essays by Eisenman and others, taken from *Oppositions*, a journal coedited by Eisenman and produced by the Institute of Architecture and Urban Studies; introductory essay by Hays contextualizes Eisenman's philosophy.

Charles Jencks and Postmodern Architecture

Jencks, Charles. *Late Modern Architecture*. New York: Rizzoli, 1980. Discussion of 1960s and 1970s architecture, building upon and departing from modern architecture.

————. *The New Paradigm in Architecture: The Language of Postmodernism*. New Haven: Yale University Press, 2002. A retrospective of postmodern architecture beginning with the 1960s.

Klotz, Heinrich. *The History of Postmodern Architecture*. Translated by Radka Donnell. Cambridge, MA: MIT Press, 1990.

Portoghesi, Paolo. *Postmodern*. Translated by Ellen Shapiro. New York: Rizzoli, 1983. Discusses postmodernism and provides dozens of architectural examples.

Demetri Porphyrios

Porphyrios, Demetri. *Classical Architecture*. London: Academy Editions 1991. 2nd ed. London: Papadakis Publishing, 2006.

————, ed. *Classicism Is Not a Style*. London: Architectural Design and Academy Editions, 1982. Essays on contemporary classical architecture by architects such as Aldo Rossi, Giorgio Grassi, Leon Krier, and Porphyrios; accompanying designs by these and other practitioners.

Juhani Pallasmaa

Holl, Steven, Juhani Pallasmaa, and Alberto Pérez-Gómez. *Questions of Perception: Phenomenology of Architecture*. Tokyo: A+U, 1994. 2nd ed., San Francisco: William K. Stout Publishers, 2006.

Pallasmaa, Juhani. *The Eyes of the Skin—Architecture and the Senses*. London: Academy Editions, 1996. 2nd ed., London: John Wiley & Sons, 2005.

Bernard Tschumi and Deconstructivist Architecture

Broadbent, Geoffrey. *Deconstruction: A Student Guide*. London: Academy Editions, 1991.

Kipnes, Jeffrey. *Perfect Acts of Architecture*. New York: MOMA; London: Thames & Hudson, 2001. Commentary on and documentation of Tschumi's *Manhattan Transcripts*, as well as Koolhaas's Exodus or Voluntary Prisoners of Architecture, Eisenman's House VI, and Libeskind's *Chamber Works: Architectural Meditations on Themes from Heraclitus*.

Tschumi, Bernard. *Architecture and Disjunction*. Cambridge, MA: MIT Press, 1997. Essays written by Tschumi between 1975 and 1991.

Rem Koolhaas

Koolhaas, Rem, and Bruce Mau. *S, M, L, XL*. New York: Monacelli Press, 1995. Collection of essays, thoughts, and projects by Koolhaas and others at OMA; often focuses on issues of complexity found in the contemporary metropolis.

Patteeuw, Véronique, ed. *Considering Rem Koolhaas and the Office for Metropolitan Architecture: What is OMA?* Rotterdam: NAi Publishers, 2003. Accompanying publication for traveling exhibition on the work of Koolhaas and OMA.

Daniel Libeskind

Kipnes, Jeffrey. *Perfect Acts of Architecture* (see Tschumi section above).

Libeskind, Daniel. *Breaking Ground: Adventures in Life and Architecture.* New York: Riverhead Books, 2004. Libeskind's autobiography.

Schneider, Bernhard. *Daniel Libeskind: Jewish Museum Berlin—Between the Lines.* Translated by John William Gabriel. Munich and New York: Prestel Publishing, 1999. Discusses the history and design of Libeskind's Jewish Museum.

Greg Lynn

Di Cristina, Giuseppa, ed. *Architecture and Science.* Chichester, West Sussex, UK: Wiley-Academy, 2001. Essays and work by architects such as Lynn, Eisenman, Gehry, and Libeskind who employ a topological approach to architecture aided by computer-based technology.

Lynn, Greg, ed. *Folding in Architecture.* Architecture Design Profile. London: Academy Editions, 1993. Revised edition, Chichester, West Sussex, UK; Hoboken, NJ: Wiley-Academy, 2004. Essays about the possibilities afforded by computer-aided design and its implications for architecture.

———. *Folds, Bodies, and Blobs: Collected Essays.* Brussels: La Lettre Volée, 1998. Writings on issues such as form, proportion, and geometry and how they are impacted by computer-aided design.

Norman Foster

Foster, Norman. *Reflections.* Munich and London: Prestel Publishing, 2006. A compilation of Foster's essays on architecture, arranged thematically.

Pawley, Martin. *Norman Foster: A Global Architecture.* New York: Universe Press, 1999. A survey of Foster's work from the beginning of his career to the late twentieth century.

Samuel Mockbee

The Home Maker: Samuel "Sambo" Mockbee. Video recording. Princeton: Films for the Humanities & Sciences, 2002. Shows footage of constructed works by Mockbee and students of the Rural Studio; commentary by Mockbee, clients, and others. Originally broadcast 7 January 2002 as a segment of *Nightline*, with host Ted Koppel.

Mockbee, Samuel. *Samuel Mockbee and the Rural Studio: Community Architecture*. Edited by David Moos and Gail Trechsel. Birmingham, Alabama: Birmingham Museum of Art; New York: Distributed Art Publishers, 2003. Exhibition catalogue.

William McDonough and Sustainable Architecture

McDonough, William. "Design, Ecology, Ethics, and the Making of Things," in *Theorizing a New Agenda for Architecture,* edited by Kate Nesbitt (see Anthologies section above). Speech given in 1993 at Cathdral of St. John the Divine in New York City.

William McDonough Architects. *The Hannover Principles: Design for Sustainability*. New York: William McDonough Architects, 1992. Recommendations for environmentally friendly and sustainable design; commissioned by city of Hannover, Germany, for the 1992 Earth Summit.

McLennan, Jason F. *The Philosophy of Sustainable Design*. Kansas City, MO: Ecotone Publishing Company, 2004. Discussion of the history and potential future of sustainable design; addresses technologies, materials, and leading practitioners and includes a list of additional readings on green design.

Todd, Nancy Jack. *A Safe and Sustainable World: The Promise of Ecological Design*. Washington, D.C.: Island Press, 2005. Written for nonspecialists, this book discusses possibilities for an environmentally friendly existence.

Andrés Duany

Bressi, Todd. *The Seaside Debate: A Critique Of The New Urbanism*. New York: Rizzoli, 2002. Discussions and critiques of New Urbanism by architects, planners, and academics.

Duany, Andrés, Elizabeth Plater-Zyberk, and Jeff Speck. *Suburban Nation: The Rise of Sprawl and the Decline of the American Dream*. New York: North Point Press, 2001. Critique of suburban problems and a reevaluation of suburban planning based on New Urbanist concepts.

Katz, Peter. *The New Urbanism: Toward an Architecture of Community*. New York: McGraw-Hill, 1993. A series of case studies, including Seaside, Florida, that demonstrate principles and techniques of New Urbanism.

Frank Gehry

Dal Co, Franceso, and Kurt W. Forster. *Frank O. Gehry: The Complete Works*. New York: Phaidon Press, 2003.

Gehry, Frank O., and J. Fiona Ragheb. *Frank Gehry, Architect*. New York: Solomon R. Guggenheim Foundation, 2003. Exhibition catalogueue.

Lindsey, Bruce. *Digital Gehry: Material Resistance, Digital Construction*. Boston: Birkhauser Press, 2002. Discussion of Gehry's use of digital technologies.

Sarah Whiting

Somol, R.E., and Sarah Whiting. "Notes around the Doppler Effect and Other Moods of Modernism." *Perspecta, The Yale Architectural Journal* 33. Cambridge, MA: MIT Press, 2002. Calls for a more projective, propositional direction for architectural practice and discourse.

Whiting, Sarah. "Bas-Relief Urbanism: Chicago's Near South Side," in *Mies in America*, edited by Phyllis Lambert. New York: Harry N. Abrams, 2001. Examines Mies's design for the campus of Illinois Institute of Technology as an urban model.

"Projective Landscape: A Conference on Projective Practice." Held at the Delft University of Technology (16–17 March 2006). http://www.projectivelandscape.nl/. Conference organized to discuss projective as opposed to critical architectural practice; website contains videos of conference lectures and discussions.

Shumon Basar

Basar, Shumon, and Markus Miessen, eds. *Did Someone Say Participate? An Atlas of Spatial Practice*. Cambridge, MA: MIT Press, 2006. Texts that address issues of space, contemporary architectural and interdisciplinary practices.

Zizek, Slavoj. *Looking Awry: An Introduction to Jacques Lacan through Popular Culture*. Cambridge, MA: MIT Press, 1991. Main psychoanalytic theories of Lacan explained and examined through investigations of popular film and literature.